Shri Guru Granth Sahib, Vol. 2 of 4

Shri Guru Granth Sahib, Vol. 2 of 4

Formatted For Educational Interest

Republished 2008 by Forgotten Books

www.forgottenbooks.org

PUBLISHER'S PREFACE

About the Book

"The Granth is the central text of Sikhism, a religion that emerged in the Punjab region of India in the 15th Century. Sikhism is a unique faith which has aspects of Islam: monotheism and iconoclasm, and Hinduism: reincarnation, karma and nirvana. However Sikhism is distinct from Hinduism and Islam. The Sikh Gurus (teachers), contemporaries of Luther and Calvin, were reformers who rejected the caste system and much of the apparatus of Hindu ritual and legalism. They promoted religious tolerance and the equality of women. The founding Guru, Shri Guru Nanak Dev Ji, (1469-1538), is noted for the saying "There is no Hindu, there is no Muslim."

The Granth, compiled by Guru Gobind Singh, contains compositions of six Gurus, namely Guru Nanak, Guru Angad, Guru Amar Das, Guru Ram Das, Guru Arjan, and Guru Teg Bahadur. The hymns are arranged by the thirty one ragas (musical forms) in which they were composed. The hymns that comprise the Granth were originally written in several different languages: Persian, mediaeval Prakrit, Hindi, Marathi, old Panjabi, Multani, and several local dialects. In addition, there are Sanskrit and Arabic portions. This makes it extrordinarily difficult to translate. The translation presented here is the Khalsa Consensus Translation, which is highly regarded by scholars.

The Granth is considered the living embodiment of the Gurus, the "eleventh guru". Printed copies of the Granth are treated with the greatest respect. This is the reason for the honorific titles that make up the full name of the book. There are protocols to be observed in while reading of the Granth. A Sikh reader suggests the following: "Out of respect, it is advised that before you do read the Sri Guru Granth Sahib, that you cover your hair." This is normally with a turban or a piece of cloth provided by the gurdwara."

(Quote from sacred-texts.com)

CONTENTS

RAAG AASAA

Section 08 - Raag Aasaa - Part 001

ONE Universal Creator God. Truth Is The Name. Creative Being Personified. No Fear. No Hatred. Image Of The Undying. Beyond Birth. Self-Existent. By Guru's Grace:

Raag Aasaa, First Mehl, First House, So Dar ~ That Gate:
What is that Gate, and what is that Home, in which You sit and take care of all?

Countless musical instruments of so many various kinds vibrate there for You; so many are the musicians there for You.

There are so many Ragas there for You, along with their accompanying harmonies; so many minstrels sing to You.

The winds sing to You, as do water and fire; the Righteous Judge of Dharma sings at Your Door.

Chitar and Gupat, the recording angels of the conscious and the subconscious, sing to You; they know, and they write, and on the basis of what they write, the Lord of Dharma passes judgement.

Shiva and Brahma and the Goddess Parvaati, so beautiful and ever adorned by You, sing to You.

The Indras, seated upon their celestial thrones, with the deities at Your Gate, sing to You.

The Siddhas in Samaadhi sing to You, and the Holy Saints, in their contemplative meditation, sing to You.

The celibates, the truthful and the patient beings sing to You, and the mighty warriors sing to You.

The scholarly Pandits sing to You, along with the holy Rishis and the readers of the Vedas throughout the ages.

The Mohinis, the heavenly beauties who entice the heart in paradise, in this world and in the nether regions, sing to You.

The fourteen priceless jewels created by You, and the sixty-eight holy places of pilgrimage, sing to You.

The mighty warriors and the divine heroes sing to You, and the four sources of creation sing to You.

The continents, the worlds and the solar systems, created and installed by Your Hand, sing to You.

They alone sing to You, who are pleasing to Your Will, and who are imbued with the nectar of Your devotional worship.

So many others sing to You, they do not come into my mind; how can Nanak think of them?

That Lord and Master - He is True, forever True; He is True, and True is His Name.

He who created the creation is True, and He shall always be True; He shall not depart, even when the creation departs.

He created the world of Maya with its various colors and species.

Having created the creation, He Himself watches over it, as it pleases His Greatness.

Whatever pleases Him, that is what He does. No one can issue any commands to Him.

Section 08 - Raag Aasaa - Part 002

He is the King, the King of Kings, the Emperor of Kings! Nanak lives in surrender to His Will. |1|1|

Aasaa, Fourth Mehl:
That Lord is Immaculate; the Lord God is Immaculate. The Lord is Unap-proachable, Unfathomable and Incomparable.

All meditate, all meditate on You, O Dear Lord, O True Creator.

All beings are Yours; You are the Giver of all beings.

So meditate on the Lord, O Saints; He is the One who takes away all pain.

The Lord Himself is the Master, and He Himself is His own servant. O Nanak, how insignificant are mortal beings! |1|

You are totally pervading within each and every heart; O Lord, You are the One Primal Being, All-permeating.

Some are givers, and some are beggars; all of this is Your wondrous play!

You Yourself are the Giver, and You Yourself are the Enjoyer. I know of no other than You.

You are the Supreme Lord God, Infinite and Eternal; what Glorious Praises of Yours should I speak and chant?

Unto those who serve, unto those who serve You, slave Nanak is a sacrifice. |2|

Those who meditate on the Lord, those who meditate on You, O Dear Lord, those humble beings dwell in peace in this world.

They are liberated, they are liberated, who meditate on the Lord; the noose of Death is cut away from them.

Those who meditate on the Fearless One, on the Fearless Lord, all their fears are dispelled.

Those who have served, those who have served my Dear Lord, are absorbed into the Being of the Lord, Har, Har.

Blessed are they, blessed are they, who have meditated on the Dear Lord; slave Nanak is a sacrifice to them. |3|

Devotion to You, devotion to You, is a treasure, overflowing, infinite and endless.

Your devotees, Your devotees praise You, O Dear Lord, in many and various ways.

For You, so many, for You, so very many, O Dear Lord, perform worship and adoration; they practice penance and endlessly chant in meditation.

For You, many - for You, so very many read the various Simritees and Shaastras; they perform religious rituals and the six ceremonies.

Those devotees, those devotees are good, O servant Nanak, who are pleasing to my Lord God. |4|

You are the Primal Being, the Unrivalled Creator Lord; there is no other as Great as You.

You are the One, age after age; forever and ever, You are One and the same. You are the Eternal, Unchanging Creator.

Whatever pleases You comes to pass. Whatever You Yourself do, happens.

You Yourself created the entire Universe, and having done so, You Yourself shall destroy it all.

Servant Nanak sings the Glorious Praises of the Creator, the Knower of all. |5|2|

One Universal Creator God. By The Grace Of The True Guru:
Raag Aasaa, First Mehl, Chaupaday, Second House:
Hearing, everyone calls You Great,
but only one who has seen You, knows just how Great You are.

Section 08 - Raag Aasaa - Part 003

No one can measure Your Worth, or describe You.
Those who describe You, remain absorbed in You. |1|

O my Great Lord and Master of Unfathomable Depth, You are the Ocean of
Excellence.
No one knows the greatness of Your expanse. |1|Pause|

All the contemplators met together and practiced contemplation;
all the appraisers met together and tried to appraise You.
The theologians, the meditators and the teachers of teachers
could not express even an iota of Your Greatness. |2|

All Truth, all austerities, all goodness,
and the greatness of the Siddhas, the beings of perfect spiritual powers
- without You, none has attained such spiritual powers.
They are obtained by Your Grace; their flow cannot be blocked. |3|

What can the helpless speaker do?
Your bounties are overflowing with Your Praises.
And the one, unto whom You give - why should he think of any other?
O Nanak, the True Lord is the Embellisher. |4|1|

Aasaa, First Mehl:
Chanting the Name, I live; forgetting it, I die.
It is so difficult to chant the True Name.
If someone feels hunger for the True Name,
then that hunger shall consume his pains. |1|

So how could I ever forget Him, O my Mother?
True is the Master, and True is His Name. |1|Pause|

People have grown weary of trying to appraise the greatness of the True
Name, but they have not been able to appraise even an iota of it.
Even if they were all to meet together and recount them,
You would not be made any greater or lesser. |2|

He does not die - there is no reason to mourn.
He continues to give, but His Provisions are never exhausted.
This Glorious Virtue is His alone - no one else is like Him;
there has never been anyone like Him, and there never shall be. |3|

As Great as You Yourself are, so Great are Your Gifts.
It is You who created day and night as well.
Those who forget their Lord and Master are vile and despicable.
O Nanak, without the Name, people are wretched outcasts. |4|2|

Aasaa, First Mehl:
If a beggar cries out at the door, the Master hears it in His Mansion.
Whether He receives him or pushes him away, it is the Gift of the Lord's Greatness. |1|

Recognize the Lord's Light within all, and do not consider social class or status; there are no classes or castes in the world hereafter. |1|Pause|

He Himself acts, and He Himself inspires us to act.
He Himself considers our complaints.
Since You, O Creator Lord, are the Doer,
why should I submit to the world? |2|

You Yourself created and You Yourself give.
You Yourself eliminate evil-mindedness;
by Guru's Grace, You come to abide in our minds,
and then, pain and darkness are dispelled from within. |3|

He Himself infuses love for the Truth.
Unto others, the Truth is not bestowed.
If He bestows it upon someone, says Nanak, then, in the world hereafter, that person is not called to account. |4|3|

Aasaa, First Mehl:
The urges of the heart are like cymbals and ankle-bells;
the drum of the world resounds with the beat.
Naarad dances to the tune of the Dark Age of Kali Yuga;
where can the celibates and the men of truth place their feet? |1|

Nanak is a sacrifice to the Naam, the Name of the Lord.
The world is blind; our Lord and Master is All-seeing. |1|Pause|

The disciple feeds on the Guru;
out of love for bread, he comes to dwell in his home.

Section 08 - Raag Aasaa - Part 004

If one were to live and eat for hundreds of years,
that day alone would be auspicious, when he recognizes his Lord and
Master. |2|

Beholding the sight of the petitioner, compassion is not aroused.
No one lives without give and take.
The king administers justice only if his palm is greased.
No one is moved by the Name of God. |3|

O Nanak, they are human beings in form and name only;
by their deeds they are dogs - this is the Command of the Lord's Court.
By Guru's Grace, if one sees himself as a guest in this world,
then he gains honor in the Court of the Lord. |4|4|

Aasaa, First Mehl:
As much as the Shabad is in the mind, so much is Your melody; as much as
the form of the universe is, so much is Your body, Lord.
You Yourself are the tongue, and You Yourself are the nose. Do not speak
of any other, O my mother. |1|

My Lord and Master is One;
He is the One and Only; O Siblings of Destiny, He is the One alone.
|1|Pause|

He Himself kills, and He Himself emancipates; He Himself gives and takes.
He Himself beholds, and He Himself rejoices; He Himself bestows His
Glance of Grace. |2|

Whatever He is to do, that is what He is doing. No one else can do
anything.
As He projects Himself, so do we describe Him; this is all Your Glorious
Greatness, Lord. |3|

The Dark Age of Kali Yuga is the bottle of wine; Maya is the sweet wine, and
the intoxicated mind continues to drink it in.
He Himself assumes all sorts of forms; thus poor Nanak speaks. |4|5|

Aasaa, First Mehl:
Make your intellect your instrument, and love your tambourine;
thus bliss and lasting pleasure shall be produced in your mind.
This is devotional worship, and this is the practice of penance.
So dance in this love, and keep the beat with your feet. |1|

Know that the perfect beat is the Praise of the Lord;
other dances produce only temporary pleasure in the mind. |1|Pause|

Play the two cymbals of truth and contentment.
Let your ankle bells be the lasting Vision of the Lord.
Let your harmony and music be the elimination of duality.
So dance in this love, and keep the beat with your feet. |2|

Let the fear of God within your heart and mind be your spinning dance,
and keep up, whether sitting or standing.
To roll around in the dust is to know that the body is only ashes.
So dance in this love, and keep the beat with your feet. |3|

Keep the company of the disciples, the students who love the teachings.
As Gurmukh, listen to the True Name.
O Nanak, chant it, over and over again.
So dance in this love, and keep the beat with your feet. |4|6|

Aasaa, First Mehl:
He created the air, and He supports the whole world; he bound water and
fire together.
The blind, ten-headed Raavan had his heads cut off, but what greatness
was obtained by killing him? |1|

What Glories of Yours can be chanted?
You are totally pervading everywhere; You love and cherish all. |1|Pause|

You created all beings, and You hold the world in Your Hands; what
greatness is it to put a ring in the nose of the black cobra, as Krishna did?

Whose Husband are You? Who is Your wife? You are subtly diffused and
pervading in all. |2|

Brahma, the bestower of blessings, entered the stem of the lotus, with his relatives, to find the extent of the universe.
Proceeding on, he could not find its limits; what glory was obtained by killing Kansa, the king? |3|

The jewels were produced and brought forth by churning the ocean of milk.
The other gods proclaimed "We are the ones who did this!"

Section 08 - Raag Aasaa - Part 005

Says Nanak, by hiding, how can the Lord be hidden? He has given each their share, one by one. |4|7|

Aasaa, First Mehl:
The vine of good actions and character has spread out, and it bears the fruit of the Lord's Name.
The Name has no form or outline; it vibrates with the unstruck Sound Current; through the Word of the Shabad, the Immaculate Lord is revealed. |1|

One can speak on this only when he knows it.
He alone drinks in the Ambrosial Nectar. |1|Pause|

Those who drink it in are enraptured; their bonds and shackles are cut away.
When one's light blends into the Divine Light, then the desire for Maya is ended. |2|

Among all lights, I behold Your Form; all the worlds are Your Maya.
Among the tumults and forms, He sits in serene detachment; He bestows His Glance of Grace upon those who are engrossed in the illusion. |3|

The Yogi who plays on the instrument of the Shabad gains the Blessed Vision of the Infinitely Beautiful Lord.
He, the Lord, is immersed in the Unstruck Shabad of the Word, says Nanak, the humble and meek. |4|8|

Aasaa, First Mehl:
My virtue is that I carry the load of my words upon my head.
The real words are the Words of the Creator Lord.

How useless are eating, drinking and laughing,
if the Lord is not cherished in the heart! |1|

Why should someone care for anything else,
if throughout his life, he gathers in that which is truly worth gathering?
|1|Pause|

The intellect of the mind is like a drunken elephant.
Whatever one utters is totally false, the most false of the false.
So what face should we put on to offer our prayer,
when both virtue and vice are close at hand as witnesses? |2|

As You make us, so we become.
Without You, there is no other at all.
As is the understanding which You bestow, so do we receive.
As it pleases Your Will, so do You lead us. |3|

The divine crystalline harmonies, their consorts, and their celestial families
- from them, the essence of Ambrosial Nectar is produced.
O Nanak, this is the wealth and property of the Creator Lord.
If only this essential reality were understood! |4|9|

Aasaa, First Mehl:
When by His Grace He came to my home, then my companions met
together to celebrate my marriage.
Beholding this play, my mind became blissful; my Husband Lord has come
to marry me. |1|

So sing - yes, sing the songs of wisdom and reflection, O brides.
My spouse, the Life of the world, has come into my home. |1|Pause|

When I was married within the Gurdwara, the Guru's Gate, I met my
Husband Lord, and I came to know Him.
The Word of His Shabad is pervading the three worlds; when my ego was
quieted, my mind became happy. |2|

He Himself arranges His own affairs; His affairs cannot be arranged by
anyone else.
By the affair of this marriage, truth, contentment, mercy and faith are
produced; but how rare is that Gurmukh who understands it! |3|

Says Nanak, that Lord alone is the Husband of all.
She, upon whom He casts His Glance of Grace, becomes the happy soul-bride. |4|10|

Aasaa, First Mehl:
Home and forest are the same, for one who dwells in the balance of intuitive peace and poise.
His evil-mindedness departs, and the Praises of God take its place.
To chant the True Name with one's mouth is the true ladder.

Section 08 - Raag Aasaa - Part 006

Serving the True Guru, one finds one's own place within the self. |1|

To conquer the mind is the knowledge of the six Shaastras.
The Divine Light of the Lord God is perfectly pervading. |1|Pause|

Excessive thirst for Maya makes people wear all sorts of religious robes.
The pain of corruption destroys the body's peace.
Sexual desire and anger steal the wealth of the self within.
But by abandoning duality, one is emancipated through the Naam, the Name of the Lord. |2|

In the Lord's Praise and adoration is intuitive peace, poise and bliss.
The Love of the Lord God is one's family and friends.
He Himself is the Doer, and He Himself is the Forgiver.
My body and mind belong to the Lord; my life is at His Command. |3|

Falsehood and corruption cause terrible suffering.
All the religious robes and social classes look just like dust.
Whoever is born, continues to come and go.
O Nanak, only the Naam and the Lord's Command are eternal and everlasting. |4|11|

Aasaa, First Mehl:
In the pool is the one incomparably beautiful lotus.
It blossoms continually; its form is pure and fragrant.
The swans pick up the bright jewels.
They take on the essence of the All-powerful Lord of the Universe. |1|

Whoever is seen, is subject to birth and death.
In the pool without water, the lotus is not seen. |1|Pause|

How rare are those who know and understand this secret.
The Vedas continually speak of the three branches.
One who merges into the knowledge of the Lord as absolute and related,
serves the True Guru and obtains the supreme status. |2|

One who is imbued with the Love of the Lord and dwells continually upon
Him is liberated.
He is the king of kings, and blossoms forth continually.
That one whom You preserve, by bestowing Your Mercy, O Lord,
even the sinking stone - You float that one across. |3|

Your Light is pervading the three worlds; I know that You are permeating
the three worlds.
When my mind turned away from Maya, I came to dwell in my own home.
Nanak falls at the feet of that person who immerses himself in the Lord's
Love, and performs devotional worship night and day. |4|12|

Aasaa, First Mehl:
Receiving the True Teachings from the Guru, arguments depart.
But through excessive cleverness, one is only plastered with dirt.
The filth of attachment is removed by the True Name of the Lord.
By Guru's Grace, one remains lovingly attached to the Lord. |1|

He is the Presence Ever-present; offer your prayers to Him.
Pain and pleasure are in the Hands of God, the True Creator. |1|Pause|

One who practices falsehood comes and goes.
By speaking and talking, His limits cannot be found.
Whatever one sees, is not understood.
Without the Name, satisfaction does not enter into the mind. |2|

Whoever is born is afflicted by disease,
tortured by the pain of egotism and Maya.
They alone are saved, who are protected by God.
Serving the True Guru, they drink in the Amrit, the Ambrosial Nectar. |3|

The unstable mind is restrained by tasting this Nectar.
Serving the True Guru, one comes to cherish the Ambrosial Nectar of the Shabad.
Through the True Word of the Shabad, the state of liberation is obtained.
O Nanak, self-conceit is eradicated from within. |4|13|

Aasaa, First Mehl:
Whatever He has done, has proved to be true.
The True Guru bestows the Ambrosial Naam, the Name of the Lord.
With the Naam in the heart, the mind is not separated from the Lord.
Night and day, one dwells with the Beloved. |1|

O Lord, please keep me in the Protection of Your Sanctuary.

Section 08 - Raag Aasaa - Part 007

By Guru's Grace, I have obtained the sublime essence of the Lord; I have received the wealth of the Naam and the nine treasures. |1|Pause|

Those whose karma and Dharma - whose actions and faith - are in the True Name of the True Lord
- I am forever a sacrifice to them.
Those who are imbued with the Lord are accepted and respected.
In their company, the supreme wealth is obtained. |2|

Blessed is that bride, who has obtained the Lord as her Husband.
She is imbued with the Lord, and she reflects upon the Word of His Shabad.
She saves herself, and saves her family and friends as well.
She serves the True Guru, and contemplates the essence of reality. |3|

The True Name is my social status and honor.
The love of the Truth is my karma and Dharma - my faith and my actions, and my self-control.
O Nanak, one who is forgiven by the Lord is not called to account.
The One Lord erases duality. |4|14|

Aasaa, First Mehl:
Some come, and after they come, they go.
Some are imbued with the Lord; they remain absorbed in Him.
Some find no place of rest at all, on the earth or in the sky.

Those who do not meditate on the Name of the Lord are the most unfortunate. |1|

From the Perfect Guru, the way to salvation is obtained.
This world is a terrifying ocean of poison; through the Word of the Guru's Shabad, the Lord helps us cross over. |1|Pause|

Those, whom God unites with Himself,
cannot be crushed by death.
The beloved Gurmukhs remain immaculately pure,
like the lotus in the water, which remains untouched. |2|

Tell me: who should we call good or bad?
Behold the Lord God; the truth is revealed to the Gurmukh.
I speak the Unspoken Speech of the Lord, contemplating the Guru's Teachings.
I join the Sangat, the Guru's Congregation, and I find God's limits. |3|

The Shaastras, the Vedas, the Simritees and all their many secrets;
bathing at the sixty-eight holy places of pilgrimage - all this is found by enshrining the sublime essence of the Lord in the heart.
The Gurmukhs are immaculately pure; no filth sticks to them.
O Nanak, the Naam, the Name of the Lord, abides in the heart, by the greatest pre-ordained destiny. |4|15|

Aasaa, First Mehl:
Bowing down, again and again, I fall at the Feet of my Guru; through Him, I have seen the Lord, the Divine Self, within.
Through contemplation and meditation, the Lord dwells within the heart; see this, and understand. |1|

So speak the Lord's Name, which shall emancipate you.
By Guru's Grace, the jewel of the Lord is found; ignorance is dispelled, and the Divine Light shines forth. |1|Pause|

By merely saying it with the tongue, one's bonds are not broken, and egotism and doubt do not depart from within.
But when one meets the True Guru, egotism departs, and then, one realizes his destiny. |2|

The Name of the Lord, Har, Har, is sweet and dear to His devotees; it is the ocean of peace - enshrine it within the heart.
The Lover of His devotees, the Life of the World, the Lord bestows the Guru's Teachings upon the intellect, and one is emancipated. |3|

One who dies fighting against his own stubborn mind finds God, and the desires of the mind are quieted.
O Nanak, if the Life of the World bestows His Mercy, one is intuitively attuned to the Love of the Lord. |4|16|

Aasaa, First Mehl:
Unto whom do they speak? Unto whom do they preach? Who understands? Let them understand themselves.
Who do they teach? Through study, they come to realize the Lord's Glorious Virtues. Through the Shabad, the Word of the True Guru, they come to dwell in contentment. |1|

Section 08 - Raag Aasaa - Part 008

Through the Guru's Teachings, realize that He is pervading in all bodies;
O my soul, vibrate on the Profound, Unfathomable Lord. |1|Pause|

Loving devotion to the Lord brings endless waves of joy and delight.
One who dwells with the Glorious Praises of the Lord, night and day, is sanctified.
The birth into the world of the faithless cynic is totally useless.
The humble devotee of the Lord remains unattached. |2|

The body which sings the Glorious Praises of the Lord is sanctified.
The soul remains conscious of the Lord, absorbed in His Love.
The Lord is the Infinite Primal Being, beyond the beyond, the priceless jewel.
My mind is totally content, imbued with my Beloved. |3|

Those who speak and babble on and on, are truly dead.
God is not far away - O God, You are right here.
I have seen that the whole world is engrossed in Maya.
O Nanak, through the Guru's Teachings, I meditate on the Naam, the Name of the Lord. |4|17|

Aasaa, First Mehl, Ti-Tukas:
One is a beggar, living on charity;
another is a king, absorbed in himself.
One receives honor, and another dishonor.
The Lord destroys and creates; He is enshrined in His meditation.
There is no other as great as You.
So whom should I present to You? Who is good enough? |1|

The Naam, the Name of the Lord, is my only Support.
You are the Great Giver, the Doer, the Creator. |1|Pause|

I have not walked on Your Path; I have followed the crooked path.
In the Court of the Lord, I find no place to sit.
I am mentally blind, in the bondage of Maya.
The wall of my body is breaking down, wearing away, growing weaker.
You have such high hopes of eating and living
- your breaths and morsels of food are already counted! |2|

Night and day they are blind - please, bless them with Your Light.
They are drowning in the terrifying world-ocean, crying out in pain.
I am a sacrifice to those who chant, hear and believe in the Name.
Nanak utters this one prayer;
soul and body, all belong to You, Lord. |3|

When You bless me, I chant Your Name.
Thus I find my seat in the Court of the Lord.
When it pleases You, evil-mindedness departs,
and the jewel of spiritual wisdom comes to dwell in the mind.
When the Lord bestows His Glance of Grace, then one comes to meet the
True Guru.
Prays Nanak, carry us across the terrifying world-ocean. |4|18|

Aasaa, First Mehl, Panch-Padas:
A cow without milk; a bird without wings; a garden without water - totally
useless!
What is an emperor, without respect? The chamber of the soul is so dark,
without the Name of the Lord. |1|

How could I ever forget You? It would be so painful!
I would suffer such pain - no, I shall not forget You! |1|Pause|

The eyes grow blind, the tongue does not taste, and the ears do not hear any sound.
He walks on his feet only when supported by someone else; without serving the Lord, such are the fruits of life. |2|

The Word is the tree; the garden of the heart is the farm; tend it, and irrigate it with the Lord's Love.
All these trees bear the fruit of the Name of the One Lord; but without the karma of good actions, how can anyone obtain it? |3|

As many living beings are there are, they are all Yours. Without selfless service, no one obtains any reward.
Pain and pleasure come by Your Will; without the Name, the soul does not even exist. |4|

To die in the Teachings is to live. Otherwise, what is life? That is not the way.

Section 08 - Raag Aasaa - Part 009

Says Nanak, He grants life to the living beings; O Lord, please keep me according to Your Will. |5|19|

Aasaa, First Mehl:
Let the body be the Brahmin, and let the mind be the loin-cloth;
let spiritual wisdom be the sacred thread, and meditation the ceremonial ring.
I seek the Name of the Lord and His Praise as my cleansing bath.
By Guru's Grace, I am absorbed into God. |1|

O Pandit, O religious scholar, contemplate God in such a way
that His Name may sanctify you, that His Name may be your study, and His Name your wisdom and way of life. |1|Pause|

The outer sacred thread is worthwhile only as long as the Divine Light is within.
So make the remembrance of the Naam, the Name of the Lord, your loin-cloth and the ceremonial mark on your forehead.
Here and hereafter, the Name alone shall stand by you.

Do not seek any other actions, except the Name. |2|

Worship the Lord in loving adoration, and burn your desire for Maya.
Behold only the One Lord, and do not seek out any other.
Become aware of reality, in the Sky of the Tenth Gate;
read aloud the Lord's Word, and contemplate it. |3|

With the diet of His Love, doubt and fear depart.
With the Lord as your night watchman, no thief will dare to break in.
Let the knowledge of the One God be the ceremonial mark on your forehead.
Let the realization that God is within you be your discrimination. |4|

Through ritual actions, God cannot be won over;
by reciting sacred scriptures, His value cannot be estimated.
The eighteen Puraanas and the four Vedas do not know His mystery.
O Nanak, the True Guru has shown me the Lord God. |5|20|

Aasaa, First Mehl:
He alone is the selfless servant, slave and humble devotee,
who as Gurmukh, becomes the slave of his Lord and Master.
He, who created the Universe, shall ultimately destroy it.
Without Him, there is no other at all. |1|

Through the Word of the Guru's Shabad, the Gurmukh reflects upon the True Name; in the True Court, he is found to be true. |1|Pause|

The true supplication, the true prayer
- within the Mansion of His Sublime Presence, the True Lord Master hears and applauds these.
He summons the truthful to His Heavenly Throne
and bestows glorious greatness upon them; that which He wills, comes to pass. |2|

The Power is Yours; You are my only Support.
The Word of the Guru's Shabad is my true password.
One who obeys the Hukam of the Lord's Command, goes to Him openly.
With the password of truth, his way is not blocked. |3|

The Pandit reads and expounds on the Vedas,

but he does not know the secret of the thing within himself.
Without the Guru, understanding and realization are not obtained;
but still God is True, pervading everywhere. |4|

What should I say, or speak or describe?
Only You Yourself know, O Lord of total wonder.
Nanak takes the Support of the Door of the One God.
There, at the True Door, the Gurmukhs sustain themselves. |5|21|

Aasaa, First Mehl:
The clay pitcher of the body is miserable; it suffers in pain through birth
and death.
How can this terrifying world-ocean be crossed over? Without the Lord -
Guru, it cannot be crossed. |1|

Without You, there is no other at all, O my Beloved; without you, there is
no other at all.
You are in all colors and forms; he alone is forgiven, upon whom You
bestow Your Glance of Grace. |1|Pause|

Maya, my mother-in-law, is evil; she does not let me live in my own home.
The vicious one does not let me meet with my Husband Lord.
I serve at the feet of my companions and friends; the Lord has showered
me with His Mercy, through Guru's Grace. |2|

Section 08 - Raag Aasaa - Part 010

Reflecting upon my self, and conquering my mind, I have seen that there is
no other friend like You.
As You keep me, so do I live. You are the Giver of peace and pleasure.
Whatever You do, comes to pass. |3|

Hope and desire have both been dispelled; I have renounced my longing for
the three qualities.
The Gurmukh obtains the state of ecstasy, taking to the Shelter of the
Saints' Congregation. |4|

All wisdom and meditation, all chanting and penance, come to one whose
heart is filled with the Invisible, Inscrutable Lord.

O Nanak, one whose mind is imbued with the Lord's Name, finds the Guru's Teachings, and intuitively serves. |5|22|

Aasaa, First Mehl, Panch-Padas:
Your attachment to your family, your attachment to all your affairs
- renounce all your attachments, for they are all corrupt. |1|

Renounce your attachments and doubts, O brother,
and dwell upon the True Name within your heart and body. |1|Pause|

When one receives the nine treasures of the True Name,
his children do not weep, and his mother does not grieve. |2|

In this attachment, the world is drowning.
Few are the Gurmukhs who swim across. |3|

In this attachment, people are reincarnated over and over again.
Attached to emotional attachment, they go to the city of Death. |4|

You have received the Guru's Teachings - now practice meditation and penance.
If attachment is not broken, no one is approved. |5|

But if He bestows His Glance of Grace, then this attachment departs.
O Nanak, then one remains merged in the Lord. |6|23|

Aasaa, First Mehl:
He Himself does everything, the True, Invisible, Infinite Lord.
I am a sinner, You are the Forgiver. |1|

By Your Will, everything come to pass.
One who acts in stubborn-mindedness is ruined in the end. |1|Pause|

The intellect of the self-willed manmukh is engrossed in falsehood.
Without the meditative remembrance of the Lord, it suffers in sin. |2|

Renounce evil-mindedness, and you shall reap the rewards.
Whoever is born, comes through the Unknowable and Mysterious Lord. |3|

Such is my Friend and Companion;

meeting with the Guru, the Lord, devotion was implanted within me. |4|

In all other transactions, one suffers loss.
The Name of the Lord is pleasing to Nanak's mind. |5|24|

Aasaa, First Mehl, Chau-Padas:
Contemplate and reflect upon knowledge, and you will become a benefactor to others.
When you conquer the five passions, then you shall come to dwell at the sacred shrine of pilgrimage. |1|

You shall hear the vibrations of the tinkling bells, when your mind is held steady.
So what can the Messenger of Death do to me hereafter? |1|Pause|

When you abandon hope and desire, then you become a true Sannyaasi.
When the Yogi practices abstinence, then he enjoys his body. |2|

Through compassion, the naked hermit reflects upon his inner self.
He slays his own self, instead of slaying others. |3|

You, O Lord, are the One, but You have so many Forms.
Nanak does not know Your wondrous plays. |4|25|

Aasaa, First Mehl:
I am not stained by only one sin, that could be washed clean by virtue.
My Husband Lord is awake, while I sleep through the entire night of my life. |1|

In this way, how can I become dear to my Husband Lord?
My Husband Lord remains awake, while I sleep through the entire night of my life. |1|Pause|

Section 08 - Raag Aasaa - Part 011

With hope and desire, I approach His Bed,
but I do not know whether He will be pleased with me or not. |2|

How do I know what will happen to me, O my mother?

Without the Blessed Vision of the Lord's Darshan, I cannot survive.
|1|Pause|

I have not tasted His Love, and my thirst is not quenched.
My beautiful youth has run away, and now I, the soul-bride, repent and regret. |3|

Even now, I am held by hope and desire.
I am depressed; I have no hope at all. |1|Pause|

She overcomes her egotism, and adorns herself;
the Husband Lord now ravishes and enjoys the soul-bride on His Bed. |4|

Then, O Nanak, the bride becomes pleasing to the Mind of her Husband Lord;
she sheds her self-conceit, and is absorbed in her Lord and Master. |1|Pause|26|

Aasaa, First Mehl:
In this world of my father's house, I, the soul-bride, have been very childish;
I did not realize the value of my Husband Lord. |1|

My Husband is the One; there is no other like Him.
If He bestows His Glance of Grace, then I shall meet Him. |1|Pause|

In the next world of my in-law's house, I, the the soul-bride, shall realize Truth;
I shall come to know the celestial peace of my Husband Lord. |2|

By Guru's Grace, such wisdom comes to me,
so that the soul-bride becomes pleasing to the Mind of the Husband Lord. |3|

Says Nanak, she who adorns herself with the Love and the Fear of God,
enjoys her Husband Lord forever on His Bed. |4|27|

Aasaa, First Mehl:
No one is anyone else's son, and no one is anyone else's mother.
Through false attachments, people wander around in doubt. |1|

O My Lord and Master, I am created by You.
If You give it to me, I will chant Your Name. |1|Pause|

That person who is filled with all sorts of sins may pray at the Lord's Door,
but he is forgiven only when the Lord so wills. |2|

By Guru's Grace, evil-mindedness is destroyed.
Wherever I look, there I find the One Lord. |3|

Says Nanak, if one comes to such an understanding,
then he is absorbed into the Truest of the True. |4|28|

Aasaa, First Mehl, Du-Padas:
In that pool of the world, the people have their homes; there, the Lord has
created water and fire.
In the mud of earthly attachment, their feet have become mired, and I
have seen them drowning there. |1|

O foolish people, why don't you remember the One Lord?
Forgetting the Lord, your virtues shall wither away. |1|Pause|

I am not a celibate, nor am I truthful, nor a scholar; I was born foolish and
ignorant.
Prays Nanak, I seek the Sanctuary of those who do not forget You, Lord.
|2|29|

Aasaa, First Mehl:
There are six systems of philosophy, six teachers, and six doctrines;
but the Teacher of teachers is the One Lord, who appears in so many
forms. |1|

That system, where the Praises of the Creator are sung
- follow that system; in it rests greatness. |1|Pause|

As the seconds, minutes, hours, days, weekdays months and seasons all
originate from the one sun,
O Nanak, so do all forms originate from the One Creator. |2|30|

Section 08 - Raag Aasaa - Part 012

One Universal Creator God. By The Grace Of The True Guru:

Aasaa, Third House, First Mehl:

You may have thousands of armies, thousands of marching bands and lances, and thousands of men to rise and salute you.

Your rule may extend over thousands of miles, and thousands of men may rise to honor you.

But, if your honor is of no account to the Lord, then all of your ostentatious show is useless. |1|

Without the Name of the Lord, the world is in turmoil.

Even though the fool may be taught again and again, he remains the blindest of the blind. |1|Pause|

You may earn thousands, collect thousands, and spend thousands of dollars; thousands may come, and thousands may go.

But, if your honor is of no account to the Lord, then where will you go to find a safe haven? |2|

Thousands of Shaastras may be explained to the mortal, and thousands of Pandits may read the Puraanas to him;

but, if his honor is of no account to the Lord, then all of this is unacceptable. |3|

Honor comes from the True Name, the Name of the Merciful Creator.

If it abides in the heart, day and night, O Nanak, then the mortal shall swim across, by His Grace. |4|1|31|

Aasaa, First Mehl:

The One Name is my lamp; I have put the oil of suffering into it.

Its flame has dried up this oil, and I have escaped my meeting with the Messenger of Death. |1|

O people, do not make fun of me.

Thousands of wooden logs, piled up together, need only a tiny flame to burn. |1|Pause|

The Lord is my festive dish, of rice balls on leafy plates; the True Name of the Creator Lord is my funeral ceremony.

Here and hereafter, in the past and in the future, this is my support. |2|

The Lord's Praise is my River Ganges and my city of Benares; my soul takes its sacred cleansing bath there.
That becomes my true cleansing bath, if night and day, I enshrine love for You. |3|

The rice balls are offered to the gods and the dead ancestors, but it is the Brahmins who eat them!
O Nanak, the rice balls of the Lord are a gift which is never exhausted. |4|2|32|

Aasaa, Fourth House, First Mehl:
One Universal Creator God. By The Grace Of The True Guru:
The Gods, yearning for the Blessed Vision of the Lord's Darshan, suffered through pain and hunger at the sacred shrines.
The yogis and the celibates live their disciplined lifestyle, while others wear saffron robes and become hermits. |1|

For Your sake, O Lord Master, they are imbued with love.
Your Names are so many, and Your Forms are endless. No one can tell how may Glorious Virtues You have. |1|Pause|

Leaving behind hearth and home, palaces, elephants, horses and native lands, mortals have journeyed to foreign lands.
The spiritual leaders, prophets, seers and men of faith renounced the world, and became acceptable. |2|

Renouncing tasty delicacies, comfort, happiness and pleasures, some have abandoned their clothes and now wear skins.
Those who suffer in pain, imbued with Your Name, have become beggars at Your Door. |3|

Some wear skins, and carry begging bowls, bearing wooden staffs, and sitting on deer skins. Others raise their hair in tufts and wear sacred threads and loin-cloths.
You are the Lord Master, I am just Your puppet. Prays Nanak, what is my social status to be? |4|1|33|

Section 08 - Raag Aasaa - Part 013

Aasaa, Fifth House, First Mehl:
One Universal Creator God. By The Grace Of The True Guru:
The five evil passions dwell hidden within the mind.
They do not remain still, but move around like wanderers. |1|

My soul does not stay held by the Merciful Lord.
It is greedy, deceitful, sinful and hypocritical, and totally attached to Maya.
|1|Pause|

I will decorate my neck with garlands of flowers.
When I meet my Beloved, then I will put on my decorations. |2|

I have five companions and one Spouse.
It is ordained from the very beginning, that the soul must ultimately depart.
|3|

The five companions will lament together.
When the soul is trapped, prays Nanak, it is called to account. |4|1|34|

One Universal Creator God. By The Grace Of The True Guru:
Aasaa, Sixth House, First Mehl:
If the pearl of the mind is strung like a jewel on the thread of the breath,
and the soul-bride adorns her body with compassion, then the Beloved
Lord will enjoy His lovely bride. |1|

O my Love, I am fascinated by Your many glories;
Your Glorious Virtues are not found in any other. |1|Pause|

If the bride wears the garland of the Lord's Name, Har, Har, around her
neck, and if she uses the toothbrush of the Lord;

and if she fashions and wears the bracelet of the Creator Lord around her
wrist, then she shall hold her consciousness steady. |2|

She should make the Lord, the Slayer of demons, her ring, and take the
Transcendent Lord as her silken clothes.
The soul-bride should weave patience into the braids of her hair, and apply
the lotion of the Lord, the Great Lover. |3|

If she lights the lamp in the mansion of her mind, and makes her body the bed of the Lord,
then, when the King of spiritual wisdom comes to her bed, He shall take her, and enjoy her. |4|1|35|

Aasaa, First Mehl:
The created being acts as he is made to act; what can be said to him, O Siblings of Destiny?
Whatever the Lord is to do, He is doing; what cleverness could be used to affect Him? |1|

The Order of Your Will is so sweet, O Lord; this is pleasing to You.
O Nanak, he alone is honored with greatness, who is absorbed in the True Name. |1|Pause|

The deeds are done according to pre-ordained destiny; no one can turn back this Order.
As it is written, so it comes to pass; no one can erase it. |2|

He who talks on and on in the Lord's Court is known as a joker.
He is not successful in the game of chess, and his chessmen do not reach their goal. |3|

By himself, no one is literate, learned or wise; no one is ignorant or evil.
When, as a slave, one praises the Lord, only then is he known as a human being. |4|2|36|

Aasaa, First Mehl:
Let the Word of the Guru's Shabad be the ear-rings in your mind, and wear the patched coat of tolerance.
Whatever the Lord does, look upon that as good; thus you shall obtain the treasure of Sehj Yoga. |1|

Section 08 - Raag Aasaa - Part 014

O father, the soul which is united in union as a Yogi, remains united in the supreme essence throughout the ages.
One who has obtained the Ambrosial Naam, the Name of the Immaculate Lord - his body enjoys the pleasure of spiritual wisdom. |1|Pause|

In the Lord's City, he sits in his Yogic posture, and he forsakes his desires and conflicts.
The sound of the horn ever rings out its beautiful melody, and day and night, he is filled with the sound current of the Naad. |2|

My cup is reflective meditation, and spiritual wisdom is my walking stick; to dwell in the Lord's Presence is the ashes I apply to my body.
The Praise of the Lord is my occupation; and to live as Gurmukh is my pure religion. |3|

My arm-rest is to see the Lord's Light in all, although their forms and colors are so numerous.
Says Nanak, listen, O Bharthari Yogi: love only the Supreme Lord God. |4|3|37|

Aasaa, First Mehl:
Make spiritual wisdom your molasses, and meditation your scented flowers; let good deeds be the herbs.
Let devotional faith be the distilling fire, and your love the ceramic cup. Thus the sweet nectar of life is distilled. |1|

O Baba, the mind is intoxicated with the Naam, drinking in its Nectar. It remains absorbed in the Lord's Love.
Night and day, remaining attached to the Love of the Lord, the celestial music of the Shabad resounds. |1|Pause|

The Perfect Lord naturally gives the cup of Truth, to the one upon whom He casts His Glance of Grace.
One who trades in this Nectar - how could he ever love the wine of the world? |2|

The Teachings of the Guru, the Ambrosial Bani - drinking them in, one becomes acceptable and renowned.
Unto the one who loves the Lord's Court, and the Blessed Vision of His Darshan, of what use is liberation or paradise? |3|

Imbued with the Lord's Praises, one is forever a Bairaagee, a renunciate, and one's life is not lost in the gamble.
Says Nanak, listen, O Bharthari Yogi: drink in the intoxicating nectar of the Lord. |4|4|38|

Aasaa, First Mehl:
Having attacked Khuraasaan, Baabar terrified Hindustan.
The Creator Himself does not take the blame, but has sent the Mugal as the messenger of death.
There was so much slaughter that the people screamed. Didn't You feel compassion, Lord? |1|

O Creator Lord, You are the Master of all.
If some powerful man strikes out against another man, then no one feels any grief in their mind. |1|Pause|

But if a powerful tiger attacks a flock of sheep and kills them, then its master must answer for it.
This priceless country has been laid waste and defiled by dogs, and no one pays any attention to the dead.
You Yourself unite, and You Yourself separate; I gaze upon Your Glorious Greatness. |2|

One may give himself a great name, and revel in the pleasures of the mind, but in the Eyes of the Lord and Master, he is just a worm, for all the corn that he eats.
Only one who dies to his ego while yet alive, obtains the blessings, O Nanak, by chanting the Lord's Name. |3|5|39|

Raag Aasaa, Second House, Third Mehl:
One Universal Creator God. By The Grace Of The True Guru:
The Blessed Vision of the Lord's Darshan is obtained by great good fortune.
Through the Word of the Guru's Shabad, true detachment is obtained.
The six systems of philosophy are pervasive,

Section 08 - Raag Aasaa - Part 015

but the Guru's system is profound and unequalled. |1|

The Guru's system is the way to liberation.
The True Lord Himself comes to dwell in the mind. |1|Pause|

Through the Guru's system, the world is saved,
if it is embraced with love and affection.

How rare is that person who truly loves the Guru's Way.
Through the Guru's system, everlasting peace is obtained. |2|

Through the Guru's system, the Door of Salvation is obtained.
Serving the True Guru, one's family is saved.
There is no salvation for those who have no Guru.
Beguiled by worthless sins, they are struck down. |3|

Through the Word of the Guru's Shabad, the body finds peace and tranquility.
The Gurmukh is not afflicted by pain.
The Messenger of Death does not come near him.
O Nanak, the Gurmukh is absorbed in the True Lord. |4|1|40|

Aasaa, Third Mehl:
One who dies in the Word of the Shabad, eradicates his self-conceit from within.
He serves the True Guru, with no iota of self-interest.
The Fearless Lord, the Great Giver, ever abides in his mind.
The True Bani of the Word is obtained only by good destiny. |1|

So gather merits, and let your demerits depart from within you.
You shall be absorbed into the Shabad, the Word of the Perfect Guru. |1|Pause|

One who purchases merits, knows the value of these merits.
He chants the Ambrosial Nectar of the Word, and the Name of the Lord.
Through the True Bani of the Word, he becomes pure.
Through merit, the Name is obtained. |2|

The invaluable merits cannot be acquired.
The pure mind is absorbed into the True Word of the Shabad.
How very fortunate are those who meditate on the Naam,
and ever enshrine in their minds the Lord, the Giver of merit. |3|

I am a sacrifice to those who gather merits.
At the Gate of Truth, I sing the Glorious Praises of the True One.
He Himself spontaneously bestows His gifts.
O Nanak, the value of the Lord cannot be described. |4|2|41|

Aasaa, Third Mehl:
Great is the greatness of the True Guru;
He merges in His Merger, those who have been separated for so long.
He Himself merges the merged in His Merger.
He Himself knows His own worth. |1|

How can anyone appraise the Lord's worth?
Through the Word of the Guru's Shabad, one may merge with the Infinite,
Unapproachable and Incomprehensible Lord. |1|Pause|

Few are the Gurmukhs who know His worth.
How rare are those who receive the Lord's Grace.
Through the Sublime Bani of His Word, one becomes sublime.
The Gurmukh chants the Word of the Shabad. |2|

Without the Name, the body suffers in pain;
but when one meets the True Guru, then that pain is removed.
Without meeting the Guru, the mortal earns only pain.
The self-willed manmukh receives only more punishment. |3|

The essence of the Lord's Name is so very sweet;
he alone drinks it, whom the Lord causes to drink it.
By Guru's Grace, the essence of the Lord is obtained.
O Nanak, imbued with the Naam, the Name of the Lord, salvation is
attained. |4|3|42|

Aasaa, Third Mehl:
My God is True, deep and profound.
Serving Him, the body acquires peace and tranquility.
Through the Word of the Shabad, His humble servants easily swim across.
I fall at their feet forever and ever. |1|

Section 08 - Raag Aasaa - Part 016

Those being whose minds are imbued and drenched with the Lord's Love
- their pains of birth and death are taken away. They are automatically
ushered into the Court of the Lord. |1|Pause|

One who has tasted the Shabad, obtains the true flavor.
The Name of the Lord abides within his mind.

The Lord God is Eternal and All-pervading.
He Himself is near, and He Himself is far away. |2|

Everyone talks and speaks through speech;
the Lord Himself forgives, and unites us with Himself.
By merely speaking and talking, He is not obtained.
By Guru's Grace, He comes to abide in the mind. |3|

The Gurmukh eradicates his self-conceit from within.
He is imbued with the Lord's Love, having discarded worldly attachment.
He contemplates the utterly Immaculate Word of the Guru's Shabad.
O Nanak, the Naam, the Name of the Lord, is our Salvation. |4|4|43|

Aasaa, Third Mehl:
Attached to the love of duality, one only incurs pain.
Without the Word of the Shabad, one's life is wasted away in vain.
Serving the True Guru, understanding is obtained,
and then, one is not attached to the love of duality. |1|

Those who hold fast to their roots, become acceptable.
Night and day, they meditate within their hearts on the Lord's Name;
through the Word of the Guru's Shabad, they know the One Lord.
|1|Pause|

One who is attached to the branch, does not receive the fruits.
For blind actions, blind punishment is received.
The blind, self-willed manmukh finds no place of rest.
He is a maggot in manure, and in manure he shall rot away. |2|

Serving the Guru, everlasting peace is obtained.
Joining the True Congregation, the Sat Sangat, the Glorious Praises of the Lord are sung.
One who contemplates the Naam, the Name of the Lord,
saves himself, and his family as well. |3|

Through the Word of the Guru's Bani, the Naam resounds;
O Nanak, through the Word of the Shabad, one finds the Mansion of the Lord's Presence within the home of the heart.
Under Guru's Instruction, bathe in the Pool of Truth, in the Water of the Lord;

thus the filth of evil-mindedness and sin shall all be washed away. |4|5|44|

Aasaa, Third Mehl:
The self-willed manmukhs are dying; they are wasting away in death.
In the love of duality, they murder their own souls.
Crying out, "Mine, mine!", they are ruined.
They do not remember their souls; they are asleep in superstition. |1|

He alone dies a real death, who dies in the Word of the Shabad.
The Guru has inspired me to realize, that praise and slander are one and the same; in this world, the profit is obtained by chanting the Name of the Lord. |1|Pause|

Those who lack the Naam, the Name of the Lord, are dissolved within the womb.
Useless is the birth of those who are lured by duality.
Without the Naam, all are burning in pain.
The Perfect True Guru has given me this understanding. |2|

The fickle mind is struck down so many times.
Having lost this opportunity, no place of rest shall be found.
Cast into the womb of reincarnation, the mortal lives in manure;
in such a home, the self-willed manmukh takes up residence. |3|

I am forever a sacrifice to my True Guru;
the light of the Gurmukh blends with the Divine Light of the Lord.
Through the Immaculate Bani of the Word, the mortal dwells within the home of his own inner self.
O Nanak, he conquers his ego, and remains forever detached. |4|6|45|

Aasaa, Third Mehl:
The Lord's slave sets aside his own social status.

Section 08 - Raag Aasaa - Part 017

He dedicates his mind and body to the True Guru, and seeks His Sanctuary.
His greatest greatness is that the Naam, the Name of the Lord, is in his heart.
The Beloved Lord God is his constant companion. |1|

He alone is the Lord's slave, who remains dead while yet alive.
He looks upon pleasure and pain alike; by Guru's Grace, he is saved through the Word of the Shabad. |1|Pause|

He does his deeds according to the Lord's Primal Command.
Without the Shabad, no one is approved.
Singing the Kirtan of the Lord's Praises, the Naam abides within the mind.
He Himself gives His gifts, without hesitation. |2|

The self-willed manmukh wanders around the world in doubt.
Without any capital, he makes false transactions.
Without any capital, he does not obtain any merchandise.
The mistaken manmukh wastes away his life. |3|

One who serves the True Guru is the Lord's slave.
His social status is exalted, and his reputation is exalted.
Climbing the Guru's Ladder, he becomes the most exalted of all.
O Nanak, through the Naam, the Name of the Lord, greatness is obtained. |4|7|46|

Aasaa, Third Mehl:
The self-willed manmukh practices falsehood, only falsehood.
He never attains the Mansion of the Lord Presence.
Attached to duality, he wanders, deluded by doubt.
Entangled in worldly attachments, he comes and goes. |1|

Behold, the decorations of the discarded bride!
Her consciousness is attached to children, spouse, wealth, and Maya, falsehood, emotional attachment, hypocrisy and corruption. |1|Pause|

She who is pleasing to God is forever a happy soul-bride.
She makes the Word of the Guru's Shabad her decoration.
Her bed is so comfortable; she enjoys her Lord, night and day.
Meeting her Beloved, the obtains eternal peace. |2|

She is a true, virtuous soul-bride, who enshrines love for the True Lord.
She keeps her Husband Lord always clasped to her heart.
She sees Him near at hand, ever-present.
My God is all-pervading everywhere. |3|

Social status and beauty will not go with you hereafter.
As are the deeds done here, so does one become.
Through the Word of the Shabad, one becomes the highest of the high.
O Nanak, he is absorbed in the True Lord. |4|8|47|

Aasaa, Third Mehl:
The Lord's humble servant is imbued with devotional love, effortlessly and
spontaneously.
Through awe and fear of the Guru, he is truly absorbed in the True One.
Without the Perfect Guru, devotional love is not obtained.
The self-willed manmukhs lose their honor, and cry out in pain. |1|

O my mind, chant the Lord's Name, and meditate on Him forever.
You shall always be in ecstasy, day and night, and you shall obtain the fruits
of your desires. |1|Pause|

Through the Perfect Guru, the Perfect Lord is obtained,
and the Shabad, the True Name, is enshrined in the mind.
One who bathes in the Pool of Ambrosial Nectar becomes immaculately
pure within.
He becomes forever sanctified, and is absorbed in the True Lord. |2|

He sees the Lord God ever-present.
By Guru's Grace, he sees the Lord permeating and pervading everywhere.
Wherever I go, there I see Him.
Without the Guru, there is no other Giver. |3|

The Guru is the ocean, the perfect treasure,
the most precious jewel and priceless ruby.
By Guru's Grace, the Great Giver blesses us;
O Nanak, the Forgiving Lord forgives us. |4|9|48|

Aasaa, Third Mehl:
The Guru is the Ocean; the True Guru is the Embodiment of Truth.
Through perfect good destiny, one serves the Guru.

Section 08 - Raag Aasaa - Part 018

He alone understands, whom the Lord Himself inspires to understand.

By Guru's Grace, one serves Him. |1|

With the jewel of spiritual wisdom, total understanding is obtained.
By Guru's Grace, ignorance is dispelled; one then remains wakeful, night and day, and beholds the True Lord. |1|Pause|

Through the Word of the Guru's Shabad, attachment and pride are burnt away.
From the Perfect Guru, true understanding is obtained.
Through the Word of the Guru's Shabad, one realizes the Lord's Presence within.
Then, one's coming and going cease, and one becomes stable, absorbed in the Naam, the Name of the Lord. |2|

The world is tied to birth and death.
The unconscious, self-willed manmukh is enveloped in the darkness of Maya and emotional attachment.
He slanders others, and practices utter falsehood.
He is a maggot in manure, and into manure he is absorbed. |3|

Joining the True Congregation, the Sat Sangat, total understanding is obtained.
Through the Word of the Guru's Shabad, devotional love for the Lord is implanted.
One who surrenders to the Lord's Will is peaceful forever.
O Nanak, he is absorbed into the True Lord. |4|10|49|

Aasaa, Third Mehl, Panch-Padas:
One who dies in the Word of the Shabad, finds eternal bliss.
He is united with the True Guru, the Guru, the Lord God.
He does not die any more, and he does not come or go.
Through the Perfect Guru, he merges with the True Lord. |1|

One who has the Naam, the Name of the Lord, written in his pre-ordained destiny,
night and day, meditates forever on the Naam; he obtains the wondrous blessing of devotional love from the Perfect Guru. |1|Pause|

Those, whom the Lord God has blended with Himself
- their sublime state cannot be described.

The Perfect True Guru has given the Glorious Greatness,
of the most exalted order, and I am absorbed into the Lord's Name. |2|

Whatever the Lord does, He does all by Himself.
In an instant, He establishes, and disestablishes.
By merely speaking, talking, shouting and preaching about the Lord, even
hundreds of times, the mortal is not approved. |3|

The Guru meets with those, who take virtue as their treasure;
they listen to the True Word of the Guru's Bani, the Shabad.
Pain departs, from that place where the Shabad abides.
By the jewel of spiritual wisdom, one is easily absorbed into the True Lord.
|4|

No other wealth is as great as the Naam.
It is bestowed only by the True Lord.
Through the Perfect Word of the Shabad, it abides in the mind.
O Nanak, imbued with the Naam, peace is obtained. |5|11|50|

Aasaa, Third Mehl:
One may dance and play numerous instruments;
but this mind is blind and deaf, so for whose benefit is this speaking and
preaching?
Deep within is the fire of greed, and the dust-storm of doubt.
The lamp of knowledge is not burning, and understanding is not obtained.
|1|

The Gurmukh has the light of devotional worship within his heart.
Understanding his own self, he meets God. |1|Pause|

The Gurmukh's dance is to embrace love for the Lord;
to the beat of the drum, he sheds his ego from within.
My God is True; He Himself is the Knower of all.
Through the Word of the Guru's Shabad, recognize the Creator Lord within
yourself. |2|

The Gurmukh is filled with devotional love for the Beloved Lord.
He intuitively reflects upon the Word of the Guru's Shabad.
For the Gurmukh, loving devotional worship is the way to the True Lord.
But the dances and the worship of the hypocrites bring only pain. |3|

Section 08 - Raag Aasaa - Part 019

True Devotion is to remain dead while yet alive.
By Guru's Grace, one crosses over the terrible world-ocean.
Through the Guru's Teachings, one's devotion is accepted,
and then, the Dear Lord Himself comes to dwell in the mind. |4|

When the Lord bestows His Mercy, He leads us to meet the True Guru.
Then, one's devotion becomes steady, and the consciousness is centered upon the Lord.
Those who are imbued with Devotion have truthful reputations.
O Nanak, imbued with the Naam, the Name of the Lord, peace is obtained. |5|12|51|

Aasaa, Eighth House, Kaafee, Third Mehl:
One Universal Creator God. By The Grace Of The True Guru:
By the Pleasure of the Lord's Will, one meets the True Guru, and true understanding is obtained.
By Guru's Grace, the Lord abides in the mind, and one comes to understand the Lord. |1|

My Husband Lord, the Great Giver, is One. There is no other at all.
By Guru's merciful favor, He abides in the mind, and then, a lasting peace ensues. |1|Pause|

In this age, the Lord's Name is fearless; it is obtained by meditative reflection upon the Guru.
Without the Name, the blind, foolish, self-willed manmukh is under Death's power. |2|

By the Pleasure of the Lord's Will, the humble being performs His service, and understands the True Lord.
By the Pleasure of the Lord's Will, He is to be praised; surrendering to His Will, peace ensues. |3|

By the Pleasure of the Lord's Will, the prize of this human birth is obtained, and the intellect is exalted.
O Nanak, praise the Naam, the Name of the Lord; as Gurmukh, you shall be emancipated. |4|39|13|52|

Aasaa, Fourth Mehl, Second House:
One Universal Creator God. By The Grace Of The True Guru:
You are the True Creator, my Lord Master.
That which is pleasing to Your Will, comes to pass. Whatever You give, that is what I receive. |1|Pause|

All are Yours; all meditate on You.
He alone, whom You bless with Your Mercy, obtains the jewel of the Naam.
The Gurmukhs obtain it, and the self-willed manmukhs lose it.
You Yourself separate the mortals, and You Yourself unite them. |1|

You are the River - all are within You.
Other than You, there is no one at all.
All beings and creatures are your play-things.
The united ones are separated, and the separated ones are re-united. |2|

That humble being, whom You inspire to understand, understands;
he continually speaks and chants the Glorious Praises of the Lord.
One who serves the Lord, obtains peace.
He is easily absorbed in the Lord's Name. |3|

You Yourself are the Creator; by Your doing, all things come to be.
Without You, there is no other at all.
You watch over the creation, and understand it.
O servant Nanak, the Lord is revealed to the Gurmukh. |4|1|53|

Section 08 - Raag Aasaa - Part 020

One Universal Creator God. By The Grace Of The True Guru:
Raag Aasaa, Second House, Fourth Mehl:
Some form alliances with friends, children and siblings.
Some form alliances with in-laws and relatives.
Some form alliances with chiefs and leaders for their own selfish motives.
My alliance is with the Lord, who is pervading everywhere. |1|

I have formed my alliance with the Lord; the Lord is my only support.
Other than the Lord, I have no other faction or alliance; I sing of the countless and endless Glorious Praises of the Lord. |1|Pause|

Those with whom you form alliances, shall perish.
Making false alliances, the mortals repent and regret in the end.
Those who practice falsehood shall not last.
I have formed my alliance with the Lord; there is no one more powerful than Him. |2|

All these alliances are mere extensions of the love of Maya.
Only fools argue over Maya.
They are born, and they die, and they lose the game of life in the gamble.
My alliance is with the Lord, who embellishes all, in this world and the next. |3|

In this Dark Age of Kali Yuga, the five thieves instigate alliances and conflicts.
Sexual desire, anger, greed, emotional attachment and self-conceit have increased.
One who is blessed by the Lord's Grace, joins the Sat Sangat, the True Congregation.
My alliance is with the Lord, who has destroyed all these alliances. |4|

In the false love of duality, people sit and form alliances.
They complain about other peoples' faults, while their own self-conceit only increases.
As they plant, so shall they harvest.
Servant Nanak has joined the Lord's alliance of Dharma, which shall conquer the whole world. |5|2|54|

Aasaa, Fourth Mehl:
Constantly listening to the Ambrosial Gurbani in the heart, it becomes pleasing to the mind.
Through Gurbani, the Incomprehensible Lord is comprehended. |1|

As Gurmukh, listen to the Naam, the Name of the Lord, O my sisters.
The One Lord is pervading and permeating deep within the heart; with your mouth, recite the Ambrosial Hymns of the Guru. |1|Pause|

My mind and body are filled with divine love, and great sadness.
By great good fortune, I have obtained the True Guru, the Primal Being. |2|

In the love of duality, the mortals wander through poisonous Maya.

The unfortunate ones do not meet the True Guru. |3|

The Lord Himself inspires us to drink in the Lord's Ambrosial Elixir.
Through the Perfect Guru, O Nanak, the Lord is obtained. |4|3|55|

Aasaa, Fourth Mehl:
The Love of the Naam, the Name of the Lord, is the Support of my mind
and body.
I chant the Naam; the Naam is the essence of peace. |1|

So chant the Naam, O my friends and companions.
Without the Naam, there is nothing else for me. By great good fortune, as
Gurmukh, I have received the Lord's Name. |1|Pause|

Without the Naam, I cannot live.
By great good fortune, the Gurmukhs obtain the Naam. |2|

Those who lack the Naam have their faces rubbed in the dirt of Maya.
Without the Naam, cursed, cursed are their lives. |3|

Section 08 - Raag Aasaa - Part 021

The Great Lord is obtained by great good destiny.
O Nanak, the Gurmukh is blessed with the Naam. |4|4|56|

Aasaa, Fourth Mehl:
I sing His Glorious Praises, and through the Word of His Bani, I speak His
Glorious Praises.
As Gurmukh, I chant and recite the Glorious Praises of the Lord. |1|

Chanting and meditating on the Naam, my mind becomes blissful.
The True Guru has implanted the True Name of the True Lord within me; I
sing His Glorious Praises, and taste the supreme ecstasy. |1|Pause|

The humble servants of the Lord sing the Lord's Glorious Praises.
By great good fortune, the detached, absolute Lord is obtained. |2|

Those without virtue are stained by Maya's filth.
Lacking virtue, the egotistical die, and suffer reincarnation. |3|

The ocean of the body yields pearls of virtue.
O Nanak, the Gurmukh churns this ocean, and discovers this essence. |4|5|57|

Aasaa, Fourth Mehl:
I listen to the Naam, the Name of the Lord; the Naam is pleasing to my mind.
By great good fortune, the Gurmukh obtains the Lord. |1|

Chant the Naam, as Gurmukh, and be exalted.
Without the Naam, I have no other support; the Naam is woven into all my breaths and morsels of food. |1|Pause|

The Naam illuminates my mind; listening to it, my mind is pleased.
One who speaks the Naam - he alone is my friend and companion. |2|

Without the Naam, the fools depart naked.
They burn away to death, chasing the poison of Maya, like the moth chasing the flame. |3|

He Himself establishes, and, having established, disestablishes.
O Nanak, the Lord Himself bestows the Naam. |4|6|58|

Aasaa, Fourth Mehl:
The vine of the Lord's Name, Har, Har, has taken root in the Gurmukh.
It bears the fruit of the Lord; its taste is so tasty! |1|

Chant the Name of the Lord, Har, Har, in endless waves of joy.
Chant and repeat the Naam; through the Guru's Teachings praise the Lord, and slay the horrible serpent of the Messenger of Death. |1|Pause|

The Lord has implanted His devotional worship in the Guru.
When the Guru is pleased, He bestows it upon His Sikh, O my siblings of Destiny. |2|

One who acts in ego, knows nothing about the Way.
He acts like an elephant, who takes a bath, and then throws dust on his head. |3|

If one's destiny is great and exalted,

O Nanak, one chants the Naam, the Name of the Immaculate, True Lord. |4|7|59|

Aasaa, Fourth Mehl:
My mind suffers hunger for the Name of the Lord, Har, Har.
Hearing the Naam, my mind is satisfied, O my Siblings of Destiny. |1|

Chant the Naam, O my friends, O GurSikhs.
Chant the Naam, and through the Naam, obtain peace; through the Guru's Teachings, enshrine the Naam in your heart and mind. |1|Pause|

Hearing the Naam, the Name of the Lord, the mind is in bliss.
Reaping the profit of the Naam, through the Guru's Teachings, my soul has blossomed forth. |2|

Without the Naam, the mortal is a leper, blinded by emotional attachment.
All his actions are fruitless; they lead only to painful entanglements. |3|

The very fortunate ones chant the Praises of the Lord, Har, Har, Har.
O Nanak, through the Guru's Teachings, one embraces love for the Naam. |4|8|60|

Section 08 - Raag Aasaa - Part 022

One Universal Creator God. By The Grace Of The True Guru:
Fourth Mehl, Raag Aasaa, 3 Of Sixth House :
You may pluck the strings with your hand, O Yogi, but your playing of the harp is in vain.
Under Guru's Instruction, chant the Glorious Praises of the Lord, O Yogi, and this mind of yours shall be imbued with the Lord's Love. |1|

O Yogi, give your intellect the Teachings of the Lord.
The Lord, the One Lord, is pervading throughout all the ages; I humbly bow down to Him. |1|Pause|

You sing in so many Ragas and harmonies, and you talk so much, but this mind of yours is only playing a game.
You work the well and irrigate the fields, but the oxen have already left to graze in the jungle. |2|

In the field of the body, plant the Lord's Name, and the Lord will sprout there, like a lush green field.
O mortal, hook up your unstable mind like an ox, and irrigate your fields with the Lord's Name, through the Guru's Teachings. |3|

The Yogis, the wandering Jangams, and all the world is Yours, O Lord. According to the wisdom which You give them, so do they follow their ways.
O Lord God of servant Nanak, O Inner-knower, Searcher of hearts, please link my mind to You. |4|9|61|

Aasaa, Fourth Mehl:
How long must one search for angle bells and cymbals, and how long must one play the guitar?
In the brief instant between coming and going, I meditate on the Naam, the Name of the Lord. |1|

Such is the devotional love which has been produced in my mind.
Without the Lord, I cannot live even for an instant, like the fish which dies without water. |1|Pause|

How long must one tune the five strings, and assemble the seven singers, and how long will they raise their voices in song?

In the time it takes to select and assemble these musicians, a moment elapses, and my mind sings the Glorious Praises of the Lord. |2|

How long must one dance and stretch out one's feet, and how long must one reach out with one's hands?

Stretching out one's hands and feet, there is a moment's delay; and then, my mind meditates on the Lord. |3|

How long must one satisfy the people, in order to obtain honor?
O servant Nanak, meditate forever in your heart on the Lord, and then everyone will congratulate you. |4|10|62|

Aasaa, Fourth Mehl:
Join the Sat Sangat, the Lord's True Congregation; joining the Company of the Holy, sing the Glorious Praises of the Lord.

With the sparkling jewel of spiritual wisdom, the heart is illumined, and ignorance is dispelled. |1|

O humble servant of the Lord, let your dancing be meditation on the Lord, Har, Har.
If only I cold meet such Saints, O my Siblings of Destiny; I would wash the feet of such servants. |1|Pause|

Meditate on the Naam, the Name of the Lord, O my mind; night and day, center your consciousness on the Lord.
You shall have the fruits of your desires, and you shall never feel hunger again. |2|

The Infinite Lord Himself is the Creator; the Lord Himself speaks, and causes us to speak.
The Saints are good, who are pleasing to Your Will; their honor is approved by You. |3|

Nanak is not satisfied by chanting the Lord's Glorious Praises; the more he chants them, the more he is at peace.
The Lord Himself has bestowed the treasure of devotional love; His customers purchase virtues, and carry them home. |4|11|63|

Section 08 - Raag Aasaa - Part 023

One Universal Creator God. By The Grace Of The True Guru:
Raag Aasaa, Eighth House, Kaafee, Fourth Mehl:
Death is ordained from the very beginning, and yet ego makes us cry.
Meditating on the Naam, as Gurmukh, one becomes stable and steady. |1|

Blessed is the Perfect Guru, through whom the way of Death is known.
The sublime people earn the profit of the Naam, the Name of the Lord; they are absorbed in the Word of the Shabad. |1|Pause|

The days of one's life are pre-ordained; they will come to their end, O mother.
One must depart, today or tomorrow, according to the Lord's Primal Order. |2|

Useless are the lives of those, who have forgotten the Naam.

They play the game of chance in this world, and lose their mind. |3|

Those who have found the Guru are at peace, in life and in death.
O Nanak, the true ones are truly absorbed into the True Lord. |4|12|64|

Aasaa, Fourth Mehl:
Having obtained the treasure of this human birth, I meditate on the Naam,
the Name of the Lord.
By Guru's Grace, I understand, and I am absorbed into the True Lord. |1|

Those who have such pre-ordained destiny practice the Naam.
The True Lord summons the truthful to the Mansion of His Presence.
|1|Pause|

Deep within is the treasure of the Naam; it is obtained by the Gurmukh.
Night and day, meditate on the Naam, and sing the Glorious Praises of the
Lord. |2|

Deep within are infinite substances, but the self-willed manmukh does not
find them.
In egotism and pride, the mortal's proud self consumes him. |3|

O Nanak, his identity consumes his identical identity.
Through the Guru's Teachings, the mind is illumined, and meets the True
Lord. |4|13|65|

Raag Aasaavaree, 2 Of Sixteenth House, Fourth Mehl, Sudhang:
One Universal Creator God. By The Grace Of The True Guru:
Night and day, I sing the Kirtan, the Praises of the Name of the Lord.
The True Guru has revealed to me the Name of the Lord; without the Lord,
I cannot live, for a moment, even an instant. |1|Pause|

My ears hear the Lord's Kirtan, and I contemplate Him; without the Lord, I
cannot live, even for an instant.
As the swan cannot live without the lake, how can the Lord's slave live
without serving Him? |1|

Some enshrine love for duality in their hearts, and some pledge love for
worldly attachments and ego.

The Lord's servant embraces love for the Lord and the state of Nirvaanaa; Nanak contemplates the Lord, the Lord God. |2|14|66|

Aasaavaree, Fourth Mehl:
O mother, my mother, tell me about my Beloved Lord.
Without the Lord, I cannot live for a moment, even an instant; I love Him, like the camel loves the vine. |1|Pause|

My mind has become sad and distant, longing for the Blessed Vision of the Lord's Darshan, my Friend.
As the bumblebee cannot live without the lotus, I cannot live without the Lord. |1|

Section 08 - Raag Aasaa - Part 024

Keep me under Your Protection, O Beloved Master of the Universe; fulfill my faith, O Lord of the World.
Servant Nanak's mind is filled with bliss, when he beholds the Blessed Vision of the Lord's Darshan, even for an instant. |2|39|13|15|67|

Raag Aasaa, Second House, Fifth Mehl:
One Universal Creator God. By The Grace Of The True Guru:
One who loves her, is ultimately devoured.
One who seats her in comfort, is totally terrified by her.
Siblings, friends and family, beholding her, argue.
But she has come under my control, by Guru's Grace. |1|

Beholding her, all are bewitched:
the strivers, the Siddhas, the demi-gods, angels and mortals. All, except the Saadhus, are deceived by her deception. |1|Pause|

Some wander around as renunciates, but they are engrossed in sexual desire.
Some grow rich as householders, but she does not belong to them.
Some call themselves men of charity, and she torments them terribly.
The Lord has saved me, by attaching me to the Feet of the True Guru. |2|

She leads astray the penitents who practice penance.
The scholarly Pandits are all seduced by greed.
The world of the three qualities is enticed, and the heavens are enticed.

The True Guru has saved me, by giving me His Hand. |3|

She is the slave of those who are spiritually wise.
With her palms pressed together, she serves them and offers her prayer:
"Whatever you wish, that is what I shall do."
O servant Nanak, she does not draw near to the Gurmukh. |4|1|

Aasaa, Fifth Mehl:
I have been separated from my Beloved by Maya (my mother-in-law).
Hope and desire (my younger brother-in-law and sister-in-law) are dying of grief.
I am no longer swayed by the fear of Death (my elder brother-in-law).
I am protected by my All-knowing, Wise Husband Lord. |1|

Listen, O people: I have tasted the elixir of love.
The evil ones are dead, and my enemies are destroyed. The True Guru has given me the Name of the Lord. |1|Pause|

First, I renounced my egotistical love of myself.
Second, I renounced the ways of the world.
Renouncing the three qualities, I look alike upon friend and enemy.
And then, the fourth state of bliss was revealed to me by the Holy One. |2|

In the cave of celestial bliss, I have obtained a seat.
The Lord of Light plays the unstruck melody of bliss.
I am in ecstasy, contemplating the Word of the Guru's Shabad.
Imbued with my Beloved Husband Lord, I am the blessed, happy soul-bride.
|3|

Servant Nanak chants the wisdom of God;
one who listens and practices it, is carried across and saved.
He is not born, and he does not die; he does not come or go.
He remains blended with the Lord. |4|2|

Aasaa, Fifth Mehl:
The bride shows such special devotion, and has such an agreeable disposition.
Her beauty is incomparable, and her character is perfect.
The house in which she dwells is such a praiseworthy house.
But rare are those who, as Gurmukh, attain that state|1|

As the soul-bride of pure actions, I have met with the Guru.

Section 08 - Raag Aasaa - Part 025

In worship, marriage and in the next world, such a soul-bride looks beautiful. |1|Pause|

As long as she lived with her father,
her Husband wandered around in sadness.
I served and surrendered to the Lord, the True Being;
the Guru brought my bride to my home, and I obtained total happiness. |2|

She is blessed with all sublime attributes, and her generations are unblemished.
Her Husband, her Lord and Master, fulfills her heart's desires.
Hope and desire (my younger brother-in-law and sister-in-law) are now totally content. |3|

She is the most noble of all the family.
She counsels and advises her hope and desire.
How blessed is that household, in which she has appeared.
O servant Nanak, she passes her time in perfect peace and comfort. |4|3|

Aasaa, Fifth Mehl:
Whatever I resolve, she does not allow it to come to pass.
She stands blocking the way of goodness and self-discipline.
She wears many disguises, and assumes many forms,
and she does not allow me to dwell in my own home. She forces me to wander around in different directions. |1|

She has become the mistress of my home, and she does not allow me to live in it.
If I try, she fights with me. |1|Pause|

In the beginning, she was sent as a helper,
but she has overwhelmed the nine continents, all places and interspaces.
She has not spared even the river banks, the sacred shrines of pilgrimage,
the Yogis and Sannyaasees,

or those who tirelessly read the Simritees and study the Vedas. |2|

Wherever I sit, she sits there with me.
She has imposed her power upon the whole world.
Seeking meager protection, I am not protected from her.
Tell me, O my friend: unto whom should I turn for protection? |3|

I heard of His Teachings, and so I have come to the True Guru.
The Guru has implanted the Mantra of the Lord's Name, Har, Har, within me.
And now, I dwell in the home of my own inner self; I sing the Glorious Praises of the Infinite Lord.
I have met God, O Nanak, and I have become care-free. |4|

My home is now my own, and she is now my mistress.
She is now my servant, and the Guru has made me intimate with the Lord. |1|Second Pause|4|4|

Aasaa, Fifth Mehl:
First, they advised me to send a letter.
Second, they advised me to send two men.
Third, they advised me to make the effort and do something.
But I have renounced everything, and I meditate only on You, God. |1|

Now, I am totally blissful, carefree and at ease.
The enemies and evil-doers have perished, and I have obtained peace. |1|Pause|

The True Guru has imparted the Teachings to me.
My soul, body and everything belong to the Lord.
Whatever I do, is by Your Almighty Power.
You are my only Support, You are my only Court. |2|

If I were to renounce You, God, unto whom could I turn?
There is no other, comparable to You.
Who else is Your servant to serve?
The faithless cynics are deluded; they wander around in the wilderness. |3|

Your Glorious Greatness cannot be described.
Wherever I am, you save me, hugging me close in Your embrace.

Nanak, Your slave, has entered Your Sanctuary.
God has preserved his honor, and congratulations are pouring in. |4|5|

Section 08 - Raag Aasaa - Part 026

Aasaa, Fifth Mehl:
Having wandered through foreign lands, I have come here to do business.
I heard of the incomparable and profitable merchandise.
I have gathered in my pockets my capital of virtue, and I have brought it here with me.
Beholding the jewel, this mind is fascinated. |1|

I have come to the door of the Trader.
Please display the merchandise, so that the business may be transacted. |1|Pause|

The Trader has sent me to the Banker.
The jewel is priceless, and the capital is priceless.
O my gentle brother, mediator and friend
- I have obtained the merchandise, and my consciousness is now steady and stable. |2|

I have no fear of thieves, of wind or water.
I have easily made my purchase, and I easily take it away.
I have earned Truth, and I shall have no pain.
I have brought this merchandise home, safe and sound. |3|

I have earned the profit, and I am happy.
Blessed is the Banker, the Perfect Bestower.
How rare is the Gurmukh who obtains this merchandise;
Nanak has brought this profitable merchandise home. |4|6|

Aasaa, Fifth Mehl:
He does not consider my merits or demerits.
He does not look at my beauty, color or decorations.
I do not know the ways of wisdom and good conduct.
But taking me by the arm, my Husband Lord has led me to His Bed. |1|

Hear, O my companions, my Husband, my Lord Master, possesses me.

Placing His Hand upon my forehead, He protects me as His Own. What do
these ignorant people know? |1|Pause|

My married life now appears so beauteous;
my Husband Lord has met me, and He sees all my pains.
Within the courtyard of my heart, the glory of the moon shines.
Night and day, I have fun with my Beloved. |2|

My clothes are dyed the deep crimson color of the poppy.
All the ornaments and garlands around my neck adorn me.
Gazing upon my Beloved with my eyes, I have obtained all treasures;
I have shaken off the power of the evil demons. |3|

I have obtained eternal bliss, and I constantly celebrate.
With the nine treasures of the Naam, the Name of the Lord, I am satisfied
in my own home.
Says Nanak, when the happy soul-bride is adorned by her Beloved,
she is forever happy with her Husband Lord. |4|7|

Aasaa, Fifth Mehl:
They give you donations and worship you.
You take from them, and then deny that they have given anything to you.
That door, through which you must ultimately go, O Brahmin
- at that door, you will come to regret and repent. |1|

Such Brahmins shall drown, O Siblings of Destiny;
they think of doing evil to the innocent. |1|Pause|

Within them is greed, and they wander around like mad dogs.
They slander others and carry loads of sin upon their heads.
Intoxicated by Maya, they do not think of the Lord.
Deluded by doubt, they wander off on many paths. |2|

Outwardly, they wear various religious robes,
but within, they are enveloped by poison.
They instruct others, but do not understand themselves.
Such Brahmins will never be emancipated. |3|

O foolish Brahmin, reflect upon God.
He watches and hears, and is always with you.

Says Nanak, if this is your destiny,
renounce your pride, and grasp the Guru's Feet. |4|8|

Aasaa, Fifth Mehl:

Section 08 - Raag Aasaa - Part 027

Pain and disease have left my body, and my mind has become pure; I sing
the Glorious Praises of the Lord, Har, Har.
I am in bliss, meeting with the Saadh Sangat, the Company of the Holy, and
now, my mind does not go wandering. |1|

My burning desires are quenched, through the Word of the Guru's Shabad,
O mother.
The fever of doubt has been totally eliminated; meeting the Guru, I am
cooled and soothed, with intuitive ease. |1|Pause|

My wandering has ended, since I have realized the One and Only Lord;
now, I have come to dwell in the eternal place.
Your Saints are the Saving Grace of the world; beholding the Blessed Vision
of their Darshan, I remain satisfied. |2|

I have left behind the sins of countless incarnations, now that I have
grasped the feet of the eternal Holy Guru.
My mind sings the celestial melody of bliss,
and death shall no longer consume it. |3|

My Lord, the Cause of all causes, is All-powerful, the Giver of peace; He is
my Lord, my Lord King.
Nanak lives by chanting Your Name, O Lord; You are my helper, with me,
through and through. |4|9|

Aasaa, Fifth Mehl:
The slanderer cries out and bewails.
He has forgotten the Supreme Lord, the Transcendent Lord; the slanderer
reaps the rewards of his own actions. |1|Pause|

If someone is his companion, then he shall be taken along with him.
Like the dragon, the slanderer carries his huge, useless loads, and burns in
his own fire. |1|

Nanak proclaims and announces what happens at the Door of the Transcendent Lord.

The humble devotees of the Lord are forever in bliss; singing the Kirtan of the Lord's Praises, they blossom forth. |2|10|

Aasaa, Fifth Mehl:
Even though I totally decorated myself,
still, my mind was not satisfied.
I applied various scented oils to my body,
and yet, I did not obtain even a tiny bit of pleasure from this.
Within my mind, I hold such a desire,
that I may live only to behold my Beloved, O my mother. |1|

O mother, what should I do? This mind cannot rest.
It is bewitched by the tender love of my Beloved. |1|Pause|

Garments, ornaments, and such exquisite pleasures
- I look upon these as of no account.
Likewise, honor, fame, dignity and greatness,
obedience by the whole world,
and a household as beautiful as a jewel.
If I am pleasing to God's Will, then I shall be blessed, and forever in bliss.
|2|

With foods and delicacies of so many different kinds,
and such abundant pleasures and entertainments,
power and property and absolute command
- with these, the mind is not satisfied, and its thirst is not quenched.
Without meeting Him, this day does not pass.
Meeting God, I find peace. |3|

By searching and seeking, I have heard this news,
that without the Saadh Sangat, the Company of the Holy, no one swims across.
One who has this good destiny written upon his forehead, finds the True Guru.
His hopes are fulfilled, and his mind is satisfied.
When one meets God, then his thirst is quenched.
Nanak has found the Lord, within his mind and body. |4|11|

Aasaa, Fifth Mehl, Panch-Padas:

Section 08 - Raag Aasaa - Part 028

First, your social status is high.
Second, you are honored in society.
Third, your home is beautiful.
But you are so ugly, with self-conceit in your mind. |1|

O beautiful, attractive, wise and clever woman:
you have been trapped by your pride and attachment. |1|Pause|

Your kitchen is so clean.
You take your bath, and worship, and apply the crimson mark upon your forehead;
with your mouth you speak wisdom, but you are destroyed by pride.
The dog of greed has ruined you in every way. |2|

You wear your robes and enjoy pleasures;
you practice good conduct to impress people;
you apply scented oils of sandalwood and musk,
but your constant companion is the demon of anger. |3|

Other people may be your water-carriers;
in this world, you may be a ruler.
Gold, silver and wealth may be yours,
but the goodness of your conduct has been destroyed by sexual promiscui-ty. |4|

That soul, upon whom the Lord has bestowed His Glance of Grace,
is delivered from bondage.
Joining the Saadh Sangat, the Company of the Holy, the Lord's sublime essence is obtained.
Says Nanak, how fruitful is that body. |5|

All graces and all comforts shall come to you, as the happy soul-bride;
you shall be supremely beautiful and wise. |1|Second Pause|12|

Aasaa, Fifth Mehl, Ik-Tukas 2 :

One who is seen to be alive, shall surely die.
But he who is dead shall remain ever-lasting. |1|

Those who die while yet alive, shall through this death, live on.
They place the Name of the Lord, Har, Har, as medicine in their mouths,
and through the Word of the Guru's Shabad, they drink in the Ambrosial
Nectar. |1|Pause|

The clay pot of the body shall be broken.
One who has eliminated the three qualities dwells in the home of his inner
self. |2|

One who climbs high, shall fall into the nether regions of the underworld.
One who lies upon the ground, shall not be touched by death. |3|

Those who continue to wander around, achieve nothing.
Those who practice the Guru's Teachings, become steady and stable. |4|

This body and soul all belong to the Lord.
O Nanak, meeting the Guru, I am enraptured. |5|13|

Aasaa, Fifth Mehl:
The puppet of the body has been fashioned with great skill.
Know for sure that it shall turn to dust. |1|

Remember your origins, O thoughtless fool.
Why are you so proud of yourself? |1|Pause|

You are a guest, given three meals a day;
other things are entrusted to you. |2|

you are just excrement, bones and blood, wrapped up in skin
- this is what you are taking such pride in! |3|

If you could understand even one thing, then you would be pure.
Without understanding, you shall be forever impure. |4|

Says Nanak, I am a sacrifice to the Guru;
through Him, I obtain the Lord, the All-knowing Primal Being. |5|14|

Aasaa, Fifth Mehl, Ik-Tukas, Chau-Padas:
One moment, one day, is for me many days.
My mind cannot survive - how can I meet my Beloved? |1|

I cannot endure one day, even one instant without Him.

Section 08 - Raag Aasaa - Part 029

My mind's desire for the Blessed Vision of His Darshan is so great. Is there any Saint who can lead me to meet my Beloved? |1|Pause|

The four watches of the day are like the four ages.
And when night comes, I think that it shall never end. |2|

The five demons have joined together, to separate me from my Husband Lord.
Wandering and rambling, I cry out and wring my hands. |3|

The Lord has revealed the Blessed Vision of His Darshan to servant Nanak; realizing his own self, he has obtained supreme peace. |4|15|

Aasaa, Fifth Mehl:
In the Lord's service, are the greatest treasures.
Serving the Lord, the Ambrosial Naam comes into one's mouth. |1|

The Lord is my Companion; He is with me, as my Help and Support.
In pain and pleasure, whenever I remember Him, He is present. How can the poor Messenger of Death frighten me now? |1|Pause|

The Lord is my Support; the Lord is my Power.
The Lord is my Friend; He is my mind's advisor. |2|

The Lord is my capital; the Lord is my credit.
As Gurmukh, I earn the wealth, with the Lord as my Banker. |3|

By Guru's Grace, this wisdom has come.
Servant Nanak has merged into the Being of the Lord. |4|16|

Aasaa, Fifth Mehl:
When God shows His Mercy, then this mind is focused on Him.

Serving the True Guru, all rewards are obtained. |1|

O my mind, why are you so sad? My True Guru is Perfect.
He is the Giver of blessings, the treasure of all comforts; His Ambrosial Pool of Nectar is always overflowing. |1|Pause|

One who enshrines His Lotus Feet within the heart,
meets the Beloved Lord; the Divine Light is revealed to him. |2|

The five companions have met together to sing the songs of joy.
The unstruck melody, the sound current of the Naad, vibrates and resounds. |3|

O Nanak, when the Guru is totally pleased, one meets the Lord, the King.
Then, the night of one's life passes in peace and natural ease. |4|17|

Aasaa, Fifth Mehl:
Showing His Mercy, the Lord has revealed Himself to me.
Meeting the True Guru, I have received the perfect wealth. |1|

Gather such a wealth of the Lord, O Siblings of Destiny.
It cannot be burned by fire, and water cannot drown it; it does not forsake society, or go anywhere else. |1|Pause|

It does not run short, and it does not run out.
Eating and consuming it, the mind remains satisfied. |2|

He is the true banker, who gathers the wealth of the Lord within his own home.
With this wealth, the whole world profits. |3|

He alone receives the Lord's wealth, who is pre-ordained to receive it.
O servant Nanak, at that very last moment, the Naam shall be your only decoration. |4|18|

Aasaa, Fifth Mehl:
Just like the farmer, He plants His crop,
and, whether it is ripe or unripe, He cuts it down. |1|

Just so, you must know this well, that whoever is born, shall die.

Only the devotee of the Lord of the Universe becomes stable and permanent. |1|Pause|

The day shall certainly be followed by the night.
And when the night passes, the morning shall again dawn. |2|

In the love of Maya, the unfortunate ones remain in sleep.
By Guru's Grace, a rare few remain awake and aware. |3|

Section 08 - Raag Aasaa - Part 030

Says Nanak, sing continually the Glorious Praises of the Lord.
Your face shall be radiant, and your consciousness shall be immaculately pure. |4|19|

Aasaa, Fifth Mehl:
The nine treasures are Yours - all treasures are Yours.
The Fulfiller of desires saves mortals in the end. |1|

You are my Beloved, so what hunger can I have?
When You dwell within my mind, pain does not touch me. |1|Pause|

Whatever You do, is acceptable to me.
O True Lord and Master, True is Your Order. |2|

When it is pleasing to Your Will, I sing the Glorious Praises of the Lord.
Within Your Home, there is justice, forever and ever. |3|

O True Lord and Master, You are unknowable and mysterious.
Nanak is committed to Your service. |4|20|

Aasaa, Fifth Mehl:
He is near at hand; He is the eternal Companion of the soul.
His Creative Power is all-pervading, in form and color. |1|

My mind does not worry; it does not grieve, or cry out.
Imperishable, Unshakable, Unapproachable and forever safe and sound is my Husband Lord. |1|Pause|

Unto whom does Your servant pay homage?

His King preserves his honor. |2|

That slave, whom God has released from the restrictions of social status
- who can now hold him in bondage? |3|

The Lord is absolutely independent, and totally care-free;
O servant Nanak, chant His Glorious Praises. |4|21|

Aasaa, Fifth Mehl:
Forsaking the Lord's sublime essence, the mortal is intoxicated with false
essences.
The substance is within the home of the self, but the mortal goes out to
find it. |1|

He cannot hear the true ambrosial discourse.
Attached to false scriptures, he is engaged in argument. |1|Pause|

He takes his wages from his Lord and Master, but he serves another.
With such sins, the mortal is engrossed. |2|

He tries to hide from the One who is always with him.
He begs from Him, again and again. |3|

Says Nanak, God is merciful to the meek.
As it pleases Him, He cherishes us. |4|22|

Aasaa, Fifth Mehl:
The Naam, the Name of the Lord, is my soul, my life, my wealth.
Here and hereafter, it is with me, to help me. |1|

Without the Lord's Name, everything else is useless.
My mind is satisfied and satiated by the Blessed Vision of the Lord's
Darshan. |1|Pause|

Gurbani is the jewel, the treasure of devotion.
Singing, hearing and acting upon it, one is enraptured. |2|

My mind is attached to the Lord's Lotus Feet.
The True Guru, in His Pleasure, has given this gift. |3|

Unto Nanak, the Guru has revealed these instructions:
recognize the Imperishable Lord God in each and every heart. |4|23|

Aasaa, Fifth Mehl:
The All-pervading Lord has established joys and celebrations.
He Himself embellishes His own works. |1|

Perfect is the Creation of the Perfect Lord Master.
His magnificent greatness is totally all-pervading. |1|Pause|

His Name is the treasure; His reputation is immaculate.
He Himself is the Creator; there is no other. |2|

All beings and creatures are in His Hands.
God is pervading in all, and is always with them. |3|

Section 08 - Raag Aasaa - Part 031

The Perfect Guru has fashioned His perfect fashion.
O Nanak, the Lord's devotees are blessed with glorious greatness. |4|24|

Aasaa, Fifth Mehl:
I have shaped this mind in the mold of the Guru's Word.
Beholding the Blessed Vision of the Guru's Darshan, I have gathered the
wealth of the Lord. |1|

O sublime understanding, come, enter into my mind,
that I may meditate and sing the Glorious Praises of the Lord of the
Universe, and love so dearly the Lord's Name. |1|Pause|

I am satisfied and satiated by the True Name.
My cleansing bath at the sixty-eight sacred shrines of pilgrimage is the dust
of the Saints. |2|

I recognize that the One Creator is contained in all.
Joining the Saadh Sangat, the Company of the Holy, my understanding is
refined. |3|

I have become the servant of all; I have renounced my ego and pride.
The Guru has given this gift to Nanak. |4|25|

Aasaa, Fifth Mehl:
My intellect has been enlightened, and my understanding is perfect.
Thus my evil-mindedness, which kept me far from Him, has been removed.
|1|

Such are the Teachings which I have received from the Guru;
while I was drowning in the pitch black well, I was saved, O my Siblings of
Destiny. |1|Pause|

The Guru is the boat to cross over the totally unfathomable ocean of fire;
He is treasure of jewels. |2|

This ocean of Maya is dark and treacherous.
The Perfect Guru has revealed the way to cross over it. |3|

I do not have the ability to chant or practice intense meditation.
Guru Nanak seeks Your Sanctuary. |4|26|

Aasaa, Fifth Mehl, Ti-Padas:
One who drinks in the Lord's sublime essence is forever imbued with it,
while other essences wear off in an instant.
Intoxicated with the Lord's sublime essence, the mind is forever in ecstasy.
Other essences bring only anxiety. |1|

One who drinks in the Lord's sublime essence, is intoxicated and enraptured;
all other essences have no effect. |1|Pause|

The value of the Lord's sublime essence cannot be described.
The Lord's sublime essence permeates the homes of the Holy.
One may spend thousands and millions, but it cannot be purchased.
He alone obtains it, who is so pre-ordained. |2|

Tasting it, Nanak is wonder-struck.
Through the Guru, Nanak has obtained this taste.
Here and hereafter, it does not leave him.
Nanak is imbued and enraptured with the Lord's subtle essence. |3|27|

Aasaa, Fifth Mehl:

If she renounces and eliminates her sexual desire, anger, greed and attachment, and her evil-mindedness and self-conceit as well;

and if, becoming humble, she serves Him, then she becomes dear to her Beloved's Heart. |1|

Listen, O beautiful soul-bride: By the Word of the Holy Saint, you shall be saved.
Your pain, hunger and doubt shall vanish, and you shall obtain peace, O happy soul-bride. |1|Pause|

Washing the Guru's feet, and serving Him, the soul is sanctified, and the thirst for sin is quenched.
If you become the slave of the slave of the Lord's slaves, then you shall obtain honor in the Court of the Lord. |2|

This is right conduct, and this is the correct lifestyle, to obey the Command of the Lord's Will; this is your devotional worship.
One who practices this Mantra, O Nanak, swims across the terrifying world-ocean. |3|28|

Section 08 - Raag Aasaa - Part 032

Aasaa, Fifth Mehl, Du-Padas:
You have been blessed with this human body.
This is your chance to meet the Lord of the Universe.
Other efforts are of no use to you.
Joining the Saadh Sangat, the Company of the Holy, vibrate and meditate on the Naam, the Name of the Lord. |1|

Make the effort, and cross over the terrifying world ocean.
This human life is passing away in vain, in the love of Maya. |1|Pause|

I have not practiced meditation, penance, self-restraint or righteous living;
I have not served the Holy Saints, and I do not know the Lord, my King.
Says Nanak, my actions are vile and despicable;
O Lord, I seek Your Sanctuary - please, preserve my honor. |2|29|

Aasaa, Fifth Mehl:
Without You, there is no other for me; You alone are in my mind.

You are my Friend and Companion, God; why should my soul be afraid? |1|

You are my support, You are my hope.
While sitting down or standing up, while sleeping or waking, with every breath and morsel of food, I never forget You. |1|Pause|

Protect me, please protect me, O God; I have come to Your Sanctuary; the ocean of fire is so horrible.
The True Guru is the Giver of peace to Nanak; I am Your child, O Lord of the World. |2|30|

Aasaa, Fifth Mehl:
The Lord God has saved me, His slave.
My mind has surrendered to my Beloved; my fever has taken poison and died. |1|Pause|

Cold and heat do not touch me at all, when I sing the Glorious Praises of the Lord.
My consciousness is not affected by the witch, Maya; I take to the Sanctuary of the Lord's Lotus Feet. |1|

By the Grace of the Saints, the Lord has shown His Mercy to me; He Himself is my Help and Support.
Nanak ever sings the Praises of the Lord, the treasure of excellence; his doubts and pains are eliminated. |2|31|

Aasaa, Fifth Mehl:
I have taken the medicine of the Name of the Lord.
I have found peace, and the seat of pain has been removed. |1|

The fever has been broken, by the Teachings of the Perfect Guru.
I am in ecstasy, and all of my sorrows have been dispelled. |1|Pause|

All beings and creatures obtain peace,
O Nanak, meditating on the Supreme Lord God. |2|32|

Aasaa, Fifth Mehl:
That time, which the mortal does not wish for, eventually comes.
Without the Lord's Command, how can understanding be understood? |1|

The body is consumed by water, fire and earth.
But the soul is neither young nor old, O Siblings of Destiny. |1|Pause|

Servant Nanak has entered the Sanctuary of the Holy.
By Guru's Grace, he has shaken off the fear of death. |2|33|

Aasaa, Fifth Mehl:
Forever and ever, the soul is illumined;
in the Saadh Sangat, the Company of the Holy, it dwells at the Feet of the Lord. |1|

Chant the Lord's Name each and every day, O my mind.
You shall find lasting peace, contentment and tranquility, and all your sins shall depart. |1|Pause|

Says Nanak, one who is blessed with perfect good karma,
meets the True Guru, and obtains the Perfect Supreme Lord God. |2|34|

Thirty-four Shabads in Second House. |

Aasaa, Fifth Mehl:
She who has the Lord God as her Friend

Section 08 - Raag Aasaa - Part 033

her pain is dispelled, and she shall not become sad again. |1|Pause|

Showing His Mercy, He joins her with His Feet,
and she attains celestial peace, joy and comfort. |1|

In the Saadh Sangat, the Company of the Holy, she sings the Glorious Praises of the Immeasurable Lord.
Remembering the Lord in meditation, O Nanak, she becomes invaluable. |2|35|

Aasaa, Fifth Mehl:
Sexual desire, anger, intoxication with Maya and jealousy - I have lost all of these in the game of chance.
Purity, contentment, compassion, faith and truthfulness - I have ushered these into the home of my self. |1|

All the loads of birth and death have been removed.
Joining the Saints' Society, my mind has become pure; the Perfect Guru has saved me in an instant. |1|Pause|

My mind has become the dust of all, and everyone seems a sweet friend to me.
My Lord and Master is contained in all. He gives His Gifts to all beings, and cherishes them. |2|

He Himself is the One and only; from the One, the One and only, came the expanse of the entire creation.
Chanting and meditating, all the humble beings have become Holy; meditating on the Naam, the Name of the Lord, so many have been saved. |3|

The Lord of the Universe is deep, profound and infinite; He has no end or limitation.
By Your Grace, Nanak sings Your Glorious Praises; meditating, meditating, he humbly bows to God. |4|36|

Aasaa, Fifth Mehl:
You are Infinite, Eternal and Incomprehensible; all this is Your Creation.
What clever games can we play, when everything is contained in You? |1|

O my True Guru, protect me, Your child, through the power of Your play.
Grant me the good sense to ever sing Your Glorious Praises, O my Inaccessible and Infinite Lord and Master. |1|Pause|

The mortal is preserved in the womb of his mother, by the Support of the Naam, the Name of the Lord;
he makes merry, and with each and every breath he remembers the Lord, and the fire does not touch him. |2|

Others' wealth, others' wives, and the slander of others - renounce your craving for these.
Serve the Lord's Lotus Feet within your heart, and hold to the Support of the Perfect Guru. |3|

Houses, mansions and palaces which you see - none of these shall go with you.

As long as you live in this Dark Age of Kali Yuga, O servant Nanak, remember the Naam, the Name of the Lord. |4|37|

Aasaa, Third House, Fifth Mehl:

One Universal Creator God. By The Grace Of The True Guru:

Power, property, youth, household, fame and the beauty of youth;

great wealth, elephants, horses and jewels, purchased with tens of thousands of dollars;

hereafter, these shall be of no avail in the Court of the Lord; the proud must depart, leaving them behind. |1|

Why center your consciousness on any other than the Lord?

Sitting down, standing up, sleeping and waking, forever and ever, meditate on the Lord. |1|Pause|

He may have the most wondrous and beautiful arenas, and be victorious on the field of battle.

Section 08 - Raag Aasaa - Part 034

He may proclaim, "I can kill anyone, I can capture anyone, and I can release anyone."

But when the Order comes from the Supreme Lord God, he departs and leaves in a day. |2|

He may perform all sorts of religious rituals and good actions, but he does not know the Creator Lord, the Doer of all.

He teaches, but does not practice what he preaches; he does not realize the essential reality of the Word of the Shabad.

Naked he came, and naked he shall depart; he is like an elephant, throwing dust on himself. |3|

O Saints, and friends, listen to me: all this world is false.

Continually claiming, "Mine, mine", the mortals are drowned; the fools waste away and die.

Meeting the Guru, O Nanak, I meditate on the Naam, the Name of the Lord; through the True Name, I am emancipated. |4|1|38|

Raag Aasaa, Fifth House, Fifth Mehl:
One Universal Creator God. By The Grace Of The True Guru:
The whole world is asleep in doubt; it is blinded by worldly entanglements.
How rare is that humble servant of the Lord who is awake and aware. |1|

The mortal is intoxicated with the great enticement of Maya, which is
dearer to him than life.
How rare is the one who renounces it. |2|

The Lord's Lotus Feet are incomparably beautiful; so is the Mantra of the
Saint.
How rare is that holy person who is attached to them. |3|

O Nanak, in the Saadh Sangat, the Company of the Holy, the love of divine
knowledge is awakened;
the Lord's Mercy is bestowed upon those who are blessed with such good
destiny. |4|1|39|

One Universal Creator God. By The Grace Of The True Guru:
Raag Aasaa, Sixth House, Fifth Mehl:
Whatever pleases You is acceptable to me; that alone brings peace and
ease to my mind.
You are the Doer, the Cause of causes, All-powerful and Infinite; there is
none other than You. |1|

Your humble servants sing Your Glorious Praises with enthusiasm and love.
That alone is good advice, wisdom and cleverness for Your humble servant,
which You do or cause to be done. |1|Pause|

Your Name is Ambrosial Nectar, O Beloved Lord; in the Saadh Sangat, the
Company of the Holy, I have obtained its sublime essence.
Those humble beings are satisfied and fulfilled, singing the Praises of the
Lord, the treasure of peace. |2|

One who has Your Support, O Lord Master, is not afflicted by anxiety.
One who is blessed by Your Kind Mercy, is the best, the most fortunate
king. |3|

Doubt, attachment, and deceit have all disappeared, since I obtained the
Blessed Vision of Your Darshan.

Dealing in the Naam, O Nanak, we become truthful, and in the Love of the Lord's Name, we are absorbed. |4|1 | 40|

Aasaa, Fifth Mehl:
He washes off the filth of other peoples' incarnations, but he obtains the rewards of his own actions.
He has no peace in this world, and he has no place in the Court of the Lord. In the City of Death, he is tortured. |1|

The slanderer loses his life in vain.
He cannot succeed in anything, and in the world hereafter, he finds no place at all. |1|Pause|

Such is the fate of the wretched slanderer - what can the poor creature do?
He is ruined there, where no one can protect him; with whom should he lodge his complaint? |2|

Section 08 - Raag Aasaa - Part 035

The slanderer shall never attain emancipation; this is the Will of the Lord and Master.
The more the Saints are slandered, the more they dwell in peace. |3|

The Saints have Your Support, O Lord and Master; You are the Saints' Help and Support.
Says Nanak, the Saints are saved by the Lord; the slanderers are drowned in the deep. |4|2|41|

Aasaa, Fifth Mehl:
He washes outwardly, but within, his mind is filthy; thus he loses his place in both worlds.
Here, he is engrossed in sexual desire, anger and emotional attachment; hereafter, he shall sigh and weep. |1|

The way to vibrate and meditate on the Lord of the Universe is different.
Destroying the snake-hole, the snake is not killed; the deaf person does not hear the Lord's Name. |1|Pause|

He renounces the affairs of Maya, but he does not appreciate the value of devotional worship.

He finds fault with the Vedas and the Shaastras, and does not know the essence of Yoga. |2|

He stands exposed, like a counterfeit coin, when inspected by the Lord, the Assayer.
The Inner-knower, the Searcher of hearts, knows everything; how can we hide anything from Him? |3|

Through falsehood, fraud and deceit, the mortal collapses in an instant - he has no foundation at all.
Truly, truly, truly, Nanak speaks; look within your own heart, and realize thIs. |4|3|42|

Aasaa, Fifth Mehl:
Making the effort, the mind becomes pure; in this dance, the self is silenced.
The five passions are kept under control, and the One Lord dwells in the mind. |1|

Your humble servant dances and sings Your Glorious Praises.
He plays upon the guitar, tambourine and cymbals, and the unstruck sound current of the Shabad resounds. |1|Pause|

First, he instructs his own mind, and then, he leads others.
He chants the Lord's Name and meditates on it in his heart; with his mouth, he announces it to all. |2|

He joins the Saadh Sangat, the Company of the Holy, and washes their feet; he applies the dust of the Saints to his body

He surrenders his mind and body, and places them before the Guru; thus, he obtains the true wealth. |3|

Whoever listens to, and beholds the Guru with faith, shall see his pains of birth and death taken away.
Such a dance eliminates hell; O Nanak, the Gurmukh remains wakeful. |4|4|43|

Aasaa, Fifth Mehl:

The lowly outcaste becomes a Brahmin, and the untouchable sweeper becomes pure and sublime.
The burning desire of the nether regions and the etheric realms is finally quenched and extinguished. |1|

The house-cat has been taught otherwise, and is terrified upon seeing the mouse.
The Guru has put the tiger under the control of the sheep, and now, the dog eats grass. |1|Pause|

Without pillars, the roof is supported, and the homeless have found a home.
Without the jeweller, the jewel has been set, and the wonderful stone shines forth. |2|

The claimant does not succeed by placing his claim, but by keeping silent, he obtains justice.
The dead sit on costly carpets, and what is seen with the eyes shall vanish. |3|

Section 08 - Raag Aasaa - Part 036

One who claims to know, is ignorant; he does not know the Knower of all.
Says Nanak, the Guru has given me the Ambrosial Nectar to drink in; savoring it and relishing it, I blossom forth in bliss. |4|5|44|

Aasaa, Fifth Mehl:
He has cut away my bonds, and overlooked my shortcomings, and so He has confirmed His nature.
Becoming merciful to me, like a mother or a father, he has come to cherish me as His own child. |1|

The GurSikhs are preserved by the Guru, by the Lord of the Universe.
He rescues them from the terrible world ocean, casting His Glance of Grace upon them. |1|Pause|

Meditating in remembrance on Him, we escape from the Messenger of Death; here and hereafter, we obtain peace.

With every breath and morsel of food, meditate, and chant with your tongue, continually, each and every day; sing the Glorious Praises of the Lord. |2|

Through loving devotional worship, the supreme status is obtained, and in the Saadh Sangat, the Company of the Holy, sorrows are dispelled.
I am not worn down, I do not die, and nothing strikes fear in me, since I have the wealth of the Lord's Immaculate Name in my purse. |3|

At the very last moment, God becomes the mortal's Help and Support; here and hereafter, He is the Savior Lord.
He is my breath of life, my friend, support and wealth; O Nanak, I am forever a sacrifice to Him. |4|6|45|

Aasaa, Fifth Mehl:
Since You are my Lord and Master, what is there for me to fear? Other than You, who else should I praise?

You are the One and only, and so do all things exist; without You, there is nothing at all for me. |1|

O Father, I have seen that the world is poison.
Save me, O Lord of the Universe! Your Name is my only Support. |1|Pause|

You know completely the condition of my mind; who else could I go to tell of it?
Without the Naam, the Name of the Lord, the whole world has gone crazy; obtaining the Naam, it finds peace. |2|

What shall I say? Unto whom shall I speak? What I have to say, I say to God. Everything which exists was created by You. You are my hope, forever and ever. |3|

If you bestow greatness, then it is Your greatness; here and hereafter, I meditate on You.
The Lord God of Nanak is forever the Giver of peace; Your Name is my only strength. |4|7|46|

Aasaa, Fifth Mehl:

Your Name is Ambrosial Nectar, O Lord Master; Your humble servant drinks in this supreme elixir.
The fearful load of sins from countless incarnations has vanished; doubt and duality are also dispelled. |1|

I live by beholding the Blessed Vision of Your Darshan.
Listening to Your Words, O True Guru, my mind and body are cooled and soothed. |1|Pause|

By Your Grace, I have joined the Saadh Sangat, the Company of the Holy; You Yourself have caused this to happen.
Holding fast to Your Feet, O God, the poison is easily neutralized. |2|

Your Name, O God, is the treasure of peace; I have received this everlasting Mantra.
Showing His Mercy, the True Guru has given it to me, and my fever and pain and hatred are annulled. |3|

Blessed is the attainment of this human body, by which God blends Himself with me.
Blessed, in this Dark Age of Kali Yuga, is the Saadh Sangat, the Company of the Holy, where the Kirtan of the Lord's Praises are sung.O Nanak, the Naam is my only Support. |4|8|47|

Section 08 - Raag Aasaa - Part 037

Aasaa, Fifth Mehl:
Everything is pre-ordained; what else can be known through study?
The errant child has been forgiven by the Supreme Lord God. |1|

My True Guru is always merciful; He has saved me, the meek one.
He has cured me of my disease, and I have obtained the greatest peace; He has placed the Ambrosial Name of the Lord in my mouth. |1|Pause|

He has washed away my countless sins; He has cut away my bonds, and I am liberated.
He has taken me by the arm, and pulled me out of the terrible, deep dark pit. |2|

I have become fearless, and all my fears have been erased. The Savior Lord has saved me.

Such is Your generosity, O my God, that You have resolved all my affairs. |3|

My mind has met with my Lord and Master, the treasure of excellence.

Taking to His Sanctuary, Nanak has become blissful. |4|9|48|

Aasaa, Fifth Mehl:

If I forget You, then everyone becomes my enemy. When You come to mind, then they serve me.

I do not know any other at all, O True, Invisible, Inscrutable Lord. |1|

When You come to mind, You are always merciful to me; what can the poor people do to me?

Tell me, who should I call good or bad, since all beings are Yours? |1|Pause|

You are my Shelter, You are my Support; giving me Your hand, You protect me.

That humble being, upon whom You bestow Your Grace, is not touched by slander or suffering. |2|

That is peace, and that is greatness, which is pleasing to the mind of the Dear Lord God.

You are all-knowing, You are forever compassionate; obtaining Your Name, I revel in it and make merry. |3|

I offer my prayer to You; my body and soul are all Yours.

Says Nanak, this is all Your greatness; no one even knows my name. |4|10|49|

Aasaa, Fifth Mehl:

Show Your Mercy, O God, O Searcher of hearts, that in the Saadh Sangat, the Company of the Holy, I might obtain You, Lord.

When You open Your Door, and reveal the Blessed Vision of Your Darshan, the mortal is not relegated to reincarnation again. |1|

Meeting with my Beloved Lord aand Master, all my pains are taken away.

I am saved and carried across, in the company of those who remember the Supreme Lord God in their hearts. |1|Pause|

This world is a great wilderness, an ocean of fire, in which mortals abide, in pleasure and pain.
Meeting with the True Guru, the mortal becomes immaculately pure; with his tongue, he chants the Ambrosial Name of the Lord. |2|

He preserves his body and wealth, and takes everything as his own; such are the subtle bonds which bind him.
By Guru's Grace, the mortal becomes liberated, meditating on the Name of the Lord, Har, Har. |3|

God, the Savior, has saved those, who are pleasing to the Will of God.
The soul and body are all Yours, O Great Giver; O Nanak, I am forever a sacrifice. |4|11|50|

Aasaa, Fifth Mehl:
You have avoided the slumber of attachment and impurity - by whose favor has this happened?
The great enticer does not affect you. Where has your laziness gone? |1|Pause|

Section 08 - Raag Aasaa - Part 038

How have you escaped from the treachery of sexual desire, anger and egotism?
The holy beings, angels and demons of the three qualities, and all the worlds have been plundered. |1|

The forest fire has burnt down so much of the grass; how rare are the plants which have remained green.
He is so All-powerful, that I cannot even describe Him; no one can chant His Praises. |2|

In the store-room of the lamp-black, I did not turn black; my color remained immaculate and pure.
The Guru has implanted the Maha Mantra, the Great Mantra, within my heart, and I have heard the wondrous Naam, the Name of the Lord. |3|

Showing His Mercy, God has looked upon me with favor, and He has attached me to His feet.
Through loving devotional worship, O Nanak, I have obtained peace; in the Saadh Sangat, the Company of the Holy, I am absorbed into the Lord. |4|12|51|

One Universal Creator God. By The Grace Of The True Guru:
Raag Aasaa, Seventh House, Fifth Mehl:
That red dress looks so beautiful on your body.
Your Husband Lord is pleased, and His heart is enticed. |1|

Whose handiwork is this red beauty of yours?
Whose love has rendered the poppy so red? |1|Pause|

You are so beautiful; you are the happy soul-bride.
Your Beloved is in your home; good fortune is in your home. |2|

You are pure and chaste, you are most distinguished.
You are pleasing to Your Beloved, and you have sublime understanding. |3|

I am pleasing to my Beloved, and so I am imbued with the deep red color.
Says Nanak, I have been totally blessed with the Lord's Glance of Grace. |4|

Listen, O companions: this is my only work;
God Himself is the One who embellishes and adorns. |1|Second Pause|1|52|

Aasaa, Fifth Mehl:
I suffered in pain, when I thought He was far away;
but now, He is Ever-present, and I receive His instructions. |1|

My pride is gone, O friends and companions;
my doubt is dispelled, and the Guru has united me with my Beloved. |1|Pause|

My Beloved has drawn me near to Him, and seated me on His Bed;
I have escaped the clutches of others. |2|

In the mansion of my heart, shines the Light of the Shabad.
My Husband Lord is blissful and playful. |3|

According to the destiny written upon my forehead, my Husband Lord has come home to me.
Servant Nanak has obtained the eternal marriage. |4|2|53|

Aasaa, Fifth Mehl:
My mind is attached to the True Name.
My dealings with other people are only superficial. |1|

Outwardly, I am on good terms with all;
but I remain detached, like the lotus upon the water. |1|Pause|

By word of mouth, I talk with everyone;
but I keep God clasped to my heart. |2|

I may appear utterly terrible,
but my mind is the dust of all men's feet.
Servant Nanak has found the Perfect Guru.

Section 08 - Raag Aasaa - Part 039

Inwardly and outwardly, He has shown me the One Lord. |4|3|54|

Aasaa, Fifth Mehl:
The mortal revels in joy, in the vigor of youth;
but without the Name, he mingles with dust. |1|

He may wear ear-rings and fine clothes,
and have a comfortable bed, and his mind may be so proud. |1|Pause|

He may have elephants to ride, and golden umbrellas over his head;
but without devotional worship to the Lord, he is buried beneath the dirt.
|2|

He may enjoy many women, of exquisite beauty;
but without the sublime essence of the Lord, all tastes are tasteless. |3|

Deluded by Maya, the mortal is led into sin and corruption.
Nanak seeks the Sanctuary of God, the All-powerful, Compassionate Lord.
|4|4|55|

Aasaa, Fifth Mehl:
There is a garden, in which so many plants have grown.
They bear the Ambrosial Nectar of the Naam as their fruit. |1|

Consider this, O wise one,
by which you may attain the state of Nirvaanaa.
All around this garden are pools of poison, but within it is the Ambrosial
Nectar, O Siblings of Destiny. |1|Pause|

There is only one gardener who tends it.
He takes care of every leaf and branch. |2|

He brings all sorts of plants and plants them there.
They all bear fruit - none is without fruit. |3|

One who receives the Ambrosial Fruit of the Naam from the Guru
- O Nanak, such a servant crosses over the ocean of Maya. |4|5|56|

Aasaa, Fifth Mehl:
The pleasures of royalty are derived from Your Name.
I attain Yoga, singing the Kirtan of Your Praises. |1|

All comforts are obtained in Your Shelter.
The True Guru has removed the veil of doubt. |1|Pause|

Understanding the Command of the Lord's Will, I revel in pleasure and joy.
Serving the True Guru, I obtain the supreme state of Nirvaanaa. |2|

One who recognizes You is recognized as a householder, and as a renunciate.
Imbued with the Naam, the Name of the Lord, he dwells in Nirvaanaa. |3|

One who has obtained the treasure of the Naam
- prays Nanak, his treasure-house is filled to overflowing. |4|6|57|

Aasaa, Fifth Mehl:
Journeying to sacred shrines of pilgrimage, I see the mortals acting in ego.
If I ask the Pandits, I find them tainted by Maya. |1|

Show me that place, O friend,
where the Kirtan of the Lord's Praises are forever sung. |1|Pause|

The Shaastras and the Vedas speak of sin and virtue;
they say that mortals are reincarnated into heaven and hell, over and over
again. |2|

In the householder's life, there is anxiety, and in the life of the renunciate,
there is egotism.
Performing religious rituals, the soul is entangled. |3|

By God's Grace, the mind is brought under control;
O Nanak, the Gurmukh crosses over the ocean of Maya. |4|

In the Saadh Sangat, the Company of the Holy, sing the Kirtan of the Lord's
Praises.
This place is found through the Guru. |1|Second Pause|7|58|

Aasaa, Fifth Mehl:
Within my home there is peace, and outwardly there is peace as well.
Remembering the Lord in meditation, all pains are erased. |1|

There is total peace, when You come into my mind.

Section 08 - Raag Aasaa - Part 040

He alone is pleasing to Your Will, who chants the Naam. |1|Pause|

My body and mind are cooled and soothed, chanting the Name of the Lord.
Meditating on the Lord, Har, Har, the house of pain is demolished. |2|

He alone, who understands the Command of the Lord's Will, is approved.
The True Shabad of the Word of God is his trademark and insignia. |3|

The Perfect Guru has implanted the Lord's Name within me.
Prays Nanak, my mind has found peace. |4|8|59|

Aasaa, Fifth Mehl:
Wherever You send me, there I go.
Whatever You give me, brings me peace. |1|

I am forever the chaylaa, the humble disciple, of the Lord of the Universe, the Sustainer of the World.
By Your Grace, I am satisfied and satiated. |1|Pause|

Whatever You give me, I wear and eat.
By Your Grace, O God, my life passes peacefully. |2|

Deep within my mind and body, I meditate on You.
I recognize none as equal to You. |3|

Says Nanak, this is my continual meditation:
that I may be emancipated, clinging to the Feet of the Saints. |4|9|60|

Aasaa, Fifth Mehl:
While standing up, and sitting down, and even while asleep, meditate on the Lord.
Walking on the Way, sing the Praises of the Lord. |1|

With your ears, listen to the Ambrosial Sermon.
Listening to it, your mind shall be filled with bliss, and the troubles and diseases of your mind shall all depart. |1|Pause|

While you work at your job, on the road and at the beach, meditate and chant.
By Guru's Grace, drink in the Ambrosial Essence of the Lord. |2|

The humble being who sings the Kirtan of the Lord's Praises, day and night, does not have to go with the Messenger of Death. |3|

One who does not forget the Lord, twenty-four hours a day, is emancipated;
O Nanak, I fall at his feet. |4|10|61|

Aasaa, Fifth Mehl:
Remembering Him in meditation, one abides in peace;
one becomes happy, and suffering is ended. |1|

Celebrate, make merry, and sing God's Glories.
Forever and ever, surrender to the True Guru. |1|Pause|

Act in accordance with the Shabad, the True Word of the True Guru.
Remain steady and stable within the home of your own self, and find God.
|2|

Do not harbor evil intentions against others in your mind,
and you shall not be troubled, O Siblings of Destiny, O friends. |3|

The Name of the Lord, Har, Har, is the Tantric exercise, and the Mantra,
given by the Guru.
Nanak knows this peace alone, night and day. |4|11|62|

Aasaa, Fifth Mehl:
That wretched being, whom no one knows
- chanting the Naam, the Name of the Lord, he is honored in the four
directions. |1|

I beg for the Blessed Vision of Your Darshan; please, give it to me, O
Beloved!
Serving You, who, who has not been saved? |1|Pause|

That person, whom no one wants to be near
- the whole world comes to wash the dirt of his feet. |2|

That mortal, who is of no use to anyone at all
- by the Grace of the Saints, he meditates on the Naam. |3|

In the Saadh Sangat, the Company of the Holy, the sleeping mind awakens.
Then, O Nanak, God seems sweet. |4|12|63|

Aasaa, Fifth Mehl:
With my eyes, I behold the One and Only Lord.
Forever and ever, I contemplate the Naam, the Name of the Lord. |1|

Section 08 - Raag Aasaa - Part 041

I sing the Praises of the Lord, Raam, Raam, Raam.
By the graceful favor of the Saints, I meditate on the Name of the Lord, Har,
Har, in the Saadh Sangat, the Company of the Holy. |1|Pause|

Everything is strung on His string.
He is contained in each and every heart. |2|

He creates and destroys in an instant.
He Himself remains unattached, and without attributes. |3|

He is the Creator, the Cause of causes, the Searcher of hearts.
Nanak's Lord and Master celebrates in bliss. |4|13|64|

Aasaa, Fifth Mehl:
My wandering through millions of births has ended.
I have won, and not lost, this human body, so difficult to obtain. |1|

My sins have been erased, and my sufferings and pains are gone.
I have been sanctified by the dust of the feet of the Saints. |1|Pause|

The Saints of God have the ability to save us;
they meet with those of us who have such pre-ordained destiny. |2|

My mind is filled with bliss, since the Guru gave me the Mantra of the Lord's Name.
My thirst has been quenched, and my mind has become steady and stable. |3|

The wealth of the Naam, the Name of the Lord, is for me the nine treasures, and the spiritual powers of the Siddhas.
O Nanak, I have obtained understanding from the Guru. |4|14|65|

Aasaa, Fifth Mehl:
My thirst, and the darkness of ignorance have been removed.
Serving the Holy Saints, countless sins are obliterated. |1|

I have obtained celestial peace and immense joy.
Serving the Guru, my mind has become immaculately pure, and I have heard the Name of the Lord, Har, Har, Har, Har. |1|Pause|

The stubborn foolishness of my mind is gone;
God's Will has become sweet to me. |2|

I have grasped the Feet of the Perfect Guru,

and the sins of countless incarnations have been washed away. |3|

The jewel of this life has become fruitful.
Says Nanak, God has shown mercy to me. |4|15|66|

Aasaa, Fifth Mehl:
I contemplate, forever and ever, the True Guru;
with my hair, I dust the feet of the Guru. |1|

Be wakeful, O my awakening mind!
Without the Lord, nothing else shall be of use to you; false is emotional attachment, and useless are worldly entanglements. |1|Pause|

Embrace love for the Word of the Guru's Bani.
When the Guru shows His Mercy, pain is destroyed. |2|

Without the Guru, there is no other place of rest.
The Guru is the Giver, the Guru gives the Name. |3|

The Guru is the Supreme Lord God; He Himself is the Transcendent Lord.
Twenty-four hours a day, O Nanak, meditate on the Guru. |4|16|67|

Aasaa, Fifth Mehl:
He Himself is the tree, and the branches extending out.
He Himself preserves His own crop. |1|

Wherever I look, I see that One Lord alone.
Deep within each and every heart, He Himself is contained. |1|Pause|

He Himself is the sun, and the rays emanating from it.
He is concealed, and He is revealed. |2|

He is said to be of the highest attributes, and without attributes.
Both converge onto His single point. |3|

Says Nanak, the Guru has dispelled my doubt and fear.
With my eyes, I perceive the Lord, the embodiment of bliss, to be everywhere. |4|17|68|

Aasaa, Fifth Mehl:

I know nothing of arguments or cleverness.

Section 08 - Raag Aasaa - Part 042

Day and night, I chant Your Name. |1|

I am worthless; I have no virtue at all.
God is the Creator, the Cause of all causes. |1|Pause|

I am foolish, stupid, ignorant and thoughtless;
Your Name is my mind's only hope. |2|

I have not practiced chanting, deep meditation, self-discipline or good actions;
but within my mind, I have worshipped God's Name. |3|

I know nothing, and my intellect is inadequate.
Prays Nanak, O God, You are my only Support. |4|18|69|

Aasaa, Fifth Mehl:
These two words, Har, Har, make up my maalaa.
Continually chanting and reciting this rosary, God has become merciful to me, His humble servant. |1|

I offer my prayer to the True Guru.
Shower Your Mercy upon me, and keep me safe in Your Sanctuary; please, give me the maalaa, the rosary of Har, Har. |1|Pause|

One who enshrines this rosary of the Lord's Name within his heart,
is freed of the pains of birth and death. |2|

The humble being who contemplates the Lord within his heart, and chants the Lord's Name, Har, Har, with his mouth,

never wavers, here or hereafter. |3|

Says Nanak, one who is imbued with the Name,
goes to the next world with the maalaa of the Lord's Name. |4|19|70|

Aasaa, Fifth Mehl:

All things belong to Him - let yourself belong to Him as well.
No stain clings to such a humble being. |1|

The Lord's servant is liberated forever.
Whatever He does, is pleasing to His servant; the way of life of His slave is immaculately pure. |1|Pause|

One who renounces everything, and enters the Lord's Sanctuary
- how can Maya cling to him? |2|

With the treasure of the Naam, the Name of the Lord, in his mind,
he suffers no anxiety, even in dreams. |3|

Says Nanak, I have found the Perfect Guru.
My doubts and attachments have been totally obliterated. |4|20|71|

Aasaa, Fifth Mehl:
When my God is totally pleased with me,
then, tell me, how can suffering or doubt draw near me? |1|

Continually listening to Your Glory, I live.
I am worthless - save me, O Lord! |1|Pause|

My suffering has been ended, and my anxiety is forgotten.
I have obtained my reward, chanting the Mantra of the True Guru. |2|

He is True, and True is His glory.
Remembering, remembering Him in meditation, keep Him clasped to your heart. |3|

Says Nanak, what action is there left to do,
by one whose mind is filled with the Lord's Name? |4|21|72|

Aasaa, Fifth Mehl:
Sexual desire, anger, and egotism lead to ruin.
Meditating on the Lord, the Lord's humble servants are redeemed. |1|

The mortals are asleep, intoxicated with the wine of Maya.
The devotees remain awake, imbued with the Lord's meditation. |1|Pause|

In emotional attachment and doubt, the mortals wander through countless incarnations.
The devotees remain ever-stable, meditating on the Lord's Lotus Feet. |2|

Bound to household and possessions, the mortals are lost in the deep, dark pit.
The Saints are liberated, knowing the Lord to be near at hand. |3|

Says Nanak, one who has taken to God's Sanctuary,
obtains peace in this world, and salvation in the world hereafter. |4|22|73|

Section 08 - Raag Aasaa - Part 043

Aasaa, Fifth Mehl:
You are my waves, and I am Your fish.
You are my Lord and Master; I wait at Your Door. |1|

You are my Creator, and I am Your servant.
I have taken to Your Sanctuary, O God, most profound and excellent. |1|Pause|

You are my life, You are my Support.
Beholding You, my heart-lotus blossoms forth. |2|

You are my salvation and honor; You make me acceptable.
You are All-powerful, You are my strength. |3|

Night and day, I chant the Naam, the Name of the Lord, the treasure of excellence.
This is Nanak's prayer to God. |4|23|74|

Aasaa, Fifth Mehl:
The mourner practices falsehood;
he laughs with glee, while mourning for others. |1|

Someone has died, while there is singing in someone else's house.
One mourns and bewails, while another laughs with glee. |1|Pause|

From childhood to old age,

the mortal does not attain his goals, and he comes to regret in the end. |2|

The world is under the influence of the three qualities.
The mortal is reincarnated, again and again, into heaven and hell. |3|

Says Nanak, one who is attached to the Naam, the Name of the Lord,
becomes acceptable, and his life becomes fruitful. |4|24|75|

Aasaa, Fifth Mehl:
She remains asleep, and does not know the news of God.
The day dawns, and then, she regrets. |1|

Loving the Beloved, the mind is filled with celestial bliss.
You yearn to meet with God, so why do you delay? |1|Pause|

He came and poured His Ambrosial Nectar into your hands,
but it slipped through your fingers, and fell onto the ground. |2|

You are burdened with desire, emotional attachment and egotism;
it is not the fault of God the Creator. |3|

In the Saadh Sangat, the Company of the Holy, the darkness of doubt is
dispelled.
O Nanak, the Creator Lord blends us with Himself. |4|25|76|

Aasaa, Fifth Mehl:
I long for the Lotus Feet of my Beloved Lord.
The wretched Messenger of Death has run away from me. |1|

You enter into my mind, by Your Kind Mercy.
Meditating on the Naam, the Name of the Lord, all diseases are destroyed.
|1|Pause|

Death gives so much pain to others,
but it cannot even come near Your slave. |2|

My mind thirsts for Your Vision;
in peaceful ease and bliss, I dwell in detachment. |3|

Hear this prayer of Nanak:

please, infuse Your Name into his heart. |4|26|77|

Aasaa, Fifth Mehl:
My mind is satisfied, and my entanglements have been dissolved.
God has become merciful to me. |1|

By the Grace of the Saints, everything has turned out well.
His House is overflowing with all things; I have met Him, the Fearless Master. |1|Pause|

By the Kind Mercy of the Holy Saints, the Naam has been implanted within me.
The most dreadful desires have been eliminated. |2|

My Master has given me a gift;
the fire has been extinguished, and my mind is now at peace. |3|

My search has ended, and my mind is absorbed in celestial bliss.

Section 08 - Raag Aasaa - Part 044

Nanak has obtained the treasure of the Naam, the Name of the Lord. |4|27|78|

Aasaa, Fifth Mehl:
Those who are attuned to their Lord and Master
are satisfied and fulfilled with the perfect food. |1|

The Lord's devotees never run short of anything.
They have plenty to eat, spend, enjoy and give. |1|Pause|

One who has the Unfathomable Lord of the Universe as his Master
- how can any mere mortal stand up to him? |2|

One who is served by the eighteen supernatural powers of the Siddhas
- grasp his feet, even for an instant. |3|

That one, upon whom You have showered Your Mercy, O my Lord Master
- says Nanak, he does not lack anything. |4|28|79|

Aasaa, Fifth Mehl:
When I meditate on my True Guru,
my mind becomes supremely peaceful. |1|

The record of my account is erased, and my doubts are dispelled.
Imbued with the Naam, the Name of the Lord, His humble servant is
blessed with good fortune. |1|Pause|

When I remember my Lord and Master,
my fears are dispelled, O my friend. |2|

When I took to Your Protection, O God,
my desires were fulfilled. |3|

Gazing upon the wonder of Your play, my mind has become encouraged.
Servant Nanak relies on You alone. |4|29|80|

Aasaa, Fifth Mehl:
Night and day, the mouse of time gnaws away at the rope of life.
Falling into the well, the mortal eats the sweet treats of Maya. |1|

Thinking and planning, the night of the life is passing away.
Thinking of the many pleasures of Maya, the mortal never remembers the
Lord, the Sustainer of the earth. |1|Pause|

Believing the shade of the tree to be permanent, he builds his house
beneath it.
But the noose of death is around his neck, and Shakti, the power of Maya,
has aimed her arrows at him. |2|

The sandy shore is being washed away by the waves,
but the fool still believes that place to be permanent. |3|

In the Saadh Sangat, the Company of the Holy, chant the Name of the Lord,
the King.
Nanak lives by singing the Glorious Praises of the Lord. |4|30|81|

Aasaa, Fifth Mehl, Du-Tukas 9:
With that, you are engaged in playful sport;
with that, I am joined to you.

With that, everyone longs for you;
without it, no one would even look at your face. |1|

Where is that detached soul now contained?
Without it, you are miserable. |1|Pause|

With that, you are the woman of the house;
with that, you are respected.
With that, you are caressed;
without it, you are reduced to dust. |2|

With that, you have honor and respect;
with that, you have relatives in the world.
With that, you are adorned in every way;
without it, you are reduced to dust. |3|

That detached soul is neither born, nor dies.
It acts according to the Command of the Lord's Will.
O Nanak, having fashioned the body, the Lord unites the soul with it, and separates them again;
He alone knows His All-powerful creative nature. |4|31|82|

Aasaa, Fifth Mehl:

Section 08 - Raag Aasaa - Part 045

He does not die, so I do not fear.
He does not perish, so I do not grieve.
He is not poor, so I do not hunger.
He is not in pain, so I do not suffer. |1|

There is no other Destroyer than Him.
He is my very life, the Giver of life. |1|Pause|

He is not bound, so I am not in bondage.
He has no occupation, so I have no entanglements.
He has no impurities, so I have no impurities.
He is in ecstasy, so I am always happy. |2|

He has no anxiety, so I have no cares.

He has no stain, so I have no pollution.
He has no hunger, so I have no thirst.
Since He is immaculately pure, I correspond to Him. |3|

I am nothing; He is the One and only.
Before and after, He alone exists.
O Nanak, the Guru has taken away my doubts and mistakes;
He and I, joining together, are of the same color. |4|32|83|

Aasaa, Fifth Mehl:
Serve Him in many different ways;
Dedicate your soul, your breath of life and your wealth to Him.
Carry water for Him, and wave the fan over Him - renounce your ego.
Make yourself a sacrifice to Him, time and time again. |1|

She alone is the happy soul-bride, who is pleasing to God.
In her company, I may meet Him, O my mother. |1|Pause|

I am the water-carrier of the slaves of His slaves.
I treasure in my soul the dust of their feet.
By that good destiny inscribed upon my forehead, I obtain their society.
Through His Love, the Lord Master meets me. |2|

I dedicate all to Him - chanting and meditation, austerity and religious
observances.
I offer all to Him - good actions, righteous conduct and incense burning.
Renouncing pride and attachment, I become the dust of the feet of the
Saints.
In their society, I behold God with my eyes. |3|

Each and every moment, I contemplate and adore Him.
Day and night, I serve Him like this.
The Lord of the Universe, the Cherisher of the World, has become merciful;
in the Saadh Sangat, the Company of the Holy, O Nanak, He forgives us.
|4|33|84|

Aasaa, Fifth Mehl:
In the Love of God, eternal peace is obtained.
In the Love of God, one is not touched by pain.
In the Love of God, the filth of ego is washed away.

In the Love of God, one becomes forever immaculate. |1|

Listen, O friend: show such love and affection to God,
the Support of the soul, the breath of life, of each and every heart.
|1|Pause|

In the Love of God, all treasures are obtained.
In the Love of God, the Immaculate Naam fills the heart.
In the Love of God, one is eternally embellished.
In the Love of God, all anxiety is ended. |2|

In the Love of God, one crosses over this terrible world-ocean.
In the Love of God, one does not fear death.
In the Love of God, all are saved.
The Love of God shall go along with you. |3|

By himself, no one is united, and no one goes astray.
One who is blessed by God's Mercy, joins the Saadh Sangat, the Company
of the Holy.
Says Nanak, I am a sacrifice to You.
O God, You are the Support and the Strength of the Saints. |4|34|85|

Aasaa, Fifth Mehl:
Becoming a king, the mortal wields his royal authority;
oppressing the people, he gathers wealth.

Section 08 - Raag Aasaa - Part 046

Gathering it and collecting it, he fills his bags.
But God takes it away from him, and gives it to another. |1|

The mortal is like an unbaked clay pot in water;
indulging in pride and egotism, he crumbles down and dissolves. |1|Pause|

Being fearless, he becomes unrestrained.
He does not think of the Creator, who is ever with him.
He raises armies, and collects arms.
But when the breath leaves him, he turns to ashes. |2|

He has lofty palaces, mansions and queens,

elephants and pairs of horses, delighting the mind;
he is blessed with a great family of sons and daughters.
But, engrossed in attachment, the blind fool wastes away to death. |3|

The One who created him destroys him.
Enjoyments and pleasures are like just a dream.
He alone is liberated, and possesses regal power and wealth,
O Nanak, whom the Lord Master blesses with His Mercy. |4|35|86|

Aasaa, Fifth Mehl:
The mortal is in love with this,
but the more he has, the more he longs for more.
It hangs around his neck, and does not leave him.
But falling at the feet of the True Guru, he is saved. |1|

I have renounced and discarded Maya, the Enticer of the world.
I have met the Absolute Lord, and congratulations are pouring in.
|1|Pause|

She is so beautiful, she captivates the mind.
On the road, and the beach, at home, in the forest and in the wilderness,
she touches us.
She seems so sweet to the mind and body.
But by Guru's Grace, I have seen her to be deceptive. |2|

Her courtiers are also great deceivers.
They do not spare even their fathers or mothers.
They have enslaved their companions.
By Guru's Grace, I have subjugated them all. |3|

Now, my mind is filled with bliss;
my fear is gone, and the noose is cut away.
Says Nanak, when I met the True Guru,
I came to dwell within my home in absolute peace. |4|36|87|

Aasaa, Fifth Mehl:
Twenty-four hours a day, he knows the Lord to be near at hand;
he surrenders to the Sweet Will of God.
The One Name is the Support of the Saints;
they remain the dust of the feet of all. |1|

Listen, to the way of life of the Saints, O my Siblings of Destiny;
their praises cannot be described. |1|Pause|

Their occupation is the Naam, the Name of the Lord.
The Kirtan, the Praise of the Lord, the embodiment of bliss, is their rest.
Friends and enemies are one and the same to them.
They know of no other than God. |2|

They erase millions upon millions of sins.
They dispel suffering; they are givers of the life of the soul.
They are so brave; they are men of their word.
The Saints have enticed Maya herself. |3|

Their company is cherished even by the gods and the angels.
Blessed is their Darshan, and fruitful is their service.
With his palms pressed together, Nanak offers his prayer:
O Lord, Treasure of Excellence, please bless me with the service of the
Saints. |4|37|88|

Aasaa, Fifth Mehl:
All peace and comforts are in the meditation of the One Name.
All righteous actions of Dharma are in the singing of the Lord's Glorious
Praises.
The Saadh Sangat, the Company of the Holy, is so very pure and sacred.

Section 08 - Raag Aasaa - Part 047

Meeting with them, love for God is embraced. |1|

By Guru's Grace, bliss is obtained.
Meditating upon Him in remembrance, the mind is illumined; his state and
condition cannot be described. |1|Pause|

Fasts, religious vows, cleansing baths, and worship to Him;
listening to the Vedas, Puraanas, and Shaastras.
Extremely pure is he, and immaculate is his place,
who meditates upon the Name of the Lord, Har, Har, in the Saadh Sangat.
|2|

That humble being becomes renowned all over the world.
Even sinners are purified, by the dust of his feet.
One who has met the Lord, the Lord our King,
his condition and state cannot be described. |3|

Twenty-four hours a day, with palms pressed together, I meditate;
I yearn to obtain the Blessed Vision of the Darshan of those Holy Saints.
Merge me, the poor one, with You, O Lord;
Nanak has come to Your Sanctuary. |4|38|89|

Aasaa, Fifth Mehl:
Twenty-four hours a day, he takes his cleansing bath in water;
he makes continual offerings to the Lord; he is a true man of wisdom.
He never leaves anything uselessly.
Again and again, he falls at the Lord's Feet. |1|

Such is the Saalagraam, the stone idol, which I serve;
such is my worship, flower-offerings and divine adoration as well.
|1|Pause|

His bell resounds to the four corners of the world.
His seat is forever in heaven.
His chauri, his fly-brush, waves over all.
His incense is ever-fragrant. |2|

He is treasured in each and every heart.
The Saadh Sangat, the Company of the Holy, is His Eternal Court.
His Aartee, his lamp-lit worship service, is the Kirtan of His Praises, which
brings lasting bliss.
His Greatness is so beautiful, and ever limitless. |3|

He alone obtains it, who is so pre-ordained;
he takes to the Sanctuary of the Saints' Feet.
I hold in my hands the Saalagraam of the Lord.
Says Nanak, the Guru has given me this Gift. |4|39|90|

Aasaa, Fifth Mehl, Panch-Pada:
That highway, upon which the water-carrier is plundered
- that way is far removed from the Saints. |1|

The True Guru has spoken the Truth.
Your Name, O Lord, is the Way to Salvation; the road of the Messenger of Death is far away. |1|Pause|

That place, where the greedy toll-collector dwells
- that path remains far removed from the Lord's humble servant. |2|

There, where so very many caravans of men are caught,
the Holy Saints remain with the Supreme Lord. |3|

Chitra and Gupat, the recording angels of the conscious and the unconscious, write the accounts of all mortal beings,

but they cannot even see the Lord's humble devotees. |4|

Says Nanak, one whose True Guru is Perfect
- the unblown bugles of ecstasy vibrate for him. |5|40|91|

Aasaa, Fifth Mehl, Du-Pada 1:
In the Saadh Sangat, the Company of the Holy, the Naam is learned;
all desires and tasks are fulfilled.
My thirst has been quenched, and I am satiated with the Lord's Praise.
I live by chanting and meditating upon the Lord, the Sustainer of the earth. |1|

I have entered the Sanctuary of the Creator, the Cause of all causes.
By Guru's Grace, I have entered the home of celestial bliss. Darkness is dispelled, and the moon of wisdom has risen. |1|Pause|

Section 08 - Raag Aasaa - Part 048

My treasure-house is overflowing with rubies and jewels;
I meditate on the Formless Lord, and so they never run short.
How rare is that humble being, who drinks in the Ambrosial Nectar of the Word of the Shabad.
O Nanak, he attains the state of highest dignity. |2|41|92|

Aasaa, Seventh House, Fifth Mehl:
Meditate continually on the Name of the Lord within your heart.
Thus you shall save all your companions and associates. |1|

My Guru is always with me, near at hand.
Meditating, meditating in remembrance on Him, I cherish Him forever.
|1|Pause|

Your actions seem so sweet to me.
Nanak begs for the treasure of the Naam, the Name of the Lord. |2|42|93|

Aasaa, Fifth Mehl:
The world is saved by the Saadh Sangat, the Company of the Holy.
The Name of the Lord is the Support of the mind. |1|

The Saints worship and adore the Lotus Feet of the Divine Guru;
they love the Beloved Lord. |1|Pause|

She who has such good destiny written upon her forehead,
says Nanak, is blessed with the eternal happy marriage with the Lord.
|2|43|94|

Aasaa, Fifth Mehl:
The Order of my Husband Lord seems so sweet to me.
My Husband Lord has driven out the one who was my rival.
My Beloved Husband has decorated me, His happy soul-bride.
He has quieted the burning thirst of my mind. |1|

It is good that I submitted to the Will of my Beloved Lord.
I have realized celestial peace and poise within this home of mine. |Pause|

I am the hand-maiden, the attendant of my Beloved Lord.
He is eternal and imperishable, inaccessible and infinite.
Holding the fan, sitting at His Feet, I wave it over my Beloved.
The five demons who tortured me have run away. |2|

I am not from a noble family, and I am not beautiful.
What do I know? Why am I pleasing to my Beloved?
I am a poor orphan, destitute and dishonored.
My Husband took me in, and made me His queen. |3|

When I saw my Beloved's face before me,
I became so happy and peaceful; my married life was blessed.

Says Nanak, my desires are fulfilled.
The True Guru has united me with God, the treasure of excellence. |4|1|95|

Aasaa, Fifth Mehl:
A frown creases her forehead, and her look is evil.
Her speech is bitter, and her tongue is rude.
She is always hungry, and she believes her Husband to be far away. |1|

Such is Maya, the woman, which the One Lord has created.
She is devouring the whole world, but the Guru has saved me, O my Siblings of Destiny. |Pause|

Administering her poisons, she has overcome the whole world.
She has bewitched Brahma, Vishnu and Shiva.
Only those Gurmukhs who are attuned to the Naam are blessed. |2|

Performing fasts, religious observances and atonements, the mortals have grown weary.
They wander over the entire planet, on pilgrimages to the banks of sacred rivers.
But they alone are saved, who seek the Sanctuary of the True Guru. |3|

Attached to Maya, the whole world is in bondage.
The foolish self-willed manmukhs are consumed by their egotism.
Taking me by the arm, Guru Nanak has saved me. |4|2|96|

Aasaa, Fifth Mehl:
Everything is painful, when one forgets the Lord Master.
Here and hereafter, such a mortal is useless. |1|

The Saints are satisfied, meditating on the Lord, Har, Har.

Section 08 - Raag Aasaa - Part 049

Bestowing Your Mercy, God, You attach us to Your Name; all peace comes by Your Will. |Pause|

The Lord is Ever-present; one who deems Him to be far away, dies again and again, repenting. |2|

The mortals do not remember the One, who has given them everything.
Engrossed in such terrible corruption, their days and nights waste away.
|3|

Says Nanak, meditate in remembrance of the One Lord God.
Salvation is obtained, in the Shelter of the Perfect Guru. |4|3|97|

Aasaa, Fifth Mehl:
Meditating on the Naam, the Name of the Lord, the mind and body are
totally rejuvenated.
All sins and sorrows are washed away. |1|

How blessed is that day, O my Siblings of Destiny,
when the Glorious Praises of the Lord are sung, and the supreme status is
obtained. |Pause|

Worshipping the feet of the Holy Saints,
troubles and hatred are eliminated from the mind. |2|

Meeting with the Perfect Guru, conflict is ended,
and the five demons are totally subdued. |3|

One whose mind is filled with the Name of the Lord,
O Nanak - I am a sacrifice to him. |4|4|98|

Aasaa, Fifth Mehl:
O singer, sing of the One,
who is the Support of the soul, the body and the breath of life.
Serving Him, all peace is obtained.
You shall no longer go to any other. |1|

My Blissful Lord Master is forever in bliss; meditate continually and forever,
on the Lord, the treasure of excellence.
I am a sacrifice to the Beloved Saints; by their kind favor, God comes to
dwell in the mind. |Pause|

His gifts are never exhausted.
In His subtle way, He easily absorbs all.
His benevolence cannot be erased.

So enshrine that True Lord within your mind. |2|

His house is filled with all sorts of articles;
God's servants never suffer pain.
Holding to His Support, the state of fearless dignity is obtained.
With each and every breath, sing of the Lord, the treasure of excellence.
|3|

He is not far from us, wherever we go.
When He shows His Mercy, we obtain the Lord, Har, Har.
I offer this prayer to the Perfect Guru.
Nanak begs for the treasure of the Lord's Name. |4|5|99|

Aasaa, Fifth Mehl:
First, the pains of the body vanish;
then, the mind becomes totally peaceful.
In His Mercy, the Guru bestows the Lord's Name.
I am a sacrifice, a sacrifice to that True Guru. |1|

I have obtained the Perfect Guru, O my Siblings of Destiny.
All illness, sorrows and sufferings are dispelled, in the Sanctuary of the True
Guru. |Pause|

The feet of the Guru abide within my heart;
I have received all the fruits of my heart's desires.
The fire is extinguished, and I am totally peaceful.
Showering His Mercy, the Guru has given this gift. |2|

The Guru has given shelter to the shelterless.
The Guru has given honor to the dishonored.
Shattering his bonds, the Guru has saved His servant.
I taste with my tongue the Ambrosial Bani of His Word. |3|

By great good fortune, I worship the Guru's feet.
Forsaking everything, I have obtained God's Sanctuary.

Section 08 - Raag Aasaa - Part 050

That humble being, O Nanak, unto whom the Guru grants His Mercy, is
forever enraptured. |4|6|100|

Aasaa, Fifth Mehl:
The True Guru has truly given a child.
The long-lived one has been born to this destiny.
He came to acquire a home in the womb,
and his mother's heart is so very glad. |1|

A son is born - a devotee of the Lord of the Universe.
This pre-ordained destiny has been revealed to all. |Pause|

In the tenth month, by the Lord's Order, the baby has been born.
Sorrow is dispelled, and great joy has ensued.
The companions blissfully sing the songs of the Guru's Bani.
This is pleasing to the Lord Master. |2|

The vine has grown, and shall last for many generations.
The Power of the Dharma has been firmly established by the Lord.
That which my mind wishes for, the True Guru has granted.
I have become carefree, and I fix my attention on the One Lord. |3|

As the child places so much faith in his father,
I speak as it pleases the Guru to have me speak.
This is not a hidden secret;
Guru Nanak, greatly pleased, has bestowed this gift. |4|7|101|

Aasaa, Fifth Mehl:
Giving His Hand, the Perfect Guru has protected the child.
The glory of His servant has become manifest. |1|

I contemplate the Guru, the Guru; I meditate on the Guru, the Guru.
I offer my heart-felt prayer to the Guru, and it is answered. |Pause|

I have taken to the Sanctuary of the True Divine Guru.
The service of His servant has been fulfilled. |2|

He has preserved my soul, body, youth and breath of life.
Says Nanak, I am a sacrifice to the Guru. |3|8|102|

Aasaa, Eighth House, Kaafee, Fifth Mehl:
One Universal Creator God. By The Grace Of The True Guru:

I am Your purchased slave, O True Lord Master.
My soul and body, and all of this, everything is Yours. |1|

You are the honor of the dishonored. O Master, in You I place my trust.
Without the True One, any other support is false - know this well.
|1|Pause|

Your Command is infinite; no one can find its limit.
One who meets with the Perfect Guru, walks in the Way of the Lord's Will.
|2|

Cunning and cleverness are of no use.
That which the Lord Master gives, by the Pleasure of His Will - that is
pleasing to me. |3|

One may perform tens of thousands of actions, but attachment to things is
not satisfied.
Servant Nanak has made the Naam his Support. He has renounced other
entanglements. |4|1|103|

Aasaa, Fifth Mehl:
I have pursued all pleasures, but none is as great as the Lord.
By the Pleasure of the Guru's Will, the True Lord Master is obtained. |1|

I am a sacrifice to my Guru; I am forever and ever a sacrifice to Him.
Please, grant me this one blessing, that I may never, even for an instant,
forget Your Name. |1|Pause|

How very fortunate are those who have the wealth of the Lord deep within
the heart.

Section 08 - Raag Aasaa - Part 051

They escape from the great noose of death; they are permeated with the
Word of the Guru's Shabad. |2|

How can I chant the Glorious Praises of the Guru? The Guru is the ocean of
Truth and clear understanding.
He is the Perfect Transcendent Lord, from the very beginning, and
throughout the ages. |3|

Meditating on the Naam, the Name of the Lord, forever and ever, my mind is filled with the Love of the Lord, Har, Har.
The Guru is my soul, my breath of life, and wealth; O Nanak, He is with me forever. |4|2|104|

Aasaa, Fifth Mehl:
If the Invisible and Infinite Lord dwells within my mind, even for a moment, then all my pains, troubles, and diseases vanish. |1|

I am a sacrifice to my Lord Master.
Meditating on Him, a great joy wells up within my mind and body. |1|Pause|

I have heard only a little bit of news about the True Lord Master.
I have obtained the peace of all peace, O my mother; I cannot estimate its worth. |2|

He is so beautiful to my eyes; beholding Him, I have been bewitched.
I am worthless, O my mother; He Himself has attached me to the hem of His robe. |3|

He is beyond the world of the Vedas, the Koran and the Bible.
The Supreme King of Nanak is immanent and manifest. |4|3|105|

Aasaa, Fifth Mehl:
Tens of thousands of devotees worship and adore You, chanting, "Beloved, Beloved."
How shall You unite me, the worthless and corrupt soul, with Yourself. |1|

You are my Support, O Merciful God, Lord of the Universe, Sustainer of the World.
You are the Master of all; the entire creation is Yours. |1|Pause|

You are the constant help and support of the Saints, who behold You Ever-present.
Those who lack the Naam, the Name of the Lord, shall die, engulfed in sorrow and pain. |2|

Those servants, who lovingly perform the Lord's service, are freed from the cycle of reincarnation.
What shall be the fate of those who forget the Naam? |3|

As are the cattle which have strayed, so is the entire world.
O God, please cut away Nanak's bonds, and unite him with Yourself. |4|4|106|

Aasaa, Fifth Mehl:
Forget all other things, and dwell upon the Lord alone.
Lay aside your false pride, and dedicate your mind and body to Him. |1|

Twenty-four hours a day, praise the Creator Lord.
I live by Your bountiful gifts - please, shower me with Your Mercy! |1|Pause|

So, do that work, by which your face shall be made radiant.
He alone becomes attached to the Truth, O Lord, unto whom You give it. |2|

So build and adorn that house, which shall never be destroyed.
Enshrine the One Lord within your consciousness; He shall never die. |3|

The Lord is dear to those, who are pleasing to the Will of God.
By Guru's Grace, Nanak describes the indescribable. |4|5|107|

Aasaa, Fifth Mehl:
What are they like - those who do not forget the Naam, the Name of the Lord?
Know that there is absolutely no difference; they are exactly like the Lord. |1|

The mind and body are enraptured, meeting with You, O Lord.
Peace is obtained, by the favor of the Lord's humble servant; all pains are taken away. |1|Pause|

As many as are the continents of the world, so many have been saved.
Those, in whose minds You Yourself dwell, O Lord, are the perfect devotees. |2|

Section 08 - Raag Aasaa - Part 052

Those whom You approve, are approved.
Such a celebrated and honored person is known everywhere. |3|

Day and night, with every breath to worship and adore the Lord
- please, O True Supreme King, fulfill this, Nanak's desire. |4|6|108|

Aasaa, Fifth Mehl:
He, my Lord Master, is fully pervading all places.
He is the One Lord Master, the roof over our heads; there is no other than Him. |1|

As it pleases Your Will, please save me, O Savior Lord.
Without You, my eyes see no other at all. |1|Pause|

God Himself is the Cherisher; He takes care of each and every heart.
That person, within whose mind You Yourself dwell, never forgets You. |2|

He does that which is pleasing to Himself.
He is known as the help and support of His devotees, throughout the ages. |3|

Chanting and meditating up the Lord's Name, the mortal never comes to regret anything.
O Nanak, I thirst for the Blessed Vision of Your Darshan; please, fulfill my desire, O Lord. |4|7|109|

Aasaa, Fifth Mehl:
Why are you sleeping, and forgetting the Name, O careless and foolish mortal?
So many have been washed away and carried off by this river of life. |1|

O mortal, get aboard the boat of the Lord's Lotus Feet, and cross over.
Twenty-four hours a day, sing the Glorious Praises of the Lord, in the Saadh Sangat, the Company of the Holy. |1|Pause|

You may enjoy various pleasures, but they are useless without the Name.
Without devotion to the Lord, you shall die in sorrow, again and again. |2|

You may dress and eat and apply scented oils to your body,
but without the meditative remembrance of the Lord, your body shall
surely turn to dust, and you shall have to depart. |3|

How very treacherous is this world-ocean; how very few realize this!
Salvation rests in the Lord's Sanctuary; O Nanak, this is your pre-ordained
destiny. |4|8|110|

Aasaa, Fifth Mehl:
No one is anyone's companion; why take any pride in others?
With the Support of the One Name, this terrible world-ocean is crossed
over. |1|

You are the True Support of me, the poor mortal, O my Perfect True Guru.
Gazing upon the Blessed Vision of Your Darshan, my mind is encouraged.
|1|Pause|

Royal powers, wealth, and worldly involvements are of no use at all.
The Kirtan of the Lord's Praise is my Support; this wealth is everlasting. |2|

As many as are the pleasures of Maya, so many are the shadows they
leave.
The Gurmukhs sing of the Naam, the treasure of peace. |3|

You are the True Lord, the treasure of excellence; O God, You are deep and
unfathomable.
The Lord Master is the hope and support of Nanak's mind. |4|9|111|

Aasaa, Fifth Mehl:
Remembering Him, suffering is removed, and celestial peace is obtained.
Night and day, with your palms pressed together, meditate on the Lord,
Har, Har. |1|

He alone is Nanak's God, unto whom all beings belong.
He is totally pervading everywhere, the Truest of the True. |1|Pause|

Inwardly and outwardly, He is my companion and my helper; He is the One
to be realized.
Adoring Him, my mind is cured of all its ailments. |2|

The Savior Lord is infinite; He saves us from the fire of the womb.

Section 08 - Raag Aasaa - Part 053

The Name of the Lord, Har, Har, is soothing and cool; remembering it in meditation, the inner fire is quenched. |3|

Peace, poise, and immense bliss, O Nanak, are obtained, when one becomes the dust of the feet of the humble servants of the Lord.
All of one's affairs are perfectly resolved, meeting with the Perfect Guru. |4|10|112|

Aasaa, Fifth Mehl:
The Lord of the Universe is the treasure of excellence; He is known only to the Gurmukh.
When He shows His Mercy and Kindness, we revel in the Lord's Love. |1|

Come, O Saints - let us join together and speak the Sermon of the Lord.
Night and day, meditate on the Naam, the Name of the Lord, and ignore the criticism of others. |1|Pause|

I live by chanting and meditating on the Naam, and so I obtain immense bliss.
Attachment to the world is useless and vain; it is false, and perishes in the end. |2|

How rare are those who embrace love for the Lord's Lotus Feet.
Blessed and beautiful is that mouth, which meditates on the Lord. |3|

The pains of birth, death and reincarnation are erased by meditating on the Lord.
That alone is Nanak's joy, which is pleasing to God. |4|11|113|

Aasaa, Fifth Mehl:
Come, O friends: let us meet together and enjoy all the tastes and flavors.
Let us join together and chant the Ambrosial Name of the Lord, Har, Har, and so wipe away our sins. |1|

Reflect upon the essence of reality, O Saintly beings, and no troubles shall afflict you.

All of the thieves shall be destroyed, as the Gurmukhs remain wakeful. |1|Pause|

Take wisdom and humility as your supplies, and burn away the poison of pride.
True is that shop, and perfect the transaction; deal only in the merchandise of the Naam, the Name of the Lord. |2|

They alone are accepted and approved, who dedicate their souls, bodies and wealth.
Those who are pleasing to their God, celebrate in happiness. |3|

Those fools, who drink in the wine of evil-mindedness, become the husbands of prostitutes.
But those who are imbued with the sublime essence of the Lord, O Nanak, are intoxicated with the Truth. |4|12|114|

Aasaa, Fifth Mehl:
I made the effort; I did it, and made a beginning.
I live by chanting and meditating on the Naam. The Guru has implanted this Mantra within me. |1|

I fall at the Feet of the True Guru, who has dispelled my doubts.
Bestowing His Mercy, God has dressed me, and decorated me with the Truth. |1|Pause|

Taking me by the hand, He made me His own, through the True Order of His Command.
That gift which God gave to me, is perfect greatness. |2|

Forever and ever, sing the Glorious Praises of the Lord, and chant the Name of the Destroyer of ego.
My vows have been honored, by the Grace of God and the True Guru, who has showered His Mercy. |3|

The Perfect Guru has given the wealth of the Naam, and the profit of singing the Lord's Glorious Praises.
The Saints are the traders, O Nanak, and the Infinite Lord God is their Banker. |4|13|115|

Aasaa, Fifth Mehl:
One who has You as His Master, O God, is blessed with great destiny.
He is happy, and forever at peace; his doubts and fears are all dispelled.
|1|

I am the slave of the Lord of the Universe; my Master is the greatest of all.
He is the Creator, the Cause of causes; He is my True Guru. |1|Pause|

There is no other whom I should fear.

Section 08 - Raag Aasaa - Part 054

Serving the Guru, the Mansion of the Lord's Presence is obtained, and the
impassable world-ocean is crossed over. |2|

By Your Glance of Grace, peace is obtained, and the treasure fills the mind.
That servant, unto whom You bestow Your Mercy, is approved and
accepted. |3|

How rare is that person who drinks in the Ambrosial Essence of the Lord's
Kirtan.
Nanak has obtained the commodity of the One Name; he lives by chanting
and meditating on it within his heart. |4|14|116|

Aasaa, Fifth Mehl:
I am God's maid-servant; He is the highest of all.
All things, big and small, are said to belong to Him. |1|

I surrender my soul, my breath of life, and my wealth, to my Lord Master.
Through His Name, I become radiant; I am known as His slave. |1|Pause|

You are Carefree, the Embodiment of Bliss. Your Name is a gem, a jewel.
One who has You as her Master, is satisfied, satiated and happy forever.
|2|

O my companions and fellow maidens, please implant that balanced
understanding within me.
Serve the Holy Saints lovingly, and find the treasure of the Lord. |3|

All are servants of the Lord Master, and all call Him their own.

She alone dwells in peace, O Nanak, whom the Lord adorns. |4|15|117|

Aasaa, Fifth Mehl:
Become the servant of the Saints, and learn this way of life.
Of all virtues, the most sublime virtue is to see your Husband Lord near at hand. |1|

So, dye this mind of yours with the color of the Lord's Love.
Renounce cleverness and cunning, and know that the Sustainer of the world is with you. |1|Pause|

Whatever your Husband Lord says, accept that, and make it your decoration.
Forget the love of duality, and chew upon this betel leaf. |2|

Make the Word of the Guru's Shabad your lamp, and let your bed be Truth.
Twenty-four hours a day, stand with your palms pressed together, and the Lord, your King, shall meet you. |3|

She alone is cultured and embellished, and she alone is of incomparable beauty.
She alone is the happy soul-bride, O Nanak, who is pleasing to the Creator Lord. |4|16|118|

Aasaa, Fifth Mehl:
As long as there are doubts in the mind, the mortal staggers and falls.
The Guru removed my doubts, and I have obtained my place of rest. |1|

Those quarrelsome enemies have been overcome, through the Guru.
I have now escaped from them, and they have run away from me. |1|Pause|

He is concerned with 'mine and yours', and so he is held in bondage.
When the Guru dispelled my ignorance, then the noose of death was cut away from my neck. |2|

As long as he does not understand the Command of God's Will, he remains miserable.
Meeting with the Guru, he comes to recognize God's Will, and then, he becomes happy. |3|

I have no enemies and no adversaries; no one is wicked to me.

That servant, who performs the Lord's service, O Nanak, is the slave of the Lord Master. |4|17|119|

Aasaa, Fifth Mehl:

Peace, celestial poise and absolute bliss are obtained, singing the Kirtan of the Lord's Praises.

Bestowing His Name, the True Guru removes the evil omens. |1|

I am a sacrifice to my Guru; forever and ever, I am a sacrifice to Him.

Section 08 - Raag Aasaa - Part 055

I am a sacrifice to the Guru; meeting Him, I am absorbed into the True Lord. |1|Pause|

Good omens and bad omens affect those who do not keep the Lord in the mind.

The Messenger of Death does not approach those who are pleasing to the Lord God. |2|

Donations to charity, meditation and penance - above all of them is the Naam.

One who chants with his tongue the Name of the Lord, Har, Har - his works are brought to perfect completion. |3|

His fears are removed, and his doubts and attachments are gone; he sees none other than God.

O Nanak, the Supreme Lord God preserves him, and no pain or sorrow afflicts him any longer. |4|18|120|

Aasaa, Ninth House, Fifth Mehl:

One Universal Creator God. By The Grace Of The True Guru:

Contemplating Him within my consciousness, I obtain total peace; but hereafter, will I be pleasing to Him or not?

There is only One Giver; all others are beggars. Who else can we turn to? |1|

When I beg from others, I am ashamed.
The One Lord Master is the Supreme King of all; who else is equal to Him?
|1|Pause|

Standing up and sitting down, I cannot live without Him. I search and search for the Blessed Vision of His Darshan.
Even Brahma and the sages Sanak, Sanandan, Sanaatan and Sanat Kumar, find it difficult to obtain the Mansion of the Lord's Presence. |2|

He is unapproachable and unfathomable; His wisdom is deep and pro-found; His value cannot be appraised.
I have taken to the Sanctuary of the True Lord, the Primal Being, and I meditate on the True Guru. |3|

God, the Lord Master, has become kind and compassionate; He has cut the noose of death away from my neck.
Says Nanak, now that I have obtained the Saadh Sangat, the Company of the Holy, I shall not have to be reincarnated again. |4|1|121|

Aasaa, Fifth Mehl:
Inwardly, I sing His Praises, and outwardly, I sing His Praises; I sing His Praises while awake and asleep.
I am a trader in the Name of the Lord of the Universe; He has given it to me as my supplies, to carry with me. |1|

I have forgotten and forsaken other things.
The Perfect Guru has given me the Gift of the Naam; this alone is my Support. |1|Pause|

I sing His Praises while suffering, and I sing His Praises while I am at peace as well. I contemplate Him while I walk along the Path.
The Guru has implanted the Naam within my mind, and my thirst has been quenched. |2|

I sing His Praises during the day, and I sing His Praises during the night; I sing them with each and every breath.
In the Sat Sangat, the True Congregation, this faith is established, that the Lord is with us, in life and in death. |3|

Bless servant Nanak with this gift, O God, that he may obtain, and enshrine in his heart, the dust of the feet of the Saints.

Hear the Lord's Sermon with your ears, and behold the Blessed Vision of His Darshan with your eyes; place your forehead upon the Guru's Feet. |4|2|122|

One Universal Creator God. By The Grace Of The True Guru: Aasaa, Tenth House, Fifth Mehl:

One Universal Creator God. By The Grace Of The True Guru: Aasaa, Tenth House, Fifth Mehl:

That which you believe to be permanent, is a guest here for only a few days.

Section 08 - Raag Aasaa - Part 056

Children, wives, homes, and all possessions - attachment to all of these is false. |1|

O mind, why do you burst out laughing?

See with your eyes, that these things are only mirages. So earn the profit of meditation on the One Lord. |1|Pause|

It is like the clothes which you wear on your body - they wear off in a few days.

How long can you run upon a wall? Ultimately, you come to its end. |2|

It is like salt, preserved in its container; when it is put into water, it dissolves.

When the Order of the Supreme Lord God comes, the soul arises, and departs in an instant. |3|

O mind, your steps are numbered, your moments spent sitting are numbered, and the breaths you are to take are numbered.

Sing forever the Praises of the Lord, O Nanak, and you shall be saved, under the Shelter of the Feet of the True Guru. |4|1|123|

Aasaa, Fifth Mehl:

That which was upside-down has been set upright; the deadly enemies and adversaries have become friends.

In the darkness, the jewel shines forth, and the impure understanding has become pure. |1|

When the Lord of the Universe became merciful,
I found peace, wealth and the fruit of the Lord's Name; I have met the True Guru. |1|Pause|

No one knew me, the miserable miser, but now, I have become famous all over the world.
Before, no one would even sit with me, but now, all worship my feet. |2|

I used to wander in search of pennies, but now, all the desires of my mind are satisfied.
I could not bear even one criticism, but now, in the Saadh Sangat, the Company of the Holy, I am cooled and soothed. |3|

What Glorious Virtues of the Inaccessible, Unfathomable, Profound Lord can one mere tongue describe?
Please, make me the slave of the slave of Your slaves; servant Nanak seeks the Lord's Sanctuary. |4|2|124|

Aasaa, Fifth Mehl:
O fool, you are so slow to earn your profits, and so quick to run up losses.
You do not purchase the inexpensive merchandise; O sinner, you are tied to your debts. |1|

O True Guru, You are my only hope.
Your Name is the Purifier of sinners, O Supreme Lord God; You are my only Shelter. |1|Pause|

Listening to the evil talk, you are caught up in it, but you are hesitant to chant the Naam, the Name of the Lord.
You are delighted by slanderous talk; your understanding is corrupt. |2|

Others' wealth, others' wives and the slander of others - eating the uneatable, you have gone crazy.
You have not enshrined love for the True Faith of Dharma; hearing the Truth, you are enraged. |3|

O God, Merciful to the meek, Compassionate Lord Master, Your Name is the Support of Your devotees.
Nanak has come to Your Sanctuary; O God, make him Your Own, and preserve his honor. |4|3|125|

Aasaa, Fifth Mehl
: They are attached to falsehood; clinging to the transitory, they are trapped in emotional attachment to Maya.
Wherever they go, they do not think of the Lord; they are blinded by intellectual egotism. |1|

O mind, O renunciate, why don't you adore Him?
You dwell in that flimsy chamber, with all the sins of corruption. |1|Pause|

Crying out, "Mine, mine", your days and nights pass away; moment by moment, your life is running out.

Section 08 - Raag Aasaa - Part 057

The sweet flavors tempt you, and you are occupied by your false and filthy business. |2|

Your senses are beguiled by sensual pleasures of sex, by anger, greed and emotional attachment.
The All-powerful Architect of Destiny has ordained that you shall be reincarnated over and over again. |3|

When the Destroyer of the pains of the poor becomes merciful, then, as Gurmukh, you shall find absolute peace.
Says Nanak, meditate on the Lord, day and night, and all your sickness shall be banished. |4|

Meditate in this way, O Siblings of Destiny, on the Lord, the Architect of Destiny.
The Destroyer of the pains of the poor has become merciful; He has removed the pains of birth and death. |1|Second Pause|4|4|126|

Aasaa, Fifth Mehl:
For a moment of sexual pleasure, you shall suffer in pain for millions of days.

For an instant, you may savor pleasure, but afterwards, you shall regret it, again and again. |1|

O blind man, meditate on the Lord, the Lord, your King.
Your day is drawing near. |1|Pause|

You are deceived, beholding with your eyes, the bitter melon and swallow-wort.
But, like the companionship of a poisonous snake, so is the desire for another's spouse. |2|

For the sake of your enemy, you commit sins, while you neglect the reality of your faith.
Your friendship is with those who abandon you, and you are angry with your friends. |3|

The entire world is entangled in this way; he alone is saved, who has the Perfect Guru.
Says Nanak, I have crossed over the terrifying world-ocean; my body has become sanctified. |4|5|127|

Aasaa, Fifth Mehl Dupadas:
O Lord, You behold whatever we do in secrecy; the fool may stubbornly deny it.
By his own actions, he is tied down, and in the end, he regrets and repents. |1|

My God knows, ahead of time, all things.
Deceived by doubt, you may hide your actions, but in the end, you shall have to confess the secrets of your mind. |1|Pause|

Whatever they are attached to, they remain joined to that. What can any mere mortal do?
Please, forgive me, O Supreme Lord Master. Nanak is forever a sacrifice to You. |2|6|128|

Aasaa, Fifth Mehl:
He Himself preserves His servants; He causes them to chant His Name.
Wherever the business and affairs of His servants are, there the Lord hurries to be. |1|

The Lord appears near at hand to His servant.
Whatever the servant asks of his Lord and Master, immediately comes to pass. |1|Pause|

I am a sacrifice to that servant, who is pleasing to his God.
Hearing of his glory, the mind is rejuvenated; Nanak comes to touch his feet. |2|7|129|

Aasaa, Eleventh House, Fifth Mehl:
One Universal Creator God. By The Grace Of The True Guru:
The actor displays himself in many disguises, but he remains just as he is.
The soul wanders through countless incarnations in doubt, but it does not come to dwell in peace. |1|

Section 08 - Raag Aasaa - Part 058

O Saints, my friends and companions, without the Lord, Har, Har, you shall perish.
Joining the Saadh Sangat, the Company of the Holy, sing the Glorious Praises of the Lord, and win this precious treasure of human life. |1|Pause|

God has created Maya of the three qualities; tell me, how can it be crossed over?
The whirlpool is awesome and unfathomable; only through the Word of the Guru's Shabad is one carried across. |2|

Searching and searching endlessly, seeking and deliberating, Nanak has realized the true essence of reality.
Meditating on the invaluable treasure of the Naam, the Name of the Lord, the jewel of the mind is satisfied. |3|1|130|

Aasaa, Fifth Mehl, Dupadas:
By Guru's Grace, He dwells within my mind; whatever I ask for, I receive.
This mind is satisfied with the Love of the Naam, the Name of the Lord; it does not go out, anywhere, anymore. |1|

My Lord and Master is the highest of all; night and day, I sing the Glories of His Praises.

In an instant, He establishes and disestablishes; through Him, I frighten you. |1|Pause|

When I behold my God, my Lord and Master, I do not pay any attention to any other.
God Himself has adorned servant Nanak; his doubts and fears have been dispelled, and he writes the account of the Lord. |2|2|131|

Aasaa, Fifth Mehl:
The four castes and social classes, and the preachers with the six Shaastras on their finger-tips,
the beautiful, the refined, the shapely and the wise - the five passions have enticed and beguiled them all. |1|

Who has seized and conquered the five powerful fighters? Is there anyone strong enough?
He alone, who conquers and defeats the five demons, is perfect in this Dark Age of Kali Yuga. |1|Pause|

They are so awesome and great; they cannot be controlled, and they do not run away. Their army is mighty and unyielding.
Says Nanak, that humble being who is under the protection of the Saadh Sangat, crushes those terrible demons. |2|3|132|

Aasaa, Fifth Mehl:
The Sublime Sermon of the Lord is the best thing for the soul. All other tastes are insipid. |1|Pause|

The worthy beings, heavenly singers, silent sages and the knowers of the six Shaastras proclaim that nothing else is worthy of consideration. |1|

It is the cure for evil passions, unique, unequalled and peace-giving; in the Saadh Sangat, the Company of the Holy, O Nanak, drink it in. |2|4|133|

Aasaa, Fifth Mehl:
My Beloved has brought forth a river of nectar. The Guru has not held it back from my mind, even for an instant. |1|Pause|

Beholding it, and touching it, I am sweetened and delighted. It is imbued with the Creator's Love. |1|

Chanting it even for a moment, I rise to the Guru; meditating on it, one is not trapped by the Messenger of Death. The Lord has placed it as a garland around Nanak's neck, and within his heart. |2|5|134|

Aasaa, Fifth Mehl:
The Saadh Sangat, the Company of the Holy, is exalted and sublime. |Pause|

Every day, hour and moment, I continually sing and speak of Govind, Govind, the Lord of the Universe. |1|

Walking, sitting and sleeping, I chant the Lord's Praises; I treasure His Feet in my mind and body. |2|

I am so small, and You are so great, O Lord and Master; Nanak seeks Your Sanctuary. |3|6|135|

Section 08 - Raag Aasaa - Part 059

Raag Aasaa, Fifth Mehl, Twelfth House:
One Universal Creator God. By The Grace Of The True Guru:
Renounce all your cleverness and remember the Supreme, Formless Lord God.
Without the One True Name, everything appears as dust. |1|

Know that God is always with you.
By Guru's Grace, one understands, and is imbued with the Love of the One Lord. |1|Pause|

Seek the Shelter of the One All-powerful Lord; there is no other place of rest.
The vast and terrifying world-ocean is crossed over, singing continually the Glorious Praises of the Lord. |2|

Birth and death are overcome, and one does not have to suffer in the City of Death.
He alone obtains the treasure of the Naam, the Name of the Lord, unto whom God shows His Mercy. |3|

The One Lord is my Anchor and Support; the One Lord alone is the power of my mind.

O Nanak, joining the Saadh Sangat, the Company of the Holy, meditate on Him; without the Lord, there is no other at all. |4|1|136|

Aasaa, Fifth Mehl:

The soul, the mind, the body and the breath of life belong to God. He has given all tastes and pleasures.

He is the Friend of the poor, the Giver of life, the Protector of those who seek His Sanctuary. |1|

O my mind, meditate on the Name of the Lord, Har, Har.

Here and hereafter, He is our Helper and Companion; embrace love and affection for the One Lord. |1|Pause|

They meditate on the Vedas and the Shaastras, to swim across the world-ocean.

The many religious rituals, good deeds of karma and Dharmic worship - above all of these is the Naam, the Name of the Lord. |2|

Sexual desire, anger, and egotism depart, meeting with the Divine True Guru.

Implant the Naam within, perform devotional worship to the Lord and serve God - this is good. |3|

I seek the Sanctuary of Your Feet, O Merciful Lord; You are the Honor of the dishonored.

You are the Support of my soul, my breath of life; O God, You are Nanak's strength. |4|2|137|

Aasaa, Fifth Mehl:

He wavers and falters, and suffers such great pain, without the Saadh Sangat, the Company of the Holy.

The profit of the sublime essence of the Lord of the Universe is obtained, by the Love of the One Supreme Lord God. |1|

Chant continually the Name of the Lord.

With each and every breath, meditate on God, and renounce other love. |1|Pause|

God is the Doer, the All-powerful Cause of causes; He Himself is the Giver of life.
So renounce all your cleverness, and meditate on God, twenty-four hours a day. |2|

He is our best friend and companion, our help and support; He is lofty, inaccessible and infinite.
Enshrine His Lotus Feet within your heart; He is the Support of the soul. |3|

Show Your Mercy, O Supreme Lord God, that I may sing Your Glorious Praises.
Total peace, and the greatest greatness, O Nanak, are obtained by living to chant the Name of the Lord. |4|3|138|

Aasaa, Fifth Mehl:
I make the effort, as You cause me to do, my Lord and Master, to behold You in the Saadh Sangat, the Company of the Holy.
I am imbued with the color of the Love of the Lord, Har, Har; God Himself has colored me in His Love. |1|

I chant the Lord's Name within my mind.
Bestow Your Mercy, and dwell within my heart; please, become my Helper. |1|Pause|

Listening continually to Your Name, O Beloved God, I yearn to behold You.

Section 08 - Raag Aasaa - Part 060

Please, be kind to me - I am just a worm. This is my object and purpose. |2|

My body and wealth are Yours; You are my God - nothing is in my power.
As You keep me, so do I live; I eat what You give me. |3|

The sins of countless incarnations are washed away, by bathing in the dust of the Lord's humble servants.
By loving devotional worship, doubt and fear depart; O Nanak, the Lord is Ever-present. |4|4|139|

Aasaa, Fifth Mehl:

The Blessed Vision of Your Darshan is unapproachable and incomprehensible; he alone obtains it, who has such good destiny recorded upon his forehead.
The Merciful Lord God has bestowed His Mercy, and the True Guru has granted the Lord's Name. |1|

The Divine Guru is the Saving Grace in this Dark Age of Kali Yuga.
Even those fools and idiots, stained with feces and urine, have all taken to Your service. |1|Pause|

You Yourself are the Creator, who established the entire world. You are contained in all.
The Righteous Judge of Dharma is wonder-struck, at the sight of everyone falling at the Lord's Feet. |2|

The Golden Age of Sat Yuga, the Silver Age of Trayta Yuga, and the Brass Age of Dwaapar Yuga are good; but the best is the Dark Age, the Iron Age, of Kali Yuga.
As we act, so are the rewards we receive; no one can take the place of another. |3|

O Dear Lord, whatever Your devotees ask for, You do. This is Your Way, Your very nature.
With my palms pressed together, O Nanak, I beg for this gift; Lord, please bless Your Saints with Your Vision. |4|5|140|

Raag Aasaa, Fifth Mehl, Thirteenth House:
One Universal Creator God. By The Grace Of The True Guru:
O True Guru, by Your Words,
even the worthless have been saved. |1|Pause|

Even the most argumentative, vicious and indecent people, have been purified in Your company. |1|

Those who have wandered in reincarnation, and those who have been consigned to hell - even their families have been redeemed. |2|

Those whom no one knew, and those whom no one respected - even they have become famous and respected at the Court of the Lord. |3|

What praise, and what greatness should I attribute to You? Nanak is a sacrifice to You, each and every moment. |4|1|141|

Aasaa, Fifth Mehl:
The crazy people are asleep. |1|Pause|

They are intoxicated with attachment to their families and sensory pleasures; they are held in the grip of falsehood. |1|

The false desires, and the dream-like delights and pleasures - these, the self-willed manmukhs call true. |2|

The wealth of the Ambrosial Naam, the Name of the Lord, is with them, but they do not find even a tiny bit of its mystery. |3|

By Your Grace, O Lord, You save those, who take to the Sanctuary of the Sat Sangat, the True Congregation. |4|2|142|

Aasaa, Fifth Mehl, Tipadas:
I seek the Love of my Beloved. |1|Pause|

Gold, jewels, giant pearls and rubies - I have no need for them. |1|

Imperial power, fortunes, royal command and mansions

Section 08 - Raag Aasaa - Part 061

- I have no desire for these. |2|

The Sanctuary of the Lord's Feet, and dedication to the Saints
- these bring me peace and pleasure.
O Nanak, my burning fire has been put out,
obtaining the Love of the Beloved. |3|3|143|

Aasaa, Fifth Mehl:
The Guru has revealed Him to my eyes. |1|Pause|

Here and there, in each and every heart, and each and every being, You, O Fascinating Lord, You exist. |1|

You are the Creator, the Cause of causes, the Support of the earth; You are the One and only, Beauteous Lord. |2|

Meeting the Saints, and beholding the Blessed Vision of their Darshan, Nanak is a sacrifice to them; he sleeps in absolute peace. |3|4|144|

Aasaa, Fifth Mehl:
The Name of the Lord, Har, Har, is priceless.
It brings peace and poise. |1|Pause|

The Lord is my Companion and Helper; He shall not forsake me or leave me. He Is unfathomable and unequalled. |1|

He is my Beloved, my brother, father and mother; He is the Support of His devotees. |2|

The Invisible Lord is seen through the Guru; O Nanak, this is the wondrous play of the Lord. |3|5|145|

Aasaa, Fifth Mehl:
Please help me sustain my devotion.
O Lord Master, I have come to You. |1|Pause|

With the wealth of the Naam, the Name of the Lord, life becomes fruitful. Lord, please place Your Feet within my heart. |1|

This is liberation, and this is the best way of life; please, keep me in the Society of the Saints. |2|

Meditating on the Naam, I am absorbed in celestial peace; O Nanak, I sing the Glorious Praises of the Lord. |3|6|146|

Aasaa, Fifth Mehl:
The Feet of my Lord and Master are so Beautiful!
The Lord's Saints obtain them. |1|Pause|

They eradicate their self-conceit and serve the Lord; drenched in His Love, they sing His Glorious Praises. |1|

They place their hopes in Him, and they thirst for the Blessed Vision of His Darshan. Nothing else is pleasing to them. |2|

This is Your Mercy, Lord; what can Your poor creatures do? Nanak is devoted, a sacrifice to You. |3|7|147|

Aasaa, Fifth Mehl:
Remember the One Lord in meditation within your mind. |1|Pause|

Meditate on the Naam, the Name of the Lord, and enshrine Him within your heart. Without Him there is no other. |1|

Entering God's Sanctuary, all rewards are obtained, and all pains are taken away. |2|

He is the Giver of all beings, the Architect of Destiny; O Nanak, He is contained in each and every heart. |3|8|148|

Aasaa, Fifth Mehl:
One who forgets the Lord is dead. |1|Pause|

One who meditates on the Naam, the Name of the Lord, obtains all rewards. That person becomes happy. |1|

One who calls himself a king, and acts in ego and pride, is caught by his doubts, like a parrot in a trap. |2|

Says Nanak, one who meets the True Guru, becomes permanent and immortal. |3|9|149|

Aasaa, Fifth Mehl, Fourteenth House:
One Universal Creator God. By The Grace Of The True Guru:
That love is forever fresh and new,
which is for the Beloved Lord. |1|Pause|

One who is pleasing to God shall not be reincarnated again.
He remains absorbed in the loving devotional worship of the Lord, in the Love of the Lord. |1|

Section 08 - Raag Aasaa - Part 062

He is blended with God, by dedicating his mind to Him.
Bless Nanak with Your Name, O Lord - please, shower Your Mercy upon him! |2|1|150|

Aasaa, Fifth Mehl:
Please, come to me, O Beloved Lord; without You, no one can comfort me. |1|Pause|

One may read the Simritees and the Shaastras, and perform all sorts of religious rituals; and yet, without the Blessed Vision of Your Darshan, God, there is no peace at all. |1|

People have grown weary of observing fasts, vows and rigorous self-discipline; Nanak abides with God, in the Sanctuary of the Saints. |2|2|151|

Aasaa, Fifth Mehl, Fifteenth House, Partaal:
One Universal Creator God. By The Grace Of The True Guru:
He sleeps, intoxicated by corruption and Maya; he does not come to realize or understand.
Seizing him by the hair, the Messenger of Death pulls him up; then, he comes to his senses. |1|

Those who are attached to the poison of greed and sin grab at the wealth of others; they only bring pain on themselves.
They are intoxicated by their pride in those things which shall be destroyed in an instant; those demons do not understand. |1|Pause|

The Vedas, the Shaastras and the holy men proclaim it, but the deaf do not hear it.
When the game of life is over, and he has lost, and he breathes his last, then the fool regrets and repents in his mind. |2|

He paid the fine, but it is in vain - in the Court of the Lord, his account is not credited.
Those deeds which would have covered him - those deeds, he has not done. |3|

The Guru has shown me the world to be thus; I sing the Kirtan of the Praises of the One Lord.

Renouncing his pride in strength and cleverness, Nanak has come to the Lord's Sanctuary. |4|1|152|

Aasaa, Fifth Mehl:
Dealing in the Name of the Lord of the Universe,
and pleasing the Saints and holy men, obtain the Beloved Lord and sing His Glorious Praises; play the sound current of the Naad with the five instruments. |1|Pause|

Obtaining His Mercy, I easily gained the Blessed Vision of His Darshan; now, I am imbued with the Love of the Lord of the Universe.
Serving the Saints, I feel love and affection for my Beloved Lord Master. |1|

The Guru has implanted spiritual wisdom within my mind, and I rejoice that I shall not have to come back again. I have obtained celestial poise, and the treasure within my mind.
I have renounced all of the affairs of my mind's desires.
It has been so long, so long, so long, so very long, since my mind has felt such a great thirst.
Please, reveal to me the Blessed Vision of Your Darshan, and show Yourself to me.
Nanak the meek has entered Your Sanctuary; please, take me in Your embrace. |2|2|153|

Aasaa, Fifth Mehl:
Who can destroy the fortress of sin,
and release me from hope, thirst, deception, attachment and doubt? |1|Pause|

How can I escape the afflictions of sexual desire, anger, greed and pride? |1|

In the Society of the Saints, love the Naam, and sing the Glorious Praises of the Lord of the Universe.
Night and day, meditate on God.
I have captured and demolished the walls of doubt.
O Nanak, the Naam is my only treasure. |2|3|154|

Aasaa, Fifth Mehl:
Renounce sexual desire, anger and greed;
remember the Name of the Lord of the Universe in your mind.
Meditation on the Lord is the only fruitful action. |1|Pause|

Section 08 - Raag Aasaa - Part 063

Renounce pride, attachment, corruption and falsehood, and chant the
Name of the Lord, Raam, Raam, Raam.
O mortal, attach yourself to the Feet of the Saints. |1|

God is the Sustainer of the world, Merciful to the meek, the Purifier of
sinners, the Transcendent Lord God. Awaken, and meditate on His Feet.
Perform His devotional worship, O Nanak, and your destiny shall be
fulfilled. |2|4|155|

Aasaa, Fifth Mehl:
Pleasure and pain, detachment and ecstasy - the Lord has revealed His Play.
|1|Pause|

One moment, the mortal is in fear, and the next moment he is fearless; in a
moment, he gets up and departs.
One moment, he enjoys pleasures, and the next moment, he leaves and
goes away. |1|

One moment, he practices Yoga and intense meditation, and all sorts of
worship; the next moment, he wanders in doubt.
One moment, O Nanak, the Lord bestows His Mercy and blesses him with
His Love, in the Saadh Sangat, the Company of the Holy. |2|5|156|

Raag Aasaa, Fifth Mehl, Seventeenth House, Aasaavaree:
One Universal Creator God. By The Grace Of The True Guru:
Meditate on the Lord, the Lord of the Universe.
Cherish the Beloved Lord, Har, Har, in your mind.
The Guru says to install it in your consciousness.
Turn away from others, and turn to Him.
Thus you shall obtain your Beloved, O my companion. |1|Pause|

In the pool of the world is the mud of attachment.
Stuck in it, his feet cannot walk towards the Lord.

The fool is stuck;
he cannot do anything else.
Only by entering the Lord's Sanctuary, O my companion, will you be released. |1|

Thus your consciousness shall be stable and steady and firm.
Wilderness and household are the same.
Deep within dwells the One Husband Lord;
outwardly, there are many distractions.
Practice Raja Yoga, the Yoga of meditation and success.
Says Nanak, this is the way to dwell with the people, and yet remain apart from them. |2|1|157|

Aasaavaree, Fifth Mehl:
Cherish one desire only:
meditate continually on the Guru.
Install the wisdom of the Saints' Mantra.
Serve the Feet of the Guru,
and you shall meet Him, by Guru's Grace, O my mind. |1|Pause|

All doubts are dispelled,
and the Lord is seen to be pervading all places.
The fear of death is dispelled,
and the primal place is obtained.
Then, all subservience is removed. |1|

One who has such destiny recorded upon his forehead, obtains it;
he crosses over the terrifying ocean of fire.
He obtains a place in the home of his own self,
and enjoys the most sublime essence of the Lord's essence.
His hunger is appeased;
Nanak, he is absorbed in celestial peace, O my mind. |2|2|158|

Aasaavaree, Fifth Mehl:
Sing the Praises of the Lord, Har, Har, Har.
Meditate on the celestial music.
The tongues of the holy Saints repeat it.
I have heard that this is the way to emancipation.
This is found by the greatest merit, O my mind. |1|Pause|

The silent sages search for Him.
God is the Master of all.
It is so difficult to find Him in this world, in this Dark Age of Kali Yuga.
He is the Dispeller of distress.
God is the Fulfiller of desires, O my mind. |1|

O my mind, serve Him.

Section 08 - Raag Aasaa - Part 064

He is unknowable and inscrutable.
Enshrine love for Him.
He does not perish, or go away, or die.
He is known only through the Guru.
Nanak, my mind is satisfied with the Lord, O my mind. |2|3|159|

Aasaavaree, Fifth Mehl:
Grab hold of the Support of the One Lord.
Chant the Word of the Guru's Shabad.
Submit to the Order of the True Lord.
Receive the treasure in your mind.
Thus you shall be absorbed in peace, O my mind. |1|Pause|

One who is dead while yet alive,
crosses over the terrifying world-ocean.
One who becomes the dust of all
- he alone is called fearless.
His anxieties are removed
by the Teachings of the Saints, O my mind. |1|

That humble being, who takes happiness in the Naam, the Name of the Lord
- pain never draws near him.
One who listens to the Praise of the Lord, Har, Har,
is obeyed by all men.
How fortunate it is that he came into the world;
Nanak, he is pleasing to God, O my mind. |2|4|160|

Aasaavaree, Fifth Mehl:
Meeting together, let us sing the Praises of the Lord,

and attain the supreme state.
Those who obtain that sublime essence,
obtain all of the spiritual powers of the Siddhas.
They remain awake and aware night and day;
Nanak, they are blessed by great good fortune, O my mind. |1|Pause|

Let us wash the feet of the Saints;
our evil-mindedness shall be cleansed.
Becoming the dust of the feet of the Lord's slaves,
one shall not be afflicted with pain.
Taking to the Sanctuary of His devotees,
he is no longer subject to birth and death.
They alone become eternal,
who chant the Name of the Lord, Har, Har, O my mind. |1|

You are my Friend, my Best Friend.
Please, implant the Naam, the Name of the Lord, within me.
Without Him, there is not any other.
Within my mind, I worship Him in adoration.
I do not forget Him, even for an instant.
How can I live without Him?
I am a sacrifice to the Guru.
Nanak, chant the Name, O my mind. |2|5|161|

Aasaavaree, Fifth Mehl:
You are the Creator, the Cause of causes.
I cannot think of any other.
Whatever You do, comes to pass.
I sleep in peace and poise.
My mind has become patient,
since I fell at God's Door, O my mind. |1|Pause|

Joining the Saadh Sangat, the Company of the Holy,
I gained perfect control over my senses.
Ever since I rid myself of my self-conceit,
my sufferings have ended.
He has showered His Mercy upon me.
The Creator Lord has preserved my honor, O my mind. |1|

Know that this is the only peace;

accept whatever the Lord does.
No one is bad.
Become the dust of the Feet of the Saints.
He Himself preserves those
who taste the Ambrosial Nectar of the Lord, O my mind. |2|

One who has no one to call his own
- God belongs to him.
God knows the state of our innermost being.
He knows everything.
Please, Lord, save the sinners.
This is Nanak's prayer, O my mind. |3|6|162|

Aasaavaree, Fifth Mehl, Ik-Tukas:
O my stranger soul,
listen to the call. |1|Pause|

Whatever you are attached to,

Section 08 - Raag Aasaa - Part 065

you shall have to leave it all behind.
These things seem like only a dream,
to one who takes the Lord's Name. |1|

Forsaking the Lord, and clinging to another,
they run toward death and reincarnation.
But those humble beings, who attach themselves to the Lord, Har, Har,
continue to live.
One who is blessed with the Lord's Mercy,
O Nanak, becomes His devotee. |2|7|163|232|

One Universal Creator God. By The Grace Of The True Guru:
Raag Aasaa, Ninth Mehl:
Who should I tell the condition of the mind?
Engrossed in greed, running around in the ten directions, you hold to your
hopes of wealth. |1|Pause|

For the sake of pleasure, you suffer such great pain, and you have to serve
each and every person.

You wander from door to door like a dog, unconscious of the Lord's meditation. |1|

You lose this human life in vain, and You are not even ashamed when others laugh at you.
O Nanak, why not sing the Lord's Praises, so that you may be rid of the body's evil disposition? |2|1|233|

Raag Aasaa, First Mehl, Ashtapadees, Second House:
One Universal Creator God. By The Grace Of The True Guru:
He descends the treacherous precipice, to bathe in the cleansing pool;
without speaking or saying anything, he sings the Glorious Praises of the Lord.
Like water vapor in the sky, he remains absorbed in the Lord.
He churns the true pleasures to obtain the supreme nectar. |1|

Listen to such spiritual wisdom, O my mind.
The Lord is totally pervading and permeating all places. |1|Pause|

One who makes Truthfulness his fast and religious vows, does not suffer the pain of death.
Through the Word of the Guru's Shabad, he burns away his anger.
He dwells in the Tenth Gate, immersed in the Samaadhi of deep meditation.
Touching the philosopher's stone, he obtains the supreme status. |2|

For the benefit of the mind, churn the true essence of reality;
bathing in the over-flowing tank of nectar, filth is washed away.
We become like the One with whom we are imbued.
Whatever the Creator does, comes to pass. |3|

The Guru is cool and soothing like ice; He puts out the fire of the mind.
Smear your body with the ashes of dedicated service,
and live in the home of peace - make this your religious order.
Let the Immaculate Bani of the Word be your playing of the flute. |4|

Spiritual wisdom within is the supreme, sublime nectar.
Contemplation of the Guru is one's bathing at holy places of pilgrimage.
Worship and adoration within is the Lord's dwelling.
He is the One who blends one's light with the Divine Light. |5|

He delights in the delightful wisdom of loving the One Lord.
He is one of the self-elect - he merges with the Lord, who occupies the throne.
He performs his works in obedience to the Will of his Lord and Master.
The Unknowable Lord cannot be understood. |6|

The lotus originates in the water, and yet it remains distinct from the water.
Just so, the Divine Light pervades and permeates the water of the world.
Who is near, and who is far away?
I sing the Glories of the Lord, the treasure of virtue; I behold Him ever-present. |7|

Inwardly and outwardly, there is none other than Him.

Section 08 - Raag Aasaa - Part 066

Whatever pleases Him, comes to pass.
Listen, O Bharthari Yogi - Nanak speaks after deliberation;
the Immaculate Name is my only Support. |8|1|

Aasaa, First Mehl:
All meditation, all austerities, and all clever tricks,
lead one to wander in the wilderness, but he does not find the Path.
Without understanding, he is not approved;
without the Naam, the Name of the Lord, ashes are thrown upon one's head. |1|

True is the Master; the world comes and goes.
The mortal is emancipated, as Gurmukh, as the Lord's slave. |1|Pause|

The world is bound by its attachments to the many desires.
Through the Guru's Teachings, some become free of desire.
Within them is the Naam, and their heart lotus blossoms forth.
They have no fear of death. |2|

The men of the world are conquered by woman; they love the ladies.
Attached to children and wife, they forget the Naam.
They waste this human life in vain, and lose the game in the gamble.

Serving the True Guru is the best occupation. |3|

One who speaks egotistically in public,
never attains liberation within.
One who burns away his attachment to Maya, by the Word of the Guru's Shabad,
meditates forever within his heart on the Immaculate Naam. |4|

He restrains his wandering mind, and keeps it under control.
The company of such a Sikh is obtained only by Grace.
Without the Guru, he goes astray and continues coming and going.
Bestowing His Mercy, the Lord unites him in Union. |5|

I cannot describe the Beauteous Lord.
I speak the unspoken; I cannot estimate His value.
All pain and pleasure come by Your Will.
All pain is eradicated by the True Name. |6|

He plays the instrument without hands, and dances without feet.
But if he understands the Word of the Shabad, then he shall behold the True Lord.
With the True Lord within the self, all happiness comes.
Showering His Mercy, the Preserving Lord preserves him. |7|

He understands the three worlds; he eliminates his self-conceit.
He understands the Bani of the Word, and he is absorbed into the True Lord.
Contemplating the Shabad, he enshrines love for the One Lord.
O Nanak, blessed is the Lord, the Embellisher. |8|2|

Aasaa, First Mehl:
There are innumerable writings; those who write them take pride in them.
When one's mind accepts the Truth, he understands, and speaks of it.
Words, spoken and read again and again, are useless loads.
There are innumerable writings, but the Infinite Lord remains unwritten. |1|

Know that such a True Lord is the One and only.
Understand that birth and death come according to the Lord's Will. |1|Pause|

Because of attachment to Maya, the world is bound by the Messenger of Death.

These bonds are released when one remembers the Naam, the Name of the Lord.

The Guru is the Giver of peace; do not look for any other.

In this world, and the next, He shall stand by you. |2|

One who dies in the Word of the Shabad, embraces love for the One Lord.

One who eats the uneatable, has his doubts dispelled.

He is Jivan Mukta - liberated while yet alive; the Naam abides in his mind.

Becoming Gurmukh, he merges into the True Lord. |3|

The One who created the earth and the Akaashic ethers of the sky,

established all; He establishes and disestablishes.

He Himself is permeating all.

He does not consult anyone; He Himself forgives. |4|

You are the Ocean, over-flowing with jewels and rubies.

You are immaculate and pure, the true treasure of virtue.

Section 08 - Raag Aasaa - Part 067

Peace is enjoyed, meeting the Guru, the Spiritual Teacher.

The Lord is the only Master; He is the only Minister. |5|

The world is held in bondage; he alone is emancipated, who conquers his ego.

How rare in the world is that wise person, who practices this.

How rare in this world is that scholar who reflects upon this.

Without meeting the True Guru, all wander in ego. |6|

The world is unhappy; only a few are happy.

The world is diseased, from its indulgences; it weeps over its lost virtue.

The world wells up, and then subsides, losing its honor.

He alone, who becomes Gurmukh, understands. |7|

His price is so costly; His weight is unbearable.

He is immovable and undeceivable; enshrine Him in your mind, through the Guru's Teachings.

Meet Him through love, become pleasing to Him, and act in fear of Him.
Nanak the lowly says this, after deep contemplation. |8|3|

Aasaa, First Mehl:
When someone dies, the five passions meet and mourn his death.
Overcoming self-conceit, he washes off his filth with the Word of the Shabad.
One who knows and understands, enters the home of peace and poise.
Without understanding, he loses all his honor. |1|

Who dies, and who weeps for him?
O Lord, Creator, Cause of causes, You are over the heads of all. |1|Pause|

Who weeps over the pain of the dead?
Those who weep, do so over their own troubles.
God knows the condition of those who are so affected.
Whatever the Creator does, comes to pass. |2|

One who remains dead while yet alive, is saved, and saves others as well.
Celebrate the Victory of the Lord; taking to His Sanctuary, the supreme status is obtained.
I am a sacrifice to the feet of the True Guru.
The Guru is the boat; through the Shabad of His Word, the terrifying world-ocean is crossed over. |3|

He Himself is Fearless; His Divine Light is contained in all.
Without the Name, the world is defiled and untouchable.
Through evil-mindedness, they are ruined; why should they cry out and weep?
They are born only to die, without hearing the music of devotional worship. |4|

Only one's true friends mourn one's death.
Those under the sway of the three dispositions continue to mourn on and on.
Disregarding pain and pleasure, center your consciousness on the Lord.
Dedicate your body and mind to the Love of the Lord. |5|

The One Lord dwells within the various and countless beings.
There are so many rituals and religious faiths, their number is innumerable.

Without the Fear of God, and devotional worship, one's life is in vain.
Singing the Glorious Praises of the Lord, the supreme wealth is obtained.
|6|

He Himself dies, and He Himself kills.
He Himself establishes, and having established, disestablishes.
He created the Universe, and by His Divine Nature, instilled His Divine Light
into it.
One who reflects upon the Word of the Shabad, meets the Lord, without
doubt. |7|

Pollution is the burning fire, which is consuming the world.
Pollution is in the water, upon the land, and everywhere.
O Nanak, people are born and die in pollution.
By Guru's Grace, they drink in the Lord's sublime elixir. |8|4|

Aasaa, First Mehl:
One who contemplates his own self, tests the worth of the jewel.
With a single glance, the Perfect Guru saves him.
When the Guru is pleased, one's mind comforts itself. |1|

He is such a banker, who tests us.
By His True Glance of Grace, we are blessed with the Love of the One Lord,
and are saved. |1|Pause|

The capital of the Naam is immaculate and sublime.
That peddler is rendered pure, who is imbued with the Truth.
Praising the Lord, in the house of poise, he attains the Guru, the Creator.
|2|

One who burns away hope and desire through the Word of the Shabad,
chants the Lord's Name, and inspires others to chant it as well.
Through the Guru, he finds the Path home, to the Mansion of the Lord's
Presence. |3|

Section 08 - Raag Aasaa - Part 068

His body becomes golden, by the Lord's Incomparable Light.
He beholds the divine beauty in all the three worlds.
That inexhaustible wealth of Truth is now in my lap. |4|

In the five elements, the three worlds, the nine regions and the four directions, the Lord is pervading.
He supports the earth and the sky, exercising His almighty power.
He turns the outgoing mind around. |5|

The fool does not realize what he sees with his eyes.
He does not taste with his tongue, and does not understand what is said.
Intoxicated with poison, he argues with the world. |6|

In the uplifting society, one is uplifted.
He chases after virtue and washes off his sins.
Without serving the Guru, celestial poise is not obtained. |7|

The Naam, the Name of the Lord, is a diamond, a jewel, a ruby.
The pearl of the mind is the inner wealth.
O Nanak, the Lord tests us, and blesses us with His Glance of Grace. |8|5|

Aasaa, First Mehl:
The Gurmukh obtains spiritual wisdom, meditation and satisfaction of the mind.
The Gurmukh realizes the Mansion of the Lord's Presence.
The Gurmukh is attuned to the Word of the Shabad, as his Insignia. |1|

Such is the loving devotional worship of the Lord's contemplation.
The Gurmukh realizes the True Name, the Destroyer of ego. |1|Pause|

Day and night, he remains immaculately pure, and abides in the sublime place.
He gains the wisdom of the three worlds.
Through the True Guru, the Command of the Lord's Will is realized. |2|

He enjoys true pleasure, and suffers no pain.
He enjoys the ambrosial wisdom, and the highest sublime essence.
He overcomes the five evil passions, and becomes the happiest of all men. |3|

Your Divine Light is contained in all; everyone belongs to You.
You Yourself join and separate again.
Whatever the Creator does, comes to pass. |4|

He demolishes, and He builds; by His Order, he merges us into Himself.
Whatever is pleasing to His Will, happens.
Without the Guru, no one obtains the Perfect Lord. |5|

In childhood and old age, he does not understand.
In the prime of youth, he is drowned in his pride.
Without the Name, what can the fool obtain? |6|

He does not know the One who blesses him with nourishment and wealth.
Deluded by doubt, he later regrets and repents.
The noose of death is around the neck of that crazy madman. |7|

I saw the world drowning, and I ran away in fear.
How very fortunate are those who have been saved by the True Guru.
O Nanak, they are attached to the feet of the Guru. |8|6|

Aasaa, First Mehl:
They sing religious songs, but their consciousness is wicked.
They sing the songs, and call themselves divine,
but without the Name, their minds are false and wicked. |1|

Where are you going? O mind, remain in your own home.
The Gurmukhs are satisfied with the Lord's Name; searching, they easily
find the Lord. |1|Pause|

Sexual desire, anger and emotional attachment fill the mind and body;
greed and egotism lead only to pain.
How can the mind be comforted without the Lord's Name? |2|

One who cleanses himself within, knows the True Lord.
The Gurmukh knows the condition of his innermost being.
Without the True Word of the Shabad, the Mansion of the Lord's Presence
is not realized. |3|

One who merges his form into the Formless Lord,
abides in the True Lord, the Powerful, beyond power.
Such a person does not enter into the womb of reincarnation again. |4|

Go there, where you may obtain the Naam, the Name of the Lord.

Section 08 - Raag Aasaa - Part 069

By Guru's Grace, perform good deeds.
Imbued with the Naam, sing the Glorious Praises of the Lord. |5|

Serving the Guru, I have come to understand myself.
The Ambrosial Naam, the Giver of Peace, abides within my mind.
Night and day, I am imbued with the Word of the Guru's Bani, and the Naam. |6|

When my God attaches someone to Him, only then is that person attached.
Conquering ego, he remains awake to the Word of the Shabad.
Here and hereafter, he enjoys lasting peace. |7|

The fickle mind does not know the way.
The filthy self-willed manmukh does not understand the Shabad.
The Gurmukh chants the Immaculate Naam. |8|

I offer my prayer to the Lord,
that I might dwell in the Saadh Sangat, the Company of the Holy.
There, sins and sufferings are erased, and one is illumined with the Lord's Name. |9|

In reflective meditation, I have come to love good conduct.
Through the Word of the True Guru, I recognize the One Lord.
O Nanak, my mind is imbued with the Lord's Name. |10|7|

Aasaa, First Mehl:
The mind of the faithless cynic is like a crazy elephant.
It wanders around the forest, distracted by attachment to Maya.
It goes here and there, hounded by death.
The Gurmukh seeks, and finds his own home. |1|

Without the Word of the Guru's Shabad, the mind finds no place of rest.
Remember in meditation the Lord's Name, the most pure and sublime; renounce your bitter egotism. |1|Pause|

Tell me, how can this stupid mind be rescued?
Without understanding, it shall suffer the pains of death.

The Lord Himself forgives us, and unites us with the True Guru.
The True Lord conquers and overcomes the tortures of death. |2|

This mind commits its deeds of karma, and this mind follows the Dharma.
This mind is born of the five elements.
This foolish mind is perverted and greedy.
Chanting the Naam, the mind of the Gurmukh becomes beautiful. |3|

The mind of the Gurmukh finds the Lord's home.
The Gurmukh comes to know the three worlds.
This mind is a Yogi, an enjoyer, a practicer of austerities.
The Gurmukh understands the Lord God Himself. |4|

This mind is a detached renunciate, forsaking egotism.
Desire and duality afflict each and every heart.
The Gurmukh drinks in the Lord's sublime essence;
at His Door, in the Mansion of the Lord's Presence, He preserves his honor.
|5|

This mind is the king, the hero of cosmic battles.
The mind of the Gurmukh becomes fearless through the Naam.
Overpowering and subduing the five passions,
holding ego in its grip, it confines them to one place. |6|

The Gurmukh renounces other songs and tastes.
The mind of the Gurmukh is awakened to devotion.
Hearing the unstruck music of the sound current, this mind contemplates
the Shabad, and accepts it.
Understanding itself, this soul becomes attuned to the Formless Lord. |7|

This mind becomes immaculately pure, in the Court and the Home of the
Lord.
The Gurmukh shows his love through loving devotional worship.
Night and day, by Guru's Grace, sing the Lord's Praises.
God dwells in each and every heart, since the very beginning of time, and
throughout the ages. |8|

This mind is intoxicated with the sublime essence of the Lord;
The Gurmukh realizes the essence of totality.
For the sake of devotional worship, he dwells at the Guru's Feet.

Nanak is the humble servant of the slave of the Lord's slaves. |9|8|

Section 08 - Raag Aasaa - Part 070

Aasaa, First Mehl:
When the body perishes, whose wealth is it?
Without the Guru, how can the Lord's Name be obtained?
The wealth of the Lord's Name is my Companion and Helper.
Night and day, center your loving attention on the Immaculate Lord. |1|

Without the Lord's Name, who is ours?
I look upon pleasure and pain alike; I shall not forsake the Naam, the Name of the Lord. The Lord Himself forgives me, and blends me with Himself. |1|Pause|

The fool loves gold and women.
Attached to duality, he has forgotten the Naam.
O Lord, he alone chants the Naam, whom You have forgiven.
Death cannot touch one who sings the Glorious Praises of the Lord. |2|

The Lord, the Guru, is the Giver; the Lord, the Sustainer of the World.
If it is pleasing to Your Will, please preserve me, O Merciful Lord.
As Gurmukh, my mind is pleased with the Lord.
My diseases are cured, and my pains are taken away. |3|

There is no other medicine, Tantric charm or mantra.
Meditative remembrance upon the Lord, Har, Har, destroys sins.
You Yourself cause us to stray from the path, and forget the Naam.
Showering Your Mercy, You Yourself save us. |4|

The mind is diseased with doubt, superstition and duality.
Without the Guru, it dwells in doubt, and contemplates duality.
The Guru reveals the Darshan, the Blessed Vision of the Primal Lord.
Without the Word of the Guru's Shabad, what use is human life? |5|

Beholding the Marvellous Lord, I am wonder-struck and astonished.
In each and every heart, of the angels and holy men, He dwells in celestial Samaadhi.
I have enshrined the All-pervading Lord within my mind.
There is no one else equal to You. |6|

For the sake of devotional worship, we chant Your Name.
The Lord's devotees dwell in the Society of the Saints.
Breaking his bonds, one comes to meditate on the Lord.
The Gurmukhs are emancipated, by the Guru-given knowledge of the Lord.
|7|

The Messenger of Death cannot touch him with pain;
the Lord's humble servant remains awake to the Love of the Naam.
The Lord is the Lover of His devotees; He dwells with His devotees.
O Nanak, they are liberated, through the Love of the Lord. |8|9|

Aasaa, First Mehl, Ik-Tukee:
One who serves the Guru, knows his Lord and Master.
His pains are erased, and he realizes the True Word of the Shabad. |1|

Meditate on the Lord, O my friends and companions.
Serving the True Guru, you shall behold God with your eyes. |1|Pause|

People are entangled with mother, father and the world.
They are entangled with sons, daughters and spouses. |2|

They are entangled with religious rituals, and religious faith, acting in ego.
They are entangled with sons, wives and others in their minds. |3|

The farmers are entangled by farming.
People suffer punishment in ego, and the Lord King exacts the penalty from them. |4|

They are entangled in trade without contemplation.
They are not satisfied by attachment to the expanse of Maya. |5|

They are entangled with that wealth, amassed by bankers.
Without devotion to the Lord, they do not become acceptable. |6|

They are entangled with the Vedas, religious discussions and egotism.
They are entangled, and perish in attachment and corruption. |7|

Nanak seeks the Sanctuary of the Lord's Name.
One who is saved by the True Guru, does not suffer entanglement. |8|10|

Section 08 - Raag Aasaa - Part 071

Raag Aasaa, First Mehl, Ashtapadees, Third House:
One Universal Creator God. By The Grace Of The True Guru:
Those heads adorned with braided hair, with their parts painted with vermillion
- those heads were shaved with scissors, and their throats were choked with dust.
They lived in palatial mansions, but now, they cannot even sit near the palaces. |1|

Hail to You, O Father Lord, Hail to You!
O Primal Lord. Your limits are not known; You create, and create, and behold the scenes. |1|Pause|

When they were married, their husbands looked so handsome beside them.
They came in palanquins, decorated with ivory;
water was sprinkled over their heads, and glittering fans were waved above them. |2|

They were given hundreds of thousands of coins when they sat, and hundreds of thousands of coins when they stood.
They ate coconuts and dates, and rested comfortably upon their beds.
But ropes were put around their necks, and their strings of pearls were broken. |3|

Their wealth and youthful beauty, which gave them so much pleasure, have now become their enemies.
The order was given to the soldiers, who dishonored them, and carried them away.
If it is pleasing to God's Will, He bestows greatness; if is pleases His Will, He bestows punishment. |4|

If someone focuses on the Lord beforehand, then why should he be punished?
The kings had lost their higher consciousness, reveling in pleasure and sensuality.

Since Baabar's rule has been proclaimed, even the princes have no food to eat. |5|

The Muslims have lost their five times of daily prayer, and the Hindus have lost their worship as well.
Without their sacred squares, how shall the Hindu women bathe and apply the frontal marks to their foreheads?

They never remembered their Lord as Raam, and now they cannot even chant Khudaa-i|6|

Some have returned to their homes, and meeting their relatives, they ask about their safety.
For some, it is pre-ordained that they shall sit and cry out in pain.
Whatever pleases Him, comes to pass. O Nanak, what is the fate of mankind? |7|11|

Aasaa, First Mehl:
Where are the games, the stables, the horses? Where are the drums and the bugles?
Where are the sword-belts and chariots? Where are those scarlet uniforms?
Where are the rings and the beautiful faces? They are no longer to be seen here. |1|

This world is Yours; You are the Lord of the Universe.
In an instant, You establish and disestablish. You distribute wealth as it pleases You. |1|Pause|

Where are the houses, the gates, the hotels and palaces? Where are those beautiful way-stations?
Where are those beautiful women, reclining on their beds, whose beauty would not allow one to sleep?
Where are those betel leaves, their sellers, and the haremees? They have vanished like shadows. |2|

For the sake of this wealth, so many were ruined; because of this wealth, so many have been disgraced.
It was not gathered without sin, and it does not go along with the dead.

Those, whom the Creator Lord would destroy - first He strips them of virtue. |3|

Millions of religious leaders failed to halt the invader, when they heard of the Emperor's invasion.

Section 08 - Raag Aasaa - Part 072

He burned the rest-houses and the ancient temples; he cut the princes limb from limb, and cast them into the dust.
None of the Mugals went blind, and no one performed any miracle. |4|

The battle raged between the Mugals and the Pat'haans, and the swords clashed on the battlefield.
They took aim and fired their guns, and they attacked with their elephants.
Those men whose letters were torn in the Lord's Court, were destined to die, O Siblings of Destiny. |5|

The Hindu women, the Muslim women, the Bhattis and the Rajputs
- some had their robes torn away, from head to foot, while others came to dwell in the cremation ground.
Their husbands did not return home - how did they pass their night? |6|

The Creator Himself acts, and causes others to act. Unto whom should we complain?
Pleasure and pain come by Your Will; unto whom should we go and cry?
The Commander issues His Command, and is pleased. O Nanak, we receive what is written in our destiny. |7|12|

One Universal Creator God. By The Grace Of The True Guru:
Aasaa, Kaafee, First Mehl, Eighth House, Ashtapadees:
As the shepherd is in the field for only a short time, so is one in the world.
Practicing falsehood, they build their homes. |1|

Wake up! Wake up! O sleepers, see that the travelling merchant is leaving. |1|Pause|

Go ahead and build your houses, if you think you will stay here forever and ever.
The body shall fall, and the soul shall depart; if only they knew this. |2|

Why do you cry out and mourn for the dead? The Lord is, and shall always be.
You mourn for that person, but who will mourn for you? |3|

You are engrossed in worldly entanglements, O Siblings of Destiny, and you are practicing falsehood.
The dead person does not hear anything at all; your cries are heard only by other people. |4|

Only the Lord, who causes the mortal to sleep, O Nanak, can awaken him again.
One who understands his true home, does not sleep. |5|

If the departing mortal can take his wealth with him,
then go ahead and gather wealth yourself. See this, reflect upon it, and understand. |6|

Make your deals, and obtain the true merchandise, or else you shall regret it later.
Abandon your vices, and practice virtue, and you shall obtain the essence of reality. |7|

Plant the seed of Truth in the soil of Dharmic faith, and practice such farming.
Only then will you be known as a merchant, if you take your profits with you. |8|

If the Lord shows His Mercy, one meets the True Guru; contemplating Him, one comes to understand.
Then, one chants the Naam, hears the Naam, and deals only in the Naam. |9|

As is the profit, so is the loss; this is the way of the world.
Whatever pleases His Will, O Nanak, is glory for me. |10|13|

Aasaa, First Mehl:
I have searched in the four directions, but no one is mine.
If it pleases You, O Lord Master, then You are mine, and I am Yours. |1|

There is no other door for me; where shall I go to worship?
You are my only Lord; Your True Name is in my mouth. |1|Pause|

Some serve the Siddhas, the beings of spiritual perfection, and some serve spiritual teachers; they beg for wealth and miraculous powers.
May I never forget the Naam, the Name of the One Lord. This is the wisdom of the True Guru. |2|

Section 08 - Raag Aasaa - Part 073

Why do the Yogis, the revellers, and the beggars wander in foreign lands?
They do not understand the Word of the Guru's Shabad, and the essence of excellence within them. |3|

The Pandits, the religious scholars, the teachers and astrologers, and those who endlessly read the Puraanas,

do not know what is within; God is hidden deep within them. |4|

Some penitents perform penance in the forests, and some dwell forever at sacred shrines.
The unenlightened people do not understand themselves - why have they become renunciates? |5|

Some control their sexual energy, and are known as celibates.
But without the Guru's Word, they are not saved, and they wander in reincarnation. |6|

Some are householders, servants, and seekers, attached to the Guru's Teachings.
They hold fast to the Naam, to charity, to cleansing and purification; they remain awake in devotion to the Lord. |7|

Through the Guru, the Gate of the Lord's Home is found, and that place is recognized.
Nanak does not forget the Naam; his mind has surrendered to the True Lord. |8|14|

Aasaa, First Mehl:

Stilling the desires of the mind, the mortal truly crosses over the terrifying world-ocean.
In the very beginning, and throughout the ages, You have been the Merciful Lord and Master; I seek Your Sanctuary. |1|

You are the Giver, and I am a mere beggar. Lord, please grant me the Blessed Vision of Your Darshan.
The Gurmukh meditates on the Naam; the temple of his mind resounds with joy. |1|Pause|

Renouncing false greed, one comes to realize the Truth.
So let yourself be absorbed in the Word of the Guru's Shabad, and know this supreme realization. |2|

This mind is a greedy king, engrossed in greed.
The Gurmukh eliminates his greed, and comes to an understanding with the Lord. |3|

Planting the seeds in the rocky soil, how can one reap a profit?
The self-willed manmukh is not pleased with Truth; the false are buried in falsehood. |4|

So renounce greed - you are blind! Greed only brings pain.
When the True Lord dwells within the mind, the poisonous ego is conquered. |5|

Renounce the evil way of duality, or you shall be plundered, O Siblings of Destiny.
Day and night, praise the Naam, in the Sanctuary of the True Guru's protection. |6|

The self-willed manmukh is a rock, a stone. His life is cursed and useless.
No matter now long a stone is kept under water, it still remains dry at its core. |7|

The Name of the Lord is the treasure; the Perfect Guru has given it to me.
O Nanak, one who does not forget the Naam, churns and drinks in the Ambrosial Nectar. |8|15|

Aasaa, First Mehl:

The travellers travel from one road to another.
The world is engrossed in its entanglements, and does not appreciate the Truth. |1|

Why wander around, and why go searching, when the Guru's Shabad reveals Him to us?
Leaving behind egotism and attachment, I have arrived at my own home. |1|Pause|

Through Truth, one meets the True One; He is not obtained through falsehood.
Centering your consciousness on the True Lord, you shall not have to come into the world again. |2|

Why do you weep for the dead? You do not know how to weep.
Weep by praising the True Lord, and recognize His Command. |3|

Blessed is the birth of one who is destined to abide by the Lord's Command.
He obtains the true profit, realizing the Lord's Command. |4|

Section 08 - Raag Aasaa - Part 074

If it pleases the Commander, one goes to His Court, robed in honor.
By His Command, God's slaves are hit over the head. |5|

The profit is earned by enshrining Truth and justice in the mind.
They obtain what is written in their destiny, and overcome pride. |6|

The self-willed manmukhs are hit over the head, and consumed by conflict.
The cheaters are plundered by falsehood; they are chained and led away. |7|

Enshrine the Lord Master in your mind, and you shall not have to repent.
He forgives our sins, when we practice the Teachings of the Guru's Word. |8|

Nanak begs for the True Name, which is obtained by the Gurmukh.
Without You, I have no other at all; please, bless me with Your Glance of Grace. |9|16|

Aasaa, First Mehl:
Why should I go searching in the forests, when the woods of my home are so green?
The True Word of the Shabad has instantaneously come and settled in my heart. |1|

Wherever I look, there He is; I know no other.
Working for the Guru, one realizes the Mansion of the Lord's Presence. |1|Pause|

The True Lord blends us with Himself, when it is pleasing to His Mind.
One who ever walks in accordance with His Will, merges into His Being. |2|

When the True Lord dwells in the mind, that mind flourishes.
He Himself grants greatness; His Gifts are never exhausted. |3|

Serving this and that person, how can one obtain the Lord's Court?
If someone embarks on a boat of stone, he shall drown with its cargo. |4|

So offer your mind, and surrender your head with it.
The Gurmukh realizes the true essence, and finds the home of his own self. |5|

People discuss birth and death; the Creator created this.
Those who conquer their selfhood and remain dead, shall never have to die again. |6|

Do those deeds which the Primal Lord has ordered for you.
If one surrenders his mind upon meeting the True Guru, who can estimate its value? |7|

That Lord Master is the Assayer of the jewel of the mind; He places the value on it.
O Nanak, True is the Glory of that one, in whose mind the Lord Master dwells. |8|17|

Aasaa, First Mehl:
Those who have forgotten the Naam, the Name of the Lord, are deluded by doubt and duality.

Those who abandon the roots and cling to the branches, shall obtain only ashes. |1|

Without the Name, how can one be emancipated? Who knows this?
One who becomes Gurmukh is emancipated; the self-willed manmukhs lose their honor. |1|Pause|

Those who serve the One Lord become perfect in their understanding, O Siblings of Destiny.
The Lord's humble servant finds Sanctuary in Him, the Immaculate One, from the very beginning, and throughout the ages. |2|

My Lord and Master is the One; there is no other, O Siblings of Destiny.
By the Grace of the True Lord, celestial peace is obtained. |3|

Without the Guru, no one has obtained Him, although many may claim to have done so.
He Himself reveals the Way, and implants true devotion within. |4|

Even if the self-willed manmukh is instructed, he stills goes into the wilderness.
Without the Lord's Name, he shall not be emancipated; he shall die, and sink into hell. |5|

He wanders through birth and death, and never chants the Lord's Name.
He never realizes his own value, without serving the Guru. |6|

Section 08 - Raag Aasaa - Part 075

Whatever service the Lord causes us to do, that is just what we do.
He Himself acts; who else should be mentioned? He beholds His own greatness. |7|

He alone serves the Guru, whom the Lord Himself inspires to do so.
O Nanak, offering his head, one is emancipated, and honored in the Court of the Lord. |8|18|

Aasaa, First Mehl:
Beautiful is the Supreme Lord and Master, and beautiful is the Word of the Guru's Bani.

By great good fortune, one meets the True Guru, and the supreme status of Nirvaanaa is obtained. |1|

I am the lowest slave of Your slaves; I am Your most humble servant.
As You keep me, I live. Your Name is in my mouth. |1|Pause|

I have such a great thirst for the Blessed Vision of Your Darshan; my mind accepts Your Will, and so You are pleased with me.
Greatness is in the Hands of my Lord and Master; by His Will, honor is obtained. |2|

Do not think that the True Lord is far away; He is deep within.
Wherever I look, there I find Him pervading; how can I estimate His value? |3|

He Himself does, and He Himself undoes. He Himself beholds His glorious greatness.
Becoming Gurmukh, one beholds Him, and so, His value is appraised. |4|

So earn your profits while you are alive, by serving the Guru.
If it is so pre-ordained, then one finds the True Guru. |5|

The self-willed manmukhs continually lose, and wander around, deluded by doubt.
The blind manmukhs do not remember the Lord; how can they obtain the Blessed Vision of His Darshan? |6|

One's coming into the world is judged worthwhile only if one lovingly attunes oneself to the True Lord.
Meeting the Guru, one becomes invaluable; his light merges into the Light. |7|

Day and night, he remains detached, and serves the Primal Lord.
O Nanak, those who are imbued with the Lord's Lotus Feet, are content with the Naam, the Name of the Lord. |8|19|

Aasaa, First Mehl:
No matter how much one may describe the Lord, His limits still cannot be known.

I am without any support; You, O Lord, are my only Support; You are my almighty power. |1|

This is Nanak's prayer, that he may be adorned with the True Name.
When self-conceit is eradicated, and understanding is obtained, one meets the Lord, through the Word of the Guru's Shabad. |1|Pause|

Abandoning egotism and pride, one obtains contemplative understanding.
When the mind surrenders to the Lord Master, He bestows the support of the Truth. |2|

Day and night, remain content with the Naam, the Name of the Lord; that is the true service.
No misfortune troubles one who follows the Command of the Lord's Will. |3|

One who follows the Command of the Lord's Will is taken into the Lord's Treasury.
The counterfeit find no place there; they are mixed with the false ones. |4|

Forever and ever, the genuine coins are treasured; with them, the true merchandise is purchased.
The false ones are not seen in the Lord's Treasury; they are seized and cast into the fire again. |5|

Those who understand their own souls, are themselves the Supreme Soul.
The One Lord is the tree of ambrosial nectar, which bears the ambrosial fruit. |6|

Those who taste the ambrosial fruit remain satisfied with Truth.
They have no doubt or sense of separation - their tongues taste the divine taste. |7|

By His Command, and through your past actions, you came into the world; walk forever according to His Will.
Please, grant virtue to Nanak, the virtueless one; bless him with the glorious greatness of the Truth. |8|20|

Aasaa, First Mehl:
One whose mind is attuned to the Lord's Name speaks the truth.

What would the people lose, if I became pleasing to You, O Lord? |1|

Section 08 - Raag Aasaa - Part 076

As long as there is the breath of life, meditate on the True Lord.
You shall receive the profit of singing the Glorious Praises of the Lord, and find peace. |1|Pause|

True is Your Service; bless me with it, O Merciful Lord.
I live by praising You; You are my Anchor and Support. |2|

I am Your servant, the gate-keeper at Your Gate; You alone know my pain.
How wonderful is Your devotional worship! It removes all pains. |3|

The Gurmukhs know that by chanting the Naam, they shall dwell in His Court, in His Presence.
True and acceptable is that time, when one recognizes the Word of the Shabad. |4|

Those who practice Truth, contentment and love, obtain the supplies of the Lord's Name.
So banish corruption from your mind, and the True One will grant you Truth. |5|

The True Lord inspires true love in the truthful.
He Himself administers justice, as it pleases His Will. |6|

True is the gift of the True, Compassionate Lord.
Day and night, I serve the One whose Name is priceless. |7|

You are so sublime, and I am so lowly, but I am called Your slave.
Please, shower Nanak with Your Glance of Grace, that he, the separated one, may merge with You again, O Lord. |8|21|

Aasaa, First Mehl:
How can coming and going, the cycle of reincarnation be ended? And how can one meet the Lord?
The pain of birth and death is so great, in constant skepticism and duality. |1|

Without the Name, what is life? Cleverness is detestable and cursed.
One who does not serve the Holy True Guru, is not pleased by devotion to the Lord. |1|Pause|

Coming and going is ended only when one finds the True Guru.
He gives the wealth and capital of the Lord's Name, and false doubt is destroyed. |2|

Joining the humble Saintly beings, let us sing the blessed, blessed Praises of the Lord.
The Primal Lord, the Infinite, is obtained by the Gurmukh. |3|

The drama of the world is staged like the show of a buffoon.
For an instant, for a moment, the show is seen, but it disappears in no time at all. |4|

The game of chance is played on the board of egotism, with the pieces of falsehood and ego.
The whole world loses; he alone wins, who reflects upon the Word of the Guru's Shabad. |5|

As is the cane in the hand of the blind man, so is the Lord's Name for me.
The Lord's Name is my Support, night and day and morning. |6|

As You keep me, Lord, I live; the Lord's Name is my only Support.
It is my only comfort in the end; the gate of salvation is found by His humble servants. |7|

The pain of birth and death is removed, by chanting and meditating on the Naam, the Name of the Lord.
O Nanak, one who does not forget the Naam, is saved by the Perfect Guru. |8|22|

Aasaa, Third Mehl, Ashtapadees, Second House:
One Universal Creator God. By The Grace Of The True Guru:
The Shaastras, the Vedas and the Simritees are contained in the ocean of Your Name; the River Ganges is held in Your Feet.
The intellect can understand the world of the three modes, but You, O Primal Lord, are totally astounding. |1|

Servant Nanak meditates on His Feet, and chants the Ambrosial Word of His Bani. |1|Pause|

Three hundred thirty million gods are Your servants. You bestow wealth, and the supernatural powers of the Siddhas; You are the Support of the breath of life.

Section 08 - Raag Aasaa - Part 077

His beauteous forms cannot be comprehended; what can anyone accomplish by discussing and debating? |2|

Throughout the ages, You are the three qualities, and the four sources of creation.
If You show Your Mercy, then one obtains the supreme status, and speaks the Unspoken Speech. |3|

You are the Creator; all are created by You. What can any mortal being do? He alone, upon whom You shower Your Grace, is absorbed into the Truth. |4|

Everyone who comes and goes chants Your Name.
When it is pleasing to Your Will, then the Gurmukh understands. Otherwise, the self-willed manmukhs wander in ignorance. |5|

You gave the four Vedas to Brahma, for him to read and read continually, and reflect upon.
The wretched one does not understand His Command, and is reincarnated into heaven and hell. |6|

In each and every age, He creates the kings, who are sung of as His Incarnations.
Even they have not found His limits; what can I speak of and contemplate? |7|

You are True, and all that You do is True. If You bless me with the Truth, I will speak on it.
One whom You inspire to understand the Truth, is easily absorbed into the Naam. |8|1|23|

Aasaa, Third Mehl:
The True Guru has dispelled my doubts.
He has enshrined the Immaculate Name of the Lord within my mind.
Focusing on the Word of the Shabad, I have obtained lasting peace. |1|

Listen, O my mind, to the essence of spiritual wisdom.
The Great Giver knows our condition completely; the Gurmukh obtains the treasure of the Naam, the Name of the Lord. |1|Pause|

The great glory of meeting the True Guru is
that it has quenched the fire of possessiveness and desire;
imbued with peace and poise, I sing the Glorious Praises of the Lord. |2|

Without the Perfect Guru, no one knows the Lord.
Attached to Maya, they are engrossed in duality.
The Gurmukh receives the Naam, and the Bani of the Lord's Word. |3|

Service to the Guru is the most excellent and sublime penance of penances.
The Dear Lord dwells in the mind, and all suffering departs.
Then, at the Gate of the True Lord, one appears truthful. |4|

Serving the Guru, one comes to know the three worlds.
Understanding his own self, he obtains the Lord.
Through the True Word of His Bani, we enter the Mansion of His Presence. |5|

Serving the Guru, all of one's generations are saved.
Keep the Immaculate Naam enshrined within your heart.
In the Court of the True Lord, you shall be adorned with True Glory. |6|

How very fortunate are they, who are committed to the Guru's service.
Night and day, they are engaged in devotional worship; the True Name is implanted within them.
Through the Naam, all of one's generations are saved. |7|

Nanak chants the true thought.
Keep the Name of the Lord enshrined within your heart.
Imbued with devotion to the Lord, the gate of salvation is found. |8|2|24|

Aasaa, Third Mehl:

Everyone lives, hoping in hope.
Understanding His Command, one becomes free of desire.
So many are asleep in hope.
He alone wakes up, whom the Lord awakens. |1|

The True Guru has led me to understand the Naam, the Name of the Lord;
without the Naam, hunger does not go away.

Section 08 - Raag Aasaa - Part 078

Through the Naam, the fire of desire is extinguished; the Naam is obtained
by His Will. |1|Pause|

In the Dark Age of Kali Yuga, realize the Word of the Shabad.
By this devotional worship, egotism is eliminated.
Serving the True Guru, one becomes approved.
So know the One, who created hope and desire. |2|

What shall we offer to one who proclaims the Word of the Shabad?
By His Grace, the Naam is enshrined within our minds.
Offer your head, and shed your self-conceit.
One who understands the Lord's Command finds lasting peace. |3|

He Himself does, and causes others to do.
He Himself enshrines His Name in the mind of the Gurmukh.
He Himself misleads us, and He Himself puts us back on the Path.
Through the True Word of the Shabad, we merge into the True Lord. |4|

True is the Shabad, and True is the Word of the Lord's Bani.
In each and every age, the Gurmukhs speak it and chant it.
The self-willed manmukhs are deluded by doubt and attachment.
Without the Name, everyone wanders around insane. |5|

Throughout the three worlds, is the one Maya.
The fool reads and reads, but holds tight to duality.
He performs all sorts of rituals, but still suffers terrible pain.
Serving the True Guru, eternal peace is obtained. |6|

Reflective meditation upon the Shabad is such sweet nectar.
Night and day, one enjoys it, subduing his ego.

When the Lord showers His Mercy, we enjoy celestial bliss.
Imbued with the Naam, love the True Lord forever. |7|

Meditate on the Lord, and read and reflect upon the Guru's Shabad.
Subdue your ego and meditate on the Lord.
Meditate on the Lord, and be imbued with fear and love of the True One.
O Nanak, enshrine the Naam within your heart, through the Guru's Teachings. |8|3|25|

One Universal Creator God. By The Grace Of The True Guru:
Raag Aasaa, Third Mehl, Ashtapadees, Eighth House, Kaafee:
Peace emanates from the Guru; He puts out the fire of desire.
The Naam, the Name of the Lord, is obtained from the Guru; it is the greatest greatness. |1|

Keep the One Name in your consciousness, O my Siblings of Destiny.
Seeing the world on fire, I have hurried to the Lord's Sanctuary. |1|Pause|

Spiritual wisdom emanates from the Guru; reflect upon the supreme essence of reality.
Through the Guru, the Lord's Mansion and His Court are attained; His devotional worship is overflowing with treasures. |2|

The Gurmukh meditates on the Naam; he achieves reflective meditation and understanding.
The Gurmukh is the Lord's devotee, immersed in His Praises; the Infinite Word of the Shabad dwells within him. |3|

Happiness emanates from the Gurmukh; he never suffers pain.
The Gurmukh conquers his ego, and his mind is immaculately pure. |4|

Meeting the True Guru, self-conceit is removed, and understanding of the three worlds is obtained.
The Immaculate Divine Light is pervading and permeating everywhere; one's light merges into the Light. |5|

The Perfect Guru instructs, and one's intellect becomes sublime.
A cooling and soothing peace comes within, and through the Naam, peace is obtained. |6|

One meets the Perfect True Guru only when the Lord bestows His Glance of Grace.
All sins and vices are eradicated, and one shall never again suffer pain or distress. |7|

Section 08 - Raag Aasaa - Part 079

Glory is in His Hands; He bestows His Name, and attaches us to it.
O Nanak, the treasure of the Naam abides within the mind, and glory is obtained. |8|4|26|

Aasaa, Third Mehl:
Listen, O mortal: enshrine His Name within your mind; He shall come to meet with you, O my Sibling of Destiny.
Night and day, center your consciousness on true devotional worship of the True Lord. |1|

Meditate on the One Naam, and you shall find peace, O my Siblings of Destiny.
Eradicate egotism and duality, and your glory shall be glorious. |1|Pause|

The angels, humans and silent sages long for this devotional worship, but without the True Guru, it cannot be attained.
The Pandits, the religious scholars, and the astrologers read their books, but they do not understand. |2|

He Himself keeps all in His Hand; nothing else can be said.
Whatever He gives, is received. The Guru has imparted this understanding to me. |3|

All beings and creatures are His; He belongs to all.
So who can we call bad, since there is no other? |4|

The Command of the One Lord is pervading throughout; duty to the One Lord is upon the heads of all.
He Himself has led them astray, and placed greed and corruption within their hearts. |5|

He has sanctified those few Gurmukhs who understand Him, and reflect upon Him.

He grants devotional worship to them, and within them is the treasure. |6|

The spiritual teachers know nothing but the Truth; they obtain true understanding.
They are led astray by Him, but they do not go astray, because they know the True Lord. |7|

Within the homes of their bodies, the five passions are pervading, but here, the five are well-behaved.
O Nanak, without the True Guru, they are not overcome; through the Naam, the ego is conquered. |8|5|27|

Aasaa, Third Mehl:
Everything is within the home of your own self; there is nothing beyond it.
By Guru's Grace, it is obtained, and the doors of the inner heart are opened wide. |1|

From the True Guru, the Lord's Name is obtained, O Siblings of Destiny.
The treasure of the Naam is within; the Perfect True Guru has shown this to me. |1|Pause|

One who is a buyer of the Lord's Name, finds it, and obtains the jewel of contemplation.
He opens the doors deep within, and through the Eyes of Divine Vision, beholds the treasure of liberation. |2|

There are so many mansions within the body; the soul dwells within them.
He obtains the fruits of his mind's desires, and he shall not have to go through reincarnation again. |3|

The appraisers cherish the commodity of the Name; they obtain under-standing from the Guru.
The wealth of the Naam is priceless; how few are the Gurmukhs who obtain it. |4|

Searching outwardly, what can anyone find? The commodity is deep within the home of the self, O Siblings of Destiny.
The entire world is wandering around, deluded by doubt; the self-willed manmukhs lose their honor. |5|

The false one leaves his own hearth and home, and goes out to another's home.
Like a thief, he is caught, and without the Naam, he is beaten and struck down. |6|

Those who know their own home, are happy, O Siblings of Destiny.
They realize God within their own hearts, through the glorious greatness of the Guru. |7|

He Himself gives gifts, and He Himself bestows understanding; unto whom can we complain?
O Nanak, meditate on the Naam, the Name of the Lord, and you shall obtain glory in the True Court. |8|6|28|

Section 08 - Raag Aasaa - Part 080

Aasaa, Third Mehl:
Those who recognize their own selves, enjoy the sweet flavor, O Siblings of Destiny.
Those who drink in the sublime essence of the Lord are emancipated; they love the Truth. |1|

The Beloved Lord is the purest of the pure; He comes to dwell in the pure mind.
Praising the Lord, through the Guru's Teachings, one remains unaffected by corruption. |1|Pause|

Without the Word of the Shabad, they do not understand themselves -they are totally blind, O Siblings of Destiny.
Through the Guru's Teachings, the heart is illuminated, and in the end, only the Naam shall be your companion. |2|

They are occupied with the Naam, and only the Naam; they deal only in the Naam.
Deep within their hearts is the Naam; upon their lips is the Naam; they contemplate the Word of God, and the Naam. |3|

They listen to the Naam, believe in the Naam, and through the Naam, they obtain glory.

They praise the Naam, forever and ever, and through the Naam, they obtain the Mansion of the Lord's Presence. |4|

Through the Naam, their hearts are illumined, and through the Naam, they obtain honor.
Through the Naam, peace wells up; I seek the Sanctuary of the Naam. |5|

Without the Naam, no one is accepted; the self-willed manmukhs lose their honor.
In the City of Death, they are tied down and beaten, and they lose their lives in vain. |6|

Those Gurmukhs who realize the Naam, all serve the Naam.
So believe in the Naam, and only the Naam; through the Naam, glorious greatness is obtained. |7|

He alone receives it, unto whom it is given. Through the Guru's Teachings, the Naam is realized.
O Nanak, everything is under the influence of the Naam; by perfect good destiny, a few obtain it. |8|7|29|

Aasaa, Third Mehl:
The deserted brides do not obtain the Mansion of their Husband's Presence, nor do they know His taste.
They speak harsh words, and do not bow to Him; they are in love with another. |1|

How can this mind come under control?
By Guru's Grace, it is held in check; instructed in spiritual wisdom, it returns to its home. |1|Pause|

He Himself adorns the happy soul-brides; they bear Him love and affection.
They live in harmony with the Sweet Will of the True Guru, naturally adorned with the Naam. |2|

They enjoy their Beloved forever, and their bed is decorated with Truth.
They are fascinated with the Love of their Husband Lord; meeting their Beloved, they obtain peace. |3|

Spiritual wisdom is the incomparable decoration of the happy soul-bride.

She is so beautiful - she is the queen of all; she enjoys the love and affection of her Husband Lord. |4|

The True Lord, the Unseen, the Infinite, has infused His Love among the happy soul-brides.
They serve their True Guru, with true love and affection. |5|

The happy soul-bride has adorned herself with the necklace of virtue.
She applies the perfume of love to her body, and within her mind is the jewel of reflective meditation. |6|

Those who are imbued with devotional worship are the most exalted. Their social standing and honor come from the Word of the Shabad.
Without the Naam, all are low class, like maggots in manure. |7|

Everyone proclaims, "Me, me!"; but without the Shabad, the ego does not depart.
O Nanak, those who are imbued with the Naam lose their ego; they remain absorbed in the True Lord. |8|8|30|

Aasaa, Third Mehl:
Those who are imbued with the True Lord are spotless and pure; their reputation is forever true.
Here, they are known in each and every home, and hereafter, they are famous throughout the ages. |1|

Section 08 - Raag Aasaa - Part 081

O beauteous and joyful mind, imbue yourself with your true color.
If you imbue yourself with the Beauteous Word of the Guru's Bani, then this color shall never fade away. |1|Pause|

I am lowly, filthy, and totally egotistical; I am attached to the corruption of duality.
But meeting with the Guru, the Philosopher's Stone, I am transformed into gold; I am blended with the Pure Light of the Infinite Lord. |2|

Without the Guru, no one is imbued with the color of the Lord's Love; meeting with the Guru, this color is applied.

Those who are imbued with the Fear, and the Love of the Guru, are absorbed in the Praise of the True Lord. |3|

Without fear, the cloth is not dyed, and the mind is not rendered pure.
Without fear, the performance of rituals is false, and one finds no place of rest. |4|

Only those whom the Lord imbues, are so imbued; they join the Sat Sangat, the True Congregation.
From the Perfect Guru, the Sat Sangat emanates, and one easily merges into the Love of the True One. |5|

Without the Sangat, the Company of the Holy, all remain like beasts and animals.
They do not know the One who created them; without the Name, all are thieves. |6|

Some purchase merits and sell off their demerits; through the Guru, they obtain peace and poise.
Serving the Guru, they obtain the Name, which comes to dwell deep within. |7|

The One Lord is the Giver of all; He assigns tasks to each and every person.
O Nanak, the Lord embellishes us with the Name; attached to the Word of the Shabad, we are merged into Him. |8|9|31|

Aasaa, Third Mehl:
Everyone longs for the Name, but he alone receives it, unto whom the Lord shows His Mercy.
Without the Name, there is only pain; he alone obtains peace, whose mind is filled with the Name. |1|

You are infinite and merciful; I seek Your Sanctuary.
From the Perfect Guru, the glorious greatness of the Naam is obtained. |1|Pause|

Inwardly and outwardly, there is only the One Lord. He has created the world, with its many varieties.
According to the Order of His Will, He makes us act. What else can we talk about, O Siblings of Destiny? |2|

Knowledge and ignorance are all your making; You have control over these. Some, You forgive, and unite with Yourself; while others, the wicked, you strike down and drive out of Your Court. |3|

Some, from the very beginning, are pure and pious; You attach them to Your Name.
Serving the Guru, peace wells up; through the True Word of the Shabad, one comes to understand. |4|

Some are crooked, filthy and vicious; the Lord Himself has led them astray from the Name.
They have no intuition, no understanding and no self-discipline; they wander around delirious. |5|

He grants faith to those whom He has blessed with His Glance of Grace.
This mind finds truth, contentment and self discipline, hearing the Immaculate Word of the Shabad. |6|

By reading books, one cannot reach Him; by speaking and talking, His limits cannot be found.
Through the Guru, His value is found; through the True Word of the Shabad, understanding is obtained. |7|

So reform this mind and body, by contemplating the Word of the Guru's Shabad.
O Nanak, within this body is the treasure of the Naam, the Name of the Lord; it is found through the Love of the Infinite Guru. |8|10|32|

Aasaa, Third Mehl:
The happy soul-brides are imbued with Truth; they are adorned with the Word of the Guru's Shabad.

Section 08 - Raag Aasaa - Part 082

They find their Husband Lord within their own home, contemplating the True Word of the Shabad. |1|

Through merits, their demerits are forgiven, and they embrace love for the Lord.

The soul-bride then obtains the Lord as her Husband; meeting the Guru, this union comes about. |1|Pause|

Some do not know the Presence of their Husband Lord; they are deluded by duality and doubt.
How can the forsaken brides meet Him? Their life night passes in pain. |2|

Those whose minds are filled with the True Lord, perform truthful actions.
Night and day, they serve the Lord with poise, and are absorbed in the True Lord. |3|

The forsaken brides wander around, deluded by doubt; telling lies, they eat poison.
They do not know their Husband Lord, and upon their deserted bed, they suffer in misery. |4|

The True Lord is the One and only; do not be deluded by doubt, O my mind.
Consult with the Guru, serve the True Lord, and enshrine the Immaculate Truth within your mind. |5|

The happy soul-bride always finds her Husband Lord; she banishes egotism and self-conceit.
She remains attached to her Husband Lord, night and day, and she finds peace upon His Bed of Truth. |6|

Those who shouted, "Mine, mine!" have departed, without obtaining anything.
The separated one does not obtain the Mansion of the Lord's Presence, and departs, repenting in the end. |7|

That Husband Lord of mine is the One and only; I am in love with the One alone.
O Nanak, if the soul-bride longs for peace, she should enshrine the Lord's Name within her mind. |8|11|33|

Aasaa, Third Mehl:
Those whom the Lord has caused to drink in the Ambrosial Nectar, naturally, intuitively, enjoy the sublime essence.
The True Lord is care-free; he does not have even an iota of greed. |1|

The True Ambrosial Nectar rains down, and trickles into the mouths of the Gurmukhs.

Their minds are forever rejuvenated, and they naturally, intuitively, sing the Glorious Praises of the Lord. |1|Pause|

The self-willed manmukhs are forever forsaken brides; they cry out and bewail at the Lord's Gate.

Those who do not enjoy the sublime taste of their Husband Lord, act according to their pre-ordained destiny. |2|

The Gurmukh plants the seed of the True Name, and it sprouts. He deals in the True Name alone.

Those whom the Lord has attached to this profitable venture, are granted the treasure of devotional worship. |3|

The Gurmukh is forever the true, happy soul-bride; she adorns herself with the fear of God and devotion to Him.

Night and day, she enjoys her Husband Lord; she keeps Truth enshrined within her heart. |4|

I am a sacrifice to those who have enjoyed their Husband Lord.

They dwell forever with their Husband Lord; they eradicate self-conceit from within. |5|

Their bodies and minds are cooled and soothed, and their faces are radiant, from the love and affection of their Husband Lord.

They enjoy their Husband Lord upon His cozy bed, having conquered their ego and desire. |6|

Granting His Grace, He comes into our homes, through our infinite Love for the Guru.

The happy soul-bride obtains the One Lord as her Husband. |7|

All of her sins are forgiven; the Uniter unites her with Himself.

O Nanak, chant such chants, that hearing them, He may enshrine love for you. |8|12|34|

Aasaa, Third Mehl:

Merit is obtained from the True Guru, when God causes us to meet Him.

Section 08 - Raag Aasaa - Part 083

Meditating on the Naam, the Name of the Lord, with intuitive ease and poise, spiritual wisdom is revealed. |1|

O my mind, do not think of the Lord as being far away; behold Him ever close at hand.
He is always listening, and always watching over us; the Word of His Shabad is all-pervading everywhere. |1|Pause|

The Gurmukhs understand their own selves; they meditate single-mindedly on the Lord.
They enjoy their Husband Lord continually; through the True Name, they find peace. |2|

O my mind, no one belongs to you; contemplate the Shabad, and see this.
So run to the Lord's Sanctuary, and find the gate of salvation. |3|

Listen to the Shabad, and understand the Shabad, and lovingly focus your consciousness on the True One.
Through the Shabad, conquer your ego, and in the True Mansion of the Lord's Presence, you shall find peace. |4|

In this age, the Naam, the Name of the Lord, is glory; without the Name, there is no glory.
The glory of this Maya lasts for only a few days; it disappears in an instant. |5|

Those who forget the Naam are already dead, and they continue dying.
They do not enjoy the sublime essence of the Lord's taste; they sink into the manure. |6|

Some are forgiven by the Lord; He unites them with Himself, and keeps them attached to the Naam, night and day.
They practice Truth, and abide in Truth; being truthful, they merge into Truth. |7|

Without the Shabad, the world does not hear, and does not see; deaf and blind, it wanders around.

Without the Naam, it obtains only misery; the Naam is received only by His Will. |8|

Those persons who link their consciousness with the Word of His Bani, are immaculately pure, and approved by the Lord.
O Nanak, they never forget the Naam, and in the Court of the Lord, they are known as true. |9|13|35|

Aasaa, Third Mehl:
Through the Word of the Shabad, the devotees are known; their words are true.
They eradicate ego from within themselves; they surrender to the Naam, the Name of the Lord, and meet with the True One. |1|

Through the Name of the Lord, Har, Har, His humble servants obtain honor.
How blessed is their coming into the world! Everyone adores them. |1|Pause|

Ego, self-centeredness, excessive anger and pride are the lot of mankind.
If one dies in the Word of the Shabad, then he is rid of this, and his light is merged into the Light of the Lord God. |2|

Meeting with the Perfect True Guru, my life has been blessed.
I have obtained the nine treasures of the Naam, and my storehouse is inexhaustible, filled to overflowing. |3|

Those who love the Naam come as dealers in the merchandise of the Naam.
Those who become Gurmukh obtain this wealth; deep within, they contemplate the Shabad. |4|

The egotistical, self-willed manmukhs do not appreciate the value of devotional worship.
The Primal Lord Himself has beguiled them; they lose their lives in the gamble. |5|

Without loving affection, devotional worship is not possible, and the body cannot be at peace.
The wealth of love is obtained from the Guru; through devotion, the mind becomes steady. |6|

He alone performs devotional worship, whom the Lord so blesses; he contemplates the Word of the Guru's Shabad.
The One Name abides in his heart, and he conquers his ego and duality. |7|

The One Name is the social status and honor of the devotees; the Lord Himself adorns them.
They remain forever in the Protection of His Sanctuary. As it pleases His Will, He arranges their affairs. |8|

Section 08 - Raag Aasaa - Part 084

The worship of the Lord is unique - it is known only by reflecting upon the Guru.
O Nanak, one whose mind is filled with the Naam, through the Lord's Fear and devotion, is embellished with the Naam. |9|14|36|

Aasaa, Third Mehl:
He wanders around, engrossed in other pleasures, but without the Naam, he suffers in pain.
He does not meet the True Guru, the Primal Being, who imparts true understanding. |1|

O my insane mind, drink in the sublime essence of the Lord, and savor its taste.
Attached to other pleasures, you wander around, and your life wastes away uselessly. |1|Pause|

In this age, the Gurmukhs are pure; they remain absorbed in the love of the True Name.
Without the destiny of good karma, nothing can be obtained; what can we say or do? |2|

He understands his own self, and dies in the Word of the Shabad; he banishes corruption from his mind.
He hurries to the Guru's Sanctuary, and is forgiven by the Forgiving Lord. |3|

Without the Name, peace is not obtained, and pain does not depart from within.

This world is engrossed in attachment to Maya; it has gone astray in duality and doubt. |4|

The forsaken soul-brides do not know the value of their Husband Lord; how can they decorate themselves?

Night and day, they continually burn, and they do not enjoy the Bed of their Husband Lord. |5|

The happy soul-brides obtain the Mansion of His Presence, eradicating their self-conceit from within.
They decorate themselves with the Word of the Guru's Shabad, and their Husband Lord unites them with Himself. |6|

He has forgotten death, in the darkness of attachment to Maya.
The self-willed manmukhs die again and again, and are reborn; they die again, and are miserable at the Gate of Death. |7|

They alone are united, whom the Lord unites with Himself; they contemplate the Word of the Guru's Shabad.
O Nanak, they are absorbed in the Naam; their faces are radiant, in that True Court. |8|22|15|37|

Aasaa, Fifth Mehl, Ashtapadees, Second House:
One Universal Creator God. By The Grace Of The True Guru:
When the five virtues were reconciled, and the five passions were estranged, I enshrined the five within myself, and cast out the other five. |1|

In this way, the village of my body became inhabited, O my Siblings of Destiny.
Vice departed, and the Guru's spiritual wisdom was implanted within me. |1|Pause|

The fence of true Dharmic religion has been built around it.
The spiritual wisdom and reflective meditation of the Guru has become its strong gate. |2|

So plant the seed of the Naam, the Name of the Lord, O friends, O Siblings of Destiny.

Deal only in the constant service of the Guru. |3|

With intuitive peace and happiness, all the shops are filled.
The Banker and the dealers dwell in the same place. |4|

There is no tax on non-believers, nor any fines or taxes at death.
The True Guru has set the Seal of the Primal Lord upon these goods. |5|

So load the merchandise of the Naam, and set sail with your cargo.
Earn your profit, as Gurmukh, and you shall return to your own home. |6|

The True Guru is the Banker, and His Sikhs are the traders.
Their merchandise is the Naam, and meditation on the True Lord is their account. |7|

One who serves the True Guru dwells in this house.
O Nanak, the Divine City is eternal. |8|1|

Section 08 - Raag Aasaa - Part 085

Aasaavaree, Fifth Mehl, Third House:
One Universal Creator God. By The Grace Of The True Guru:
My mind is in love with the Lord.
In the Saadh Sangat, the Company of the Holy, I meditate on the Lord, Har, Har; my lifestyle is pure and true. |1|Pause|

I have such a great thirst for the Blessed Vision of His Darshan; I think of him in so many ways.
So be Merciful, O Supreme Lord; shower Your Mercy upon me, O Lord, Destroyer of pride. |1|

My stranger soul has come to join the Saadh Sangat.
That commodity, which I longed for, I have found in the Love of the Naam, the Name of the Lord. |2|

There are so many pleasures and delights of Maya, but they pass away in an instant.
Your devotees are imbued with Your Name; they enjoy peace everywhere. |3|

The entire world is seen to be passing away; only the Lord's Name is lasting and stable.

So make friends with the Holy Saints, so that you may obtain a lasting place of rest. |4|

Friends, acquaintances, children and relatives - none of these shall be your companion.

The Lord's Name alone shall go with you; God is the Master of the meek. |5|

The Lord's Lotus Feet are the Boat; attached to Them, you shall cross over the world-ocean.

Meeting with the Perfect True Guru, I embrace True Love for God. |6|

The prayer of Your Holy Saints is, "May I never forget You, for even one breath or morsel of food."

Whatever is pleasing to Your Will is good; by Your Sweet Will, my affairs are adjusted. |7|

I have met my Beloved, the Ocean of Peace, and Supreme Bliss has welled up within me.

Says Nanak, all my pains have been eradicated, meeting with God, the Lord of Supreme Bliss. |8|1|2|

Aasaa, Fifth Mehl, Birharray ~ Songs Of Separation, To Be Sung In The Tune Of The Chhants. Fourth House:

One Universal Creator God. By The Grace Of The True Guru:

Remember the Supreme Lord God, O Beloved, and make yourself a sacrifice to the Blessed Vision of His Darshan. |1|

Remembering Him, sorrows are forgotten, O Beloved; how can one forsake Him? |2|

I would sell this body to the Saint, O Beloved, if he would lead me to my Dear Lord. |3|

The pleasures and adornments of corruption are insipid and useless; I have forsaken and abandoned them, O my Mother. |4|

Lust, anger and greed left me, O Beloved, when I fell at the Feet of the True Guru. |5|

Those humble beings who are imbued with the Lord, O Beloved, do not go anywhere else. |6|

Those who have tasted the Lord's sublime essence, O Beloved, remain satisfied and satiated. |7|

One who grasps the Hem of the Gown of the Holy Saint, O Nanak, crosses over the terrible world-ocean. |8|1|3|

The pains of birth and death are removed, O Beloved, when the mortal meets with the Lord, the King. |1|

God is so Beautiful, so Refined, so Wise - He is my very life! Reveal to me Your Darshan! |2|

Those beings who are separated from You, O Beloved, are born only to die; they eat the poison of corruption. |3|

He alone meets You, whom You cause to meet, O Beloved; I fall at his feet. |4|

That happiness which one receives by beholding Your Darshan, O Beloved, cannot be described in words. |5|

True Love cannot be broken, O Beloved; throughout the ages, it remains. |6|

Section 08 - Raag Aasaa - Part 086

Whatever pleases You is good, O Beloved; Your Will is Eternal. |7|

Nanak, those who are imbued with the Love of the All-Pervading Lord, O Beloved, remain intoxicated with His Love, in natural ease. |8|2|4|

You know all about my condition, O Beloved; who can I speak to about it? |1|

You are the Giver of all beings; they eat and wear what You give them. |2|

Pleasure and pain come by Your Will, O Beloved; they do not come from any other. |3|

Whatever You cause me to do, that I do, O Beloved; I cannot do anything else. |4|

All my days and nights are blessed, O Beloved, when I chant and meditate on the Lord's Name. |5|

He does the deeds, O Beloved, which are pre-ordained, and inscribed upon his forehead. |6|

The One is Himself prevailing everywhere, O Beloved; He is pervading in each and every heart. |7|

Lift me up out of the deep pit of the world, O Beloved; Nanak has taken to Your Sanctuary. |8|3|22|15|2|42|

Raag Aasaa, First Mehl, Patee Likhee ~ The Poem Of The Alphabet:
One Universal Creator God. By The Grace Of The True Guru:
Sassa: He who created the world, is the One Lord and Master of all.
Those whose consciousness remains committed to His Service - blessed is their birth and their coming into the world. |1|

O mind, why forget Him? You foolish mind!
When your account is adjusted, O brother, only then shall you be judged wise. |1|Pause|

Eevree: The Primal Lord is the Giver; He alone is True.
No accounting is due from the Gurmukh who understands the Lord through these letters. |2|

Ooraa: Sing the Praises of the One whose limit cannot be found.
Those who perform service and practice truth, obtain the fruits of their rewards. |3|

Nganga: One who understands spiritual wisdom becomes a Pandit, a religious scholar.

One who recognizes the One Lord among all beings does not talk of ego.
|4|

Kakka: When the hair grows grey, then it shines without shampoo.
The hunters of the King of Death come, and bind him in the chains of Maya.
|5|

Khakha: The Creator is the King of the world; He enslaves by giving nourishment.
By His Binding, all the world is bound; no other Command prevails. |6|

Gagga: One who renounces the singing of the songs of the Lord of the Universe, becomes arrogant in his speech.
One who has shaped the pots, and made the world the kiln, decides when to put them in it. |7|

Ghagha: The servant who performs service, remains attached to the Word of the Guru's Shabad.
One who recognizes bad and good as one and the same - in this way he is absorbed into the Lord and Master. |8|

Chacha: He created the four Vedas, the four sources of creation, and the four ages
- through each and every age, He Himself has been the Yogi, the enjoyer, the Pandit and the scholar. |9|

Section 08 - Raag Aasaa - Part 087

Chhachha: Ignorance exists within everyone; doubt is Your doing, O Lord.
Having created doubt, You Yourself cause them to wander in delusion; those whom You bless with Your Mercy meet with the Guru. |10|

Jajja: That humble being who begs for wisdom has wandered begging through 8.4 million incarnations.
The One Lord takes away, and the One Lord gives; I have not heard of any other. |11|

Jhajha: O mortal being, why are you dying of anxiety? Whatever the Lord is to give, He shall keep on giving.

He gives, and gives, and watches over us; according to the Orders which He issues, His beings receive nourishment. |12|

Nyanya: When the Lord bestows His Glance of Grace, then I do not behold any other.
The One Lord is totally pervading everywhere; the One Lord abides within the mind. |13|

Tatta: Why do you practice hypocrisy, O mortal? In a moment, in an instant, you shall have to get up and depart.
Don't lose your life in the gamble - hurry to the Lord's Sanctuary. |14|

T'hat'ha: Peace pervades within those who link their consciousness to the Lord's Lotus Feet.
Those humble beings, whose consciousness is so linked, are saved; by Your Grace, they obtain peace. |15|

Dadda: Why do you make such ostentatious shows, O mortal? Whatever exists, shall all pass away.
So serve Him, who is contained and pervading among everyone, and you shall obtain peace. |16|

Dhadha: He Himself establishes and disestablishes; as it pleases His Will, so does He act.
Having created the creation, He watches over it; He issues His Commands, and emancipates those, upon whom He casts His Glance of Grace. |17|

Nanna: One whose heart is filled with the Lord, sings His Glorious Praises.
One whom the Creator Lord unites with Himself, is not consigned to reincarnation. |18|

Tatta: The terrible world-ocean is so very deep; its limits cannot be found.
I do not have a boat, or even a raft; I am drowning - save me, O Savior King! |19|

T'hat'ha: In all places and interspaces, He is; everything which exists, is by His doing.
What is doubt? What is called Maya? Whatever pleases Him is good. |20|

Dadda: Do not blame anyone else; blame instead your own actions.

Whatever I did, for that I have suffered; I do not blame anyone else. |21|

Dhadha: His power established and upholds the earth; the Lord has imparted His color to everything.
His gifts are received by everyone; all act according to His Command. |22|

Nanna: The Husband Lord enjoys eternal pleasures, but He is not seen or understood.
I am called the happy soul-bride, O sister, but my Husband Lord has never met me. |23|

Pappa: The Supreme King, the Transcendent Lord, created the world, and watches over it.
He sees and understands, and knows everything; inwardly and outwardly, he is fully pervading. |24|

Faffa: The whole world is caught in the noose of Death, and all are bound by its chains.
By Guru's Grace, they alone are saved, who hurry to enter the Lord's Sanctuary. |25|

Babba: He set out to play the game, on the chess-board of the four ages.

Section 08 - Raag Aasaa - Part 088

He made all beings and creatures his chessmen, and He Himself threw the dice. |26|

Bhabha: Those who search, find the fruits of their rewards; by Guru's Grace, they live in the Fear of God.
The self-willed manmukhs wander around, and they do not remember the Lord; the fools are consigned to the cycle of 8.4 million incarnations. |27|

Mamma: In emotional attachment, he dies; he only thinks of the Lord, the Love of Nectar, when he dies.
As long as the body is alive, he reads other things, and forgets the letter 'm', which stands for marnaa - death. |28|

Yaya: He is never reincarnated again, if he recognizes the True Lord.

The Gurmukh speaks, the Gurmukh understands, and the Gurmukh knows only the One Lord. |29|

Rarra: The Lord is contained among all; He created all beings.
Having created His beings, He has put them all to work; they alone remember the Naam, upon whom He bestows His Grace. |30|

Lalla: He has assigned people to their tasks, and made the love of Maya seem sweet to them.
We eat and drink; we should endure equally whatever occurs, by His Will, by His Command. |31|

Wawa: The all-pervading Transcendent Lord beholds the world; He created the form it wears.
He beholds, tastes, and knows everything; He is pervading and permeating inwardly and outwardly. |32|

Rarra: Why do you quarrel, O mortal? Meditate on the Imperishable Lord, and be absorbed into the True One. Become a sacrifice to Him. |33|

Haha: There is no other Giver than Him; having created the creatures, He gives them nourishment.
Meditate on the Lord's Name, be absorbed into the Lord's Name, and night and day, reap the Profit of the Lord's Name. |34|

Airaa: He Himself created the world; whatever He has to do, He continues to do.
He acts, and causes others to act, and He knows everything; so says Nanak, the poet. |35|1|

Raag Aasaa, Third Mehl, Patee - The Alphabet:
One Universal Creator God. By The Grace Of The True Guru:
Ayo, Angai: The whole world which was created - Kaahkai, Ghangai: It shall pass away.
Reeree, Laalee: People commit sins, and falling into vice, forget virtue. |1|

O mortal, why have you studied such an account,
which shall call you to answer for payment? |1|Pause|

Sidhan, Ngaayiyai: You do not remember the Lord. Nanna: You do not take the Lord's Name.
Chhachha: You are wearing away, every night and day; you fool, how will you find release? You are held in the grip of death. |2|

Babba: You do not understand, you fool; deluded by doubt, you are wasting your life.
Without justification, you call yourself a teacher; thus you take on the loads of others. |3|

Jajja: You have been robbed of your Light, you fool; in the end, you shall have to depart, and you shall regret and repent.
You have not remembered the One Word of the Shabad, and so you shall have to enter the womb over and over again. |4|

Read that which is written on your forehead, O Pandit, and do not teach wickedness to others.

Section 08 - Raag Aasaa - Part 089

First, the teacher is tied down, and then, the noose is placed around the pupil's neck. |5|

Sassa: You have lost your self-discipline, you fool, and you have accepted an offering under false pretenses.
The daughter of the alms-giver is just like your own; by accepting this payment for performing the wedding ceremony, you have cursed your own life. |6|

Mamma: You have been cheated out your intellect, you fool, and you are afflicted with the great disease of ego.
Within your innermost self, you do not recognize God, and you compromise yourself for the sake of Maya. |7|

Kakka: You wander around in sexual desire and anger, you fool; attached to possessiveness, you have forgotten the Lord.
You read, and reflect, and proclaim out loud, but without understanding, you are drowned to death. |8|

Tatta: In anger, you are burnt, you fool. T'hat'ha: That place where you live, is cursed.
Ghagha: You go begging from door to door, you fool. Dadda: But still, you do not receive the gift. |9|

Pappa: You shall not be able to swim across, you fool, since you are engrossed in worldly affairs.
The True Lord Himself has ruined you, you fool; this is the destiny written on your forehead. |10|

Bhabha: You have drowned in the terrifying world-ocean, you fool, and you have become engrossed in Maya.
One who comes to know the One Lord, by Guru's Grace, is carried across in an instant. |11|

Wawa: Your turn has come, you fool, but you have forgotten the Lord of Light.
This opportunity shall not come again, you fool; you shall fall under the power of the Messenger of Death. |12|

Jhajha: You shall never have to regret and repent, you fool, if you listen to the Teachings of the True Guru, for even an instant.
Without the True Guru, there is no Guru at all; one who is without a Guru has a bad reputation. |13|

Dhadha: Restrain your wandering mind, you fool; deep within you the treasure is to be found.
When one becomes Gurmukh, then he drinks in the sublime essence of the Lord; throughout the ages, he continues to drink it in. |14|

Gagga: Keep the Lord of the Universe in your mind, you fool; by mere words, no one has ever attained Him.
Enshrine the Guru's feet within your heart, you fool, and all your past sins shall be forgiven. |15|

Haha: Understand the Lord's Sermon, you fool; only then shall you attain eternal peace.
The more the self-willed manmukhs read, the more pain they suffer. Without the True Guru, liberation is not obtained. |16|

Rarra: Center your consciousness on the Lord, you fool; abide with those whose hearts are filled with the Lord.

By Guru's Grace, those who recognize the Lord, understand the absolute Lord. |17|

Your limits cannot be known; the indescribable Lord cannot be described.

O Nanak, whose who have met the True Guru, have their accounts settled. |18|1|2|

Raag Aasaa, First Mehl, Chhant, First House:

One Universal Creator God. By The Grace Of The True Guru:

O beautiful young bride, my Beloved Lord is very playful.

When the bride enshrines great love for her Husband Lord, He becomes merciful, and loves her in return.

Section 08 - Raag Aasaa - Part 090

The soul-bride meets her Husband Lord, when the Lord Master Himself showers His favor upon her.

Her bed is decorated in the company of her Beloved, and her seven pools are filled with ambrosial nectar.

Be kind and compassionate to me, O Merciful True Lord, that I may obtain the Word of the Shabad, and sing Your Glorious Praises.

O Nanak, gazing upon her Husband Lord, the soul-bride is delighted, and her mind is filled with joy. |1|

O bride of natural beauty, offer your loving prayers to the Lord.

The Lord is pleasing to my mind and body; I am intoxicated in my Lord God's Company.

Imbued with the Love of God, I pray to the Lord, and through the Lord's Name, I abide in peace.

If you recognize His Glorious Virtues, then you shall come to know God; thus virtue shall dwell in you, and sin shall run away.

Without You, I cannot survive, even for an instant; by merely talking and listening about You, I am not satisfied.

Nanak proclaims, "O Beloved, O Beloved!" His tongue and mind are drenched with the Lord's sublime essence. |2|

O my companions and friends, my Husband Lord is the merchant.

I have purchased the Lord's Name; its sweetness and value are unlimited.

His value is invaluable; the Beloved dwells in His true home. If it is pleasing to God, then He blesses His bride.

Some enjoy sweet pleasures with the Lord, while I stand crying at His door.

The Creator, the Cause of causes, the All-powerful Lord Himself arranges our affairs.

O Nanak, blessed is the soul-bride, upon whom He casts His Glance of Grace; she enshrines the Word of the Shabad in her heart. |3|

In my home, the true songs of rejoicing resound; the Lord God, my Friend, has come to me.

He enjoys me, and imbued with His Love, I have captivated His heart, and given mine to Him.

I gave my mind, and obtained the Lord as my Husband; as it pleases His Will, He enjoys me.

I have placed my body and mind before my Husband Lord, and through the Shabad, I have been blessed. Within the home of my own self, I have obtained the ambrosial fruit.

He is not obtained by intellectual recitation or great cleverness; only by love does the mind obtain Him.

O Nanak, the Lord Master is my Best Friend; I am not an ordinary person. |4|1|

Aasaa, First Mehl:

The unstruck melody of the sound current resounds with the vibrations of the celestial instruments.

My mind, my mind is imbued with the Love of my Darling Beloved.

Night and day, my detached mind remains absorbed in the Lord, and I obtain my home in the profound trance of the celestial void.

The True Guru has revealed to me the Primal Lord, the Infinite, my Beloved, the Unseen.

The Lord's posture and His seat are permanent; my mind is absorbed in reflective contemplation upon Him.

O Nanak, the detached ones are imbued with His Name, the unstruck melody, and the celestial vibrations. |1|

Tell me, how can I reach that unreachable, that unreachable city?

By practicing truthfulness and self-restraint, by contemplating His Glorious Virtues, and living the Word of the Guru's Shabad.

Practicing the True Word of the Shabad, one comes to the home of his own inner being, and obtains the treasure of virtue.

He has no stems, roots, leaves or branches, but He is the Supreme Lord over the heads of all.

Practicing intensive meditation, chanting and self-discipline, people have grown weary; stubbornly practicing these rituals, they still have not found Him.

O Nanak, through spiritual wisdom, the Lord, the Life of the world, is met; the True Guru imparts this understanding. |2|

The Guru is the ocean, the mountain of jewels, overflowing with jewels.

Section 08 - Raag Aasaa - Part 091

Take your bath in the seven seas, O my mind, and become pure.

One bathes in the water of purity when it is pleasing to God, and obtains the five virtues by reflective meditation.

Renouncing sexual desire, anger, deceit and corruption, he enshrines the True Name in his heart.

When the waves of ego, greed and avarice subside, he finds the Lord Master, Merciful to the meek.

O Nanak, there is no place of pilgrimage comparable to the Guru; the True Guru is the Lord of the world. |3|

I have searched the jungles and forests, and looked upon all the fields.

You created the three worlds, the entire universe, everything.

You created everything; You alone are permanent. Nothing is equal to You.

You are the Giver - all are Your beggars; without You, who should we praise?

You bestow Your gifts, even when we do not ask for them, O Great Giver; devotion to You is a treasure over-flowing.

Without the Lord's Name, there is no liberation; so says Nanak, the meek. |4|2|

Aasaa, First Mehl:

My mind, my mind is attuned to the Love of my Beloved Lord.

The True Lord Master, the Primal Being, the Infinite One, is the Support of the earth.

He is unfathomable, unapproachable, infinite and incomparable. He is the Supreme Lord God, the Lord above all.

He is the Lord, from the beginning, throughout the ages, now and forevermore; know that all else is false.

If one does not appreciate the value of good deeds and Dharmic faith, how can one obtain clarity of consciousness and liberation?

O Nanak, the Gurmukh realizes the Word of the Shabad; night and day, he meditates on the Naam, the Name of the Lord. |1|

My mind, my mind has come to accept, that the Naam is our only Friend.
Egotism, worldly attachment, and the lures of Maya shall not go with you.
Mother, father, famliy, children, cleverness, property and spouses - none of these shall go with you.
I have renounced Maya, the daughter of the ocean; reflecting upon reality, I have trampled it under my feet.
The Primal Lord has revealed this wondrous show; wherever I look, there I see Him.
O Nanak, I shall not forsake the Lord's devotional worship; in the natural course, what shall be, shall be. |2|

My mind, my mind has become immaculately pure, contemplating the True Lord.
I have dispelled my vices, and now I walk in the company of the virtuous.
Discarding my vices, I do good deeds, and in the True Court, I am judged as true.
My coming and going has come to an end; as Gurmukh, I reflect upon the nature of reality.
O my Dear Friend, You are my all-knowing companion; grant me the glory of Your True Name.
O Nanak, the jewel of the Naam has been revealed to me; such are the Teachings I have received from the Guru. |3|

I have carefully applied the healing ointment to my eyes, and I am attuned to the Immaculate Lord.
He is permeating my mind and body, the Life of the world, the Lord, the Great Giver.
My mind is imbued with the Lord, the Great Giver, the Life of the world; I have merged and blended with Him, with intuitive ease.
In the Company of the Holy, and the Saints' Society, by God's Grace, peace is obtained.
The renunciates remain absorbed in devotional worship to the Lord; they are rid of emotional attachment and desire.

O Nanak, how rare is that unattached servant, who conquers his ego, and remains pleased with the Lord. |4|3|

Section 08 - Raag Aasaa - Part 092

Raag Aasaa, First Mehl, Chhant, Second House:
One Universal Creator God. By The Grace Of The True Guru:
You are everywhere, wherever I go, O True Creator Lord.
You are the Giver of all, the Architect of Destiny, the Dispeller of distress.
The Lord Master is the Dispeller of distress; all that happens is by His doing.
Millions upon millions of sins, He destroys in an instant.
He calls a swan a swan, and a crane a crane; He contemplates each and every heart.
You are everywhere, wherever I go, O True Creator Lord. |1|

Those who meditate on Him single-mindedly obtain peace; how rare are they in this world.
The Messenger of Death does not draw near those who live the Guru's Teachings; they never return defeated.
Those who appreciate the Glorious Praises of the Lord, Har, Har, never suffer defeat; the Messenger of Death does not even approach them.
Birth and death are ended for those who are attached to the feet of the Lord.
Through the Guru's Teachings, they obtain the sublime essence of the Lord, and the fruit of the Lord; they enshrine the Name of the Lord, Har, Har, in their hearts.
Those who meditate on Him single-mindedly obtain peace; how rare are they in this world. |2|

He who created the world and assigned all to their tasks - unto Him I am a sacrifice.
So serve Him, and gather profit, and you shall obtain honor in the Court of the Lord.
That humble being, who recognizes the One Lord alone, obtains honor in the Court of the Lord.
One who meditates on the Lord, through the Guru's Teachings, obtains the nine treasures; he chants and repeats continually the Glorious Praises of the Lord.
Day and night, take the Naam, the Name of the Lord, the most sublime Primal Being.

The One who created the world and assigned all to their tasks - I am a sacrifice to Him. |3|

Those who chant the Naam look beautiful; they obtain the fruit of peace. Those who believe in the Name win the game of life.
Their blessings are not exhausted, if it pleases the Lord, even though numerous ages may pass.
Even though numerous ages may pass, O Lord Master, their blessings are not exhausted.
They do not age, they do not die and fall into hell, if they meditate on the Naam, the Name of the Lord.
Those who chant the Lord's Name, Har, Har, do not wither, O Nanak; they are not afflicted by pain.
Those who chant the Naam look beautiful; they obtain the fruit of peace. Those who believe in the Name win the game of life. |4|1|4|

One Universal Creator God. By The Grace Of The True Guru:
Aasaa, First Mehl, Chhant, Third House:
Listen, O black deer: why are you so attached to the orchard of passion?
The fruit of sin is sweet for only a few days, and then it grows hot and bitter.
That fruit which intoxicated you has now become bitter and painful, without the Naam.

Section 08 - Raag Aasaa - Part 093

It is temporary, like the waves on the sea, and the flash of lightning.
Without the Lord, there is no other protector, but you have forgotten Him.
Nanak speaks the Truth. Reflect upon it, O mind; you shall die, O black deer. |1|

O bumble bee, you wander among the flowers, but terrible pain awaits you.
I have asked my Guru for true understanding.
I have asked my True Guru for understanding about the bumble bee, who is so involved with the flowers of the garden.
When the sun rises, the body will fall, and it will be cooked in hot oil.
You shall be bound and beaten on the road of Death, without the Word of the Shabad, O madman.

Nanak speaks the Truth. Reflect upon it, O mind; you shall die, O bumble bee. |2|

O my stranger soul, why do you fall into entanglements?
The True Lord abides within your mind; why are you trapped by the noose of Death?
The fish leaves the water with tearful eyes, when the fisherman casts his net.
The love of Maya is sweet to the world, but in the end, this delusion is dispelled.
So perform devotional worship, link your consciousness to the Lord, and dispel anxiety from your mind.
Nanak speaks the Truth; focus your consciousness on the Lord, O my stranger soul. |3|

The rivers and streams which separate may sometime be united again.
In age after age, that which is sweet, is full of poison; how rare is the Yogi who understands this.
That rare person who centers his consciousness on the True Guru, knows intuitively and realizes the Lord.
Without the Naam, the Name of the Lord, the thoughtless fools wander in doubt, and are ruined.
Those whose hearts are not touched by devotional worship and the Name of the True Lord, shall weep and wail loudly in the end.
Nanak speaks the Truth; through the True Word of the Shabad, those long separated from the Lord, are united once again. |4|1|5|

One Universal Creator God. By The Grace Of The True Guru:
Aasaa, Third Mehl, Chhant, First House:
Within my home, the true wedding songs of rejoicing are sung; my home is adorned with the True Word of the Shabad.
The soul-bride has met her Husband Lord; God Himself has consummated this union.
God Himself has consummated this union; the soul-bride enshrines Truth within her mind, intoxicated with peaceful poise.
Embellished with the Word of the Guru's Shabad, and beautified with Truth, she enjoys her Beloved forever, imbued with His Love.
Eradicating her ego, she obtains her Husband Lord, and then, the sublime essence of the Lord dwells within her mind.

Says Nanak, fruitful and prosperous is her entire life; she is embellished with the Word of the Guru's Shabad. |1|

The soul-bride who has been led astray by duality and doubt, does not attain her Husband Lord.
That soul-bride has no virtue, and she wastes her life in vain.
The self-willed, ignorant and disgraceful manmukh wastes her life in vain, and in the end, she comes to grief.
But when she serves her True Guru, she obtains peace, and then she meets her Husband Lord, face to face.
Beholding her Husband Lord, she blossoms forth; her heart is delighted, and she is beautified by the True Word of the Shabad.
O Nanak, without the Name, the soul-bride wanders around, deluded by doubt. Meeting her Beloved, she obtains peace. |2|

Section 08 - Raag Aasaa - Part 094

The soul-bride knows that her Husband Lord is with her; the Guru unites her in this union.
Within her heart, she is merged with the Shabad, and the fire of her desire is easily extinguished.
The Shabad has quenched the fire of desire, and within her heart, peace and tranquility have come; she tastes the Lord's essence with intuitive ease.
Meeting her Beloved, she enjoys His Love continually, and her speech rings with the True Shabad.
Reading and studying continually, the Pandits, the religious scholars, and the silent sages have grown weary; wearing religious robes, liberation is not obtained.
O Nanak, without devotional worship, the world has gone insane; through the True Word of the Shabad, one meets the Lord. |3|

Bliss permeates the mind of the soul-bride, who meets her Beloved Lord.
The soul-bride is enraptured with the sublime essence of the Lord, through the incomparable Word of the Guru's Shabad.
Through the incomparable Word of the Guru's Shabad, she meets her Beloved; she continually contemplates and enshrines His Glorious Virtues in her mind.
Her bed was adorned when she enjoyed her Husband Lord; meeting with her Beloved, her demerits were erased.

That house, within which the Lord's Name is continually meditated upon, resounds with the wedding songs of rejoicing, throughout the four ages.

O Nanak, imbued with the Naam, we are in bliss forever; meeting the Lord, our affairs are resolved. |4|1|6|

One Universal Creator God. By The Grace Of The True Guru:

Aasaa, Third Mehl, Chhant, Third House:

O my beloved friend, dedicate yourself to the devotional worship of your Husband Lord.

Serve your Guru constantly, and obtain the wealth of the Naam.

Dedicate yourself to the worship of your Husband Lord; this is pleasing to your Beloved Husband.

If you walk in accordance with your own will, then your Husband Lord will not be pleased with you.

This path of loving devotional worship is very difficult; how rare are those who find it, through the Gurdwara, the Guru's Gate.

Says Nanak, that one, upon whom the Lord casts His Glance of Grace, links his consciousness to the worship of the Lord. |1|

O my detached mind, unto whom do you show your detachment?

Those who sing the Glorious Praises of the Lord live in the joy of the Lord, forever and ever.

So become detached, and renounce hypocrisy; Your Husband Lord knows everything.

The One Lord is pervading the water, the land and the sky; the Gurmukh realizes the Command of His Will.

One who realizes the Lord's Command, obtains all peace and comforts.

Thus says Nanak: such a detached soul remains absorbed in the Lord's Love, day and night. |2|

Wherever you wander, O my mind, the Lord is there with you.

Renounce your cleverness, O my mind, and reflect upon the Word of the Guru's Shabad.

Your Husband Lord is always with you, if you remember the Lord's Name, even for an instant.

The sins of countless incarnations shall be washed away, and in the end, you shall obtain the supreme status.

You shall be linked to the True Lord, and as Gurmukh, remember Him forever.

Thus says Nanak: wherever you go, O my mind, the Lord is there with you.
|3|

Meeting the True Guru, the wandering mind is held steady; it comes to abide in its own home.
It purchases the Naam, chants the Naam, and remains absorbed in the Naam.

Section 08 - Raag Aasaa - Part 095

The outgoing, wandering soul, upon meeting the True Guru, opens the Tenth Gate.
There, Ambrosial Nectar is food and the celestial music resounds; the world is held spell-bound by the music of the Word.
The many strains of the unstruck melody resound there, as one merges in Truth.
Thus says Nanak: by meeting the True Guru, the wandering soul becomes steady, and comes to dwell in the home of its own self. |4|

O my mind, you are the embodiment of the Divine Light - recognize your own origin.
O my mind, the Dear Lord is with you; through the Guru's Teachings, enjoy His Love.
Acknowledge your origin, and then you shall know your Husband Lord, and so understand death and birth.
By Guru's Grace, know the One; then, you shall not love any other.
Peace comes to the mind, and gladness resounds; then, you shall be acclaimed.
Thus says Nanak: O my mind, you are the very image of the Luminous Lord; recognize the true origin of your self. |5|

O mind, you are so full of pride; loaded with pride, you shall depart.
The fascinating Maya has fascinated you, over and over again, and lured you into reincarnation.
Clinging to pride, you shall depart, O foolish mind, and in the end, you shall regret and repent.
You are afflicted with the diseases of ego and desire, and you are wasting your life away in vain.
The foolish self-willed manmukh does not remember the Lord, and shall regret and repent hereafter.

Thus says Nanak: O mind, you are full of pride; loaded with pride, you shall depart. |6|

O mind, don't be so proud of yourself, as if you know it all; the Gurmukh is humble and modest.
Within the intellect are ignorance and ego; through the True Word of the Shabad, this filth is washed off.
So be humble, and surrender to the True Guru; do not attach your identity to your ego.
The world is consumed by ego and self-identity; see this, lest you lose your own self as well.
Make yourself follow the Sweet Will of the True Guru; remain attached to His Sweet Will.
Thus says Nanak: renounce your ego and self-conceit, and obtain peace; let your mind abide in humility. |7|

Blessed is that time, when I met the True Guru, and my Husband Lord came into my consciousness.
I became so very blissful, and my mind and body found such a natural peace.
My Husband Lord came into my consciousness; I enshrined Him within my mind, and I renounced all vice.
When it pleased Him, virtues appeared in me, and the True Guru Himself adorned me.
Those humble beings become acceptable, who cling to the One Name and renounce the love of duality.
Thus says Nanak: blessed is the time when I met the True Guru, and my Husband Lord came into my consciousness. |8|

Some people wander around, deluded by doubt; their Husband Lord Himself has misled them.
They wander around in the love of duality, and they do their deeds in ego.
Their Husband Lord Himself has misled them, and put them on the path of evil. Nothing lies in their power.
You alone know their ups and downs, You, who created the creation.
The Command of Your Will is very strict; how rare is the Gurmukh who understands.
Thus says Nanak: what can the poor creatures do, when You mislead them into doubt? |9|

Section 08 - Raag Aasaa - Part 096

O My True Lord Master, True is Your glorious greatness.

You are the Supreme Lord God, the Infinite Lord and Master. Your creative power cannot be described.

True is Your glorious greatness; when You enshrine it within the mind, one sings Your Glorious Praises forever.

He sings Your Glorious Praises, when it is pleasing to You, O True Lord; he centers his consciousness on You.

One whom You unite with Yourself, as Gurmukh, remains absorbed in You.

Thus says Nanak: O my True Lord Master, True is Your Glorious Greatness. |10|2|7|5|2|7|

Raag Aasaa, Chhant, Fourth Mehl, First House:

One Universal Creator God. By The Grace Of The True Guru:

Life - I have found real life, as Gurmukh, through His Love.

The Lord's Name - He has given me the Lord's Name, and enshrined it within my breath of life.

He has enshrined the Name of the Lord, Har, Har within my breath of life, and all my doubts and sorrows have departed.

I have meditated on the invisible and unapproachable Lord, through the Guru's Word, and I have obtained the pure, supreme status.

The unstruck melody resounds, and the instruments ever vibrate, singing the Bani of the True Guru.

O Nanak, God the Great Giver has given me a gift; He has blended my light into the Light. |1|

The self-willed manmukhs die in their self-willed stubbornness, declaring that the wealth of Maya is theirs.

They attach their consciousness to the foul-smelling pile of filth, which comes for a moment, and departs in an instant.

They attach their consciousness to the foul-smelling pile of filth, which is transitory, like the fading color of the safflower.

One moment, they are facing east, and the next instant, they are facing west; they continue spinning around, like the potter's wheel.

In sorrow, they eat, and in sorrow, they gather things and try to enjoy them, but they only increase their stores of sorrow.

O Nanak, one easily crosses over the terrifying world-ocean, when he comes to the Sanctuary of the Guru. |2|

My Lord, my Lord Master is sublime, unapproachable and unfathomable.

The wealth of the Lord - I seek the wealth of the Lord, from my True Guru, the Divine Banker.

I seek the wealth of the Lord, to purchase the Naam; I sing and love the Glorious Praises of the Lord.

I have totally renounced sleep and hunger, and through deep meditation, I am absorbed into the Absolute Lord.

The traders of one kind come and take away the Name of the Lord as their profit.

O Nanak, dedicate your mind and body to the Guru; one who is so destined, attains it. |3|

The great ocean is full of the treasures of jewels upon jewels.

Those who are committed to the Word of the Guru's Bani, see them come into their hands.

This priceless, incomparable jewel comes into the hands of those who are committed to the Word of the Guru's Bani.

They obtain the immeasurable Name of the Lord, Har, Har; their treasure is overflowing with devotional worship.

I have churned the ocean of the body, and I have seen the incomparable thing come into view.

The Guru is God, and God is the Guru, O Nanak; there is no difference between the two, O Siblings of Destiny. |4|1|8|

Aasaa, Fourth Mehl:

Slowly, slowly, slowly, very slowly, the drops of Ambrosial Nectar trickle down.

Section 08 - Raag Aasaa - Part 097

As Gurmukh, the Gurmukh beholds the Lord, the Beloved Lord.

The Name of the Lord, the Emancipator of the world, is dear to him; the Name of the Lord is his glory.

In this Dark Age of Kali Yuga, the Lord's Name is the boat, which carries the Gurmukh across.

This world, and the world hereafter, are adorned with the Lord's Name; the Gurmukh's lifestyle is the most excellent.

O Nanak, bestowing His kindness, the Lord gives the gift of His emancipating Name. |1|

I chant the Name of the Lord, Raam, Raam, which destroys my sorrows and erases my sins.

Associating with the Guru, associating with the Guru, I practice meditation; I have enshrined the Lord within my heart.

I enshrined the Lord within my heart, and obtained the supreme status, when I came to the Sanctuary of the Guru.

My boat was sinking under the weight of greed and corruption, but it was uplifted when the True Guru implanted the Naam, the Name of the Lord, within me.

The Perfect Guru has given me the gift of spiritual life, and I center my consciousness on the Lord's Name.

The Merciful Lord Himself has mercifully given this gift to me; O Nanak, I take to the Sanctuary of the Guru. |2|

Hearing the Bani of the Lord's Name, all my affairs were brought to perfection and embellished.

With each and every hair, with each and every hair, as Gurmukh, I meditate on the Lord.

I meditate on the Lord's Name, and become pure; He has no form or shape.

The Name of the Lord, Raam, Raam, is permeating my heart deep within, and all of my desire and hunger has disappeared.

My mind and body are totally adorned with peace and tranquility; through the Guru's Teachings, the Lord has been revealed to me.

The Lord Himself has shown His kind mercy to Nanak; He has made me the slave of the slaves of His slaves. |3|

Those who forget the Name of the Lord, Raam, Raam, are foolish, unfortunate, self-willed manmukhs.

Within, they are engrossed in emotional attachment; each and every moment, Maya clings to them.

The filth of Maya clings to them, and they become unfortunate fools - they do not love the Lord's Name.

The egotistical and proud perform all sorts of rituals, but they shy away from the Lord's Name.

The path of Death is very arduous and painful; it is stained with the darkness of emotional attachment.

O Nanak, the Gurmukh meditates on the Naam, and finds the gate of salvation. |4|

The Name of the Lord, Raam, Raam, and the Lord Guru, are known by the Gurmukh.

One moment, this mind is in the heavens, and the next, it is in the nether regions; the Guru brings the wandering mind back to one-pointedness.

When the mind returns to one-pointedness, one totally understands the value of salvation, and enjoys the subtle essence of the Lord's Name.

The Lord's Name preserves the honor of His servant, as He preserved and emancipated Prahlaad.

So repeat continually the Name of the Lord, Raam, Raam; chanting His Glorious Virtues, His limit cannot be found.

Nanak is drenched in happiness, hearing the Name of the Lord; he is merged in the Name of the Lord. |5|

Those beings, whose minds are filled the Lord's Name, forsake all anxiety.

They obtain all wealth, and all Dharmic faith, and the fruits of their minds' desires.

They obtain the fruits of their hearts' desires, meditating on the Lord's Name, and singing the Glorious Praises of the Lord's Name.

Evil-mindedness and duality depart, and their understanding is enlightened. They attach their minds to the Name of the Lord.

Section 08 - Raag Aasaa - Part 098

Their lives and bodies become totally blessed and fruitful; the Lord's Name illumines them.

O Nanak, by continually vibrating upon the Lord, day and night, the Gurmukhs abide in the home of the inner self. |6|

Those who place their faith in the Lord's Name, do not attach their consciousness to another.

Even if the entire earth were to be transformed into gold, and given to them, without the Naam, they love nothing else.

The Lord's Name is pleasing to their minds, and they obtain supreme peace; when they depart in the end, it shall go with them as their support.

I have gathered the capital, the wealth of the Lord's Name; it does not sink, and does not depart.

The Lord's Name is the only true support in this age; the Messenger of Death does not draw near it.

O Nanak, the Gurmukhs recognize the Lord; in His Mercy, He unites them with Himself. |7|

True, True is the Name of the Lord, Raam, Raam; the Gurmukh knows the Lord.

The Lord's servant is the one who commits himself to the Guru's service, and dedicates his mind and body as an offering to Him.

He dedicates his mind and body to Him, placing great faith in Him; the Guru lovingly unites His servant with Himself.

The Master of the meek, the Giver of souls, is obtained through the Perfect Guru.

The Guru's Sikh, and the Sikh's Guru, are one and the same; both spread the Guru's Teachings.

The Mantra of the Lord's Name is enshrined within the heart, O Nanak, and we merge with the Lord so easily. |8|2|9|

One Universal Creator God. By The Grace Of The True Guru:

Aasaa, Chhant, Fourth Mehl, Second House:

The Creator Lord, Har, Har, is the Destroyer of distress; the Name of the Lord is the Purifier of sinners.

One who lovingly serves the Lord, obtains the supreme status. Service to the Lord, Har, Har, is more exalted than anything.

Chanting the Name of the Lord is the most exalted occupation; chanting the Name of the Lord, one becomes immortal.

The pains of both birth and death are eradicated, and one comes to sleep in peaceful ease.

O Lord, O Lord and Master, shower Your Mercy upon me; within my mind, I chant the Name of the Lord.

The Creator Lord, Har, Har, is the Destroyer of distress; the Name of the Lord is the Purifier of sinners. |1|

The wealth of the Lord's Name is the most exalted in this Dark Age of Kali Yuga; chant the Lord's Name according to the Way of the True Guru.

As Gurmukh, read of the Lord; as Gurmukh, hear of the Lord. Chanting and listening to the Lord's Name, pain departs.

Chanting the Name of the Lord, Har, Har, pains are removed. Through the Name of the Lord, supreme peace is obtained.

The spiritual wisdom of the True Guru illumines the heart; this Light dispels the darkness of spiritual ignorance.

They alone meditate on the Lord's Name, Har, Har, upon whose foreheads such destiny is written.

The wealth of the Lord's Name is the most exalted in this Dark Age of Kali Yuga; chant the Lord's Name according to the Way of the True Guru. |2|

One whose mind loves the Lord, Har, Har, obtains supreme peace. He reaps the profit of the Lord's Name, the state of Nirvaanaa.
He embraces love for the Lord, and the Lord's Name becomes his companion. His doubts, and his comings and goings are ended.

Section 08 - Raag Aasaa - Part 099

His comings and goings, doubts and fears come to an end, and he sings the Glorious Praises of the Lord, Har, Har, Har.
The sins and pains of countless incarnations are washed away, and he merges into the Name of the Lord, Har, Har.
Those who are blessed by such pre-ordained destiny, meditate on the Lord, and their lives become fruitful and approved.
One whose mind loves the Lord, Har, Har, obtains supreme peace. He reaps the profit of the Lord's Name, the state of Nirvaanaa. |3|

Celebrated are those people, unto whom the Lord seems sweet; how exalted are those people of the Lord, Har, Har.
The Lord's Name is their glorious greatness; the Lord's Name is their companion and helper. Through the Word of the Guru's Shabad, they enjoy the sublime essence of the Lord.
They enjoy the sublime essence of the Lord, and remain totally detached. By great good fortune, they obtain the sublime essence of the Lord.
So very blessed and truly perfect are those, who through Guru's Instruction meditate on the Naam, the Name of the Lord.
Servant Nanak begs for the dust of the feet of the Holy; his mind is rid of sorrow and separation.
Celebrated are those people, unto whom the Lord seems sweet; how exalted are those people of the Lord, Har, Har. |4|3|10|

Aasaa, Fourth Mehl:
In the Golden Age of Sat Yuga, everyone embodied contentment and meditation; religion stood upon four feet.
With mind and body, they sang of the Lord, and attained supreme peace. In their hearts was the spiritual wisdom of the Lord's Glorious Virtues.
Their wealth was the spiritual wisdom of the Lord's Glorious Virtues; the Lord was their success, and to live as Gurmukh was their glory.

Inwardly and outwardly, they saw only the One Lord God; for them there was no other second.

They centered their consciousness lovingly on the Lord, Har, Har. The Lord's Name was their companion, and in the Court of the Lord, they obtained honor.

In the Golden Age of Sat Yuga, everyone embodied contentment and meditation; religion stood upon four feet. |1|

Then came the Silver Age of Trayta Yuga; men's minds were ruled by power, and they practiced celibacy and self-discipline.

The fourth foot of religion dropped off, and three remained. Their hearts and minds were inflamed with anger.

Their hearts and minds were filled with the horribly poisonous essence of anger. The kings fought their wars and obtained only pain.

Their minds were afflicted with the illness of egotism, and their self-conceit and arrogance increased.

If my Lord, Har, Har, shows His Mercy, my Lord and Master eradicates the poison by the Guru's Teachings and the Lord's Name.

Then came the Silver Age of Trayta Yuga; men's minds were ruled by power, and they practiced celibacy and self-discipline. |2|

The Brass Age of Dwaapar Yuga came, and people wandered in doubt. The Lord created the Gopis and Krishna.

The penitents practiced penance, they offered sacred feasts and charity, and performed many rituals and religious rites.

They performed many rituals and religious rites; two legs of religion dropped away, and only two legs remained.

So many heroes waged great wars; in their egos they were ruined, and they ruined others as well.

The Lord, Compassionate to the poor, led them to meet the Holy Guru. Meeting the True Guru, their filth is washed away.

The Brass Age of Dwaapar Yuga came, and the people wandered in doubt. The Lord created the Gopis and Krishna. |3|

Section 08 - Raag Aasaa - Part 100

The Lord ushered in the Dark Age, the Iron Age of Kali Yuga; three legs of religion were lost, and only the fourth leg remained intact.

Acting in accordance with the Word of the Guru's Shabad, the medicine of the Lord's Name is obtained. Singing the Kirtan of the Lord's Praises, divine peace is obtained.

The season of singing the Lord's Praise has arrived; the Lord's Name is glorified, and the Name of the Lord, Har, Har, grows in the field of the body.

In the Dark Age of Kali Yuga, if one plants any other seed than the Name, all profit and capital is lost.

Servant Nanak has found the Perfect Guru, who has revealed to him the Naam within his heart and mind.

The Lord ushered in the Dark Age, the Iron Age of Kali Yuga; three legs of religion were lost, and only the fourth leg remained intact. |4|4|11|

Aasaa, Fourth Mehl:

One whose mind is pleased with the Kirtan of the Lord's Praises, attains the supreme status; the Lord seems so sweet to her mind and body.

She obtains the sublime essence of the Lord, Har, Har; through the Guru's Teachings, she meditates on the Lord, and the destiny written on her forehead is fulfilled.

By that high destiny written on her forehead, she chants the Name of the Lord, her Husband, and through the Name of the Lord, she sings the Lord's Glorious Praises.

The jewel of immense love sparkles on her forehead, and she is adorned with the Name of the Lord, Har, Har.

Her light blends with the Supreme Light, and she obtains God; meeting the True Guru, her mind is satisfied.

One whose mind is pleased with the Kirtan of the Lord's Praises, attains the supreme status; the Lord seems sweet to her mind and body. |1|

Those who sing the Praises of the Lord, Har, Har, obtain the supreme status; they are the most exalted and acclaimed people.

I bow at their feet; each and every moment, I wash the feet of those, unto whom the Lord seems sweet.

The Lord seems sweet to them, and they obtain the supreme status; their faces are radiant and beautiful with good fortune.

Under Guru's Instruction, they sing the Lord's Name, and wear the garland of the Lord's Name around their necks; they keep the Lord's Name in their throats.

They look upon all with equality, and recognize the Supreme Soul, the Lord, pervading among all.

Those who sing the Praises of the Lord, Har, Har, obtain the supreme status; they are the most exalted and acclaimed people. |2|

One whose mind is pleased with the Sat Sangat, the True Congregation, savors the sublime essence of the Lord; in the Sangat, is this essence of the Lord.
He meditates in adoration upon the Lord, Har, Har, and through the Word of the Guru's Shabad, he blossoms forth. He plants no other seed.
There is no Nectar, other than the Lord's Ambrosial Nectar. One who drinks it in, knows the way.
Hail, hail to the Perfect Guru; through Him, God is found. Joining the Sangat, the Naam Is understood.
I serve the Naam, and I meditate on the Naam. Without the Naam, there is no other at all.
One whose mind is pleased with the Sat Sangat, savors the sublime essence of the Lord; in the Sangat, is this essence of the Lord. |3|

O Lord God, shower Your Mercy upon me; I am just a stone. Please, carry me across, and lift me up with ease, through the Word of the Shabad.
I am stuck in the swamp of emotional attachment, and I am sinking. O Lord God, please, take me by the arm.
God took me by the arm, and I obtained the highest understanding; as His slave, I grasped the Guru's feet.

Section 08 - Raag Aasaa - Part 101

I chant and meditate in adoration upon the Name of the Lord, Har, Har, according to the good destiny written upon my forehead.
The Lord has showered His Mercy upon servant Nanak, and the Name of the Lord, Har, Har, seems so sweet to his mind.
O Lord God, shower Your Mercy upon me; I am just a stone. Please, carry me across, and lift me up with ease, through the Word of the Shabad. |4|5|12|

Aasaa, Fourth Mehl:
One who chants the Naam, the Name of the Lord, Har, Har in his mind - the Lord is pleasing to his mind. In the mind of the devotees there is a great yearning for the Lord.

Those humble beings who remain dead while yet alive, drink in the Ambrosial Nectar; through the Guru's Teachings, their minds embrace love for the Lord.

Their minds love the Lord, Har, Har, and the Guru is Merciful to them. They are Jivan Mukta - liberated while yet alive, and they are at peace.

Their birth and death, through the Name of the Lord, are illustrious, and in their hearts and minds, the Lord, Har, Har, abides.

The Name of the Lord, Har, Har, abides in their minds, and through the Guru's Teachings, they savor the Lord, Har, Har; they drink in the sublime essence of the Lord with abandon.

One who chants the Naam, the Name of the Lord, Har, Har, in his mind - the Lord is pleasing to his mind. In the mind of the devotees there is such a great yearning for the Lord. |1|

The people of the world do not like death; they try to hide from it. They are afraid that the Messenger of Death may catch them and take them away.

Inwardly and outwardly, the Lord God is the One and Only; this soul cannot be concealed from Him.

How can one keep one's soul, when the Lord wishes to have it? All things belong to Him, and He shall take them away.

The self-willed manmukhs wander around in pathetic lamentation, trying all medicines and remedies.

God, the Master, unto whom all things belong, shall take them away; the Lord's servant is redeemed by living the Word of the Shabad.

The people of the world do not like death; they try to hide from it. They are afraid that the Messenger of Death may catch them and take them away. |2|

Death is pre-ordained; the Gurmukhs look beauteous, and the humble beings are saved, meditating on the Lord, Har, Har.

Through the Lord they obtain honor, and through the Lord's Name, glorious greatness. In the Court of the Lord, they are robed in honor.

Robed in honor in the Court of the Lord, in the perfection of the Lord's Name, they obtain peace through the Lord's Name.

The pains of both birth and death are eliminated, and they merge into the Name of the Lord.

The Lord's servants meet with God and merge into Oneness. The Lord's servant and God are one and the same.

Death is pre-ordained; the Gurmukhs look beauteous, and the humble beings are saved, meditating on the Lord, Har, Har. |3|

The people of the world are born, only to perish, and perish, and perish again. Only by attaching oneself to the Lord as Gurmukh, does one become permanent.

The Guru implants His Mantra within the heart, and one savors the sublime essence of the Lord; the Ambrosial Nectar of the Lord trickles into his mouth.

Obtaining the Ambrosial Essence of the Lord, the dead are restored to life, and do not die again.

Through the Name of the Lord, Har, Har, one obtains the immortal status, and merges into the Lord's Name.

The Naam, the Name of the Lord, is the only Support and Anchor of servant Nanak; without the Naam, there is nothing else at all.

The people of the world are born, only to perish, and perish, and perish again. Only by attaching oneself to the Lord as Gurmukh, does one become permanent. |4|6|13|

Section 08 - Raag Aasaa - Part 102

Aasaa, Fourth Mehl, Chhant:
My Lord of the Universe is great, unapproachable, unfathomable, primal, immaculate and formless.

His condition cannot be described; His Glorious Greatness is immeasurable. My Lord of the Universe is invisible and infinite.

The Lord of the Universe is invisible, infinite and unlimited. He Himself knows Himself.

What should these poor creatures say? How can they speak of and describe You?

That Gurmukh who is blessed by Your Glance of Grace contemplates You.

My Lord of the Universe is great, unapproachable, unfathomable, primal, immaculate and formless. |1|

You, O Lord, O Primal Being, are the Limitless Creator; Your limits cannot be found.

You are pervading and permeating each and every heart, everywhere, You are contained in all.

Within the heart is the Transcendent, Supreme Lord God, whose limits cannot be found.

He has no form or shape; He is unseen and unknown. The Gurmukh sees the unseen Lord.

He remains in continual ecstasy, day and night, and is spontaneously absorbed into the Naam.

You, O Lord, O Primal Being, are the Limitless Creator; Your limits cannot be found. |2|

You are the True, Transcendent Lord, forever imperishable. The Lord, Har, Har, is the treasure of virtue.

The Lord God, Har, Har, is the One and only; there is no other at all. You Yourself are the all-knowing Lord.

You are the all-knowing Lord, the most exalted and auspicious; there is no other as great as You.

The Word of Your Shabad is pervading in all; whatever You do, comes to pass.

The One Lord God is permeating all; the Gurmukh comes to understand the Lord's Name.

You are the True, Transcendent Lord, forever imperishable. The Lord, Har, Har, is the treasure of virtue. |3|

You are the Creator of all, and all greatness is Yours. As it pleases Your Will, so do we act.

As it pleases Your Will, so do we act. All are merged into Your Shabad.

When it pleases Your Will, we obtain greatness through Your Shabad.

The Gurmukh obtains wisdom, and eliminates his self-conceit, and remains absorbed in the Shabad.

The Gurmukh obtains Your incomprehensible Shabad; O Nanak, he remains merged in the Naam.

You are the Creator of all, and all greatness is Yours. As it pleases Your Will, so do we act. |4|7|14|

One Universal Creator God. By The Grace Of The True Guru:

Aasaa, Fourth Mehl, Chhant, Fourth House:

My eyes are wet with the Nectar of the Lord, and my mind is imbued with His Love, O Lord King.

The Lord applied His touch-stone to my mind, and found it one hundred per cent gold.

As Gurmukh, I am dyed in the deep red of the poppy, and my mind and body are drenched with His Love.

Section 08 - Raag Aasaa - Part 103

Servant Nanak is drenched with His Fragrance; blessed, blessed is his entire life. |1|

The Bani of the Lord's Love is the pointed arrow, which has pierced my mind, O Lord King.
Only those who feel the pain of this love, know how to endure it.
Those who die, and remain dead while yet alive, are said to be Jivan Mukta, liberated while yet alive.
O Lord, unite servant Nanak with the True Guru, that he may cross over the terrifying world-ocean. |2|

I am foolish and ignorant, but I have taken to His Sanctuary; may I merge in the Love of the Lord of the Universe, O Lord King.
Through the Perfect Guru, I have obtained the Lord, and I beg for the one blessing of devotion to the Lord.
My mind and body blossom forth through the Word of the Shabad; I meditate on the Lord of infinite waves.
Meeting with the humble Saints, Nanak finds the Lord, in the Sat Sangat, the True Congregation. |3|

O Merciful to the meek, hear my prayer, O Lord God; You are my Master, O Lord King.
I beg for the Sanctuary of the Lord's Name, Har, Har; please, place it in my mouth.
It is the Lord's natural way to love His devotees; O Lord, please preserve my honor!
Servant Nanak has entered His Sanctuary, and has been saved by the Name of the Lord. |4|8|15|

Aasaa, Fourth Mehl:
As Gurmukh, I searched and searched, and found the Lord, my Friend, my Sovereign Lord King.
Within the walled fortress of my golden body, the Lord, Har, Har, is revealed.
The Lord, Har, Har, is a jewel, a diamond; my mind and body are pierced through.
By the great good fortune of pre-ordained destiny, I have found the Lord.
Nanak is permeated with His sublime essence. |1|

I stand by the roadside, and ask the way; I am just a youthful bride of the Lord King.

The Guru has caused me to remember the Name of the Lord, Har, Har; I follow the Path to Him.

The Naam, the Name of the Lord, is the Support of my mind and body; I have burnt away the poison of ego.

O True Guru, unite me with the Lord, unite me with the Lord, adorned with garlands of flowers. |2|

O my Love, come and meet me as Gurmukh; I have been separated from You for so long, Lord King.

My mind and body are sad; my eyes are wet with the Lord's sublime essence.

Show me my Lord God, my Love, O Guru; meeting the Lord, my mind is pleased.

I am just a fool, O Nanak, but the Lord has appointed me to perform His service. |3|

The Guru's body is drenched with Ambrosial Nectar; He sprinkles it upon me, O Lord King.

Those whose minds are pleased with the Word of the Guru's Bani, drink in the Ambrosial Nectar again and again.

As the Guru is pleased, the Lord is obtained, and you shall not be pushed around any more.

The Lord's humble servant becomes the Lord, Har, Har; O Nanak, the Lord and His servant are one and the same. |4|9|16|

Aasaa, Fourth Mehl:

The treasure of Ambrosial Nectar, the Lord's devotional service, is found through the Guru, the True Guru, O Lord King.

The Guru, the True Guru, is the True Banker, who gives to His Sikh the capital of the Lord.

Blessed, blessed is the trader and the trade; how wonderful is the Banker, the Guru!

O servant Nanak, they alone obtain the Guru, who have such pre-ordained destiny written upon their foreheads. |1|

You are my True Banker, O Lord; the whole world is Your trader, O Lord King.

You fashioned all vessels, O Lord, and that which dwells within is also Yours.

Whatever You place in that vessel, that alone comes out again. What can the poor creatures do?

Section 08 - Raag Aasaa - Part 104

The Lord has given the treasure of His devotional worship to servant Nanak. |2|

What Glorious Virtues of Yours can I describe, O Lord and Master? You are the most infinite of the infinite, O Lord King.

I praise the Lord's Name, day and night; this alone is my hope and support.

I am a fool, and I know nothing. How can I find Your limits?

Servant Nanak is the slave of the Lord, the water-carrier of the slaves of the Lord. |3|

As it pleases You, You save me; I have come seeking Your Sanctuary, O God, O Lord King.

I am wandering around, ruining myself day and night; O Lord, please save my honor!

I am just a child; You, O Guru, are my father. Please give me understanding and instruction.

Servant Nanak is known as the Lord's slave; O Lord, please preserve his honor! |4|10|17|

Aasaa, Fourth Mehl:

Those who have the blessed pre-ordained destiny of the Lord written on their foreheads, meet the True Guru, the Lord King.

The Guru removes the darkness of ignorance, and spiritual wisdom illuminates their hearts.

They find the wealth of the jewel of the Lord, and then, they do not wander any longer.

Servant Nanak meditates on the Naam, the Name of the Lord, and in meditation, he meets the Lord. |1|

Those who have not kept the Lord's Name in their consciousness - why did they bother to come into the world, O Lord King?

It is so difficult to obtain this human incarnation, and without the Naam, it is all futile and useless.

Now, in this most fortunate season, he does not plant the seed of the Lord's Name; what will the hungry soul eat, in the world hereafter?

The self-willed manmukhs are born again and again. O Nanak, such is the Lord's Will. |2|

You, O Lord, belong to all, and all belong to You. You created all, O Lord King.

Nothing is in anyone's hands; all walk as You cause them to walk.

They alone are united with You, O Beloved, whom You cause to be so united; they alone are pleasing to Your Mind.

Servant Nanak has met the True Guru, and through the Lord's Name, he has been carried across. |3|

Some sing of the Lord, through musical Ragas and the sound current of the Naad, through the Vedas, and in so many ways. But the Lord, Har, Har, is not pleased by these, O Lord King.

Those who are filled with fraud and corruption within - what good does it do for them to cry out?

The Creator Lord knows everything, although they may try to hide their sins and the causes of their diseases.

O Nanak, those Gurmukhs whose hearts are pure, obtain the Lord, Har, Har, by devotional worship. |4|11|18|

Aasaa, Fourth Mehl:

Those whose hearts are filled with the love of the Lord, Har, Har, are the wisest and most clever people, O Lord King.

Even if they misspeak outwardly, they are still very pleasing to the Lord.

The Lord's Saints have no other place. The Lord is the honor of the dishonored.

The Naam, the Name of the Lord, is the Royal Court for servant Nanak; the Lord's power is his only power. |1|

Wherever my True Guru goes and sits, that place is beautiful, O Lord King.

The Guru's Sikhs seek out that place; they take the dust and apply it to their faces.

The works of the Guru's Sikhs, who meditate on the Lord's Name, are approved.

Those who worship the True Guru, O Nanak - the Lord causes them to be worshipped in turn. |2|

The Guru's Sikh keeps the Love of the Lord, and the Name of the Lord, in his mind. He loves You, O Lord, O Lord King.

Section 08 - Raag Aasaa - Part 105

He serves the Perfect True Guru, and his hunger and self-conceit are eliminated.
The hunger of the Gursikh is totally eliminated; indeed, many others are satisfied through them.
Servant Nanak has planted the Seed of the Lord's Goodness; this Goodness of the Lord shall never be exhausted. |3|

The minds of the Gursikhs rejoice, because they have seen my True Guru, O Lord King.
If someone recites to them the story of the Lord's Name, it seems so sweet to the mind of those Gursikhs.
The Gursikhs are robed in honor in the Court of the Lord; my True Guru is very pleased with them.
Servant Nanak has become the Lord, Har, Har; the Lord, Har, Har, abides within his mind. |4|12|19|

Aasaa, Fourth Mehl:
Those who meet my Perfect True Guru - He implants within them the Name of the Lord, the Lord King.
Those who meditate on the Lord's Name have all of their desire and hunger removed.
Those who meditate on the Name of the Lord, Har, Har - the Messenger of Death cannot even approach them.
O Lord, shower Your Mercy upon servant Nanak, that he may ever chant the Name of the Lord; through the Name of the Lord, he is saved. |1|

Those who, as Gurmukh, meditate on the Naam, meet no obstacles in their path, O Lord King.
Those who are pleasing to the almighty True Guru are worshipped by everyone.
Those who serve their Beloved True Guru obtain eternal peace.

Those who meet the True Guru, O Nanak - the Lord Himself meets them. |2|

Those Gurmukhs, who are filled with His Love, have the Lord as their Saving Grace, O Lord King.
How can anyone slander them? The Lord's Name is dear to them.
Those whose minds are in harmony with the Lord - all their enemies attack them in vain.
Servant Nanak meditates on the Naam, the Name of the Lord, the Lord Protector. |3|

In each and every age, He creates His devotees and preserves their honor, O Lord King.
The Lord killed the wicked Harnaakhash, and saved Prahlaad.
He turned his back on the egotists and slanderers, and showed His Face to Naam Dayv.
Servant Nanak has so served the Lord, that He will deliver him in the end. |4|13|20|

Aasaa, Fourth Mehl, Chhant, Fifth House:
One Universal Creator God. By The Grace Of The True Guru:
O my dear beloved stranger mind, please come home!
Meet with the Lord-Guru, O my dear beloved, and He will dwell in the home of your self.
Revel in His Love, O my dear beloved, as the Lord bestows His Mercy.
As Guru Nanak is pleased, O my dear beloved, we are united with the Lord. |1|

I have not tasted divine love, O my dear beloved, within my heart.
The mind's desires are not quenched, O my dear beloved, but I still hold out hope.
Youth is passing away, O my dear beloved, and death is stealing away the breath of life.
The virtuous bride realizes the good fortune of her destiny, O my dear beloved; O Nanak, she enshrines the Lord within her heart. |2|

Section 08 - Raag Aasaa - Part 106

My eyes are drenched with the Love of my Husband Lord, O my dear beloved, like the song-bird with the rain drop.

My mind is cooled and soothed, O my dear beloved, by drinking in the rain drops of the Lord.

Separation from my Lord keeps my body awake, O my dear beloved; I cannot sleep at all.

Nanak has found the Lord, the True Friend, O my dear beloved, by loving the Guru. |3|

In the month of Chayt, O my dear beloved, the pleasant season of spring begins.

But without my Husband Lord, O my dear beloved, my courtyard is filled with dust.

But my sad mind is still hopeful, O my dear beloved; my eyes are both fixed upon Him.

Beholding the Guru, Nanak is filled with wondrous joy, like a child, gazing upon his mother. |4|

The True Guru has preached the sermon of the Lord, O my dear beloved.

I am a sacrifice to the Guru, O my dear beloved, who has united me with the Lord.

The Lord has fulfilled all my hopes, O my dear beloved; I have obtained the fruits of my heart's desires.

When the Lord is pleased, O my dear beloved, servant Nanak is absorbed into the Naam. |5|

Without the Beloved Lord, there is no play of love.

How can I find the Guru? Grasping hold of Him, I behold my Beloved.

O Lord, O Great Giver, let me meet the Guru; as Gurmukh, may I merge with You.

Nanak has found the Guru, O my dear beloved; such was the destiny inscribed upon his forehead. |6|14|21|

One Universal Creator God. By The Grace Of The True Guru:

Raag Aasaa, Fifth Mehl, Chhant, First House:

Joy - great joy! I have seen the Lord God!

Tasted - I have tasted the sweet essence of the Lord.

The sweet essence of the Lord has rained down in my mind; by the pleasure of the True Guru, I have attained peaceful ease.

I have come to dwell in the home of my own self, and I sing the songs of joy; the five villains have fled.

I am soothed and satisfied with the Ambrosial Bani of His Word; the friendly Saint is my advocate.

Says Nanak, my mind is in harmony with the Lord; I have seen God with my eyes. |1|

Adorned - adorned are my beauteous gates, O Lord.

Guests - my guests are the Beloved Saints, O Lord.

The Beloved Saints have resolved my affairs; I humbly bowed to them, and committed myself to their service.

He Himself is the groom's party, and He Himself the bride's party; He Himself is the Lord and Master; He Himself is the Divine Lord.

He Himself resolves His own affairs; He Himself sustains the Universe.

Says Nanak, my Bridegroom is sitting in my home; the gates of my body are beautifully adorned. |2|

The nine treasures - the nine treasures come into my home, Lord.

Everything - I obtain everything, meditating on the Naam, the Name of the Lord.

Meditating on the Naam, the Lord of the Universe becomes the one's eternal companion, and he dwells in peaceful ease.

His calculations are ended, his wanderings cease, and his mind is no longer afflicted with anxiety.

When the Lord of the Universe reveals Himself, and the unstruck melody of the sound current vibrates, the drama of wondrous splendor is enacted.

Says Nanak, when my Husband Lord is with me, I obtain the nine treasures. |3|

Over-joyed - over-joyed are all my brothers and friends.

Section 08 - Raag Aasaa - Part 107

Meeting the Guru, I have won the most arduous battle in the arena of life.

Meeting the Guru, I am victorious; praising the Lord, Har, Har, the walls of the fortress of doubt have been destroyed.

I have obtained the wealth of so many treasures; the Lord Himself has stood by my side.

He is the man of spiritual wisdom, and he is the leader, whom God has made His own.

Says Nanak, when the Lord and Master is on my side, then my brothers and friends rejoice. |4|1|

Aasaa, Fifth Mehl:

Inexpressible is the sermon of the inexpressible Lord; it cannot be known at all.

The demi-gods, mortal beings, angels and silent sages express it in their peaceful poise.

In their poise, they recite the Ambrosial Bani of the Lord's Word; they embrace love for the Lord's Lotus Feet.

Meditating on the One incomprehensible and immaculate Lord, they obtain the fruits of their heart's desires.

Renouncing self-conceit, emotional attachment, corruption and duality, their light merges into the Light.

Prays Nanak, by Guru's Grace, one enjoys the Lord's Love forever. |1|

The Lord's Saints - the Lord's Saints are my friends, my best friends and helpers.

By great good fortune, by great good fortune, I have obtained the Sat Sangat, the True Congregation.

By great good fortune, I obtained it, and I meditate on the Naam, the Name of the Lord; my pains and sufferings have been taken away.

I have grasped the Guru's Feet, and my doubts and fears are gone. He Himself has erased my self-conceit.

Granting His Grace, God has united me with Himself; no longer do I suffer the pains of separation, and I shall not have to go anywhere.

Prays Nanak, I am forever Your slave, Lord; I seek Your Sanctuary. |2|

The Lord's Gate - at the Lord's Gate, Your beloved devotees look beautiful.

I am a sacrifice, a sacrifice, again and again a sacrifice to them.

I am forever a sacrifice, and I humbly bow to them; meeting them, I know God.

The Perfect and All-powerful Lord, the Architect of Destiny, is contained in each and every heart, everywhere.

Meeting the Perfect Guru, we meditate on the Naam, and do not lose this life in the gamble.

Prays Nanak, I seek Your Sanctuary; please, shower Your Mercy upon me, and protect me. |3|

Innumerable - innumerable are Your Glorious Virtues; how many of them can I sing?

The dust of Your feet, of Your feet, I have obtained, by great good fortune.

Bathing in the Lord's dust, my filth has been washed away, and the pains of birth and death have departed.

Inwardly and outwardly, the Transcendent Lord God is ever-present, always with us.

Suffering departs, and there is peace; singing the Kirtan of the Lord's Praises, one is not consigned to reincarnation again.

Prays Nanak, in the Guru's Sanctuary, one swims across, and is pleasing to God. |4|2|

Aasaa, Chhant, Fifth Mehl, Fourth House:

One Universal Creator God. By The Grace Of The True Guru:

My mind is pierced by the Lord's Lotus Feet; He alone is sweet to my mind, the Lord King.

Joining the Society of the Saints, I meditate on the Lord in adoration; I behold the Lord King in each and every heart.

I behold the Lord in each and every heart, and the Ambrosial Nectar rains down upon me; the pains of birth and death are gone.

Singing the Praises of the Lord, the treasure of virtue, all my pains are erased, and the knot of ego has been untied.

Section 08 - Raag Aasaa - Part 108

My Beloved shall not leave me to go anywhere - this is His natural way; my mind is imbued with the lasting color of the Lord's Love.

The Lotus Feet of the Lord have pierced Nanak's mind, and now, nothing else seems sweet to him. |1|

Just like the fish which revels in water, I am intoxicated with the sublime essence of the Lord, my Lord King.

The Perfect Guru has instructed me, and blessed me with salvation in my life; I love the Lord, my King.

The Lord Master, the Searcher of hearts, blesses me with salvation in my life; He Himself attaches me to His Love.

The Lord is the treasure of jewels, the perfect manifestation; He shall not forsake us to go anywhere else.

God, the Lord Master, is so accomplished, beauteous, and all-knowing; His gifts are never exhausted.

As the fish is enraptured by the water, so is Nanak intoxicated by the Lord. |2|

As the song-bird yearns for the rain-drop, the Lord, the Lord my King, is the Support of my breath of life.

My Lord King is more beloved than all wealth, treasure, children, siblings and friends.

The absolute Lord, the Primal Being, is more beloved than all; His condition cannot be known.

I shall never forget the Lord, for an instant, for a single breath; through the Word of the Guru's Shabad, I enjoy His Love.

The Primal Lord God is the Life of the Universe; His Saints drink in the Lord's sublime essence. Meditating on Him, doubts, attachments and pains are shaken off.

As the song-bird yearns for the rain-drop, so does Nanak love the Lord. |3|

Meeting the Lord, my Lord King, my desires are fulfilled.

The walls of doubt have been torn down, meeting the Brave Guru, O Lord King.

The Perfect Guru is obtained by perfect pre-ordained destiny; God Is the Giver of all treasures - He is merciful to the meek.

In the beginning, in the middle, and in the end, is God, the most beautiful Guru, the Sustainer of the World.

The dust of the feet of the Holy purifies sinners, and brings great joy, bliss and ecstasy.

The Lord, the Infinite Lord, has met with Nanak, and his desires are fulfilled. |4|1|3|

Aasaa, Fifth Mehl, Chhant, Sixth House:
One Universal Creator God. By The Grace Of The True Guru:
Shalok:
Those beings, unto whom the Lord God shows His Mercy, meditate on the Lord, Har, Har.

O Nanak, they embrace love for the Lord, meeting the Saadh Sangat, the Company of the Holy. |1|

Chhant:
Just like water, which loves milk so much that it will not let it burn - O my mind, so love the Lord.

The bumble bee becomes enticed by the lotus, intoxicated by its fragrance, and does not leave it, even for a moment.

Do not let up your love for the Lord, even for an instant; dedicate all your decorations and pleasures to Him.

Where painful cries are heard, and the Way of Death is shown, there, in the Saadh Sangat, the Company of the Holy, you shall not be afraid.

Sing the Kirtan, the Praises of the Lord of the Universe, and all sins and sorrows shall depart.

Says Nanak, chant the Hymns of the Lord, the Lord of the Universe, O mind, and enshrine love for the Lord; love the Lord this way in your mind. |1|

As the fish loves the water, and is not content even for an instant outside it, O my mind, love the Lord in this way.

Section 08 - Raag Aasaa - Part 109

Like the song-bird, thirsting for the rain-drops, chirping each and every moment to the beautiful rain clouds.

So love the Lord, and give to Him this mind of yours; totally focus your consciousness on the Lord.

Do not take pride in yourself, but seek the Sanctuary of the Lord, and make yourself a sacrifice to the Blessed Vision of His Darshan.

When the Guru is totally pleased, the separated soul-bride is re-united with her Husband Lord; she sends the message of her true love.

Says Nanak, chant the Hymns of the Infinite Lord Master; O my mind, love Him and enshrine such love for Him. |2|

The chakvi bird is in love with the sun, and thinks of it constantly; her greatest longing is to behold the dawn.

The cuckoo is in love with the mango tree, and sings so sweetly. O my mind, love the Lord in this way.

Love the Lord, and do not take pride in yourself; everyone is a guest for a single night.

Now, why are you entangled in pleasures, and engrossed in emotional attachment? Naked we come, and naked we go.

Seek the eternal Sanctuary of the Holy and fall at their feet, and the attachments which you feel shall depart.

Says Nanak, chant the Hymns of the Merciful Lord God, and enshrine love for the Lord, O my mind; otherwise, how will you come to behold the dawn? |3|

Like the deer in the night, who hears the sound of the bell and gives his heart - O my mind, love the Lord in this way.

Like the wife, who is bound by love to her husband, and serves her beloved - like this, give your heart to the Beloved Lord.

Give your heart to your Beloved Lord, and enjoy His bed, and enjoy all pleasure and bliss.

I have obtained my Husband Lord, and I am dyed in the deep crimson color of His Love; after such a long time, I have met my Friend.

When the Guru became my advocate, then I saw the Lord with my eyes. No one else looks like my Beloved Husband Lord.

Says Nanak, chant the Hymns of the merciful and fascinating Lord, O mind. Grasp the lotus feet of the Lord, and enshrine such love for Him in your mind. |4|1|4|

Aasaa, Fifth Mehl|

Shalok:
From forest to forest, I wandered searching; I am so tired of taking baths at sacred shrines of pilgrimage.

O Nanak, when I met the Holy Saint, I found the Lord within my mind. |1|

Chhant:
Countless silent sages and innumerable ascetics seek Him;

millions of Brahmas meditate and adore Him; the spiritual teachers meditate and chant His Name.

Through chanting, deep meditation, strict and austere self-discipline, religious rituals, sincere worship, endless purifications and humble salutations,

wandering all over the earth and bathing at sacred shrines of pilgrimage, people seek to meet the Pure Lord.

Mortals, forests, blades of grass, animals and birds all meditate on You.

The Merciful Beloved Lord, the Lord of the Universe is found; O Nanak, joining the Saadh Sangat, the Company of the Holy, salvation is attained. |1|

Millions of incarnations of Vishnu and Shiva, with matted hair yearn for You, O Merciful Lord; their minds and bodies are filled with infinite longing.

The Lord Master, the Lord of the Universe, is infinite and unapproachable; God is the all-pervading Lord of all.

The angels, the Siddhas, the beings of spiritual perfection, the heavenly heralds and celestial singers meditate on You. The Yakhsha demons, the guards of the divine treasures, and the Kinnars, the dancers of the god of wealth chant Your Gl

Millions of Indras and countless gods and super-human beings meditate on the Lord Master and celebrate His Praises.
The Merciful Lord is the Master of the masterless, O Nanak; joining the Saadh Sangat, the Company of the Holy, one is saved. |2|

Millions of gods and goddesses of wealth serve Him in so many ways.

Section 08 - Raag Aasaa - Part 110

The invisible and visible beings worship Him in adoration, along with wind and water, day and night.
The stars, the moon and the sun meditate on Him; the earth and the sky sing to Him.
All the sources of creation, and all languages meditate on Him, forever and ever.
The Simritees, the Puraanas, the four Vedas and the six Shaastras meditate on Him.
He is the Purifier of sinners, the Lover of His Saints; O Nanak, He is met in the Society of the Saints. |3|

As much as God has revealed to us, that much we can speak with our tongues.
Those unknown ones who serve You cannot be counted.
Imperishable, incalculable, and unfathomable is the Lord and Master; He is everywhere, inside and out.
We are all beggars, He is the One and only Giver; He is not far away, but is with us, ever-present.
He is in the power of His devotees; those whose souls are united with Him - how can their praises be sung?

May Nanak receive this gift and honor, of placing his head on the feet of the Holy Saints. |4|2|5|

Aasaa, Fifth Mehl,
Shalok:

Make the effort, O very fortunate ones, and meditate on the Lord, the Lord King.

O Nanak, remembering Him in meditation, you shall obtain total peace, and your pains and troubles and doubts shall depart. |1|

Chhant:
Chant the Naam, the Name of the Lord of the Universe; don't be lazy.

Meeting with the Saadh Sangat, the Company of the Holy, you shall not have to go to the City of Death.

Pain, trouble and fear will not afflict you; meditating on the Naam, a lasting peace is found.

WIth each and every breath, worship the Lord in adoration; meditate on the Lord God in your mind and with your mouth.

O kind and compassionate Lord, O treasure of sublime essence, treasure of excellence, please link me to Your service.

Prays Nanak: may I meditate on the Lord's lotus feet, and not be lazy in chanting the Naam, the Name of the Lord of the Universe. |1|

The Purifier of sinners is the Naam, the Pure Name of the Immaculate Lord.

The darkness of doubt is removed by the healing ointment of the Guru's spiritual wisdom.

By the healing ointment of the Guru's spiritual wisdom, one meets the Immaculate Lord God, who is totally pervading the water, the land and the sky.

If He dwells within the heart, for even an instant, sorrows are forgotten.

The wisdom of the all-powerful Lord and Master is incomprehensible; He is the Destroyer of the fears of all.

Prays Nanak, I meditate on the Lord's lotus feet. The Purifier of sinners is the Naam, the Pure Name of the Immaculate Lord. |2|

I have grasped the protection of the merciful Lord, the Sustainer of the Universe, the treasure of grace.

I take the support of Your lotus feet, and in the protection of Your Sanctuary, I attain perfection.

The Lord's lotus feet are the cause of causes; the Lord Master saves even the sinners.

So many are saved; they cross over the terrifying world-ocean, contemplating the Naam, the Name of the Lord.

In the beginning and in the end, countless are those who seek the Lord. I have heard that the Society of the Saints is the way to salvation.

Prays Nanak, I meditate on the Lord's lotus feet, and grasp the protection of the Lord of the Universe, the merciful, the ocean of kindness. |3|

The Lord is the Lover of His devotees; this is His natural way.
Wherever the Saints worship the Lord in adoration, there He is revealed.
God blends Himself with His devotees in His natural way, and resolves their affairs.
In the ecstasy of the Lord's Praises, they obtain supreme joy, and forget all their sorrows.

Section 08 - Raag Aasaa - Part 111

The brilliant flash of the One Lord is revealed to them - they behold Him in the ten directions.
Prays Nanak, I meditate on the Lord's lotus feet; the Lord is the Lover of His devotees; this is His natural way. |4|3|6|

Aasaa, Fifth Mehl:
The Husband Lord of the Saints is eternal; He does not die or go away.
She, whose home is blessed by her Husband Lord, enjoys Him forever.
God is eternal and immortal, forever young and immaculately pure.
He is not far away, He is ever-present; the Lord and Master fills the ten directions, forever and ever.
He is the Lord of souls, the source of salvation and wisdom. The Love of my Dear Beloved is pleasing to me.
Nanak speaks what the Guru's Teachings have led him to know. The Husband Lord of the Saints is eternal; He does not die or go away. |1|

One who has the Lord as her Husband enjoys great bliss.
That soul-bride is happy, and her glory is perfect.
She obtains honor, greatness and happiness, singing the Praise of the Lord.
God, the Great Being, is always with her.
She attains total perfection and the nine treasures; her home lacks nothing.
- everything is there.
Her speech is so sweet; she obeys her Beloved Lord; her marriage is permanent and everlasting.
Nanak chants what he knows through the Guru's Teachings: One who has the Lord as her Husband enjoys great bliss. |2|

Come, O my companions, let us dedicate ourselves to serving the Saints.

Let us grind their corn, wash their feet and so renounce our self-conceit.

Let us shed our egos, and our troubles shall be removed; let us not display ourselves.

Let us take to His Sanctuary and obey Him, and be happy with whatever He does.

Let us become the slaves of His slaves, and shed our sadness, and with our palms pressed together, remain wakeful day and night.

Nanak chants what he knows through the Guru's Teachings; come, O my companions, let us dedicate ourselves to serving the Saints. |3|

One who has such good destiny written upon his forehead, dedicates himself to His service.

One who attains the Saadh Sangat, the Company of the Holy, has his desires fulfilled.

In the Saadh Sangat, immerse yourself in the Love of the Lord; remember the Lord of the Universe in meditation.

Doubt, emotional attachment, sin and duality - he renounces them all.

Peace, poise and tranquility fill his mind, and he sings the Lord's Glorious Praises with joy and delight.

Nanak chants what he knows through the Guru's Teachings: one who has such good destiny written upon his forehead, dedicates himself to His service. |4|4|7|

Aasaa, Fifth Mehl,
Shalok:

If you chant the Naam, the Name of the Lord, Har, Har, the Messenger of Death will have nothing to say to you.

O Nanak, the mind and body will be at peace, and in the end, you shall merge with the Lord of the world. |1|

Chhant:

Let me join the Society of the Saints - save me, Lord!

With my palms pressed together, I offer my prayer: give me Your Name, O Lord, Har, Har.

I beg for the Lord's Name, and fall at His feet; I renounce my self-conceit, by Your kindness.

I shall not wander anywhere else, but take to Your Sanctuary. O God, embodiment of mercy, have mercy on me.

O all-powerful, indescribable, infinite and immaculate Lord Master, listen to this, my prayer.

With palms pressed together, Nanak begs for this blessing: O Lord, let my cycle of birth and death come to an end. |1|

Section 08 - Raag Aasaa - Part 112

I am a sinner, devoid of wisdom, worthless, destitute and vile.
I am deceitful, hard-hearted, lowly and entangled in the mud of emotional attachment.
I am stuck in the filth of doubt and egotistical actions, and I try not to think of death.
In ignorance, I cling to the pleasures of woman and the joys of Maya.
My youth is wasting away, old age is approaching, and Death, my companion, is counting my days.
Prays Nanak, my hope is in You, Lord; please preserve me, the lowly one, in the Sanctuary of the Holy. |2|

I have wandered through countless incarnations, suffering terrible pain in these lives.
I am entangled in sweet pleasures and gold.
After wandering around with such great loads of sin, I have come, after wandering through so many foreign lands.
Now, I have taken the protection of God, and I have found total peace in the Name of the Lord.
God, my Beloved, is my protector; nothing was done, or will ever be done, by myself alone.
I have found peace, poise and bliss, O Nanak; by Your mercy, I swim across the world-ocean. |3|

You saved those who only pretended to believe, so what doubts should Your true devotees have?
By every means possible, listen to the Praises of the Lord with your ears.
Listen with your ears to the Word of the Lord's Bani, the hymns of spiritual wisdom; thus you shall obtain the treasure in your mind.
Attuned to the Love of the Lord God, the Architect of Destiny, sing the Glorious Praises of the Lord.
The earth is the paper, the forest is the pen and the wind is the writer,
but still, the end of the endless Lord cannot be found. O Nanak, I have taken to the Sanctuary of His lotus feet. |4|5|8|

Aasaa, Fifth Mehl:

The Primal Lord is the Lord God of all beings. I have taken to His Sanctuary.

My life has become fearless, and all my anxieties have been removed.

I know the Lord as my mother, father, son, friend, well-wisher and close relative.

The Guru has led me to embrace Him; the Saints chant His Pure Praises.

His Glorious Virtues are infinite, and His greatness is unlimited. His value cannot be described at all.

God is the One and only, the Unseen Lord and Master; O Nanak, I have grasped His protection. |1|

The world is a pool of nectar, when the Lord becomes our helper.

One who wears the necklace of the Lord's Name - his days of suffering are ended.

His state of doubt, attachment and sin is erased, and the cycle of reincarnation into the womb is totally ended.

The ocean of fire becomes cool, when one grasps the hem of the robe of the Holy Saint.

The Lord of the Universe, the Sustainer of the World, the merciful all-powerful Lord - the Holy Saints proclaim the victory of the Lord.

O Nanak, meditating on the Naam, in the perfect Saadh Sangat, the Company of the Holy, I have obtained the supreme status. |2|

Wherever I look, there I find the One Lord permeating and pervading all.

In each and every heart, He Himself dwells, but how rare is that person who realizes this.

The Lord is permeating and pervading the water, the land and the sky; He is contained in the ant and the elephant.

In the beginning, in the middle and in the end, He exists. By Guru's Grace, He is known.

God created the expanse of the universe, God created the play of the world. His humble servants call Him the Lord of the Universe, the treasure of virtue.

Meditate in remembrance on the Lord Master, the Searcher of hearts; O Nanak, He is the One, pervading and permeating all. |3|

Day and night, become beauteous by remembering the Naam, the Name of the Lord.

Section 08 - Raag Aasaa - Part 113

In love with the Lord's Lotus Feet, corruption and sin depart.

Pain, hunger and poverty run away, and the path is clearly revealed.

Joining the Saadh Sangat, the Company of the Holy, one is attuned to the Naam, and obtains the desires of the mind.

Beholding the Blessed Vision of the Lord's Darshan, desires are fulfilled; all one's family and relatives are saved.

Day and night, he is in bliss, night and day, remembering the Lord in meditation, O Nanak. |4|6|9|

Aasaa, Fifth Mehl, Chhant, Seventh House:

One Universal Creator God. By The Grace Of The True Guru:

Shalok:

It is the most sublime contemplation, to speak of the Lord of the Universe in the pure Saadh Sangat, the Company of the Holy.

O Nanak, never the Naam, even for a moment; bless me with Your Grace, Lord God! |1|

Chhant:

The night is wet with dew, and the stars twinkle in the heavens.

The Saints remain wakeful; they are the Beloveds of my Lord.

The Beloveds of the Lord remain ever wakeful, remembering the Naam, the Name of the Lord, day and night.

In their hearts, they meditate on the lotus feet of God; they do not forget Him, even for an instant.

They renounce their pride, emotional attachment and mental corruption, and burn away the pain of wickedness.

Prays Nanak, the Saints, the beloved servants of the Lord, remain ever wakeful. |1|

My bed is adorned in splendor.

My mind is filled with bliss, since I heard that God is coming.

Meeting God, the Lord and Master, I have entered the realm of peace; I am filled with joy and delight.

He is joined to me, in my very fiber; my sorrows have departed, and my body, mind and soul are all rejuvenated.

I have obtained the fruits of my mind's desires, meditating on God; the day of my wedding is auspicious.

Prays Nanak, when I meet the Lord of excellence, I came to experience all pleasure and bliss. |2|

I meet with my companions and say, "Show me the insignia of my Husband Lord."

I am filled with the sublime essence of His Love, and I do not know how to say anything.

The Glorious Virtues of the Creator are profound, mysterious and infinite; even the Vedas cannot find His limits.

With loving devotion, I meditate on the Lord Master, and sing the Glorious Praises of the Lord forever.

Filled with all virtues and spiritual wisdom, I have become pleasing to my God.

Prays Nanak, imbued with the color of the Lord's Love, I am imperceptibly absorbed into Him. |3|

When I began to sing the songs of rejoicing to the Lord, my friends became glad, and my troubles and enemies departed.

My peace and happiness increased; I rejoiced in the Naam, the Name of the Lord, and God Himself blessed me with His mercy.

I have grasped the Lord's feet, and remaining ever wakeful, I have met the Lord, the Creator.

The appointed day came, and I attained peace and poise; all treasures are in the feet of God.

Prays Nanak, the Lord's humble servants always seek the Sanctuary of the Lord and Master. |4|1|10|

Aasaa, Fifth Mehl:
Rise up and go forth, O traveller; why do you delay?

Your allotted time is now complete - why are you engrossed in falsehood?

You desire that which is false; deceived by Maya, you commit innumerable sins.

Your body shall become a pile of dust; the Messenger of Death has spotted you, and will conquer you.

Section 08 - Raag Aasaa - Part 114

Abandoning your wealth and youth, you will have to leave, without any food or clothing.

O Nanak, only your actions shall go with you; the consequences of your actions cannot be erased. |1|

Like the deer, captured on a moon-lit night,

so does the constant commission of sins turn pleasure into pain.

The sins you have committed shall not leave you; placing the noose around your neck, they shall lead you away.

Beholding an illusion, you are deceived, and on your bed, you enjoy a false lover.

You are intoxicated with greed, avarice and egotism; you are engrossed in self-conceit.

O Nanak, like the deer, you are being destroyed by your ignorance; your comings and goings shall never end. |2|

The fly is caught in the sweet candy - how can it fly away?

The elephant has fallen into the pit - how can it escape?

It shall be so difficult to swim across, for one who does not remember the Lord and Master, even for an instant.

His sufferings and punishments are beyond reckoning; he receives the consequences of his own actions.

His secret deeds are exposed, and he is ruined here and hereafter.

O Nanak, without the True Guru, the self-willed egotistical manmukh is defrauded. |3|

The Lord's slaves live by holding on to God's feet.

The Lord and Master embraces those who seek His Sanctuary.

He blesses them with power, wisdom, knowledge and meditation; He Himself inspires them to chant His Name.

He Himself is the Saadh Sangat, the Company of the Holy, and He Himself saves the world.

The Preserver preserves those whose actions are always pure.

O Nanak, they never have to go to hell; the Lord's Saints are under the Lord's Protection. |4|2|11|

Aasaa, Fifth Mehl:

Be gone, O my laziness, that I may pray to the Lord.

I enjoy my Husband Lord, and look beautiful with my God.

I look beautiful in the Company of my Husband Lord; I enjoy my Lord Master day and night.

I live by remembering God with each and every breath, beholding the Lord, and singing His Glorious Praises.

The pain of separation has grown shy, for I have obtained the Blessed Vision of His Darshan; His Ambrosial Glance of Grace has filled me with bliss.

Prays Nanak, my desires are fulfilled; I have met the One I was seeking. ||1||

Run away, O sins; the Creator has entered my home.
The demons within me have been burnt; the Lord of the Universe has revealed Himself to me.
The Beloved Lord of the Universe, the Lord of the World has revealed Himself; in the Saadh Sangat, the Company of the Holy, I chant His Name.
I have seen the Wondrous Lord; He showers His Ambrosial Nectar upon me, and by Guru's Grace, I know Him.
My mind is at peace, resounding with the music of bliss; the Lord's limits cannot be found.
Prays Nanak, God brings us to union with Himself, in the poise of celestial peace. ||2||

They do not have to see hell, if they remember the Lord in meditation.
The Righteous Judge of Dharma applauds them, and the Messenger of Death runs away from them.
Dharmic faith, patience, peace and poise are obtained by vibrating upon the Lord in the Saadh Sangat, the Company of the Holy.
Showering His Blessings, He saves those who renounce all attachments and egotism.
The Lord embraces us; the Guru unites us with Him. Meditating on the Lord of the Universe, we are satisfied.
Prays Nanak, remembering the Lord and Master in meditation, all hopes are fulfilled. ||3||

Section 08 - Raag Aasaa - Part 115

Grasping the Lord's Feet, the treasure of the Siddhas, what suffering can I feel?
Everything is in His Power - He is my God.
Holding me the the the arm, He blesses me with His Name; placing His Hand upon my forehead, He saves me.
The world-ocean does not trouble me, for I have drunk the sublime elixir of the Lord.
In the Saadh Sangat, imbued with the Naam, the Name of the Lord, I am victorious on the great battlefield of life.
Prays Nanak, I have entered the Sanctuary of the Lord and Master; the Messenger of Death shall not destroy me again. ||4||3||12||

Aasaa, Fifth Mehl:

Those actions you perform, day and night, are recorded upon your forehead.

And the One, from whom you hide these actions - He sees them, and is always with you.

The Creator Lord is with you; He sees you, so why commit sins?

So perform good deeds, and chant the Naam, the Name of the Lord; you shall never have to go to hell.

Twenty-four hours a day, dwell upon the Lord's Name in meditation; it alone shall go along with you.

So vibrate continually in the Saadh Sangat, the Company of the Holy, O Nanak, and the sins you committed shall be erased. |1|

Practicing deceit, you fill your belly, you ignorant fool!

The Lord, the Great Giver, continues to give you everything.

The Great Giver is always merciful. Why should we forget the Lord Master from our minds?

Join the Saadh Sangat, and vibrate fearlessly; all your relations shall be saved.

The Siddhas, the seekers, the demi-gods, the silent sages and the devotees, all take the Naam as their support.

Prays Nanak, vibrate continually upon God, the One Creator Lord. |2|

Do not practice deception - God is the Assayer of all.

Those who practice falsehood and deceit are reincarnated in the world.

Those who meditate on the One Lord, cross over the world-ocean.

Renouncing sexual desire, anger, flattery and slander, they enter the Sanctuary of God.

The lofty, inaccessible and infinite Lord and Master is pervading the water, the land and the sky.

Prays Nanak, He is the support of His servants; His Lotus Feet are their only sustenance. |3|

Behold - the world is a mirage; nothing here is permanent.

The pleasures of Maya which are here, shall not go with you.

The Lord, your companion, is always with you; remember Him day and night.

Without the One Lord, there is no other; burn away the love of duality.

Know in your mind, that the One God is your friend, youth, wealth and everything.

Prays Nanak, by great good fortune, we find the Lord, and merge in peace and celestial poise. |4|4|13|

Aasaa, Fifth Mehl, Chhant, Eighth House:
One Universal Creator God. By The Grace Of The True Guru:
Maya is the wall of doubt - Maya is the wall of doubt. It is such a powerful and destructive intoxicant; it corrupts and wastes away one's life.
In the terrible, impenetrable world-forest - in the terrible, impenetrable world-forest, the thieves are plundering man's house in broad daylight; night and day, this life is being consumed.
The days of your life are being consumed; they are passing away without God. So meet God, the Merciful Lord.

Section 08 - Raag Aasaa - Part 116

I passed through so many births and deaths; without Union with the Beloved, I did not obtain salvation.
I am without the status of high birth, beauty, glory or spiritual wisdom; without You, who is mine, O Mother?

With my palms pressed together, O Nanak, I enter the Lord's Sanctuary; O beloved almighty Lord and Master, please, save me! |1|

Like a fish out of water - like a fish out of water, separated from the Lord, the mind and body perish; how can I live, without my Beloved?

Facing the arrow head-on - facing the arrow head-on, the deer surrenders his mind, body and breath of life; he is struck by the hunter's soothing music.
I have enshrined love for my Beloved. In order to meet Him, I have become a renunciate. Cursed is that body which remains without Him, even for an instant.
My eyelids do not close, for I am absorbed in the love of my Beloved. Day and night, my mind thinks only of God.
Attuned to the Lord, intoxicated with the Naam, fear, doubt and duality have all left me.
Bestow Your mercy and compassion, O merciful and perfect Lord, that Nanak may be intoxicated with Your Love. |2|

The bumble-bee is buzzing - the bumble-bee is buzzing, intoxicated with the honey, the flavor and the fragrance; because of its love for the lotus, it entangles itself.

The mind of the rainbird thirsts - the mind of the rainbird thirsts; its mind longs for the beautiful rain-drops from the clouds. Drinking them in, its fever departs.

O Destroyer of fever, Remover of pain, please unite me with You. My mind and body have such great love for You.

O my beautiful, wise and all-knowing Lord and Master, with what tongue should I chant Your Praises?

Take me by the arm, and grant me Your Name. One who is blessed with Your Glance of Grace, has his sins erased.

Nanak meditates on the Lord, the Purifier of sinners; beholding His Vision, he suffers no more. |3|

I focus my consciousness on the Lord - I focus my consciousness upon the Lord; I am helpless - please, keep me under Your Protection. I yearn to meet You, my soul hungers for You.

I meditate on Your beautiful body - I meditate on Your beautiful body; my mind is fascinated by Your spiritual wisdom, O Lord of the world. Please, preserve the honor of Your humble servants and beggars.

God bestows perfect honor and destroys pain; He has fulfilled all my desires.

How very blessed was that day when the Lord embraced me; meeting my Husband Lord, my bed was beautified.

When God granted His Grace and met me, all my sins were erased.

Prays Nanak, my hopes are fulfilled; I have met the Lord, the Lord of Lakshmi, the treasure of excellence. |4|1|14|

One Universal Creator God. Truth Is The Name. Creative Being Personified. No Fear. No Hatred. Image Of The Undying. Beyond Birth. Self-Existent. By Guru's Grace:

Aasaa, First Mehl:
Vaar With Shaloks, And Shaloks Written By The First Mehl. To Be Sung To The Tune Of 'Tunda-Asraajaa':
Shalok, First Mehl:
A hundred times a day, I am a sacrifice to my Guru;
He made angels out of men, without delay. |1|

Section 08 - Raag Aasaa - Part 117

Second Mehl:
If a hundred moons were to rise, and a thousand suns appeared,
even with such light, there would still be pitch darkness without the Guru.
|2|

First Mehl:
O Nanak, those who do not think of the Guru, and who think of themselves as clever,
shall be left abandoned in the field, like the scattered sesame.
They are abandoned in the field, says Nanak, and they have a hundred masters to please.
The wretches bear fruit and flower, but within their bodies, they are filled with ashes. |3|

Pauree:
He Himself created Himself; He Himself assumed His Name.
Secondly, He fashioned the creation; seated within the creation, He beholds it with delight.
You Yourself are the Giver and the Creator; by Your Pleasure, You bestow Your Mercy.
You are the Knower of all; You give life, and take it away again with a word.
Seated within the creation, You behold it with delight. |1|

Shalok, First Mehl:
True are Your worlds, True are Your solar Systems.
True are Your realms, True is Your creation.
True are Your actions, and all Your deliberations.
True is Your Command, and True is Your Court.
True is the Command of Your Will, True is Your Order.
True is Your Mercy, True is Your Insignia.
Hundreds of thousands and millions call You True.
In the True Lord is all power, in the True Lord is all might.
True is Your Praise, True is Your Adoration.
True is Your almighty creative power, True King.
O Nanak, true are those who meditate on the True One.
Those who are subject to birth and death are totally false. |1|

First Mehl:

Great is His greatness, as great as His Name.

Great is His greatness, as True is His justice.

Great is His greatness, as permanent as His Throne.

Great is His greatness, as He knows our utterances.

Great is His greatness, as He understands all our affections.

Great is His greatness, as He gives without being asked.

Great is His greatness, as He Himself is all-in-all.

O Nanak, His actions cannot be described.

Whatever He has done, or will do, is all by His Own Will. |2|

Second Mehl:

This world is the room of the True Lord; within it is the dwelling of the True Lord.

By His Command, some are merged into Him, and some, by His Command, are destroyed.

Some, by the Pleasure of His Will, are lifted up out of Maya, while others are made to dwell within it.

No one can say who will be rescued.

O Nanak, he alone is known as Gurmukh, unto whom the Lord reveals Himself. |3|

Pauree:

O Nanak, having created the souls, the Lord installed the Righteous Judge of Dharma to read and record their accounts.

There, only the Truth is judged true; the sinners are picked out and separated.

The false find no place there, and they go to hell with their faces blackened.

Those who are imbued with Your Name win, while the cheaters lose.

The Lord installed the Righteous Judge of Dharma to read and record the accounts. |2|

Shalok, First Mehl:

Wonderful is the sound current of the Naad, wonderful is the knowledge of the Vedas.

Wonderful are the beings, wonderful are the species.

Wonderful are the forms, wonderful are the colors.

Wonderful are the beings who wander around naked.

Section 08 - Raag Aasaa - Part 118

Wonderful is the wind, wonderful is the water.
Wonderful is fire, which works wonders.
Wonderful is the earth, wonderful the sources of creation.
Wonderful are the tastes to which mortals are attached.
Wonderful is union, and wonderful is separation.
Wonderful is hunger, wonderful is satisfaction.
Wonderful is His Praise, wonderful is His adoration.
Wonderful is the wilderness, wonderful is the path.
Wonderful is closeness, wonderful is distance.
How wonderful to behold the Lord, ever-present here.
Beholding His wonders, I am wonder-struck.
O Nanak, those who understand this are blessed with perfect destiny. |1|

First Mehl:
By His Power we see, by His Power we hear; by His Power we have fear, and the essence of happiness.
By His Power the nether worlds exist, and the Akaashic ethers; by His Power the entire creation exists.
By His Power the Vedas and the Puraanas exist, and the Holy Scriptures of the Jewish, Christian and Islamic religions. By His Power all deliberations exist.
By His Power we eat, drink and dress; by His Power all love exists.
- By His Power come the species of all kinds and colors; by His Power the living beings of the world exist.
By His Power virtues exist, and by His Power vices exist. By His Power come honor and dishonor.
By His Power wind, water and fire exist; by His Power earth and dust exist.
Everything is in Your Power, Lord; You are the all-powerful Creator. Your Name is the Holiest of the Holy.
O Nanak, through the Command of His Will, He beholds and pervades the creation; He is absolutely unrivalled. |2|

Pauree:
Enjoying his pleasures, one is reduced to a pile of ashes, and the soul passes away.
He may be great, but when he dies, the chain is thrown around his neck, and he is led away.
There, his good and bad deeds are added up; sitting there, his account is read.
He is whipped, but finds no place of rest, and no one hears his cries of pain.

The blind man has wasted his life away. |3|

Shalok, First Mehl:
In the Fear of God, the wind and breezes ever blow.
In the Fear of God, thousands of rivers flow.
In the Fear of God, fire is forced to labor.
In the Fear of God, the earth is crushed under its burden.
In the Fear of God, the clouds move across the sky.
In the Fear of God, the Righteous Judge of Dharma stands at His Door.
In the Fear of God, the sun shines, and in the Fear of God, the moon reflects.
They travel millions of miles, endlessly.
In the Fear of God, the Siddhas exist, as do the Buddhas, the demi-gods and Yogis.
In the Fear of God, the Akaashic ethers are stretched across the sky.
In the Fear of God, the warriors and the most powerful heroes exist.
In the Fear of God, multitudes come and go.
God has inscribed the Inscription of His Fear upon the heads of all.
O Nanak, the Fearless Lord, the Formless Lord, the True Lord, is One. |1|

First Mehl:
O Nanak, the Lord is fearless and formless; myriads of others, like Rama, are mere dust before Him.
There are so many stories of Krishna, so many who reflect over the Vedas.
So many beggars dance, spinning around to the beat.
The magicians perform their magic in the market place, creating a false illusion.
They sing as kings and queens, and speak of this and that.
They wear earrings, and necklaces worth thousands of dollars.
Those bodies on which they are worn, O Nanak, those bodies turn to ashes.

Section 08 - Raag Aasaa - Part 119

Wisdom cannot be found through mere words. To explain it is as hard as iron.
When the Lord bestows His Grace, then alone it is received; other tricks and orders are useless. |2|

Pauree:
If the Merciful Lord shows His Mercy, then the True Guru is found.

This soul wandered through countless incarnations, until the True Guru instructed it in the Word of the Shabad.

There is no giver as great as the True Guru; hear this, all you people.

Meeting the True Guru, the True Lord is found; He removes self-conceit from within,

and instructs us in the Truth of Truths. |4|

Shalok, First Mehl:

All the hours are the milk-maids, and the quarters of the day are the Krishnas.

The wind, water and fire are the ornaments; the sun and moon are the Incarnations.

All of the earth, property, wealth and articles are all entanglements.

O Nanak, without divine knowledge, one is plundered, and devoured by the Messenger of Death. |1|

First Mehl:

The disciples play the music, and the gurus dance.

They move their feet and roll their heads.

The dust flies and falls upon their hair.

Beholding them, the people laugh, and then go home.

They beat the drums for the sake of bread.

They throw themselves upon the ground.

They sing of the milk-maids, they sing of the Krishnas.

They sing of Sitas, and Ramas and kings.

The Lord is fearless and formless; His Name is True.

The entire universe is His Creation.

Those servants, whose destiny is awakened, serve the Lord.

The night of their lives is cool with dew; their minds are filled with love for the Lord.

Contemplating the Guru, I have been taught these teachings;

granting His Grace, He carries His servants across.

The oil-press, the spinning wheel, the grinding stones, the potter's wheel,

the numerous, countless whirlwinds in the desert,

the spinning tops, the churning sticks, the threshers,

the breathless tumblings of the birds,

and the men moving round and round on spindles

- O Nanak, the tumblers are countless and endless.

The Lord binds us in bondage - so do we spin around.

According to their actions, so do all people dance.

Those who dance and dance and laugh, shall weep on their ultimate departure.

They do not fly to the heavens, nor do they become Siddhas.

They dance and jump around on the urgings of their minds.

O Nanak, those whose minds are filled with the Fear of God, have the love of God in their minds as well. |2|

Pauree:

Your Name is the Fearless Lord; chanting Your Name, one does not have to go to hell.

Soul and body all belong to Him; asking Him to give us sustenance is a waste.

If you yearn for goodness, then perform good deeds and feel humble.

Even if you remove the signs of old age, old age shall still come in the guise of death.

No one remains here when the count of the breaths is full. |5|

Shalok, First Mehl:

The Muslims praise the Islamic law; they read and reflect upon it.

The Lord's bound servants are those who bind themselves to see the Lord's Vision.

The Hindus praise the Praiseworthy Lord; the Blessed Vision of His Darshan, His form is incomparable.

They bathe at sacred shrines of pilgrimage, making offerings of flowers, and burning incense before idols.

The Yogis meditate on the absolute Lord there; they call the Creator the Unseen Lord.

Section 08 - Raag Aasaa - Part 120

But to the subtle image of the Immaculate Name, they apply the form of a body.

In the minds of the virtuous, contentment is produced, thinking about their giving.

They give and give, but ask a thousand-fold more, and hope that the world will honor them.

The thieves, adulterers, perjurers, evil-doers and sinners

- after using up what good karma they had, they depart; have they done any good deeds here at all?

There are beings and creatures in the water and on the land, in the worlds and universes, form upon form.

Whatever they say, You know; You care for them all.

O Nanak, the hunger of the devotees is to praise You; the True Name is their only support.

They live in eternal bliss, day and night; they are the dust of the feet of the virtuous. |1|

First Mehl:

The clay of the Muslim's grave becomes clay for the potter's wheel.

Pots and bricks are fashioned from it, and it cries out as it burns.

The poor clay burns, burns and weeps, as the fiery coals fall upon it.

O Nanak, the Creator created the creation; the Creator Lord alone knows. |2|

Pauree:

Without the True Guru, no one has obtained the Lord; without the True Guru, no one has obtained the Lord.

He has placed Himself within the True Guru; revealing Himself, He declares this openly.

Meeting the True Guru, eternal liberation is obtained; He has banished attachment from within.

This is the highest thought, that one's consciousness is attached to the True Lord.

Thus the Lord of the World, the Great Giver is obtained. |6|

Shalok, First Mehl:

In ego they come, and in ego they go.

In ego they are born, and in ego they die.

In ego they give, and in ego they take.

In ego they earn, and in ego they lose.

In ego they become truthful or false.

In ego they reflect on virtue and sin.

In ego they go to heaven or hell.

In ego they laugh, and in ego they weep.

In ego they become dirty, and in ego they are washed clean.

In ego they lose social status and class.

In ego they are ignorant, and in ego they are wise.

They do not know the value of salvation and liberation.

In ego they love Maya, and in ego they are kept in darkness by it.

Living in ego, mortal beings are created.
When one understands ego, then the Lord's gate is known.
Without spiritual wisdom, they babble and argue.
O Nanak, by the Lord's Command, destiny is recorded.
As the Lord sees us, so are we seen. |1|

Second Mehl:
This is the nature of ego, that people perform their actions in ego.
This is the bondage of ego, that time and time again, they are reborn.
Where does ego come from? How can it be removed?
This ego exists by the Lord's Order; people wander according to their past actions.
Ego is a chronic disease, but it contains its own cure as well.
If the Lord grants His Grace, one acts according to the Teachings of the Guru's Shabad.
Nanak says, listen, people: in this way, troubles depart. |2|

Pauree:
Those who serve are content. They meditate on the Truest of the True.

Section 08 - Raag Aasaa - Part 121

They do not place their feet in sin, but do good deeds and live righteously in Dharma.
They burn away the bonds of the world, and eat a simple diet of grain and water.
You are the Great Forgiver; You give continually, more and more each day.
By His greatness, the Great Lord is obtained. |7|

Shalok, First Mehl:
Men, trees, sacred shrines of pilgrimage, banks of sacred rivers, clouds, fields,
islands, continents, worlds, solar systems, and universes;
the four sources of creation - born of eggs, born of the womb, born of the earth and born of sweat;
oceans, mountains, and all beings - O Nanak, He alone knows their condition.
O Nanak, having created the living beings, He cherishes them all.
The Creator who created the creation, takes care of it as well.
He, the Creator who formed the world, cares for it.

Unto Him I bow and offer my reverence; His Royal Court is eternal.
O Nanak, without the True Name, of what use is the frontal mark of the Hindus, or their sacred thread? |1|

First Mehl:
Hundreds of thousands of virtues and good actions, and hundreds of thousands of blessed charities,
hundreds of thousands of penances at sacred shrines, and the practice of Sehj Yoga in the wilderness,
hundreds of thousands of courageous actions and giving up the breath of life on the field of battle,
hundreds of thousands of divine understandings, hundreds of thousands of divine wisdoms and meditations and readings of the Vedas and the Puraanas

- before the Creator who created the creation, and who ordained coming and going,
O Nanak, all these things are false. True is the Insignia of His Grace. |2|

Pauree:
You alone are the True Lord. The Truth of Truths is pervading everywhere.
He alone receives the Truth, unto whom You give it; then, he practices Truth.
Meeting the True Guru, Truth is found. In His Heart, Truth is abiding.
The fools do not know the Truth. The self-willed manmukhs waste their lives away in vain.
Why have they even come into the world? |8|

Shalok, First Mehl:
You may read and read loads of books; you may read and study vast multitudes of books.
You may read and read boat-loads of books; you may read and read and fill pits with them.
You may read them year after year; you may read them as many months are there are.
You may read them all your life; you may read them with every breath.
O Nanak, only one thing is of any account: everything else is useless babbling and idle talk in ego. |1|

First Mehl:

The more one write and reads,
the more one burns.
The more one wanders at sacred shrines of pilgrimage,
the more one talks uselessly.
The more one wears religious robes, the more pain he causes his body.
O my soul, you must endure the consequences of your own actions.
One who does not eat the corn, misses out on the taste.
One obtains great pain, in the love of duality.
One who does not wear any clothes,
suffers night and day.
Through silence, he is ruined.
How can the sleeping one be awakened without the Guru?
One who goes barefoot
suffers by his own actions.
One who eats filth and throws ashes on his head
- the blind fool loses his honor.
Without the Name, nothing is of any use.
One who lives in the wilderness, in cemeteries and cremation grounds
- that blind man does not know the Lord; he regrets and repents in the end.

Section 08 - Raag Aasaa - Part 122

One who meets the True Guru finds peace.
He enshrines the Name of the Lord in his mind.
O Nanak, when the Lord grants His Grace, He is obtained.
He becomes free of hope and fear, and burns away his ego with the Word of the Shabad. |2|

Pauree:
Your devotees are pleasing to Your Mind, Lord. They look beautiful at Your door, singing Your Praises.
O Nanak, those who are denied Your Grace, find no shelter at Your Door; they continue wandering.
Some do not understand their origins, and without cause, they display their self-conceit.
I am the Lord's minstrel, of low social status; others call themselves high caste.
I seek those who meditate on You. |9|

Shalok, First Mehl:

False is the king, false are the subjects; false is the whole world.
False is the mansion, false are the skyscrapers; false are those who live in them.
False is gold, and false is silver; false are those who wear them.
False is the body, false are the clothes; false is incomparable beauty.
False is the husband, false is the wife; they mourn and waste away.
The false ones love falsehood, and forget their Creator.
With whom should I become friends, if all the world shall pass away?
False is sweetness, false is honey; through falsehood, boat-loads of men have drowned.
Nanak speaks this prayer: without You, Lord, everything is totally false. |1|

First Mehl:
One knows the Truth only when the Truth is in his heart.
The filth of falsehood departs, and the body is washed clean.
One knows the Truth only when he bears love to the True Lord.
Hearing the Name, the mind is enraptured; then, he attains the gate of salvation.
One knows the Truth only when he knows the true way of life.
Preparing the field of the body, he plants the Seed of the Creator.
One knows the Truth only when he receives true instruction.
Showing mercy to other beings, he makes donations to charities.
One knows the Truth only when he dwells in the sacred shrine of pilgrimage of his own soul.
He sits and receives instruction from the True Guru, and lives in accordance with His Will.
Truth is the medicine for all; it removes and washes away our sins.
Nanak speaks this prayer to those who have Truth in their laps. |2|

Pauree:
The gift I seek is the dust of the feet of the Saints; if I were to obtain it, I would apply it to my forehead.
Renounce false greed, and meditate single-mindedly on the unseen Lord.
As are the actions we commit, so are the rewards we receive.
If it is so pre-ordained, then one obtains the dust of the feet of the Saints.
But through small-mindedness, we forfeit the merits of selfless service. |10|

Shalok, First Mehl:

There is a famine of Truth; falsehood prevails, and the blackness of the Dark Age of Kali Yuga has turned men into demons.

Those who planted their seed have departed with honor; now, how can the shattered seed sprout?

If the seed is whole, and it is the proper season, then the seed will sprout.

O Nanak, without treatment, the raw fabric cannot be dyed.

In the Fear of God it is bleached white, if the treatment of modesty is applied to the cloth of the body.

O Nanak, if one is imbued with devotional worship, his reputation is not false. |1|

First Mehl:
Greed and sin are the king and prime minister; falsehood is the treasurer.

Sexual desire, the chief advisor, is summoned and consulted; they all sit together and contemplate their plans.

Section 08 - Raag Aasaa - Part 123

Their subjects are blind, and without wisdom, they try to please the will of the dead.

The spiritually wise dance and play their musical instruments, adorning themselves with beautiful decorations.

They shout out loud, and sing epic poems and heroic stories.

The fools call themselves spiritual scholars, and by their clever tricks, they love to gather wealth.

The righteous waste their righteousness, by asking for the door of salvation.

They call themselves celibate, and abandon their homes, but they do not know the true way of life.

Everyone calls himself perfect; none call themselves imperfect.

If the weight of honor is placed on the scale, then, O Nanak, one sees his true weight. |2|

First Mehl:
Evil actions become publicly known; O Nanak, the True Lord sees every-thing.

Everyone makes the attempt, but that alone happens which the Creator Lord does.

In the world hereafter, social status and power mean nothing; hereafter, the soul is new.

Those few, whose honor is confirmed, are good. |3|

Pauree:
Only those whose karma You have pre-ordained from the very beginning, O Lord, meditate on You.
Nothing is in the power of these beings; You created the various worlds.
Some, You unite with Yourself, and some, You lead astray.
By Guru's Grace You are known; through Him, You reveal Yourself.
We are easily absorbed in You. |11|

Shalok, First Mehl:
Suffering is the medicine, and pleasure the disease, because where there is pleasure, there is no desire for God.
You are the Creator Lord; I can do nothing. Even if I try, nothing happens. |1|

I am a sacrifice to Your almighty creative power which is pervading everywhere.
Your limits cannot be known. |1|Pause|

Your Light is in Your creatures, and Your creatures are in Your Light; Your almighty power is pervading everywhere.
You are the True Lord and Master; Your Praise is so beautiful. One who sings it, is carried across.
Nanak speaks the stories of the Creator Lord; whatever He is to do, He does. |2|

Second Mehl:
The Way of Yoga is the Way of spiritual wisdom; the Vedas are the Way of the Brahmins.
The Way of the Khshatriya is the Way of bravery; the Way of the Shudras is service to others.
The Way of all is the Way of the One; Nanak is a slave to one who knows this secret; he himself is the Immaculate Divine Lord. |3|

Second Mehl:
The One Lord Krishna is the Divine Lord of all; He is the Divinity of the individual soul.
Nanak is a slave to anyone who understands this mystery of the all-pervading Lord; he himself is the Immaculate Divine Lord. |4|

First Mehl:
Water remains confined within the pitcher, but without water, the pitcher could not have been formed;
just so, the mind is restrained by spiritual wisdom, but without the Guru, there is no spiritual wisdom. |5|

Pauree:
If an educated person is a sinner, then the illiterate holy man is not to be punished.
As are the deeds done, so is the reputation one acquires.
So do not play such a game, which will bring you to ruin at the Court of the Lord.
The accounts of the educated and the illiterate shall be judged in the world hereafter.
One who stubbornly follows his own mind shall suffer in the world hereafter. |12|

Section 08 - Raag Aasaa - Part 124

Shalok, First Mehl:
O Nanak, the soul of the body has one chariot and one charioteer.
In age after age they change; the spiritually wise understand this.
In the Golden Age of Sat Yuga, contentment was the chariot and righteousness the charioteer.
In the Silver Age of Traytaa Yuga, celibacy was the chariot and power the charioteer.
In the Brass Age of Dwaapar Yuga, penance was the chariot and truth the charioteer.
In the Iron Age of Kali Yuga, fire is the chariot and falsehood the charioteer. |1|

First Mehl:
The Sama Veda says that the Lord Master is robed in white; in the Age of Truth, everyone desired Truth, abided in Truth, and was merged in the Truth.
The Rig Veda says that God is permeating and pervading everywhere;
among the deities, the Lord's Name is the most exalted.
Chanting the Name, sins depart;
O Nanak, then, one obtains salvation.

In the Jujar Veda, Kaan Krishna of the Yaadva tribe seduced Chandraavali by force.

He brought the Elysian Tree for his milk-maid, and revelled in Brindaaban.

In the Dark Age of Kali Yuga, the Atharva Veda became prominent; Allah became the Name of God.

Men began to wear blue robes and garments; Turks and Pat'haans assumed power.

The four Vedas each claim to be true.

Reading and studying them, four doctrines are found.

With loving devotional worship, abiding in humility, O Nanak, salvation is attained. |2|

Pauree:
I am a sacrifice to the True Guru; meeting Him, I have come to cherish the Lord Master.

He has taught me and given me the healing ointment of spiritual wisdom, and with these eyes, I behold the world.

Those dealers who abandon their Lord and Master and attach themselves to another, are drowned.

The True Guru is the boat, but few are those who realize this.

Granting His Grace, He carries them across. |13|

Shalok, First Mehl:
The simmal tree is straight as an arrow; it is very tall, and very thick.

But those birds which visit it hopefully, depart disappointed.

Its fruits are tasteless, its flowers are nauseating, and its leaves are useless.

Sweetness and humility, O Nanak, are the essence of virtue and goodness.

Everyone bows down to himself; no one bows down to another.

When something is placed on the balancing scale and weighed, the side which descends is heavier.

The sinner, like the deer hunter, bows down twice as much.

But what can be achieved by bowing the head, when the heart is impure? |1|

First Mehl:
You read your books and say your prayers, and then engage in debate;
you worship stones and sit like a stork, pretending to be in Samaadhi.

With your mouth you utter falsehood, and you adorn yourself with precious decorations;
you recite the three lines of the Gayatri three times a day.

Around your neck is a rosary, and on your forehead is a sacred mark;
upon your head is a turban, and you wear two loin cloths.
If you knew the nature of God,
you would know that all of these beliefs and rituals are in vain.
Says Nanak, meditate with deep faith;
without the True Guru, no one finds the Way. |2|

Pauree:
Abandoning the world of beauty, and beautiful clothes, one must depart.
He obtains the rewards of his good and bad deeds.
He may issue whatever commands he wishes, but he shall have to take to
the narrow path hereafter.

Section 08 - Raag Aasaa - Part 125

He goes to hell naked, and he looks hideous then.
He regrets the sins he committed. |14|

Shalok, First Mehl:
Make compassion the cotton, contentment the thread, modesty the knot
and truth the twist.
This is the sacred thread of the soul; if you have it, then go ahead and put it
on me.
It does not break, it cannot be soiled by filth, it cannot be burnt, or lost.
Blessed are those mortal beings, O Nanak, who wear such a thread around
their necks.
You buy the thread for a few shells, and seated in your enclosure, you put it
on.
Whispering instructions into others' ears, the Brahmin becomes a guru.
But he dies, and the sacred thread falls away, and the soul departs without
it. |1|

First Mehl:
He commits thousands of robberies, thousands of acts of adultery,
thousands of falsehoods and thousands of abuses.
He practices thousands of deceptions and secret deeds, night and day,
against his fellow beings.
The thread is spun from cotton, and the Brahmin comes and twists it.
The goat is killed, cooked and eaten, and everyone then says, "Put on the
sacred thread."

When it wears out, it is thrown away, and another one is put on.

O Nanak, the thread would not break, if it had any real strength. |2|

First Mehl:

Believing in the Name, honor is obtained. The Lord's Praise is the true sacred thread.

Such a sacred thread is worn in the Court of the Lord; it shall never break. |3|

First Mehl:

There is no sacred thread for the sexual organ, and no thread for woman.

The man's beard is spat upon daily.

There is no sacred thread for the feet, and no thread for the hands;

no thread for the tongue, and no thread for the eyes.

The Brahmin himself goes to the world hereafter without a sacred thread.

Twisting the threads, he puts them on others.

He takes payment for performing marriages;

reading their horoscopes, he shows them the way.

Hear, and see, O people, this wondrous thing.

He is mentally blind, and yet his name is wisdom. |4|

Pauree:

One, upon whom the Merciful Lord bestows His Grace, performs His service.

That servant, whom the Lord causes to obey the Order of His Will, serves Him.

Obeying the Order of His Will, he becomes acceptable, and then, he obtains the Mansion of the Lord's Presence.

One who acts to please His Lord and Master, obtains the fruits of his mind's desires.

Then, he goes to the Court of the Lord, wearing robes of honor. |15|

Shalok, First Mehl:

They tax the cows and the Brahmins, but the cow-dung they apply to their kitchen will not save them.

They wear their loin cloths, apply ritual frontal marks to their foreheads, and carry their rosaries, but they eat food with the Muslims.

O Siblings of Destiny, you perform devotional worship indoors, but read the Islamic sacred texts, and adopt the Muslim way of life.

Renounce your hypocrisy!

Taking the Naam, the Name of the Lord, you shall swim across. |1|

First Mehl:
The man-eaters say their prayers.
Those who wield the knife wear the sacred thread around their necks.
In their homes, the Brahmins sound the conch.
They too have the same taste.
False is their capital, and false is their trade.
Speaking falsehood, they take their food.
The home of modesty and Dharma is far from them.
O Nanak, they are totally permeated with falsehood.
The sacred marks are on their foreheads, and the saffron loin-cloths are around their waists;
in their hands they hold the knives - they are the butchers of the world!

Section 08 - Raag Aasaa - Part 126

Wearing blue robes, they seek the approval of the Muslim rulers.
Accepting bread from the Muslim rulers, they still worship the Puraanas.
They eat the meat of the goats, killed after the Muslim prayers are read over them,
but they do not allow anyone else to enter their kitchen areas.
They draw lines around them, plastering the ground with cow-dung.
The false come and sit within them.
They cry out, "Do not touch our food, or it will be polluted!"
But with their polluted bodies, they commit evil deeds.
With filthy minds, they try to cleanse their mouths.
Says Nanak, meditate on the True Lord.
If you are pure, you will obtain the True Lord. |2|

Pauree:
All are within Your mind; You see and move them under Your Glance of Grace, O Lord.
You Yourself grant them glory, and You Yourself cause them to act.
The Lord is the greatest of the great; great is His world. He enjoins all to their tasks.
If he should cast an angry glance, He can transform kings into blades of grass.
Even though they may beg from door to door, no one will give them charity. |16|

Shalok, First Mehl:
The thief robs a house, and offers the stolen goods to his ancestors.
In the world hereafter, this is recognized, and his ancestors are considered thieves as well.
The hands of the go-between are cut off; this is the Lord's justice.
O Nanak, in the world hereafter, that alone is received, which one gives to the needy from his own earnings and labor. |1|

First Mehl:
As a woman has her periods, month after month,
so does falsehood dwell in the mouth of the false; they suffer forever, again and again.
They are not called pure, who sit down after merely washing their bodies.
Only they are pure, O Nanak, within whose minds the Lord abides. |2|

Pauree:
With saddled horses, as fast as the wind, and harems decorated in every way;
in houses and pavilions and lofty mansions, they dwell, making ostentatious shows.
They act out their minds' desires, but they do not understand the Lord, and so they are ruined.
Asserting their authority, they eat, and beholding their mansions, they forget about death.
But old age comes, and youth is lost. |17|

Shalok, First Mehl:
If one accepts the concept of impurity, then there is impurity everywhere.
In cow-dung and wood there are worms.
As many as are the grains of corn, none is without life.
First, there is life in the water, by which everything else is made green.
How can it be protected from impurity? It touches our own kitchen.
O Nanak, impurity cannot be removed in this way; it is washed away only by spiritual wisdom. |1|

First Mehl:
The impurity of the mind is greed, and the impurity of the tongue is falsehood.

The impurity of the eyes is to gaze upon the beauty of another man's wife, and his wealth.

The impurity of the ears is to listen to the slander of others.

O Nanak, the mortal's soul goes, bound and gagged to the city of Death. |2|

First Mehl:

All impurity comes from doubt and attachment to duality.

Birth and death are subject to the Command of the Lord's Will; through His Will we come and go.

Eating and drinking are pure, since the Lord gives nourishment to all.

O Nanak, the Gurmukhs, who understand the Lord, are not stained by impurity. |3|

Section 08 - Raag Aasaa - Part 127

Pauree:

Praise the Great True Guru; within Him is the greatest greatness.

When the Lord causes us to meet the Guru, then we come to see them.

When it pleases Him, they come to dwell in our minds.

By His Command, when He places His hand on our foreheads, wickedness departs from within.

When the Lord is thoroughly pleased, the nine treasures are obtained. |18|

Shalok, First Mehl:

First, purifying himself, the Brahmin comes and sits in his purified enclosure.

The pure foods, which no one else has touched, are placed before him.

Being purified, he takes his food, and begins to read his sacred verses.

But it is then thrown into a filthy place - whose fault is this?

The corn is sacred, the water is sacred; the fire and salt are sacred as well; when the fifth thing, the ghee, is added,

then the food becomes pure and sanctified.

Coming into contact with the sinful human body, the food becomes so impure that is is spat upon.

That mouth which does not chant the Naam, and without the Name eats tasty foods

- O Nanak, know this: such a mouth is to be spat upon. |1|

First Mehl:
From woman, man is born; within woman, man is conceived; to woman he is engaged and married.
Woman becomes his friend; through woman, the future generations come.
When his woman dies, he seeks another woman; to woman he is bound.
So why call her bad? From her, kings are born.
From woman, woman is born; without woman, there would be no one at all.
O Nanak, only the True Lord is without a woman.
That mouth which praises the Lord continually is blessed and beautiful.
O Nanak, those faces shall be radiant in the Court of the True Lord. |2|

Pauree:
All call You their own, Lord; one who does not own You, is picked up and thrown away.
Everyone receives the rewards of his own actions; his account is adjusted accordingly.
Since one is not destined to remain in this world anyway, why should he ruin himself in pride?
Do not call anyone bad; read these words, and understand.
Don't argue with fools. |19|

Shalok, First Mehl:
O Nanak, speaking insipid words, the body and mind become insipid.
He is called the most insipid of the insipid; the most insipid of the insipid is his reputation.
The insipid person is discarded in the Court of the Lord, and the insipid one's face is spat upon.
The insipid one is called a fool; he is beaten with shoes in punishment. |1|

First Mehl:
Those who are false within, and honorable on the outside, are very common in this world.
Even though they may bathe at the sixty-eight sacred shrines of pilgrimage, still, their filth does not depart.
Those who have silk on the inside and rags on the outside, are the good ones in this world.
They embrace love for the Lord, and contemplate beholding Him.
In the Lord's Love, they laugh, and in the Lord's Love, they weep, and also keep silent.

They do not care for anything else, except their True Husband Lord.

Sitting, waiting at the Lord's Door, they beg for food, and when He gives to them, they eat.

There is only One Court of the Lord, and He has only one pen; there, you and I shall meet.

In the Court of the Lord, the accounts are examined; O Nanak, the sinners are crushed, like oil seeds in the press. |2|

Section 08 - Raag Aasaa - Part 128

Pauree:

You Yourself created the creation; You Yourself infused Your power into it.

You behold Your creation, like the losing and winning dice of the earth.

Whoever has come, shall depart; all shall have their turn.

He who owns our soul, and our very breath of life - why should we forget that Lord and Master from our minds?

With our own hands, let us resolve our own affairs. |20|

Shalok, Second Mehl:

What sort of love is this, which clings to duality?

O Nanak, he alone is called a lover, who remains forever immersed in absorption.

But one who feels good only when good is done for him, and feels bad when things go badly

- do not call him a lover. He trades only for his own account. |1|

Second Mehl:

One who offers both respectful greetings and rude refusal to his master, has gone wrong from the very beginning.

O Nanak, both of his actions are false; he obtains no place in the Court of the Lord. |2|

Pauree:

Serving Him, peace is obtained; meditate and dwell upon that Lord and Master forever.

Why do you do such evil deeds, that you shall have to suffer so?

Do not do any evil at all; look ahead to the future with foresight.

So throw the dice in such a way, that you shall not lose with your Lord and Master.

Do those deeds which shall bring you profit. |21|

Shalok, Second Mehl:
If a servant performs service, while being vain and argumentative,
he may talk as much as he wants, but he shall not be pleasing to his Master.
But if he eliminates his self-conceit and then performs service, he shall be honored.
O Nanak, if he merges with the one with whom he is attached, his attachment becomes acceptable. |1|

Second Mehl:
Whatever is in the mind, comes forth; spoken words by themselves are just wind.
He sows seeds of poison, and demands Ambrosial Nectar. Behold - what justice is this? |2|

Second Mehl:
Friendship with a fool never works out right.
As he knows, he acts; behold, and see that it is so.
One thing can be absorbed into another thing, but duality keeps them apart.
No one can issue commands to the Lord Master; offer instead humble prayers.
Practicing falsehood, only falsehood is obtained. O Nanak, through the Lord's Praise, one blossoms forth. |3|

Second Mehl:
Friendship with a fool, and love with a pompous person,
are like lines drawn in water, leaving no trace or mark. |4|

Second Mehl:
If a fool does a job, he cannot do it right.
Even if he does something right, he does the next thing wrong. |5|

Pauree:
If a servant, performing service, obeys the Will of his Master,
his honor increases, and he receives double his wages.
But if he claims to be equal to his Master, he earns his Master's displeasure.

He loses his entire salary, and is also beaten on his face with shoes.

Let us all celebrate Him, from whom we receive our nourishment.

O Nanak, no one can issue commands to the Lord Master; let us offer prayers instead. |22|

Shalok, Second Mehl:

What sort of gift is this, which we receive only by our own asking?

Section 08 - Raag Aasaa - Part 129

O Nanak, that is the most wonderful gift, which is received from the Lord, when He is totally pleased. |1|

Second Mehl:

What sort of service is this, by which the fear of the Lord Master does not depart?

O Nanak, he alone is called a servant, who merges with the Lord Master. |2|

Pauree:

O Nanak, the Lord's limits cannot be known; He has no end or limitation.

He Himself creates, and then He Himself destroys.

Some have chains around their necks, while some ride on many horses.

He Himself acts, and He Himself causes us to act. Unto whom should I complain?

O Nanak, the One who created the creation - He Himself takes care of it. |23|

Shalok, First Mehl:

He Himself fashioned the vessel of the body, and He Himself fills it.

Into some, milk is poured, while others remain on the fire.

Some lie down and sleep on soft beds, while others remain watchful.

He adorns those, O Nanak, upon whom He casts His Glance of Grace. |1|

Second Mehl:

He Himself creates and fashions the world, and He Himself keeps it in order.

Having created the beings within it, He oversees their birth and death.

Unto whom should we speak, O Nanak, when He Himself is all-in-all? |2|

Pauree:
The description of the greatness of the Great Lord cannot be described.
He is the Creator, all-lowerful and benevolent; He gives sustenance to all beings.
The mortal does that work, which has been pre-destined from the very beginning.
O Nanak, except for the One Lord, there is no other place at all.
He does whatever He wills. |24|1|

Sudh|One Universal Creator God. Truth Is The Name. Creative Being Personified. No Fear. No Hatred. Image Of The Undying. Beyond Birth. Self-Exlstent. By Guru's Grace:

Raag Aasaa, The Word Of The Devotees:
Kabeer, Naam Dayv And Ravi Daas.
Aasaa, Kabeer Jee:
Falling at the Feet of the Guru, I pray, and ask Him, "Why was man created? What deeds cause the world to come into being, and be destroyed? Tell me, that I may understand."|1|

O Divine Guru, please, show Mercy to me, and place me on the right path, by which the bonds of fear may be cut away.
The pains of birth and death come from past actions and karma; peace comes when the soul finds release from reincarnation. |1|Pause|

The mortal does not break free from the bonds of the noose of Maya, and he does not seek the shelter of the profound, absolute Lord.
He does not realize the dignity of the self, and Nirvaanaa; because of this, his doubt does not depart. |2|

The soul is not born, even though he thinks it is born; it is free from birth and death.
When the mortal gives up his ideas of birth and death, he remains constantly absorbed in the Lord's Love. |3|

As the reflection of an object blends in the water when the pitcher is broken,
says Kabeer, just so virtue dispels doubt, and then the soul is absorbed in the profound, absolute Lord. |4|1|

Section 08 - Raag Aasaa - Part 130

Aasaa:
They wear loin cloths, three and a half yards long, and triple-wound sacred threads.
They have rosaries around their necks, and they carry glittering jugs in their hands.
They are not called Saints of the Lord - they are thugs of Benares. |1|

Such 'saints' are not pleasing to me;
they eat the trees along with the branches. |1|Pause|

They wash their pots and pans before putting them on the stove, and they wash the wood before lighting it.
They dig up the earth and make two fireplaces, but they eat the whole person! |2|

Those sinners continually wander in evil deeds, while they call themselves touch-nothing saints.
They wander around forever and ever in their self-conceit, and all their families are drowned. |3|

He is attached to that, to which the Lord has attached him, and he acts accordingly.
Says Kabeer, one who meets the True Guru, is not reincarnated again. |4|2|

Aasaa:
My Father has comforted me. He has given me a cozy bed, and placed His Ambrosial Nectar in my mouth.
How could I forget that Father from my mind?
When I go to the world hereafter, I shall not lose the game. |1|

Maya is dead, O mother, and I am very happy.
I do not wear the patched coat, nor do I feel the chill. |1|Pause|

I am a sacrifice to my Father, who gave me life.
He put an end to my association with the five deadly sins.
I have conquered those five demons, and trampled them underfoot.

Remembering the Lord in meditation, my mind and body are drenched with His Love. |2|

My Father is the Great Lord of the Universe.
How shall I go to that Father?
When I met the True Guru, He showed me the Way.
The Father of the Universe is pleasing to my mind. |3|

I am Your son, and You are my Father.
We both dwell in the same place.
Says Kabeer, the Lord's humble servant knows only the One.
By Guru's Grace, I have come to know everything. |4|3|

Aasaa:
In one pot, they put a boiled chicken, and in the other pot, they put wine.
The five Yogis of the Tantric ritual sit there, and in their midst sits the noseless one, the shameless queen. |1|

The bell of the shameless queen, Maya, rings in both worlds.
Some rare person of discriminating wisdom has cut off your nose. |1|Pause|

Within all dwells the noseless Maya, who kills all, and destroys them.
She says, "I am the sister, and the daughter of the sister of everyone; I am the hand-maiden of one who marries me." |2|

My Husband is the Great One of discriminating wisdom; He alone is called a Saint.
He stands by me, and no one else comes near me. |3|

I have cut off her nose, and cut off her ears, and cutting her into bits, I have expelled her.
Says Kabeer, she is the darling of the three worlds, but the enemy of the Saints. |4|4|

Aasaa:
The Yogis, celibates, penitents and Sannyaasees make pilgrimages to all the sacred places.
The Jains with shaven heads, the silent ones, the beggars with matted hair - in the end, they all shall die. |1|

Meditate, therefore, on the Lord.
What can the Messenger of Death do to one whose tongue loves the Name of the Lord? |1|Pause|

Those who know the Shaastras and the Vedas, astrology and the rules of grammar of many languages;

Section 08 - Raag Aasaa - Part 131

those who know Tantras and mantras and all medicines - even they shall die in the end. |2|

Those who enjoy regal power and rule, royal canopies and thrones, many beautiful women,
betel nuts, camphor and fragrant sandalwood oil - in the end, they too shall die. |3|

I have searched all the Vedas, Puraanas and Simritees, but none of these can save anyone.
Says Kabeer, meditate on the Lord, and eliminate birth and death. |4|5|

Aasaa:
The elephant is the guitar player, the ox is the drummer, and the crow plays the cymbals.
Putting on the skirt, the donkey dances around, and the water buffalo performs devotional worship. |1|

The Lord, the King, has cooked the cakes of ice,
but only the rare man of understanding eats them. |1|Pause|

Sitting in his den, the lion prepares the betel leaves, and the muskrat brings the betel nuts.
Going from house to house, the mouse sings the songs of joy, and the turtle blows on the conch-shell. |2|

The son of the sterile woman goes to get married, and the golden canopy is spread out for him.
He marries a beautiful and enticing young woman; the rabbit and the lion sing their praises. |3|

Says Kabeer, listen, O Saints - the ant has eaten the mountain.
The turtle says, "I need a burning coal, also." Listen to this mystery of the Shabad. |4|6|

Aasaa:
The body is a bag with seventy-two chambers, and one opening, the Tenth Gate.
He alone is a real Yogi on this earth, who asks for the primal world of the nine regions. |1|

Such a Yogi obtains the nine treasures.
He lifts his soul up from below, to the skies of the Tenth Gate. |1|Pause|

He makes spiritual wisdom his patched coat, and meditation his needle. He twists the thread of the Word of the Shabad.
Making the five elements his deer skin to sit on, he walks on the Guru's Path. |2|

He makes compassion his shovel, his body the firewood, and he kindles the fire of divine vision.
He places love within his heart, and he remains in deep meditation throughout the four ages. |3|

All Yoga is in the Name of the Lord; the body and the breath of life belong to Him.
Says Kabeer, if God grants His Grace, He bestows the insignia of Truth. |4|7|

Aasaa:
Where have the Hindus and Muslims come from? Who put them on their different paths?
Think of this, and contemplate it within your mind, O men of evil intentions. Who will go to heaven and hell? |1|

O Qazi, which book have you read?
Such scholars and students have all died, and none of them have discovered the inner meaning. |1|Pause|

Because of the love of woman, circumcision is done; I don't believe in it, O Siblings of Destiny.
If God wished me to be a Muslim, it would be cut off by itself. |2|

If circumcision makes one a Muslim, then what about a woman?
She is the other half of a man's body, and she does not leave him, so he remains a Hindu. |3|

Give up your holy books, and remember the Lord, you fool, and stop oppressing others so badly.
Kabeer has grasped hold of the Lord's Support, and the Muslims have utterly failed. |4|8|

Aasaa:
As long as the oil and the wick are in the lamp, everything is illuminated.

Section 08 - Raag Aasaa - Part 132

But when the oil is burnt, the wick goes out, and the mansion becomes desolate. |1|

O mad-man, no one will keep you, for even a moment.
Meditate on the Name of that Lord. |1|Pause|

Tell me, whose mother is that, whose father is that, and which man has a wife?
When the pitcher of the body breaks, no one cares for you at all. Everyone says, "Take him away, take him away!"|2|

Sitting on the threshold, his mother cries, and his brothers take away the coffin.
Taking down her hair, his wife cries out in sorrow, and the swan-soul departs all alone. |3|

Says Kabeer, listen, O Saints, about the terrifying world-ocean.
This human suffers torture and the Messenger of Death will not leave him alone, O Lord of the World. |4|9|

Du-Tukas
One Universal Creator God. By The Grace Of The True Guru:

Aasaa Of Kabeer Jee, Chau-Padas, Ik-Tukas:
Sanak and Sanand, the sons of Brahma, could not find the Lord's limits.
Brahma wasted his life away, continually reading the Vedas. |1|

Churn the churn of the Lord, O my Siblings of Destiny.
Churn it steadily, so that the essence, the butter, may not be lost.
|1|Pause|

Make your body the churning jar, and use the stick of your mind to churn it.
Gather the curds of the Word of the Shabad. |2|

The churning of the Lord is to reflect upon Him within your mind.
By Guru's Grace, the Ambrosial Nectar flows into us. |3|

Says Kabeer, if the Lord, our King casts His Glance of Grace,
one is carried across to the other side, holding fast to the Lord's Name.
|4|1|10|

Aasaa:
The wick has dried up, and the oil is exhausted.
The drum does not sound, and the actor has gone to sleep. |1|

The fire has gone out, and no smoke is produced.
The One Lord is pervading and permeating everywhere; there is no other
second. |1|Pause|

The string has broken, and the guitar makes no sound.
He mistakenly ruins his own affairs. |2|

When one comes to understand, he forgets his preaching, ranting and
raving, and arguing. |3|

Says Kabeer, the state of supreme dignity is never far from those who
conquer the five demons of the body passions. |4|2|11|

Aasaa:
As many mistakes as the son commits,
his mother does not hold them against him in her mind. |1|

O Lord, I am Your child.

Why not destroy my sins? |1|Pause|

If the son, in anger, runs away,
even then, his mother does not hold it against him in her mind. |2|

My mind has fallen into the whirlpool of anxiety.
Without the Naam, how can I cross over to the other side? |3|

Please, bless my body with pure and lasting understanding, Lord;
in peace and poise, Kabeer chants the Praises of the Lord. |4|3|12|

Aasaa:
My pilgrimage to Mecca is on the banks of the Gomati River;
the spiritual teacher in his yellow robes dwells there. |1|

Waaho! Waaho! Hail! Hail! How wondrously he sings.
The Name of the Lord is pleasing to my mind. |1|Pause|

Section 08 - Raag Aasaa - Part 133

Naarada the sage, and Shaarada the goddess of knowledge, serve the Lord.
The goddess Lakhshmi sits by Him as His slave. |2|

The mala is around my neck, and the Lord's Name is upon my tongue.
I repeat the Naam, the Name of the Lord, a thousand times, and bow in
reverence to Him. |3|

Says Kabeer, I sing the Glorious Praises of the Lord;
I teach both Hindus and Muslims. |4|4|13|

Aasaa, Kabeer Jee, 9 Panch-Padas, 5 Du-Tukas:
One Universal Creator God. By The Grace Of The True Guru:
You tear off the leaves, O gardener, but in each and every leaf, there is life.
That stone idol, for which you tear off those leaves - that stone idol is
lifeless. |1|

In this, you are mistaken, O gardener.
The True Guru is the Living Lord. |1|Pause|

Brahma is in the leaves, Vishnu is in the branches, and Shiva is in the flowers.
When you break these three gods, whose service are you performing? |2|

The sculptor carves the stone and fashions it into an idol, placing his feet upon its chest.
If this stone god was true, it would devour the sculptor for this! |3|

Rice and beans, candies, cakes and cookies
- the priest enjoys these, while he puts ashes into the mouth of the idol. |4|

The gardener is mistaken, and the world is mistaken, but I am not mistaken.
Says Kabeer, the Lord preserves me; the Lord, my King, has showered His Blessings upon me. |5|1|14|

Aasaa:
Twelve years pass in childhood, and for another twenty years, he does not practice self-discipline and austerity.
For another thirty years, he does not worship God in any way, and then, when he is old, he repents and regrets. |1|

His life wastes away as he cries out, "Mine, mine!"
The pool of his power has dried up. |1|Pause|

He makes a dam around the dried-up pool, and with his hands, he makes a fence around the harvested field.
When the thief of Death comes, he quickly carries away what the fool had tried to preserve as his own. |2|

His feet and head and hands begin to tremble, and the tears flow copiously from his eyes.
His tongue has not spoken the correct words, but now, he hopes to practice religion! |3|

If the Dear Lord shows His Mercy, one enshrines love for Him, and obtains the Profit of the Lord's Name.
By Guru's Grace, he receives the wealth of the Lord's Name, which alone shall go with him, when he departs in the end. |4|

Says Kabeer, listen, O Saints - he shall not take any other wealth with him.
When the summons comes from the King, the Lord of the Universe, the
mortal departs, leaving behind his wealth and mansions. |5|2|15|

Aasaa:
To some, the Lord has given silks and satins, and to some, beds decorated
with cotton ribbons.
Some do not even have a poor patched coat, and some live in thatched
huts. |1|

Do not indulge in envy and bickering, O my mind.
By continually doing good deeds, these are obtained, O my mind.
|1|Pause|

The potter works the same clay, and colors the pots in different ways.
Into some, he sets pearls, while to others, he attaches filth. |2|

God gave wealth to the miser for him to preserve, but the fool calls it his
own.

Section 08 - Raag Aasaa - Part 134

When the Messenger of Death strikes him with his club, in an instant,
everything is settled. |3|

The Lord's humble servant is called the most exalted Saint; he obeys the
Command of the Lord's Order, and obtains peace.
Whatever is pleasing to the Lord, he accepts as True; he enshrines the
Lord's Will within his mind. |4|

Says Kabeer, listen, O Saints - it is false to call out, "Mine, mine."
Breaking the bird cage, death takes the bird away, and only the torn
threads remain. |5|3|16|

Aasaa:
I am Your humble servant, Lord; Your Praises are pleasing to my mind.
The Lord, the Primal Being, the Master of the poor, does not ordain that
they should be oppressed. |1|

O Qazi, it is not right to speak before Him. |1|Pause|

Keeping your fasts, reciting your prayers, and reading the Kalma, the Islamic creed, shall not take you to paradise.
The Temple of Mecca is hidden within your mind, if you only knew it. |2|

That should be your prayer, to administer justice. Let your Kalma be the knowledge of the unknowable Lord.
Spread your prayer mat by conquering your five desires, and you shall recognize the true religion. |3|

Recognize Your Lord and Master, and fear Him within your heart; conquer your egotism, and make it worthless.
As you see yourself, see others as well; only then will you become a partner in heaven. |4|

The clay is one, but it has taken many forms; I recognize the One Lord within them all.
Says Kabeer, I have abandoned paradise, and reconciled my mind to hell. |5|4|17|

Aasaa:
From the city of the Tenth Gate, the sky of the mind, not even a drop rains down. Where is the music of the sound current of the Naad, which was contained in it?

The Supreme Lord God, the Transcendent Lord, the Master of wealth has taken away the Supreme Soul. |1|

O Father, tell me: where has it gone? It used to dwell within the body, and dance in the mind, teaching and speaking. |1|Pause|

Where has the player gone - he who made this temple his own?
No story, word or understanding is produced; the Lord has drained off all the power. |2|

The ears, your companions, have gone deaf, and the power of your organs is exhausted.
Your feet have failed, your hands have gone limp, and no words issue forth from your mouth. |3|

Having grown weary, the five enemies and all the thieves have wandered away according to their own will.
The elephant of the mind has grown weary, and the heart has grown weary as well; through its power, it used to pull the strings. |4|

He is dead, and the bonds of the ten gates are opened; he has left all his friends and brothers.
Says Kabeer, one who meditates on the Lord, breaks his bonds, even while yet alive. |5|5|18|

Aasaa, 4 Ik-Tukas:
No one is more powerful than the she-serpent Maya,
who deceived even Brahma, Vishnu and Shiva. |1|

Having bitten and struck them down, she now sits in the immaculate waters.
By Guru's Grace, I have seen her, who has bitten the three worlds. |1|Pause|

O Siblings of Destiny, why is she called a she-serpent?
One who realizes the True Lord, devours the she-serpent. |2|

No one else is more frivolous than this she-serpent.
When the she-serpent is overcome, what can the Messengers of the King of Death do? |3|

Section 08 - Raag Aasaa - Part 135

This she-serpent is created by Him.
What power or weakness does she have by herself? |4|

If she abides with the mortal, then his soul abides in his body.
By Guru's Grace, Kabeer has easily crossed over. |5|6|19|

Aasaa:
Why bother to read the Simritees to a dog?
Why bother to sing the Lord's Praises to the faithless cynic? |1|

Remain absorbed in the Lord's Name, Raam, Raam, Raam.

Do not bother to speak of it to the faithless cynic, even by mistake. |1|Pause|

Why offer camphor to a crow?
Why give the snake milk to drink? |2|

Joining the Sat Sangat, the True Congregation, discriminating understanding is attained.
That iron which touches the Philosopher's Stone becomes gold. |3|

The dog, the faithless cynic, does everything as the Lord causes him to do.
He does the deeds pre-ordained from the very beginning. |4|

If you take Ambrosial Nectar and irrigate the neem tree with it,
still, says Kabeer, its natural qualities are not changed. |5|7|20|

Aasaa:
A fortress like that of Sri Lanka, with the ocean as a moat around it
- there is no news about that house of Raavan. |1|

What shall I ask for? Nothing is permanent.
I see with my eyes that the world is passing away. |1|Pause|

Thousands of sons and thousands of grandsons
- but in that house of Raavan, the lamps and wicks have gone out. |2|

The moon and the sun cooked his food.
The fire washed his clothes. |3|

Under Guru's Instructions, one whose mind is filled with the Lord's Name,
becomes permanent, and does not go anywhere. |4|

Says Kabeer, listen, people:
without the Lord's Name, no one is liberated. |5|8|21|

Aasaa:
First, the son was born, and then, his mother.
The guru falls at the feet of the disciple. |1|

Listen to this wonderful thing, O Siblings of Destiny!

I saw the lion herding the cows. |1|Pause|

The fish of the water gives birth upon a tree.
I saw a cat carrying away a dog. |2|

The branches are below, and the roots are above.
The trunk of that tree bears fruits and flowers. |3|

Riding a horse, the buffalo takes him out to graze.
The bull is away, while his load has come home. |4|

Says Kabeer, one who understands this hymn,
and chants the Lord's Name, comes to understand everything. |5|9|22|

22 Chau-Padas And Panch-Padas, Aasaa Of Kabeer Jee, 8 Tri-Padas, 7 Du-Tukas, 1 Ik-Tuka:
One Universal Creator God. By The Grace Of The True Guru:
The Lord created the body from sperm, and protected it in the fire pit.
For ten months He preserved you in your mother's womb, and then, after you were born, you became attached to Maya. |1|

O mortal, why have you attached yourself to greed, and lost the jewel of life?
You did not plant the seeds of good actions in the earth of your past lives. |1|Pause|

From an infant, you have grown old. That which was to happen, has happened.
When the Messenger of Death comes and grabs you by your hair, why do you cry out then? |2|

Section 08 - Raag Aasaa - Part 136

You hope for long life, while Death counts your breaths.
The world is a game, O Kabeer, so throw the dice consciously. |3|1|23|

Aasaa:
I make my body the dying vat, and within it, I dye my mind. I make the five elements my marriage guests.

I take my marriage vows with the Lord, my King; my soul is imbued with His Love. |1|

Sing, sing, O brides of the Lord, the marriage songs of the Lord.
The Lord, my King, has come to my house as my Husband. |1|Pause|

Within the lotus of my heart, I have made my bridal pavilion, and I have spoken the wisdom of God.
I have obtained the Lord King as my Husband - such is my great good fortune. |2|

The angles, holy men, silent sages, and the 330,000,000 deities have come in their heavenly chariots to see this spectacle.
Says Kabeer, I have been taken in marriage by the One Supreme Being, the Lord God. |3|2|24|

Aasaa:
I am bothered by my mother-in-law, Maya, and loved by my father-in-law, the Lord. I fear even the name of my husband's elder brother, Death.
O my mates and companions, my husband's sister, misunderstanding has seized me, and I am burning with the pain of separation from my husband's younger brother, divine knowledge. |1|

My mind has gone insane, since I forgot the Lord. How can I lead a virtuous lifestyle?
He rests in the bed of my mind, but I cannot see Him with my eyes. Unto whom should I tell my sufferings? |1|Pause|

My step-father, egotism, fights with me, and my mother, desire, is always intoxicated.
When I stayed with my elder brother, meditation, then I was loved by my Husband Lord. |2|

Says Kabeer, the five passions argue with me, and in these arguments, my life is wasting away.
The false Maya has bound the whole world, but I have obtained peace, chanting the Name of the Lord. |3|3|25|

Aasaa:

In my house, I constantly weave the thread, while you wear the thread around your neck, O Brahmin.
You read the Vedas and sacred hymns, while I have enshrined the Lord of the Universe in my heart. |1|

Upon my tongue, within my eyes, and within my heart, abides the Lord, the Lord of the Universe.
When you are interrogated at Death's door, O mad-man, what will you say then? |1|Pause|

I am a cow, and You are the herdsman, the Sustainer of the World. You are my Saving Grace, lifetime after lifetime.
You have never taken me across to graze there - what sort of a herdsman are You? |2|

You are a Brahmin, and I am a weaver of Benares; can You understand my wisdom?
You beg from emperors and kings, while I meditate on the Lord. |3|4|26|

Aasaa:
The life of the world is only a dream; life is just a dream.
Believing it to be true, I grasped at it, and abandoned the supreme treasure. |1|

O Father, I have enshrined love and affection for Maya,
which has taken the jewel of spiritual wisdom away from me. |1|Pause|

The moth sees with its eyes, but it still becomes entangled; the insect does not see the fire.
Attached to gold and woman, the fool does not think of the noose of Death. |2|

Reflect upon this, and abandon sin; the Lord is a boat to carry you across.
Says Kabeer, such is the Lord, the Life of the World; there is no one equal to Him. |3|5|27|

Aasaa:

Section 08 - Raag Aasaa - Part 137

In the past, I have taken many forms, but I shall not take form again.
The strings and wires of the musical instrument are worn out, and I am in the power of the Lord's Name. |1|

Now, I no longer dance to the tune.
My mind no longer beats the drum. |1|Pause|

I have burnt away sexual desire, anger and attachment to Maya, and the pitcher of my desires has burst.
The gown of sensuous pleasures is worn out, and all my doubts have been dispelled. |2|

I look upon all beings alike, and my conflict and strife are ended.
Says Kabeer, when the Lord showed His Favor, I obtained Him, the Perfect One. |3|6|28|

Aasaa:
You keep your fasts to please Allah, while you murder other beings for pleasure.
You look after your own interests, and so not see the interests of others. What good is your word? |1|

O Qazi, the One Lord is within you, but you do not behold Him by thought or contemplation.
You do not care for others, you are a religious fanatic, and your life is of no account at all. |1|Pause|

Your holy scriptures say that Allah is True, and that he is neither male nor female.
But you gain nothing by reading and studying, O mad-man, if you do not gain the understanding in your heart. |2|

Allah is hidden in every heart; reflect upon this in your mind.
The One Lord is within both Hindu and Muslim; Kabeer proclaims this out loud. |3|7|29|

Aasaa, Ti-Pada, Ik-Tuka:
I have decorated myself to meet my Husband Lord.
But the Lord, the Life of the Word, the Sustainer of the Universe, has not come to meet me. |1|

The Lord is my Husband, and I am the Lord's bride.
The Lord is so great, and I am infinitesimally small. |1|Pause|

The bride and the Groom dwell together.
They lie upon the one bed, but their union is difficult. |2|

Blessed is the soul-bride, who is pleasing to her Husband Lord.
Says Kabeer, she shall not have to be reincarnated again. |3|8|30|

Aasaa Of Kabeer Jee, Du-Padas:
One Universal Creator God. By The Grace Of The True Guru:
When the Diamond of the Lord pierces the diamond of my mind, the fickle
mind waving in the wind is easily absorbed into Him.
This Diamond fills all with Divine Light; through the True Guru's Teachings, I
have found Him. |1|

The sermon of the Lord is the unstruck, endless song.
Becoming a swan, one recognizes the Diamond of the Lord. |1|Pause|

Says Kabeer, I have seen such a Diamond, permeating and pervading the
world.
The hidden diamond became visible, when the Guru revealed it to me.
|2|1|31|

Aasaa:
My first wife, ignorance, was ugly, of low social status and bad character;
she was evil in my home, and in her parents' home.
My present bride, divine understanding, is beautiful, wise and well-
behaved; I have taken her to my heart. |1|

It has turned out so well, that my first wife has died.
May she, whom I have now married, live throughout the ages. |1|Pause|

Says Kabeer, when the younger bride came, the elder one lost her
husband.
The younger bride is with me now, and the elder one has taken another
husband. |2|2|32|

Section 08 - Raag Aasaa - Part 138

Aasaa:
My daughter-in-law was first called Dhannia, the woman of wealth,
but now she is called Raam-jannia, the servant of the Lord. |1|

These shaven-headed saints have ruined my house.
They have caused my son to start chanting the Lord's Name. |1|Pause|

Says Kabeer, listen, O mother:
these shaven-headed saints have done away with my low social status.
|2|3|33|

Aasaa:
Stay, stay, O daughter-in-law - do not cover your face with a veil.
In the end, this shall not bring you even half a shell. |1|Pause|

The one before you used to veil her face;
do not follow in her footsteps. |1|

The only merit in veiling your face is
that for a few days, people will say, "What a noble bride has come". |2|

Your veil shall be true only if
you skip, dance and sing the Glorious Praises of the Lord. |3|

Says Kabeer, the soul-bride shall win,
only if she passes her life singing the Lord's Praises. |4|1|34|

Aasaa:
I would rather be cut apart by a saw, than have You turn Your back on me.
Hug me close, and listen to my prayer. |1|

I am a sacrifice to You - please, turn Your face to me, O Beloved Lord.
Why have You turned Your back to me? Why have You killed me?
|1|Pause|

Even if You cut my body apart, I shall not pull my limbs away from You.
Even if my body falls, I shall not break my bonds of love with You. |2|

Between You and I, there is no other.

You are the Husband Lord, and I am the soul-bride. |3|

Says Kabeer, listen, O people:
now, I place no reliance in you. |4|2|35|

Aasaa:
No one knows the secret of God, the Cosmic Weaver.
He has stretched out the fabric of the whole world. |1|Pause|

When you listen to the Vedas and the Puraanas,
you shall know that the whole world is only a small piece of His woven fabric. |1|

He has made the earth and sky His loom.
Upon it, He moves the two bobbins of the sun and the moon. |2|

Placing my feet together, I have accomplished one thing - my mind is pleased with that Weaver.
I have come to understand my own home, and recognize the Lord within my heart. |3|

Says Kabeer, when my body workshop breaks,
the Weaver shall blend my thread with His thread. |4|3|36|

Aasaa:
With filth within the heart, even if one bathes at sacred places of pilgrimage, still, he shall not go to heaven.
Nothing is gained by trying to please others - the Lord cannot be fooled. |1|

Worship the One Divine Lord.
The true cleansing bath is service to the Guru. |1|Pause|

If salvation can be obtained by bathing in water, then what about the frog, which is always bathing in water?

As is the frog, so is that mortal; he is reincarnated, over and over again. |2|

If the hard-hearted sinner dies in Benaares, he cannot escape hell.

And even if the Lord's Saint dies in the cursed land of Haramba, still, he saves all his family. |3|

Where there is neither day nor night, and neither Vedas nor Shaastras, there, the Formless Lord abides.
Says Kabeer, meditate on Him, O mad-men of the world. |4|4|37|

Section 08 - Raag Aasaa - Part 139

One Universal Creator God. By The Grace Of The True Guru:
Aasaa, The Word Of The Reverend Naam Dayv Jee:
In the one and in the many, He is pervading and permeating; wherever I look, there He is.
The marvellous image of Maya is so fascinating; how few understand this. |1|

God is everything, God is everything. Without God, there is nothing at all.
As one thread holds hundreds and thousands of beads, He is woven into His creation. |1|Pause|

The waves of the water, the foam and bubbles, are not distinct from the water.
This manifested world is the playful game of the Supreme Lord God; reflecting upon it, we find that it is not different from Him. |2|

False doubts and dream objects - man believes them to be true.
The Guru has instructed me to try to do good deeds, and my awakened mind has accepted this. |3|

Says Naam Dayv, see the Creation of the Lord, and reflect upon it in your heart.
In each and every heart, and deep within the very nucleus of all, is the One Lord. |4|1|

Aasaa:
Bringing the pitcher, I fill it with water, to bathe the Lord.
But 4.2 million species of beings are in the water - how can I use it for the Lord, O Siblings of Destiny? |1|

Wherever I go, the Lord is there.

He continually plays in supreme bliss. |1|Pause|

I bring flowers to weave a garland, in worshipful adoration of the Lord.
But the bumble bee has already sucked out the fragrance - how can I use it for the Lord, O Siblings of Destiny? |2|

I carry milk and cook it to make pudding, with which to feed the Lord.
But the calf has already tasted the milk - how can I use it for the Lord, O Siblings of Destiny? |3|

The Lord is here, the Lord is there; without the Lord, there is no world at all.
Prays Naam Dayv, O Lord, You are totally permeating and pervading all places and interspaces. |4|2|

Aasaa:
My mind is the yardstick, and my tongue is the scissors.
I measure it out and cut off the noose of death. |1|

What do I have to do with social status? What do I have to with ancestry?
I meditate on the Name of the Lord, day and night. |1|Pause|

I dye myself in the color of the Lord, and sew what has to be sewn.
Without the Lord's Name, I cannot live, even for a moment. |2|

I perform devotional worship, and sing the Glorious Praises of the Lord.
Twenty-four hours a day, I meditate on my Lord and Master. |3|

My needle is gold, and my thread is silver.
Naam Dayv's mind is attached to the Lord. |4|3|

Aasaa:
The snake sheds its skin, but does not lose its venom.
The heron appears to be meditating, but it is concentrating on the water. |1|

Why do you practice meditation and chanting,
when your mind is not pure? |1|Pause|

That man who feeds like a lion,

is called the god of thieves. |2|

Naam Dayv's Lord and Master has settled my inner conflicts.

Section 08 - Raag Aasaa - Part 140

Drink in the sublime elixir of the Lord, O deceitful one. |3|4|

Aasaa:
One who recognizes the Supreme Lord God, dislikes other desires.
He focuses his consciousness on the Lord's devotional worship, and keeps his mind free of anxiety. |1|

O my mind, how will you cross over the world-ocean, if you are filled with the water of corruption?
Gazing upon the falseness of Maya, you have gone astray, O my mind. |1|Pause|

You have given me birth in the house of a calico-printer, but I have found the Teachings of the Guru.
By the Grace of the Saint, Naam Dayv has met the Lord. |2|5|

Aasaa, The Word Of The Reverend Ravi Daas Jee:
One Universal Creator God. By The Grace Of The True Guru:
The deer, the fish, the bumble bee, the moth and the elephant are destroyed, each for a single defect.
So the one who is filled with the five incurable vices - what hope is there for him? |1|

O Lord, he is in love with ignorance.
His lamp of clear wisdom has grown dim. |1|Pause|

The creeping creatures live thoughtless lives, and cannot discriminate between good and evil.
It is so difficult to obtain this human incarnation, and yet, they keep company with the low. |2|

Wherever the beings and creatures are, they are born according to the karma of their past actions.

The noose of death is unforgiving, and it shall catch them; it cannot be warded off. |3|

O servant Ravi Daas, dispel your sorrow and doubt, and know that Guru-given spiritual wisdom is the penance of penances.
O Lord, Destroyer of the fears of Your humble devotees, make me supremely blissful in the end. |4|1|

Aasaa:
Your Saints are Your body, and their company is Your breath of life.
By the True Guru-given spiritual wisdom, I know the Saints as the gods of gods. |1|

O Lord, God of gods, grant me the Society of the Saints, the sublime essence of the Saints' conversation, and the Love of the Saints. |1|Pause|

The Character of the Saints, the lifestyle of the Saints, and the service of the servant of the Saints. |2|

I ask for these, and for one thing more - devotional worship, which shall fulfill my desires.
Do not show me the wicked sinners. |3|

Says Ravi Daas, he alone is wise, who knows this:
there is no difference between the Saints and the Infinite Lord. |4|2|

Aasaa:
You are sandalwood, and I am the poor castor oil plant, dwelling close to you.
From a lowly tree, I have become exalted; Your fragrance, Your exquisite fragrance now permeates me. |1|

O Lord, I seek the Sanctuary of the company of Your Saints;
I am worthless, and You are so benevolent. |1|Pause|

You are the white and yellow threads of silk, and I am like a poor worm.
O Lord, I seek to live in the Company of the Saints, like the bee with its honey. |2|

My social status is low, my ancestry is low, and my birth is low as well.

I have not performed the service of the Lord, the Lord, says Ravi Daas the cobbler. |3|3|

Aasaa:
What would it matter, if my body were cut into pieces?
If I were to lose Your Love, Lord, then Your humble servant would be afraid. |1|

Your lotus feet are the home of my mind.
Drinking in Your Nectar, I have obtained the wealth of the Lord. |1|Pause|

Prosperity, adversity, property and wealth are just Maya.

Section 08 - Raag Aasaa - Part 141

Your humble servant is not engrossed in them. |2|

Your humble servant is tied by the rope of Your Love.
Says Ravi Daas, what benefit would I get by escaping from it? |3|4|

Aasaa:
The Lord, Har, Har, Har, Har, Har, Har, Haray.
Meditating on the Lord, the humble are carried across to salvation. |1|Pause|

Through the Lord's Name, Kabeer became famous and respected.
The accounts of his past incarnations were torn up. |1|

Because of Naam Dayv's devotion, the Lord drank the milk he offered.
He shall not have to suffer the pains of reincarnation into the world again. |2|

Servant Ravi Daas is imbued with the Lord's Love.
By Guru's Grace, he shall not have to go to hell. |3|5|

How does the puppet of clay dance?
He looks and listens, hears and speaks, and runs around. |1|Pause|

When he acquires something, he is inflated with ego.
But when his wealth is gone, then he cries and bewails. |1|

In thought, word and deed, he is attached to the sweet and tangy flavors. When he dies, no one knows where he has gone. |2|

Says Ravi Daas, the world is just a dramatic play, O Siblings of Destiny. I have enshrined love for the Lord, the star of the show. |3|6|

Aasaa, The Word Of Devotee Dhanna Jee:
One Universal Creator God. By The Grace Of The True Guru:
I wandered through countless incarnations, but mind, body and wealth never remain stable.
Attached to, and stained by the poisons of sexual desire and greed, the mind has forgotten the jewel of the Lord. |1|Pause|

The poisonous fruit seems sweet to the demented mind, which does not know the difference between good and evil.
Turning away from virtue, his love for other things increases, and he weaves again the web of birth and death. |1|

He does not know the way to the Lord, who dwells within his heart; burning in the trap, he is caught by the noose of death.
Gathering the poisonous fruits, he fills his mind with them, and he forgets God, the Supreme Being, from his mind. |2|

The Guru has given the wealth of spiritual wisdom; practicing meditation, the mind becomes one with Him.
Embracing loving devotional worship for the Lord, I have come to know peace; satisfied and satiated, I have been liberated. |3|

One who is filled with the Divine Light, recognizes the undeceivable Lord God.
Dhanna has obtained the Lord, the Sustainer of the World, as his wealth; meeting the humble Saints, he merges in the Lord. |4|1|

Fifth Mehl:
Naam Dayv's mind was absorbed into God, Gobind, Gobind, Gobind.
The calico-printer, worth half a shell, became worth millions. |1|Pause|

Abandoning weaving and stretching thread, Kabeer enshrined love for the Lord's lotus feet.

A weaver from a lowly family, he became an ocean of excellence. |1|

Ravi Daas, who used to carry dead cows every day, renounced the world of Maya.
He became famous in the Saadh Sangat, the Company of the Holy, and obtained the Blessed Vision of the Lord's Darshan. |2|

Sain, the barber, the village drudge, became famous in each and every house.
The Supreme Lord God dwelled in his heart, and he was counted among the devotees. |3|

Section 08 - Raag Aasaa - Part 142

Hearing this, Dhanna the Jaat applied himself to devotional worship.
The Lord of the Universe met him personally; Dhanna was so very blessed. |4|2|

O my consciousness, why don't you remain conscious of the Merciful Lord? How can you recognize any other?

You may run around the whole universe, but that alone happens which the Creator Lord does. |1|Pause|

In the water of the mother's womb, He fashioned the body with ten gates.
He gives it sustenance, and preserves it in fire - such is my Lord and Master. |1|

The mother turtle is in the water, and her babies are out of the water. She has no wings to protect them, and no milk to feed them.
The Perfect Lord, the embodiment of supreme bliss, the Fascinating Lord takes care of them. See this, and understand it in your mind|2|

The worm lies hidden under the stone - there is no way for him to escape.
Says Dhanna, the Perfect Lord takes care of him. Fear not, O my soul. |3|3|

Aasaa, The Word Of Shaykh Fareed Jee:
One Universal Creator God. By The Grace Of The True Guru:
They alone are true, whose love for God is deep and heart-felt.

Those who have one thing in their heart, and something else in their mouth, are judged to be false. |1|

Those who are imbued with love for the Lord, are delighted by His Vision. Those who forget the Naam, the Name of the Lord, are a burden on the earth. |1|Pause|

Those whom the Lord attaches to the hem of His robe, are the true dervishes at His Door. Blessed are the mothers who gave birth to them, and fruitful is their coming into the world. |2|

O Lord, Sustainer and Cherisher, You are infinite, unfathomable and endless. Those who recognize the True Lord - I kiss their feet. |3|

I seek Your Protection - You are the Forgiving Lord. Please, bless Shaykh Fareed with the bounty of Your meditative worship. |4|1|

Aasaa: Says Shaykh Fareed, O my dear friend, attach yourself to the Lord. This body shall turn to dust, and its home shall be a neglected graveyard. |1|

You can meet the Lord today, O Shaykh Fareed, if you restrain your bird-like desires which keep your mind in turmoil. |1|Pause|

If I had known that I was to die, and not return again, I would not have ruined myself by clinging to the world of falsehood. |2|

So speak the Truth, in righteousness, and do not speak falsehood. The disciple ought to travel the route, pointed out by the Guru. |3|

Seeing the youths being carried across, the hearts of the beautiful young soul-brides are encouraged. Those who side with the glitter of gold, are cut down with a saw. |4|

O Shaykh, no one's life is permanent in this world.

That seat, upon which we now sit - many others sat on it and have since departed. |5|

As the swallows appear in the month of Katik, forest fires in the month of Chayt, and lightning in Saawan,

and as the bride's arms adorn her husband's neck in winter; |6|

Just so, the transitory human bodies pass away. Reflect upon this in your mind.
It takes six months to form the body, but it breaks in an instant. |7|

O Fareed, the earth asks the sky, "Where have the boatmen gone?"
Some have been cremated, and some lie in their graves; their souls are suffering rebukes. |8|2|

RAAG GOOJAREE

Section 09 - Raag Goojaree - Part 001

ONE Universal Creator God. Truth Is The Name. Creative Being Personified. No Fear. No Hatred. Image Of The Undying. Beyond Birth. Self-Existent. By Guru's Grace:

Raag Goojaree, First Mehl, Chau-Padas, First House:
I would make Your Name the sandalwood, and my mind the stone to rub it on;
for saffron, I would offer good deeds; thus, I perform worship and adoration within my heart. |1|

Perform worship and adoration by meditating on the Naam, the Name of the Lord; without the Name, there is no worship and adoration. |1|Pause|

If one were to wash his heart inwardly, like the stone idol which is washed on the outside,
his filth would be removed, his soul would be cleansed, and he would be liberated when he departs. |2|

Even beasts have value, as they eat grass and give milk.
Without the Naam, the mortal's life is cursed, as are the actions he performs. |3|

The Lord is hear at hand - do not think that He is far away. He always cherishes us, and remembers us.
Whatever He gives us, we eat; says Nanak, He is the True Lord. |4|1|

Goojaree, First Mehl:
From the lotus of Vishnu's navel, Brahma was born; He chanted the Vedas with a melodious voice.
He could not find the Lord's limits, and he remained in the darkness of coming and going. |1|

Why should I forget my Beloved? He is the support of my very breath of life.
The perfect beings perform devotional worship to Him. The silent sages serve Him through the Guru's Teachings. |1|Pause|

His lamps are the sun and the moon; the One Light of the Destroyer of ego fills the three worlds.
One who becomes Gurmukh remains immaculately pure, day and night, while the self-willed manmukh is enveloped by the darkness of night. |2|

The Siddhas in Samaadhi are continually in conflict; what can they see with their two eyes?
One who has the Divine Light within his heart, and is awakened to the melody of the Word of the Shabad - the True Guru settles his conflicts. |3|

O Lord of angels and men, infinite and unborn, Your True Mansion is incomparable.
Nanak merges imperceptibly into the Life of the world; shower Your mercy upon him, and save him. |4|2|

Section 09 - Raag Goojaree - Part 002

Raag Goojaree, Third Mehl, First House:
One Universal Creator God. By The Grace Of The True Guru:
Cursed is that life, in which the Lord's Love is not obtained.
Cursed is that occupation, in which the Lord is forgotten, and one becomes attached to duality. |1|

Serve such a True Guru, O my mind, that by serving Him, God's Love may be produced, and all others may be forgotten.
Your consciousness shall remain attached to the Lord; there shall be no fear of old age, and the supreme status shall be obtained. |1|Pause|

A divine peace wells up from God's Love; behold, it comes from devotional worship.
When my identity consumed my identical identity, then my mind became immaculately pure, and my light was blended with the Divine Light. |2|

Without good fortune, such a True Guru cannot be found, no matter how much all may yearn for Him.

If the veil of falsehood is removed from within, then lasting peace is obtained. |3|

O Nanak, what service can the servant perform for such a True Guru? He should offer his life, his very soul, to the Guru.
If he focuses his consciousness on the Will of the True Guru, then the True Guru Himself will bless him. |4|1|3|

Goojaree, Third Mehl:
Serve the Lord; do not serve anyone else.
Serving the Lord, you shall obtain the fruits of your heart's desires; serving another, your life shall pass away in vain. |1|

The Lord is my Love, the Lord is my way of life, the Lord is my speech and conversation.
By Guru's Grace, my mind is saturated with the Lord's Love; this is what makes up my service. |1|Pause|

The Lord is my Simritees, the Lord is my Shaastras; the Lord is my relative and the Lord is my brother.
I am hungry for the Lord; my mind is satisfied with the Name of the Lord. The Lord is my relation, my helper in the end. |2|

Without the Lord, other assets are false. They do not go with the mortal when he departs.
The Lord is my wealth, which shall go with me; wherever I go, it will go. |3|

One who is attached to falsehood is false; false are the deeds he does.
Says Nanak, everything happens according to the Will of the Lord; no one has any say in this at all. |4|2|4|

Goojaree, Third Mehl:
It is so difficult to obtain the Naam, the Name of the Lord, in this age; only the Gurmukh obtains it.
Without the Name, no one is liberated; let anyone make other efforts, and see. |1|

I am a sacrifice to my Guru; I am forever a sacrifice to Him.
Meeting the True Guru, the Lord comes to dwell in the mind, and one remains absorbed in Him. |1|Pause|

When God instills His fear, a balanced detachment springs up in the mind. Through this detachment, the Lord is obtained, and one remains absorbed in the Lord. |2|

He alone is liberated, who conquers his mind; Maya does not stick to him again.
He dwells in the Tenth Gate, and obtains the understanding of the three worlds. |3|

O Nanak, through the Guru, one becomes the Guru; behold, His Wondrous Will.

Section 09 - Raag Goojaree - Part 003

This deed was done by the Creator Lord; one's light merges into the Light. |4|3|5|

Goojaree, Third Mehl:
Everyone chants the Lord's Name, Raam, Raam; but by such chanting, the Lord is not obtained.
By Guru's Grace, the Lord comes to dwell in the mind, and then, the fruits are obtained. |1|

One who enshrines love for God within his mind,
never forgets the Lord; he continually chants the Lord's Name, Har, Har, in his conscious mind. |1|Pause|

Those whose hearts are filled with hypocrisy, who are called saints only for their outward show
- their desires are never satisfied, and they depart grieving in the end. |2|

Although one may bathe at many places of pilgrimage, still, his ego never departs.
That man, whose sense of duality does not depart - the Righteous Judge of Dharma shall punish him. |3|

That humble being, unto whom God showers His Mercy, obtains Him; how few are the Gurmukhs who understand Him.

O Nanak, if one conquers his ego within, then he comes to meet the Lord. |4|4|6|

Goojaree, Third Mehl:
That humble being who eliminates his ego is at peace; he is blessed with an ever-stable intellect.
That humble being is immaculately pure, who, as Gurmukh, understands the Lord, and focuses his consciousness on the Lord's Feet. |1|

O my unconscious mind, remain conscious of the Lord, and you shall obtain the fruits of your desires.
By Guru's Grace, you shall obtain the sublime elixir of the Lord; by continually drinking it in, you shall have eternal peace. |1|Pause|

When one meets the True Guru, he becomes the philosopher's stone, with the ability to transform others, inspiring them to worship the Lord.
One who worships the Lord in adoration, obtains his rewards; instructing others, he reveals the Truth. |2|

Without becoming the philosopher's stone, he does not inspire others to worship the Lord; without instructing his own mind, how can he instruct others?

The ignorant, blind man calls himself the guru, but to whom can he show the way? |3|

O Nanak, without His Mercy, nothing can be obtained. One upon whom He casts His Glance of Grace, obtains Him.
By Guru's Grace, God bestows greatness, and projects the Word of His Shabad. |4|5|7|

Goojaree, Third Mehl, Panch-Padas:
Wisdom is not produced in Benares, nor is wisdom lost in Benares.
Meeting the True Guru, wisdom is produced, and then, one obtains this understanding. |1|

Listen to the sermon of the Lord, O mind, and enshrine the Shabad of His Word within your mind.
If your intellect remains stable and steady, then doubt shall depart from within you. |1|Pause|

Enshrine the Lord's lotus feet within your heart, and your sins shall be erased.

If your soul overcomes the five elements, then you shall come to have a home at the true place of pilgrimage. |2|

This mind of the self-centered manmukh is so stupid; it does not obtain any understanding at all.

It does not understand the Name of the Lord; it departs repenting in the end. |3|

In this mind are found Benares, all sacred shrines of pilgrimage and the Shaastras; the True Guru has explained this.

The sixty-eight places of pilgrimage remain with one, whose heart is filled with the Lord. |4|

O Nanak, upon meeting the True Guru, the Order of the Lord's Will is understood, and the One Lord comes to dwell in the mind.

Those who are pleasing to You, O True Lord, are true. They remain absorbed in You. |5|6|8|

Section 09 - Raag Goojaree - Part 004

Goojaree, Third Mehl:

The One Name is the treasure, O Pandit. Listen to these True Teachings.

No matter what you read in duality, reading and contemplating it, you shall only continue to suffer. |1|

So grasp the Lord's lotus feet; through the Word of the Guru's Shabad, you shall come to understand.

With your tongue, taste the sublime elixir of the Lord, and your mind shall be rendered immaculately pure. |1|Pause|

Meeting the True Guru, the mind becomes content, and then, hunger and desire will not trouble you any longer.

Obtaining the treasure of the Naam, the Name of the Lord, one does not go knocking at other doors. |2|

The self-willed manmukh babbles on and on, but he does not understand.

One whose heart is illumined, by Guru's Teachings, obtains the Name of the Lord. |3|

You may listen to the Shaastras, but you do not understand, and so you wander from door to door.
He is a fool, who does not understand his own self, and who does not enshrine love for the True Lord. |4|

The True Lord has fooled the world - no one has any say in this at all.
O Nanak, He does whatever He pleases, according to His Will. |5|7|9|

One Universal Creator God. By The Grace Of The True Guru:
Raag Goojaree, Fourth Mehl, Chau-Padas, First House:
O Servant of the Lord, O True Guru, O True Primal Being, I offer my prayers to You, O Guru.
I am an insect and a worm; O True Guru, I seek Your Sanctuary; please, be merciful and bestow upon me the Light of the Naam, the Name of the Lord. |1|

O my Best Friend, O Divine Guru, please illuminate me with the Light of the Lord.
By Guru's Instructions, the Naam is my breath of life, and the Praise of the Lord is my occupation. |1|Pause|

The Lord's servants have the greatest good fortune; they have faith in the Lord, Har, Har, and a thirst for the Lord.
Obtaining the Name of the Lord, Har, Har, they are satisfied; joining the Company of the Holy, their virtues shine forth. |2|

Those who have not obtained the essence of the Name of the Lord, Har, Har, are most unfortunate; they are taken away by the Messenger of Death.
Those who have not sought the Sanctuary of the True Guru and the Company of the Holy - cursed are their lives, and cursed are their hopes of life. |3|

Those humble servants of the Lord, who have obtained the Company of the True Guru, have such pre-ordained destiny written on their foreheads.

Blessed, blessed is the Sat Sangat, the True Congregation, where the sublime essence of the Lord is obtained. Meeting with His humble servant, O Nanak, the Naam shines forth. |4|1|

Goojaree, Fourth Mehl:
The Lord, the Lord of the Universe is the Beloved of the minds of those who join the Sat Sangat, the True Congregation. The Shabad of His Word fascinates their minds.
Chant, and meditate on the Lord, the Lord of the Universe; God is the One who gives gifts to all. |1|

O my Siblings of Destiny, the Lord of the Universe, Govind, Govind, Govind, has enticed and fascinated my mind.
I sing the Glorious Praises of the Lord of the Universe, Govind, Govind, Govind; joining the Holy Society of the Guru, Your humble servant is beautified. |1|Pause|

Devotional worship to the Lord is an ocean of peace; through the Guru's Teachings, wealth, prosperity and the spiritual powers of the Siddhas fall at our feet.
The Lord's Name is the Support of His humble servant; he chants the Lord's Name, and with the Lord's Name he is adorned. |2|

Section 09 - Raag Goojaree - Part 005

Evil-minded, unfortunate and shallow-minded are those who feel anger in their minds, when they hear the Naam, the Name of the Lord.
You may place ambrosial nectar before crows and ravens, but they will be satisfied only by eating manure and dung with their mouths. |3|

The True Guru, the Speaker of Truth, is the pool of Ambrosial Nectar; bathing within it, the crow becomes a swan.
O Nanak, blessed, blessed and very fortunate are those who, through the Guru's Teachings, with the Naam, wash away the filth of their hearts. |4|2|

Goojaree, Fourth Mehl:
The humble servants of the Lord are exalted, and exalted is their speech. With their mouths, they speak for the benefit of others.
Those who listen to them with faith and devotion, are blessed by the Lord; showering His Mercy, He saves them. |1|

Lord, please, let me meet the beloved servants of the Lord.
The True Guru, the Perfect Guru, is my Beloved, my very breath of life; the Guru has saved me, the sinner. |1|Pause|

The Gurmukhs are fortunate, so very fortunate; their Support is the Name of the Lord, Har, Har.
They obtain the Ambrosial Nectar of the Name of the Lord, Har, Har; through the Guru's Teachings, they obtain this treasure-house of devotional worship. |2|

Those who do not obtain the Blessed Vision of the Darshan of the True Guru, the True Primal Being, are most unfortunate; they are destroyed by the Messenger of Death.
They are like dogs, pigs and jackasses; they are cast into the womb of reincarnation, and the Lord strikes them down as the worst of murderers. |3|

O Lord, Kind to the poor, please shower Your mercy upon Your humble servant, and save him.
Servant Nanak has entered the Lord's Sanctuary; if it pleases You, Lord, please save him. |4|3|

Goojaree, Fourth Mehl:
Be Merciful and attune my mind, so that I might meditate continually on the Lord's Name, night and day.
The Lord is all peace, all virtue and all wealth; remembering Him, all misery and hunger depart. |1|

O my mind, the Lord's Name is my companion and brother.
Under Guru's Instruction, I sing the Praises of the Lord's Name; it shall be my help and support in the end, and it shall deliver me in the Court of the Lord. |1|Pause|

You Yourself are the Giver, O God, Inner-knower, Searcher of hearts; by Your Grace, You have infused longing for You in my mind.
My mind and body long for the Lord; God has fulfilled my longing. I have entered the Sanctuary of the True Guru. |2|

Human birth is obtained through good actions; without the Name, it is cursed, totally cursed, and it passes away in vain.
Without the Naam, the Name of the Lord, one obtains only suffering for his delicacies to eat. His mouth is insipid, and his face is spat upon, again and again. |3|

Those humble beings, who have entered the Sanctuary of the Lord God, Har, Har, are blessed with glory in the Court of the Lord, Har, Har.
Blessed, blessed and congratulations, says God to His humble servant. O servant Nanak, He embraces him, and blends him with Himself. |4|4|

Goojaree, Fourth Mehl:
O Gurmukhs, O my friends and companions, give me the gift of the Lord's Name, the life of my very life.
I am the slave, the servant of the Guru's Sikhs, who meditate on the Lord God, the Primal Being, night and day. |1|

Within my mind and body, I have enshrined love for the feet of the Guru's Sikhs.
O my life-mates, O Sikhs of the Guru, O Siblings of Destiny, instruct me in the Teachings, that I might merge in the Lord's Merger. |1|Pause|

Section 09 - Raag Goojaree - Part 006

When it pleases the Lord God, he causes us to meet the Gurmukhs; the Hymns of the Guru, the True Guru, are very sweet to their minds.
Very fortunate are the beloved Sikhs of the Guru; through the Lord, they attain the supreme state of Nirvaanaa. |2|

The Sat Sangat, the True Congregation of the Guru, is loved by the Lord. The Naam, the Name of the Lord, Har, Har, is sweet and pleasing to their minds.
One who does not obtain the Association of the True Guru, is a most unfortunate sinner; he is consumed by the Messenger of Death. |3|

If God, the Kind Master, Himself shows His kindness, then the Lord causes the Gurmukh to merge into Himself.
Servant Nanak chants the Glorious Words of the Guru's Bani; through them, one is absorbed into the Naam, the Name of the Lord. |4|5|

Goojaree, Fourth Mehl:
One who has found the Lord God through the True Guru, has made the Lord seem so sweet to me, through the His Teachings.
My mind and body have been cooled and soothed, and totally rejuvenated; by great good fortune, I meditate on the Name of the Lord. |1|

O Siblings of Destiny, let anyone who can implant the Lord's Name within me, come and meet with me.
Unto my Beloved, I give my mind and body, and my very breath of life. He speaks to me of the sermon of my Lord God. |1|Pause|

Through the Guru's Teachings, I have obtained courage, faith and the Lord.
He keeps my mind focused continually on the Lord, and the Name of the Lord.
The Words of the True Guru's Teachings are Ambrosial Nectar; this Amrit trickles into the mouth of the one who chants them. |2|

Immaculate is the Naam, which cannot be stained by filth. Through the Guru's Teachings, chant the Naam with love.
That man who has not found the wealth of the Naam is most unfortunate; he dies over and over again. |3|

The source of bliss, the Life of the world, the Great Giver brings bliss to all who meditate on the Lord.
You are the Great Giver, all beings belong to You. O servant Nanak, You forgive the Gurmukhs, and merge them into Yourself. |4|6|

One Universal Creator God. By The Grace Of The True Guru:
Goojaree, Fourth Mehl, Third House:
Mother, father and sons are all made by the Lord;
the relationships of all are established by the Lord. |1|

I have given up all my strength, O my brother.
The mind and body belong to the Lord, and the human body is entirely under His control. |1|Pause|

The Lord Himself infuses devotion into His humble devotees.
In the midst of family life, they remain unattached. |2|

When inner love is established with the Lord,

then whatever one does, is pleasing to my Lord God. |3|

I do those deeds and tasks which the Lord has set me to;
I do that which He makes me to do. |4|

Those whose devotional worship is pleasing to my God
- O Nanak, those humble beings center their minds lovingly on the Lord's
Name. |5|1|7|16|

Section 09 - Raag Goojaree - Part 007

Goojaree, Fifth Mehl, Chau-Padas, First House:
One Universal Creator God. By The Grace Of The True Guru:
Why, O mind, do you contrive your schemes, when the Dear Lord Himself
provides for your care?
From rocks and stones, He created the living beings, and He places before
them their sustenance. |1|

O my Dear Lord of Souls, one who meets with the Sat Sangat, the True
Congregation, is saved.
By Guru's Grace, he obtains the supreme status, and the dry branch
blossoms forth in greenery. |1|Pause|

Mother, father, friends, children, and spouse - no one is the support of any
other.
For each and every individual, the Lord and Master provides sustenance;
why do you fear, O my mind? |2|

The flamingoes fly hundreds of miles, leaving their young ones behind.
Who feeds them, and who teaches them to feed themselves? Have you
ever thought of this in your mind? |3|

All treasures and the eighteen supernatural spiritual powers of the Siddhas
are held by the Lord and Master in the palm of His hand.
Servant Nanak is devoted, dedicated, and forever a sacrifice to You - Your
vast expanse has no limit. |4|1|

Goojaree, Fifth Mehl, Chau-Padas, Second House:
One Universal Creator God. By The Grace Of The True Guru:

They perform the four rituals and six religious rites; the world is engrossed in these.
They are not cleansed of the filth of their ego within; without the Guru, they lose the game of life. |1|

O my Lord and Master, please, grant Your Grace and preserve me.
Out of millions, hardly anyone is a servant of the Lord. All the others are mere traders. |1|Pause|

I have searched all the Shaastras, the Vedas and the Simritees, and they all affirm one thing:
without the Guru, no one obtains liberation; see, and reflect upon this in your mind. |2|

Even if one takes cleansing baths at the sixty-eight sacred shrines of pilgrimage, and wanders over the whole planet,

and performs all the rituals of purification day and night, still, without the True Guru, there is only darkness. |3|

Roaming and wandering around, I have travelled over the whole world, and now, I have arrived at the Lord's Door.
The Lord has eliminated my evil-mindedness, and enlightened my intellect; O servant Nanak, the Gurmukhs are saved. |4|1|2|

Goojaree, Fifth Mehl:
The wealth of the Lord is my chanting, the wealth of the Lord is my deep meditation; the wealth of the Lord is the food I enjoy.
I do not forget the Lord, Har, Har, from my mind, even for an instant; I have found Him in the Saadh Sangat, the Company of the Holy. |1|

O mother, your son has returned home with a profit:
the wealth of the Lord while walking, the wealth of the Lord while sitting, and the wealth of the Lord while waking and sleeping. |1|Pause|

The wealth of the Lord is my cleansing bath, the wealth of the Lord is my wisdom; I center my meditation on the Lord.
The wealth of the Lord is my raft, the wealth of the Lord is my boat; the Lord, Har, Har, is the ship to carry me across. |2|

Section 09 - Raag Goojaree - Part 008

Through the wealth of the Lord, I have forgotten my anxiety; through the wealth of the Lord, my doubt has been dispelled.
From the wealth of the Lord, I have obtained the nine treasures; the true essence of the Lord has come into my hands. |3|

No matter how much I eat and expend this wealth, it is not exhausted; here and hereafter, it remains with me.
Loading the treasure, Guru Nanak has given it, and this mind is imbued with the Lord's Love. |4|2|3|

Goojaree, Fifth Mehl:
Remembering Him, all sins are erased, and ones generations are saved.
So meditate continually on the Lord, Har, Har; He has no end or limitation. |1|

O son, this is your mother's hope and prayer,
that you may never forget the Lord, Har, Har, even for an instant. May you ever vibrate upon the Lord of the Universe. |1|Pause|

May the True Guru be kind to you, and may you love the Society of the Saints.
May the preservation of your honor by the Transcendent Lord be your clothes, and may the singing of His Praises be your food. |2|

So drink in forever the Ambrosial Nectar; may you live long, and may the meditative remembrance of the Lord give you infinite delight.
May joy and pleasure be yours; may your hopes be fulfilled, and may you never be troubled by worries. |3|

Let this mind of yours be the bumble bee, and let the Lord's feet be the lotus flower.
Says servant Nanak, attach your mind to them, and blossom forth like the song-bird, upon finding the rain-drop. |4|3|4|

Goojaree, Fifth Mehl:
He decides to go to the west, but the Lord leads him away to the east.
In an instant, He establishes and disestablishes; He holds all matters in His hands. |1|

Cleverness is of no use at all.
Whatever my Lord and Master deems to be right - that alone comes to pass. |1|Pause|

In his desire to acquire land and accumulate wealth, one's breath escapes him.
He must leave all his armies, assistants and servants; rising up, he departs to the City of Death. |2|

Believing himself to be unique, he clings to his stubborn mind, and shows himself off.
That food, which the blameless people have condemned and discarded, he eats again and again. |3|

One, unto whom the Lord shows His natural mercy, has the noose of Death cut away from him.
Says Nanak, one who meets the Perfect Guru, is celebrated as a house-holder as well as a renunciate. |4|4|5|

Goojaree, Fifth Mehl:
Those humble beings who chant the treasure of the Naam, the Name of the Lord, have their bonds broken.
Sexual desirer, anger, the poison of Maya and egotism - they are rid of these afflictions. |1|

One who joins the Saadh Sangat, the Company of the Holy, and chants the Praises of the Lord,
has his mind purified, by Guru's Grace, and he obtains the joy of all joys. |1|Pause|

Whatever the Lord does, he sees that as good; such is the devotional service he performs.
He sees friends and enemies as all the same; this is the sign of the Way of Yoga. |2|

The all-pervading Lord is fully filling all places; why should I go anywhere else?
He is permeating and pervading within each and every heart; I am immersed in His Love, dyed in the color of His Love. |3|

When the Lord of the Universe becomes kind and compassionate, then one enters the home of the Fearless Lord.

Section 09 - Raag Goojaree - Part 009

His troubles and worries are ended in an instant; O Nanak, he merges in celestial peace. |4|5|6|

Goojaree, Fifth Mehl:
Whoever I approach to ask for help, I find him full of his own troubles.
One who worships in his heart the Supreme Lord God, crosses over the terrifying world-ocean. |1|

No one, except the Guru-Lord, can dispel our pain and sorrow.
Forsaking God, and serving another, one's honor, dignity and reputation are decreased. |1|Pause|

Relatives, relations and family bound through Maya are of no avail.
The Lord's servant, although of lowly birth, is exalted. Associating with him, one obtains the fruits of his mind's desires. |2|

Through corruption, one may obtain thousands and millions of enjoyments, but even so, his desires are not satisfied through them.
Remembering the Naam, the Name of the Lord, millions of lights appear, and the incomprehensible is understood. |3|

Wandering and roaming around, I have come to Your Door, Destroyer of fear, O Lord King.
Servant Nanak yearns for the dust of the feet of the Holy; in it, he finds peace. |4|6|7|

Goojaree, Fifth Mehl, Panch-Pada, Second House:
One Universal Creator God. By The Grace Of The True Guru:
First, he came to dwell in his mother's womb; leaving it, he came into the world.
Splendid mansions, beautiful gardens and palaces - none of these shall go with him. |1|

All other greeds of the greedy are false.

The Perfect Guru has given me the Name of the Lord, which my soul has come to treasure. |1|Pause|

Surrounded by dear friends, relatives, children, siblings and spouse, he laughs playfully.
But when the very last moment arrives, Death seizes him, while they merely look on. |2|

By continual oppression and exploitation, he accumulates wealth, gold, silver and money,
but the load-bearer gets only paltry wages, while the rest of the money passes on to others. |3|

He grabs and collects horses, elephants and chariots, and claims them as his own.
But when he sets out on the long journey, they will not go even one step with him. |4|

The Naam, the Name of the Lord, is my wealth; the Naam is my princely pleasure; the Naam is my family and helper.
The Guru has given Nanak the wealth of the Naam; it neither perishes, nor comes or goes. |5|1|8|

Goojaree, Fifth Mehl, Ti-Padas, Second House:
One Universal Creator God. By The Grace Of The True Guru:
My sorrows are ended, and I am filled with peace. The fire of desire within me has been quenched.
The True Guru has implanted the treasure of the Naam, the Name of the Lord, within me; it neither dies, nor goes anywhere. |1|

Meditating on the Lord, the bonds of Maya are cut away.
When my God becomes kind and compassionate, one joins the Saadh Sangat, the Company of the Holy, and is emancipated. |1|Pause|

Section 09 - Raag Goojaree - Part 010

Twenty-four hours a day, he sings the Glorious Praises of the Lord, absorbed in loving devotional worship.
He remains unaffected by both fortune and misfortune, and he recognizes the Creator Lord. |2|

The Lord saves those who belong to Him, and all pathways are opened to them.

Says Nanak, the value of the Merciful Lord God cannot be described. |3|1|9|

Goojaree, Fifth Mehl, Du-Padas, Second House:

One Universal Creator God. By The Grace Of The True Guru:

The Lord has sanctified the sinners and made them His own; all bow in reverence to Him.

No one asks about their ancestry and social status; instead, they yearn for the dust of their feet. |1|

O Lord Master, such is Your Name.

You are called the Lord of all creation; You give Your unique support to Your servant. |1|Pause|

In the Saadh Sangat, the Company of the Holy, Nanak has obtained understanding; singing the Kirtan of the Lord's Praises is his only support.

The Lord's servants, Naam Dayv, Trilochan, Kabeer and Ravi Daas the shoe-maker have been liberated. |2|1|10|

Goojaree, Fifth Mehl:

No one understands the Lord; who can understand His plans?

Shiva, Brahma and all the silent sages cannot understand the state of the Lord. |1|

God's sermon is profound and unfathomable.

He is heard to be one thing, but He is understood to be something else again; He is beyond description and explanation. |1|Pause|

He Himself is the devotee, and He Himself is the Lord and Master; He is imbued with Himself.

Nanak's God is pervading and permeating everywhere; wherever he looks, He is there. |2|2|11|

Goojaree, Fifth Mehl:

The humble servant of the Lord has no plans, politics or other clever tricks.

Whenever the occasion arises, there, he meditates on the Lord. |1|

It is the very nature of God to love His devotees;
He cherishes His servant, and caresses him as His own child. |1|Pause|

The Lord's servant sings the Kirtan of His Praises as his worship, deep meditation, self-discipline and religious observances.
Nanak has entered the Sanctuary of his Lord and Master, and has received the blessings of fearlessness and peace. |2|3|12|

Goojaree, Fifth Mehl:
Worship the Lord in adoration, day and night, O my dear - do not delay for a moment.
Serve the Saints with loving faith, and set aside your pride and stubbornness. |1|

The fascinating, playful Lord is my very breath of life and honor.
He abides in my heart; beholding His playful games, my mind is fascinated. |1|Pause|

Remembering Him, my mind is in bliss, and the rust of my mind is removed.
The great honor of meeting the Lord cannot be described; O Nanak, it is infinite, beyond measure. |2|4|13|

Goojaree, Fifth Mehl:
They call themselves silent sages, Yogis and scholars of the Shaastras, but Maya has has them all under her control.
The three gods, and the 330,000,000 demi-gods, were astonished. |1|

Section 09 - Raag Goojaree - Part 011

The power of Maya is pervading everywhere.
Her secret is known only by Guru's Grace - no one else knows it. |1|Pause|

Conquering and conquering, she has conquered everywhere, and she clings to the whole world.
Says Nanak, she surrenders to the Holy Saint; becoming his servant, she falls at his feet. |2|5|14|

Goojaree, Fifth Mehl:
With my palms pressed together, I offer my prayer, meditating on my Lord and Master.

Giving me His hand, the Transcendent Lord has saved me, and erased all my sins. |1|

The Lord and Master Himself has become merciful.
I have been emancipated, the embodiment of bliss; I am the child of the Lord of the Universe - He has carried me across. |1|Pause|

Meeting her Husband, the soul-bride sings the songs of joy, and celebrates her Lord and Master.
Says Nanak, I am a sacrifice to the Guru, who has emancipated everyone. |2|6|15|

Goojaree, Fifth Mehl:
Mother, father, siblings, children and relatives - their power is insignificant.
I have seen the many pleasures of Maya, but none goes with them in the end. |1|

O Lord Master, other than You, no one is mine.
I am a worthless orphan, devoid of merit; I long for Your Support. |1|Pause|

I am a sacrifice, a sacrifice, a sacrifice, a sacrifice to Your lotus feet; here and hereafter, Yours is the only power.
In the Saadh Sangat, the Company of the Holy, Nanak has obtained the Blessed Vision of Your Darshan; my obligations to all others are annulled. |2|7|16|

Goojaree, Fifth Mehl:
He rids us of entanglements, doubt and emotional attachment, and leads us to love God.
He implants this instruction in our minds, for us to sing the Glorious Praises of the Lord, in peace and poise. |1|

O friend, the Saintly Guru is such a helper.
Meeting Him, the bonds of Maya are released, and one never forgets the Lord. |1|Pause|

Practicing, practicing various actions in so many ways, I came to recognize this as the best way.

Joining the Company of the Holy, Nanak sings the Glorious Praises of the Lord, and crosses over the terrifying world-ocean. |2|8|17|

Goojaree, Fifth Mehl:
In an instant, He establishes and disestablishes; His value cannot be described.
He turns the king into a beggar in an instant, and He infuses splendor into the lowly. |1|

Meditate forever on Your Lord.
Why should I feel worry or anxiety, when I am here for only a short time. |1|Pause|

You are my support, O my Perfect True Guru; my mind has taken to the protection of Your Sanctuary.
Nanak, I am a foolish and ignorant child; reach out to me with Your hand, Lord, and save me. |2|9|18|

Goojaree, Fifth Mehl:
You are the Giver of all beings; please, come to dwell within my mind.
That heart, within which Your lotus feet are enshrined, suffers no darkness or doubt. |1|

O Lord Master, wherever I remember You, there I find You.
Show Mercy to me, O God, Cherisher of all, that I may sing Your Praises forever. |1|Pause|

With each and every breath, I contemplate Your Name; O God, I long for You alone.
O Nanak, my support is the Creator Lord; I have renounced all other hopes. |2|10|19|

Section 09 - Raag Goojaree - Part 012

Goojaree, Fifth Mehl:
Show Mercy to me, and grant me the Blessed Vision of Your Darshan. I sing Your Praises night and day.
With my hair, I wash the feet of Your slave; this is my life's purpose. |1|

O Lord and Master, without You, there is no other at all.

O Lord, in my mind I remain conscious of You; with my tongue I worship You, and with my eyes, I gaze upon You. |1|Pause|

O Merciful Lord, O Lord and Master of all, with my palms pressed together I pray to You.
Nanak, Your slave, chants Your Name, and is redeemed in the twinkling of an eye. |2|11|20|

Goojaree, Fifth Mehl:
Overwhelming the realm of Brahma, the realm of Shiva and the realm of Indra, Maya has come running here.
But she cannot touch the Saadh Sangat, the Company of the Holy; she washes and massages their feet. |1|

Now, I have come and entered the Lord's Sanctuary.
This awful fire has burned so many; the True Guru has cautioned me about it. |1|Pause|

It clings to the necks of the Siddhas, and the seekers, the demi-gods, angels and mortals.
Servant Nanak has the support of God the Creator, who has millions of slaves like her. |2|12|21|

Goojaree, Fifth Mehl:
His bad reputation is erased, he is acclaimed all over the world, and he obtains a seat in the Court of the Lord.
The fear of death is removed in an instant, and he goes to the Lord's House in peace and bliss. |1|

His works do not go in vain.
Twenty-four hours a day, remember your God in meditation; meditate on Him continually in your mind and body. |1|Pause|

I seek Your Sanctuary, O Destroyer of the pains of the poor; whatever You give me, God, that is what I receive.
Nanak is imbued with the love of Your lotus feet; O Lord, please preserve the honor of Your slave. |2|13|22|

Goojaree, Fifth Mehl:

The all-sustaining Lord is the Giver of all beings; His devotional worship is an overflowing treasure.
Service to Him is not wasted; in an instant, He emancipates. |1|

O my mind, immerse yourself in the Lord's lotus feet.
Seek from Him, who is worshipped by all beings. |1|Pause|

Nanak has entered Your Sanctuary, O Creator Lord; You, O God, are the support of my breath of life.
He who is protected by You, O Helper Lord - what can the world do to him? |2|14|23|

Goojaree, Fifth Mehl:
The Lord Himself has protected the honor of His humble servant.
The Guru has given the medicine of the Lord's Name, Har, Har, and all afflictions are gone. |1|Pause|

The Transcendent Lord, in His Mercy, has preserved Har Gobind.
The disease is over, and there is joy all around; we ever contemplate the Glories of God. |1|

My Creator Lord has made me His own; such is the glorious greatness of the Perfect Guru.
Guru Nanak laid the immovable foundation, which grows higher and higher each day. |2|15|24|

Goojaree, Fifth Mehl:
You never focused your consciousness on the Lord.

Section 09 - Raag Goojaree - Part 013

You have spent your life engaged in worldly pursuits; you have not sung the Glorious Praises of the treasure of the Naam. |1|Pause|

Shell by shell, you accumulate money; in various ways, you work for this.
Forgetting God, you suffer awful pain beyond measure, and you are consumed by the Great Enticer, Maya. |1|

Show Mercy to me, O my Lord and Master, and do not hold me to account for my actions.

O merciful and compassionate Lord God, ocean of peace, Nanak has taken to Your Sanctuary, Lord. |2|16|25|

Goojaree, Fifth Mehl:
With your tongue, chant the Lord's Name, Raam, Raam.
Renounce other false occupations, and vibrate forever on the Lord God. |1|Pause|

The One Name is the support of His devotees; in this world, and in the world hereafter, it is their anchor and support.
In His mercy and kindness, the Guru has given me the divine wisdom of God, and a discriminating intellect. |1|

The all-powerful Lord is the Creator, the Cause of causes; He is the Master of wealth - I seek His Sanctuary.
Liberation and worldly success come from the dust of the feet of the Holy Saints; Nanak has obtained the Lord's treasure. |2|17|26|

Goojaree, Fifth Mehl, Fourth House, Chau-Padas:
One Universal Creator God. By The Grace Of The True Guru:
Give up all your clever tricks, and seek the Sanctuary of the Holy Saint.
Sing the Glorious Praises of the Supreme Lord God, the Transcendent Lord. |1|

O my consciousness, contemplate and adore the Lotus Feet of the Lord.
You shall obtain total peace and salvation, and all troubles shall depart. |1|Pause|

Mother, father, children, friends and siblings - without the Lord, none of them are real.
Here and hereafter, He is the companion of the soul; He is pervading everywhere. |2|

Millions of plans, tricks, and efforts are of no use, and serve no purpose.
In the Sanctuary of the Holy, one becomes immaculate and pure, and obtains salvation, through the Name of God. |3|

God is profound and merciful, lofty and exalted; He gives Sanctuary to the Holy.

He alone obtains the Lord, O Nanak, who is blessed with such pre-ordained destiny to meet Him. |4|1|27|

Goojaree, Fifth Mehl:
Serve your Guru forever, and chant the Glorious Praises of the Lord of the Universe.
With each and every breath, worship the Lord, Har, Har, in adoration, and the anxiety of your mind will be dispelled. |1|

O my mind, chant the Name of God.
You shall be blessed with peace, poise and pleasure, and you shall find the immaculate place. |1|Pause|

In the Saadh Sangat, the Company of the Holy, redeem your mind, and adore the Lord, twenty-four hours a day.
Sexual desire, anger and egotism will be dispelled, and all troubles shall end. |2|

The Lord Master is immovable, immortal and inscrutable; seek His Sanctuary.
Worship in adoration the lotus feet of the Lord in your heart, and center your consciousness lovingly on Him alone. |3|

The Supreme Lord God has shown mercy to me, and He Himself has forgiven me.
The Lord has given me His Name, the treasure of peace; O Nanak, meditate on that God. |4|2|28|

Goojaree, Fifth Mehl:
By Guru's Grace, I meditate on God, and my doubts are gone.

Section 09 - Raag Goojaree - Part 014

Pain, ignorance and fear have left me, and my sins have been dispelled. |1|

My mind is filled with love for the Name of the Lord, Har, Har.
Meeting the Holy Saint, under His Instruction, I meditate on the Lord of the Universe, in the most immaculate way. |1|Pause|

Chanting, deep meditation and various rituals are contained in the fruitful meditative remembrance of the Naam, the Name of the Lord.
Showing His Mercy, the Lord Himself has protected me, and all my works have been brought to fruition. |2|

With each and every breath, may I never forget You, O God, Almighty Lord and Master.
How can my tongue describe Your countless virtues? They are uncountable, and forever indescribable. |3|

You are the Remover of the pains of the poor, the Savior, the Compassionate Lord, the Bestower of Mercy.
Remembering the Naam in meditation, the state of eternal dignity is obtained; Nanak has grasped the protection of the Lord, Har, Har. |4|3|29|

Goojaree, Fifth Mehl:
Intellectual egotism and great love for Maya are the most serious chronic diseases.
The Lord's Name is the medicine, which is potent to cure everything. The Guru has given me the Naam, the Name of the Lord. |1|

My mind and body yearn for the dust of the Lord's humble servants.
With it, the sins of millions of incarnations are obliterated. O Lord of the Universe, please fulfill my desire. |1|Pause|

In the beginning, in the middle, and in the end, one is hounded by dreadful desires.
Through the Guru's spiritual wisdom, we sing the Kirtan of the Praises of the Lord of the Universe, and the noose of death is cut away. |2|

Those who are cheated by sexual desire, anger, greed and emotional attachment suffer reincarnation forever.
By loving devotional worship to God, and meditative remembrance of the Lord of the World, one's wandering in reincarnation is ended. |3|

Friends, children, spouses and well-wishers are burnt by the three fevers.
Chanting the Name of the Lord, Raam, Raam, one's miseries are ended, as one meets the Saintly servants of the Lord. |4|

Wandering around in all directions, they cry out, "Nothing can save us!"
Nanak has entered the Sanctuary of the Lotus Feet of the Infinite Lord; he
holds fast to their Support. |5|4|30|

Goojaree, Fifth Mehl, Fourth House, Du-Padas:
One Universal Creator God. By The Grace Of The True Guru:
Worship and adore the Lord of wealth, the fulfilling vision, the Almighty
Cause of causes.
Uttering His Praises, and hearing of His infinite glory, you shall never suffer
separation from Him again. |1|

O my mind, worship the Lord's Lotus Feet.
Meditating in remembrance, strife and sorrow are ended, and the noose of
the Messenger of Death is snapped. |1|Pause|

Chant the Name of the Lord, and your enemies shall be consumed; there is
no other way.
Show Mercy, O my God, and bestow upon Nanak the taste of the Naam,
the Name of the Lord. |2|1|31|

Goojaree, Fifth Mehl:
You are the Almighty Lord, the Giver of Sanctuary, the Destroyer of pain,
the King of happiness.
Troubles depart, and fear and doubt are dispelled, singing the Glorious
Praises of the Immaculate Lord God. |1|

O Lord of the Universe, without You, there is no other place.
Show Mercy to me, O Supreme Lord Master, that I may chant Your Name.
|Pause|

Serving the True Guru, I am attached to the Lord's Lotus Feet; by great
good fortune, I have embraced love for Him.

Section 09 - Raag Goojaree - Part 015

My heart lotus blossoms forth in the Saadh Sangat, the Company of the
Holy; I have renounced evil-mindedness and intellectualism. |2|

One who sings the Glorious Praises of the Lord, twenty-four hours a day,
and remembers the Lord in meditation, who is Kind to the poor,

saves himself, and redeems all his generations; all of his bonds are released. |3|

I take the Support of Your Feet, O God, O Lord and Master; you are with me through and through, God.
Nanak has entered Your Sanctuary, God; giving him His hand, the Lord has protected him. |4|2|32|

Goojaree, Ashtapadees, First Mehl, First House:
One Universal Creator God. By The Grace Of The True Guru:
In the one village of the body, live the five thieves; they have been warned, but they still go out stealing.
One who keeps his assets safe from the three modes and the ten passions, O Nanak, attains liberation and emancipation. |1|

Center your mind on the all-pervading Lord, the Wearer of garlands of the jungles.
Let your rosary be the chanting of the Lord's Name in your heart. |1|Pause|

Its roots extend upwards, and its branches reach down; the four Vedas are attached to it.
He alone reaches this tree with ease, O Nanak, who remains wakeful in the Love of the Supreme Lord God. |2|

The Elysian Tree is the courtyard of my house; in it are the flowers, leaves and stems of reality.
Meditate on the self-existent, immaculate Lord, whose Light is pervading everywhere; renounce all your worldly entanglements. |3|

Listen, O seekers of Truth - Nanak begs you to renounce the traps of Maya.
Reflect within your mind, that by enshrining love for the One Lord, you shall not be subject to birth and death again. |4|

He alone is said to be a Guru, he alone is said to be a Sikh, and he alone is said to be a physician, who knows the patient's illness.
He is not affected by actions, responsibilities and entanglements; in the entanglements of his household, he maintains the detachment of Yoga. |5|

He renounces sexual desire, anger, egotism, greed, attachment and Maya. Within his mind, he meditates on the reality of the Imperishable Lord; by Guru's Grace he finds Him. |6|

Spiritual wisdom and meditation are all said to be God's gifts; all of the demons are turned white before him.
He enjoys the taste of the honey of God's lotus; he remains awake, and does not fall asleep. |7|

This lotus is very deep; its leaves are the nether regions, and it is connected to the whole universe.
Under Guru's Instruction, I shall not have to enter the womb again; I have renounced the poison of corruption, and I drink in the Ambrosial Nectar. |8|1|

Goojaree, First Mehl:
Those who beg of God the Great Giver - their numbers cannot be counted.
You, Almighty True Lord, fulfill the desires within their hearts. |1|

O Dear Lord, chanting, deep meditation, self-discipline and truth are my foundations.
Bless me with Your Name, Lord, that I may find peace. Your devotional worship is a treasure over-flowing. |1|Pause|

Some remain absorbed in Samaadhi, their minds fixed lovingly on the One Lord; they reflect only on the Word of the Shabad.
In that state, there is no water, land, earth or sky; only the Creator Lord Himself exists. |2|

There is no intoxication of Maya there, and no shadow, nor the infinite light of the sun or the moon.
The eyes within the mind which see everything - with one glance, they see the three worlds. |3|

Section 09 - Raag Goojaree - Part 016

He created air, water and fire, Brahma, Vishnu and Shiva - the whole creation.
All are beggars; You alone are the Great Giver, God. You give Your gifts according to Your own considerations. |4|

Three hundred thirty million gods beg of God the Master; even as He gives, His treasures are never exhausted.

Nothing can be contained in a vessel turned upside-down; Ambrosial Nectar pours into the upright one. |5|

The Siddhas in Samaadhi beg for wealth and miracles, and proclaim His victory.

As is the thirst within their minds, so is the water which You give to them. |6|

The most fortunate ones serve their Guru; there is no difference between the Divine Guru and the Lord.

The Messenger of Death cannot see those who come to realize within their minds the contemplative meditation of the Word of the Shabad. |7|

I shall never ask anything else of the Lord; please, bless me with the Love of Your Immaculate Name.

Nanak, the song-bird, begs for the Ambrosial Water; O Lord, shower Your Mercy upon him, and bless him with Your Praise. |8|2|

Goojaree, First Mehl:

O Dear One, he is born, and then dies; he continues coming and going; without the Guru, he is not emancipated.

Those mortals who become Gurmukhs are attuned to the Naam, the Name of the Lord; through the Name, they obtain salvation and honor. |1|

O Siblings of Destiny, focus your consciousness lovingly on the Lord's Name.

By Guru's Grace, one begs of the Lord God; such is the glorious greatness of the Naam. |1|Pause|

O Dear One, so many wear various religious robes, for begging and filling their bellies.

Without devotional worship to the Lord, O mortal, there can be no peace. Without the Guru, pride does not depart. |2|

O Dear One, death hangs constantly over his head. Incarnation after incarnation, it is his enemy.

Those who are attuned to the True Word of the Shabad are saved. The True Guru has imparted this understanding. |3|

In the Guru's Sanctuary, the Messenger of Death cannot see the mortal, or torture him.
I am imbued with the Imperishable and Immaculate Lord Master, and lovingly attached to the Fearless Lord. |4|

O Dear One, implant the Naam within me; lovingly attached to the Naam, I lean on the True Guru's Support.
Whatever pleases Him, He does; no one can erase His actions. |5|

O Dear One, I have hurried to the Sanctuary of the Guru; I have no love for any other except You.
I constantly call upon the One Lord; since the very beginning, and through-out the ages, He has been my help and support. |6|

O Dear One, please preserve the Honor of Your Name; I am hand and glove with You.
Bless me with Your Mercy, and reveal to me the Blessed Vision of Your Darshan, O Guru. Through the Word of the Shabad, I have burnt away my ego. |7|

O Dear One, what should I ask of You? Nothing appears permanent; whoever comes into this world shall depart.
Bless Nanak with the wealth of the Naam, to adorn his heart and neck. |8|3|

Goojaree, First Mehl:
O Dear One, I am not high or low or in the middle. I am the Lord's slave, and I seek the Lord's Sanctuary.
Imbued with the Naam, the Name of the Lord, I am detached from the world; I have forgotten sorrow, separation and disease. |1|

O Siblings of Destiny, by Guru's Grace, I perform devotional worship to my Lord and Master.

Section 09 - Raag Goojaree - Part 017

One whose heart is filled with the Hymns of the True Guru, obtains the Pure Lord. He is not under the power of the Messenger of Death, nor does he owe Death anything. |1|Pause|

He chants the Glorious Praises of the Lord with his tongue, and abides with God; he does whatever pleases the Lord.
Without the Lord's Name, life passes in vain in the world, and every moment is useless. |2|

The false have no place of rest, either inside or outside; the slanderer does not find salvation.
Even if one is resentful, God does not withhold His blessings; day by day, they increase. |3|

No one can take away the Guru's gifts; my Lord and Master Himself has given them.
The black-faced slanderers, with slander in their mouths, do not appreciate the Guru's gifts. |4|

God forgives and blends with Himself those who take to His Sanctuary; He does not delay for an instant.
He is the source of bliss, the Greatest Lord; through the True Guru, we are united in His Union. |5|

Through His Kindness, the Kind Lord pervades us; through Guru's Teachings, our wanderings cease.
Touching the philosopher's stone, metal is transformed into gold. Such is the glorious greatness of the Society of the Saints. |6|

The Lord is the immaculate water; the mind is the bather, and the True Guru is the bath attendant, O Siblings of Destiny.
That humble being who joins the Sat Sangat shall not be consigned to reincarnation again; his light merges into the Light. |7|

You are the Great Primal Lord, the infinite tree of life; I am a bird perched on Your branches.
Grant to Nanak the Immaculate Naam; throughout the ages, he sings the Praises of the Shabad. |8|4|

Goojaree, First Mehl, Fourth House:

One Universal Creator God. By The Grace Of The True Guru:
The devotees worship the Lord in loving adoration. They thirst for the True Lord, with infinite affection.
They tearfully beg and implore the Lord; in love and affection, their consciousness is at peace. |1|

Chant the Naam, the Name of the Lord, O my mind, and take to His Sanctuary.
The Lord's Name is the boat to cross over the world-ocean. Practice such a way of life. |1|Pause|

O mind, even death wishes you well, when you remember the Lord through the Word of the Guru's Shabad.
The intellect receives the treasure, the knowledge of reality and supreme bliss, by repeating the Lord's Name in the mind. |2|

The fickle consciousness wanders around chasing after wealth; it is intoxicated with worldly love and emotional attachment.
Devotion to the Naam is permanently implanted within the mind, when it is attuned to the Guru's Teachings and His Shabad. |3|

Wandering around, doubt is not dispelled; afflicted by reincarnation, the world is being ruined.
The Lord's eternal throne is free of this affliction; he is truly wise, who takes the Naam as his deep meditation. |4|

This world is engrossed in attachment and transitory love; it suffers the terrible pains of birth and death.
Run to the Sanctuary of the True Guru, chant the Lord's Name in your heart, and you shall swim across. |5|

Following the Guru's Teaching, the mind becomes stable; the mind accepts it, and reflects upon it in peaceful poise.
That mind is pure, which enshrines Truth within, and the most excellent jewel of spiritual wisdom. |6|

By the Fear of God, and Love of God, and by devotion, man crosses over the terrifying world-ocean, focusing his consciousness on the Lord's Lotus Feet.

Section 09 - Raag Goojaree - Part 018

The Name of the Lord, the most pure and sacred, is within my heart; this body is Your Sanctuary, Lord. |7|

The waves of greed and avarice are subdued, by treasuring the Lord's Name in the mind.
Subdue my mind, O Pure Immaculate Lord; says Nanak, I have entered Your Sanctuary. |8|1|5|

Goojaree, Third Mehl, First House:
One Universal Creator God. By The Grace Of The True Guru:
I dance, and make this mind dance as well.
By Guru's Grace, I eliminate my self-conceit.
One who keeps his consciousness focused on the Lord is liberated; he obtains the fruits of his desires. |1|

So dance, O mind, before your Guru.
If you dance according to the Guru's Will, you shall obtain peace, and in the end, the fear of death shall leave you. |Pause|

One whom the Lord Himself causes to dance, is called a devotee. He Himself links us to His Love.
He Himself sings, He Himself listens, and He puts this blind mind on the right path. |2|

One who dances night and day, and banishes Shakti's Maya, enters the House of the Lord Shiva, where there is no sleep.
The world is asleep in Maya, the house of Shakti; it dances, jumps and sings in duality. The self-willed manmukh has no devotion. |3|

The angels, mortals, renunciates, ritualists, silent sages and beings of spiritual wisdom dance.
The Siddhas and seekers, lovingly focused on the Lord, dance, as do the Gurmukhs, whose minds dwell in reflective meditation. |4|

The planets and solar systems dance in the three qualities, as do those who bear love for You, Lord.
The beings and creatures all dance, and the four sources of creation dance. |5|

They alone dance, who are pleasing to You, and who, as Gurmukhs, embrace love for the Word of the Shabad.
They are devotees, with the essence of spiritual wisdom, who obey the Hukam of His Command. |6|

This is devotional worship, that one loves the True Lord; without service, one cannot be a devotee.
If one remains dead while yet alive, he reflects upon the Shabad, and then, he obtains the True Lord. |7|

So many people dance for the sake of Maya; how rare are those who contemplate reality.
By Guru's Grace, that humble being obtains You, Lord, upon whom You show Mercy. |8|

If I forget the True Lord, even for an instant, that time passes in vain.
With each and every breath, constantly remember the Lord; He Himself shall forgive you, according to His Will. |9|

They alone dance, who are pleasing to Your Will, and who, as Gurmukhs, contemplate the Word of the Shabad.
Says Nanak, they alone find celestial peace, whom You bless with Your Grace. |10|1|6|

Goojaree, Fourth Mehl, Second House:
One Universal Creator God. By The Grace Of The True Guru:
Without the Lord, my soul cannot survive, like an infant without milk.
The inaccessible and incomprehensible Lord God is obtained by the Gurmukh; I am a sacrifice to my True Guru. |1|

O my mind, the Kirtan of the Lord's Praise is a boat to carry you across.
The Gurmukhs obtain the Ambrosial Water of the Naam, the Name of the Lord. You bless them with Your Grace. |Pause|

Section 09 - Raag Goojaree - Part 019

Sanak, Sanandan and Naarad the sage serve You; night and day, they continue to chant Your Name, O Lord of the jungle.
Slave Prahlaad sought Your Sanctuary, and You saved his honor. |2|

The One unseen immaculate Lord is pervading everywhere, as is the Light of the Lord.

All are beggars, You alone are the Great Giver. Reaching out our hands, we beg from You. |3|

The speech of the humble devotees is sublime; they sing continually the wondrous, Unspoken Speech of the Lord.

Their lives become fruitful; they save themselves, and all their generations. |4|

The self-willed manmukhs are engrossed in duality and evil-mindedness; within them is the darkness of attachment.

They do not love the sermon of the humble Saints, and they are drowned along with their families. |5|

By slandering, the slanderer washes the filth off others; he is an eater of filth, and a worshipper of Maya.

He indulges in the slander of the humble Saints; he is neither on this shore, nor the shore beyond. |6|

All this worldly drama is set in motion by the Creator Lord; He has infused His almighty strength into all.

The thread of the One Lord runs through the world; when He pulls out this thread, the One Creator alone remains. |7|

With their tongues, they sing the Glorious Praises of the Lord, and savor Them. They place the sublime essence of the Lord upon their tongues, and savor it.

O Nanak, other than the Lord, I ask for nothing else; I am in love with the Love of the Lord's sublime essence. |8|1|7|

Goojaree, Fifth Mehl, Second House:
One Universal Creator God. By The Grace Of The True Guru:
Among kings, You are called the King. Among land-lords, You are the Land-lord.

Among masters, You are the Master. Among tribes, Yours is the Supreme Tribe. |1|

My Father is wealthy, deep and profound.

What praises should I chant, O Creator Lord? Beholding You, I am wonder-struck. |1|Pause|

Among the peaceful, You are called the Peaceful One. Among givers, You are the Greatest Giver.
Among the glorious, You are said to be the Most Glorious. Among revellers, You are the Reveller. |2|

Among warriors, You are called the Warrior. Among indulgers, You are the Indulger.
Among householders, You are the Great Householder. Among yogis, You are the Yogi. |3|

Among creators, You are called the Creator. Among the cultured, You are the Cultured One.
Among bankers, You are the True Banker. Among merchants, You are the Merchant. |4|

Among courts, Yours is the Court. Yours is the Most Sublime of Sanctuaries. The extent of Your wealth cannot be determined. Your Coins cannot be counted. |5|

Among names, Your Name, God, is the most respected. Among the wise, You are the Wisest.
Among ways, Yours, God, is the Best Way. Among purifying baths, Yours is the Most Purifying. |6|

Among spiritual powers, Yours, O God, are the Spiritual Powers. Among actions, Yours are the Greatest Actions.
Among wills, Your Will, God, is the Supreme Will. Of commands, Yours is the Supreme Command. |7|

Section 09 - Raag Goojaree - Part 020

As You cause me to speak, so do I speak, O Lord Master. What other power do I have?
In the Saadh Sangat, the Company of the Holy, O Nanak, sing His Praises; they are so very dear to God. |8|1|8|

Goojaree, Fifth Mehl, Fourth House:

One Universal Creator God. By The Grace Of The True Guru:
O Lord, Man-lion Incarnate, Companion to the poor, Divine Purifier of sinners;
O Destroyer of fear and dread, Merciful Lord Master, Treasure of Excellence, fruitful is Your service. |1|

O Lord, Cherisher of the World, Guru-Lord of the Universe.
I seek the Sanctuary of Your Feet, O Merciful Lord. Carry me across the terrifying world-ocean. |1|Pause|

O Dispeller of sexual desire and anger, Eliminator of intoxication and attachment, Destroyer of ego, Honey of the mind;

set me free from birth and death, O Sustainer of the earth, and preserve my honor, O Embodiment of supreme bliss. |2|

The many waves of desire for Maya are burnt away, when the Guru's spiritual wisdom is enshrined in the heart, through the Guru's Mantra.
Destroy my egotism, O Merciful Lord; dispel my anxiety, O Infinite Primal Lord. |3|

Remember in meditation the Almighty Lord, every moment and every instant; meditate on God in the celestial peace of Samaadhi.
O Merciful to the meek, perfectly blissful Lord, I beg for the dust of the feet of the Holy. |4|

Emotional attachment is false, desire is filthy, and longing is corrupt.
Please, preserve my faith, dispel these doubts from my mind, and save me, O Formless Lord. |5|

They have become wealthy, loaded with the treasures of the Lord's riches; they were lacking even clothes.
The idiotic, foolish and senseless people have become virtuous and patient, receiving the Gracious Glance of the Lord of wealth. |6|

Become Jivan-Mukta, liberated while yet alive, by meditating on the Lord of the Universe, O mind, and maintaining faith in Him in your heart.
Show kindness and mercy to all beings, and realize that the Lord is pervading everywhere; this is the way of life of the enlightened soul, the supreme swan. |7|

He grants the Blessed Vision of His Darshan to those who listen to His Praises, and who, with their tongues, chant His Name.

They are part and parcel, life and limb with the Lord God; O Nanak, they feel the Touch of God, the Savior of sinners. |8|1|2|5|1|1|2|57|

Goojaree Ki Vaar, Third Mehl, Sung In The Tune Of The Vaar Of Sikandar & Biraahim:

One Universal Creator God. By The Grace Of The True Guru:

Shalok, Third Mehl:

This world perishing in attachment and possessiveness; no one knows the way of life.

One who walks in harmony with the Guru's Will, obtains the supreme status of life.

Those humble beings who focus their consciousness on the Lord's Feet, live forever and ever.

O Nanak, by His Grace, the Lord abides in the minds of the Gurmukhs, who merge in celestial bliss. |1|

Third Mehl:

Within the self is the pain of doubt; engrossed in worldly affairs, they are killing themselves.

Asleep in the love of duality, they never wake up; they are in love with, and attached to Maya.

They do not think of the Naam, the Name of the Lord, and they do not contemplate the Word of the Shabad. This is the conduct of the self-willed manmukhs.

Section 09 - Raag Goojaree - Part 021

They do not obtain the Lord's Name, and they waste away their lives in vain; O Nanak, the Messenger of Death punishes and dishonors them. |2|

Pauree:

He created Himself - at that time, there was no other.

He consulted Himself for advice, and what He did came to pass.

At that time, there were no Akaashic Ethers, no nether regions, nor the three worlds.

At that time, only the Formless Lord Himself existed - there was no creation.

As it pleased Him, so did He act; without Him, there was no other. |1|

Shalok, Third Mehl:
My Master is eternal. He is seen by practicing the Word of the Shabad.
He never perishes; He does not come or go in reincarnation.
So serve Him, forever and ever; He is contained in all.
Why serve another who is born, and then dies?
Fruitless is the life of those who do not know their Lord and Master, and who center their consciousness on others.
O Nanak, it cannot be known, how much punishment the Creator shall inflict on them. |1|

Third Mehl:
Meditate on the True Name; the True Lord is pervading everywhere.
O Nanak, by understanding the Hukam of the Lord's Command, one becomes acceptable, and then obtains the fruit of Truth.
He wanders around babbling and speaking, but he does not understand the Lord's Command at all. He is blind, the falsest of the false. |2|

Pauree:
Creating union and separation, He laid the foundations of the Universe.
By His Command, the Lord of Light fashioned the Universe, and infused His Divine Light into it.
From the Lord of Light, all light originates. The True Guru proclaims the Word of the Shabad.
Brahma, Vishnu and Shiva, under the influence of the three dispositions, were put to their tasks.
He created the root of Maya, and the peace obtained in the fourth state of consciousness. |2|

Shalok, Third Mehl:
That alone is chanting, and that alone is deep meditation, which is pleasing to the True Guru.
Pleasing the True Guru, glorious greatness is obtained.
O Nanak, renouncing self-conceit, one merges into the Guru. |1|

Third Mehl:
How rare are those who receive the Guru's Teachings.
O Nanak, he alone receives it, whom the Lord Himself blesses with glorious greatness. |2|

Pauree:
Emotional attachment to Maya is spiritual darkness; it is very difficult and such a heavy load.
Loaded with so very many stones of sin, how can the boat cross over?
Those who are attuned to the Lord's devotional worship night and day are carried across.
Under the Instruction of the Guru's Shabad, one sheds egotism and corruption, and the mind becomes immaculate.
Meditate on the Name of the Lord, Har, Har; the Lord, Har, Har, is our Saving Grace. |3|

Shalok:
O Kabeer, the gate of liberation is narrow, less than one-tenth of a mustard seed.
The mind has become as big as an elephant; how can it pass through this gate?
If one meets such a True Guru, by His Pleasure, He shows His Mercy.
Then, the gate of liberation becomes wide open, and the soul easily passes through. |1|

Third Mehl:
O Nanak, the gate of liberation is very narrow; only the very tiny can pass through.
Through egotism, the mind has become bloated. How can it pass through?
Meeting the True Guru, egotism departs, and one is filled with the Divine Light.

Section 09 - Raag Goojaree - Part 022

Then, this soul is liberated forever, and it remains absorbed in celestial bliss. |2|

Pauree:
God created the Universe, and He keeps it under His power.
God cannot be obtained by counting; the mortal wanders in doubt.
Meeting the True Guru, one remains dead while yet alive; understanding Him, he is absorbed in the Truth.
Through the Word of the Shabad, egotism is eradicated, and one is united in the Lord's Union.

He knows everything, and Himself does everything; beholding His Creation, He rejoices. |4|

Shalok, Third Mehl:
One who has not focused his consciousness on the True Guru, and into whose mind the Naam does not come

- cursed is such a life. What has he gained by coming into the world?
Maya is false capital; in an instant, its false covering falls off.
When it slips from his hand, his body turns black, and his face withers away.
Those who focus their consciousness on the True Guru - peace comes to abide in their minds.
They meditate on the Name of the Lord with love; they are lovingly attuned to the Name of the Lord.
O Nanak, the True Guru has bestowed upon them the wealth, which remains contained within their hearts.
They are imbued with supreme love; its color increases day by day. |1|

Third Mehl:
Maya is a serpent, clinging to the world.
Whoever serves her, she ultimately devours.
The Gurmukh is a snake-charmer; he has trampled her and thrown her down, and crushed her underfoot.
O Nanak, they alone are saved, who remain lovingly absorbed in the True Lord. |2|

Pauree:
The minstrel cries out, and God hears him.
He is comforted within his mind, and he obtains the Perfect Lord.
Whatever destiny is pre-ordained by the Lord, those are the deeds he does.
When the Lord and Master becomes Merciful, then one obtains the Mansion of the Lord's Presence as his home.
That God of mine is so very great; as Gurmukh, I have met Him. |5|

Shalok, Third Mehl:
There is One Lord God of all; He remains ever-present.
O Nanak, if one does not obey the Hukam of the Lord's Command, then within one's own home, the Lord seems far away.

They alone obey the Lord's Command, upon whom He casts His Glance of Grace.

Obeying His Command, one obtains peace, and becomes the happy, loving soul-bride. |1|

Third Mehl:
She who does not love her Husband Lord, burns and wastes away all through the night of her life.

O Nanak, the soul-brides dwell in peace; they have the Lord, their King, as their Husband. |2|

Pauree:
Roaming over the entire world, I have seen that the Lord is the only Giver.

The Lord cannot be obtained by any device at all; He is the Architect of Karma.

Through the Word of the Guru's Shabad, the Lord comes to dwell in the mind, and the Lord is easily revealed within.

The fire of desire within is quenched, and one bathes in the Lord's Pool of Ambrosial Nectar.

The great greatness of the great Lord God - the Gurmukh speaks of this. |6|

Shalok, Third Mehl:
What love is this between the body and soul, which ends when the body falls?

Why feed it by telling lies? When you leave, it does not go with you.

Section 09 - Raag Goojaree - Part 023

The body is merely blind dust; go, and ask the soul.

The soul answers, "I am enticed by Maya, and so I come and go, again and again."

O Nanak, I do not know my Lord and Master's Command, by which I would merge in the Truth. |1|

Third Mehl:
The Naam, the Name of the Lord, is the only permanent wealth; all other wealth comes and goes.

Thieves cannot steal this wealth, nor can robbers take it away.

This wealth of the Lord is embedded in the soul, and with the soul, it shall depart.

It is obtained from the Perfect Guru; the self-willed manmukhs do not receive it.

Blessed are the traders, O Nanak, who have come to earn the wealth of the Naam. |2|

Pauree:

My Master is so very great, true, profound and unfathomable.

The whole world is under His power; everything is the projection of Him.

By Guru's Grace, the eternal wealth is obtained, bringing peace and patience to the mind.

By His Grace, the Lord dwells in the mind, and one meets the Brave Guru.

The virtuous praise the ever-stable, permanent, perfect Lord. |7|

Shalok, Third Mehl:

Cursed is the life of those who forsake and throw away the peace of the Lord's Name, and suffer pain instead by practicing ego and sin.

The ignorant self-willed manmukhs are engrossed in the love of Maya; they have no understanding at all.

In this world and in the world beyond, they do not find peace; in the end, they depart regretting and repenting.

By Guru's Grace, one may meditate on the Naam, the Name of the Lord, and egotism departs from within him.

O Nanak, one who has such pre-ordained destiny, comes and falls at the Guru's Feet. |1|

Third Mehl:

The self-willed manmukh is like the inverted lotus; he has neither devotional worship, nor the Lord's Name.

He remains engrossed in material wealth, and his efforts are false.

His consciousness is not softened within, and the words from his mouth are insipid.

He does not mingle with the righteous; within him are falsehood and selfishness.

O Nanak, the Creator Lord has arranged things, so that the self-willed manmukhs are drowned by telling lies, while the Gurmukhs are saved by chanting the Lord's Name. |2|

Pauree:

Without understanding, one must wander around the cycle of reincarnation, and continue coming and going.

One who has not served the True Guru, shall depart regretting and repenting in the end.

But if the Lord shows His Mercy, one finds the Guru, and ego is banished from within.

Hunger and thirst depart from within, and peace comes to dwell in the mind.

Forever and ever, praise Him with love in your heart. |8|

Shalok, Third Mehl:
One who serves his True Guru, is worshipped by everyone.

Of all efforts, the supreme effort is the attainment of the Lord's Name.

Peace and tranquility come to dwell within the mind; meditating within the heart, there comes a lasting peace.

The Ambrosial Amrit is his food, and the Ambrosial Amrit is his clothes; O Nanak, through the Naam, the Name of the Lord, greatness is obtained. |1|

Third Mehl:
O mind, listen to the Guru's Teachings, and you shall obtain the treasure of virtue.

Section 09 - Raag Goojaree - Part 024

The Lord, the Giver of peace, shall dwell in your mind, and your egotism and pride shall depart.

O Nanak, when the Lord bestows His Glance of Grace, then, night and day, one centers his meditation on the Lord. |2|

Pauree:
The Gurmukh is totally truthful, content and pure.

Deception and wickedness have departed from within him, and he easily conquers his mind.

There, the Divine Light and the essence of bliss are manifest, and ignorance is eliminated.

Night and day, he sings the Glorious Praises of the Lord, and manifests the excellence of the Lord.

The One Lord is the Giver of all; the Lord alone is our friend. |9|

Shalok, Third Mehl:

One who understands God, who lovingly centers his mind on the Lord night and day, is called a Brahmin.

Consulting the True Guru, he practices Truth and self-restraint, and he is rid of the disease of ego.

He sings the Glorious Praises of the Lord, and gathers in His Praises; his light is blended with the Light.

In this world, one who knows God is very rare; eradicating ego, he is absorbed in God.

O Nanak, meeting him, peace is obtained; night and day, he meditates on the Lord's Name. |1|

Third Mehl:
Within the ignorant self-willed manmukh is deception; with his tongue, he speaks lies.

Practicing deception, he does not please the Lord God, who always sees and hears with natural ease.

In the love of duality, he goes to instruct the world, but he is engrossed in the poison of Maya and attachment to pleasure.

By doing so, he suffers in constant pain; he is born and then dies, and comes and goes again and again.

His doubts do not leave him at all, and he rots away in manure.

One, unto whom my Lord Master shows His Mercy, listens to the Guru's Teachings.

He meditates on the Lord's Name, and sings the Lord's Name; in the end, the Lord's Name will deliver him. |2|

Pauree:
Those who obey the Hukam of the Lord's Command, are the perfect persons in the world.

They serve their Lord Master, and reflect upon the Perfect Word of the Shabad.

They serve the Lord, and love the True Word of the Shabad.

They attain the Mansion of the Lord's Presence, as they eradicate egotism from within.

O Nanak, the Gurmukhs remain united with Him, chanting the Name of the Lord, and enshrining it within their hearts. |10|

Shalok, Third Mehl:
The Gurmukh meditates on the Lord; the celestial sound-current resounds within him, and he focuses his consciousness on the True Name.

The Gurmukh remains imbued with the Lord's Love, night and day; his mind is pleased with the Name of the Lord.

The Gurmukh beholds the Lord, the Gurmukh speaks of the Lord, and the Gurmukh naturally loves the Lord.

O Nanak, the Gurmukh attains spiritual wisdom, and the pitch-black darkness of ignorance is dispelled.

One who is blessed by the Perfect Lord's Grace - as Gurmukh, he meditates on the Lord's Name. |1|

Third Mehl:
Those who do not serve the True Guru do not embrace love for the Word of the Shabad.

They do not meditate on the Celestial Naam, the Name of the Lord - why did they even bother to come into the world?

Time and time again, they are reincarnated, and they rot away forever in manure.

They are attached to false greed; they are not on this shore, nor on the one beyond.

Section 09 - Raag Goojaree - Part 025

O Nanak, the Gurmukhs are saved; the Creator Lord unites them with Himself. |2|

Pauree:
The devotees look beauteous in the True Court of the Lord; they abide in the True Word of the Shabad.

The Lord's Love wells up in them; they are attracted by the Lord's Love.

They abide in the Lord's Love, they remain imbued with the Lord's Love forever, and with their tongues, they drink in the sublime essence of the Lord.

Fruitful are the lives of those Gurmukhs who recognize the Lord and enshrine Him in their hearts.

Without the Guru, they wander around crying out in misery; in the love of duality, they are ruined. |11|

Shalok, Third Mehl:
In the Dark Age of Kali Yuga, the devotees earn the treasure of the Naam, the Name of the Lord; they obtain the supreme status of the Lord.

Serving the True Guru, they enshrine the Lord's Name in their minds, and they meditate on the Naam, night and day.

Within the home of their own selves, they remain unattached, through the Guru's Teachings; they burn away egotism and emotional attachment.

They save themselves, and they save the whole world. Blessed are the mothers who gave birth to them.

He alone finds such a True Guru, upon whose forehead the Lord inscribed such pre-ordained destiny.

Servant Nanak is a sacrifice to his Guru; when he was wandering in doubt, He placed him on the Path. |1|

Third Mehl:

Beholding Maya with her three dispositions, he goes astray; he is like the moth, which sees the flame, and is consumed.

The mistaken, deluded Pandits gaze upon Maya, and watch to see whether anyone has offered them something.

In the love of duality, they read continually about sin, while the Lord has withheld His Name from them.

The Yogis, the wandering hermits and the Sannyaasees have gone astray; their egotism and arrogance have increased greatly.

They do not accept the true donations of clothes and food, and their lives are ruined by their stubborn minds.

Among these, he alone is a man of poise, who, as Gurmukh, meditates on the Naam, the Name of the Lord.

Unto whom should servant Nanak speak and complain? All act as the Lord causes them to act. |2|

Pauree:

Emotional attachment to Maya, sexual desire, anger and egotism are demons.

Because of them, mortals are subject to death; above their heads hangs the heavy club of the Messenger of Death.

The self-willed manmukhs, in love with duality, are led onto the path of Death.

In the City of Death, they are tied up and beaten, and no one hears their cries.

One who is blessed by the Lord's Grace meets the Guru; as Gurmukh, he is emancipated. |12|

Shalok, Third Mehl:

By egotism and pride, the self-willed manmukhs are enticed, and consumed.

Those who center their consciousness on duality are caught in it, and remain stuck.

But when it is burnt away by the Word of the Guru's Shabad, only then does it depart from within.

The body and mind become radiant and bright, and the Naam, the Name of the Lord, comes to dwell within the mind.

O Nanak, the Lord's Name is the antidote to Maya; the Gurmukh obtains it. |1|

Third Mehl:

This mind has wandered through so many ages; it has not remained stable - it continues coming and going.

When it is pleasing to the Lord's Will, then He causes the soul to wander; He has set the world-drama in motion.

When the Lord forgives, then one meets the Guru, and becoming stable, he remains absorbed in the Lord.

Section 09 - Raag Goojaree - Part 026

O Nanak, through the mind, the mind is satisfied, and then, nothing comes or goes. |2|

Pauree:

The body is the fortress of the Infinite Lord; it is obtained only by destiny.

The Lord Himself dwells within the body; He Himself is the Enjoyer of pleasures.

He Himself remains detached and unaffected; while unattached, He is still attached.

He does whatever He pleases, and whatever He does, comes to pass.

The Gurmukh meditates on the Lord's Name, and separation from the Lord is ended. |13|

Shalok, Third Mehl:

Waaho! Waaho! The Lord Himself causes us to praise Him, through the True Word of the Guru's Shabad.

Waaho! Waaho! is His Eulogy and Praise; how rare are the Gurmukhs who understand this.

Waaho! Waaho! is the True Word of His Bani, by which we meet our True Lord.

O Nanak, chanting Waaho! Waaho! God is attained; by His Grace, He is obtained. |1|

Third Mehl:

Chanting Waaho! Waaho! the tongue is adorned with the Word of the Shabad.

Through the Perfect Shabad, one comes to meet God.

How very fortunate are those, who with their mouths, chant Waaho! Waaho!

How beautiful are those persons who chant Waaho! Waaho! ; people come to venerate them.

Waaho! Waaho! is obtained by His Grace; O Nanak, honor is obtained at the Gate of the True Lord. |2|

Pauree:

Within the fortress of body, are the hard and rigid doors of falsehood, deception and pride.

Deluded by doubt, the blind and ignorant self-willed manmukhs cannot see them.

They cannot be found by any efforts; wearing their religious robes, the wearers have grown weary of trying.

The doors are opened only by the Word of the Guru's Shabad, and then, one chants the Name of the Lord.

The Dear Lord is the Tree of Ambrosial Nectar; those who drink in this Nectar are satisfied. |14|

Shalok, Third Mehl:

Chanting Waaho! Waaho! the night of one's life passes in peace.

Chanting Waaho! Waaho! I am in eternal bliss, O my mother!

Chanting Waaho! Waaho!, I have fallen in love with the Lord.

Waaho! Waaho! Through the karma of good deeds, I chant it, and inspire others to chant it as well.

Chanting Waaho! Waaho!, one obtains honor.

O Nanak, Waaho! Waaho! is the Will of the True Lord. |1|

Third Mehl:

Waaho! Waaho! is the Bani of the True Word. Searching, the Gurmukhs have found it.

Waaho! Waaho! They chant the Word of the Shabad. Waaho! Waaho! They enshrine it in their hearts.

Chanting Waaho! Waaho! the Gurmukhs easily obtain the Lord, after searching.

O Nanak, very fortunate are those who reflect upon the Lord, Har, Har, within their hearts. |2|

Pauree:

O my utterly greedy mind, you are constantly engrossed in greed.

In your desire for the enticing Maya, you wander in the ten directions.

Your name and social status shall not go with you hereafter; the self-willed manmukh is consumed by pain.

Your tongue does not taste the sublime essence of the Lord; it utters only insipid words.

Those Gurmukhs who drink in the Ambrosial Nectar are satisfied. |15|

Shalok, Third Mehl:

Chant Waaho! Waaho! to the Lord, who is True, profound and unfathomable.

Chant Waaho! Waaho! to the Lord, who is the Giver of virtue, intelligence and patience.

Section 09 - Raag Goojaree - Part 027

Chant Waaho! Waaho! to the Lord, who is permeating and pervading in all.

Chant Waaho! Waaho! to the Lord, who is the Giver of sustenance to all.

O Nanak, Waaho! Waaho! - praise the One Lord, revealed by the True Guru. |1|

Third Mehl:

Waaho! Waaho! The Gurmukhs praise the Lord continually, while the self-willed manmukhs eat poison and die.

They have no love for the Lord's Praises, and they pass their lives in misery.

The Gurmukhs drink in the Ambrosial Nectar, and they center their consciousness on the Lord's Praises.

O Nanak, those who chant Waaho! Waaho! are immaculate and pure; they obtain the knowledge of the three worlds. |2|

Pauree:

By the Lord's Will, one meets the Guru, serves Him, and worships the Lord.

By the Lord's Will, the Lord comes to dwell in the mind, and one easily drinks in the sublime essence of the Lord.

By the Lord's Will, one finds peace, and continually earns the Lord's Profit.

He is seated on the Lord's throne, and he dwells continually in the home of his own being.

He alone surrenders to the Lord's Will, who meets the Guru. |16|

Shalok, Third Mehl:

Waaho! Waaho! Those humble beings ever praise the Lord, unto whom the Lord Himself grants understanding.

Chanting Waaho! Waaho!, the mind is purified, and egotism departs from within.

The Gurmukh who continually chants Waaho! Waaho! attains the fruits of his heart's desires.

Beauteous are those humble beings who chant Waaho! Waaho! O Lord, let me join them!

Within my heart, I chant Waaho! Waaho!, and with my mouth, Waaho! Waaho!

O Nanak, those who chant Waaho! Waaho! - unto them I dedicate my body and mind. |1|

Third Mehl:

Waaho! Waaho! is the True Lord Master; His Name is Ambrosial Nectar.

Those who serve the Lord are blessed with the fruit; I am a sacrifice to them.

Waaho! Waaho! is the treasure of virtue; he alone tastes it, who is so blessed.

Waaho! Waaho! The Lord is pervading and permeating the oceans and the land; the Gurmukh attains Him.

Waaho! Waaho! Let all the Gursikhs continually praise Him. Waaho! Waaho! The Perfect Guru is pleased with His Praises.

O Nanak, one who chants Waaho! Waaho! with his heart and mind - the Messenger of Death does not approach him. |2|

Pauree:

The Dear Lord is the Truest of the True; True is the Word of the Guru's Bani.

Through the True Guru, the Truth is realized, and one is easily absorbed in the True Lord.

Night and day, they remain awake, and do not sleep; in wakefulness, the night of their lives passes.

Those who taste the sublime essence of the Lord, through the Guru's Teachings, are the most worthy persons.

Without the Guru, no one has obtained the Lord; the ignorant rot away and die. |17|

Shalok, Third Mehl:

Waaho! Waaho! is the Bani, the Word, of the Formless Lord. There is no other as great as He is.

Waaho! Waaho! The Lord is unfathomable and inaccessible. Waaho! Waaho! He is the True One.

Waaho! Waaho! He is the self-existent Lord. Waaho! Waaho! As He wills, so it comes to pass.

Waaho! Waaho! is the Ambrosial Nectar of the Naam, the Name of the Lord, obtained by the Gurmukh.

Waaho! Waaho! This is realized by His Grace, as He Himself grants His Grace.

Section 09 - Raag Goojaree - Part 028

O Nanak, Waaho! Waaho! This is obtained by the Gurmukhs, who hold tight to the Naam, night and day. |1|

Third Mehl:

Without serving the True Guru, peace is not obtained, and the sense of duality does not depart.

No matter how much one may wish, without the Lord's Grace, He is not found.

Those who are filled with greed and corruption are ruined by the love of duality.

They cannot escape birth and death, and with egotism within them, they suffer in misery.

Those who center their consciousness on the True Guru, never go empty-handed.

They are not summoned by the Messenger of Death, and they do not suffer in pain.

O Nanak, the Gurmukhs are saved; they merge in the True Lord. |2|

Pauree:

He alone is called a minstrel, who enshrines love for his Lord and Master.

Standing at the Lord's Door, he serves the Lord, and reflects upon the Word of the Guru's Shabad.

The minstrel attains the Lord's Gate and Mansion, and he keeps the True Lord clasped to his heart.

The status of the minstrel is exalted; he loves the Name of the Lord.

The service of the minstrel is to meditate on the Lord; he is emancipated by the Lord. |18|

Shalok, Third Mehl:

The milkmaid's status is very low, but she attains her Husband Lord when she reflects upon the Word of the Guru's Shabad, and chants the Lord's Name, night and day.

She who meets the True Guru, lives in the Fear of God; she is a woman of noble birth.

She alone realizes the Hukam of her Husband Lord's Command, who is blessed by the Creator Lord's Mercy.

She who is of little merit and ill-mannered, is discarded and forsaken by her Husband Lord.

By the Fear of God, filth is washed off, and the body becomes immaculately pure.

The soul is enlightened, and the intellect is exalted, meditating on the Lord, the ocean of excellence.

One who dwells in the Fear of God, lives in the Fear of God, and acts in the Fear of God.

He obtains peace and glorious greatness here, in the Lord's Court, and at the Gate of Salvation.

Through the Fear of God, the Fearless Lord is obtained, and one's light merges in the Infinite Light.

O Nanak, that bride alone is good, who is pleasing to her Lord and Master, and whom the Creator Lord Himself forgives. |1|

Third Mehl:

Praise the Lord, forever and ever, and make yourself a sacrifice to the True Lord.

O Nanak, let that tongue be burnt, which renounces the One Lord, and attaches itself to another. |2|

Pauree:

From a single particle of His greatness, He created His incarnations, but they indulged in the love of duality.

They ruled like kings, and fought for pleasure and pain.

Those who serve Shiva and Brahma do not find the limits of the Lord.

The Fearless, Formless Lord is unseen and invisible; He is revealed only to the Gurmukh.

There, one does not suffer sorrow or separation; he becomes stable and immortal in the world. |19|

Shalok, Third Mehl:

All these things come and go, all these things of the world.

One who knows this written account is acceptable and approved.

O Nanak, anyone who takes pride in himself is foolish and unwise. |1|

Third Mehl:

The mind is the elephant, the Guru is the elephant-driver, and knowledge is the whip. Wherever the Guru drives the mind, it goes.

O Nanak, without the whip, the elephant wanders into the wilderness, again and again. |2|

Pauree:

I offer my prayer to the One, from whom I was created.

Section 09 - Raag Goojaree - Part 029

Serving my True Guru, I have obtained all the fruits.

I meditate continually on the Ambrosial Name of the Lord.

In the Society of the Saints, I am rid of my pain and suffering.

O Nanak, I have become care-free; I have obtained the imperishable wealth of the Lord. |20|

Shalok, Third Mehl:

Raising the embankments of the mind's field, I gaze at the heavenly mansion.

When devotion comes to the mind of the soul-bride, she is visited by the friendly guest.

O clouds, if you are going to rain, then go ahead and rain; why rain after the season has passed?

Nanak is a sacrifice to those Gurmukhs who obtain the Lord in their minds. |1|

Third Mehl:

That which is pleasing is sweet, and one who is sincere is a friend.
O Nanak, he is known as a Gurmukh, whom the Lord Himself enlightens. |2|

Pauree:
O God, Your humble servant offers his prayer to You; You are my True Master.
You are my Protector, forever and ever; I meditate on You.
All the beings and creatures are Yours; You are pervading and permeating in them.
One who slanders Your slave is crushed and destroyed.
Falling at Your Feet, Nanak has renounced his cares, and has become care-free. |21|

Shalok, Third Mehl:
Building up its hopes, the world dies, but its hopes do not die or depart.
O Nanak, hopes are fulfilled only by attaching one's consciousness to the True Lord. |1|

Third Mehl:
Hopes and desires shall die only when He, who created them, takes them away.
O Nanak, nothing is permanent, except the Name of the Lord. |2|

Pauree:
He Himself created the world, with His perfect workmanship.
He Himself is the true banker, He Himself is the merchant, and He Himself is the store.
He Himself is the ocean, He Himself is the boat, and He Himself is the boatman.
He Himself is the Guru, He Himself is the disciple, and He Himself shows the destination.
O servant Nanak, meditate on the Naam, the Name of the Lord, and all your sins shall be eradicated. |22|1|SUDH|

Raag Goojaree, Vaar, Fifth Mehl:
One Universal Creator God. By The Grace Of The True Guru:
Shalok, Fifth Mehl:
Deep within yourself, worship the Guru in adoration, and with your tongue, chant the Guru's Name.

Let your eyes behold the True Guru, and let your ears hear the Guru's Name.

Attuned to the True Guru, you shall receive a place of honor in the Court of the Lord.

Says Nanak, this treasure is bestowed on those who are blessed with His Mercy.

In the midst of the world, they are known as the most pious - they are rare indeed. |1|

Fifth Mehl:

O Savior Lord, save us and take us across.

Falling at the feet of the Guru, our works are embellished with perfection.

You have become kind, merciful and compassionate; we do not forget You from our minds.

In the Saadh Sangat, the Company of the Holy, we are carried across the terrifying world-ocean.

In an instant, You have destroyed the faithless cynics and slanderous enemies.

That Lord and Master is my Anchor and Support; O Nanak, hold firm in your mind.

Section 09 - Raag Goojaree - Part 030

Remembering Him in meditation, happiness comes, and all sorrows and pains simply vanish. |2|

Pauree:

He is without relatives, immaculate, all-powerful, unapproachable and infinite.

Truly, the True Lord is seen to be the Truest of the True.

Nothing established by You appears to be false.

The Great Giver gives sustenance to all those He has created.

He has strung all on only one thread; He has infused His Light in them.

By His Will, some drown in the terrifying world-ocean, and by His Will, some are carried across.

O Dear Lord, he alone meditates on You, upon whose forehead such blessed destiny is inscribed.

Your condition and state cannot be known; I am a sacrifice to You. |1|

Shalok, Fifth Mehl:

When You are pleased, O Merciful Lord, you automatically come to dwell within my mind.

When You are pleased, O Merciful Lord, I find the nine treasures within the home of my own self.

When You are pleased, O Merciful Lord, I act according to the Guru's Instructions.

When You are pleased, O Merciful Lord, then Nanak is absorbed in the True One. |1|

Fifth Mehl:

Many sit on thrones, to the sounds of musical instruments.

O Nanak, without the True Name, no one's honor is safe. |2|

Pauree:

The followers of the Vedas, the Bible and the Koran, standing at Your Door, meditate on You.

Uncounted are those who fall at Your Door.

Brahma meditates on You, as does Indra on his throne.

Shiva and Vishnu, and their incarnations, chant the Lord's Praise with their mouths,

as do the Pirs, the spiritual teachers, the prophets and the Shaykhs, the silent sages and the seers.

Through and through, the Formless Lord is woven into each and every heart.

One is destroyed through falsehood; through righteousness, one prospers.

Whatever the Lord links him to, to that he is linked. |2|

Shalok, Fifth Mehl:

He is reluctant to do good, but eager to practice evil.

O Nanak, today or tomorrow, the feet of the careless fool shall fall into the trap. |1|

Fifth Mehl:

No matter how evil my ways are, still, Your Love for me is not concealed.

Nanak: You, O Lord, conceal my short-comings and dwell within my mind; You are my true friend. |2|

Pauree:

I beg of You, O Merciful Lord: please, make me the slave of Your slaves.

I obtain the nine treasures and royalty; chanting Your Name, I live.

The great ambrosial treasure, the Nectar of the Naam, is in the home of the Lord's slaves.

In their company, I am in ecstasy, listening to Your Praises with my ears. Serving them, my body is purified.

I wave the fans over them, and carry water for them; I grind the corn for them, and washing their feet, I am over-joyed.

By myself, I can do nothing; O God, bless me with Your Glance of Grace.

I am worthless - please, bless me with a seat in the place of worship of the Saints. |3|

Shalok, Fifth Mehl:
O Friend, I pray that I may remain forever the dust of Your Feet.
Nanak has entered Your Sanctuary, and beholds You ever-present. |1|

Fifth Mehl:
Countless sinners become pure, by fixing their minds on the Feet of the Lord.
The Name of God is the sixty-eight holy places of pilgrimage, O Nanak, for one who has such destiny written upon his forehead. |2|

Pauree:
With every breath and morsel of food, chant the Name of the Lord, the Cherisher.
The Lord does not forget one upon whom He has bestowed His Grace.
He Himself is the Creator, and He Himself destroys.

Section 09 - Raag Goojaree - Part 031

The Knower knows everything; He understands and contemplates.
By His creative power, He assumes numerous forms in an instant.
One whom the Lord attaches to the Truth is redeemed.
One who has God on his side is never conquered.
His Court is eternal and imperishable; I humbly bow to Him. |4|

Shalok, Fifth Mehl:
Renounce sexual desire, anger and greed, and burn them in the fire.
As long as you are alive, O Nanak, meditate continually on the True Name. |1|

Fifth Mehl:

Meditating, meditating in remembrance on my God, I have obtained all the fruits.

O Nanak, I worship the Naam, the Name of the Lord; the Perfect Guru has united me with the Lord. |2|

Pauree:
One who has been instructed by the Guru is liberated in this world.

He avoids disaster, and his anxiety is dispelled.

Beholding the blessed vision of his Darshan, the world is over-joyed.

In the company of the Lord's humble servants, the world is over-joyed, and the filth of sin is washed away.

There, they meditate on the Ambrosial Nectar of the True Name.

The mind becomes content, and its hunger is satisfied.

One whose heart is filled with the Name, has his bonds cut away.

By Guru's Grace, some rare person earns the wealth of the Lord's Name. |5|

Shalok, Fifth Mehl:
Within my mind, I think thoughts of always rising early, and making the effort.

O Lord, my Friend, please bless Nanak with the habit of singing the Kirtan of the Lord's Praises. |1|

Fifth Mehl:
Casting His Glance of Grace, God has saved me; my mind and body are imbued with the Primal Being.

O Nanak, those who are pleasing to God, have their cries of suffering taken away. |2|

Pauree:
When your soul is feeling sad, offer your prayers to the Guru.

Renounce all your cleverness, and dedicate your mind and body to Him.

Worship the Feet of the Guru, and your evil-mindedness shall be burnt away.

Joining the Saadh Sangat, the Company of the Holy, you shall cross over the terrifying and difficult world-ocean.

Serve the True Guru, and in the world hereafter, you shall not die of fear.

In an instant, he shall make you happy, and the empty vessel shall be filled to overflowing.

The mind becomes content, meditating forever on the Lord.

He alone dedicates himself to the Guru's service, unto whom the Lord has granted His Grace. |6|

Shalok, Fifth Mehl:
I am attached to the right place; the Uniter has united me.
O Nanak, there are hundreds and thousands of waves, but my Husband Lord does not let me drown. |1|

Fifth Mehl:
In the dreadful wilderness, I have found the one and only companion; the Name of the Lord is the Destroyer of distress.
I am a sacrifice, a sacrifice to the Beloved Saints, O Nanak; through them, my affairs have been brought to fulfillment. |2|

Pauree:
All treasures are obtained, when we are attuned to Your Love.
One does not have to suffer regret and repentance, when he meditates on You.
No one can equal Your humble servant, who has Your Support.
Waaho! Waaho! How wonderful is the Perfect Guru! Cherishing Him in my mind, I obtain peace.
The treasure of the Lord's Praise comes from the Guru; by His Mercy, it is obtained.
When the True Guru bestows His Glance of Grace, one does not wander any more.
The Merciful Lord preserves him - He makes him His own slave.
Listening, hearing the Name of the Lord, Har, Har, Har, Har, I live. |7|

Section 09 - Raag Goojaree - Part 032

Shalok, Fifth Mehl:
O Husband Lord, You have given me the silk gown of Your Love to cover and protect my honor.
You are all-wise and all-knowing, O my Master; Nanak: I have not appreciated Your value, Lord. |1|

Fifth Mehl:
By Your meditative remembrance, I have found everything; nothing seems difficult to me.

One whose honor the True Lord Master has preserved - O Nanak, no one can dishonor him. |2|

Pauree:
Meditating on the Lord, there comes a great peace.
Multitudes of illnesses vanish, singing the Glorious Praises of the Lord.
Utter peace pervades within, when God comes to mind.
One's hopes are fulfilled, when one's mind is filled with the Name.
No obstacles stand in the way, when one eliminates his self-conceit.
The intellect attains the blessing of spiritual wisdom from the Guru.
He receives everything, unto whom the Lord Himself gives.
You are the Lord and Master of all; all are under Your Protection. |8|

Shalok, Fifth Mehl:
Crossing the stream, my foot does not get stuck - I am filled with love for You.
O Lord, my heart is attached to Your Feet; the Lord is Nanak's raft and boat. |1|

Fifth Mehl:
The sight of them banishes my evil-mindedness; they are my only true friends.
I have searched the whole world; O servant Nanak, how rare are such persons! |2|

Pauree:
You come to mind, O Lord and Master, when I behold Your devotees.
The filth of my mind is removed, when I dwell in the Saadh Sangat, the Company of the Holy.
The fear of birth and death is dispelled, meditating on the Word of His humble servant.
The Saints untie the bonds, and all the demons are dispelled.
They inspire us to love Him, the One who established the entire universe.
The seat of the inaccessible and infinite Lord is the highest of the high.
Night and day, with your palms pressed together, with each and every breath, meditate on Him.
When the Lord Himself becomes merciful, then we attain the Society of His devotees. |9|

Shalok, Fifth Mehl:

In this wondrous forest of the world, there is chaos and confusion; shrieks emanate from the highways.

I am in love with You, O my Husband Lord; O Nanak, I cross the jungle joyfully. |1|

Fifth Mehl:

The true society is the company of those who meditate on the Name of the Lord.

Do not associate with those, O Nanak, who look out only for their own interests. |2|

Pauree:

Approved is that time, when one meets the True Guru.

Joining the Saadh Sangat, the Company of the Holy, he does not suffer pain again.

When he attains the eternal place, he does not have to enter the womb again.

He comes to see the One God everywhere.

He focuses his meditation on the essence of spiritual wisdom, and withdraws his attention from other sights.

All chants are chanted by one who chants them with his mouth.

Realizing the Hukam of the Lord's Command, he becomes happy, and he is filled with peace and tranquility.

Those who are assayed, and placed in the Lord's treasury, are not declared counterfeit again. |10|

Shalok, Fifth Mehl:

The pincers of separation are so painful to endure.

If only the Master would come to meet me! O Nanak, I would then obtain all the true comforts. |1|

Section 09 - Raag Goojaree - Part 033

Fifth Mehl:

The earth is in the water, and the fire is contained in the wood.

O Nanak, yearn for that Lord, who is the Support of all. |2|

Pauree:

The works which You have done, O Lord, could only have been performed by You.

That alone happens in the world, which You, O Master, have done.

I am wonderstruck beholding the wonder of Your Almighty Creative Power.

I seek Your Sanctuary - I am Your slave; if it is Your Will, I shall be emancipated.

The treasure is in Your Hands; according to Your Will, You bestow it.

One, upon whom You have bestowed Your Mercy, is blessed with the Lord's Name.

You are unapproachable, unfathomable and infinite; Your limits cannot be found.

One, unto whom You have been compassionate, meditates on the Naam, the Name of the Lord. |11|

Shalok, Fifth Mehl:

The ladles cruise through the food, but they do not know the taste of it.

I long to see the faces of those, O Nanak, who are imbued with the essence of the Lord's Love. |1|

Fifth Mehl:

Through the Tracker, I discovered the tracks of those who ruined my crops.

You, O Lord, have put up the fence; O Nanak, my fields shall not be plundered again. |2|

Pauree:

Worship in adoration that True Lord; everything is under His Power.

He Himself is the Master of both ends; in an instant, He adjusts our affairs.

Renounce all your efforts, and hold fast to His Support.

Run to His Sanctuary, and you shall obtain the comfort of all comforts.

The karma of good deeds, the righteousness of Dharma and the essence of spiritual wisdom are obtained in the Society of the Saints.

Chanting the Ambrosial Nectar of the Naam, no obstacle shall block your way.

The Lord abides in the mind of one who is blessed by His Kindness.

All treasures are obtained, when the Lord and Master is pleased. |12|

Shalok, Fifth Mehl:

I have found the object of my search - my Beloved took pity on me.

There is One Creator; O Nanak, I do not see any other. |1|

Fifth Mehl:

Take aim with the arrow of Truth, and shoot down sin.

Cherish the Words of the Guru's Mantra, O Nanak, and you shall not suffer in pain. |2|

Pauree:
Waaho! Waaho! The Creator Lord Himself has brought about peace and tranquility.
He is Kind to all beings and creatures; meditate forever on Him.
The all-powerful Lord has shown Mercy, and my cries of suffering are ended.
My fevers, pains and diseases are gone, by the Grace of the Perfect Guru.
The Lord has established me, and protected me; He is the Cherisher of the poor.
He Himself has delivered me, breaking all my bonds.
My thirst is quenched, my hopes are fulfilled, and my mind is contented and satisfied.
The greatest of the great, the Infinite Lord and Master - He is not affected by virtue and vice. |13|

Shalok, Fifth Mehl:
They alone meditate on the Lord God, Har, Har, unto whom the Lord is Merciful.
O Nanak, they enshrine love for the Lord, meeting the Saadh Sangat, the Company of the Holy. |1|

Fifth Mehl:
Contemplate the Lord, O very fortunate ones; He is pervading in the water, the land and the sky.
O Nanak, worshipping the Naam, the Name of the Lord, the mortal encounters no misfortune. |2|

Pauree:
The speech of the devotees is approved; it is accepted in the Court of the Lord.
Your devotees take to Your Support; they are imbued with the True Name.
One unto whom You are Merciful, has his sufferings depart.

Section 09 - Raag Goojaree - Part 034

O Merciful Lord, You bless Your devotees with Your Grace.
Suffering, pain, terrible disease and Maya do not afflict them.

This is the Support of the devotees, that they sing the Glorious Praises of the Lord of the Universe.

Forever and ever, day and night, they meditate on the One and Only Lord.

Drinking in the Ambrosial Amrit of the Naam, the Name of the Lord, His humble servants remain satisfied with the Naam. |14|

Shalok, Fifth Mehl:

Millions of obstacles stand in the way of one who forgets the Name.

O Nanak, night and day, he croaks like a raven in a deserted house. |1|

Fifth Mehl:

Beauteous is that season, when I am united with my Beloved.

I do not forget Him for a moment or an instant; O Nanak, I contemplate Him constantly. |2|

Pauree:

Even brave and mighty men cannot withstand the powerful and over-whelming army which the five passions have gathered.

The ten organs of sensation attach even detached renunciates to sensory pleasures.

They seek to conquer and overpower them, and so increase their following.

The world of the three dispositions is under their influence; no one can stand against them.

So tell me - how can the fort of doubt and the moat of Maya be overcome?

Worshipping the Perfect Guru, this awesome force is subdued.

I stand before Him, day and night, with my palms pressed together. |15|

Shalok, Fifth Mehl:

All sins are washed away, by continually singing the Lord's Glories.

Millions of afflictions are produced, O Nanak, when the Name is forgotten. |1|

Fifth Mehl:

O Nanak, meeting the True Guru, one comes to know the Perfect Way.

While laughing, playing, dressing and eating, he is liberated. |2|

Pauree:

Blessed, blessed is the True Guru, who has demolished the fortress of doubt.

Waaho! Waaho! - Hail! Hail! to the True Guru, who has united me with the Lord.

The Guru has given me the medicine of the inexhaustible treasure of the Naam.

He has banished the great and terrible disease.

I have obtained the great treasure of the wealth of the Naam.

I have obtained eternal life, recognizing my own self.

The Glory of the all-powerful Divine Guru cannot be described.

The Guru is the Supreme Lord God, the Transcendent Lord, infinite, unseen and unknowable. |16|

Shalok, Fifth Mehl:

Make the effort, and you shall live; practicing it, you shall enjoy peace.

Meditating, you shall meet God, O Nanak, and your anxiety shall vanish. |1|

Fifth Mehl:

Bless me with sublime thoughts, O Lord of the Universe, and contemplation in the immaculate Saadh Sangat, the Company of the Holy.

O Nanak, may I never forget the Naam, the Name of the Lord, for even an instant; be merciful to me, Lord God. |2|

Pauree:

Whatever happens is according to Your Will, so why should I be afraid?

Meeting Him, I meditate on the Name - I offer my soul to Him.

When the Infinite Lord comes to mind, one is enraptured.

Who can touch one who has the Formless Lord on his side?

Everything is under His control; no one is beyond Him.

He, the True Lord, dwells in the minds of His devotees.

Your slaves meditate on You; You are the Savior, the Protector Lord.

Section 09 - Raag Goojaree - Part 035

You are the Almighty Overlord of all; You bless us with Your Glance of Grace. |17|

Shalok, Fifth Mehl:

Take away my sexual desire, anger, pride, greed, emotional attachment and evil desires.

Protect me, O my God; Nanak is forever a sacrifice to You. |1|

Fifth Mehl:
By eating and eating, the mouth is worn out; by wearing clothes, the limbs grow weary.
O Nanak, cursed are the lives of those who are not attuned to the Love of the True Lord. |2|

Pauree:
As is the Hukam of Your Command, so do things happen.
Wherever You keep me, there I go and stand.
With the Love of Your Name, I wash away my evil-mindedness.
By continually meditating on You, O Formless Lord, my doubts and fears are dispelled.
Those who are attuned to Your Love, shall not be trapped in reincarnation.
Inwardly and outwardly, they behold the One Lord with their eyes.
Those who recognize the Lord's Command never weep.
O Nanak, they are blessed with the gift of the Name, woven into the fabric of their minds. |18|

Shalok, Fifth Mehl:
Those who do not remember the Lord while they are alive, shall mix with the dust when they die.
O Nanak, the foolish and filthy faithless cynic passes his life engrossed in the world. |1|

Fifth Mehl:
One who remembers the Lord while he is alive, shall be imbued with the Lord's Love when he dies.
The precious gift of his life is redeemed, O Nanak, in the Saadh Sangat, the Company of the Holy. |2|

Pauree:
From the beginning, and through the ages, You have been our Protector and Preserver.
True is Your Name, O Creator Lord, and True is Your Creation.
You do not lack anything; You are filling each and every heart.
You are merciful and all-powerful; You Yourself cause us to serve You.
Those whose minds in which You dwell are forever at peace.
Having created the creation, You Yourself cherish it.
You Yourself are everything, O infinite, endless Lord.

Nanak seeks the Protection and Support of the Perfect Guru. |19|

Shalok, Fifth Mehl:
In the beginning, in the middle and in the end, the Transcendent Lord has saved me.
The True Guru has blessed me with the Lord's Name, and I have tasted the Ambrosial Nectar.
In the Saadh Sangat, the Company of the Holy, I chant the Glorious Praises of the Lord, night and day.
I have obtained all my objectives, and I shall not wander in reincarnation again.
Everything is in the Hands of the Creator; He does what is done.
Nanak begs for the gift of the dust of the feet of the Holy, which shall deliver him. |1|

Fifth Mehl:
Enshrine Him in your mind, the One who created you.
Whoever meditates on the Lord and Master obtains peace.
Fruitful is the birth, and approved is the coming of the Gurmukh.
One who realizes the Hukam of the Lord's Command shall be blessed - so has the Lord and Master ordained.
One who is blessed with the Lord's Mercy does not wander.
Whatever the Lord and Master gives him, with that he is content.
O Nanak, one who is blessed with the kindness of the Lord, our Friend, realizes the Hukam of His Command.
But those whom the Lord Himself causes to wander, continue to die, and take reincarnation again. |2|

Pauree:
The slanderers are destroyed in an instant; they are not spared for even a moment.
God will not endure the sufferings of His slaves, but catching the slanderers, He binds them to the cycle of reincarnation.

Section 09 - Raag Goojaree - Part 036

Grabbing them by the hair on their heads, the Lord throws them down, and leaves them on the path of Death.
They cry out in pain, in the darkest of hells.

But hugging His slaves close to His Heart, O Nanak, the True Lord saves them. |20|

Shalok, Fifth Mehl:
Meditate on the Lord, O fortunate ones; He is pervading the waters and the earth.
O Nanak, meditate on the Naam, the Name of the Lord, and no misfortune shall strike you. |1|

Fifth Mehl:
Millions of misfortunes block the way of one who forgets the Name of the Lord.
O Nanak, like a crow in a deserted house, he cries out, night and day. |2|

Pauree:
Meditating, meditating in remembrance of the Great Giver, one's heart's desires are fulfilled.
The hopes and desires of the mind are realized, and sorrows are forgotten.
The treasure of the Naam, the Name of the Lord, is obtained; I have searched for it for so long.
My light is merged into the Light, and my labors are over.
I abide in that house of peace, poise and bliss.
My comings and goings have ended - there is no birth or death there.
The Master and the servant have become one, with no sense of separation.
By Guru's Grace, Nanak is absorbed in the True Lord. |21|1|2|SUDH|

Raag Goojaree, The Words Of The Devotees:
One Universal Creator God. By The Grace Of The True Guru:
Chau-Padas Of Kabeer Jee, Second House:
With four feet, two horns and a mute mouth, how could you sing the Praises of the Lord?
Standing up and sitting down, the stick shall still fall on you, so where will you hide your head? |1|

Without the Lord, you are like a stray ox;
with your nose torn, and your shoulders injured, you shall have only the straw of coarse grain to eat. |1|Pause|

All day long, you shall wander in the forest, and even then, your belly will not be full.

You did not follow the advice of the humble devotees, and so you shall obtain the fruits of your actions. |2|

Enduring pleasure and pain, drowned in the great ocean of doubt, you shall wander in numerous reincarnations.
You have lost the jewel of human birth by forgetting God; when will you have such an opportunity again? |3|

You turn on the wheel of reincarnation, like an ox at the oil-press; the night of your life passes away without salvation.
Says Kabeer, without the Name of the Lord, you shall pound your head, and regret and repent. |4|1|

GOOJAREE, THIRD HOUSE:
Kabeer's mother sobs, cries and bewails
- O Lord, how will my grandchildren live? |1|

Kabeer has given up all his spinning and weaving,
and written the Name of the Lord on his body. |1|Pause|

As long as I pass the thread through the bobbin,
I forget the Lord, my Beloved. |2|

My intellect is lowly - I am a weaver by birth,
but I have earned the profit of the Name of the Lord. |3|

Says Kabeer, listen, O my mother
- the Lord alone is the Provider, for me and my children. |4|2|

Section 09 - Raag Goojaree - Part 037

Goojaree, Padas Of Naam Dayv Jee, First House:
One Universal Creator God. By The Grace Of The True Guru:
If You gave me an empire, then what glory would be in it for me?
If You made me beg for charity, what would it take away from me? |1|

Meditate and vibrate upon the Lord, O my mind, and you shall obtain the state of Nirvaanaa.
You shall not have to come and go in reincarnation any longer. |1|Pause|

You created all, and You lead them astray in doubt.
They alone understand, unto whom You give understanding. |2|

Meeting the True Guru, doubt is dispelled.
Who else should I worship? I can see no other. |3|

One stone is lovingly decorated,
while another stone is walked upon.
If one is a god, then the other must also be a god.
Says Naam Dayv, I serve the Lord. |4|1|

GOOJAREE, FIRST HOUSE:
He does not have even a trace of impurity - He is beyond impurity. He is
fragrantly scented - He has come to take His Seat in my mind.
No one saw Him come - who can know Him, O Siblings of Destiny? |1|

Who can describe Him? Who can understand Him? The all-pervading Lord
has no ancestors, O Siblings of Destiny. |1|Pause|

As the path of a bird's flight across the sky cannot be seen,
and the path of a fish through the water cannot be seen; |2|

As the mirage leads one to mistake the sky for a pitcher filled with water
- so is God, the Lord and Master of Naam Dayv, who fits these three
comparisons. |3|2|

Goojaree, Padas Of Ravi Daas Jee, Third House:
One Universal Creator God. By The Grace Of The True Guru:
The calf has contaminated the milk in the teats.
The bumble bee has contaminated the flower, and the fish the water. |1|

O mother, where shall I find any offering for the Lord's worship?
I cannot find any other flowers worthy of the incomparable Lord.
|1|Pause|

The snakes encircle the sandalwood trees.
Poison and nectar dwell there together. |2|

Even with incense, lamps, offerings of food and fragrant flowers,
how are Your slaves to worship You? |3|

I dedicate and offer my body and mind to You.
By Guru's Grace, I attain the immaculate Lord. |4|

I cannot worship You, nor offer You flowers.
Says Ravi Daas, what shall my condition be hereafter? |5|1|

Goojaree, Padas Of Trilochan Jee, First House:
One Universal Creator God. By The Grace Of The True Guru:
You have not cleansed the filth from within yourself, although outwardly,
you wear the dress of a renunciate.
In the heart-lotus of your self, you have not recognized God - why have you
become a Sannyaasee? |1|

Section 09 - Raag Goojaree - Part 038

Deluded by doubt, O Jai Chand,
you have not realized the Lord, the embodiment of supreme bliss.
|1|Pause|

You eat in each and every house, fattening your body; you wear the
patched coat and the ear-rings of the beggar, for the sake of wealth.
You apply the ashes of cremation to your body, but without a Guru, you
have not found the essence of reality. |2|

Why bother to chant your spells? Why bother to practice austerities? Why
bother to churn water?
Meditate on the Lord of Nirvaanaa, who has created the 8.4 million species
of beings. |3|

Why bother to carry the water-pot, O saffron-robed Yogi? Why bother to
visit the sixty-eight holy places of pilgrimage?

Says Trilochan, listen, mortal: you have no corn - what are you trying to
thresh? |4|1|

GOOJAREE:
At the very last moment, one who thinks of wealth, and dies in such
thoughts,
shall be reincarnated over and over again, in the form of serpents. |1|

O sister, do not forget the Name of the Lord of the Universe. |Pause|

At the very last moment, he who thinks of women, and dies in such thoughts,
shall be reincarnated over and over again as a prostitute. |2|

At the very last moment, one who thinks of his children, and dies in such thoughts,
shall be reincarnated over and over again as a pig. |3|

At the very last moment, one who thinks of mansions, and dies in such thoughts,
shall be reincarnated over and over again as a goblin. |4|

At the very last moment, one who thinks of the Lord, and dies in such thoughts,
says Trilochan, that man shall be liberated; the Lord shall abide in his heart. |5|2|

Goojaree, Padas Of Jai Dayv Jee, Fourth House:
One Universal Creator God. By The Grace Of The True Guru:
In the very beginning, was the Primal Lord, unrivalled, the Lover of Truth and other virtues.
He is absolutely wonderful, transcending creation; remembering Him, all are emancipated. |1|

Dwell only upon the beauteous Name of the Lord,
the embodiment of ambrosial nectar and reality.
Remembering Him in meditation, the fear of birth, old age and death will not trouble you. |1|Pause|

If you desire to escape the fear of the Messenger of Death, then praise the Lord joyfully, and do good deeds.
In the past, present and future, He is always the same; He is the embodiment of supreme bliss. |2|

If you seek the path of good conduct, forsake greed, and do not look upon other men's property and women.

Renounce all evil actions and evil inclinations, and hurry to the Sanctuary of the Lord. |3|

Worship the immaculate Lord, in thought, word and deed.
What is the good of practicing Yoga, giving feasts and charity, and practicing penance? |4|

Meditate on the Lord of the Universe, the Lord of the Universe, O man; He is the source of all the spiritual powers of the Siddhas.
Jai Dayv has openly come to Him; He is the salvation of all, in the past, present and future. |5|1|

RAAG DAYV

Section 10 - Raag Dayv-Gandhaaree - Part 001

ONE Universal Creator God. Truth Is The Name. Creative Being Personified. No Fear. No Hatred. Image Of The Undying. Beyond Birth. Self-Existent. By Guru's Grace:

Raag Dayv-Gandhaaree, Fourth Mehl, First House:
Those who become the humble servants of the Lord and Master, lovingly focus their minds on Him.
Those who chant Your Praises, through the Guru's Teachings, have great good fortune recorded upon their foreheads. |1|Pause|

The bonds and shackles of Maya are shattered, by lovingly focusing their minds on the Name of the Lord.
My mind is enticed by the Guru, the Enticer; beholding Him, I am wonder-struck. |1|

I slept through the entire dark night of my life, but through the tiniest bit of the Guru's Grace, I have been awakened.
O Beautiful Lord God, Master of servant Nanak, there is none comparable to You. |2|1|

DAYV-GANDHAAREE:
Tell me - on what path will I find my Beauteous Lord?
O Saints of the Lord, show me the Way, and I shall follow. |1|Pause|

I cherish in my heart the Words of my Beloved; this is the best way.
The bride may be hunch-backed and short, but if she is loved by her Lord Master, she becomes beautiful, and she melts in the Lord's embrace. |1|

There is only the One Beloved - we are all soul-brides of our Husband Lord.
She who is pleasing to her Husband Lord is good.
What can poor, helpless Nanak do? As it pleases the Lord, so does he walk. |2|2|

DAYV-GANDHAAREE:
O my mind, chant the Name of the Lord, Har, Har, Har.
The Gurmukh is imbued with the deep red color of the poppy. His shawl is saturated with the Lord's Love. |1|Pause|

I wander around here and there, like a madman, bewildered, seeking out my Darling Lord.
I shall be the slave of the slave of whoever unites me with my Darling Beloved. |1|

So align yourself with the Almighty True Guru; drink in and savor the Ambrosial Nectar of the Lord.
By Guru's Grace, servant Nanak has obtained the wealth of the Lord within. |2|3|

DAYV-GANDHAAREE:
Now, I have come, exhausted, to my Lord and Master.
Now that I have come seeking Your Sanctuary, God, please, either save me, or kill me. |1|Pause|

Section 10 - Raag Dayv-Gandhaaree - Part 002

I have burnt in the fire the clever devices and praises of the world.
Some speak good of me, and some speak ill of me, but I have surrendered my body to You. |1|

Whoever comes to Your Sanctuary, O God, Lord and Master, You save by Your Merciful Grace.
Servant Nanak has entered Your Sanctuary, Dear Lord; O Lord, please, protect his honor! |2|4|

DAYV-GANDHAAREE:
I am a sacrifice to one who sings the Glorious Praises of the Lord.
I live by continuously beholding the Blessed Vision of the Holy Guru's Darshan; within His Mind is the Name of the Lord. |1|Pause|

You are pure and immaculate, O God, Almighty Lord and Master; how can I, the impure one, meet You?

I have one thing in my mind, and another thing on my lips; I am such a poor, unfortunate liar! |1|

I appear to chant the Lord's Name, but within my heart, I am the most wicked of the wicked.
As it pleases You, save me, O Lord and Master; servant Nanak seeks Your Sanctuary. |2|5|

DAYV-GANDHAAREE:
Without the Name of the Lord, the beautiful are just like the noseless ones.
Like the son, born into the house of a prostitute, his name is cursed. |1|Pause|

Those who do not have the Name of their Lord and Master within their hearts, are the most wretched, deformed lepers.
Like the person who has no Guru, they may know many things, but they are cursed in the Court of the Lord. |1|

Those, unto whom my Lord Master becomes Merciful, long for the feet of the Holy.
O Nanak, the sinners become pure, joining the Company of the Holy; following the Guru, the True Guru, they are emancipated. |2|6| First Set of Six|

Dayv-Gandhaaree, Fifth Mehl, Second House:
One Universal Creator God. By The Grace Of The True Guru:
O mother, I focus my consciousness on the Guru's feet.
As God shows His Mercy, the lotus of my heart blossoms, and forever and ever, I meditate on the Lord. |1|Pause|

The One Lord is within, and the One Lord is outside; the One Lord is contained in all.
Within the heart, beyond the heart, and in all places, God, the Perfect One, is seen to be permeating. |1|

So many of Your servants and silent sages sing Your Praises, but no one has found Your limits.
O Giver of peace, Destroyer of pain, Lord and Master - servant Nanak is forever a sacrifice to You. |2|1|

DAYV-GANDHAAREE:

O mother, whatever is to be, shall be.

God pervades His pervading creation; one gains, while another loses. |1|Pause|

Sometimes he blossoms in bliss, while at other times, he suffers in mourning. Sometimes he laughs, and sometimes he weeps.

Sometimes he is filled with the filth of ego, while at other times, he washes it off in the Saadh Sangat, the Company of the Holy. |1|

No one can erase the actions of God; I cannot see any other like Him.

Says Nanak, I am a sacrifice to the Guru; by His Grace, I sleep in peace. |2|2|

Section 10 - Raag Dayv-Gandhaaree - Part 003

DAYV-GANDHAAREE:

O mother, I hear of death, and think of it, and I am filled with fear.

Renouncing 'mine and yours' and egotism, I have sought the Sanctuary of the Lord and Master. |1|Pause|

Whatever He says, I accept that as good. I do not say "No" to what He says.

Let me not forget Him, even for an instant; forgetting Him, I die. |1|

The Giver of peace, God, the Perfect Creator, endures my great ignorance.

I am worthless, ugly and of low birth, O Nanak, but my Husband Lord is the embodiment of bliss. |2|3|

DAYV-GANDHAAREE:

O my mind, chant forever the Kirtan of the Lord's Praises.

By singing, hearing and meditating on Him, all, whether of high or low status, are saved. |1|Pause|

He is absorbed into the One from which he originated, when he understands the Way.

Wherever this body was fashioned, it was not allowed to remain there. |1|

Peace comes, and fear and doubt are dispelled, when God becomes Merciful.

Says Nanak, my hopes have been fulfilled, renouncing my greed in the Saadh Sangat, the Company of the Holy. |2|4|

DAYV-GANDHAAREE:
O my mind, act as it pleases God.
Become the lowest of the low, the very least of the tiny, and speak in utmost humility. |1|Pause|

The many ostentatious shows of Maya are useless; I withhold my love from these.
As something pleases my Lord and Master, in that I find my glory. |1|

I am the slave of His slaves; becoming the dust of the feet of his slaves, I serve His humble servants.
I obtain all peace and greatness, O Nanak, living to chant His Name with my mouth. |2|5|

DAYV-GANDHAAREE:
Dear God, by Your Grace, my doubts have been dispelled.
By Your Mercy, all are mine; I reflect upon this in my mind. |1|Pause|

Millions of sins are erased, by serving You; the Blessed Vision of Your Darshan drives away sorrow.
Chanting Your Name, I have obtained supreme peace, and my anxieties and diseases have been cast out. |1|

Sexual desire, anger, greed, falsehood and slander are forgotten, in the Saadh Sangat, the Company of the Holy.
The ocean of mercy has cut away the bonds of Maya; O Nanak, He has saved me. |2|6|

DAYV-GANDHAAREE:
All the cleverness of my mind is gone.
The Lord and Master is the Doer, the Cause of causes; Nanak holds tight to His Support. |1|Pause|

Erasing my self-conceit, I have entered His Sanctuary; these are the Teachings spoken by the Holy Guru.
Surrendering to the Will of God, I attain peace, and the darkness of doubt is dispelled. |1|

I know that You are all-wise, O God, my Lord and Master; I seek Your Sanctuary.

In an instant, You establish and disestablish; the value of Your Almighty Creative Power cannot be estimated. |2|7|

Dayv-Gandhaaree, Fifth Mehl:
The Lord God is my praanaa, my breath of life; He is the Giver of peace.
By Guru's Grace, only a few know Him. |1|Pause|

Your Saints are Your Beloveds; death does not consume them.
They are dyed in the deep crimson color of Your Love, and they are intoxicated with the sublime essence of the Lord's Name. |1|

Section 10 - Raag Dayv-Gandhaaree - Part 004

The greatest sins, and millions of pains and diseases are destroyed by Your Gracious Glance, O God.
While sleeping and waking, Nanak sings the Lord's Name, Har, Har, Har; he falls at the Guru's feet. |2|8|

Dayv-Gandhaaree, Fifth Mehl:
I have seen that God with my eyes everywhere.
The Giver of peace, the Giver of souls, His Speech is Ambrosial Nectar. |1|Pause|

The Saints dispel the darkness of ignorance; the Guru is the Giver of the gift of life.
Granting His Grace, the Lord has made me His own; I was on fire, but now I am cooled. |1|

The karma of good deeds, and the Dharma of righteous faith, have not been produced in me, in the least; nor has pure conduct welled up in me.
Renouncing cleverness and self-mortification, O Nanak, I fall at the Guru's feet. |2|9|

Dayv-Gandhaaree, Fifth Mehl:
Chant the Lord's Name, and earn the profit.
You shall attain salvation, peace, poise and bliss, and the noose of Death shall be cut away. |1|Pause|

Searching, searching, searching and reflecting, I have found that the Lord's Name is with the Saints.

They alone obtain this treasure, who have such pre-ordained destiny. |1|

They are very fortunate and honorable; they are the perfect bankers.

They are beautiful, so very wise and handsome; O Nanak, purchase the Name of the Lord, Har, Har. |2|10|

Dayv-Gandhaaree, Fifth Mehl:

O mind, why are you so puffed up with egotism?

Whatever is seen in this foul, impure and filthy world, is only ashes. |1|Pause|

Remember the One who created you, O mortal; He is the Support of your soul, and the breath of life.

One who forsakes Him, and attaches himself to another, dies to be reborn; he is such an ignorant fool! |1|

I am blind, mute, crippled and totally lacking in understanding; O God, Preserver of all, please preserve me!

The Creator, the Cause of causes is all-powerful; O Nanak, how helpless are His beings! |2|11|

Dayv-Gandhaaree, Fifth Mehl:

God is the nearest of the near.

Remember Him, meditate on Him, and sing the Glorious Praises of the Lord of the Universe, day and night, evening and morning. |1|Pause|

Redeem your body in the invaluable Saadh Sangat, the Company of the Holy, chanting the Name of the Lord, Har, Har.

Do not delay for an instant, even for a moment. Death is keeping you constantly in his vision. |1|

Lift me up out of the dark dungeon, O Creator Lord; what is there which is not in Your home?

Bless Nanak with the Support of Your Name, that he may find great happiness and peace. |2|12|

Second Set of Six|

Dayv-Gandhaaree, Fifth Mehl:
O mind, meet with the Guru, and worship the Naam in adoration.
You shall obtain peace, poise, bliss, joy and pleasure, and lay the foundation of eternal life. |1|Pause|

Showing His Mercy, the Lord has made me His slave, and shattered the bonds of Maya.
Through loving devotion, and singing the Glorious Praises of the Lord of the Universe, I have escaped the Path of Death. |1|

When he became Merciful, the rust was removed, and I found the priceless treasure.
O Nanak, I am a sacrifice, a hundred thousand times, to my unapproachable, unfathomable Lord and Master. |2|13|

Section 10 - Raag Dayv-Gandhaaree - Part 005

Dayv-Gandhaaree, Fifth Mehl:
O mother, how fruitful is the birth of one who sings the Glories of God, and enshrines love for the Supreme Lord God. |1|Pause|

Beautiful, wise, brave and divine is one who obtains the Saadh Sangat, the Company of the Holy.
He chants the Naam, the Name of the Lord, with his tongue, and does not have to wander in reincarnation again. |1|

The Perfect Lord God pervades his mind and body; he does not look upon any other.
Hell and disease do not afflict one who joins the Company of the Lord's humble servants, O Nanak; the Lord attaches him to the hem of His robe. |2|14|

Dayv-Gandhaaree, Fifth Mehl:
His fickle mind is entangled in a dream.
He does not even understand this much, that someday he shall have to depart; he has gone crazy with Maya. |1|Pause|

He is engrossed in the delight of the flower's color; he strives only to indulge in corruption.
Hearing about greed, he feels happy in his mind, and he runs after it. |1|

Wandering and roaming all around, I have endured great pain, but now, I have come to the door of the Saint.
Granting His Grace, the Supreme Lord Master has blended Nanak with Himself. |2|15|

Dayv-Gandhaaree, Fifth Mehl:
All peace is found in the Guru's feet.
They drive away my sins and purify my mind; their Support carries me across. |1|Pause|

This is the labor which I perform: worship, flower-offerings, service and devotion.
My mind blossoms forth and is enlightened, and I am not cast into the womb again. |1|

I behold the fruitful vision of the Saint; this is the meditation I have taken.
The Lord Master has become Merciful to Nanak, and he has entered the Sanctuary of the Holy. |2|16|

Dayv-Gandhaaree, Fifth Mehl:
Offer your prayer to your Lord.
You shall obtain the four blessings, and the treasures of bliss, pleasure, peace, poise and the spiritual powers of the Siddhas. |1|Pause|

Renounce your self-conceit, and grasp hold of the Guru's feet; hold tight to the hem of God's robe.
The heat of the ocean of fire does not affect one who longs for the Lord and Master's Sanctuary. |1|

Again and again, God puts up with the millions of sins of the supremely ungrateful ones.
The embodiment of mercy, the Perfect Transcendent Lord - Nanak longs for His Sanctuary. |2|17|

Dayv-Gandhaaree, Fifth Mehl:
Place the Guru's feet within your heart,

and all illness, sorrow and pain shall be dispelled; all suffering shall come to an end. |1|Pause|

The sins of countless incarnations are erased, as if one has taken purifying baths at millions of sacred shrines.
The treasure of the Naam, the Name of the Lord, is obtained by singing the Glorious Praises of the Lord of the Universe, and centering one's mind in meditation on Him. |1|

Showing His Mercy, the Lord has made me His slave; breaking my bonds, He has saved me.
I live by chanting and meditating on the Naam, and the Bani of Your Word; slave Nanak is a sacrifice to You. |2|18|

Third Set of Six|

Dayv-Gandhaaree, Fifth Mehl:
O mother, I long to see the Feet of God.

Section 10 - Raag Dayv-Gandhaaree - Part 006

Be Merciful to me, O my Lord and Master, that I might never forsake them from my mind. |1|Pause|

Applying the dust of the feet of the Holy to my face and forehead, I burn away the poison of sexual desire and anger.
I judge myself to be the lowest of all; in this way, I instill peace within my mind. |1|

I sing the Glorious Praises of the Imperishable Lord and Master, and I shake off all my sins.
I have found the gift of the treasure of the Naam, O Nanak; I hug it close, and enshrine it in my heart. |2|19|

Dayv-Gandhaaree, Fifth Mehl:
Dear God, I long to behold the Blessed Vision of Your Darshan.
I cherish this beautiful meditation day and night; You are dearer to me than my soul, dearer than life itself. |1|Pause|

I have studied and contemplated the essence of the Shaastras, the Vedas and the Puraanas.
Protector of the meek, Lord of the breath of life, O Perfect One, carry us across the terrifying world-ocean. |1|

Since the very beginning, and throughout the ages, the humble devotees have been Your servants; in the midst of the world of corruption, You are their Support.
Nanak longs for the dust of the feet of such humble beings; the Transcendent Lord is the Giver of all. |2|20|

Dayv-Gandhaaree, Fifth Mehl:
Your humble servant, O Lord, is intoxicated with Your sublime essence.
One who obtains the treasure of the Nectar of Your Love, does not renounce it to go somewhere else. |1|Pause|

While sitting, he repeats the Lord's Name, Har, Har; while sleeping, he repeats the Lord's Name, Har, Har; he eats the Nectar of the Lord's Name as his food.
Bathing in the dust of the feet of the Holy is equal to taking cleansing baths at the sixty-eight sacred shrines of pilgrimage. |1|

How fruitful is the birth of the Lord's humble servant; the Creator is his Father.
O Nanak, one who recognizes the Perfect Lord God, takes all with him, and saves everyone. |2|21|

Dayv-Gandhaaree, Fifth Mehl:
O mother, without the Guru, spiritual wisdom is not obtained.
They wander around, weeping and crying out in various ways, but the Lord of the World does not meet them. |1|Pause|

The body is tied up with emotional attachment, disease and sorrow, and so it is lured into countless reincarnations.
He finds no place of rest without the Saadh Sangat, the Company of the Holy; to whom should he go and cry? |1|

When my Lord and Master shows His Mercy, we lovingly focus our consciousness on the feet of the Holy.

The most horrible agonies are dispelled in an instant, O Nanak, and we merge in the Blessed Vision of the Lord. |2|22|

Dayv-Gandhaaree, Fifth Mehl:
The Lord and Master Himself has become Merciful.
I have been emancipated, and I have become the embodiment of bliss; I am the Lord's child - He has saved me. |Pause|

With my palms pressed together, I offer my prayer; within my mind, I meditate on the Supreme Lord God.
Giving me His hand, the Transcendent Lord has eradicated all my sins. |1|

Husband and wife join together in rejoicing, celebrating the Victory of the Lord Master.
Says Nanak, I am a sacrifice to the humble servant of the Lord, who emancipates everyone. |2|23|

Section 10 - Raag Dayv-Gandhaaree - Part 007

One Universal Creator God. By The Grace Of The True Guru:
Dayv-Gandhaaree, Fifth Mehl:
I offer my prayer to my True Guru.
The Destroyer of distress has become kind and merciful, and all my anxiety is over. |Pause|

I am a sinner, hypocritical and greedy, but still, He puts up with all of my merits and demerits.
Placing His hand on my forehead, He has exalted me. The wicked ones who wanted to destroy me have been killed. |1|

He is generous and benevolent, the beautifier of all, the embodiment of peace; the Blessed Vision of His Darshan is so fruitful!

Says Nanak, He is the Giver to the unworthy; I enshrine His Lotus Feet within my heart. |2|24|

Dayv-Gandhaaree, Fifth Mehl:
My God is the Master of the masterless.
I have come to the Sanctuary of the Savior Lord. |Pause|

Protect me on all sides, O Lord;
protect me in the future, in the past, and at the very last moment. |1|

Whenever something comes to mind, it is You.
Contemplating Your virtues, my mind is sanctified. |2|

I hear and sing the Hymns of the Guru's Word.
I am a sacrifice, a sacrifice to the Blessed Vision of the Darshan of the Holy.
|3|

Within my mind, I have the Support of the One Lord alone.
O Nanak, my God is the Creator of all. |4|25|

Dayv-Gandhaaree, Fifth Mehl:
God, this is my heart's desire:
O treasure of kindness, O Merciful Lord, please make me the slave of your
Saints. |Pause|

In the early hours of the morning, I fall at the feet of Your humble servants;
night and day, I obtain the Blessed Vision of their Darshan.
Dedicating my body and mind, I serve the humble servant of the Lord; with
my tongue, I sing the Glorious Praises of the Lord. |1|

With each and every breath, I meditate in remembrance on my God; I live
continually in the Society of the Saints.
The Naam, the Name of the Lord, is my only support and wealth; O Nanak,
from this, I obtain bliss. |2|26|

Raag Dayv-Gandhaaree, Fifth Mehl, Third House:
One Universal Creator God. By The Grace Of The True Guru:
O friend, such is the Dear Lord whom I have obtained.
He does not leave me, and He always keeps me company. Meeting the
Guru, night and day, I sing His Praises. |1|Pause|

I met the Fascinating Lord, who has blessed me with all comforts; He does
not leave me to go anywhere else.
I have seen the mortals of many and various types, but they are not equal
to even a hair of my Beloved. |1|

His palace is so beautiful! His gate is so wonderful! The celestial melody of the sound current resounds there.

Says Nanak, I enjoy eternal bliss; I have obtained a permanent place in the home of my Beloved. |2|1|27|

Dayv-Gandhaaree, Fifth Mehl:
My mind longs for the Blessed Vision of the Lord's Darshan, and His Name.
I have wandered everywhere, and now I have come to follow the Saint. |1|Pause|

Whom should I serve? Whom should I worship in adoration? Whoever I see shall pass away.

Section 10 - Raag Dayv-Gandhaaree - Part 008

I have sought the Sanctuary of the Saadh Sangat, the Company of the Holy; my mind longs for the dust of their Feet. |1|

I do not know the way, and I have no virtue. It is so difficult to escape from Maya!
Nanak has come and fallen at the Guru's feet; all of his evil inclinations have vanished. |2|2|28|

Dayv-Gandhaaree, Fifth Mehl:
O Beloved, Your Words are Ambrosial Nectar.
O supremely beautiful Enticer, O Beloved, You are among all, and yet distinct from all. |1|Pause|

I do not seek power, and I do not seek liberation. My mind is in love with Your Lotus Feet.
Brahma, Shiva, the Siddhas, the silent sages and Indra - I seek only the Blessed Vision of my Lord and Master's Darshan. |1|

I have come, helpless, to Your Door, O Lord Master; I am exhausted - I seek the Sanctuary of the Saints.
Says Nanak, I have met my Enticing Lord God; my mind is cooled and soothed - it blossoms forth in joy. |2|3|29|

Dayv-Gandhaaree, Fifth Mehl:
Meditating on the Lord, His servant swims across to salvation.

When God becomes merciful to the meek, then one does not have to suffer reincarnation, only to die again. |1|Pause|

In the Saadh Sangat, the Company of the Holy, he sings the Glorious Praises of the Lord, and he does not lose the jewel of this human life.
Singing the Glories of God, he crosses over the ocean of poison, and saves all his generations as well. |1|

The Lotus Feet of the Lord abide within his heart, and with every breath and morsel of food, he chants the Lord's Name.
Nanak has grasped the Support of the Lord of the Universe; again and again, he is a sacrifice to Him. |2|4|30|

Raag Dayv-Gandhaaree, Fifth Mehl, Fourth House:
One Universal Creator God. By The Grace Of The True Guru:
Some wander around the forests, wearing religious robes, but the Fascinating Lord remains distant from them. |1|Pause|

They talk, preach, and sing their lovely songs, but within their minds, the filth of their sins remains. |1|

They may be very beautiful, extremely clever, wise and educated, and they may speak very sweetly. |2|

To forsake pride, emotional attachment, and the sense of 'mine and yours', is the path of the double-edged sword. |3|

Says Nanak, they alone swim across the terrifying world-ocean, who, by God's Grace, join the Society of the Saints. |4|1|31|

Raag Dayv-Gandhaaree, Fifth Mehl, Fifth House:
One Universal Creator God. By The Grace Of The True Guru:
I have seen the Lord to be on high; the Fascinating Lord is the highest of all.
No one else is equal to Him - I have made the most extensive search on this. |1|Pause|

Utterly infinite, exceedingly great, deep and unfathomable - He is lofty, beyond reach.
His weight cannot be weighed, His value cannot be estimated. How can the Enticer of the mind be obtained? |1|

Millions search for Him, on various paths, but without the Guru, none find Him.

Says Nanak, the Lord Master has become Merciful. Meeting the Holy Saint, I drink in the sublime essence. |2|1|32|

Section 10 - Raag Dayv-Gandhaaree - Part 009

Dayv-Gandhaaree, Fifth Mehl:
I have looked in so many ways, but there is no other like the Lord.
On all the continents and islands, He is permeating and fully pervading; He is in all worlds. |1|Pause|

He is the most unfathomable of the unfathomable; who can chant His Praises? My mind lives by hearing news of Him.
People in the four stages of life, and in the four social classes are liberated, by serving You, Lord. |1|

The Guru has implanted the Word of His Shabad within me; I have attained the supreme status. My sense of duality has been dispelled, and now, I am at peace.
Says Nanak, I have easily crossed over the terrifying world-ocean, obtaining the treasure of the Lord's Name. |2|2|33|

Raag Dayv-Gandhaaree, Fifth Mehl, Sixth House:
One Universal Creator God. By The Grace Of The True Guru:
Know that there is One and only One Lord.
O Gurmukh, know that He is One. |1|Pause|

Why are you wandering around? O Siblings of Destiny, don't wander around; He is permeating and pervading everywhere. |1|

As the fire in the forest, without control, cannot serve any purpose
- just so, without the Guru, one cannot attain the Gate of the Lord.
Joining the Society of the Saints, renounce your ego; says Nanak, in this way, the supreme treasure is obtained. |2|1|34|

Dayv-Gandhaaree, Fifth Mehl:
His state cannot be known. |1|Pause|

How can I behold Him through clever tricks? Those who tell this story are wonder-struck and amazed. |1|

The servants of God, the celestial singers, the Siddhas and the seekers,
the angelic and divine beings, Brahma and those like Brahma,
and the four Vedas proclaim, day and night,
that the Lord and Master is inaccessible, unapproachable and unfathomable.
Endless, endless are His Glories, says Nanak; they cannot be described - they are beyond our reach. |2|2|35|

Dayv-Gandhaaree, Fifth Mehl:
I meditate, and sing of the Creator Lord.
I have become fearless, and I have found peace, poise and bliss, remembering the infinite Lord. |1|Pause|

The Guru, of the most fruitful image, has placed His hand upon my forehead.
Wherever I look, there, I find Him with me.
The Lotus Feet of the Lord are the Support of my very breath of life. |1|

My God is all-powerful, unfathomable and utterly vast.
The Lord and Master is close at hand - He dwells in each and every heart.
Nanak seeks the Sanctuary and the Support of God, who has no end or limitation. |2|3|36|

Dayv-Gandhaaree, Fifth Mehl:
Turn away, O my mind, turn away.
Turn away from the faithless cynic.
False is the love of the false one; break the ties, O my mind, and your ties shall be broken. Break your ties with the faithless cynic. |1|Pause|

One who enters a house filled with soot is blackened.
Run far away from such people! One who meets the Guru escapes from the bondage of the three dispositions. |1|

I beg this blessing of You, O Merciful Lord, ocean of mercy - please, don't bring me face to face with the faithless cyincs.

Section 10 - Raag Dayv-Gandhaaree - Part 010

Make servant Nanak the slave of Your slave; let his head roll in the dust under the feet of the Holy. |2|4|37|

Raag Dayv-Gandhaaree, Fifth Mehl, Seventh House:
One Universal Creator God. By The Grace Of The True Guru:
You are all-powerful, at all times; You show me the Way; I am a sacrifice, a sacrifice to You.
Your Saints sing to You with love; I fall at their feet. |1|Pause|

O Praiseworthy Lord, Enjoyer of celestial peace, Embodiment of mercy, One Infinite Lord, Your place is so beautiful. |1|

Riches, supernatural spiritual powers and wealth are in the palm of Your hand. O Lord, Life of the World, Master of all, infinite is Your Name.
Show Kindness, Mercy and Compassion to Nanak; hearing Your Praises, I live. |2|1|38|6|44|

One Universal Creator God. By The Grace Of The True Guru:
Raag Dayv-Gandhaaree, Ninth Mehl:
This mind does not follow my advice one tiny bit.
I am so tired of giving it instructions - it will not refrain from its evil-mindedness. |1|Pause|

It has gone insane with the intoxication of Maya; it does not chant the Lord's Praise.
Practicing deception, it tries to cheat the world, and so it fills its belly. |1|

Like a dog's tail, it cannot be straightened; it will not listen to what I tell it.
Says Nanak, vibrate forever the Name of the Lord, and all your affairs shall be adjusted. |2|1|

Raag Dayv-Gandhaaree, Ninth Mehl:
All things are mere diversions of life:
mother, father, siblings, children, relatives and the wife of your home. |1|Pause|

When the soul is separated from the body, then they will cry out, calling you a ghost.

No one will let you stay, for even half an hour; they drive you out of the house. |1|

The created world is like an illusion, a mirage - see this, and reflect upon it in your mind.
Says Nanak, vibrate forever the Name of the Lord, which shall deliver you. |2|2|

Raag Dayv-Gandhaaree, Ninth Mehl:
In this world, I have seen love to be false.
Whether they are spouses or friends, all are concerned only with their own happiness. |1|Pause|

All say, "Mine, mine", and attach their consciousness to you with love.
But at the very last moment, none shall go along with you. How strange are the ways of the world! |1|

The foolish mind has not yet reformed itself, although I have grown weary of continually instructing it.
O Nanak, one crosses over the terrifying world-ocean, singing the Songs of God. |2|3|6|38|47|

RAAG BIHAAGRA

Section 11 - Raag Bihaagra - Part 001

ONE Universal Creator God. Truth Is The Name. Creative Being Personified. No Fear. No Hatred. Image Of The Undying. Beyond Birth. Self-Existent. By Guru's Grace:

Raag Bihaagraa, Chau-Padas, Fifth Mehl, Second House:
To associate with your arch enemies,
is to live with poisonous snakes;
I have made the effort to shake them off. |1|

Then, I repeated the Name of the Lord, Har, Har,
and I obtained celestial peace. |1|Pause|

False is the love of the many emotional attachments,
which suck the mortal into the whirlpool of reincarnation. |2|

All are travellers,
who have gathered under the world-tree,
and are bound by their many bonds. |3|

Eternal is the Company of the Holy,
where the Kirtan of the Lord's Praises are sung.
Nanak seeks this Sanctuary. |4|1|

One Universal Creator God. By The Grace Of The True Guru:
Raag Bihaagraa, Ninth Mehl:
No one knows the state of the Lord.
The Yogis, the celibates, the penitents, and all sorts of clever people have failed. |1|Pause|

In an instant, He changes the beggar into a king, and the king into a beggar.
He fills what is empty, and empties what is full - such are His ways. |1|

He Himself spread out the expanse of His Maya, and He Himself beholds it.

He assumes so many forms, and plays so many games, and yet, He remains detached from it all. |2|

Incalculable, infinite, incomprehensible and immaculate is He, who has misled the entire world.
Cast off all your doubts; prays Nanak, O mortal, focus your consciousness on His Feet. |3|1|2|

Raag Bihaagraa, Chhant, Fourth Mehl, First House:
One Universal Creator God. By The Grace Of The True Guru:
Meditate on the Name of the Lord, Har, Har, O my soul; as Gurmukh, meditate on the invaluable Name of the Lord.
My mind is pierced through by the sublime essence of the Lord's Name.
The Lord is dear to my mind. With the sublime essence of the Lord's Name, my mind is washed clean.

Section 11 - Raag Bihaagra - Part 002

Under Guru's Instructions, hold your mind steady; O my soul, do not let it wander anywhere.
One who utters the Bani of the Praises of the Lord God, O Nanak, obtains the fruits of his heart's desires. |1|

Under Guru's Instruction, the Ambrosial Name abides within the mind, O my soul; with your mouth, utter the words of ambrosia.
The Words of the devotees are Ambrosial Nectar, O my soul; hearing them in the mind, embrace loving affection for the Lord.
Separated for so very long, I have found the Lord God; He holds me close in His loving embrace.
Servant Nanak's mind is filled with bliss, O my soul; the unstruck sound-current of the Shabad vibrates within. |2|

If only my friends and companions would come and unite me with my Lord God, O my soul.
I offer my mind to the one who recites the sermon of my Lord God, O my soul.
As Gurmukh, ever worship the Lord in adoration, O my soul, and you shall obtain the fruits of your heart's desires.
O Nanak, hurry to the Lord's Sanctuary; O my soul, those who meditate on the Lord's Name are very fortunate. |3|

By His Mercy, God comes to meet us, O my soul; through the Guru's Teachings, He reveals His Name.

Without the Lord, I am so sad, O my soul - as sad as the lotus without water.

The Perfect Guru has united me, O my soul, with the Lord, my best friend, the Lord God.

Blessed, blessed is the Guru, who has shown me the Lord, O my soul; servant Nanak blossoms forth in the Name of the Lord. |4|1|

Raag Bihaagraa, Fourth Mehl:

The Name of the Lord, Har, Har, is Ambrosial Nectar, O my soul; through the Guru's Teachings, this Nectar is obtained.

Pride in Maya is poison, O my soul; through the Ambrosial Nectar of the Name, this poison is eradicated.

The dry mind is rejuvenated, O my soul, meditating on the Name of the Lord, Har, Har.

The Lord has given me the pre-ordained blessing of high destiny, O my soul; servant Nanak merges in the Naam, the Name of the Lord. |1|

My mind is attached to the Lord, O my soul, like the infant, sucking his mother's milk.

Without the Lord, I find no peace, O my soul; I am like the song-bird, crying out without the rain drops.

Go, and seek the Sanctuary of the True Guru, O my soul; He shall tell you of the Glorious Virtues of the Lord God.

Servant Nanak has merged into the Lord, O my soul; the many melodies of the Shabad resound within his heart. |2|

Through egotism, the self-willed manmukhs are separated, O my soul; bound to poison, they are burnt by egotism.

Like the pigeon, which itself falls into the trap, O my soul, all the self-willed manmukhs fall under the influence of death.

Those self-willed manmukhs who focus their consciousness on Maya, O my soul, are foolish, evil demons.

Section 11 - Raag Bihaagra - Part 003

The Lord's humble servants beseech and implore Him, and enter His Sanctuary, O my soul; Guru Nanak becomes their Divine Protector. |3|

The Lord's humble servants are saved, through the Love of the Lord, O my soul; by their pre-ordained good destiny, they obtain the Lord.

The Name of the Lord, Har, Har, is the ship, O my soul, and the Guru is the helmsman. Through the Word of the Shabad, He ferries us across.

The Lord, Har, Har, is all-powerful and very kind, O my soul; through the Guru, the True Guru, He seems so sweet.

Shower Your Mercy upon me, and hear my prayer, O Lord, Har, Har; please, let servant Nanak meditate on Your Name. |4|2|

Bihaagraa, Fourth Mehl:

In this world, the best occupation is to sing the Praises of the Naam, O my soul. Singing the Praises of the Lord, the Lord is enshrined in the mind.

The Name of the Lord, Har, Har, is immaculate and pure, O my soul. Chanting the Name of the Lord, Har, Har, one is saved.

All sins and errors are erased, O my soul; with the Naam, the Gurmukh washes off this filth.

By great good fortune, servant Nanak meditates on the Lord; even fools and idiots like me have been saved. |1|

Those who meditate on the Lord's Name, O my soul, overpower the five passions.

The nine treasures of the Naam are within, O my soul; the Great Guru has made me see the unseen Lord.

The Guru has fulfilled my hopes and desires, O my soul; meeting the Lord, all my hunger is satisfied.

O servant Nanak, he alone sings the Glorious Praises of the Lord, O my soul, upon whose forehead God has inscribed such pre-ordained destiny. |2|

I am a deceitful sinner, O my soul, a cheat, and a robber of others' wealth.

But, by great good fortune, I have found the Guru, O my soul; through the Perfect Guru, I have found the way to salvation.

The Guru has poured the Ambrosial Nectar of the Lord's Name into my mouth, O my soul, and now, my dead soul has come to life again.

O servant Nanak: those who meet the True Guru, O my soul, have all of their pains taken away. |3|

The Name of the Lord is sublime, O my soul; chanting it, one's sins are washed away.

The Guru, the Lord, has purified even the sinners, O my soul; now, they are famous and respected in the four directions and throughout the four ages.

The filth of egotism is totally wiped away, O my soul, by bathing in the Ambrosial Pool of the Lord's Name.

Even sinners are carried across, O my soul, if they are imbued with the Lord's Name, even for an instant, O servant Nanak. |4|3|

Bihaagraa, Fourth Mehl:

I am a sacrifice, O my soul, to those who take the Support of the Name of the Lord, Har, Har.

The Guru, the True Guru, implanted the Name within me, O my soul, and He has carried me across the terrifying world-ocean of poison.

Those who have meditated one-pointedly on the Lord, O my soul - I proclaim the Victory of those saintly beings.

Section 11 - Raag Bihaagra - Part 004

Nanak has found peace, meditating on the Lord, O my soul; the Lord is the Destroyer of all pain. |1|

Blessed, blessed is that tongue, O my soul, which sings the Glorious Praises of the Lord God.

Sublime and splendid are those ears, O my soul, which listen to the Kirtan of the Lord's Praises.

Sublime, pure and pious is that head, O my soul, which falls at the Guru's Feet.

Nanak is a sacrifice to that Guru, O my soul; the Guru has placed the Name of the Lord, Har, Har, in my mind. |2|

Blessed and approved are those eyes, O my soul, which gaze upon the Holy True Guru.

Sacred and sanctified are those hands, O my soul, which write the Praises of the Lord, Har, Har.

I worship continually the feet of that humble being, O my soul, who walks on the Path of Dharma - the path of righteousness.

Nanak is a sacrifice to those, O my soul, who hear of the Lord, and believe in the Lord's Name. |3|

The earth, the nether regions of the underworld, and the Akaashic ethers, O my soul, all meditate on the Name of the Lord, Har, Har.

Wind, water and fire, O my soul, continually sing the Praises of the Lord, Har, Har, Har.

The woods, the meadows and the whole world, O my soul, chant with their mouths the Lord's Name, and meditate on the Lord.

O Nanak, one who, as Gurmukh, focuses his consciousness on the Lord's devotional worship - O my soul, he is robed in honor in the Court of the Lord. |4|4|

Bihaagraa, Fourth Mehl:

Those who do not remember the Name of the Lord, Har, Har, O my soul - those self-willed manmukhs are foolish and ignorant.

Those who attach their consciousness to emotional attachment and Maya, O my soul, depart regretfully in the end.

They find no place of rest in the Court of the Lord, O my soul; those self-willed manmukhs are deluded by sin.

O servant Nanak, those who meet the Guru are saved, O my soul; chanting the Name of the Lord, they are absorbed in the Name of the Lord. |1|

Go, everyone, and meet the True Guru; O my soul, He implants the Name of the Lord, Har, har, within the heart.

Do not hesitate for an instant - meditate on the Lord, O my soul; who knows whether he shall draw another breath?

That time, that moment, that instant, that second is so fruitful, O my soul, when my Lord comes into my mind.

Servant Nanak has meditated on the Naam, the Name of the Lord, O my soul, and now, the Messenger of Death does not draw near him. |2|

The Lord continually watches, and hears everything, O my soul; he alone is afraid, who commits sins.

One whose heart is pure within, O my soul, casts off all his fears.

One who has faith in the Fearless Name of the Lord, O my soul - all his enemies and attackers speak against him in vain.

Section 11 - Raag Bihaagra - Part 005

Nanak has served the Perfect Guru, O my soul, who causes all to fall at His feet. |3|

Serve such a Lord continuously, O my soul, who is the Great Lord and Master of all.

Those who single-mindedly worship Him in adoration, O my soul, are not subservient to anyone.

Serving the Guru, I have obtained the Mansion of the Lord's Presence, O my soul; all the slanderers and trouble-makers bark in vain.

Servant Nanak has meditated on the Name, O my soul; such is the pre-ordained destiny which the Lord written on his forehead. |4|5|

Bihaagraa, Fourth Mehl:

All beings are Yours - You permeate them all. O my Lord God, You know what they do in their hearts.

The Lord is with them, inwardly and outwardly, O my soul; He sees everything, but the mortal denies the Lord in his mind.

The Lord is far away from the self-willed manmukhs, O my soul; all their efforts are in vain.

Servant Nanak, as Gurmukh, meditates on the Lord, O my soul; he beholds the Lord ever-present. |1|

They are devotees, and they are servants, O my soul, who are pleasing to the Mind of my God.

They are robed in honor in the Court of the Lord, O my soul; night and day, they remain absorbed in the True Lord.

In their company, the filth of one's sins is washed away, O my soul; imbued with the Lord's Love, one comes to bear the Mark of His Grace.

Nanak offers his prayer to God, O my soul; joining the Saadh Sangat, the Company of the Holy, he is satisfied. |2|

O tongue, chant the Name of God; O my soul, chanting the Name of the Lord, Har, Har, your desires shall be extinguished.

He, unto whom my Supreme Lord God shows Mercy, O my soul, enshrines the Name in his mind.

One who meets the Perfect True Guru, O my soul, obtains the treasure of the Lord's wealth.

By great good fortune, one joins the Company of the Holy, O my soul. O Nanak, sing the Glorious Praises of the Lord. |3|

In the places and interspaces, O my soul, the Supreme Lord God, the Great Giver, is pervading.

His limits cannot be found, O my soul; He is the Perfect Architect of Destiny.

He cherishes all beings, O my soul, as the mother and father cherish their child.

By thousands of clever tricks, He cannot be obtained, O my soul; servant Nanak, as Gurmukh, has come to know the Lord. |4|6|

First Set of Six|

Bihaagraa, Fifth Mehl, Chhant, First House:

One Universal Creator God. By The Grace Of The True Guru:

I have seen one miracle of the Lord, O my Dear Beloved - whatever He does is righteous and just.

The Lord has fashioned this beautiful arena, O my Dear Beloved, where all come and go.

Section 11 - Raag Bihaagra - Part 006

The One who fashioned the world causes them to come and go.

Some meet the True Guru - the Lord invites them into the Mansion of His Presence; others wander around, deluded by doubt.

You alone know Your limits; You are contained in all.

Nanak speaks the Truth: listen, Saints - the Lord dispenses even-handed justice. |1|

Come and join me, O my beautiful dear beloveds; let's worship the Name of the Lord, Har, Har.

Let's serve the Perfect True Guru, O my dear beloveds, and clear away the Path of Death.

Having cleared the treacherous path, as Gurmukhs, we shall obtain honor in the Court of the Lord.

Those who have such pre-ordained destiny, lovingly focus their consciousness on the Lord, night and day.

Self-conceit, egotism and emotional attachment are eradicated when one joins the Saadh Sangat, the Company of the Holy.

Says servant Nanak, one who contemplates the Name of the Lord, Har, Har, is liberated. |2|

Let's join hands, O Saints; let's come together, O my dear beloveds, and worship the imperishable, Almighty Lord.

I sought Him through uncounted forms of adoration, O my dear beloveds; now, I dedicate my entire mind and body to the Lord.

The mind, body and all wealth belong to God; so what can anyone offer to Him in worship?

He alone merges in the lap of God, unto whom the Merciful Lord Master becomes compassionate.

One who has such pre-ordained destiny written on his forehead, comes to bear love for the Guru.

Says servant Nanak, joining the Saadh Sangat, the Company of the Holy, let's worship the Name of the Lord, Har, Har. |3|

I wandered around, searching in the ten directions, O my dear beloveds, but I came to find the Lord in the home of my own being.

The Dear Lord has fashioned the body as the temple of the Lord, O my dear beloveds; the Lord continues to dwell there.

The Lord and Master Himself is pervading everywhere; through the Guru, He is revealed.

Darkness is dispelled, and pains are removed, when the sublime essence of the Lord's Ambrosial Nectar trickles down.

Wherever I look, the Lord and Master is there. The Supreme Lord God is everywhere.

Says servant Nanak, meeting the True Guru, I have found the Lord, within the home of my own being. |4|1|

Raag Bihaagraa, Fifth Mehl:
He is dear to me; He fascinates my mind; He is the ornament of my heart, the support of the breath of life.

The Glory of the Beloved, Merciful Lord of the Universe is beautiful; He is infinite and without limit.

O Compassionate Sustainer of the World, Beloved Lord of the Universe, please, join with Your humble soul-bride.

My eyes long for the Blessed Vision of Your Darshan; the night passes, but I cannot sleep.

I have applied the healing ointment of spiritual wisdom to my eyes; the Naam, the Name of the Lord, is my food. These are all my decorations.

Prays Nanak, let's meditate on the Saint, that he may unite us with our Husband Lord. |1|

I endure thousands of reprimands, and still, my Lord has not met with me.
I make the effort to meet with my Lord, but none of my efforts work.

Unsteady is my consciousness, and unstable is my wealth; without my Lord, I cannot be consoled.

Section 11 - Raag Bihaagra - Part 007

Food, drink and decorations are useless; without my Husband Lord, how can I survive?
I yearn for Him, and desire Him night and day. I cannot live without Him, even for an instant.
Prays Nanak, O Saint, I am Your slave; by Your Grace, I meet my Husband Lord. |2|

I share a bed with my Beloved, but I do not behold the Blessed Vision of His Darshan.
I have endless demerits - how can my Lord call me to the Mansion of His Presence?
The worthless, dishonored and orphaned soul-bride prays, "Meet with me, O God, treasure of mercy."
The wall of doubt has been shattered, and now I sleep in peace, beholding God, the Lord of the nine treasures, even for an instant.
If only I could come into the Mansion of my Beloved Lord's Presence! Joining with Him, I sing the songs of joy.
Prays Nanak, I seek the Sanctuary of the Saints; please, reveal to me the Blessed Vision of Your Darshan. |3|

By the Grace of the Saints, I have obtained the Lord, Har, Har.
My desires are fulfilled, and my mind is at peace; the fire within has been quenched.
Fruitful is that day, and beauteous is that night, and countless are the joys, celebrations and pleasures.
The Lord of the Universe, the Beloved Sustainer of the World, has been revealed. With what tongue can I speak of His Glory?

Doubt, greed, emotional attachment and corruption are taken away; joining with my companions, I sing the songs of joy.
Prays Nanak, I meditate on the Saint, who has led me to merge with the Lord, Har, Har. |4|2|

Bihaagraa, Fifth Mehl:

Shower Your Mercy upon me, O Guru, O Perfect Supreme Lord God, that I might chant the Naam, the Name of the Lord, night and day.

I speak the Ambrosial Words of the Guru's Bani, praising the Lord. Your Will is sweet to me, Lord.

Show kindness and compassion, O Sustainer of the Word, Lord of the Universe; without You, I have no other.

Almighty, sublime, infinite, perfect Lord - my soul, body, wealth and mind are Yours.

I am foolish, stupid, masterless, fickle, powerless, lowly and ignorant.

Prays Nanak, I seek Your Sanctuary - please save me from coming and going in reincarnation. |1|

In the Sanctuary of the Holy Saints, I have found the Dear Lord, and I constantly sing the Glorious Praises of the Lord.

Applying the dust of the devotees to the mind and body, O Dear Lord, all sinners are sanctified.

The sinners are sanctified in the company of those who have met the Creator Lord.

Imbued with the Naam, the Name of the Lord, they are given the gift of the life of the soul; their gifts increase day by day.

Wealth, the supernatural spiritual powers of the Siddhas, and the nine treasures come to those who meditate on the Lord, and conquer their own soul.

Prays Nanak, it is only by great good fortune that the Holy Saints, the Lord's companions, are found, O friends. |2|

Those who deal in Truth, O Dear Lord, are the perfect bankers.

They possess the great treasure, O Dear Lord, and they reap the profit of the Lord's Praise.

Sexual desire, anger and greed do not cling to those who are attuned to God.

They know the One, and they believe in the One; they are intoxicated with the Lord's Love.

They fall at the Feet of the Saints, and seek their Sanctuary; their minds are filled with joy.

Prays Nanak, those who have the Naam in their laps are the true bankers. |3|

O Nanak, meditate on that Dear Lord, who supports all by His almighty strength.

Section 11 - Raag Bihaagra - Part 008

In their minds, the Gurmukhs do not forget the Dear Lord, the Primal Creator Lord.

Pain, disease and fear do not cling to those who meditate on the Lord, Har, Har.

By the Grace of the Saints, they cross over the terrifying world-ocean, and obtain their pre-ordained destiny.

They are congratulated and applauded, their minds are at peace, and they meet the infinite Lord God.

Prays Nanak, by meditating in remembrance on the Lord, Har, Har, my desires are fulfilled. |4|3|

Bihaagraa, Fifth Mehl, Second House:

One Universal Creator God. By The Grace Of The True Guru:

O peaceful night, grow longer - I have come to enshrine love for my Beloved.

O painful sleep, grow shorter, so that I may constantly grasp His Feet.

I long for the dust of His Feet, and beg for His Name; for His Love, I have renounced the world.

I am imbued with the Love of my Beloved, and I am naturally intoxicated with it; I have forsaken my awful evil-mindedness.

He has taken me by the arm, and I am saturated with His Love; I have met my Beloved on the Path of Truth.

Prays Nanak, please Lord, shower Your Mercy on me, that I may remain attached to Your Feet. |1|

O my friends and companions, let us remain attached to the Feet of God.

Within my mind is great love for my Beloved; I beg for the Lord's devotional worship.

The Lord's devotional worship is obtained, meditating on God. Let us go and meet the humble servants of the Lord.

Renounce pride, emotional attachment and corruption, and dedicate this body, wealth and mind to Him.

The Lord God is great, perfect, glorious, absolutely perfect; meeting the Lord, Har, Har, the wall of doubt is torn down.

Prays Nanak, hear these teachings, O friends - chant the Lord's Name constantly, over and over again. |2|

The Lord's bride is a happy wife; she enjoys all pleasures.

She does not sit around like a widow, because the Lord God lives forever.

She does not suffer pain - she meditates on God. She is blessed, and very fortunate.

She sleeps in peaceful ease, her sins are erased, and she wakes to the joy and love of the Naam.

She remains absorbed in her Beloved - the Lord's Name is her ornament. The Words of her Beloved are sweet and pleasing to her.

Prays Nanak, I have obtained my mind's desires; I have met my eternal Husband Lord. |3|

The songs of bliss resound, and millions of pleasures are found in that house;

the mind and body are permeated by God, the Lord of supreme bliss.

My Husband Lord is infinite and merciful; He is the Lord of wealth, the Lord of the Universe, the Saving Grace of sinners.

God, the Giver of mercy, the Lord, the Destroyer of pride, carries us across the terrifying world-ocean of poison.

The Lord lovingly embraces whoever comes to the Lord's Sanctuary - this is the way of the Lord and Master.

Prays Nanak, I have met my Husband Lord, who plays with me forever. |4|1|4|

Bihaagraa, Fifth Mehl:
The Lord's Feet are the Pools of Ambrosial Nectar; your dwelling is there, O my mind.

Section 11 - Raag Bihaagra - Part 009

Take your cleansing bath in the Ambrosial Pool of the Lord, and all of your sins shall be wiped away, O my soul.

Take your cleansing ever in the Lord God, O friends, and the pain of darkness shall be dispelled.

Birth and death shall not touch you, and the noose of Death shall be cut away.

So join the Saadh Sangat, the Company of the Holy, and be imbued with the Naam, the Name of the Lord; there, your hopes shall be fulfilled.

Prays Nanak, shower Your Mercy upon me, O Lord, that I might dwell at Your Lotus Feet. |1|

There is bliss and ecstasy there always, and the unstruck celestial melody resounds there.

Meeting together, the Saints sing God's Praises, and celebrate His Victory.

Meeting together, the Saints sing the Praises of the Lord Master; they are pleasing to the Lord, and saturated with the sublime essence of His love and affection.

They obtain the profit of the Lord, eliminate their self-conceit, and meet Him, from whom they were separated for so long.

Taking them by the arm, He makes them His own; God, the One, inaccessible and infinite, bestows His kindness.

Prays Nanak, forever immaculate are those who sing the Praises of the True Word of the Shabad. |2|

Listen, O most fortunate ones, to the Ambrosial Bani of the Word of the Lord.

He alone, whose karma is so pre-ordained, has it enter into his heart.

He alone knows the Unspoken Speech, unto whom God has shown His Mercy.

He becomes immortal, and shall not die again; his troubles, disputes and pains are dispelled.

He finds the Sanctuary of the Lord; he does not forsake the Lord, and does not leave. God's Love is pleasing to his mind and body.

Prays Nanak, sing forever the Sacred Ambrosial Bani of His Word. |3|

My mind and body are intoxicated - this state cannot be described.

We originated from Him, and into Him we shall merge once again.

I merge into God's Light, through and through, like water merging into water.

The One Lord permeates the water, the land and the sky - I do not see any other.

He is totally permeating the woods, meadows and the three worlds. I cannot express His worth.

Prays Nanak, He alone knows - He who created this creation. |4|2|5|

Bihaagraa, Fifth Mehl:

The Saints go around, searching for God, the support of their breath of life.

They lose the strength of their bodies, if they do not merge with their Beloved Lord.

O God, my Beloved, please, bestow Your kindness upon me, that I may merge with You; by Your Mercy, attach me to the hem of Your robe.

Bless me with Your Name, that I may chant it, O Lord and Master; beholding the Blessed Vision of Your Darshan, I live.

He is all-powerful, perfect, eternal and unchanging, exalted, unapproachable and infinite.

Prays Nanak, bestow Your Mercy upon me, O Beloved of my soul, that I may merge with You. |1|

I have practiced chanting, intensive meditation and fasting, to see Your Feet, O Lord.

But still, my burning is not quenched, without the Sanctuary of the Lord Master.

I seek Your Sanctuary, God - please, cut away my bonds and carry me across the world-ocean.

I am masterless, worthless, and I know nothing; please do not count up my merits and demerits.

O Lord, Merciful to the meek, Sustainer of the world, O Beloved, Almighty Cause of causes.

Nanak, the song-bird, begs for the rain-drop of the Lord's Name; meditating on the Feet of the Lord, Har, Har, he lives. |2|

Section 11 - Raag Bihaagra - Part 010

Drink in the Ambrosial Nectar from the pool of the Lord; chant the Name of the Lord, Har, Har.

In the Society of the Saints, one meets the Lord; meditating on Him, one's affairs are resolved.

God is the One who accomplishes everything; He is the Dispeller of pain. Never forget Him from your mind, even for an instant.

He is blissful, night and day; He is forever True. All Glories are contained in the Lord in the Universe.

Incalculable, lofty and infinite is the Lord and Master. Unapproachable is His home.

Prays Nanak, my desires are fulfilled; I have met the Lord, the Greatest Lover. |3|

The fruits of many millions of charitable feasts come to those who listen to and sing the Lord's Praise.

Chanting the Name of the Lord, Har, Har, all one's generations are carried across.

Chanting the Name of the Lord, one is beautified; what Praises of His can I chant?

I shall never forget the Lord; He is the Beloved of my soul. My mind constantly yearns for the Blessed Vision of His Darshan.

Auspicious is that day, when God, the lofty, inaccessible and infinite, hugs me close in His embrace.

Prays Nanak, everything is fruitful - I have met my supremely beloved Lord God. |4|3|6|

Bihaagraa, Fifth Mehl, Chhant:

Why are you imbued with the love of another? That path is very dangerous. O sinner, no one is your friend.

No one shall be your friend, and you shall forever regret your actions.

You have not chanted with your tongue the Praises of the Sustainer of the World; when will these days come again?

The leaf, separated from the branch, shall not be joined with it again; all alone, it falls on its way to death.

Prays Nanak, without the Lord's Name, the soul wanders, forever suffering. |1|

You are practicing deception secretly, but the Lord, the Knower, knows all.

When the Righteous Judge of Dharma reads your account, you shall be squeezed like a sesame seed in the oil-press.

For the actions you committed, you shall suffer the penalty; you shall be consigned to countless reincarnations.

Imbued with the love of Maya, the great enticer, you shall lose the jewel of this human life.

Except for the One Name of the Lord, you are clever in everything else.

Prays Nanak, those who have such pre-ordained destiny are attracted to doubt and emotional attachment. |2|

No one advocates for the ungrateful person, who is separated from the Lord.

The hard-hearted Messenger of Death comes and seizes him.

He seizes him, and leads him away, to pay for his evil deeds; he was imbued with Maya, the great enticer.

He was not Gurmukh - he did not chant the Glorious Praises of the Lord of the Universe; and now, the hot irons are put to his chest.

He is ruined by sexual desire, anger and egotism; deprived of spiritual wisdom, he comes to regret.

Prays Nanak, by his cursed destiny he has gone astray; with his tongue, he does not chant the Name of the Lord. |3|

Without You, God, no one is our savior.

It is Your Nature, Lord, to save the sinners.

O Savior of sinners, I have entered Your Sanctuary, O Lord and Master, Compassionate Ocean of Mercy.

Please, rescue me from the deep, dark pit, O Creator, Cherisher of all hearts.

I seek Your Sanctuary; please, cut away these heavy bonds, and give me the Support of the One Name.

Section 11 - Raag Bihaagra - Part 011

Prays Nanak, please, give me Your Hand and save me, O Lord of the Universe, Merciful to the meek. |4|

That day is judged to be fruitful, when I merged with my Lord.

Total happiness was revealed, and pain was taken far away.

Peace, tranquility, joy and eternal happiness come from constantly singing the Glorious Praises of the Sustainer of the World.

Joining the Saadh Sangat, the Company of the Holy, I lovingly remember the Lord; I shall not wander again in reincarnation.

He has naturally hugged me close in His Loving Embrace, and the seed of my primal destiny has sprouted.

Prays Nanak, He Himself has met me, and He shall never again leave me. |5|4|7|

Bihaagraa, Fifth Mehl, Chhant:

Listen to my prayer, O my Lord and Master.

I am filled with millions of sins, but still, I am Your slave.

O Destroyer of pain, Bestower of Mercy, Fascinating Lord, Destroyer of sorrow and strife,

I have come to Your Sanctuary; please preserve my honor. You are all-pervading, O Immaculate Lord.

He hears and beholds all; God is with us, the nearest of the near.

O Lord and Master, hear Nanak's prayer; please save the servants of Your household. |1|

You are eternal and all-powerful; I am a mere beggar, Lord.

I am intoxicated with the love of Maya - save me, Lord!

Bound down by greed, emotional attachment and corruption, I have made so many mistakes.

The creator is both attached and detached from entanglements; one obtains the fruits of his own actions.

Show kindness to me, O Purifier of sinners; I am so tired of wandering through reincarnation.

Prays Nanak, I am the slave of the Lord; God is the Support of my soul, and my breath of life. |2|

You are great and all-powerful; my understanding is so inadequate, O Lord.

You cherish even the ungrateful ones; Your Glance of Grace is perfect, Lord.

Your wisdom is unfathomable, O Infinite Creator. I am lowly, and I know nothing.

Forsaking the jewel, I have saved the shell; I am a lowly, ignorant beast.

I have kept that which forsakes me, and is very fickle, continually committing sins, again and again.

Nanak seeks Your Sanctuary, Almighty Lord and Master; please, preserve my honor. |3|

I was separated from Him, and now, He has united me with Himself.

In the Saadh Sangat, the Company of the Holy, I sing the Glorious Praises of the Lord.

Singing the Praises of the Lord of the Universe, the ever-sublime blissful Lord is revealed to me.

My bed is adorned with God; my God has made me His own.

Abandoning anxiety, I have become carefree, and I shall not suffer in pain any longer.

Nanak lives by beholding the Blessed Vision of His Darshan, singing the Glorious Praises of the Lord of the Universe, the ocean of excellence. |4|5|8|

Bihaagraa, Fifth Mehl, Chhant:

O you of sublime faith, chant the Lord's Name; why do you remain silent?

with your eyes, you have seen the treacherous ways of Maya.

Nothing shall go along with you, except the Name of the Lord of the Universe.

Land, clothes, gold and silver - all of these things are useless.

Children, spouse, worldly honors, elephants, horses and other corrupting influences shall not go with you.

Prays Nanak, without the Saadh Sangat, the Company of the Holy, the whole world is false. |1|

Section 11 - Raag Bihaagra - Part 012

O king, why are you sleeping? Why don't you wake up to reality?

It is useless to cry and whine about Maya, but so many cry out and bewail.

So many cry out for Maya, the great enticer, but without the Name of the Lord, there is no peace.

Thousands of clever tricks and efforts will not succeed. One goes wherever the Lord wills him to go.

In the beginning, in the middle, and in the end, He is all-pervading everywhere; He is in each and every heart.

Prays Nanak, those who join the Saadh Sangat go to the house of the Lord with honor. |2|

O king of mortals, know that your palaces and wise servants shall be of no use in the end.

You shall certainly have to separate yourself from them, and their attachment shall make you feel regret.

Beholding the phantom city, you have gone astray; how can you now find stability?

Absorbed in things other than the Name of the Lord, this human life is wasted in vain.

Indulging in egotistical actions, your thirst is not quenched. Your desires are not fulfilled, and you do not attain spiritual wisdom.

Prays Nanak, without the Name of the Lord, so many have departed with regret. |3|

Showering His blessings, the Lord has made me His own.

Grasping me by the arm, He has pulled me out of the mud, and He has blessed me with the Saadh Sangat, the Company of the Holy.

Worshipping the Lord in the Saadh Sangat, all my sins and sufferings are burnt away.

This is the greatest religion, and the best act of charity; this alone shall go along with you.

My tongue chants in adoration the Name of the One Lord and Master; my mind and body are drenched in the Lord's Name.

O Nanak, whoever the Lord unites with Himself, is filled with all virtues. |4|6|9|

Vaar Of Bihaagraa, Fourth Mehl:
One Universal Creator God. By The Grace Of The True Guru:
Shalok, Third Mehl:
Serving the Guru, peace is obtained; do not search for peace anywhere else.
The soul is pierced by the Word of the Guru's Shabad. The Lord dwells ever with the soul.
O Nanak, they alone obtain the Naam, the Name of the Lord, who are blessed by the Lord with His Glance of Grace. |1|

Third Mehl:
The treasure of the Lord's Praise is such a blessed gift; he alone obtains it to spend, unto whom the Lord bestows it.
Without the True Guru, it does not come to hand; all have grown weary of performing religious rituals.
O Nanak, the self-willed manmukhs of the world lack this wealth; when they are hungry in the next world, what will they have to eat there? |2|

Pauree:
All are Yours, and You belong to all. You created all.
You are pervading within all - all meditate on You.
You accept the devotional worship of those who are pleasing to Your Mind.
Whatever pleases the Lord God happens; all act as You cause them to act.
Praise the Lord, the greatest of all; He preserves the honor of the Saints. |1|

Shalok, Third Mehl:
O Nanak, the spiritually wise one has conquered all others.
Through the Name, his affairs are brought to perfection; whatever happens is by His Will.
Under Guru's Instruction, his mind is held steady; no one can make him waver.
The Lord makes His devotee His own, and his affairs are adjusted.

Section 11 - Raag Bihaagra - Part 013

The self-willed manmukhs have been led astray from the very beginning; within them lurks greed, avarice and ego.

Their nights and days pass in argument, and they do not reflect upon the Word of the Shabad.

The Creator has taken away their subtle intellect, and all their speech is corrupt.

No matter what they are given, they are not satisfied; within them is desire, and the great darkness of ignorance.

O Nanak, it is right to break with the self-willed manmukhs; to them, the love of Maya is sweet. |1|

Third Mehl:
What can fear and doubt do to those, who have given their heads to the Creator, and to the True Guru?

He who has preserved honor from the beginning of time, He shall preserve their honor as well.

Meeting their Beloved, they find peace; they reflect upon the True Word of the Shabad.

O Nanak, I serve the Giver of Peace; He Himself is the Assessor. |2|

Pauree:
All beings are Yours; You are the wealth of all.

One unto whom You give, obtains everything; there is no one else to rival You.

You alone are the Great Giver of all; I offer my prayer unto You, Lord.

One with whom You are pleased, is accepted by You; how blessed is such a person!

Your wondrous play is pervading everywhere. I place my pain and pleasure before You. |2|

Shalok, Third Mehl:
The Gurmukhs are pleasing to the True Lord; they are judged to be true in the True Court.

The minds of such friends are filled with bliss, as they reflect upon the Word of the Guru's Shabad.

They enshrine the Shabad within their hearts; their pain is dispelled, and the Creator blesses them with the Divine Light.

O Nanak, the Savior Lord shall save them, and shower them with His Mercy. |1|

Third Mehl:
Serve the Guru, and wait upon Him; as you work, maintain the Fear of God.
As you serve Him, you will become like Him, as you walk according to His Will.
O Nanak, He Himself is everything; there is no other place to go. |2|

Pauree:
You alone know Your greatness - no one else is as great as You.
If there were some other rival as great as You, then I would speak of him. You alone are as great as You are.
One who serves You obtains peace; who else can compare to You?
You are all-powerful to destroy and create, O Great Giver; with palms pressed together, all stand begging before You.
I see none as great as You, O Great Giver; You give in charity to the beings of all the continents, worlds, solar systems, nether regions and universes. |3|

Shalok, Third Mehl:
O mind, you have no faith, and you have not embraced love for the Celestial Lord;
you do not enjoy the sublime taste of the Word of the Shabad - what Praises of the Lord will you stubborn-mindedly sing?

O Nanak, his coming alone is approved, who, as Gurmukh, merges into the True Lord. |1|

Third Mehl:
The fool does not understand his own self; he annoys others with his speech.
His underlying nature does not leave him; separated from the Lord, he suffers cruel blows.
Through the fear of the True Guru, he has not changed and reformed himself, so that he might merge in the lap of God.

Section 11 - Raag Bihaagra - Part 014

Night and day, his doubts never stop; without the Word of the Shabad, he suffers in pain.
Sexual desire, anger and greed are so powerful within him; he passes his life constantly entangled in worldly affairs.

His feet, hands, eyes and ears are exhausted; his days are numbered, and his death is immanent.

The True Name does not seem sweet to him - the Name by which the nine treasures are obtained.

But if he remains dead while yet alive, then by so dying, he truly lives; thus, he attains liberation.

But if he is not blessed with such pre-ordained karma, then without this karma, what can he obtain?

Meditate in remembrance on the Word of the Guru's Shabad, you fool; through the Shabad, you shall obtain salvation and wisdom.

O Nanak, he alone finds the True Guru, who eliminates self-conceit from within. |2|

Pauree:

One whose consciousness is filled with my Lord Master - why should he feel anxious about anything?

The Lord is the Giver of Peace, the Lord of all things; why would we turn our faces away from His meditation, even for a moment, or an instant?

One who meditates on the Lord obtains all pleasures and comforts; let us go each and every day, to sit in the Saints' Society.

All the pain, hunger, and disease of the Lord's servant are eradicated; the bonds of the humble beings are torn away.

By the Lord's Grace, one becomes the Lord's devotee; beholding the face of the Lord's humble devotee, the whole world is saved and carried across. |4|

Shalok, Third Mehl:

Let that tongue, which has not tasted the Name of the Lord, be burnt.

O Nanak, one whose mind is filled with the Name of the Lord, Har, Har - his tongue savors the Word of the Shabad. |1|

Third Mehl:

Let that tongue, which has forgotten the Name of the Lord, be burnt.

O Nanak, the tongue of the Gurmukh chants the Lord's Name, and loves the Name of the Lord. |2|

Pauree:

The Lord Himself is the Master, the servant and the devotee; the Lord Himself is the Cause of causes.

The Lord Himself beholds, and He Himself rejoices. As He wills, so does He enjoin us.

The Lord places some on the Path, and the Lord leads others into the wilderness.

The Lord is the True Master; True is His justice. He arranges and beholds all His plays.

By Guru's Grace, servant Nanak speaks and sings the Glorious Praises of the True Lord. |5|

Shalok, Third Mehl:

How rare is the dervish, the Saintly renunciate, who understands renunciation.

Cursed is the life, and cursed are the clothes, of one who wanders around, begging from door to door.

But, if he abandons hope and anxiety, and as Gurmukh receives the Name as his charity,

then Nanak washes his feet, and is a sacrifice to him. |1|

Third Mehl:

O Nanak, the tree has one fruit, but two birds are perched upon it.

They are not seen coming or going; these birds have no wings.

One enjoys so many pleasures, while the other, through the Word of the Shabad, remains in Nirvaanaa.

Imbued with the subtle essence of the fruit of the Lord's Name, O Nanak, the soul bears the True Insignia of God's Grace. |2|

Pauree:

He Himself is the field, and He Himself is the farmer. He Himself grows and grinds the corn.

He Himself cooks it, He Himself puts the food in the dishes, and He Himself sits down to eat.

Section 11 - Raag Bihaagra - Part 015

He Himself is the water, He Himself gives the tooth-pick, and He Himself offers the mouthwash.

He Himself calls and seats the congregation, and He Himself bids them goodbye.

One whom the Lord Himself blesses with His Mercy - the Lord causes him to walk according to His Will. |6|

Shalok, Third Mehl:
Rituals and religions are all just entanglements; bad and good are bound up with them.
Those things done for the sake of children and spouse, in ego and attachment, are just more bonds.
Wherever I look, there I see the noose of attachment to Maya.
O Nanak, without the True Name, the world is engrossed in blind entanglements. |1|

Fourth Mehl:
The blind receive the Divine Light, when they merge with the Will of the True Guru.
They break their bonds, and dwell in Truth, and the darkness of ignorance is dispelled.
They see that everything belongs to the One who created and fashioned the body.
Nanak seeks the Sanctuary of the Creator - the Creator preserves his honor. |2|

Pauree:
When the Creator, sitting all by Himself, created the Universe, he did not consult with any of His servants;

so what can anyone take, and what can anyone give, when He did not create any other like Himself?
Then, after fashioning the world, the Creator blessed all with His blessings.
He Himself instructs us in His service, and as Gurmukh, we drink in His Ambrosial Nectar.
He Himself is formless, and He Himself is formed; whatever He Himself does, comes to pass. |7|

Shalok, Third Mehl:
The Gurmukhs serve God forever; night and day, they are steeped in the Love of the True Lord.
They are in bliss forever, singing the Glorious Praises of the True Lord; in this world and in the next, they keep Him clasped to their hearts.
Their Beloved dwells deep within; the Creator pre-ordained this destiny.
O Nanak, He blends them into Himself; He Himself showers His Mercy upon them. |1|

Third Mehl:

By merely talking and speaking, He is not found. Night and day, sing His Glorious Praises continually.

Without His Merciful Grace, no one finds Him; many have died barking and bewailing.

When the mind and body are saturated with the Word of the Guru's Shabad, the Lord Himself comes to dwell in his mind.

O Nanak, by His Grace, He is found; He unites us in His Union. |2|

Pauree:

He Himself is the Vedas, the Puraanas and all the Shaastras; He Himself chants them, and He Himself is pleased.

He Himself sits down to worship, and He Himself creates the world.

He Himself is a householder, and He Himself is a renunciate; He Himself utters the Unutterable.

He Himself is all goodness, and He Himself causes us to act; He Himself remains detached.

He Himself grants pleasure and pain; the Creator Himself bestows His gifts. |8|

Shalok, Third Mehl:

O Shaykh, abandon your cruel nature; live in the Fear of God and give up your madness.

Through the Fear of the Guru, many have been saved; in this fear, find the Fearless Lord.

Pierce your stone heart with the Word of the Shabad; let peace and tranquility come to abide in your mind.

If good deeds are done in this state of peace, they are approved by the Lord and Master.

O Nanak, through sexual desire and anger, no one has ever found God - go, and ask any wise man. |1|

Third Mehl:

Section 11 - Raag Bihaagra - Part 016

The self-willed manmukh is emotionally attached to Maya - he has no love for the Naam.

He practices falsehood, gathers in falsehood, and makes falsehood his sustenance.

He collects the poisonous wealth of Maya, and then dies; in the end, it is all reduced to ashes.

He practices religious rituals, purity and austere self-discipline, but within, there is greed and corruption.

O Nanak, whatever the self-willed manmukh does, is not acceptable; in the Court of the Lord, he is dishonored. |2|

Pauree:

He Himself created the four sources of creation, and He Himself fashioned speech; He Himself formed the worlds and solar systems.

He Himself is the ocean, and He Himself is the sea; He Himself puts the pearls in it.

By His Grace, the Lord enables the Gurmukh to find these pearls.

He Himself is the terrifying world-ocean, and He Himself is the boat; He Himself is the boatman, and He Himself ferries us across.

The Creator Himself acts, and causes us to act; no one else can equal You, Lord. |9|

Shalok, Third Mehl:

Fruitful is service to the True Guru, if one does so with a sincere mind.

The treasure of the Naam, is obtained, and the mind comes to be free of anxiety.

The pains of birth and death are eradicated, and the mind is rid of egotism and self-conceit.

One achieves the ultimate state, and remains absorbed in the True Lord.

O Nanak, the True Guru comes and meets those who have such pre-ordained destiny. |1|

Third Mehl:

The True Guru is imbued with the Naam, the Name of the Lord; He is the boat in this Dark Age of Kali Yuga.

One who becomes Gurmukh crosses over; the True Lord dwells within him.

He remembers the Naam, he gathers in the Naam, and he obtains honor through the Naam.

Nanak has found the True Guru; by His Grace, the Name is obtained. |2|

Pauree:

He Himself is the Philosopher's Stone, He Himself is the metal, and He Himself is transformed into gold.

He Himself is the Lord and Master, He Himself is the servant, and He Himself is the Destroyer of sins.

He Himself enjoys every heart; the Lord Master Himself is the basis of all illusion.

He Himself is the discerning one, and He Himself is the Knower of all; He Himself breaks the bonds of the Gurmukhs.

Servant Nanak is not satisfied by merely praising You, O Creator Lord; You are the Great Giver of peace. |10|

Shalok, Fourth Mehl:
Without serving the True Guru, the deeds which are done are only chains binding the soul.

Without serving the True Guru, they find no place of rest. They die, only to be born again - they continue coming and going.

Without serving the True Guru, their speech is insipid. They do not enshrine the Naam, the Name of the Lord, in the mind.

O Nanak, without serving the True Guru, they are bound and gagged, and beaten in the City of Death; they depart with blackened faces. |1|

Third Mehl:
Some wait upon and serve the True Guru; they embrace love for the Lord's Name.

O Nanak, they reform their lives, and redeem their generations as well. |2|

Pauree:
He Himself is the school, He Himself is the teacher, and He Himself brings the students to be taught.

He Himself is the father, He Himself is the mother, and He Himself makes the children wise.

In one place, He teaches them to read and understand everything, while in another place, He Himself makes them ignorant.

Some, You summon to the Mansion of Your Presence within, when they are pleasing to Your Mind, O True Lord.

Section 11 - Raag Bihaagra - Part 017

That Gurmukh, whom You have blessed with greatness - that humble being is known in Your True Court. |11|

Shalok, Mardaanaa:

The Dark Age of Kali Yuga is the vessel, filled with the wine of sexual desire; the mind is the drunkard.

Anger is the cup, filled with emotional attachment, and egotism is the server.

Drinking too much in the company of falsehood and greed, one is ruined.

So let good deeds be your distillery, and Truth your molasses; in this way, make the most excellent wine of Truth.

Make virtue your bread, good conduct the ghee, and modesty the meat to eat.

As Gurmukh, these are obtained, O Nanak; partaking of them, one's sins depart. |1|

MARDAANAA:

The human body is the vat, self-conceit is the wine, and desire is the company of drinking buddies.

The cup of the mind's longing is overflowing with falsehood, and the Messenger of Death is the cup-bearer.

Drinking in this wine, O Nanak, one takes on countless sins and corruptions.

So make spiritual wisdom your molasses, the Praise of God your bread, and the Fear of God the meat you eat.

O Nanak, this is the true food; let the True Name be your only Support. |2|

If the human body is the vat, and self-realization is the wine, then a stream of Ambrosial Nectar is produced.

Meeting with the Society of the Saints, the cup of the Lord's Love is filled with this Ambrosial Nectar; drinking it in, one's corruptions and sins are wiped away. |3|

Pauree:

He Himself is the angelic being, the heavenly herald, and the celestial singer. He Himself is the one who explains the six schools of philosophy.

He Himself is Shiva, Shankara and Mahaysh; He Himself is the Gurmukh, who speaks the Unspoken Speech.

He Himself is the Yogi, He Himself is the Sensual Enjoyer, and He Himself is the Sannyaasee, wandering through the wilderness.

He discusses with Himself, and He teaches Himself; He Himself is discrete, graceful and wise.

Staging His own play, He Himself watches it; He Himself is the Knower of all beings. |12|

Shalok, Third Mehl:
That evening prayer alone is acceptable, which brings the Lord God to my consciousness.
Love for the Lord wells up within me, and my attachment to Maya is burnt away.
By Guru's Grace, duality is conquered, and the mind becomes stable; I have made contemplative meditation my evening prayer.
O Nanak, the self-willed manmukh may recite his evening prayers, but his mind is not centered on it; through birth and death, he is ruined. |1|

Third Mehl:
I wandered over the whole world, crying out, "Love, O Love!", but my thirst was not quenched.
O Nanak, meeting the True Guru, my desires are satisfied; I found my Beloved, when I returned to my own home. |2|

Pauree:
He Himself is the supreme essence, He Himself is the essence of all. He Himself is the Lord and Master, and He Himself is the servant.
He Himself created the people of the eighteen castes; God Himself acquired His domain.
He Himself kills, and He Himself redeems; He Himself, in His Kindness, forgives us. He is infallible
- He never errs; the justice of the True Lord is totally True.
Those whom the Lord Himself instructs as Gurmukh - duality and doubt depart from within them. |13|

Shalok, Fifth Mehl:
That body, which does not remember the Lord's Name in meditation in the Saadh Sangat, the Company of the Holy, shall be reduced to dust.
Cursed and insipid is that body, O Nanak, which does not know the One who created it. |1|

Section 11 - Raag Bihaagra - Part 018

Fifth Mehl:

Let the Lotus Feet of the Lord abide within your heart, and with your tongue, chant God's Name.

O Nanak, meditate in remembrance on God, and nurture this body. |2|

Pauree:

The Creator Himself is the sixty-eight sacred places of pilgrimage; He Himself takes the cleansing bath in them.

He Himself practices austere self-discipline; the Lord Master Himself causes us to chant His Name.

He Himself becomes merciful to us; the Destroyer of fear Himself gives in charity to all.

One whom He has enlightened and made Gurmukh, ever obtains honor in His Court.

One whose honor the Lord Master has preserved, comes to know the True Lord. |14|

Shalok, Third Mehl:

O Nanak, without meeting the True Guru, the world is blind, and it does blind deeds.

It does not focus its consciousness on the Word of the Shabad, which would bring peace to abide in the mind.

Always afflicted with the dark passions of low energy, it wanders around, passing its days and nights burning.

Whatever pleases Him, comes to pass; no one has any say in this. |1|

Third Mehl:

The True Guru has commanded us to do this:

through the Guru's Gate, meditate on the Lord Master.

The Lord Master is ever-present. He tears away the veil of doubt, and installs His Light within the mind.

The Name of the Lord is Ambrosial Nectar - take this healing medicine!

Enshrine the Will of the True Guru in your consciousness, and make the True Lord's Love your self-discipline.

O Nanak, you shall be kept in peace here, and hereafter, you shall celebrate with the Lord. |2|

Pauree:

He Himself is the vast variety of Nature, and He Himself makes it bear fruit.

He Himself is the Gardener, He Himself irrigates all the plants, and He Himself puts them in His mouth.

He Himself is the Creator, and He Himself is the Enjoyer; He Himself gives, and causes others to give.

He Himself is the Lord and Master, and He Himself is the Protector; He Himself is permeating and pervading everywhere.

Servant Nanak speaks of the greatness of the Lord, the Creator, who has no greed at all. |15|

Shalok, Third Mehl:

One person brings a full bottle, and another fills his cup.

Drinking the wine, his intelligence departs, and madness enters his mind; he cannot distinguish between his own and others, and he is struck down by his Lord and Master.

Drinking it, he forgets his Lord and Master, and he is punished in the Court of the Lord.

Do not drink the false wine at all, if it is in your power.

O Nanak, the True Guru comes and meets the mortal; by His Grace, one obtains the True Wine.

He shall dwell forever in the Love of the Lord Master, and obtain a seat in the Mansion of His Presence. |1|

Third Mehl:

When this world comes to understand, it remains dead while yet alive.

When the Lord puts him to sleep, he remains asleep; when He wakes him up, he regains consciousness.

O Nanak, when the Lord casts His Glance of Grace, He causes him to meet the True Guru.

By Guru's Grace, remain dead while yet alive, and you shall not have to die again. |2|

Pauree:

By His doing, everything happens; what does He care for anyone else?

O Dear Lord, everyone eats whatever You give - all are subservient to You.

Section 11 - Raag Bihaagra - Part 019

One who praises You obtains everything; You bestow Your Mercy upon him, O Immaculate Lord.

He alone is a true banker and trader, who loads the merchandise of the wealth of the Your Name, O Lord.

O Saints, let everyone praise the Lord, who has destroyed the pile of the love of duality. |16|

Shalok:
Kabeer, the world is dying - dying to death, but no one knows how to truly die.
Whoever dies, let him die such a death, that he does not have to die again. |1|

Third Mehl:
What do I know? How will I die? What sort of death will it be?
If I do not forget the Lord Master from my mind, then my death will be easy.
The world is terrified of death; everyone longs to live.
By Guru's Grace, one who dies while yet alive, understands the Lord's Will.
O Nanak, one who dies such a death, lives forever. |2|

Pauree:
When the Lord Master Himself becomes merciful, the Lord Himself causes His Name to be chanted.
He Himself causes us to meet the True Guru, and blesses us with peace. His servant is pleasing to the Lord.
He Himself preserves the honor of His servants; He causes others to fall at the feet of His devotees.
The Righteous Judge of Dharma is a creation of the Lord; he does not approach the humble servant of the Lord.
One who is dear to the Lord, is dear to all; so many others come and go in vain. |17|

Shalok, Third Mehl:
The entire world roams around, chanting, "Raam, Raam, Lord, Lord", but the Lord cannot be obtained like this.
He is inaccessible, unfathomable and so very great; He is unweighable, and cannot be weighed.
No one can evaluate Him; He cannot be purchased at any price.
Through the Word of the Guru's Shabad, His mystery is known; in this way, He comes to dwell in the mind.
O Nanak, He Himself is infinite; by Guru's Grace, He is known to be permeating and pervading everywhere.
He Himself comes to blend, and having blended, remains blended. |1|

Third Mehl:

O my soul, this is the wealth of the Naam; through it, comes peace, forever and ever.

It never brings any loss; through it, one earns profits forever.

Eating and spending it, it never decreases; He continues to give, forever and ever.

One who has no skepticism at all never suffers humiliation.

O Nanak, the Gurmukh obtains the Name of the Lord, when the Lord bestows His Glance of Grace. |2|

Pauree:

He Himself is deep within all hearts, and He Himself is outside them.

He Himself is prevailing unmanifest, and He Himself is manifest.

For thirty-six ages, He created the darkness, abiding in the void.

There were no Vedas, Puraanas or Shaastras there; only the Lord Himself existed.

He Himself sat in the absolute trance, withdrawn from everything.

Only He Himself knows His state; He Himself is the unfathomable ocean. |18|

Shalok, Third Mehl:

In egotism, the world is dead; it dies and dies, again and again.

Section 11 - Raag Bihaagra - Part 020

As long as there is breath in the body, he does not remember the Lord; what will he do in the world hereafter?

One who remembers the Lord is a spiritual teacher; the ignorant one acts blindly.

O Nanak, whatever one does in this world, determines what he shall receive in the world hereafter. |1|

Third Mehl:

From the very beginning, it has been the Will of the Lord Master, that He cannot be remembered without the True Guru.

Meeting the True Guru, he realizes that the Lord is permeating and pervading deep within him; he remains forever absorbed in the Lord's Love.

With each and every breath, he constantly remembers the Lord in meditation; not a single breath passes in vain.

His fears of birth and death depart, and he obtains the honored state of eternal life.

O Nanak, He bestows this rank upon that mortal, upon whom He showers His Mercy. |2|

Pauree:
He Himself is all-wise and all-knowing; He Himself is supreme.

He Himself reveals His form, and He Himself enjoins us to His meditation.

He Himself poses as a silent sage, and He Himself speaks spiritual wisdom.

He does not seem bitter to anyone; He is pleasing to all.

His Praises cannot be described; forever and ever, I am a sacrifice to Him. |19|

Shalok, First Mehl:
In this Dark Age of Kali Yuga, O Nanak, the demons have taken birth.

The son is a demon, and the daughter is a demon; the wife is the chief of the demons. |1|

First Mehl:
The Hindus have forgotten the Primal Lord; they are going the wrong way.

As Naarad instructed them, they are worshipping idols. They are blind and mute, the blindest of the blind.

The ignorant fools pick up stones and worship them.

But when those stones themselves sink, who will carry you across? |2|

Pauree:
Everything is in Your power; You are the True King.

The devotees are imbued with the Love of the One Lord; they have perfect faith in Him.

The Name of the Lord is the ambrosial food; His humble servants eat their fill.

All treasures are obtained - meditative remembrance on the Lord is the true profit.

The Saints are very dear to the Supreme Lord God, O Nanak; the Lord is unapproachable and unfathomable. |20|

Shalok, Third Mehl:
Everything comes by the Lord's Will, and everything goes by the Lord's Will.

If some fool believes that he is the creator, he is blind, and acts in blindness.

O Nanak, the Gurmukh understands the Hukam of the Lord's Command; the Lord showers His Mercy upon him. |1|

Third Mehl:

He alone is a Yogi, and he alone finds the Way, who, as Gurmukh, obtains the Naam.

In the body-village of that Yogi are all blessings; this Yoga is not obtained by outward show.

O Nanak, such a Yogi is very rare; the Lord is manifest in his heart. |2|

Pauree:

He Himself created the creatures, and He Himself supports them.

He Himself is seen to be subtle, and He Himself is obvious.

He Himself remains a solitary recluse, and He Himself has a huge family.

Nanak asks for the gift of the dust of the feet of the Saints of the Lord.

I cannot see any other Giver; You alone are the Giver, O Lord. |21|1| Sudh|

RAAG WADAHANS

Section 12 - Raag Wadahans - Part 001

ONE Universal Creator God. Truth Is The Name. Creative Being Personified. No Fear. No Hatred. Image Of The Undying. Beyond Birth. Self-Existent. By Guru's Grace:

Raag Wadahans, First Mehl, First House:
To the addict, there is nothing like the drug; to the fish, there is nothing else like water.
Those who are attuned to their Lord - everyone is pleasing to them. |1|

I am a sacrifice, cut apart into pieces, a sacrifice to Your Name, O Lord Master. |1|Pause|

The Lord is the fruitful tree; His Name is ambrosial nectar.
Those who drink it in are satisfied; I am a sacrifice to them. |2|

You are not visible to me, although You dwell with everyone.
How can the thirst of the thirsty be quenched, with that wall between me and the pond? |3|

Nanak is Your merchant; You, O Lord Master, are my merchandise.
My mind is cleansed of doubt, only when I praise You, and pray to You. |4|1|

Wadahans, First Mehl:
The virtuous bride enjoys her Husband Lord; why does the unworthy one cry out?
If she were to become virtuous, then she too could enjoy her Husband Lord. |1|

My Husband Lord is loving and playful; why should the soul-bride enjoy anyone else? |1|Pause|

If the soul-bride does good deeds, and strings them on the thread of her mind,
she obtains the jewel, which cannot be purchased for any price, strung upon the thread of her consciousness. |2|

I ask, but do not follow the way shown to me; still, I claim to have reached my destination.
I do not speak with You, O my Husband Lord; how then can I come to have a place in Your home? |3|

O Nanak, without the One Lord, there is no other at all.
If the soul-bride remains attached to You, then she shall enjoy her Husband Lord. |4|2|

Wadahans, First Mehl, Second House:
The peacocks are singing so sweetly, O sister; the rainy season of Saawan has come.
Your beauteous eyes are like a string of charms, fascinating and enticing the soul-bride.
I would cut myself into pieces for the Blessed Vision of Your Darshan; I am a sacrifice to Your Name.
I take pride in You; without You, what could I be proud of?
So smash your bracelets along with your bed, O soul-bride, and break your arms, along with the arms of your couch.
In spite of all the decorations which you have made, O soul-bride, your Husband Lord is enjoying someone else.

Section 12 - Raag Wadahans - Part 002

You don't have the bracelets of gold, nor the good crystal jewelry; you haven't dealt with the true jeweller.
Those arms, which do not embrace the neck of the Husband Lord, burn in anguish.
All my companions have gone to enjoy their Husband Lord; which door should I, the wretched one, go to?

O friend, I may look very attractive, but I am not pleasing to my Husband Lord at all.
I have woven my hair into lovely braids, and saturated their partings with vermillion;

but when I go before Him, I am not accepted, and I die, suffering in anguish.

I weep; the whole world weeps; even the birds of the forest weep with me.

The only thing which doesn't weep is my body's sense of separateness, which has separated me from my Lord.

In a dream, He came, and went away again; I cried so many tears.

I can't come to You, O my Beloved, and I can't send anyone to You.

Come to me, O blessed sleep - perhaps I will see my Husband Lord again.

One who brings me a message from my Lord and Master - says Nanak, what shall I give to Him?

Cutting off my head, I give it to Him to sit upon; without my head, I shall still serve Him.

Why haven't I died? Why hasn't my life just ended? My Husband Lord has become a stranger to me. |1|3|

Wadahans, Third Mehl, First House:
One Universal Creator God. By The Grace Of The True Guru:
When the mind is filthy, everything is filthy; by washing the body, the mind is not cleaned.

This world is deluded by doubt; how rare are those who understand this. |1|

O my mind, chant the One Name.
The True Guru has given me this treasure. |1|Pause|

Even if one learns the Yogic postures of the Siddhas, and holds his sexual energy in check,
still, the filth of the mind is not removed, and the filth of egotism is not eliminated. |2|

This mind is not controlled by any other discipline, except the Sanctuary of the True Guru.
Meeting the True Guru, one is transformed beyond description. |3|

Prays Nanak, one who dies upon meeting the True Guru, shall be rejuvenated through the Word of the Guru's Shabad.
The filth of his attachment and possessiveness shall depart, and his mind shall become pure. |4|1|

Wadahans, Third Mehl:

By His Grace, one serves the True Guru; by His Grace, service is performed.
By His grace, this mind is controlled, and by His Grace, it becomes pure. |1|

O my mind, think of the True Lord.
Think of the One Lord, and you shall obtain peace; you shall never suffer in sorrow again. |1|Pause|

By His Grace, one dies while yet alive, and by His Grace, the Word of the Shabad is enshrined in the mind.
By His Grace, one understands the Hukam of the Lord's Command, and by His Command, one merges into the Lord. |2|

That tongue, which does not savor the sublime essence of the Lord - may that tongue be burned off!
It remains attached to other pleasures, and through the love of duality, it suffers in pain. |3|

The One Lord grants His Grace to all; He Himself makes distinctions.
O Nanak, meeting the True Guru, the fruits are obtained, and one is blessed with the Glorious Greatness of the Naam. |4|2|

Section 12 - Raag Wadahans - Part 003

Wadahans, Third Mehl:
Emotional attachment to Maya is darkness; without the Guru, there is no wisdom.
Those who are attached to the Word of the Shabad understand; duality has ruined the people. |1|

O my mind, under Guru's Instruction, do good deeds.
Dwell forever and ever upon the Lord God, and you shall find the gate of salvation. |1|Pause|

The Lord alone is the treasure of virtue; He Himself gives, and then one receives.
Without the Name, all are separated from the Lord; through the Word of the Guru's Shabad, one meets the Lord. |2|

Acting in ego, they lose, and nothing comes into their hands.

Meeting the True Guru, they find Truth, and merge into the True Name. |3|

Hope and desire abide in this body, but the Lord's Light shines within as well.
O Nanak, the self-willed manmukhs remain in bondage; the Gurmukhs are liberated. |4|3|

Wadahans, Third Mehl:
The faces of the happy soul-brides are radiant forever; through the Guru, they are peacefully poised.
They enjoy their Husband Lord constantly, eradicating their ego from within. |1|

O my mind, meditate on the Name of the Lord, Har, Har.
The True Guru has led me to understand the Lord. |1|Pause|

The abandoned brides cry out in their suffering; they do not attain the Mansion of the Lord's Presence.
In the love of duality, they appear so ugly; they suffer in pain as they go to the world beyond. |2|

The virtuous soul-bride constantly chants the Glorious Praises of the Lord; she enshrines the Naam, the Name of the Lord, within her heart.
The unvirtuous woman suffers, and cries out in pain. |3|

The One Lord and Master is the Husband Lord of all; His Praises cannot be expressed.
O Nanak, He has separated some from Himself, while others are to His Name. |4|4|

Wadahans, Third Mehl:
The Ambrosial Nectar of the Naam is always sweet to me; through the Word of the Guru's Shabad, I come to taste it.
Through the True Word of the Guru's Bani, I am merged in peace and poise; the Dear Lord is enshrined in the mind. |1|

The Lord, showing His Mercy, has caused me to meet the True Guru.
Through the Perfect True Guru, I meditate on the Name of the Lord. |1|Pause|

Through Brahma, the hymns of the Vedas were revealed, but the love of Maya spread.
The wise one, Shiva, remains absorbed in himself, but he is engrossed in dark passions and excessive egotism. |2|

Vishnu is always busy reincarnating himself - who will save the world?
The Gurmukhs are imbued with spiritual wisdom in this age; they are rid of the darkness of emotional attachment. |3|

Serving the True Guru, one is emancipated; the Gurmukh crosses over the world-ocean.
The detached renunciates are imbued with the True Name; they attain the gate of salvation. |4|

The One True Lord is pervading and permeating everywhere; He cherishes everyone.
O Nanak, without the One Lord, I do not know any other; He is the Merciful Master of all. |5|5|

Wadahans, Third Mehl:
The Gurmukh practices true self-discipline, and attains the essence of wisdom.
The Gurmukh meditates on the True Lord. |1|

Section 12 - Raag Wadahans - Part 004

As Gurmukh, O my mind, remember the Naam, the Name of the Lord.
It shall stand by you always, and go with you. |Pause|

The True Lord is the social status and honor of the Gurmukh.
Within the Gurmukh, is God, his friend and helper. |2|

He alone becomes Gurmukh, whom the Lord so blesses.
He Himself blesses the Gurmukh with greatness. |3|

The Gurmukh lives the True Word of the Shabad, and practices good deeds.
The Gurmukh, O Nanak, emancipates his family and relations. |4|6|

Wadahans, Third Mehl:

My tongue is intuitively attracted to the taste of the Lord.
My mind is satisfied, meditating on the Name of the Lord. |1|

Lasting peace is obtained, contemplating the Shabad, the True Word of God.
I am forever a sacrifice to my True Guru. |1|Pause|

My eyes are content, lovingly focused on the One Lord.
My mind is content, having forsaken the love of duality. |2|

The frame of my body is at peace, through the Shabad, and the Name of the Lord.
The fragrance of the Naam permeates my heart. |3|

O Nanak, one who has such great destiny written upon his forehead,
through the Bani of the Guru's Word, easily and intuitively becomes free of desire. |4|7|

Wadahans, Third Mehl:
From the Perfect Guru, the Naam is obtained.
Through the Shabad, the True Word of God, one merges in the True Lord. |1|

O my soul, obtain the treasure of the Naam,
by submitting to the Will of your Guru. |1|Pause|

Through the Word of the Guru's Shabad, filth is washed away from within.
The Immaculate Naam comes to abide within the mind. |2|

Deluded by doubt, the world wanders around.
It dies, and is born again, and is ruined by the Messenger of Death. |3|

O Nanak, very fortunate are those who meditate on the Name of the Lord.
By Guru's Grace, they enshrine the Name within their minds. |4|8|

Wadahans, Third Mehl:
Ego is opposed to the Name of the Lord; the two do not dwell in the same place.
In egotism, selfless service cannot be performed, and so the soul goes unfulfilled. |1|

O my mind, think of the Lord, and practice the Word of the Guru's Shabad.
If you submit to the Hukam of the Lord's Command, then you shall meet with the Lord; only then will your ego depart from within. |Pause|

Egotism is within all bodies; through egotism, we come to be born.
Egotism is total darkness; in egotism, no one can understand anything. |2|

In egotism, devotional worship cannot be performed, and the Hukam of the Lord's Command cannot be understood.
In egotism, the soul is in bondage, and the Naam, the Name of the Lord, does not come to abide in the mind. |3|

O Nanak, meeting with the True Guru, egotism is eliminated, and then, the True Lord comes to dwell in the mind|

One starts practicing truth, abides in truth and by serving the True One gets absorbed in Him. |4|9|12|

Wadahans, Fourth Mehl, First House:
One Universal Creator God. By The Grace Of The True Guru:
There is one bed, and One Lord God.
The Gurmukh enjoys the Lord, the ocean of peace. |1|

My mind longs to meet my Beloved Lord.

Section 12 - Raag Wadahans - Part 005

The Perfect Guru leads me to meet my Beloved; I am a sacrifice, a sacrifice to my Guru. |1|Pause|

My body is over-flowing with corruption;
how can I meet my Perfect Beloved? |2|

The virtuous ones obtain my Beloved;
I do not have these virtues. How can I meet Him, O my mother? |3|

I am so tired of making all these efforts.
Please protect Nanak, the meek one, O my Lord. |4|1|

Wadahans, Fourth Mehl:
My Lord God is so beautiful. I do not know His worth.
Abandoning my Lord God, I have become entangled in duality. |1|

How can I meet with my Husband? I don't know.
She who pleases her Husband Lord is a happy soul-bride. She meets with her Husband Lord - she is so wise. |1|Pause|

I am filled with faults; how can I attain my Husband Lord?
You have many loves, but I am not in Your thoughts, O my Husband Lord. |2|

She who enjoys her Husband Lord, is the good soul-bride.
I don't have these virtues; what can I, the discarded bride, do? |3|

The soul-bride continually, constantly enjoys her Husband Lord.
I have no good fortune; will He ever hold me close in His embrace? |4|

You, O Husband Lord, are meritorious, while I am without merit.
I am worthless; please forgive Nanak, the meek. |5|2|

Wadahans, Fourth Mehl, Second House:
One Universal Creator God. By The Grace Of The True Guru:
Within my mind there is such a great yearning; how will I attain the Blessed Vision of the Lord's Darshan?

I go and ask my True Guru; with the Guru's advice, I shall teach my foolish mind.
The foolish mind is instructed in the Word of the Guru's Shabad, and meditates forever on the Lord, Har, Har.
O Nanak, one who is blessed with the Mercy of my Beloved, focuses his consciousness on the Lord's Feet. |1|

I dress myself in all sorts of robes for my Husband, so that my True Lord God will be pleased.
But my Beloved Husband Lord does not even cast a glance in my direction; how can I be consoled?
For His sake, I adorn myself with adornments, but my Husband is imbued with the love of another.

O Nanak, blessed, blessed, blessed is that soul-bride, who enjoys her True, Sublime Husband Lord. |2|

I go and ask the fortunate, happy soul-bride, "How did you attain Him - your Husband Lord, my God?"
She answers, "My True Husband blessed me with His Mercy; I abandoned the distinction between mine and yours.
Dedicate everything, mind, body and soul, to the Lord God; this is the Path to meet Him, O sister."
If her God gazes upon her with favor, O Nanak, her light merges into the Light. |3|

I dedicate my mind and body to the one who brings me a message from my Lord God.
I wave the fan over him every day, serve him and carry water for him.
Constantly and continuously, I serve the Lord's humble servant, who recites to me the sermon of the Lord, Har, Har.

Section 12 - Raag Wadahans - Part 006

Hail, hail unto the Guru, the Guru, the Perfect True Guru, who fulfills Nanak's heart's desires. |4|

O Lord, let me meet the Guru, my best friend; meeting Him, I meditate on the Lord's Name.
I seek the Lord's sermon from the Guru, the True Guru; joining with Him, I sing the Glorious Praises of the Lord.
Each and every day, forever, I sing the Lord's Praises; my mind lives by hearing Your Name.
O Nanak, that moment when I forget my Lord and Master - at that moment, my soul dies. |5|

Everyone longs to see the Lord, but he alone sees Him, whom the Lord causes to see Him.
One upon whom my Beloved bestows His Glance of Grace, cherishes the Lord, Har, Har forever.
He alone cherishes the Lord, Har, Har, forever and ever, who meets my Perfect True Guru.
O Nanak, the Lord's humble servant and the Lord become One; meditating on the Lord, he blends with the Lord. |6|1|3|

Wadahans, Fifth Mehl, First House:
One Universal Creator God. By The Grace Of The True Guru:
His Darbaar, His Court, is the most lofty and exalted.
It has no end or limitations.
Millions, millions, tens of millions seek,
but they cannot find even a tiny bit of His Mansion. |1|

What is that auspicious moment, when God is met? |1|Pause|

Tens of thousands of devotees worship Him in adoration.
Tens of thousands of ascetics practice austere discipline.
Tens of thousands of Yogis practice Yoga.
Tens of thousands of pleasure seekers seek pleasure. |2|

He dwells in each and every heart, but only a few know this.
Is there any friend who can rip apart the screen of separation?
I can only make the effort, if the Lord is merciful to me.
I sacrifice my body and soul to Him. |3|

After wandering around for so long, I have finally come to the Saints;
all of my pains and doubts have been eradicated.
God summoned me to the Mansion of His Presence, and blessed me with
the Ambrosial Nectar of His Name.
Says Nanak, my God is lofty and exalted. |4|1|

Wadahans, Fifth Mehl:
Blessed is that time, when the Blessed Vision of His Darshan is given;
I am a sacrifice to the feet of the True Guru. |1|

You are the Giver of souls, O my Beloved God.
My soul lives by reflecting upon the Name of God. |1|Pause|

True is Your Mantra, Ambrosial is the Bani of Your Word.
Cooling and soothing is Your Presence, all-knowing is Your gaze. |2|

True is Your Command; You sit upon the eternal throne.
My eternal God does not come or go. |3|

You are the Merciful Master; I am Your humble servant.

O Nanak, the Lord and Master is totally permeating and pervading everywhere. |4|2|

Wadahans, Fifth Mehl:
You are infinite - only a few know this.
By Guru's Grace, some come to understand You through the Word of the Shabad. |1|

Your servant offers this prayer, O Beloved:

Section 12 - Raag Wadahans - Part 007

I live by meditating on Your Feet, God. |1|Pause|

O my Merciful and Almighty God, O Great Giver,
he alone knows You, whom You so bless. |2|

Forever and ever, I am a sacrifice to You.
Here and hereafter, I seek Your Protection. |3|

I am without virtue; I know none of Your Glorious Virtues.
O Nanak, seeing the Holy Saint, my mind is imbued with You. |4|3|

Wadahans, Fifth Mehl:
God is perfect - He is the Inner-knower, the Searcher of hearts.
He blesses us with the gift of the dust of the feet of the Saints. |1|

Bless me with Your Grace, God, O Merciful to the meek.
I seek Your Protection, O Perfect Lord, Sustainer of the World. |1|Pause|

He is totally pervading and permeating the water, the land and the sky.
God is near at hand, not far away. |2|

One whom He blesses with His Grace, meditates on Him.
Twenty-four hours a day, he sings the Glorious Praises of the Lord. |3|

He cherishes and sustains all beings and creatures.
Nanak seeks the Sanctuary of the Lord's Door. |4|4|

Wadahans, Fifth Mehl:

You are the Great Giver, the Inner-knower, the Searcher of hearts.
God, the Perfect Lord and Master, is permeating and pervading in all. |1|

The Name of my Beloved God is my only support.
I live by hearing, continually hearing Your Name. |1|Pause|

I seek Your Sanctuary, O my Perfect True Guru.
My mind is purified by the dust of the Saints. |2|

I have enshrined His Lotus Feet within my heart.
I am a sacrifice to the Blessed Vision of Your Darshan. |3|

Show mercy unto me, that I may sing Your Glorious Praises.
O Nanak, chanting the Naam, the Name of the Lord, I obtain peace. |4|5|

Wadahans, Fifth Mehl:
In the Saadh Sangat, the Company of the Holy, drink in the Ambrosial Nectar of the Lord.
The soul does not die, nor does it ever waste away. |1|

By great good fortune, one meets the Perfect Guru.
By Guru's Grace, one meditates on God. |1|Pause|

The Lord is the jewel, the pearl, the gem, the diamond.
Meditating, meditating in remembrance on God, I am in ecstasy. |2|

Wherever I look, I see the Sanctuary of the Holy.
Singing the Glorious Praises of the Lord, my soul becomes immaculately pure. |3|

Within each and every heart, dwells my Lord and Master.
O Nanak, one obtains the Naam, the Name of the Lord, when God bestows His Mercy. |4|6|

Wadahans, Fifth Mehl:
Do not forget me, O God, Merciful to the meek.
I seek Your Sanctuary, O Perfect, Compassionate Lord. |1|Pause|

Wherever You come to mind, that place is blessed.
The moment I forget You, I am stricken with regret. |1|

All beings are Yours; You are their constant companion.
Please, give me Your hand, and pull me up out of this world-ocean. |2|

Coming and going are by Your Will.
One whom You save is not afflicted by suffering. |3|

You are the One and only Lord and Master; there is no other.
Nanak offers this prayer with his palms pressed together. |4|7|

Wadahans, Fifth Mehl:
When You allow Yourself to be known, then we know You.
We chant Your Name, which You have given to us. |1|

You are wonderful! Your creative potency is amazing! |1|Pause|

Section 12 · Raag Wadahans - Part 008

You Yourself are the Cause of causes, You Yourself are the Creator.
By Your Will, we are born, and by Your Will, we die. |2|

Your Name is the Support of our mind and body.
This is Your blessing to Nanak, Your slave. |3|8|

Wadahans, Fifth Mehl, Second House:
One Universal Creator God. By The Grace Of The True Guru:
Deep within me, there is a longing to meet my Beloved; how can I attain
my Perfect Guru?
Even though a baby may play hundreds of games, he cannot survive
without milk.
The hunger within me is not satisfied, O my friend, even though I am
served hundreds of dishes.
My mind and body are filled with love for my Beloved; how can my soul
find relief, without the Blessed Vision of the Lord's Darshan? |1|

Listen, O my dear friends and siblings - lead me to my True Friend, the
Giver of peace.
He knows all the troubles of my soul; every day, he tells me stories of the
Lord.

I cannot live without Him, even for an instant. I cry out for Him, just as the song-bird cries for the drop of water.
Which of Your Glorious Virtues should I sing? You save even worthless beings like me. |2|

I have become depressed, waiting for my Husband Lord, O my friend; when shall my eyes behold my Husband?

I have forgotten how to enjoy all pleasures; without my Husband Lord, they are of no use at all.
These clothes do not please my body; I cannot dress myself.
I bow to those friends of mine, who have enjoyed their Beloved Husband Lord. |3|

I have adorned myself with all sorts of decorations, O my friend, but without my Husband Lord, they are of no use at all.
When my Husband does not care for me, O my friend, then my youth passes, totally useless.
Blessed, blessed are the happy soul-brides, O my friend, who are blended with their Husband Lord.
I am a sacrifice to those happy soul-brides; I wash their feet again and again. |4|

As long as I suffered from duality and doubt, O my friend, I thought God was far away.
But when I met the Perfect True Guru, O my friend, then all my hopes and desires were fulfilled.
I have obtained all pleasures and comforts, O my friend; my Husband Lord is all-pervading everywhere.
Servant Nanak enjoys the Lord's Love, O my friend; I fall at the feet of the Guru, the True Guru. |5|1|9|

Wadahans, Third Mehl, Ashtapadees:
One Universal Creator God. By The Grace Of The True Guru:
True is the Bani of His Word, and True is the melody; True is contemplative meditation on the Word of the Shabad.
Night and day, I praise the True Lord. Blessed, blessed is my great good fortune. |1|

O my mind, let yourself be a sacrifice to the True Name.

If you become the slave of the Lord's slaves, you shall obtain the True Name. |1|Pause|

Section 12 - Raag Wadahans - Part 009

True is the tongue which is imbued with Truth, and true are the mind and body.
By praising any other than the True Lord, one's whole life is wasted. |2|

Let Truth be the farm, Truth the seed, and Truth the merchandise you trade.
Night and day, you shall earn the profit of the Lord's Name; you shall have the treasure overflowing with the wealth of devotional worship. |3|

Let Truth be your food, and let Truth be your clothes; let your True Support be the Name of the Lord.
One who is so blessed by the Lord, obtains a seat in the Mansion of the Lord's Presence. |4|

In Truth we come, and in Truth we go, and then, we are not consigned to reincarnation again.
The Gurmukhs are hailed as True in the True Court; they merge in the True Lord. |5|

Deep within they are True, and their minds are True; they sing the Glorious Praises of the True Lord.
In the true place, they praise the True Lord; I am a sacrifice to the True Guru. |6|

True is the time, and true is the moment, when one falls in love with the True Lord.
Then, he sees Truth, and speaks the Truth; he realizes the True Lord pervading the entire Universe. |7|

O Nanak, one merges with the True Lord, when He merges with Himself.
As it pleases Him, He preserves us; He Himself ordains His Will. |8|1|

Wadahans, Third Mehl:
His mind wanders in the ten directions - how can he sing the Glorious Praises of the Lord?

The sensory organs are totally engrossed in sensuality; sexual desire and anger constantly afflict him. |1|

Waaho! Waaho! Hail! Hail! Chant His Glorious Praises.
The Lord's Name is so difficult to obtain in this age; under Guru's Instruction, drink in the subtle essence of the Lord. |1|Pause|

Remembering the Word of the Shabad, the mind becomes immaculately pure, and then, one sings the Glorious Praises of the Lord.
Under Guru's Instruction, one comes to understand his own self, and then, he comes to dwell in the home of his inner self. |2|

O my mind, be imbued forever with the Lord's Love, and sing forever the Glorious Praises of the Lord.
The Immaculate Lord is forever the Giver of peace; from Him, one receives the fruits of his heart's desires. |3|

I am lowly, but I have been exalted, entering the Sanctuary of the Lord.
He has lifted up the sinking stone; True is His glorious greatness. |4|

From poison, I have been transformed into Ambrosial Nectar; under Guru's Instruction, I have obtained wisdom.
From bitter herbs, I have been transformed into sandalwood; this fragrance permeates me deep within. |5|

This human birth is so precious; one must earn the right to come into the world.
By perfect destiny, I met the True Guru, and I meditate on the Lord's Name. |6|

The self-willed manmukhs are deluded; attached to corruption, they waste away their lives in vain.
The Name of the Lord is forever an ocean of peace, but the manmukhs do not love the Word of the Shabad. |7|

Everyone can chant the Name of the Lord, Har, Har with their mouths, but only a few enshrine it within their hearts.
O Nanak, those who enshrine the Lord within their hearts, attain liberation and emancipation. |8|2|

Wadahans, First Mehl, Chhant:

One Universal Creator God. By The Grace Of The True Guru:

Why bother to wash the body, polluted by falsehood?

One's cleansing bath is only approved, if he practices Truth.

When there is Truth within the heart, then one becomes True, and obtains the True Lord.

Section 12 - Raag Wadahans - Part 010

Without pre-ordained destiny, understanding is not attained; talking and babbling, one wastes his life away.

Wherever you go and sit, speak well, and write the Word of the Shabad in your consciousness.

Why bother to wash the body which is polluted by falsehood? |1|

When I have spoken, I spoke as You made me speak.

The Ambrosial Name of the Lord is pleasing to my mind.

The Naam, the Name of the Lord, seems so sweet to my mind; it has destroyed the dwelling of pain.

Peace came to dwell in my mind, when You gave the Order.

It is Yours to bestow Your Grace, and it is mine to speak this prayer; You created Yourself.

When I have spoken, I spoke as You made me speak. |2|

The Lord and Master gives them their turn, according to the deeds they have done.

Do not speak ill of others, or get involved in arguments.

Do not get into arguments with the Lord, or you shall ruin yourself.

If you challenge the One, with whom you must abide, you will cry in the end.

Be satisfied with what God gives you; tell your mind not to complain uselessly.

The Lord and Master gives them their turn, according to the deeds they have done. |3|

He Himself created all, and He blesses then with His Glance of Grace.

No one asks for that which is bitter; everyone asks for sweets.

Let everyone ask for sweets, and behold, it is as the Lord wills.

Giving donations to charity, and performing various religious rituals are not equal to the contemplation of the Naam.

O Nanak, those who are blessed with the Naam have had such good karma pre-ordained.
He Himself created all, and He blesses them with His Glance of Grace. |4|1|

Wadahans, First Mehl:
Show mercy to me, that I may chant Your Name.
You Yourself created all, and You are pervading among all.
You Yourself are pervading among all, and You link them to their tasks.
Some, You have made kings, while others go about begging.
You have made greed and emotional attachment seem sweet; they are deluded by this delusion.
Be ever merciful to me; only then can I chant Your Name. |1|

Your Name is True, and ever pleasing to my mind.
My pains are dispelled, and I am permeated with peace.
The angels, the mortals and the silent sages sing of You.
The angels, the mortals and the silent sages sing of You; they are pleasing to Your Mind.
Enticed by Maya, they do not remember the Lord, and they waste away their lives in vain.
Some fools and idiots never think of the Lord; whoever has come, shall have to go.
Your Name is True, and ever pleasing to my mind. |2|

Beauteous is Your time, O Lord; the Bani of Your Word is Ambrosial Nectar.
Your servants serve You with love; these mortals are attached to Your essence.
Those mortals are attached to Your essence, who are blessed with the Ambrosial Name.
Those who are imbued with Your Name, prosper more and more, day by day.
Some do not practice good deeds, or live righteously; nor do they practice self-restraint. They do not realize the One Lord.
Ever beauteous is Your time, O Lord; the Bani of Your Word is Ambrosial Nectar. |3|

I am a sacrifice to the True Name.

Section 12 - Raag Wadahans - Part 011

Your rule shall never end.

Your rule is eternal and unchanging; it shall never come to an end.

He alone becomes Your servant, who contemplates You in peaceful ease.

Enemies and pains shall never touch him, and sin shall never draw near him.

I am forever a sacrifice to the One Lord, and Your Name. |4|

Throughout the ages, Your devotees sing the Kirtan of Your Praises, O Lord Master, at Your Door.

They meditate on the One True Lord.

Only then do they meditate on the True Lord, when they enshrine Him in their minds.

Doubt and delusion are Your making; when these are dispelled,

then, by Guru's Grace, You grant Your Grace, and save them from the noose of Death.

Throughout the ages, they are Your devotees. |5|

O my Great Lord and Master, You are unfathomable and infinite.

How should I make and offer my prayer? I do not know what to say.

If You bless me with Your Glance of Grace, I realize the Truth.

Only then do I come to realize the Truth, when You Yourself instruct me.

The pain and hunger of the world are Your making; dispel this doubt.

Prays Nanak, ones skepticism is taken away, when he understands the Guru's wisdom.

The Great Lord Master is unfathomable and infinite. |6|

Your eyes are so beautiful, and Your teeth are delightful.

Your nose is so graceful, and Your hair is so long.

Your body is so precious, cast in gold.

His body is cast in gold, and He wears Krishna's mala; meditate on Him, O sisters.

You shall not have to stand at Death's door, O sisters, if you listen to these teachings.

From a crane, you shall be transformed into a swan, and the filth of your mind shall be removed.

Your eyes are so beautiful, and Your teeth are delightful. |7|

Your walk is so graceful, and Your speech is so sweet.

You coo like a songbird, and your youthful beauty is alluring.

Your youthful beauty is so alluring; it pleases You, and it fulfills the heart's desires.

Like an elephant, You step with Your Feet so carefully; You are satisfied with Yourself.

She who is imbued with the Love of such a Great Lord, flows intoxicated, like the waters of the Ganges.

Prays Nanak, I am Your slave, O Lord; Your walk is so graceful, and Your speech is so sweet. |8|2|

Wadahans, Third Mehl, Chhant:
One Universal Creator God. By The Grace Of The True Guru:
Let yourself be imbued with the Love of your Husband Lord, O beautiful, mortal bride.

Let yourself remain merged in the True Word of the Shabad, O mortal bride; savor and enjoy the Love of your Beloved Husband Lord.

The Husband Lord embellishes His beloved bride with His True Love; she is in love with the Lord, Har, Har.

Renouncing her self-centeredness, she attains her Husband Lord, and remains merged in the Word of the Guru's Shabad.

That soul bride is adorned, who is attracted by His Love, and who treasures the Love of her Beloved within her heart.

O Nanak, the Lord blends that soul bride with Himself; the True King adorns her. |1|

O worthless bride, see your Husband Lord ever-present.

One who, as Gurmukh, enjoys her Husband Lord, O mortal bride, knows Him to be all-pervading everywhere.

Section 12 - Raag Wadahans - Part 012

The Lord is all-pervading everywhere; behold Him ever-present. Through-out the ages, know Him as the One.

The young, innocent bride enjoys her Husband Lord; she meets Him, the Architect of karma.

One who tastes the sublime essence of the Lord, and utters the sublime Word of the Shabad, remains immersed in the Lord's Ambrosial Pool.

O Nanak, that soul bride is pleasing to her Husband Lord, who, through the Shabad, remains in His Presence. |2|

Go and ask the happy soul-brides, O mortal bride, who have eradicated their self-conceit from within.

Those who have not eradicated their self-conceit, O mortal bride, do not realize the Hukam of their Husband Lord's Command.

Those who eradicate their self-conceit, obtain their Husband Lord; they delight in His Love.

Ever imbued with His Love, in perfect poise and grace, she repeats His Name, night and day.

Very fortunate is that bride, who focuses her consciousness on Him; her Lord's Love is so sweet to her.

O Nanak, that soul-bride who is adorned with Truth, is imbued with her Lord's Love, in the state of perfect poise. |3|

Overcome your egotism, O mortal bride, and walk in the Guru's Way.

Thus you shall ever enjoy your Husband Lord, O mortal bride, and obtain an abode in the home of your own inner being.

Obtaining an abode in the home of her inner being, she vibrates the Word of the Shabad, and is a happy soul-bride forever.

The Husband Lord is delightful, and forever young; night and day, He embellishes His bride.

Her Husband Lord activates the destiny written on her forehead, and she is adorned with the True Shabad.

O Nanak, the soul-bride is imbued with the Love of the Lord, when she walks according to the Will of the True Guru. |4|1|

Wadahans, Third Mehl:

All dealings of the Gurmukh are good, if they are accomplished with poise and grace.

Night and day, he repeats the Naam, the Name of the Lord, and he earns his profits, drinking in the subtle essence of the Lord.

He earns the profit of the subtle essence of the Lord, meditating on the Lord, and repeating the Naam, night and day.

He gathers in merits, and eliminates demerits, and realizes his own self.

Under Guru's Instruction, he is blessed with glorious greatness; he drinks in the essence of the True Word of the Shabad.

O Nanak, devotional worship of the Lord is wonderful, but only a few Gurmukhs perform it. |1|

As Gurmukh, plant the crop of the Lord within the field of your body, and let it grow.

Within the home of your own being, enjoy the Lord's subtle essence, and earn profits in the world hereafter.

This profit is earned by enshrining the Lord within your mind; blessed is this farming and trade.

Meditating on the Lord's Name, and enshrining Him within your mind, you shall come to understand the Guru's Teachings.

The self-willed manmukhs have grown weary of this farming and trade; their hunger and thirst will not go away.

O Nanak, plant the seed of the Name within your mind, and adorn yourself with the True Word of the Shabad. |2|

Those humble beings engage in the Lord's Trade, who have the jewel of such pre-ordained destiny upon their foreheads.

Under Guru's Instruction, the soul dwells in the home of the self; through the True Word of the Shabad, she becomes unattached.

By the destiny written upon their foreheads, they become truly unattached, and by reflective meditation, they are imbued with Truth.

Without the Naam, the Name of the Lord, the whole world is insane; through the Shabad, the ego is conquered.

Attached to the True Word of the Shabad, wisdom comes forth. The Gurmukh obtains the Naam, the Name of the Husband Lord.

Section 12 - Raag Wadahans - Part 013

O Nanak, through the Shabad, one meets the Lord, the Destroyer of fear, and by the destiny written on her forehead, she enjoys Him. |3|

All farming and trading is by Hukam of His Will; surrendering to the Lord's Will, glorious greatness is obtained.

Under Guru's Instruction, one comes to understand the Lord's Will, and by His Will, he is united in His Union.

By His Will, one merges and easily blends with Him. The Shabads of the Guru are incomparable.

Through the Guru, true greatness is obtained, and one is embellished with Truth.

He finds the Destroyer of fear, and eradicates his self-conceit; as Gurmukh, he is united in His Union.

Says Nanak, the Name of the immaculate, inaccessible, unfathomable Commander is permeating and pervading everywhere. |4|2|

Wadahans, Third Mehl:
O my mind, contemplate the True Lord forever.
Dwell in peace in the home of your own self, and the Messenger of Death shall not touch you.
The noose of the Messenger of Death shall not touch you, when you embrace love for the True Word of the Shabad.
Ever imbued with the True Lord, the mind becomes immaculate, and its coming and going is ended.
The love of duality and doubt have ruined the self-willed manmukh, who is lured away by the Messenger of Death.
Says Nanak, listen, O my mind: contemplate the True Lord forever. |1|

O my mind, the treasure is within you; do not search for it on the outside.
Eat only that which is pleasing to the Lord, and as Gurmukh, receive the blessing of His Glance of Grace.
As Gurmukh, receive the blessing of His Glance of Grace, O my mind; the Name of the Lord, your help and support, is within you.
The self-willed manmukhs are blind, and devoid of wisdom; they are ruined by the love of duality.
Without the Name, no one is emancipated. All are bound by the Messenger of Death.
O Nanak, the treasure is within you; do not search for it on the outside. |2|

O my mind, obtaining the blessing of this human birth, some are engaged in the trade of Truth.
They serve their True Guru, and the Infinite Word of the Shabad resounds within them.
Within them is the Infinite Shabad, and the Beloved Naam, the Name of the Lord; through the Naam, the nine treasures are obtained.
The self-willed manmukhs are engrossed in emotional attachment to Maya; they suffer in pain, and through duality, they lose their honor.
But those who conquer their ego, and merge in the True Shabad, are totally imbued with Truth.
O Nanak, it is so difficult to obtain this human life; the True Guru imparts this understanding. |3|

O my mind, those who serve their True Guru are the most fortunate beings.
Those who conquer their minds are beings of renunciation and detachment.

They are beings of renunciation and detachment, who lovingly focus their consciousness on the True Lord; they realize and understand their own selves.

Their intellect is steady, deep and profound; as Gurmukh, they naturally chant the Naam, the Name of the Lord.

Some are lovers of beautiful young women; emotional attachment to Maya is very dear to them. The unfortunate self-willed manmukhs remain asleep.

O Nanak, those who intuitively serve their Guru, have perfect destiny. |4|3|

Wadahans, Third Mehl:

Purchase the jewel, the invaluable treasure; the True Guru has given this understanding.

The profit of profits is the devotional worship of the Lord; one's virtues merge into the virtues of the Lord.

Section 12 - Raag Wadahans - Part 014

One's virtues merge into the virtues of the Lord; he comes to understand his own self. He earns the profit of devotional worship in this world.

Without devotion, there is no peace; through duality, one's honor is lost, but under Guru's Instruction, he is blessed with the Support of the Naam.

He ever earns the profit of the merchandise of the Naam, whom the Lord employs in this Trade.

He purchases the jewel, the invaluable treasure, unto whom the True Guru has given this understanding. |1|

The love of Maya is totally painful; this is a bad deal.

Speaking falsehood, one eats poison, and the evil within increases greatly.

The evil within increases greatly, in this world of doubt; without the Name, one's honor is lost.

Reading and studying, the religious scholars argue and debate; but without understanding, there is no peace.

Their comings and goings never end; emotional attachment to Maya is dear to them.

The love of Maya is totally painful; this is a bad deal. |2|

The counterfeit and the genuine are all assayed in the Court of the True Lord.

The counterfeit are cast out of the Court, and they stand there, crying out in misery.

They stand there, crying out in misery; the foolish, idiotic, self-willed manmukhs have wasted their lives.

Maya is the poison which has deluded the world; it does not love the Naam, the Name of the Lord.

The self-willed manmukhs are resentful toward the Saints; they harvest only pain in this world.

The counterfeit and the genuine are assayed in that True Court of the Lord. |3|

He Himself acts; who else should I ask? No one else can do anything.

As He pleases, He engages us; such is His glorious greatness.

Such is His glorious greatness - He Himself causes all to act; no one is a warrior or a coward.

The Life of the World, the Great Giver, the Architect of karma - He Himself grants forgiveness.

By Guru's Grace, self-conceit is eradicated, O Nanak, and through the Naam, honor is obtained.

He Himself acts; who else should I ask? No one else can do anything. |4|4|

Wadahans, Third Mehl:

The True merchandise is the Lord's Name. This is the true trade.

Under Guru's Instruction, we trade in the Lord's Name; its value is very great.

The value of this true trade is very great; those who are engaged in the true trade are very fortunate.

Inwardly and outwardly, they are imbued with devotion, and they enshrine love for the True Name.

One who is blessed with the Lord's Favor, obtains Truth, and reflects upon the Word of the Guru's Shabad.

O Nanak, those who are imbued with the Name find peace; they deal only in the True Name. |1|

Egotistical involvement in Maya is filth; Maya is overflowing with filth.

Under Guru's Instruction, the mind is made pure and the tongue tastes the subtle essence of the Lord.

The tongue tastes the subtle essence of the Lord, and deep within, the heart is drenched with His Love, contemplating the True Word of the Shabad.

Deep within, the well of the heart is overflowing with the Lord's Ambrosial Nectar; the water-carrier draws and drinks in the water of the Shabad.

One who is blessed with the Lord's favor is attuned to the Truth; with his tongue, he chants the Lord's Name.

O Nanak, those who are attuned to the Naam, the Name of the Lord, are immaculate. The others are full of the filth of egotism. |2|

All the religious scholars and astrologers read and study, and argue and shout. Who are they trying to teach?

Section 12 - Raag Wadahans - Part 015

The filth of attachment to Maya clings to their hearts; they deal in Maya alone.

They love to deal in Maya in this world; coming and going, they suffer in pain.

The worm of poison is addicted to poison; it is immersed in manure.

He does what is pre-ordained for him; no one can erase his destiny.

O Nanak, imbued with the Naam, the Name of the Lord, lasting peace is found; the ignorant fools die screaming. |3|

Their minds are colored by emotional attachment to Maya; because of this emotional attachment, they do not understand.

The soul of the Gurmukh is imbued with the Lord's Love; the love of duality departs.

The love of duality departs, and the soul merges in Truth; the warehouse is overflowing with Truth.

One who becomes Gurmukh, comes to understand; the Lord embellishes him with Truth.

He alone merges with the Lord, whom the Lord causes to merge; nothing else can be said or done.

O Nanak, without the Name, one is deluded by doubt; but some, imbued with the Name, enshrine love for the Lord. |4|5|

Wadahans, Third Mehl:

O my mind, the world comes and goes in birth and death; only the True Name shall emancipate you in the end.

When the True Lord Himself grants forgiveness, then one does not have to enter the cycle of reincarnation again.

He does not have to enter the cycle of reincarnation again, and he is emancipated in the end; as Gurmukh, he obtains glorious greatness.

Imbued with love for the True Lord, he is intoxicated with celestial bliss, and he remains absorbed in the Celestial Lord.

The True Lord is pleasing to his mind; he enshrines the True Lord in his mind; attuned to the Word of the Shabad, he is emancipated in the end.

O Nanak, those who are imbued with the Naam, merge in the True Lord; they are not cast into the terrifying world-ocean again. |1|

Emotional attachment to Maya is total madness; through the love of duality, one is ruined.

Mother and father - all are subject to this love; in this love, they are entangled.

They are entangled in this love, on account of their past actions, which no one can erase.

The One who created the Universe, beholds it; no other is as great as He.

The blind, self-willed manmukh is consumed by his burning rage; without the Word of the Shabad, peace is not obtained.

O Nanak, without the Name, everyone is deluded, ruined by emotional attachment to Maya. |2|

Seeing that this world on fire, I have hurried to the Sanctuary of the Lord.

I offer my prayer to the Perfect Guru: please save me, and bless me with Your glorious greatness.

Preserve me in Your Sanctuary, and bless me with the glorious greatness of the Name of the Lord; there is no other Giver as great as You.

Those who are engaged in serving You are very fortunate; throughout the ages, they know the One Lord.

You may practice celibacy, truth, austere self-discipline and rituals, but without the Guru, you shall not be emancipated.

O Nanak, he alone understands the Word of the Shabad, who goes and seeks the Lord's Sanctuary. |3|

That understanding, imparted by the Lord, wells up; there is no other understanding.

Deep within, and beyond as well, You alone are, O Lord; You Yourself impart this understanding.

One whom He Himself blesses with this understanding, does not love any other. As Gurmukh, he tastes the subtle essence of the Lord.

In the True Court, he is forever True; with love, he chants the True Word of the Shabad.

Section 12 - Raag Wadahans - Part 016

Within his home, he finds the home of his own being; the True Guru blesses him with glorious greatness.
O Nanak, those who are attuned to the Naam find the Mansion of the Lord's Presence; their understanding is true, and approved. |4|6|

Wadahans, Fourth Mehl, Chhant:
One Universal Creator God. By The Grace Of The True Guru:
My mind, my mind - the True Guru has blessed it with the Lord's Love.
He has enshrined the Name of the Lord, Har, Har, Har, Har, within my mind.
The Name of the Lord, Har, Har, dwells within my mind; He is the Destroyer of all pain.
By great good fortune, I have obtained the Blessed Vision of the Guru's Darshan; blessed, blessed is my True Guru.
While standing up and sitting down, I serve the True Guru; serving Him, I have found peace.
My mind, my mind - the True Guru has blessed it with the Lord's Love. |1|

I live, I live, and I blossom forth, beholding the True Guru.
The Name of the Lord, the Name of the Lord, He has implanted within me; chanting the Name of the Lord, Har, Har, I blossom forth.
Chanting the Name of the Lord, Har, Har, the heart-lotus blossoms forth, and through the Name of the Lord, I have obtained the nine treasures.
The disease of egotism has been eradicated, suffering has been eliminated, and I have entered the Lord's state of celestial Samaadhi.
I have obtained the glorious greatness of Name of the Lord from the True Guru; beholding the Divine True Guru, my mind is at peace.
I live, I live, and I blossom forth, beholding the True Guru. |2|

If only someone would come, if only someone would come, and lead me to meet my Perfect True Guru.
My mind and body, my mind and body - I cut my body into pieces, and I dedicate these to Him.
Cutting my mind and body apart, cutting them into pieces, I offer these to the one, who recites to me the Words of the True Guru.

My unattached mind has renounced the world; obtaining the Blessed Vision of the Guru's Darshan, it has found peace.

O Lord, Har, Har, O Giver of Peace, please, grant Your Grace, and bless me with the dust of the feet of the True Guru.

If only someone would come, if only someone would come, and lead me to meet my Perfect True Guru. |3|

A Giver as great as the Guru, as great as the Guru - I cannot see any other.

He blesses me with the gift of the Lord's Name, the gift of the Lord's Name; He is the Immaculate Lord God.

Those who worship in adoration the Name of the Lord, Har, Har - their pain, doubts and fears are dispelled.

Through their loving service, those very fortunate ones, whose minds are attached to the Guru's Feet, meet Him.

Says Nanak, the Lord Himself causes us to meet the Guru; meeting the Almighty True Guru, peace is obtained.

A Giver as great as the Guru, as great as the Guru - I cannot see any other. |4|1|

Wadahans, Fourth Mehl:
Without the Guru, I am - without the Guru, I am totally dishonored.

The Life of the World, the Life of the World, the Great Giver has led me to meet and merge with the Guru.

Meeting with the True Guru, I have merged into the Naam, the Name of the Lord. I chant the Name of the Lord, Har, Har, and meditate on it.

I was seeking and searching for Him, the Lord, my best friend, and I have found Him within the home of my own being.

Section 12 - Raag Wadahans - Part 017

I see the One Lord, and I know the One Lord; I realize Him within my soul.

Without the Guru, I am - without the Guru, I am totally dishonored. |1|

Those who have found the True Guru, the True Guru, the Lord God unites them in His Union.

Their feet, their feet, I adore; I fall at their feet.

O Lord, Har, Har, I adore the feet of those who meditate on the True Guru, and the Almighty Lord God.

You are the Greatest Giver, the Inner-knower, the Searcher of hearts; please, reward my faith, O Lord King.

Meeting the Gursikh, my faith is rewarded; night and day, I sing the Glorious Praises of the Lord.

Those who have found the True Guru, the True Guru, the Lord God unites them in His Union. |2|

I am a sacrifice, I am a sacrifice to the Gursikhs, my dear friends.

They chant the Lord's Name, the Lord's Name; the Beloved Naam, the Name of the Lord, is my only Support.

The Name of the Lord, Har, Har, is the companion of my breath of life; without it, I cannot live for an instant or a moment.

The Lord, Har, Har, the Giver of peace, shows His Mercy, and the Gurmukh drinks in the Ambrosial Nectar.

The Lord blesses him with faith, and unites him in His Union; He Himself adorns him.

I am a sacrifice, I am a sacrifice to the Gursikhs, my dear friends. |3|

The Lord Himself, the Lord Himself, is the Immaculate Almighty Lord God.

The Lord Himself, the Lord Himself, unites us with Himself; that which He does, comes to pass.

Whatever is pleasing to the Lord God, that alone comes to pass; nothing else can be done.

Even by very clever tricks, He cannot be obtained; all have grown weary of practicing cleverness.

By Guru's Grace, servant Nanak beholds the Lord; without the Lord, I have no other at all.

The Lord Himself, the Lord Himself, is the Immaculate Almighty Lord God. |4|2|

Wadahans, Fourth Mehl:

The Lord, the True Guru, the Lord, the True Guru - if only I could meet the Lord, the True Guru; His Lotus Feet are so pleasing to me.

The darkness of my ignorance was dispelled, when the Guru applied the healing ointment of spiritual wisdom to my eyes.

The True Guru has applied the healing ointment of spiritual wisdom to my eyes, and the darkness of ignorance has been dispelled.

Serving the Guru, I have obtained the supreme status; I meditate on the Lord with every breath, and every morsel of food.

Those, upon whom the Lord God has bestowed His Grace, are committed to the service of the True Guru.

The Lord, the True Guru, the Lord, the True Guru - if only I could meet the Lord, the True Guru; His Lotus Feet are so pleasing to me. |1|

My True Guru, my True Guru is my Beloved; without the Guru, I cannot live. He gives me the Name of the Lord, the Name of the Lord, my only companion in the end.

The Name of the Lord, Har, Har, is my only companion in the end; the Guru, the True Guru, has implanted the Naam, the Name of the Lord, within me.

There, where neither child nor spouse shall accompany you, the Name of the Lord, Har, Har shall emancipate you.

Blessed, blessed is the True Guru, the Immaculate, Almighty Lord God; meeting Him, I meditate on the Name of the Lord.

My True Guru, my True Guru is my Beloved; without the Guru, I cannot live. |2|

Section 12 - Raag Wadahans - Part 018

Those who have not obtained the Blessed Vision, the Blessed Vision of the Darshan of the True Guru, the Almighty Lord God,

they have fruitlessly, fruitlessly wasted their whole lives in vain.

They have wasted away their whole lives in vain; those faithless cynics die a regretful death.

They have the jewel-treasure in their own homes, but still, they are hungry; those unlucky wretches are far away from the Lord.

O Lord, please, let me not see those who do not meditate on the Name of the Lord, Har, Har,

and who have not obtained the Blessed Vision, the Blessed Vision of the Darshan of the True Guru, the Almighty Lord God. |3|

I am a song-bird, I am a meek song-bird; I offer my prayer to the Lord.

If only I could meet the Guru, meet the Guru, O my Beloved; I dedicate myself to the devotional worship of the True Guru.

I worship the Lord, Har, Har, and the True Guru; the Lord God has granted His Grace.

Without the Guru, I have no other friend. The Guru, the True Guru, is my very breath of life.

Says Nanak, the Guru has implanted the Naam within me; the Name of the Lord, Har, Har, the True Name.

I am a song-bird, I am a meek song-bird; I offer my prayer to the Lord. |4|3|

Wadahans, Fourth Mehl:
O Lord, show Your Mercy, show Your Mercy, and let me meet the True Guru, the Giver of peace.
I go and ask, I go and ask from the True Guru, about the sermon of the Lord.
I ask about the sermon of the Lord from the True Guru, who has obtained the treasure of the Naam.
I bow at His Feet constantly, and pray to Him; the Guru, the True Guru, has shown me the Way.
He alone is a devotee, who looks alike upon pleasure and pain; he is imbued with the Name of the Lord, Har, Har.
O Lord, show Your Mercy, show Your Mercy, and let me meet the True Guru, the Giver of peace. |1|

Listen as Gurmukh, listen as Gurmukh, to the Naam, the Name of the Lord; all egotism and sins are eradicated.
Chanting the Name of the Lord, Har, Har, chanting the Name of the Lord, Har, Har, the troubles of the world vanish.
Those who contemplate the Name of the Lord, Har, Har, are rid of their suffering and sins.
The True Guru has placed the sword of spiritual wisdom in my hands; I have overcome and slain the Messenger of Death.
The Lord God, the Giver of peace, has granted His Grace, and I am rid of pain, sin and disease.
Listen as Gurmukh, listen as Gurmukh, to the Naam, the Name of the Lord; all egotism and sins are eradicated. |2|

Chanting the Name of the Lord, Har, Har, chanting the Name of the Lord, Har, Har, is so pleasing to my mind.
Speaking as Gurmukh, speaking as Gurmukh, chanting the Naam, all disease is eradicated.
As Gurmukh, chanting the Naam, all disease is eradicated, and the body becomes free of disease.
Night and day, one remains absorbed in the Perfect Poise of Samaadhi; meditate on the Name of the Lord, the inaccessible and unfathomable Lord.

Whether of high or low social status, one who meditates on the Naam obtains the supreme treasure.

Chanting the Name of the Lord, Har, Har, chanting the Name of the Lord, Har, Har, is pleasing to my mind. |3|

Section 12 - Raag Wadahans - Part 019

Grant Your Grace, grant Your Grace, O Lord, and save me.

I am a sinner, I am a worthless sinner, I am meek, but I am Yours, O Lord.

I am a worthless sinner, and I am meek, but I am Yours; I seek Your Sanctuary, O Merciful Lord.

You are the Destroyer of pain, the Giver of absolute peace; I am a stone - carry me across and save me.

Meeting the True Guru, servant Nanak has obtained the subtle essence of the Lord; through the Naam, the Name of the Lord, he is saved.

Grant Your Grace, grant Your Grace, Lord, and save me. |4|4|

Wadahans, Fourth Mehl, Ghorees ~ The Wedding Procession Songs:

One Universal Creator God. By The Grace Of The True Guru:

This body-horse was created by the Lord.

Blessed is human life, which is obtained by virtuous actions.

Human life is obtained only by the most virtuous actions; this body is radiant and golden.

The Gurmukh is imbued with the deep red color of the poppy; he is imbued with the new color of the Lord's Name, Har, Har, Har.

This body is so very beautiful; it chants the Name of the Lord, and it is adorned with the Name of the Lord, Har, Har.

By great good fortune, the body is obtained; the Naam, the Name of the Lord, is its companion; O servant Nanak, the Lord has created it. |1|

I place the saddle on the body-horse, the saddle of realization of the Good Lord.

Riding this horse, I cross over the terrifying world-ocean.

The terrifying world-ocean is rocked by countless waves, but the Gurmukh is carried across.

Embarking upon the boat of the Lord, the very fortunate ones cross over; the Guru, the Boatman, carries them across through the Word of the Shabad.

Night and day, imbued with the Lord's Love, singing the Glorious Praises of the Lord, the Lord's lover loves the Lord.

Servant Nanak has obtained the state of Nirvaanaa, the state of ultimate goodness, the state of the Lord. |2|

For a bridle in my mouth, the Guru has implanted spiritual wisdom within me.
He has applied the whip of the Lord's Love to my body.
Applying the whip of the Lord's Love to his body, the Gurmukh conquers his mind, and wins the battle of life.
He trains his untrained mind with the Word of the Shabad, and drinks in the rejuvenating essence of the Lord's Nectar.
Listen with your ears to the Word, uttered by the Guru, and attune your body-horse to the Lord's Love.
Servant Nanak has crossed over the long and treacherous path. |3|

The transitory body-horse was created by the Lord.
Blessed, blessed is that body-horse which meditates on the Lord God.
Blessed and acclaimed is that body-horse which meditates on the Lord God; it is obtained by the merits of past actions.
Riding the body-horse, one crosses over the terrifying world ocean; the Gurmukh meets the Lord, the embodiment of supreme bliss.
The Lord, Har, Har, has perfectly arranged this wedding; the Saints have come together as a marriage party.
Servant Nanak has obtained the Lord as his Spouse; joining together, the Saints sing the songs of joy and congratulations. |4|1|5|

Wadahans, Fourth Mehl:
The body is the Lord's horse; the Lord imbues it with the fresh and new color.
From the Guru, I ask for the Lord's spiritual wisdom.

Section 12 - Raag Wadahans - Part 020

I ask for the Lord's spiritual wisdom, and the Lord's sublime sermon; through the Name of the Lord, I have come to know His value and His state.
The Creator has made my life totally fruitful; I chant the Name of the Lord.
The Lord's humble servant begs for the Lord's Name, for the Lord's Praises, and for devotional worship of the Lord God.
Says servant Nanak, listen, O Saints: devotional worship of the Lord, the Lord of the Universe, is sublime and good. |1|

The golden body is saddled with the saddle of gold.

It is adorned with the jewel of the Name of the Lord, Har, Har.

Adorned with the jewel of the Naam, one obtains the Lord of the Universe; he meets the Lord, sings the Glorious Praises of the Lord, and obtains all sorts of comforts.

He obtains the Word of the Guru's Shabad, and he meditates on the Name of the Lord; by great good fortune, he assumes the color of the Lord's Love.

He meets his Lord and Master, the Inner-knower, the Searcher of hearts; His body is ever-new, and His color is ever-fresh.

Nanak chants and realizes the Naam; he begs for the Name of the Lord, the Lord God. |2|

The Guru has placed the reins in the mouth of the body-horse.

The mind-elephant is overpowered by the Word of the Guru's Shabad.

The bride obtains the supreme status, as her mind is brought under control; she is the beloved of her Husband Lord.

Deep within her inner self, she is in love with her Lord; in His home, she is beautiful - she is the bride of her Lord God.

Imbued with the Lord's Love, she is intuitively absorbed in bliss; she obtains the Lord God, Har, Har.

Servant Nanak, the Lord's slave, says that only the very fortunate meditate on the Lord, Har, Har. |3|

The body is the horse, upon which one rides to the Lord.

Meeting with the True Guru, one sings the songs of joy.

Sing the songs of joy to the Lord, serve the Name of the Lord, and become the servant of His servants.

You shall go and enter the Mansion of the Beloved Lord's Presence, and lovingly enjoy His Love.

I sing the Glorious Praises of the Lord, so pleasing to my mind; following the Guru's Teachings, I meditate on the Lord within my mind.

The Lord has showered His Mercy upon servant Nanak; mounting the body-horse, he has found the Lord. |4|2|6|

Raag Wadahans, Fifth Mehl, Chhant, Fourth House:

One Universal Creator God. By The Grace Of The True Guru:

Meeting with the Guru, I have found my Beloved Lord God.

I have made this body and mind a sacrifice, a sacrificial offering to my Lord.

Dedicating my body and mind, I have crossed over the terrifying world-ocean, and shaken off the fear of death.

Drinking in the Ambrosial Nectar, I have become immortal; my comings and goings have ceased.

I have found that home, of celestial Samaadhi; the Name of the Lord is my only Support.

Says Nanak, I enjoy peace and pleasure; I bow in reverence to the Perfect Guru. |1|

Listen, O my friend and companion
- the Guru has given the Mantra of the Shabad, the True Word of God.

Meditating on this True Shabad, I sing the songs of joy, and my mind is rid of anxiety.

I have found God, who never leaves; forever and ever, He sits with me.

One who is pleasing to God receives true honor. The Lord God blesses him with wealth.

Section 12 - Raag Wadahans - Part 021

Says Nanak, I am a sacrifice to such a humble being. O Lord, You bless all with Your bountiful blessings. |2|

When it pleases You, then I am satisfied and satiated.

My mind is soothed and calmed, and all my thirst is quenched.

My mind is soothed and calmed, the burning has ceased, and I have found so many treasures.

All the Sikhs and servants partake of them; I am a sacrifice to my True Guru.

I have become fearless, imbued with the Love of my Lord Master, and I have shaken off the fear of death.

Slave Nanak, Your humble servant, lovingly embraces Your meditation; O Lord, be with me always. |3|

My hopes and desires have been fulfilled, O my Lord.

I am worthless, without virtue; all virtues are Yours, O Lord.

All virtues are Yours, O my Lord and Master; with what mouth should I praise You?

You did not consider my merits and demerits; you forgave me in an instant.

I have obtained the nine treasures, congratulations are pouring in, and the unstruck melody resounds.

Says Nanak, I have found my Husband Lord within my own home, and all my anxiety is forgotten. |4|1|

Shalok:

Why do you listen to falsehood? It shall vanish like a gust of wind.

O Nanak, those ears are acceptable, which listen to the True Master. |1|

Chhant:

I am a sacrifice to those who listen with their ears to the Lord God.

Blissful and comfortable are those, who with their tongues chant the Name of the Lord, Har, Har.

They are naturally embellished, with priceless virtues; they have come to save the world.

God's Feet are the boat, which carries so many across the terrifying world-ocean.

Those who are blessed with the favor of my Lord and Master, are not asked to render their account.

Says Nanak, I am a sacrifice to those who listen to God with their ears. |1|

Shalok:

With my eyes, I have seen the Light of the Lord, but my great thirst is not quenched.

O Nanak, those eyes are different, which behold my Husband Lord. |1|

Chhant:

I am a sacrifice to those who have seen the Lord God.

In the True Court of the Lord, they are approved.

They are approved by their Lord and Master, and acclaimed as supreme; they are imbued with the Lord's Love.

They are satiated with the sublime essence of the Lord, and they merge in celestial peace; in each and every heart, they see the all-pervading Lord.

They alone are the friendly Saints, and they alone are happy, who are pleasing to their Lord and Master.

Says Nanak, I am forever a sacrifice to those who have seen the Lord God. |2|

Shalok:

The body is blind, totally blind and desolate, without the Naam.

O Nanak, fruitful is the life of that being, within whose heart the True Lord and Master abides. |1|

Chhant:

I am cut into pieces as a sacrifice, to those who have seen my Lord God.

His humble servants partake of the Sweet Ambrosial Nectar of the Lord, Har, Har, and are satiated.

The Lord seems sweet to their minds; God is merciful to them, His Ambrosial Nectar rains down upon them, and they are at peace.

Pain is eliminated and doubt is dispelled from the body; chanting the Name of the Lord of the World, their victory is celebrated.

They are rid of emotional attachment, their sins are erased, and their association with the five passions is broken off.

Section 12 - Raag Wadahans - Part 022

Says Nanak, I am every bit a sacrifice to those, within whose hearts my Lord God abides. |3|

Shalok:
Those who long for the Lord, are said to be His servants.
Nanak knows this Truth, that the Lord is not different from His Saint. |1|

Chhant:
As water mixes and blends with water,
so does one's light mix and blend with the Lord's Light.
Merging with the perfect, all-powerful Creator, one comes to know his own self.
Then, he enters the celestial state of absolute Samaadhi, and speaks of the One and Only Lord.
He Himself is unmanifest, and He Himself is liberated; He Himself speaks of Himself.
O Nanak, doubt, fear and the limitations of the three qualities are dispelled, as one merges into the Lord, like water blending with water. |4|2|

Wadahans, Fifth Mehl:
God is the all-powerful Creator, the Cause of causes.
He preserves the whole world, reaching out with His hand.
He is the all-powerful, safe Sanctuary, Lord and Master, Treasure of mercy, Giver of peace.
I am a sacrifice to Your slaves, who recognize only the One Lord.
His color and shape cannot be seen; His description is indescribable.
Prays Nanak, hear my prayer, O God, Almighty Creator, Cause of causes. |1|

These beings are Yours; You are their Creator.

God is the Destroyer of pain, suffering and doubt.

Eliminate my doubt, pain and suffering in an instant, and preserve me, O Lord, Merciful to the meek.

You are mother, father and friend, O Lord and Master; the whole world is Your child, O Lord of the World.

One who comes seeking Your Sanctuary, obtains the treasure of virtue, and does not have to enter the cycle of birth and death again.

Prays Nanak, I am Your slave. All beings are Yours; You are their Creator. |2|

Meditating on the Lord, twenty-four hours a day,

the fruits of the heart's desires are obtained.

Your heart's desires are obtained, meditating on God, and the fear of death is dispelled.

I sing of the Lord of the Universe in the Saadh Sangat, the Company of the Holy, and my hopes are fulfilled.

Renouncing egotism, emotional attachment and all corruption, we become pleasing to the Mind of God.

Prays Nanak, day and night, meditate forever on the Lord, Har, Har. |3|

At the Lord's Door, the unstruck melody resounds.

In each and every heart, the Lord, the Lord of the Universe, sings.

The Lord of the Universe sings, and abides forever; He is unfathomable, profoundly deep, lofty and exalted.

His virtues are infinite - none of them can be described. No one can reach Him.

He Himself creates, and He Himself sustains; all beings and creatures are fashioned by Him.

Prays Nanak, happiness comes from devotional worship of the Naam; at His Door, the unstruck melody resounds. |4|3|

Raag Wadahans, First Mehl, Fifth House, Alaahanees ~ Songs Of Mourning:

One Universal Creator God. By The Grace Of The True Guru:

Blessed is the Creator, the True King, who has linked the whole world to its tasks.

When one's time is up, and the measure is full, this dear soul is caught, and driven off.

Section 12 - Raag Wadahans - Part 023

This dear soul is driven off, when the pre-ordained Order is received, and all the relatives cry out in mourning.

The body and the swan-soul are separated, when one's days are past and done, O my mother.

As is one's pre-ordained Destiny, so does one receive, according to one's past actions.

Blessed is the Creator, the True King, who has linked the whole world to its tasks. |1|

Meditate in remembrance on the Lord and Master, O my Siblings of Destiny; everyone has to pass this way.

These false entanglements last for only a few days; then, one must surely move on to the world hereafter.

He must surely move on to the world hereafter, like a guest; so why does he indulge in ego?

Chant the Name of the Lord; serving Him, you shall obtain peace in His Court.

In the world hereafter, no one's commands will be obeyed. According to their actions, each and every person proceeds.

Meditate in remembrance on the Lord and Master, O my Siblings of Destiny; everyone has to pass this way. |2|

Whatever pleases the Almighty Lord, that alone comes to pass; this world is an opportunity to please Him.

The True Creator Lord is pervading and permeating the water, the land and the air.

The True Creator Lord is invisible and infinite; His limits cannot be found.

Fruitful is the coming of those, who meditate single-mindedly on Him.

He destroys, and having destroyed, He creates; by His Order, He adorns us.

Whatever pleases the Almighty Lord, that alone comes to pass; this world is an opportunity to please Him. |3|

Nanak: he alone truly weeps, O Baba, who weeps in the Lord's Love.

One who weeps for the sake of worldly objects, O Baba, weeps totally in vain.

This weeping is all in vain; the world forgets the Lord, and weeps for the sake of Maya.

He does not distinguish between good and evil, and wastes away this life in vain.

Everyone who comes here, shall have to leave; to act in ego is false.

Nanak: he alone truly weeps, O Baba, who weeps in the Lord's Love. |4|1|

Wadahans, First Mehl:

Come, O my companions - let us meet together and dwell upon the True Name.

Let us weep over the body's separation from the Lord and Master; let us remember Him in contemplation.

Let us remember the Lord and Master in contemplation, and keep a watchful eye on the Path. We shall have to go there as well.

He who has created, also destroys; whatever happens is by His Will.

Whatever He has done, has come to pass; how can we command Him?

Come, O my companions - let us meet together and dwell upon the True Name. |1|

Death would not be called bad, O people, if one knew how to truly die.

Serve your Almighty Lord and Master, and your path in the world hereafter will be easy.

Take this easy path, and you shall obtain the fruits of your rewards, and receive honor in the world hereafter.

Go there with your offering, and you shall merge in the True Lord; your honor shall be confirmed.

You shall obtain a place in the Mansion of the Lord Master's Presence; being pleasing to Him, you shall enjoy the pleasures of His Love.

Death would not be called bad, O people, if one knew how to truly die. |2|

The death of brave heroes is blessed, if it is approved by God.

Section 12 - Raag Wadahans - Part 024

They alone are acclaimed as brave warriors in the world hereafter, who receive true honor in the Court of the Lord.

They are honored in the Court of the Lord; they depart with honor, and they do not suffer pain in the world hereafter.

They meditate on the One Lord, and obtain the fruits of their rewards. Serving the Lord, their fear is dispelled.

Do not indulge in egotism, and dwell within your own mind; the Knower Himself knows everything.

The death of brave heroes is blessed, if it is approved by God. |3|

Nanak: for whom should we mourn, O Baba? This world is merely a play.
The Lord Master beholds His work, and contemplates His creative potency.
He contemplates His creative potency, having established the Universe. He who created it, He alone knows.
He Himself beholds it, and He Himself understands it. He Himself realizes the Hukam of His Command.
He who created these things, He alone knows. His subtle form is infinite.
Nanak: for whom should we mourn, O Baba? This world is merely a play. |4|2|

Wadahans, First Mehl, Dakhanee:
The True Creator Lord is True - know this well; He is the True Sustainer.
He Himself fashioned His Own Self; the True Lord is invisible and infinite.
He brought together, and then separated, the two grinding stones of the earth and the sky; without the Guru, there is only pitch darkness.
He created the sun and the moon; night and day, they move according to His Thought. |1|

O True Lord and Master, You are True. O True Lord, bless me with Your Love. |Pause|

You created the Universe; You are the Giver of pain and pleasure.
You created woman and man, the love of poison, and emotional attachment to Maya.
The four sources of creation, and the power of the Word, are also of Your making. You give Support to all beings.
You have made the Creation as Your Throne; You are the True Judge. |2|

You created comings and goings, but You are ever-stable, O Creator Lord.
In birth and death, in coming and going, this soul is held in bondage by corruption.
The evil person has forgotten the Naam; he has drowned - what can he do now?
Forsaking merit, he has loaded the poisonous cargo of demerits; he is a trader of sins. |3|

The beloved soul has received the Call, the Command of the True Creator Lord.

The soul, the husband, has become separated from the body, the bride. The Lord is the Re-uniter of the separated ones.

No one cares for your beauty, O beautiful bride.; the Messenger of Death is bound only by the Lord Commander's Command.

He does not distinguish between young children and old people; he tears apart love and affection. |4|

The nine doors are closed by the True Lord's Command, and the swan-soul takes flight into the skies.

The body-bride is separated, and defrauded by falsehood; she is now a widow - her husband's body lies dead in the courtyard.

The widow cries out at the door, "The light of my mind has gone out, O my mother, with his death."

So cry out, O soul-brides of the Husband Lord, and dwell on the Glorious Praises of the True Lord. |5|

Her loved one is cleansed, bathed in water, and dressed in silken robes.

The musicians play, and the Bani of the True Lord's Words are sung; the five relatives feel as if they too are dead, so deadened are their minds.

"Separation from my beloved is like death to me!" cries the widow. "My life in this world is cursed and worthless!"

But she alone is approved, who dies, while yet still alive; she lives for the sake of the Love of her Beloved. |6|

So cry out in mourning, you who have come to mourn; this world is false and fraudulent.

Section 12 - Raag Wadahans - Part 025

I too have been defrauded, chasing after worldly entanglements; my Husband Lord has forsaken me - I practice the evil deeds of a wife without a spouse.

In each and every home, are the brides of the Husband Lord; they gaze upon their Handsome Lord with love and affection.

I sing the Praises of my True Husband Lord, and through the Naam, the Name of my Husband Lord, I blossom forth. |7|

Meeting with the Guru, the soul-bride's dress is transformed, and she is adorned with Truth.

Come and meet with me, O brides of the Lord; let's meditate in remembrance on the Creator Lord.

Through the Naam, the soul-bride becomes the Lord's favorite; she is adorned with Truth.

Do not sing the songs of separation, O Nanak; reflect upon God. |8|3|

Wadahans, First Mehl:

The One who creates and dissolves the world - that Lord and Master alone knows His creative power.

Do not search for the True Lord far away; recognize the Word of the Shabad in each and every heart.

Recognize the Shabad, and do not think that the Lord is far away; He created this creation.

Meditating on the Naam, the Name of the Lord, one obtains peace; without the Naam, he plays a losing game.

The One who established the Universe, He alone knows the Way; what can anyone say?

The One who established the world cast the net of Maya over it; accept Him as your Lord and Master. |1|

O Baba, he has come, and now he must get up and depart; this world is only a way-station.

Upon each and every head, the True Lord writes their destiny of pain and pleasure, according to their past actions.

He bestows pain and pleasure, according to the deeds done; the record of these deeds stays with the soul.

He does those deeds which the Creator Lord causes him to do; he attempts no other actions.

The Lord Himself is detached, while the world is entangled in conflict; by His Command, He emancipates it.

He may put this off today, but tomorrow he is seized by death; in love with duality, he practices corruption. |2|

The path of death is dark and dismal; the way cannot be seen.

There is no water, no quilt or mattress, and no food there.

He receives no food there, no honor or water, no clothes or decorations.

The chain is put around his neck, and the Messenger of Death standing over his head strikes him; he cannot see the door of his home.

The seeds planted on this path do not sprout; bearing the weight of his sins upon his head, he regrets and repents.

Without the True Lord, no one is his friend; reflect upon this as true. |3|

O Baba, they alone are known to truly weep and wail, who meet together and weep, chanting the Praises of the Lord.
Defrauded by Maya and worldly affairs, the weepers weep.
They weep for the sake of worldly affairs, and they do not wash off their own filth; the world is merely a dream.
Like the juggler, deceiving by his tricks, one is deluded by egotism, falsehood and illusion.
The Lord Himself reveals the Path; He Himself is the Doer of deeds.
Those who are imbued with the Naam, are protected by the Perfect Guru, O Nanak; they merge in celestial bliss. |4|4|

Wadahans, First Mehl:
O Baba, whoever has come, will rise up and leave; this world is merely a false show.
One's true home is obtained by serving the True Lord; real Truth is obtained by being truthful.
By falsehood and greed, no place of rest is found, and no place in the world hereafter is obtained.
No one invites him to come in and sit down. He is like a crow in a deserted home.
Trapped by birth and death, he is separated from the Lord for such a long time; the whole world is wasting away.
Greed, worldly entanglements and Maya deceive the world. Death hovers over its head, and causes it to weep. |1|

Section 12 - Raag Wadahans - Part 026

Come, O Baba, and Siblings of Destiny - let's join together; take me in your arms, and bless me with your prayers.
O Baba, union with the True Lord cannot be broken; bless me with your prayers for union with my Beloved.
Bless me with your prayers, that I may perform devotional worship service to my Lord; for those already united with Him, what is there to unite?

Some have wandered away from the Name of the Lord, and lost the Path. The Word of the Guru's Shabad is the true game.
Do not go on Death's path; remain merged in the Word of the Shabad, the true form throughout the ages.

Through good fortune, we meet such friends and relatives, who meet with the Guru, and escape the noose of Death. |2|

O Baba, we come into the world naked, into pain and pleasure, according to the record of our account.
The call of our pre-ordained destiny cannot be altered; it follows from our past actions.
The True Lord sits and writes of ambrosial nectar, and bitter poison; as the Lord attaches us, so are we attached.
The Charmer, Maya, has worked her charms, and the multi-colored thread is around everyone's neck.
Through shallow intellect, the mind becomes shallow, and one eats the fly, along with the sweets.
Contrary to custom, he comes into the Dark Age of Kali Yuga naked, and naked he is bound down and sent away again. |3|

O Baba, weep and mourn if you must; the beloved soul is bound and driven off.
The pre-ordained record of destiny cannot be erased; the summons has come from the Lord's Court.
The messenger comes, when it pleases the Lord, and the mourners begin to mourn.
Sons, brothers, nephews and very dear friends weep and wail.
Let him weep, who weeps in the Fear of God, cherishing the virtues of God. No one dies with the dead.
O Nanak, throughout the ages, they are known as wise, who weep, remembering the True Lord. |4|5|

Wadahans, Third Mehl:
One Universal Creator God. By The Grace Of The True Guru:
Praise God, the True Lord; He is all-powerful to do all things.
The soul-bride shall never be a widow, and she shall never have to endure suffering.
She shall never suffer - night and day, she enjoys pleasures; that soul-bride merges in the Mansion of her Lord's Presence.
She knows her Beloved, the Architect of karma, and she speaks words of ambrosial sweetness.
The virtuous soul-brides dwell on the Lord's virtues; they keep their Husband Lord in their remembrance, and so they never suffer separation from Him.

So praise your True Husband Lord, who is all-powerful to do all things. |1|

The True Lord and Master is realized through the Word of His Shabad; He blends all with Himself.

That soul-bride is imbued with the Love of her Husband Lord, who banishes her self-conceit from within.

Eradicating her ego from within herself, death shall not consume her again; as Gurmukh, she knows the One Lord God.

The desire of the soul-bride is fulfilled; deep within herself, she is drenched in His Love. She meets the Great Giver, the Life of the World.

Imbued with love for the Shabad, she is like a youth intoxicated; she merges into the very being of her Husband Lord.

The True Lord Master is realized through the Word of His Shabad. He blends all with Himself. |2|

Those who have realized their Husband Lord - I go and ask those Saints about Him.

Section 12 - Raag Wadahans - Part 027

Renouncing ego, I serve them; thus I meet my True Husband Lord, with intuitive ease.

The True Husband Lord comes to meet the soul-bride who practices Truth, and is imbued with the True Word of the Shabad.

She shall never become a widow; she shall always be a happy bride. Deep within herself, she dwells in the celestial bliss of Samaadhi.

Her Husband Lord is fully pervading everywhere; beholding Him ever-present, she enjoys His Love, with intuitive ease.

Those who have realized their Husband Lord - I go and ask those Saints about Him. |3|

The separated ones also meet with their Husband Lord, if they fall at the Feet of the True Guru.

The True Guru is forever merciful; through the Word of His Shabad, demerits are burnt away.

Burning away her demerits through the Shabad, the soul-bride eradicates her love of duality, and remains absorbed in the True, True Lord.

Through the True Shabad, everlasting peace is obtained, and egotism and doubt are dispelled.

The Immaculate Husband Lord is forever the Giver of peace; O Nanak, through the Word of His Shabad, He is met.

The separated ones also meet with their Husband Lord, if they fall at the feet of the True Guru. |4|1|

Wadahans, Third Mehl:

Listen, O brides of the Lord: serve your Beloved Husband Lord, and contemplate the Word of His Shabad.

The worthless bride does not know her Husband Lord - she is deluded; forgetting her Husband Lord, she weeps and wails.

She weeps, thinking of her Husband Lord, and she cherishes His virtues; her Husband Lord does not die, and does not leave.

As Gurmukh, she knows the Lord; through the Word of His Shabad, He is realized; through True Love, she merges with Him.

She who does not know her Husband Lord, the Architect of karma, is deluded by falsehood - she herself is false.

Listen, O brides of the Lord: serve your Beloved Husband Lord, and contemplate the Word of His Shabad. |1|

He Himself created the whole world; the world comes and goes.

The love of Maya has ruined the world; people die, to be re-born, over and over again.

People die to be re-born, over and over again, while their sins increase; without spiritual wisdom, they are deluded.

Without the Word of the Shabad, the Husband Lord is not found; the worthless, false bride wastes her life away, weeping and wailing.

He is my Beloved Husband Lord, the Life of the World - for whom should I weep? They alone weep, who forget their Husband Lord.

He Himself created the whole world; the world comes and goes. |2|

That Husband Lord is True, forever True; He does not die, and He does not leave.

The ignorant soul-bride wanders in delusion; in the love of duality, she sits like a widow.

She sits like a widow, in the love of duality; through emotional attachment to Maya, she suffers in pain. She is growing old, and her body is withering away.

Whatever has come, all that shall pass away; through the love of duality, they suffer in pain.

They do not see the Messenger of Death; they long for Maya, and their consciousness is attached to greed.

That Husband Lord is True, forever True; He does not die, and He does not leave. |3|

Some weep and wail, separated from their Husband Lord; the blind ones do not know that their Husband is with them.

By Guru's Grace, they may meet with their True Husband, and cherish Him always deep within.

She cherishes her Husband deep within herself - He is always with her; the self-willed manmukhs think that He is far away.

This body rolls in the dust, and is totally useless; it does not realize the Presence of the Lord and Master.

Section 12 - Raag Wadahans - Part 028

O Nanak, that soul-bride is united in Union; she cherishes her Beloved Husband forever, deep within herself.

Some weep and wail, separated from their Husband Lord; the blind ones do not know that their Husband is with them. |4|2|

Wadahans, Third Mehl:

Those who are separated from their Beloved Husband Lord weep and wail, but my True Husband Lord is always with me.

Those who know that they must depart, serve the True Guru, and dwell upon the Naam, the Name of the Lord.

They dwell constantly upon the Naam, and the True Guru is with them; they serve the True Guru, and so obtain peace.

Through the Shabad, they kill death, and enshrine the True Lord within their hearts; they shall not have to come and go again.

True is the Lord and Master, and True is His Name; bestowing His Gracious Glance, one is enraptured.

Those who are separated from their Beloved Husband Lord weep and wail, but my True Husband Lord is always with me. |1|

God, my Lord and Master, is the highest of all; how can I meet my Dear Beloved?

When the True Guru united me, then I was naturally united with my Husband Lord, and now, I keep Him clasped to my heart.

I constantly, lovingly cherish my Beloved within my heart; through the True Guru, I see my Beloved.

The cloak of Maya's love is false; wearing it, one slips and loses his footing.

That cloak is true, which is dyed in the color of the Love of my Beloved; wearing it, my inner thirst is quenched.

God, my Lord and Master, is the highest of all; how can I meet my Dear Beloved? |2|

I have realized my True Lord God, while the other worthless ones have gone astray.

I dwell constantly upon my Beloved Husband Lord, and reflect upon the True Word of the Shabad.

The bride reflects upon the True Shabad, and is imbued with His Love; she meets with the True Guru, and finds her Beloved.

Deep within, she is imbued with His Love, and intoxicated with delight; her enemies and sufferings are all taken away.

Surrender body and soul to your Guru, and then you shall become happy; your thirst and pain shall be taken away.

I have realized my True Lord God, while the other worthless ones have gone astray. |3|

The True Lord Himself created the world; without the Guru, there is only pitch darkness.

He Himself unites, and causes us to unite with Him; He Himself blesses us with His Love.

He Himself blesses us with His Love, and deals in celestial peace; the life of the Gurmukh is reformed.

Blessed is his coming into the world; he banishes his self-conceit, and is acclaimed as true in the Court of the True Lord.

The light of the jewel of spiritual wisdom shines within his heart, O Nanak, and he loves the Naam, the Name of the Lord.

The True Lord Himself created the world; without the Guru, there is only pitch darkness. |4|3|

Wadahans, Third Mehl:

This body is frail; old age is overtaking it.

Those who are protected by the Guru are saved, while others die, to be reincarnated; they continue coming and going.

Others die, to be reincarnated; they continue coming and going, and in the end, they depart regretfully. Without the Name, there is no peace.

As one acts here, so does he obtain his rewards; the self-willed manmukh loses his honor.

In the City of Death, there is pitch darkness, and huge clouds of dust; neither sister nor brother is there.

This body is frail; old age is overtaking it. |1|

The body becomes like gold, when the True Guru unites one with Himself.

Section 12 - Raag Wadahans - Part 029

Doubt and Maya have been removed from within me, and I am merged in the Naam, the True Name of the Lord.

Merged in the True Name of the Lord, I sing the Glorious Praises of the Lord; meeting my Beloved, I have found peace.

I am in constant bliss, day and night; egotism has been dispelled from within me.

I fall at the feet of those who enshrine the Naam within their consciousness.

The body becomes like gold, when the True Guru unites one with Himself. |2|

We truly praise the True Lord, when the True Guru imparts understanding.

Without the True Guru, they are deluded by doubt; going to the world hereafter, what face will they display?

What face will they show, when they go there? They will regret and repent for their sins; their actions will bring them only pain and suffering.

Those who are imbued with the Naam are dyed in the deep crimson color of the Lord's Love; they merge into the Being of their Husband Lord.

I can conceive of no other as great as the Lord; unto whom should I go and speak?

We truly praise the True Lord, when the True Guru imparts understanding. |3|

I fall at the feet of those who praise the Truest of the True.

Those humble beings are true, and immaculately pure; meeting them, all filth is washed off.

Meeting them, all filth is washed off; bathing in the Pool of Truth, one becomes truthful, with intuitive ease.

The True Guru has given me the realization of the Naam, the Immaculate Name of the Lord, the unfathomable, the imperceptible.

Those who perform devotional worship to the Lord night and day, are imbued with His Love; O Nanak, they are absorbed in the True Lord.

I fall at the feet of those who meditate on the Truest of the True. |4|4|

Vaar Of Wadahans, Fourth Mehl: To Be Sung In The Tune Of Lalaa-Behleemaa:

One Universal Creator God. By The Grace Of The True Guru:

Shalok, Third Mehl:

The great swans are imbued with the Word of the Shabad; they enshrine the True Name within their hearts.

They gather Truth, remain always in Truth, and love the True Name.

They are always pure and immaculate - filth does not touch them; they are blessed with the Grace of the Creator Lord.

O Nanak, I am a sacrifice to those who, night and day, meditate on the Lord. |1|

Third Mehl:

I thought that he was a great swan, so I associated with him.

If I had known that he was only a wretched heron from birth, I would not have touched him. |2|

Third Mehl:

Seeing the swans swimming, the herons became envious.

But the poor herons drowned and died, and floated with their heads down, and their feet above. |3|

Pauree:

You Yourself are Yourself, all by Yourself; You Yourself created the creation.

You Yourself are Yourself the Formless Lord; there is no other than You.

You are the all-powerful Cause of causes; what You do, comes to be.

You give gifts to all beings, without their asking.

Everyone proclaims, "Waaho! Waaho! Blessed, blessed is the True Guru, who has given the supreme gift of the Name of the Lord. |1|

Section 12 - Raag Wadahans - Part 030

Shalok, Third Mehl:

The entire universe is in fear; only the Dear Lord is fearless.

Serving the True Guru, the Lord comes to dwell in the mind, and then, fear cannot stay there.

Enemies and pain cannot come close, and no one can touch him.

The Gurmukh reflects upon the Lord in his mind; whatever pleases the Lord - that alone comes to pass.

O Nanak, He Himself preserves one's honor; He alone resolves our affairs. |1|-

Third Mehl:

Some friends are leaving, some have already left, and those remaining will eventually leave.

Those who do not serve the True Guru, come and go regretting.

O Nanak, those who are attuned to Truth are not separated; serving the True Guru, they merge into the Lord. |2|

Pauree:

Meet with that True Guru, the True Friend, within whose mind the Lord, the virtuous One, abides.

Meet with that Beloved True Guru, who has subdued ego from within himself.

Blessed, blessed is the Perfect True Guru, who has given the Lord's Teachings to reform the whole world.

O Saints, meditate constantly on the Lord's Name, and cross over the terrifying, poisonous world-ocean.

The Perfect Guru has taught me about the Lord; I am forever a sacrifice to the Guru. |2|

Shalok, Third Mehl:

Service to, and obedience to the True Guru, is the essence of comfort and peace.

Doing so, one obtains honor here, and the door of salvation in the Court of the Lord.

In this way, perform the tasks of Truth, wear Truth, and take the Support of the True Name.

Associating with Truth, obtain Truth, and love the True Name.

Through the True Word of the Shabad, be always happy, and you shall be acclaimed as True in the True Court.

O Nanak, he alone serves the True Guru, whom the Creator has blessed with His Glance of Grace. |1|

Third Mehl:

Cursed is the life, and cursed is the dwelling, of those who serve another.

Abandoning the Ambrosial Nectar, they turn to poison; they earn poison, and poison is their only wealth.

Poison is their food, and poison is their dress; they fill their mouths with morsels of poison.

In this world, they earn only pain and suffering, and dying, they go to abide in hell.

The self-willed manmukhs have filthy faces; they do not know the Word of the Shabad; in sexual desire and anger they waste away.

They forsake the Fear of the True Guru, and because of their stubborn ego, their efforts do not come to fruition.

In the City of Death, they are bound and beaten, and no one hears their prayers.

O Nanak, they act according to their pre-ordained destiny; the Gurmukh abides in the Naam, the Name of the Lord. |2|

Pauree:

Serve the True Guru, O Holy people; He implants the Name of the Lord, Har, Har, in our minds.

Worship the True Guru day and night; He leads us the meditate on the Lord of the Universe, the Master of the Universe.

Behold the True Guru, each and every moment; He shows us the Divine Path of the Lord.

Let everyone fall at the feet of the True Guru; He has dispelled the darkness of emotional attachment.

Let everyone hail and praise the True Guru, who has led us to find the treasure of the Lord's devotional worship. |3|

Shalok, Third Mehl:

Meeting with the True Guru, hunger departs; by wearing the robes of a beggar, hunger does not depart.

Section 12 - Raag Wadahans - Part 031

Afflicted with pain, he wanders from house to house, and in the world hereafter, he receives double punishment.

Peace does not come to his heart - he is not content to eat what comes his way.

With his stubborn mind, he begs, and grabs, and annoys those who give.

Instead of wearing these beggar's robes, it is better to be a householder, and give to others.

Those who are attuned to the Word of the Shabad, acquire understanding; the others wander, deluded by doubt.

They act according to their past actions; it is useless to talk to them.

O Nanak, those who are pleasing unto the Lord are good; He upholds their honor. |1|

Third Mehl:

Serving the True Guru, one finds a lasting peace; the pains of birth and death are removed.

He is not troubled by anxiety, and the carefree Lord comes to dwell in the mind.

Deep within himself, is the sacred shrine of spiritual wisdom, revealed by the True Guru.

His filth is removed, and his soul becomes immaculately pure, bathing in the sacred shrine, the pool of Ambrosial Nectar.

The friend meets with the True Friend, the Lord, through the love of the Shabad.

Within the home of his own being, he finds the Divine Self, and his light blends with the Light.

The Messenger of Death does not leave the hypocrite; he is led away in dishonor.

O Nanak, those who are imbued with the Naam are saved; they are in love with the True Lord. |2|

Pauree:

Go, and sit in the Sat Sangat, the True Congregation, where the Name of the Lord is churned.

In peace and poise, contemplate the Lord's Name - don't lose the essence of the Lord.

Chant the Name of the Lord, Har, Har, constantly, day and night, and you shall be accepted in the Court of the Lord.

He alone finds the Perfect True Guru, on whose forehead such a pre-ordained destiny is written.

Let everyone bow in worship to the Guru, who utters the sermon of the Lord. |4|

Shalok, Third Mehl:

The friends who love the True Guru, meet with the Lord, the True Friend.

Meeting their Beloved, they meditate on the True Lord with love and affection.

Their minds are appeased by their own minds, through the incomparable Word of the Guru's Shabad.

These friends are united, and will not be separated again; they have been united by the Creator Lord Himself.

Some do not believe in the Blessed Vision of the Guru's Darshan; they do not contemplate the Shabad.

The separated ones are in love with duality - what more separation can they suffer?

Friendship with the self-willed manmukhs lasts for only a few short days.

This friendship is broken in an instant; this friendship leads to corruption.

They do not fear the True Lord within their hearts, and they do not love the Naam.

O Nanak, why become friends with those whom the Creator Lord Himself has misled? |1|

Third Mehl:

Some remain constantly imbued with the Lord's Love; I am forever a sacrifice to them.

I dedicate my mind, soul and wealth to them; bowing low, I fall at their feet.

Meeting them, the soul is satisfied, and one's hunger and thirst all depart.

O Nanak, those who are attuned to the Naam are happy forever; they lovingly focus their minds on the True Lord. |2|

Pauree:

I am a sacrifice to the Guru, who recites the sermon of the Lord's Teachings.

Section 12 - Raag Wadahans - Part 032

I am forever a sacrifice to that Guru, who has led me to serve the Lord.

That Beloved True Guru is always with me; wherever I may be, He will save me.

Most blessed is that Guru, who imparts understanding of the Lord.

O Nanak, I am a sacrifice to the Guru, who has given me the Lord's Name, and fulfilled the desires of my mind. |5|

Shalok, Third Mehl:

Consumed by desires, the world is burning and dying; burning and burning, it cries out.

But if it meets with the cooling and soothing True Guru, it does not burn any longer.

O Nanak, without the Name, and without contemplating the Word of the Shabad, no one becomes fearless. |1|

Third Mehl:

Wearing ceremonial robes, the fire is not quenched, and the mind is filled with anxiety.

Destroying the snake's hole, the snake is not killed; it is just like doing deeds without a Guru.

Serving the Giver, the True Guru, the Shabad comes to abide in the mind.

The mind and body are cooled and soothed; peace ensues, and the fire of desire is quenched.

The supreme comforts and lasting peace are obtained, when one eradicates ego from within.

He alone becomes a detached Gurmukh, who lovingly focuses his consciousness on the True Lord.

Anxiety does not affect him at all; he is satisfied and satiated with the Name of the Lord.

O Nanak, without the Naam, no one is saved; they are utterly ruined by egotism. |2|

Pauree:

Those who meditate on the Lord, Har, Har, obtain all peace and comforts.

Fruitful is the entire life of those, who hunger for the Name of the Lord in their minds.

Those who worship the Lord in adoration, through the Word of the Guru's Shabad, forget all their pains and suffering.

Those Gursikhs are good Saints, who care for nothing other than the Lord.

Blessed, blessed is their Guru, whose mouth tastes the Ambrosial Fruit of the Lord's Name. |6|

Shalok, Third Mehl:

In the Dark Age of Kali Yuga, the Messenger of Death is the enemy of life, but he acts according to the Lord's Command.

Those who are protected by the Guru are saved, while the self-willed manmukhs receive their punishment.

The world is under the control, and in the bondage of the Messenger of Death; no one can hold him back.

So serve the One who created Death; as Gurmukh, no pain shall touch you.

O Nanak, Death serves the Gurmukhs; the True Lord abides in their minds. |1|

Third Mehl:

This body is filled with disease; without the Word of the Shabad, the pain of the disease of ego does not depart.

When one meets the True Guru, then he becomes immaculately pure, and he enshrines the Lord's Name within his mind.

O Nanak, meditating on the Naam, the Name of the Peace-Giving Lord, his pains are automatically forgotten. |2|

Pauree:

I am forever a sacrifice to the Guru, who has taught me about the Lord, the Life of the World.

I am every bit a sacrifice to the Guru, the Lover of Nectar, who has revealed the Name of the Lord.

I am a sacrifice to the Guru, who has totally cured me of the fatal disease of egotism.

Glorious and great are the virtues of the Guru, who has eradicated evil, and instructed me in virtue.

Section 12 - Raag Wadahans - Part 033

The True Guru meets with those upon whose foreheads such blessed destiny is recorded. |7|

Shalok, Third Mehl:

They alone worship the Lord, who remain dead while yet alive; the Gurmukhs worship the Lord continually.

The Lord blesses them with the treasure of devotional worship, which no one can destroy.

They obtain the treasure of virtue, the One True Lord, within their minds.

O Nanak, the Gurmukhs remain united with the Lord; they shall never be separated again. |1|

Third Mehl:

He does not serve the True Guru; how can he reflect upon the Lord?

He does not appreciate the value of the Shabad; the fool wanders in corruption and sin.

The blind and ignorant perform all sorts of ritualistic actions; they are in love with duality.

Those who take unjustified pride in themselves, are punished and humiliated by the Messenger of Death.

O Nanak, who else is there to ask? The Lord Himself is the Forgiver. |2|

Pauree:

You, O Creator, know all things; all beings belong to You.

Those who are pleasing to You, You unite with Yourself; what can the poor creatures do?

You are all-powerful, the Cause of causes, the True Creator Lord.

Only those unite with you, Beloved Lord, whom you approve and who meditate on Guru's Word.

I am a sacrifice to my True Guru, who has allowed me to see my unseen Lord. |8|

Shalok, Third Mehl:

He is the Assayer of jewels; He contemplates the jewel.

He is ignorant and totally blind - he does not appreciate the value of the jewel.

The Jewel is the Word of the Guru's Shabad; the Knower alone knows it.

The fools take pride in themselves, and are ruined in birth and death.

O Nanak, he alone obtains the jewel, who, as Gurmukh, enshrines love for it.

Chanting the Naam, the Name of the Lord, forever and ever, make the Name of the Lord your daily occupation.

If the Lord shows His Mercy, then I keep Him enshrined within my heart. |1|

Third Mehl:

They do not serve the True Guru, and they do not embrace love for the Lord's Name.

Do not even think that they are alive - the Creator Lord Himself has killed them.

Egotism is such a terrible disease; in the love of duality, they do their deeds.

O Nanak, the self-willed manmukhs are in a living death; forgetting the Lord, they suffer in pain. |2|

Pauree:

Let all bow in reverence, to that humble being whose heart is pure within.

I am a sacrifice to that humble being whose mind is filled with the treasure of the Naam.

He has a discriminating intellect; he meditates on the Name of the Lord.

That True Guru is a friend to all; everyone is dear to Him.

The Lord, the Supreme Soul, is pervading everywhere; reflect upon the wisdom of the Guru's Teachings. |9|

Shalok, Third Mehl:

Without serving the True Guru, the soul is in the bondage of deeds done in ego.

Without serving the True Guru, one finds no place of rest; he dies, and is reincarnated, and continues coming and going.

Without serving the True Guru, one's speech is vapid and insipid; the Naam, the Name of the Lord, does not abide in his mind.

Section 12 - Raag Wadahans - Part 034

O Nanak, without serving the True Guru, they are bound and beaten in the City of Death; they arise and depart with blackened faces. |1|

First Mehl:

Burn away those rituals which lead you to forget the Beloved Lord.

O Nanak, sublime is that love, which preserves my honor with my Lord Master. |2|

Pauree:

Serve the One Lord, the Great Giver; meditate on the One Lord.

Beg from the One Lord, the Great Giver, and you shall obtain your heart's desires.

But if you beg from another, then you shall be shamed and destroyed.

One who serves the Lord obtains the fruits of his rewards; all of his hunger is satisfied.

Nanak is a sacrifice to those, who night and day, meditate within their hearts on the Name of the Lord. |10|

Shalok, Third Mehl:

He Himself is pleased with His humble devotees; my Beloved Lord attaches them to Himself.

The Lord blesses His humble devotees with royalty; He fashions the true crown upon their heads.

They are always at peace, and immaculately pure; they perform service for the True Guru.

They are not said to be kings, who die in conflict, and then enter again the cycle of reincarnation.

O Nanak, without the Name of the Lord, they wander about with their noses cut off in disgrace; they get no respect at all. |1|

Third Mehl:

Hearing the teachings, he does not appreciate them, as long as he is not Gurmukh, attached to the Word of the Shabad.

Serving the True Guru, the Naam comes to abide in the mind, and doubts and fears run away.

As he knows the True Guru, so he is transformed, and then, he lovingly focuses his consciousness on the Naam.

O Nanak, through the Naam, the Name of the Lord, greatness is obtained; he shall be resplendent in the Court of the Lord hereafter. |2|

Pauree:

The minds of the Gursikhs are filled with the love of the Lord; they come and worship the Guru.

They trade lovingly in the Lord's Name, and depart after earning the profit of the Lord's Name.

The faces of the Gursikhs are radiant; in the Court of the Lord, they are approved.

The Guru, the True Guru, is the treasure of the Lord's Name; how very fortunate are the Sikhs who share in this treasure of virtue.

I am a sacrifice to those Gursikhs who, sitting and standing, meditate on the Lord's Name. |11|

Shalok, Third Mehl:

O Nanak, the Naam, the Name of the Lord, is the treasure, which the Gurmukhs obtain.

The self-willed manmukhs are blind; they do not realize that it is within their own home. They die barking and crying. |1|

Third Mehl:

That body is golden and immaculate, which is attached to the True Name of the True Lord.

The Gurmukh obtains the Pure Light of the Luminous Lord, and his doubts and fears run away.

O Nanak, the Gurmukhs find lasting peace; night and day, they remain detached, while in the Love of the Lord. |2|

Pauree:

Blessed, blessed are those Gursikhs, who, with their ears, listen to the Guru's Teachings about the Lord.

The Guru, the True Guru, implants the Naam within them, and their egotism and duality are silenced.

There is no friend, other than the Name of the Lord; the Lord's humble servants reflect upon this and see.

Section 12 - Raag Wadahans - Part 035

Those Gursikhs, with whom the Lord is pleased, accept the Word of the True Guru.

Those Gurmukhs who meditate on the Naam are imbued with the four-fold color of the Lord's Love. |12|

Shalok, Third Mehl:

The self-willed manmukh is cowardly and ugly; lacking the Name of the Lord, his nose is cut off in disgrace.

Night and day, he is engrossed in worldly affairs, and even in his dreams, he finds no peace.

O Nanak, if he becomes Gurmukh, then he shall be saved; otherwise, he is held in bondage, and suffers in pain. |1|

Third Mehl:

The Gurmukhs always look beautiful in the Court of the Lord; they practice the Word of the Guru's Shabad.

There is a lasting peace and happiness deep within them; at the Court of the True Lord, they receive honor.

O Nanak, the Gurmukhs are blessed with the Name of the Lord; they merge imperceptibly into the True Lord. |2|

Pauree:

As Gurmukh, Prahlaad meditated on the Lord, and was saved.

As Gurmukh, Janak lovingly centered his consciousness on the Lord's Name.

As Gurmukh, Vashisht taught the Teachings of the Lord.

Without the Guru, no one has found the Lord's Name, O my Siblings of Destiny.

The Lord blesses the Gurmukh with devotion. |13|

Shalok, Third Mehl:

One who has no faith in the True Guru, and who does not love the Word of the Shabad,

shall find no peace, even though he may come and go hundreds of times.

O Nanak, the Gurmukh meets the True Lord with natural ease; he is in love with the Lord. |1|

Third Mehl:

O mind, search for such a True Guru, by serving whom the pains of birth and death are dispelled.

Doubt shall never afflict you, and your ego shall be burnt away through the Word of the Shabad.

The veil of falsehood shall be torn down from within you, and Truth shall come to dwell in the mind.

Peace and happiness shall fill your mind deep within, if you act according to truth and self-discipline.

O Nanak, by perfect good karma, you shall meet the True Guru, and then the Dear Lord, by His Sweet Will, shall bless you with His Mercy. |2|

Pauree:

The whole world comes under the control of one whose home is filled with the Lord, the King.

He is subject to no one else's rule, and the Lord, the King, causes everyone to fall at his feet.

One may run away from the courts of other men, but where can one go to escape the Lord's Kingdom?

The Lord is such a King, who abides in the hearts of His devotees; He brings the others, and makes them stand before His devotees.

The glorious greatness of the Lord's Name is obtained only by His Grace; how few are the Gurmukhs who meditate on Him. |14|

Shalok, Third Mehl:

Without serving the True Guru, the people of the world are dead; they waste their lives away in vain.

In love with duality, they suffer terrible pain; they die, and are reincarnated, and continue coming and going.

They live in manure, and are reincarnated again and again.

O Nanak, without the Name, the Messenger of Death punishes them; in the end, they depart regretting and repenting. |1|

Third Mehl:

In this world, there is one Husband Lord; all other beings are His brides.

Section 12 - Raag Wadahans - Part 036

He enjoys the hearts of all, and yet He remains detached; He is unseen; He cannot be described.

The Perfect Guru reveals Him, and through the Word of His Shabad, we come to understand Him.

Those who serve their Husband Lord, become like Him; their egos are burnt away by His Shabad.

He has no rival, no attacker, no enemy.

His rule is unchanging and eternal; He does not come or go.

Night and day, His servant serves Him, singing the Glorious Praises of the True Lord.

Beholding the Glorious Greatness of the True Lord, Nanak blossoms forth. |2|

Pauree:

Those whose hearts are forever filled with the Name of the Lord, have the Name of the Lord as their Protector.

The Lord's Name is my father, the Lord's Name is my mother; the Lord's Name is my helper and friend.

My conversation is with the Lord's Name, and my counseling is with the Lord's Name; the Lord's Name always takes care of me.

The Lord's Name is my most beloved society, the Lord's Name is my ancestry, and the Lord's Name is my family.

The Guru, the Lord Incarnate, has bestowed upon servant Nanak the Name of the Lord; in this world, and in the next, the Lord ever saves me. |15|

Shalok, Third Mehl:

Those who meet the True Guru, ever sing the Kirtan of the Lord's Praises.

The Lord's Name naturally fills their minds, and they are absorbed in the Shabad, the Word of the True Lord.

They redeem their generations, and they themselves obtain the state of liberation.

The Supreme Lord God is pleased with those who fall at the Guru's Feet.

Servant Nanak is the Lord's slave; by His Grace, the Lord preserves his honor. |1|

Third Mehl:

In egotism, one is assailed by fear; he passes his life totally troubled by fear.

Egotism is such a terrible disease; he dies, to be reincarnated - he continues coming and going.

Those who have such pre-ordained destiny meet with the True Guru, God Incarnate.

O Nanak, by Guru's Grace, they are redeemed; their egos are burnt away through the Word of the Shabad. |2|

Pauree:

The Lord's Name is my immortal, unfathomable, imperishable Creator Lord, the Architect of Destiny.

I serve the Lord's Name, I worship the Lord's Name, and my soul is imbued with the Lord's Name.

I know of no other as great as the Lord's Name; the Lord's Name shall deliver me in the end.

The Generous Guru has given me the Lord's Name; blessed, blessed are the Guru's mother and father.

I ever bow in humble reverence to my True Guru; meeting Him, I have come to know the Lord's Name. |16|

Shalok, Third Mehl:

One who does not serve the Guru as Gurmukh, who does not love the Lord's Name,

and who does not savor the taste of the Shabad, shall die, and be reborn, over and over again.

The blind, self-willed manmukh does not think of the Lord; why did he even come into the world?

O Nanak, that Gurmukh, upon whom the Lord casts His Glance of Grace, crosses over the world-ocean. |1|

Third Mehl:

Only the Guru is awake; the rest of the world is asleep in emotional attachment and desire.
Those who serve the True Guru and remain wakeful, are imbued with the True Name, the treasure of virtue.

Section 12 - Raag Wadahans - Part 037

The blind, self-willed manmukhs do not think of the Lord; they are ruined through birth and death.
O Nanak, the Gurmukhs meditate on the Naam, the Name of the Lord; this is their destiny, pre-ordained by the Primal Lord God. |2|

Pauree:
The Lord's Name is my food; eating the thirty-six varieties of it, I am satisfied and satiated.
The Lord's Name is my clothing; wearing it, I shall never be naked again, and my desire to wear other clothing is gone.
The Lord's Name is my business, the Lord's Name is my commerce; the True Guru has blessed me with its use.
I record the account of the Lord's Name, and I shall not be subject to death again.
Only a few, as Gurmukh, meditate on the Lord's Name; they are blessed by the Lord, and receive their pre-ordained destiny. |17|

Shalok, Third Mehl:
The world is blind and ignorant; in the love of duality, it engages in actions.
But those actions which are performed in the love of duality, cause only pain to the body.
By Guru's Grace, peace wells up, when one acts according to the Word of the Guru's Shabad.
He acts according to the True Word of the Guru's Bani; night and day, he meditates on the Naam, the Name of the Lord.
O Nanak, as the Lord Himself engages him, so is he engaged; no one has any say in this matter. |1|

Third Mehl:
Within the home of my own being, is the everlasting treasure of the Naam; it is a treasure house, overflowing with devotion.
The True Guru is the Giver of the life of the soul; the Great Giver lives forever.

Night and day, I continually sing the Kirtan of the Lord's Praise, through the Infinite Word of the Guru's Shabad.

I recite continually the Guru's Shabads, which have been effective throughout the ages.

This mind ever abides in peace, dealing in peace and poise.

Deep within me is the Guru's Wisdom, the Lord's jewel, the Bringer of liberation.

O Nanak, one who is blessed by the Lord's Glance of Grace obtains this, and is judged to be True in the Court of the Lord. |2|

Pauree:

Blessed, blessed is that Sikh of the Guru, who goes and falls at the Feet of the True Guru.

Blessed, blessed is that Sikh of the Guru, who with his mouth, utters the Name of the Lord.

Blessed, blessed is that Sikh of the Guru, whose mind, upon hearing the Lord's Name, becomes blissful.

Blessed, blessed is that Sikh of the Guru, who serves the True Guru, and so obtains the Lord's Name.

I bow forever in deepest respect to that Sikh of the Guru, who walks in the Way of the Guru. |18|

Shalok, Third Mehl:

No one has ever found the Lord through stubborn-mindedness. All have grown weary of performing such actions.

Through their stubborn-mindedness, and by wearing their disguises, they are deluded; they suffer in pain from the love of duality.

Riches and the supernatural spiritual powers of the Siddhas are all emotional attachments; through them, the Naam, the Name of the Lord, does not come to dwell in the mind.

Serving the Guru, the mind becomes immaculately pure, and the darkness of spiritual ignorance is dispelled.

The jewel of the Naam is revealed in the home of one's own being; O Nanak, one merges in celestial bliss. |1|

Third Mehl:

Section 12 - Raag Wadahans - Part 038

One who does not savor the taste of the Shabad, who does not love the Naam, the Name of the Lord,
and who speaks insipid words with his tongue, is ruined, again and again.
O Nanak, he acts according to the karma of his past actions, which no one can erase. |2|

Pauree:
Blessed, blessed is the True Being, my True Guru; meeting Him, I have found peace.
Blessed, blessed is the True Being, my True Guru; meeting Him, I have attained the Lord's devotional worship.
Blessed, blessed is the Lord's devotee, my True Guru; serving Him, I have come to enshrine love for the Name of the Lord.
Blessed, blessed is the Knower of the Lord, my True Guru; He has taught me to look upon friend and foe alike.
Blessed, blessed is the True Guru, my best friend; He has led me to embrace love for the Name of the Lord. |19|

Shalok, First Mehl:
The soul-bride is at home, while the Husband Lord is away; she cherishes His memory, and mourns His absence.
She shall meet Him without delay, if she rids herself of duality. |1|

First Mehl:
O Nanak, false is the speech of one who acts without loving the Lord.
He judges things to be good, only as long as the Lord gives and he receives. |2|

Pauree:
The Lord, who created the creatures, also protects them.
I have tasted the food of Ambrosial Nectar, the True Name.
I am satisfied and satiated, and my hunger is appeased.
The One Lord is pervading in all, but rare are those who realize this.
Servant Nanak is enraptured, in the Protection of God. |20|

Shalok, Third Mehl:
All the living beings of the world behold the True Guru.
One is not liberated by merely seeing Him, unless one contemplates the Word of His Shabad.

The filth of ego is not removed, and he does not enshrine love for the Naam.

The Lord forgives some, and unites them with Himself; they forsake their duality and sinful ways.

O Nanak, some behold the Blessed Vision of the True Guru's Darshan, with love and affection; conquering their ego, they meet with the Lord. |1|

Third Mehl:

The foolish, blind clown does not serve the True Guru.

In love with duality, he endures terrible suffering, and burning, he cries out in pain.

He forgets the Guru, for the sake of mere objects, but they will not come to his rescue in the end.

Through the Guru's Instructions, Nanak has found peace; the Forgiving Lord has forgiven him. |2|

Pauree:

You Yourself, all by Yourself, are the Creator of all. If there were any other, then I would speak of another.

The Lord Himself speaks, and causes us to speak; He Himself is pervading the water and the land.

The Lord Himself destroys, and the Lord Himself saves. O mind, seek and remain in the Lord's Sanctuary.

Other than the Lord, no one can kill or rejuvenate. O mind, do not be anxious - remain fearless.

While standing, sitting, and sleeping, forever and ever, meditate on the Lord's Name; O servant Nanak, as Gurmukh, you shall attain the Lord. |21|1|SUDH|

RAAG SORAT'H

Section 13 - Raag Sorat'h - Part 001

ONE Universal Creator God. Truth Is The Name. Creative Being Personified. No Fear. No Hatred. Image Of The Undying. Beyond Birth. Self-Existent. By Guru's Grace:

Sorat'h, First Mehl, First House, Chau-Padas:
Death comes to all, and all must suffer separation.
Go and ask the clever people, whether they shall meet in the world hereafter.
Those who forget my Lord and Master shall suffer in terrible pain. |1|

So praise the True Lord,
by whose Grace peace ever prevails. |Pause|

Praise Him as great; He is, and He shall ever be.
You alone are the Great Giver; mankind cannot give anything.
Whatever pleases Him, comes to pass; what good does it do to cry out in protest? |2|

Many have proclaimed their sovereignty over millions of fortresses on the earth, but they have now departed.
And those, whom even the sky could not contain, had ropes put through their noses.
O mind, if you only knew the torment in your future, you would not relish the sweet pleasures of the present. |3|

O Nanak, as many as are the sins one commits, so many are the chains around his neck.
If he possesses virtues, then the chains are cut away; these virtues are his brothers, his true brothers.
Going to the world hereafter, those who have no Guru are not accepted; they are beaten, and expelled. |4|1|

Sorat'h, First Mehl, First House:

Make your mind the farmer, good deeds the farm, modesty the water, and your body the field.

Let the Lord's Name be the seed, contentment the plow, and your humble dress the fence.

Doing deeds of love, the seed shall sprout, and you shall see your home flourish. |1|

O Baba, the wealth of Maya does not go with anyone.

This Maya has bewitched the world, but only a rare few understand this. |Pause|

Make your ever-decreasing life your shop, and make the Lord's Name your merchandise.

Make understanding and contemplation your warehouse, and in that warehouse, store the Lord's Name.

Deal with the Lord's dealers, earn your profits, and rejoice in your mind. |2|

Let your trade be listening to scripture, and let Truth be the horses you take to sell.

Gather up merits for your travelling expenses, and do not think of tomorrow in your mind.

When you arrive in the land of the Formless Lord, you shall find peace in the Mansion of His Presence. |3|

Let your service be the focusing of your consciousness, and let your occupation be the placing of faith in the Naam.

Section 13 - Raag Sorat'h - Part 002

Let your work be restraint from sin; only then will people call you blessed.

O Nanak, the Lord shall look upon you with His Glance of Grace, and you shall be blessed with honor four times over. |4|2|

Sorat'h, First Mehl, Chau-Tukas:

The son is dear to his mother and father; he is the wise son-in-law to his father-in-law.

The father is dear to his son and daughter, and the brother is very dear to his brother.

By the Order of the Lord's Command, he leaves his house and goes outside, and in an instant, everything becomes alien to him.

The self-willed manmukh does not remember the Name of the Lord, does not give in charity, and does not cleanse his consciousness; his body rolls in the dust. |1|

The mind is comforted by the Comforter of the Naam.

I fall at the Guru's feet - I am a sacrifice to Him; He has given me to understand the true understanding. |Pause|

The mind is impressed with the false love of the world; he quarrels with the Lord's humble servant.

Infatuated with Maya, night and day, he sees only the worldly path; he does not chant the Naam, and drinking poison, he dies.

He is imbued and infatuated with vicious talk; the Word of the Shabad does not come into his consciousness.

He is not imbued with the Lord's Love, and he is not impressed by the taste of the Name; the self-willed manmukh loses his honor. |2|

He does not enjoy celestial peace in the Company of the Holy, and there is not even a bit of sweetness on his tongue.

He calls his mind, body and wealth his own; he has no knowledge of the Court of the Lord.

Closing his eyes, he walks in darkness; he cannot see the home of his own being, O Siblings of Destiny.

Tied up at Death's door, he finds no place of rest; he receives the rewards of his own actions. |3|

When the Lord casts His Glance of Grace, then I see Him with my own eyes; He is indescribable, and cannot be described.

With my ears, I continually listen to the Word of the Shabad, and I praise Him; His Ambrosial Name abides within my heart.

He is Fearless, Formless and absolutely without vengeance; I am absorbed in His Perfect Light.

O Nanak, without the Guru, doubt is not dispelled; through the True Name, glorious greatness is obtained. |4|3|

Sorat'h, First Mehl, Du-Tukas:

In the realm of land, and in the realm of water, Your seat is the chamber of the four directions.

Yours is the one and only form of the entire universe; Your mouth is the mint to fashion all. |1|

O my Lord Master, Your play is so wonderful!
You are pervading and permeating the water, the land and the sky; You Yourself are contained in all. |Pause|

Wherever I look, there I see Your Light, but what is Your form?
You have one form, but it is unseen; there is none like any other. |2|

The beings born of eggs, born of the womb, born of the earth and born of sweat, all are created by You.
I have seen one glory of Yours, that You are pervading and permeating in all. |3|

Your Glories are so numerous, and I do not know even one of them; I am such a fool - please, give me some of them!

Prays Nanak, listen, O my Lord Master: I am sinking like a stone - please, save me! |4|4|

Sorat'h, First Mehl:
I am a wicked sinner and a great hypocrite; You are the Immaculate and Formless Lord.
Tasting the Ambrosial Nectar, I am imbued with supreme bliss; O Lord and Master, I seek Your Sanctuary. |1|

O Creator Lord, You are the honor of the dishonored.
In my lap is the honor and glory of the wealth of the Name; I merge into the True Word of the Shabad. |Pause|

You are perfect, while I am worthless and imperfect. You are profound, while I am trivial.

Section 13 - Raag Sorat'h - Part 003

My mind is imbued with You, day and night and morning, O Lord; my tongue chants Your Name, and my mind meditates on You. |2|

You are True, and I am absorbed into You; through the mystery of the Shabad, I shall ultimately become True as well.

Those who are imbued with the Naam day and night are pure, while those who die to be reborn are impure. |3|

I do not see any other like the Lord; who else should I praise? No one is equal to Him.

Prays Nanak, I am the slave of His slaves; by Guru's Instruction, I know Him. |4|5|

Sorat'h, First Mehl:

He is unknowable, infinite, unapproachable and imperceptible. He is not subject to death or karma.

His caste is casteless; He is unborn, self-illumined, and free of doubt and desire. |1|

I am a sacrifice to the Truest of the True.

He has no form, no color and no features; through the True Word of the Shabad, He reveals Himself. |Pause|

He has no mother, father, sons or relatives; He is free of sexual desire; He has no wife.

He has no ancestry; He is immaculate. He is infinite and endless; O Lord, Your Light is pervading all. |2|

Deep within each and every heart, God is hidden; His Light is in each and every heart.

The heavy doors are opened by Guru's Instructions; one becomes fearless, in the trance of deep meditation. |3|

The Lord created all beings, and placed death over the heads of all; all the world is under His Power.

Serving the True Guru, the treasure is obtained; living the Word of the Shabad, one is emancipated. |4|

In the pure vessel, the True Name is contained; how few are those who practice true conduct.

The individual soul is united with the Supreme Soul; Nanak seeks Your Sanctuary, Lord. |5|6|

Sorat'h, First Mehl:
Like a fish without water is the faithless cynic, who dies of thirst.
So shall you die, O mind, without the Lord, as your breath goes in vain. |1|

O mind, chant the Lord's Name, and praise Him.
Without the Guru, how will you obtain this juice? The Guru shall unite you with the Lord. |Pause|

For the Gurmukh, meeting with the Society of the Saints is like making a pilgrimage to a sacred shrine.
The benefit of bathing at the sixty-eight sacred shrines of pilgrimage is obtained by the Blessed Vision of the Guru's Darshan. |2|

Like the Yogi without abstinence, and like penance without truth and contentment,
so is the body without the Lord's Name; death will slay it, because of the sin within. |3|

The faithless cynic does not obtain the Lord's Love; the Lord's Love is obtained only through the True Guru.
One who meets with the Guru, the Giver of pleasure and pain, says Nanak, is absorbed in the Lord's Praise. |4|7|

Sorat'h, First Mehl:
You, God, are the Giver of gifts, the Lord of perfect understanding; I am a mere beggar at Your Door.
What should I beg for? Nothing remains permanent; O Lord, please, bless me with Your Beloved Name. |1|

In each and every heart, the Lord, the Lord of the forest, is permeating and pervading.
In the water, on the land, and in the sky, He is pervading but hidden; through the Word of the Guru's Shabad, He is revealed. |Pause|

In this world, in the nether regions of the underworld, and in the Akaashic Ethers, the Guru, the True Guru, has shown me the Lord; He has showered me with His Mercy.
He is the unborn Lord God; He is, and shall ever be. Deep within your heart, behold Him, the Destroyer of ego. |2|

Section 13 - Raag Sorat'h - Part 004

This wretched world is caught in birth and death; in the love of duality, it has forgotten devotional worship of the Lord.
Meeting the True Guru, the Guru's Teachings are obtained; the faithless cynic loses the game of life. |3|

Breaking my bonds, the True Guru has set me free, and I shall not be cast into the womb of reincarnation again.
O Nanak, the jewel of spiritual wisdom shines forth, and the Lord, the Formless Lord, dwells within my mind. |4|8|

Sorat'h, First Mehl:
The treasure of the Name, for which you have come into the world - that Ambrosial Nectar is with the Guru.
Renounce costumes, disguises and clever tricks; this fruit is not obtained by duplicity. |1|

O my mind, remain steady, and do not wander away.
By searching around on the outside, you shall only suffer great pain; the Ambrosial Nectar is found within the home of your own being. |Pause|

Renounce corruption, and seek virtue; committing sins, you shall only come to regret and repent.
You do not know the difference between good and evil; again and again, you sink into the mud. |2|

Within you is the great filth of greed and falsehood; why do you bother to wash your body on the outside?

Chant the Immaculate Naam, the Name of the Lord always, under Guru's Instruction; only then will your innermost being be emancipated. |3|

Let greed and slander be far away from you, and renounce falsehood; through the True Word of the Guru's Shabad, you shall obtain the true fruit.
As it pleases You, You preserve me, Dear Lord; servant Nanak sings the Praises of Your Shabad. |4|9|

Sorat'h, First Mehl, Panch-Padas:

You cannot save your own home from being plundered; why do you spy on the houses of others?
That Gurmukh who joins himself to the Guru's service, saves his own home, and tastes the Lord's Nectar. |1|

O mind, you must realize what your intellect is focused on.
Forgetting the Naam, the Name of the Lord, one is involved with other tastes; the unfortunate wretch shall come to regret it in the end. |Pause|

When things come, he is pleased, but when they go, he weeps and wails; this pain and pleasure remains attached to him.
The Lord Himself causes him to enjoy pleasure and endure pain; the Gurmukh, however, remains unaffected. |2|

What else can be said to be above the subtle essence of the Lord? One who drinks it in is satisfied and satiated.
One who is lured by Maya loses this juice; that faithless cynic is tied to his evil-mindedness. |3|

The Lord is the life of the mind, the Master of the breath of life; the Divine Lord is contained in the body.
If You so bless us, Lord, then we sing Your Praises; the mind is satisfied and fulfilled, lovingly attached to the Lord. |4|

In the Saadh Sangat, the Company of the Holy, the subtle essence of the Lord is obtained; meeting the Guru, the fear of death departs.
O Nanak, chant the Name of the Lord, as Gurmukh; you shall obtain the Lord, and realize your pre-ordained destiny. |5|10|

Sorat'h, First Mehl:
Destiny, pre-ordained by the Lord, looms over the heads of all beings; no one is without this pre-ordained destiny.
Only He Himself is beyond destiny; creating the creation by His creative power, He beholds it, and causes His Command to be followed. |1|

O mind, chant the Name of the Lord, and be at peace.
Day and night, serve at the Guru's feet; the Lord is the Giver, and the Enjoyer. |Pause|

Section 13 - Raag Sorat'h - Part 005

He is within - see Him outside as well; there is no one, other than Him.
As Gurmukh, look upon all with the single eye of equality; in each and every heart, the Divine Light is contained. |2|

Restrain your fickle mind, and keep it steady within its own home; meeting the Guru, this understanding is obtained.
Seeing the unseen Lord, you shall be amazed and delighted; forgetting your pain, you shall be at peace. |3|

Drinking in the ambrosial nectar, you shall attain the highest bliss, and dwell within the home of your own self.
So sing the Praises of the Lord, the Destroyer of the fear of birth and death, and you shall not be reincarnated again. |4|

The essence, the immaculate Lord, the Light of all - I am He and He is me - there is no difference between us.
The Infinite Transcendent Lord, the Supreme Lord God - Nanak has met with Him, the Guru. |5|11|

Sorat'h, First Mehl, Third House:
One Universal Creator God. By The Grace Of The True Guru:
When I am pleasing to Him, then I sing His Praises.
Singing His Praises, I receive the fruits of my rewards.
The rewards of singing His Praises are obtained when He Himself gives them. |1|

O my mind, through the Word of the Guru's Shabad, the treasure is obtained;
this is why I remain immersed in the True Name. |Pause|

When I awoke within myself to the Guru's Teachings,
then I renounced my fickle intellect.
When the Light of the Guru's Teachings dawned,
and then all darkness was dispelled. |2|

When the mind is attached to the Guru's Feet,
then the Path of Death recedes.
Through the Fear of God, one attains the Fearless Lord;
then, one enters the home of celestial bliss. |3|

Prays Nanak, how rare are those who reflect and understand,
the most sublime action in this world.
The noblest deed is to sing the Lord's Praises,
and so meet the Lord Himself. |4|1|12|

Sorat'h, Third Mehl, First House:
One Universal Creator God. By The Grace Of The True Guru:
All of Your servants, who relish the Word of Your Shabad, serve You.
By Guru's Grace, they become pure, eradicating self-conceit from within.
Night and day, they continually sing the Glorious Praises of the True Lord;
they are adorned with the Word of the Guru's Shabad. |1|

O my Lord and Master, I am Your child; I seek Your Sanctuary.
You are the One and Only Lord, the Truest of the True; You Yourself are the
Destroyer of ego. |Pause|

Those who remain wakeful obtain God; through the Word of the Shabad,
they conquer their ego.
Immersed in family life, the Lord's humble servant ever remains detached;
he reflects upon the essence of spiritual wisdom.
Serving the True Guru, he finds eternal peace, and he keeps the Lord
enshrined in his heart. |2|

This mind wanders in the ten directions; it is consumed by the love of
duality.

Section 13 - Raag Sorat'h - Part 006

The foolish self-willed manmukh does not remember the Lord's Name; he
wastes away his life in vain.
But when he meets the True Guru, then he obtains the Name; he sheds
egotism and emotional attachment. |3|

The Lord's humble servants are True - they practice Truth, and reflect upon
the Word of the Guru's Shabad.
The True Lord God unites them with Himself, and they keep the True Lord
enshrined in their hearts.
O Nanak, through the Name, I have obtained salvation and understanding;
this alone is my wealth. |4|1|

Sorat'h, Third Mehl:

The True Lord has blessed His devotees with the treasure of devotional worship, and the wealth of the Lord's Name.

The wealth of the Naam, shall never be exhausted; no one can estimate its worth.

With the wealth of the Naam, their faces are radiant, and they attain the True Lord. |1|

O my mind, through the Word of the Guru's Shabad, the Lord is found.

Without the Shabad, the world wanders around, and receives its punishment in the Court of the Lord. |Pause|

Within this body dwell the five thieves: sexual desire, anger, greed, emotional attachment and egotism.

They plunder the Nectar, but the self-willed manmukh does not realize it; no one hears his complaint.

The world is blind, and its dealings are blind as well; without the Guru, there is only pitch darkness. |2|

Indulging in egotism and possessiveness, they are ruined; when they depart, nothing goes along with them.

But one who becomes Gurmukh meditates on the Naam, and ever contemplates the Lord's Name.

Through the True Word of Gurbani, he sings the Glorious Praises of the Lord; blessed with the Lord's Glance of Grace, he is enraptured. |3|

The spiritual wisdom of the True Guru is a steady light within the heart. The Lord's decree is over the heads of even kings.

Night and day, the Lord's devotees worship Him; night and day, they gather in the true profit of the Lord's Name.

O Nanak, through the Lord's Name, one is emancipated; attuned to the Shabad, he finds the Lord. |4|2|

Sorat'h, Third Mehl:

If one becomes the slave of the Lord's slaves, then he finds the Lord, and eradicates ego from within.

The Lord of bliss is his object of devotion; night and day, he sings the Glorious Praises of the Lord.

Attuned to the Word of the Shabad, the Lord's devotees remain ever as one, absorbed in the Lord. |1|

O Dear Lord, Your Glance of Grace is True.
Show mercy to Your slave, O Beloved Lord, and preserve my honor. |Pause|

Continually praising the Word of the Shabad, I live; under Guru's Instruction, my fear has been dispelled.
My True Lord God is so beautiful! Serving the Guru, my consciousness is focused on Him.
One who chants the True Word of the Shabad, and the Truest of the True, the Word of His Bani, remains wakeful, day and night. |2|

He is so very deep and profound, the Giver of eternal peace; no one can find His limit.
Serving the Perfect Guru, one becomes carefree, enshrining the Lord within the mind.
The mind and body become immaculately pure, and a lasting peace fills the heart; doubt is eradicated from within. |3|

The Way of the Lord is always such a difficult path; only a few find it, contemplating the Guru.
Imbued with the Lord's Love, and intoxicated with the Shabad, he renounces ego and corruption.
O Nanak, imbued with the Naam, and the Love of the One Lord, he is embellished with the Word of the Shabad. |4|3|

Section 13 - Raag Sorat'h - Part 007

Sorat'h, Third Mehl:
Dear Beloved Lord, I praise You continually, as long as there is the breath within my body.
If I were to forget You, for a moment, even for an instant, O Lord Master, it would be like fifty years for me.
I was always such a fool and an idiot, O Siblings of Destiny, but now, through the Word of the Guru's Shabad, my mind is enlightened. |1|

Dear Lord, You Yourself bestow understanding.

Dear Lord, I am forever a sacrifice to You; I am dedicated and devoted to Your Name. |Pause|

I have died in the Word of the Shabad, and through the Shabad, I am dead while yet alive, O Siblings of Destiny; through the Shabad, I have been liberated.
Through the Shabad, my mind and body have been purified, and the Lord has come to dwell within my mind.
The Guru is the Giver of the Shabad; my mind is imbued with it, and I remain absorbed in the Lord. |2|

Those who do not know the Shabad are blind and deaf; why did they even bother to come into the world?

They do not obtain the subtle essence of the Lord's elixir; they waste away their lives, and are reincarnated over and over again.
The blind, idiotic, self-willed manmukhs are like maggots in manure, and in manure they rot away. |3|

The Lord Himself creates us, watches over us, and places us on the Path, O Siblings of Destiny; there is no one other than Him.
No one can erase that which is pre-ordained, O Siblings of Destiny; whatever the Creator wills, comes to pass.
O Nanak, the Naam, the Name of the Lord, abides deep within the mind; O Siblings of Destiny, there is no other at all. |4|4|

Sorat'h, Third Mehl:
The Gurmukhs practice devotional worship, and become pleasing to God; night and day, they chant the Naam, the Name of the Lord.
You Yourself protect and take care of Your devotees, who are pleasing to Your Mind.
You are the Giver of virtue, realized through the Word of Your Shabad. Uttering Your Glories, we merge with You, O Glorious Lord. |1|

O my mind, remember always the Dear Lord.
At the very last moment, He alone shall be your best friend; He shall always stand by you. |Pause|

The gathering of the wicked enemies shall always practice falsehood; they do not contemplate understanding.

Who can obtain fruit from the slander of evil enemies? Remember that Harnaakhash was torn apart by the Lord's claws.

Prahlaad, the Lord's humble servant, constantly sang the Glorious Praises of the Lord, and the Dear Lord saved him. |2|

The self-willed manmukhs see themselves as being very virtuous; they have absolutely no understanding at all.

They indulge in slander of the humble spiritual people; they waste their lives away, and then they have to depart.

They never think of the Lord's Name, and in the end, they depart, regretting and repenting. |3|

The Lord makes the lives of His devotees fruitful; He Himself links them to the Guru's service.

Imbued with the Word of the Shabad, and intoxicated with celestial bliss, night and day, they sing the Glorious Praises of the Lord.

Slave Nanak utters this prayer: O Lord, please, let me fall at their feet. |4|5|

Sorat'h, Third Mehl:
He alone is a Sikh, a friend, a relative and a sibling, who walks in the Way of the Guru's Will.

One who walks according to his own will, O Siblings of Destiny, suffers separation from the Lord, and shall be punished.

Without the True Guru, peace is never obtained, O Siblings of Destiny; again and again, he regrets and repents. |1|

The Lord's slaves are happy, O Siblings of Destiny.

Section 13 - Raag Sorat'h - Part 008

The sins and sorrows of countless lifetimes are eradicated; the Lord Himself unites them in His Union. |Pause|

All of these relatives are like chains upon the soul, O Siblings of Destiny; the world is deluded by doubt.

Without the Guru, the chains cannot be broken; the Gurmukhs find the door of salvation.

One who performs rituals without realizing the Word of the Guru's Shabad, shall die and be reborn, again and again. |2|

The world is entangled in egotism and possessiveness, O Siblings of Destiny, but no one belongs to anyone else.

The Gurmukhs attain the Mansion of the Lord's Presence, singing the Glories of the Lord; they dwell in the home of their own inner being.

One who understands here, realizes himself; the Lord God belongs to him. |3|

The True Guru is forever merciful, O Siblings of Destiny; without good destiny, what can anyone obtain?

He looks alike upon all with His Glance of Grace, but people receive the fruits of their rewards according to their love for the Lord.

O Nanak, when the Naam, the Name of the Lord, comes to dwell within the mind, then self-conceit is eradicated from within. |4|6|

Sorat'h, Third Mehl, Chau-Tukas:
True devotional worship is obtained only through the True Guru, when the True Word of His Bani is in the heart.

Serving the True Guru, eternal peace is obtained; egotism is obliterated through the Word of the Shabad.

Without the Guru, there is no true devotion; otherwise, people wander around, deluded by ignorance.

The self-willed manmukhs wander around, suffering in constant pain; they drown and die, even without water. |1|

O Siblings of Destiny, remain forever in the Lord's Sanctuary, under His Protection.

Bestowing His Glance of Grace, He preserves our honor, and blesses us with the glory of the Lord's Name. |Pause|

Through the Perfect Guru, one comes to understand himself, contemplating the True Word of the Shabad.

The Lord, the Life of the world, ever abides in his heart, and he renounces sexual desire, anger and egotism.

The Lord is ever-present, permeating and pervading all places; the Name of the Infinite Lord is enshrined within the heart.

Throughout the ages, through the Word of His Bani, His Shabad is realized, and the Name becomes so sweet and beloved to the mind. |2|

Serving the Guru, one realizes the Naam, the Name of the Lord; fruitful is his life, and his coming into the world.

Tasting the sublime elixir of the Lord, his mind is satisfied and satiated forever; singing the Glories of the Glorious Lord, he is fulfilled and satisfied.

The lotus of his heart blossoms forth, he is ever imbued with the Lord's Love, and the unstruck melody of the Shabad resounds within him.

His body and mind become immaculately pure; his speech becomes immaculate as well, and he merges in the Truest of the True. |3|

No one knows the state of the Lord's Name; through the Guru's Teachings, it comes to abide in the heart.

One who becomes Gurmukh, understands the Path; his tongue savors the sublime essence of the Lord's Nectar.

Meditation, austere self-discipline and self-restraint are all obtained from the Guru; the Naam, the Name of the Lord, comes to abide within the heart.

O Nanak, those humble beings who praise the Naam are beautiful; they are honored in the Court of the True Lord. |4|7|

Sorat'h, Third Mehl, Du-Tukas:

Meeting the True Guru, one turns away from the world, O Siblings of Destiny; when he remains dead while yet alive, he obtains true understanding.

He alone is the Guru, and he alone is a Sikh, O Siblings of Destiny, whose light merges in the Light. |1|

O my mind, be lovingly attuned to the Name of the Lord, Har, Har.

Chanting the Name of the Lord, it seems so sweet to the mind, O Siblings of Destiny; the Gurmukhs obtain a place in the Court of the Lord. |Pause|

Section 13 - Raag Sorat'h - Part 009

Without the Guru, love for the Lord does not well up, O Siblings of Destiny; the self-willed manmukhs are engrossed in the love of duality.

Actions performed by the manmukh are like the threshing of the chaff - they obtain nothing for their efforts. |2|

Meeting the Guru, the Naam comes to permeate the mind, O Siblings of Destiny, with true love and affection.

He always sings the Glorious Praises of the Lord, O Siblings of Destiny, with infinite love for the Guru. |3|

How blessed and approved is his coming into the world, O Siblings of Destiny, who focuses his mind on serving the Guru.
O Nanak, the Name of the Lord is obtained, O Siblings of Destiny, through the Word of the Guru's Shabad, and we merge with the Lord. |4|8|

Sorat'h, Third Mehl, First House:
The three worlds are entangled in the three qualities, O Siblings of Destiny; the Guru imparts understanding.
Attached to the Lord's Name, one is emancipated, O Siblings of Destiny; go and ask the wise ones about this. |1|

O mind, renounce the three qualities, and focus your consciousness on the fourth state.
The Dear Lord abides in the mind, O Siblings of Destiny; ever sing the Glorious Praises of the Lord. |Pause|

From the Naam, everyone originated, O Siblings of Destiny; forgetting the Naam, they die away.
The ignorant world is blind, O Siblings of Destiny; those who sleep are plundered. |2|

Those Gurmukhs who remain awake are saved, O Siblings of Destiny; they cross over the terrifying world-ocean.
In this world, the Name of the Lord is the true profit, O Siblings of Destiny; keep it enshrined within your heart. |3|

In the Guru's Sanctuary, O Siblings of Destiny, you shall be saved; be lovingly attuned to the Lord's Name.
O Nanak, the Name of the Lord is the boat, and the Name is the raft, O Siblings of Destiny; setting out on it, the Lord's humble servant crosses over the world-ocean. |4|9|

Sorat'h, Third Mehl, First House:
The True Guru is the ocean of peace in the world; there is no other place of rest and peace.
The world is afflicted with the painful disease of egotism; dying, only to be reborn, it cries out in pain. |1|

O mind, serve the True Guru, and obtain peace.
If you serve the True Guru, you shall find peace; otherwise, you shall depart, after wasting away your life in vain. |Pause|

Led around by the three qualities, he does many deeds, but he does not come to taste and savor the subtle essence of the Lord.
He says his evening prayers, and makes offerings of water, and recites his morning prayers, but without true understanding, he still suffers in pain. |2|

One who serves the True Guru is very fortunate; as the Lord so wills, he meets with the Guru.
Drinking in the sublime essence of the Lord, His humble servants remain ever satisfied; they eradicate self-conceit from within themselves. |3|

This world is blind, and all act blindly; without the Guru, no one finds the Path.
O Nanak, meeting with the True Guru, one sees with his eyes, and finds the True Lord within the home of his own being. |4|10|

Sorat'h, Third Mehl:
Without serving the True Guru, he suffers in terrible pain, and throughout the four ages, he wanders aimlessly.
I am poor and meek, and throughout the ages, You are the Great Giver - please, grant me the understanding of the Shabad. |1|

O Dear Beloved Lord, please show mercy to me.
Unite me in the Union of the True Guru, the Great Giver, and give me the support of the Lord's Name. |Pause|

Conquering my desires and duality, I have merged in celestial peace, and I have found the Naam, the Name of the Infinite Lord.
I have tasted the sublime essence of the Lord, and my soul has become immaculately pure; the Lord is the Destroyer of sins. |2|

Section 13 - Raag Sorat'h - Part 010

Dying in the Word of the Shabad, you shall live forever, and you shall never die again.

The Ambrosial Nectar of the Naam is ever-sweet to the mind; but how few are those who obtain the Shabad. |3|

The Great Giver keeps His Gifts in His Hand; He gives them to those with whom He is pleased.
O Nanak, imbued with the Naam, they find peace, and in the Court of the Lord, they are exalted. |4|11|

Sorat'h, Third Mehl:
Serving the True Guru, the divine melody wells up within, and one is blessed with wisdom and salvation.
The True Name of the Lord comes to abide in the mind, and through the Name, one merges in the Name. |1|

Without the True Guru, the whole world is insane.
The blind, self-willed manmukhs do not realize the Word of the Shabad; they are deluded by false doubts. |Pause|

The three-faced Maya had led them astray in doubt, and they are snared by the noose of egotism.
Birth and death hang over their heads, and being reborn from the womb, they suffer in pain. |2|

The three qualities permeate the whole world; acting in ego, it loses its honor.
But one who becomes Gurmukh comes to realize the fourth state of celestial bliss; he finds peace through the Name of the Lord. |3|

The three qualities are all Yours, O Lord; You Yourself created them. Whatever You do, comes to pass.
O Nanak, through the Lord's Name, one is emancipated; through the Shabad, he is rid of egotism. |4|12|

Sorat'h, Fourth Mehl, First House:
One Universal Creator God. By The Grace Of The True Guru:
My Beloved Lord Himself pervades and permeates all; He Himself is, all by Himself.
My Beloved Himself is the trader in this world; He Himself is the true banker.

My Beloved Himself is the trade and the trader; He Himself is the true credit. |1|

O mind, meditate on the Lord, Har, Har, and praise His Name.
By Guru's Grace, the Beloved, Ambrosial, unapproachable and unfathomable Lord is obtained. |Pause|

The Beloved Himself sees and hears everything; He Himself speaks through the mouths of all beings.
The Beloved Himself leads us into the wilderness, and He Himself shows us the Way.
The Beloved Himself is Himself all-in-all; He Himself is carefree. |2|

The Beloved Himself, all by Himself, created everything; He Himself links all to their tasks.
The Beloved Himself creates the Creation, and He Himself destroys it.
He Himself is the wharf, and He Himself is the ferryman, who ferries us across. |3|

The Beloved Himself is the ocean, and the boat; He Himself is the Guru, the boatman who steers it
. The Beloved Himself sets sail and crosses over; He, the King, beholds His wondrous play.
The Beloved Himself is the Merciful Master; O servant Nanak, He forgives and blends with Himself. |4|1|

Sorat'h, Fourth Mehl:
He Himself is born of the egg, from the womb, from sweat and from the earth; He Himself is the continents and all the worlds.
He Himself is the thread, and He Himself is the many beads; through His Almighty Power, He has strung the worlds.

Section 13 - Raag Sorat'h - Part 011

He holds the thread, and when He withdraws the thread, the beads scatter into heaps. |1|

O my mind, there is no other than the Lord for me.
The treasure of the Beloved Naam is within the True Guru; in His Mercy, he pours the Ambrosial Nectar into my mouth. |Pause|

The Beloved Himself is in all the oceans and lands; whatever God does, comes to pass.

The Beloved brings nourishment to all; there is no other than Him.

The Beloved Himself plays, and whatever He Himself does, comes to pass. |2|

The Beloved Himself, all by Himself, is immaculate and pure; He Himself is immaculate and pure.

The Beloved Himself determines the value of all; whatever He does comes to pass.

The Beloved Himself is unseen - He cannot be seen; He Himself causes us to see. |3|

The Beloved Himself is deep and profound and unfathomable; there is no other as great as He.

The Beloved Himself enjoys every heart; He is contained within every woman and man.

O Nanak, the Beloved is pervading everywhere, but He is hidden; through the Guru, He is revealed. |4|2|

Sorat'h, Fourth Mehl:

He Himself, the Beloved, is Himself all-in-all; He Himself establishes and disestablishes.

The Beloved Himself beholds, and rejoices; God Himself works wonders, and beholds them.

The Beloved Himself is contained in all the woods and meadows; as Gurmukh, He reveals Himself. |1|

Meditate, O mind, on the Lord, Har, Har; through the sublime essence of Lord's Name, you shall be satisfied.

The Ambrosial Nectar of the Naam, is the sweetest juice; through the Word of the Guru's Shabad, its taste is revealed. |Pause|

The Beloved is Himself the place of pilgrimage and the raft; God Himself ferries Himself across.

The Beloved Himself casts the net over all the world; the Lord Himself is the fish.

The Beloved Himself is infallible; He makes no mistakes. There is no other like Him to be seen. |2|

The Beloved Himself is the Yogi's horn, and the sound current of the Naad; He Himself plays the tune.

The Beloved Himself is the Yogi, the Primal Being; He Himself practices intense meditation.

He Himself is the True Guru, and He Himself is the disciple; God Himself imparts the Teachings. |3|

The Beloved Himself inspires us to chant His Name, and He Himself practices meditation.

The Beloved Himself is the Ambrosial Nectar; He Himself is the juice of it.

The Beloved Himself praises Himself; servant Nanak is satisfied, with the sublime essence of the Lord. |4|3|

Sorat'h, Fourth Mehl:
God Himself is the balance scale, He Himself is the weigher, and He Himself weighs with the weights.

He Himself is the banker, He Himself is the trader, and He Himself makes the trades.

The Beloved Himself fashioned the world, and He Himself counter-balances it with a gram. |1|

My mind meditates on the Lord, Har, Har, and finds peace.

The Name of the Beloved Lord, Har, Har, is a treasure; the Perfect Guru has made it seem sweet to me. |Pause|

The Beloved Himself is the earth, and He Himself is the water; He Himself acts, and causes others to act.

The Beloved Himself issues His Commands, and keeps the water and the land bound down.

The Beloved Himself instills the Fear of God; He binds the tiger and the goat together. |2|

Section 13 - Raag Sorat'h - Part 012

The Beloved Lord Himself is the firewood, and He Himself keeps the fire within the wood.

The Beloved Lord Himself, all by Himself, permeates them, and because of the Fear of God, the fire cannot burn the wood.

The Beloved Himself kills and revives; all draw the breath of life, given by Him. |3|

The Beloved Himself is power and presence; He Himself engages us in our work.
As the Beloved makes me walk, I walk, as it pleases my Lord God.
The Beloved Himself is the musician, and the musical instrument; servant Nanak vibrates His vibration. |4|4|

Sorat'h, Fourth Mehl:
The Beloved Himself created the Universe; He made the light of the sun and the moon.
The Beloved Himself is the power of the powerless; He Himself is the honor of the dishonored.
The Beloved Himself grants His Grace and protects us; He Himself is wise and all-knowing. |1|

O my mind, chant the Name of the Lord, and receive His Insignia.
Join the Sat Sangat, the True Congregation, and meditate on the Lord, Har, Har; you shall not have to come and go in reincarnation again. |Pause|

The Beloved Himself pervades His Glorious Praises, and He Himself approves them.
The Beloved Himself grants His forgiveness, and He Himself bestows the Insignia of Truth.
The Beloved Himself obeys His Will, and He Himself issues His Command. |2|

The Beloved Himself is the treasure of devotion; He Himself gives His gifts.
The Beloved Himself commits some to His service, and He Himself blesses them with honor.
The Beloved Himself is absorbed in Samaadhi; He Himself is the treasure of excellence. |3|

The Beloved Himself is the greatest; He Himself is supreme.
The Beloved Himself appraises the value; He Himself is the scale, and the weights.
The Beloved Himself is unweighable - He weighs Himself; servant Nanak is forever a sacrifice to Him. |4|5|

Sorat'h, Fourth Mehl:

The Beloved Himself commits some to His service; He Himself blesses them with the joy of devotional worship.

The Beloved Himself causes us to sing His Glorious Praises; He Himself is absorbed in the Word of His Shabad.

He Himself is the pen, and He Himself is the scribe; He Himself inscribes His inscription. |1|

O my mind, joyfully chant the Name of the Lord.

Those very fortunate ones are in ecstasy night and day; through the Perfect Guru, they obtain the profit of the Lord's Name. |Pause|

The Beloved Himself is the milk-maid and Krishna; He Himself herds the cows in the woods.

The Beloved Himself is the blue-skinned, handsome one; He Himself plays on His flute.

The Beloved Himself took the form of a child, and destroyed Kuwalia-peer, the mad elephant. |2|

The Beloved Himself sets the stage; He performs the plays, and He Himself watches them.

The Beloved Himself assumed the form of the child, and killed the demons Chandoor, Kansa and Kaysee.

The Beloved Himself, by Himself, is the embodiment of power; He shatters the power of the fools and idiots. |3|

The Beloved Himself created the whole world. In His hands He holds the power of the ages.

Section 13 - Raag Sorat'h - Part 013

The Beloved Himself puts the chains around their necks; as God pulls them, must they go.

Whoever harbors pride shall be destroyed, O Beloved; meditating on the Lord, Nanak is absorbed in devotional worship. |4|6|

Sorat'h, Fourth Mehl, Du-Tukas:

Separated from the Lord for countless lifetimes, the self-willed manmukh suffers in pain, engaged in acts of egotism.

Beholding the Holy Saint, I found God; O Lord of the Universe, I seek Your Sanctuary. |1|

The Love of God is very dear to me.
When I joined the Sat Sangat, the Company of the Holy People, the Lord, the embodiment of peace, came into my heart. |Pause|

You dwell, hidden, within my heart day and night, Lord; but the poor fools do not understand Your Love.
Meeting with the Almighty True Guru, God was revealed to me; I sing His Glorious Praises, and reflect upon His Glories. |2|

As Gurmukh, I have become enlightened; peace has come, and evil-mindedness has been dispelled from my mind.
Understanding the relationship of the individual soul with God, I have found peace, in Your Sat Sangat, Your True Congregation, O Lord. |3|

Those who are blessed by Your Kind Mercy, meet the Almighty Lord, and find the Guru.
Nanak has found the immeasurable, celestial peace; night and day, he remains awake to the Lord, the Master of the Forest of the Universe. |4|7|

Sorat'h, Fourth Mehl:
The inner depths of my mind are pierced by love for the Lord; I cannot live without the Lord.
Just as the fish dies without water, I die without the Lord's Name. |1|

O my God, please bless me with the water of Your Name.
I beg for Your Name, deep within myself, day and night; through the Name, I find peace. |Pause|

The song-bird cries out for lack of water - without water, its thirst cannot be quenched.
The Gurmukh obtains the water of celestial bliss, and is rejuvenated, blossoming forth through the blessed Love of the Lord. |2|

The self-willed manmukhs are hungry, wandering around in the ten directions; without the Name, they suffer in pain.
They are born, only to die, and enter into reincarnation again; in the Court of the Lord, they are punished. |3|

But if the Lord shows His Mercy, then one comes to sing His Glorious Praises; deep within the nucleus of his own self, he finds the sublime essence of the Lord's elixir.
The Lord has become Merciful to meek Nanak, and through the Word of the Shabad, his desires are quenched. |4|8|

Sorat'h, Fourth Mehl, Panch-Padas:
If one eats the uneatable, then he becomes a Siddha, a being of perfect spirituality; through this perfection, he obtains wisdom.
When the arrow of the Lord's Love pierces his body, then his doubt is eradicated. |1|

O my Lord of the Universe, please bless Your humble servant with glory.
Under Guru's Instructions, enlighten me with the Lord's Name, that I may dwell forever in Your Sanctuary. |Pause|

This whole world is engrossed in coming and going; O my foolish and ignorant mind, be mindful of the Lord.
O Dear Lord, please, take pity upon me, and unite me with the Guru, that I may merge in the Lord's Name. |2|

Only one who has it knows God; he alone has it, to whom God has given it - so very beautiful, unapproachable and unfathomable. Through the Perfect Guru, the unknowable is known. |3|

Only one who tastes it knows it, like the mute, who tastes the sweet candy, but cannot speak of it.

Section 13 - Raag Sorat'h - Part 014

The jewel is concealed, but it is not concealed, even though one may try to conceal it. |4|

Everything is Yours, O Inner-knower, Searcher of hearts; You are the Lord God of all.
He alone receives the gift, unto whom You give it; O servant Nanak, there is no one else. |5|9|

Sorat'h, Fifth Mehl, First House, Ti-Tukas:

One Universal Creator God. By The Grace Of The True Guru:
Who should I ask? Who should I worship? All were created by Him.
Whoever appears to be the greatest of the great, shall ultimately be mixed with the dust.
The Fearless, Formless Lord, the Destroyer of Fear bestows all comforts, and the nine treasures. |1|

O Dear Lord, Your gifts alone satisfy me.
Why should I praise the poor helpless man? Why should I feel subservient to him? |Pause|

All things come to one who meditates on the Lord; the Lord satisfies his hunger.
The Lord, the Giver of peace, bestows such wealth, that it can never be exhausted.
I am in ecstasy, absorbed in celestial peace; the True Guru has united me in His Union. |2|

O mind, chant the Naam, the Name of the Lord; worship the Naam, night and day, and recite the Naam.
Listen to the Teachings of the Holy Saints, and all fear of death will be dispelled.
Those blessed by God's Grace are attached to the Word of the Guru's Bani. |3|

Who can estimate Your worth, God? You are kind and compassionate to all beings.
Everything which You do, prevails; I am just a poor child - what can I do?
Protect and preserve Your servant Nanak; be kind to him, like a father to his son. |4|1|

Sorat'h, Fifth Mehl, First House, Chau-Tukas:
Praise the Guru, and the Lord of the Universe, O Siblings of Destiny; enshrine Him in your mind, body and heart.
Let the True Lord and Master abide in your mind, O Siblings of Destiny; this is the most excellent way of life.
Those bodies, in which the Name of the Lord does not well up, O Siblings of Destiny - those bodies are reduced to ashes.
I am a sacrifice to the Saadh Sangat, the Company of the Holy, O Siblings of Destiny; they take the Support of the One and Only Lord. |1|

So worship and adore that True Lord, O Siblings of Destiny; He alone does everything.

The Perfect Guru has taught me, O Siblings of Destiny, that without Him, there is no other at all. |Pause|

Without the Naam, the Name of the Lord, they putrefy and die, O Siblings of Destiny; their numbers cannot be counted.

Without Truth, purity cannot be achieved, O Siblings of Destiny; the Lord is true and unfathomable.

Coming and going do not end, O Siblings of Destiny; pride in worldly valuables is false.

The Gurmukh saves millions of people, O Siblings of Destiny, blessing them with even a particle of the Name. |2|

I have searched through the Simritees and the Shaastras, O Siblings of Destiny - without the True Guru, doubt does not depart.

They are so tired of performing their many deeds, O Siblings of Destiny, but they fall into bondage again and again.

I have searched in the four directions, O Siblings of Destiny, but without the True Guru, there is no place at all.

Section 13 - Raag Sorat'h - Part 015

By great good fortune, I found the Guru, O Siblings of Destiny, and I meditate on the Name of the Lord, Har, Har. |3|

The Truth is forever pure, O Siblings of Destiny; those who are true are pure.

When the Lord bestows His Glance of Grace, O Siblings of Destiny, then one obtains Him.

Among millions, O Siblings of Destiny, hardly one humble servant of the Lord is found.

Nanak is imbued with the True Name, O Siblings of Destiny; hearing it, the mind and body become immaculately pure. |4|2|

Sorat'h, Fifth Mehl, Du-Tukas:
As long as this person believes in love and hate, it is difficult for him to meet the Lord.

As long as he discriminates between himself and others, he will distance himself from the Lord. |1|

O Lord, grant me such understanding,
that I might serve the Holy Saints, and seek the protection of their feet, and not forget them, for a moment, even an instant. |Pause|

O foolish, thoughtless and fickle mind, such understanding did not come into your heart.
Renouncing the Lord of Life, you have become engrossed in other things, and you are involved with your enemies. |2|

Sorrow does not afflict one who does not harbor self-conceit; in the Saadh Sangat, the Company of the Holy, I have attained this understanding.
Know that the babbling of the faithless cynic is like wind passing by. |3|

This mind is inundated by millions of sins - what can I say?
Nanak, Your humble servant has come to Your Sanctuary, God; please, erase all his accounts. |4|3|

Sorat'h, Fifth Mehl:
Children, spouses, men and women in one's household, are all bound by Maya.
At the very last moment, none of them shall stand by you; their love is totally false. |1|

O man, why do you pamper your body so?
It shall disperse like a cloud of smoke; vibrate upon the One, the Beloved Lord. |Pause|

There are three ways in which the body can be consumed - it can be thrown into water, given to the dogs, or cremated to ashes.
He considers himself to be immortal; he sits in his home, and forgets the Lord, the Cause of causes. |2|

In various ways, the Lord has fashioned the beads, and strung them on a slender thread.
The thread shall break, O wretched man, and then, you shall repent and regret. |3|

He created you, and after creating you, He adorned you - meditate on Him day and night.
God has showered His Mercy upon servant Nanak; I hold tight to the Support of the True Guru. |4|4|

Sorat'h, Fifth Mehl:
I met the True Guru, by great good fortune, and my mind has been enlightened.
No one else can equal me, because I have the loving support of my Lord and Master. |1|

I am a sacrifice to my True Guru.
I am at peace in this world, and I shall be in celestial peace in the next; my home is filled with bliss. |Pause|

He is the Inner-knower, the Searcher of hearts, the Creator, my Lord and Master.
I have become fearless, attached to the Guru's feet; I take the Support of the Name of the One Lord. |2|

Fruitful is the Blessed Vision of His Darshan; the Form of God is deathless; He is and shall always be.
He hugs His humble servants close, and protects and preserves them; their love for Him is sweet to Him. |3|

Great is His glorious greatness, and wondrous is His magnificence; through Him, all affairs are resolved.

Section 13 - Raag Sorat'h - Part 016

Nanak has met with the Perfect Guru; all his sorrows have been dispelled. |4|5|

Sorat'h, Fifth Mehl:
To the happy person, everyone seems happy; to the sick person, everyone seems sick.
The Lord and Master acts, and causes us to act; union is in His Hands. |1|

O my mind, no one appears to be mistaken, to one who has dispelled his own doubts; he realizes that everyone is God. |Pause|

One whose mind is comforted in the Society of the Saints, believes that all are joyful.
One whose mind is afflicted by the disease of egotism, cries out in birth and death. |2|

Everything is clear to one whose eyes are blessed with the ointment of spiritual wisdom.
In the darkness of spiritual ignorance, he sees nothing at all; he wanders around in reincarnation, over and over again. |3|

Hear my prayer, O Lord and Master; Nanak begs for this happiness:
whereever Your Holy Saints sing the Kirtan of Your Praises, let my mind be attached to that place. |4|6|

Sorat'h, Fifth Mehl:
My body belongs to the Saints, my wealth belongs to the Saints, and my mind belongs to the Saints.
By the Grace of the Saints, I meditate on the Lord's Name, and then, all comforts come to me. |1|

Without the Saints, there are no other givers.
Whoever takes to the Sanctuary of the Holy Saints, is carried across. |Pause|

Millions of sins are erased by serving the humble Saints, and singing the Glorious Praises of the Lord with love.
One finds peace in this world, and one's face is radiant in the next world, by associating with the humble Saints, through great good fortune. |2|

I have only one tongue, and the Lord's humble servant is filled with countless virtues; how can I sing his praises?

The inaccessible, unapproachable and eternally unchanging Lord is obtained in the Sanctuary of the Saints. |3|

I am worthless, lowly, without friends or support, and full of sins; I long for the Shelter of the Saints.
I am drowning in the deep, dark pit of household attachments - please save me, Lord! |4|7|

Sorat'h, Fifth Mehl, First House:
O Creator Lord, You fulfill the desires of those, within whose heart You abide.
Your slaves do not forget You; the dust of Your feet is pleasing to their minds. |1|

Your Unspoken Speech cannot be spoken.
O treasure of excellence, Giver of peace, Lord and Master, Your greatness is the highest of all. |Pause|

The mortal does those deeds, and those alone, which You ordained by destiny.
Your servant, whom You bless with Your service, is satisfied and fulfilled, beholding the Blessed Vision of Your Darshan. |2|

You are contained in all, but he alone realizes this, whom You bless with understanding.
By Guru's Grace, his spiritual ignorance is dispelled, and he is respected everywhere. |3|

He alone is spiritually enlightened, he alone is a meditator, and he alone is a man of good nature.
Says Nanak, one unto whom the Lord becomes Merciful, does not forget the Lord from his mind. |4|8|

Sorat'h, Fifth Mehl:
The whole creation is engrossed in emotional attachment; sometimes, one is high, and at other times, low.
No one can be purified by any rituals or devices; they cannot reach their goal. |1|

Section 13 - Raag Sorat'h - Part 017

O my mind, emancipation is attained in the Sanctuary of the Holy Saints.
Without the Perfect Guru, births and deaths do not cease, and one comes and goes, over and over again. |Pause|

The whole world is entangled in what is called the delusion of doubt.

The perfect devotee of the Primal Lord God remains detached from everything. |2|

Don't indulge in slander for any reason, for everything is the creation of the Lord and Master.
One who is blessed with the Mercy of my God, dwells on the Name in the Saadh Sangat, the Company of the Holy. |3|

The Supreme Lord God, the Transcendent Lord, the True Guru, saves all.
Says Nanak, without the Guru, no one crosses over; this is the perfect essence of all contemplation. |4|9|

Sorat'h, Fifth Mehl:
I have searched and searched and searched, and found that the Lord's Name is the most sublime reality.
Contemplating it for even an instant, sins are erased; the Gurmukh is carried across and saved. |1|

Drink in the sublime essence of the Lord's Name, O man of spiritual wisdom.
Listening to the Ambrosial Words of the Holy Saints, the mind finds absolute fulfillment and satisfaction. |Pause|

Liberation, pleasures, and the true way of life are obtained from the Lord, the Giver of all peace.
The Perfect Lord, the Architect of Destiny, blesses His slave with the gift of devotional worship. |2|

Hear with your ears, and sing with your tongue, and meditate within your heart on Him.
The Lord and Master is all-powerful, the Cause of causes; without Him, there is nothing at all. |3|

By great good fortune, I have obtained the jewel of human life; have mercy on me, O Merciful Lord.
In the Saadh Sangat, the Company of the Holy, Nanak sings the Glorious Praises of the Lord, and contemplates Him forever in meditation. |4|10|

Sorat'h, Fifth Mehl:

After taking your cleansing bath, remember your God in meditation, and your mind and body shall be free of disease.

Millions of obstacles are removed, in the Sanctuary of God, and good fortune dawns. |1|

The Word of God's Bani, and His Shabad, are the best utterances.

So constantly sing them, listen to them, and read them, O Siblings of Destiny, and the Perfect Guru shall save you. |Pause|

The glorious greatness of the True Lord is immeasurable; the Merciful Lord is the Lover of His devotees.

He has preserved the honor of His Saints; from the very beginning of time, His Nature is to cherish them. |2|

So eat the Ambrosial Name of the Lord as your food; put it into your mouth at all times.

The pains of old age and death shall all depart, when you constantly sing the Glorious Praises of the Lord of the Universe. |3|

My Lord and Master has heard my prayer, and all my affairs have been resolved.

The glorious greatness of Guru Nanak is manifest, throughout all the ages. |4|11|

Sorat'h, Fifth Mehl, Second House, Chau-Padas:
One Universal Creator God. By The Grace Of The True Guru:
The One God is our father; we are the children of the One God. You are our Guru.
Listen, friends: my soul is a sacrifice, a sacrifice to You; O Lord, reveal to me the Blessed Vision of Your Darshan. |1|

Section 13 - Raag Sorat'h - Part 018

Listen, friends: I am a sacrifice to the dust of Your feet.
This mind is yours, O Siblings of Destiny. |Pause|

I wash your feet, I massage and clean them; I give this mind to you.
Listen, friends: I have come to Your Sanctuary; teach me, that I might unite with God. |2|

Do not be proud; seek His Sanctuary, and accept as good all that He does.
Listen, friends: dedicate your soul, body and your whole being to Him; thus you shall receive the Blessed Vision of His Darshan. |3|

He has shown mercy to me, by the Grace of the Saints; the Lord's Name is sweet to me.
The Guru has shown mercy to servant Nanak; I see the casteless, immaculate Lord everywhere. |4|1|12|

Sorat'h, Fifth Mehl:
God is the Lord and Master of millions of universes; He is the Giver of all beings.
He ever cherishes and cares for all beings, but the fool does not appreciate any of His virtues. |1|

I do not know how to worship the Lord in adoration.
I can only repeat, "Lord, Lord, Guru, Guru."
O Dear Lord, I go by the name of the Lord's slave. |Pause|

The Compassionate Lord is Merciful to the meek, the ocean of peace; He fills all hearts.
He sees, hears, and is always with me; but I am a fool, and I think that He is far away. |2|

The Lord is limitless, but I can only describe Him within my limitations; what do I know, about what He is like?

I offer my prayer to my True Guru; I am so foolish - please, teach me! |3|

I am just a fool, but millions of sinners just like me have been saved.
Those who have heard, and seen Guru Nanak, do not descend into the womb of reincarnation again. |4|2|13|

Sorat'h, Fifth Mehl:
Those things, which caused me such anxiety, have all vanished.
Now, I sleep in peace and tranquility, and my mind is in a state of deep and profound peace; the inverted lotus of my heart has blossomed forth. |1|

Behold, a wondrous miracle has happened!

That Lord and Master, whose wisdom is said to be unfathomable, has been enshrined within my heart, by the Guru. |Pause|

The demons which tormented me so much, have themselves become terrified.
They pray: please, save us from your Lord Master; we seek your protection. |2|

When the treasure of the Lord of the Universe is opened, those who are pre-destined, receive it.
The Guru has given me the one jewel, and my mind and body have become peaceful and tranquil. |3|

The Guru has blessed me with the one drop of Ambrosial Nectar, and so I have become stable, unmoving and immortal - I shall not die.
The Lord blessed Guru Nanak with the treasure of devotional worship, and did not call him to account again. |4|3|14|

Sorat'h, Fifth Mehl:
Those whose minds are attached to the lotus feet of the Lord - those humble beings are satisfied and fulfilled.
But those, within whose hearts the priceless virtue does not abide - those men remain thirsty and unsatisfied. |1|

Worshipping the Lord in adoration, one becomes happy, and free of disease.
But one who forgets my Dear Lord - know him to be afflicted with tens of thousands of illnesses. |Pause|

Section 13 - Raag Sorat'h - Part 019

Those who hold tightly to Your Support, God, are happy in Your Sanctuary.
But those humble beings who forget the Primal Lord, the Architect of Destiny, are counted among the most miserable beings. |2|

One who has faith in the Guru, and who is lovingly attached to God, enjoys the delights of supreme ecstasy.
One who forgets God and forsakes the Guru, falls into the most horrible hell. |3|

As the Lord engages someone, so he is engaged, and so does he perform. Nanak has taken to the Shelter of the Saints; his heart is absorbed in the Lord's feet. |4|4|15|

Sorat'h, Fifth Mehl:
As the king is entangled in kingly affairs, and the egotist in his own egotism, and the greedy man is enticed by greed, so is the spiritually enlightened being absorbed in the Love of the Lord. |1|

This is what befits the Lord's servant.
Beholding the Lord near at hand, he serves the True Guru, and he is satisfied through the Kirtan of the Lord's Praises. |Pause|

The addict is addicted to his drug, and the landlord is in love with his land. As the baby is attached to his milk, so the Saint is in love with God. |2|

The scholar is absorbed in scholarship, and the eyes are happy to see. As the tongue savors the tastes, so does the humble servant of the Lord sing the Glorious Praises of the Lord. |3|

As is the hunger, so is the fulfiller; He is the Lord and Master of all hearts. Nanak thirsts for the Blessed Vision of the Lord's Darshan; he has met God, the Inner-knower, the Searcher of hearts. |4|5|16|

Sorat'h, Fifth Mehl:
We are filthy, and You are immaculate, O Creator Lord; we are worthless, and You are the Great Giver.
We are fools, and You are wise and all-knowing. You are the knower of all things. |1|

O Lord, this is what we are, and this is what You are.
We are sinners, and You are the Destroyer of sins. Your abode is so beautiful, O Lord and Master. |Pause|

You fashion all, and having fashioned them, You bless them. You bestow upon them soul, body and the breath of life.
We are worthless - we have no virtue at all; please, bless us with Your gift, O Merciful Lordand Master. |2|

You do good for us, but we do not see it as good; You are kind and compassionate, forever and ever.
You are the Giver of peace, the Primal Lord, the Architect of Destiny; please, save us, Your children! |3|

You are the treasure, eternal Lord King; all beings and creatures beg of You.
Says Nanak, such is our condition; please, Lord, keep us on the Path of the Saints. |4|6|17|

Sorat'h, Fifth Mehl, Second House:
In our mother's womb, You blessed us with Your meditative remembrance, and You preserved us there.
Through the countless waves of the ocean of fire, please, carry us across and save us, O Savior Lord! |1|

O Lord, You are the Master above my head.
Here and hereafter, You alone are my Support. |Pause|

He looks upon the creation like a mountain of gold, and sees the Creator as a blade of grass.
You are the Great Giver, and we are all mere beggars; O God, You give gifts according to Your Will. |2|

In an instant, You are one thing, and in another instant, You are another. Wondrous are Your ways!
You are beautiful, mysterious, profound, unfathomable, lofty, inaccessible and infinite. |3|

Section 13 - Raag Sorat'h - Part 020

When You brought me to the Saadh Sangat, the Company of the Holy, then I heard the Bani of Your Word.
Nanak is in ecstasy, beholding the Glory of the Primal Lord of Nirvaanaa. |4|7|18|

Sorat'h, Fifth Mehl:
I am the dust of the feet of the Beloved Saints; I seek the Protection of their Sanctuary.
The Saints are my all-powerful Support; the Saints are my ornament and decoration. |1|

I am hand and glove with the Saints.
I have realized my pre-ordained destiny.
This mind is yours, O Siblings of Destiny. |Pause|

My dealings are with the Saints, and my business is with the Saints.
I have earned the profit with the Saints, and the treasure filled to over-flowing with devotion to the Lord. |2|

The Saints entrusted to me the capital, and my mind's delusion was dispelled.
What can the Righteous Judge of Dharma do now? All my accounts have been torn up. |3|

I have found the greatest bliss, and I am at peace, by the Grace of the Saints.
Says Nanak, my mind is reconciled with the Lord; it is imbued with the wondrous Love of the Lord. |4|8|19|

Sorat'h, Fifth Mehl:
All the things that you see, O man, you shall have to leave behind.
Let your dealings be with the Lord's Name, and you shall attain the state of Nirvaanaa. |1|

O my Beloved, You are the Giver of peace.
The Perfect Guru has given me these Teachings, and I am attuned to You. |Pause|

In sexual desire, anger, greed, emotional attachment and self-conceit, peace is not to be found.
So be the dust of the feet of all, O my mind, and then you shall find bliss, joy and peace. |2|

He knows the condition of your inner self, and He will not let your work go in vain - serve Him, O mind.
Worship Him, and dedicate this mind unto Him, the Image of the Undying Lord, the Divine Guru. |3|

He is the Lord of the Universe, the Compassionate Lord, the Supreme Lord God, the Formless Lord.

The Naam is my merchandise, the Naam is my nourishment; the Naam, O Nanak, is the Support of my breath of life. |4|9|20|

Sorat'h, Fifth Mehl:
He infuses the breath into the dead bodies, and he reunited the separated ones.
Even beasts, demons and fools become attentive listeners, when He sings the Praises of the Lord's Name. |1|

Behold the glorious greatness of the Perfect Guru.
His worth cannot be described. |Pause|

He has demolished the abode of sorrow and disease, and brought bliss, joy and happiness.
He effortlessly awards the fruits of the mind's desire, and all works are brought to perfection. |2|

He finds peace in this world, and his face is radiant in the world hereafter; his comings and goings are finished.
He becomes fearless, and his heart is filled with the Naam, the Name of the Lord; his mind is pleasing to the True Guru. |3|

Standing up and sitting down, he sings the Glorious Praises of the Lord; his pain, sorrow and doubt are dispelled.
Says Nanak, his karma is perfect; his mind is attached to the Guru's feet. |4|10|21|

Sorat'h, Fifth Mehl:
Forsaking the jewel, he is attached to the shell; nothing will come of it.

Section 13 - Raag Sorat'h - Part 021

O my mind, meditate forever on the Perfect, Supreme Lord God, the Transcendent Lord. |1|

Meditate in remembrance on the Name of the Lord, Har, Har, O mortal.
Your frail body shall perish, you ignorant fool. |Pause|

Illusions and dream-objects possess nothing of greatness.

Without meditating on the Lord, nothing succeeds, and nothing will go along with you. |2|

Acting in egotism and pride, his life passes away, and he does nothing for his soul.
Wandering and wandering all around, he is never satisfied; he does not remember the Name of the Lord. |3|

Intoxicated with the taste of corruption, cruel pleasures and countless sins, he is consigned to the cycle of reincarnation.
Nanak offers his prayer to God, to eradicate his demerits. |4|11|22|

Sorat'h, Fifth Mehl:
Sing the Glorious Praises of the Perfect, Imperishable Lord, and the poison of sexual desire and anger shall be burnt away.
You shall cross over the awesome, arduous ocean of fire, in the Saadh Sangat, the Company of the Holy. |1|

The Perfect Guru has dispelled the darkness of doubt.
Remember God with love and devotion; He is near at hand. |Pause|

Drink in the sublime essence, the treasure of the Name of the Lord, Har, Har, and your mind and body shall remain satisfied.
The Transcendent Lord is totally permeating and pervading everywhere; where would He come from, and where would He go? |2|

One whose mind is filled with the Lord, is a person of meditation, penance, self-restraint and spiritual wisdom, and a knower of reality.
The Gurmukh obtains the jewel of the Naam; his efforts come to perfect fruition. |3|

All his struggles, sufferings and pains are dispelled, and the noose of death is cut away from him.
Says Nanak, God has extended His Mercy, and so his mind and body blossom forth. |4|12|23|

Sorat'h, Fifth Mehl:
God is the Doer, the Cause of causes, the Great Giver; God is the Supreme Lord and Master.

The Merciful Lord created all beings; God is the Inner-knower, the Searcher of hearts. |1|

My Guru is Himself my friend and support.
I am in celestial peace, bliss, joy, pleasure and wondrous glory. |Pause|

Seeking the Sanctuary of the Guru, my fears have been dispelled, and I am accepted in the Court of the True Lord.
Singing His Glorious Praises, and worshipping in adoration the Name of the Lord, I have reached my destination. |2|

Everyone applauds and congratulates me; the Saadh Sangat, the Company of the Holy, is dear to me.
I am forever a sacrifice to my God, who has totally protected and preserved my honor. |3|

They are saved, who receive the Blessed Vision of His Darshan; they listen to the spiritual dialogue of the Naam.
Nanak's God has become Merciful to him; he has arrived home in ecstasy. |4|13|24|

Sorat'h, Fifth Mehl:
In God's Sanctuary, all fears depart, suffering disappears, and peace is obtained.
When the Supreme Lord God and Master becomes merciful, we meditate on the Perfect True Guru. |1|

O Dear God, You are my Lord Master and Great Giver.
By Your Mercy, O God, Merciful to the meek, imbue me with Your Love, that I might sing Your Glorious Praises. |Pause|

The True Guru has implanted the treasure of the Naam within me, and all my anxieties have been dispelled.

Section 13 - Raag Sorat'h - Part 022

By His Mercy, He has made me His own, and the imperishable Lord has come to dwell within my mind. |2|

No misfortune afflicts one who is protected by the True Guru.

The Lotus Feet of God come to abide within his heart, and he savors the sublime essence of the Lord's Ambrosial Nectar. |3|

So, as a servant, serve your God, who fulfills your mind's desires.
Slave Nanak is a sacrifice to the Perfect Lord, who has protected and preserved his honor. |4|14|25|

Sorat'h, Fifth Mehl:
Infatuated with the darkness of emotional attachment to Maya, he does not know the Lord, the Great Giver.
The Lord created his body and fashioned his soul, but he claims that his power is his own. |1|

O foolish mind, God, your Lord and Master is watching over you.
Whatever you do, He knows; nothing can remain concealed from Him. |Pause|

You are intoxicated with the tastes of the tongue, with greed and pride; countless sins spring from these.
You wandered in pain through countless incarnations, weighed down by the chains of egotism. |2|

Behind closed doors, hidden by many screens, the man takes his pleasure with another man's wife.
When Chitr and Gupt, the celestial accountants of the conscious and subconscious, call for your account, who will screen you then? |3|

O Perfect Lord, Merciful to the meek, Destroyer of pain, without You, I have no shelter at all.
Please, lift me up out of the world-ocean; O God, I have come to Your Sanctuary. |4|15|26|

Sorat'h, Fifth Mehl:
The Supreme Lord God has become my helper and friend; His sermon and the Kirtan of His Praises have brought me peace.
Chant the Word of the Perfect Guru's Bani, and be ever in bliss, O mortal. |1|

Remember the True Lord in meditation, O Siblings of Destiny.

In the Saadh Sangat, the Company of the Holy, eternal peace is obtained, and the Lord is never forgotten. |Pause|

Your Name, O Transcendent Lord, is Ambrosial Nectar; whoever meditates on it, lives.
One who is blessed with God's Grace - that humble servant becomes immaculate and pure. |2|

Obstacles are removed, and all pains are eliminated; my mind is attached to the Guru's feet.
Singing the Glorious Praises of the immovable and imperishable Lord, one remains awake to the Lord's Love, day and night. |3|

He obtains the fruits of his mind's desires, listening to the comforting sermon of the Lord.
In the beginning, in the middle, and in the end, God is Nanak's best friend. |4|16|27|

Sorat'h, Fifth Mehl, Panch-Padas:
May my emotional attachment, my sense of mine and yours, and my self-conceit be dispelled. |1|

O Saints, show me such a way,
by which my egotism and pride might be eliminated. |1|Pause|

I see the Supreme Lord God in all beings, and I am the dust of all. |2|

I see God always with me, and the wall of doubt has been shattered. |3|

The medicine of the Naam, and the Immaculate Water of Ambrosial Nectar, are obtained through the Guru's Gate. |4|

Says Nanak, one who has such pre-ordained destiny inscribed upon his forehead, meets with the Guru, and his diseases are cured. |5|17|28|

Section 13 - Raag Sorat'h - Part 023

Sorat'h, Fifth Mehl, Second House, Du-Padas:
One Universal Creator God. By The Grace Of The True Guru:
Fire is contained in all firewood, and butter is contained in all milk.

God's Light is contained in the high and the low; the Lord is in the hearts of all beings. |1|

O Saints, He is pervading and permeating each and every heart.
The Perfect Lord is completely permeating everyone, everywhere; He is diffused in the water and the land. |1|Pause|

Nanak sings the Praises of the Lord, the treasure of excellence; the True Guru has dispelled his doubt.
The Lord is pervading everywhere, permeating all, and yet, He is unattached from all. |2|1|29|

Sorat'h, Fifth Mehl:
Meditating on Him, one is in ecstasy; the pains of birth and death and fear are removed.
The four cardinal blessings, and the nine treasures are received; you shall never feel hunger or thirst again. |1|

Chanting His Name, you shall be at peace.
With each and every breath, meditate on the Lord and Master, O my soul, with mind, body and mouth. |1|Pause|

You shall find peace, and your mind shall be soothed and cooled; the fire of desire shall not burn within you.
The Guru has revealed God to Nanak, in the three worlds, in the water, the earth and the woods. |2|2|30|

Sorat'h, Fifth Mehl:
Sexual desire, anger, greed, falsehood and slander - please, save me from these, O Lord.
Please eradicate these from within me, and call me to come close to You. |1|

You alone teach me Your Ways.
With the Lord's humble servants, I sing His Praises. |1|Pause|

May I never forget the Lord within my heart; please, instill such understanding within my mind.
By great good fortune, servant Nanak has met with the Perfect Guru, and now, he will not go anywhere else. |2|3|31|

Sorat'h, Fifth Mehl:
Meditating in remembrance on Him, all things are obtained, and one's efforts shall not be in vain.
Forsaking God, why do you attach yourself to another? He is contained in everything. |1|

O Saints, meditate in remembrance on the World-Lord, Har, Har.
Joining the Saadh Sangat, the Company of the Holy, meditate on the Naam, the Name of the Lord; your efforts shall be rewarded. |1|Pause|

He ever preserves and cherishes His servant; with Love, He hugs him close.
Says Nanak, forgetting You, O God, how can the world find life? |2|4|32|

Sorat'h, Fifth Mehl:
He is imperishable, the Giver of all beings; meditating on Him, all filth is removed.
He is the treasure of excellence, the object of His devotees, but rare are those who find Him. |1|

O my mind, meditate on the Guru, and God, the Cherisher of the world.
Seeking His Sanctuary, one finds peace, and he shall not suffer in pain again. |1|Pause|

By great good fortune, one obtains the Saadh Sangat, the Company of the Holy. Meeting them, evil-mindedness is eliminated.

Section 13 - Raag Sorat'h - Part 024

Slave Nanak yearns for the dust of the feet of those, who have woven the Lord's Name into their hearts. |2|5|33|

Sorat'h, Fifth Mehl:
He dispels the pains of countless incarnations, and lends support to the dry and shrivelled mind.
Beholding the Blessed Vision of His Darshan, one is enraptured, contemplating the Name of the Lord. |1|

My physician is the Guru, the Lord of the Universe.

He places the medicine of the Naam into my mouth, and cuts away the noose of Death. |1|Pause|

He is the all-powerful, Perfect Lord, the Architect of Destiny; He Himself is the Doer of deeds.
The Lord Himself saves His slave; Nanak takes the Support of the Naam. |2|6|34|

Sorat'h, Fifth Mehl:
Only You know the state of my innermost self; You alone can judge me.
Please forgive me, O Lord God Master; I have committed thousands of sins and mistakes. |1|

O my Dear Lord God Master, You are always near me.
O Lord, please bless Your disciple with the shelter of Your feet. |1|Pause|

Infinite and endless is my Lord and Master; He is lofty, virtuous and profoundly deep.
Cutting away the noose of death, the Lord has made Nanak His slave, and now, what does he owe to anyone else? |2|7|35|

Sorat'h, Fifth Mehl:
The Guru, the Lord of the Universe, became merciful to me, and I obtained all of my mind's desires.
I have become stable and steady, touching the Lord's Feet, and singing the Glorious Praises of the Lord of the Universe. |1|

It is a good time, a perfectly auspicious time.
I am in celestial peace, tranquility and ecstasy, chanting the Naam, the Name of the Lord; the unstruck melody of the sound current vibrates and resounds. |1|Pause|

Meeting with my Beloved Lord and Master, my home has become a mansion filled with happiness.
Servant Nanak has attained the treasure of the Lord's Name; all his desires have been fulfilled. |2|8|36|

Sorat'h, Fifth Mehl:
The Guru's feet abide within my heart; God has blessed me with good fortune.

The Perfect Transcendent Lord became merciful to me, and I found the treasure of the Naam within my mind. |1|

My Guru is my Saving Grace, my only best friend.
Over and over again, He blesses me with double, even four-fold, greatness. |1|Pause|

God saves all beings and creatures, giving them the Blessed Vision of His Darshan.
Wondrous is the glorious greatness of the Perfect Guru; Nanak is forever a sacrifice to Him. |2|9|37|

Sorat'h, Fifth Mehl:
I gather in and collect the immaculate wealth of the Naam; this commodity is inaccessible and incomparable.
Revel in it, delight in it, be happy and enjoy peace, and live long, O Sikhs and brethren. |1|

I have the support of the Lotus Feet of the Lord.
By the Grace of the Saints, I have found the boat of Truth; embarking on it, I sail across the ocean of poison. |1|Pause|

The perfect, imperishable Lord has become merciful; He Himself has taken care of me.
Beholding, beholding His Vision, Nanak has blossomed forth in ecstasy. O Nanak, He is beyond estimation. |2|10|38|

Sorat'h, Fifth Mehl:
The Perfect Guru has revealed His power, and compassion has welled up in every heart.
Blending me with Himself, He has blessed me with glorious greatness, and I have found pleasure and happiness. |1|

The Perfect True Guru is always with me.

Section 13 - Raag Sorat'h - Part 025

Meditating on the Supreme Lord God, I am forever in ecstasy. |Pause|

Inwardly and outwardly, in all places and interspaces, wherever I look, He is there.
Nanak has found the Guru, by great good fortune; no one else is as great as He. |2|11|39|

Sorat'h, Fifth Mehl:
I have been blessed with peace, pleasure, bliss, and the celestial sound current, gazing upon the feet of God.
The Savior has saved His child, and the True Guru has cured his fever. |1|

I have been saved, in the True Guru's Sanctuary;
service to Him does not go in vain. |1|Pause|

There is peace within the home of one's heart, and there is peace outside as well, when God becomes kind and compassionate.
O Nanak, no obstacles block my way; my God has become gracious and merciful to me. |2|12|40|

Sorat'h, Fifth Mehl:
In the Saadh Sangat, the Company of the Holy, my mind became excited, and I sang the Praises of the jewel of the Naam.
My anxiety was dispelled, meditating in remembrance on the Infinite Lord; I have crossed over the world ocean, O Siblings of Destiny. |1|

I enshrine the Lord's Feet within my heart.
I have found peace, and the celestial sound current resounds within me; countless diseases have been eradicated. |Pause|

Which of Your Glorious Virtues can I speak and describe? Your worth cannot be estimated.
O Nanak, the Lord's devotees become imperishable and immortal; their God becomes their friend and support. |2|13|41|

Sorat'h, Fifth Mehl:
My sufferings have come to an end, and all diseases have been eradicated.
God has showered me with His Grace. Twenty-four hours a day, I worship and adore my Lord and Master; my efforts have come to fruition. |1|

O Dear Lord, You are my peace, wealth and capital.
Please, save me, O my Beloved! I offer this prayer to my God. |Pause|

Whatever I ask for, I receive; I have total faith in my Master.
Says Nanak, I have met with the Perfect Guru, and all my fears have been dispelled. |2|14|42|

Sorat'h, Fifth Mehl:
Meditating, meditating in remembrance on my Guru, the True Guru, all pains have been eradicated.
The fever and the disease are gone, through the Word of the Guru's Teachings, and I have obtained the fruits of my mind's desires. |1|

My Perfect Guru is the Giver of peace.
He is the Doer, the Cause of causes, the Almighty Lord and Master, the Perfect Primal Lord, the Architect of Destiny. |Pause|

Sing the Glorious Praises of the Lord in bliss, joy and ecstasy; Guru Nanak has become kind and compassionate.
Shouts of cheers and congratulations ring out all over the world; the Supreme Lord God has become my Savior and Protector. |2|15|43|

Sorat'h, Fifth Mehl:
He did not take my accounts into account; such is His forgiving nature.
He gave me His hand, and saved me and made me His own; forever and ever, I enjoy His Love. |1|

The True Lord and Master is forever merciful and forgiving.
My Perfect Guru has bound me to Him, and now, I am in absolute ecstasy. |Pause|

The One who fashioned the body and placed the soul within, who gives you clothing and nourishment
- He Himself preserves the honor of His slaves. Nanak is forever a sacrifice to Him. |2|16|44|

Section 13 - Raag Sorat'h - Part 026

Sorat'h, Fifth Mehl:
The Lord God Himself has rid the whole world of its sins, and saved it.
The Supreme Lord God extended His mercy, and confirmed His innate nature. |1|

I have attained the Protective Sanctuary of the Lord, my King.
In celestial peace and ecstasy, I sing the Glorious Praises of the Lord, and my mind, body and being are at peace. |Pause|

My True Guru is the Savior of sinners; I have placed my trust and faith in Him.
The True Lord has heard Nanak's prayer, and He has forgiven everything. |2|17|45|

Sorat'h, Fifth Mehl:
The Supreme Lord God, the Transcendent Lord, has forgiven me, and all diseases have been cured.
Those who come to the Sanctuary of the True Guru are saved, and all their affairs are resolved. |1|

The Lord's humble servant meditates in remembrance on the Naam, the Name of the Lord; this is his only support.
The Perfect True Guru extended His Mercy, and the fever has been dispelled. |Pause|

So celebrate and be happy, my beloveds - the Guru has saved Hargobind.
Great is the glorious greatness of the Creator, O Nanak; True is the Word of His Shabad, and True is the sermon of His Teachings. |2|18|46|

Sorat'h, Fifth Mehl:
My Lord and Master has become Merciful, in His True Court.
The True Guru has taken away the fever, and the whole world is at peace, O Siblings of Destiny.
The Lord Himself protects His beings and creatures, and the Messenger of Death is out of work. |1|

Enshrine the Lord's feet within your heart.
Forever and ever, meditate in remembrance on God, O Siblings of Destiny.
He is the Eradicator of suffering and sins. |1|Pause|

He fashioned all beings, O Siblings of Destiny, and His Sanctuary saves them.
He is the Almighty Creator, the Cause of causes, O Siblings of Destiny; He, the True Lord, is True.

Nanak: meditate on God, O Siblings of Destiny, and your mind and body shall be cool and calm. |2|19|47|

Sorat'h, Fifth Mehl:
O Saints, meditate on the Name of the Lord, Har, Har.
Never forget God, the ocean of peace; thus you shall obtain the fruits of your mind's desires. |1|Pause|

Extending His Mercy, the Perfect True Guru has dispelled the fever.
The Supreme Lord God has become kind and compassionate, and my whole family is now free of pain and suffering. |1|

The Treasure of absolute joy, sublime elixir and beauty, the Name of the Lord is my only Support.
O Nanak, the Transcendent Lord has preserved my honor, and saved the whole world. |2|20|48|

Sorat'h, Fifth Mehl:
My True Guru is my Savior and Protector.
Showering us with His Mercy and Grace, God extended His Hand, and saved Hargobind, who is now safe and secure. |1|Pause|

The fever is gone - God Himself eradicated it, and preserved the honor of His servant.
I have obtained all blessings from the Saadh Sangat, the Company of the Holy; I am a sacrifice to the True Guru. |1|

God has saved me, both here and hereafter. He has not taken my merits and demerits into account.

Section 13 - Raag Sorat'h - Part 027

Your Word is eternal, O Guru Nanak; You placed Your Hand of blessing upon my forehead. |2|21|49|

Sorat'h, Fifth Mehl:
All beings and creatures were created by Him; He alone is the support and friend of the Saints.
He Himself preserves the honor of His servants; their glorious greatness becomes perfect. |1|

The Perfect Supreme Lord God is always with me.
The Perfect Guru has perfectly and totally protected me, and now everyone is kind and compassionate to me. |1|Pause|

Night and day, Nanak meditates on the Naam, the Name of the Lord; He is the Giver of the soul, and the breath of life itself.
He hugs His slave close in His loving embrace, like the mother and father hug their child. |2|22|50|

Sorat'h, Fifth Mehl, Third House, Chau-Padas:
One Universal Creator God. By The Grace Of The True Guru:
Meeting with the council, my doubts were not dispelled.
The chiefs did not give me satisfaction.
I presented my dispute to the noblemen as well.
But it was only settled by meeting with the King, my Lord. |1|

Now, I do not go searching anywhere else,
because I have met the Guru, the Lord of the Universe. |Pause|

When I came to God's Darbaar, His Holy Court,
then all of my cries and complaints were settled.
Now that I have attained what I had sought,
where should I come and where should I go? |2|

There, true justice is administered.
There, the Lord Master and His disciple are one and the same.
The Inner-knower, the Searcher of hearts, knows.
Without our speaking, He understands. |3|

He is the King of all places.
There, the unstruck melody of the Shabad resounds.
Of what use is cleverness when dealing with Him?
Meeting with Him, O Nanak, one loses his self-conceit. |4|1|51|

Sorat'h, Fifth Mehl:
Enshrine the Naam, the Name of the Lord, within your heart;
sitting within your own home, meditate on the Guru.
The Perfect Guru has spoken the Truth;
the True Peace is obtained only from the Lord. |1|

My Guru has become merciful.
In bliss, peace, pleasure and joy, I have returned to my own home, after my
purifying bath. |Pause|

True is the glorious greatness of the Guru;
His worth cannot be described.
He is the Supreme Overlord of kings.
Meeting with the Guru, the mind is enraptured. |2|

All sins are washed away,
meeting with the Saadh Sangat, the Company of the Holy.
The Lord's Name is the treasure of excellence;
chanting It, one's affairs are perfectly resolved. |3|

The Guru has opened the door of liberation,
and the entire world applauds Him with cheers of victory.
O Nanak, God is always with me;
my fears of birth and death are gone. |4|2|52|

Sorat'h, Fifth Mehl:
The Perfect Guru has granted His Grace,
and God has fulfilled my desire.
After taking my bath of purification, I returned to my home,
and I found bliss, happiness and peace. |1|

O Saints, salvation comes from the Lord's Name.
While standing up and sitting down, meditate on the Lord's Name. Night
and day, do good deeds. |1|Pause|

Section 13 - Raag Sorat'h - Part 028

The way of the Saints is the ladder of righteous living, found only by great
good fortune.
The sins of millions of incarnations are washed away, by focusing your
consciousness on the Lord's feet. |2|

So sing the Praises of your God forever; His almighty power is perfect.
All beings and creatures are purified, listening to the True Teachings of the
True Guru. |3|

The True Guru has implanted the Naam, the Name of the Lord, within me; it is the Eliminator of obstructions, the Destroyer of all pains.
All of my sins were erased, and I have been purified; servant Nanak has returned to his home of peace. |4|3|53|

Sorat'h, Fifth Mehl:
O Lord Master, You are the ocean of excellence.
My home and all my possessions are Yours.
The Guru, the Lord of the world, is my Savior.
All beings have become kind and compassionate to me. |1|

Meditating on the Guru's feet, I am in bliss.
There is no fear at all, in God's Sanctuary. |Pause|

You dwell in the hearts of Your slaves, Lord.
God has laid the eternal foundation.
You are my strength, wealth and support.
You are my Almighty Lord and Master. |2|

Whoever finds the Saadh Sangat, the Company of the Holy,
is saved by God Himself.
By His Grace, He has blessed me with the sublime essence of the Naam.
All joy and pleasure then came to me. |3|

God became my helper and my best friend;
everyone rises up and bows down at my feet.
With each and every breath, meditate on God;
O Nanak, sing the songs of joy to the Lord. |4|4|54|

Sorat'h, Fifth Mehl:
Celestial peace and bliss have come,
meeting God, who is so pleasing to my mind.
The Perfect Guru showered me with His Mercy,
and I attained salvation. |1|

My mind is absorbed in loving devotional worship of the Lord,
and the unstruck melody of the celestial sound current ever resounds within me. |Pause|

The Lord's feet are my all-powerful shelter and support;
my dependence on other people is totally finished.
I have found the Life of the world, the Great Giver;
in joyful rapture, I sing the Glorious Praises of the Lord. |2|

God has cut away the noose of death.
My mind's desires have been fulfilled;
wherever I look, He is there.
Without the Lord God, there is no other at all. |3|

In His Mercy, God has protected and preserved me.
I am rid of all the pains of countless incarnations.
I have meditated on the Naam, the Name of the Fearless Lord;
O Nanak, I have found eternal peace. |4|5|55|

Sorat'h, Fifth Mehl:
The Creator has brought utter peace to my home;
the fever has left my family.
The Perfect Guru has saved us.
I sought the Sanctuary of the True Lord. |1|

The Transcendent Lord Himself has become my Protector.
Tranquility, intuitive peace and poise welled up in an instant, and my mind
was comforted forever. |Pause|

The Lord, Har, Har, gave me the medicine of His Name,
which has cured all disease.
He extended His Mercy to me,
and resolved all these affairs. |2|

God confirmed His loving nature;
He did not take my merits or demerits into account.
The Word of the Guru's Shabad has become manifest,

Section 13 - Raag Sorat'h - Part 029

and through it, my honor was totally preserved. |3|

I speak as You cause me to speak;
O Lord and Master, You are the ocean of excellence.

Nanak chants the Naam, the Name of the Lord, according to the Teachings of Truth.
God preserves the honor of His slaves. |4|6|56|

Sorat'h, Fifth Mehl:
The Creator Lord Himself stood between us,
and not a hair upon my head was touched.
The Guru made my cleansing bath successful;
meditating on the Lord, Har, Har, my sins were erased. |1|

O Saints, the purifying pool of Ram Das is sublime.
Whoever bathes in it, his family and ancestry are saved, and his soul is saved as well. |1|Pause|

The world sings cheers of victory,
and the fruits of his mind's desires are obtained.
Whoever comes and bathes here, and meditates on his God, is safe and sound. |2|

One who bathes in the healing pool of the Saints,
that humble being obtains the supreme status.
He does not die, or come and go in reincarnation;
he meditates on the Name of the Lord, Har, Har. |3|

He alone knows this about God,
whom God blesses with His kindness.
Baba Nanak seeks the Sanctuary of God;
all his worries and anxieties are dispelled. |4|7|57|

Sorat'h, Fifth Mehl:
The Supreme Lord God has stood by me and fulfilled me,
and nothing is left unfinished.
Attached to the Guru's feet, I am saved;
I contemplate and cherish the Name of the Lord, Har, Har. |1|

He is forever the Savior of His slaves.
Bestowing His Mercy, He made me His own and preserved me; like a mother or father, He cherishes me. |1|Pause|

By great good fortune, I found the True Guru,

who obliterated the path of the Messenger of Death.
My consciousness is focused on loving, devotional worship of the Lord.
One who lives in this meditation is very fortunate indeed. |2|

He sings the Ambrosial Word of the Guru's Bani,
and bathes in the dust of the feet of the Holy.
He Himself bestows His Name.
God, the Creator, saves us. |3|

The Blessed Vision of the Lord's Darshan is the support of the breath of life.
This is the perfect, pure wisdom.
The Inner-knower, the Searcher of hearts, has granted His Mercy;
slave Nanak seeks the Sanctuary of his Lord and Master. |4|8|58|

Sorat'h, Fifth Mehl:
The Perfect Guru has attached me to His feet.
I have obtained the Lord as my companion, my support, my best friend.
Wherever I go, I am happy there.
By His Kind Mercy, God united me with Himself. |1|

So sing forever the Glorious Praises of the Lord with loving devotion.
You shall obtain all the fruits of your mind's desires, and the Lord shall become the companion and the support of your soul. |1|Pause|

The Lord is the support of the breath of life.
I am the dust of the feet of the Holy people.
I am a sinner, but the Lord made me pure.
By His Kind Mercy, the Lord blessed me with His Praises. |2|

The Supreme Lord God cherishes and nurtures me.
He is always with me, the Protector of my soul.
Singing the Kirtan of the Lord's Praises day and night,
I shall not be consigned to reincarnation again. |3|

One who is blessed by the Primal Lord, the Architect of Destiny,
realizes the subtle essence of the Lord.
The Messenger of Death does not come near him.
In the Lord's Sanctuary, Nanak has found peace. |4|9|59|

Section 13 - Raag Sorat'h - Part 030

Sorat'h, Fifth Mehl:
The Perfect Guru has made me perfect.
God is totally pervading and permeating everywhere.
With joy and pleasure, I take my purifying bath.
I am a sacrifice to the Supreme Lord God. |1|

I enshrine the lotus feet of the Guru within my heart.
Not even the tiniest obstacle blocks my way; all my affairs are resolved.
|1|Pause|

Meeting with the Holy Saints, my evil-mindedness was eradicated.
All the sinners are purified.
Bathing in the sacred pool of Guru Ram Das,
all the sins one has committed are washed away. |2|

So sing forever the Glorious Praises of the Lord of the Universe;
joining the Saadh Sangat, the Company of the Holy, meditate on Him.
The fruits of your mind's desires are obtained
by meditating on the Perfect Guru within your heart. |3|

The Guru, the Lord of the World, is blissful;
chanting, meditating on the Lord of supreme bliss, He lives.
Servant Nanak meditates on the Naam, the Name of the Lord.
God has confirmed His innate nature. |4|10|60|

Sorat'h, Fifth Mehl:
In the ten directions, the clouds cover the sky like a canopy; through the
dark clouds, lightning flashes, and I am terrified.
By bed is empty, and my eyes are sleepless; my Husband Lord has gone far
away. |1|

Now, I receive no messages from Him, O mother!
When my Beloved used to go even a mile away, He would send me four
letters. |Pause|

How could I forget this Dear Beloved of mine? He is the Giver of peace, and
all virtues.
Ascending to His Mansion, I gaze upon His path, and my eyes are filled with
tears. |2|

The wall of egotism and pride separates us, but I can hear Him nearby.
There is a veil between us, like the wings of a butterfly; without being able
to see Him, He seems so far away. |3|

The Lord and Master of all has become merciful; He has dispelled all my
sufferings.
Says Nanak, when the Guru tore down the wall of egotism, then, I found
my Merciful Lord and Master. |4|

All my fears have been dispelled, O mother!
Whoever I seek, the Guru leads me to find.
The Lord, our King, is the treasure of all virtue. |Second Pause|11|61|

Sorat'h, Fifth Mehl:
The Restorer of what was taken away, the Liberator from captivity; the
Formless Lord, the Destroyer of pain.
I do not know about karma and good deeds; I do not know about Dharma
and righteous living. I am so greedy, chasing after Maya.
I go by the name of God's devotee; please, save this honor of Yours. |1|

O Dear Lord, You are the honor of the dishonored.
You make the unworthy ones worthy, O my Lord of the Universe; I am a
sacrifice to Your almighty creative power. |Pause|

Like the child, innocently making thousands of mistakes
- his father teaches him, and scolds him so many times, but still, he hugs
him close in his embrace.
Please forgive my past actions, God, and place me on Your path for the
future. |2|

The Lord, the Inner-knower, the Searcher of hearts, knows all about my
state of mind; so who else should I go to and speak to?

The Lord, the Lord of the Universe, is not pleased by mere recitation of
words; if it is pleasing to His Will, He preserves our honor.
I have seen all other shelters, but Yours alone remains for me. |3|

Section 13 - Raag Sorat'h - Part 031

Becoming kind and compassionate, God the Lord and Master Himself listens to my prayer.

He unites me in Union with the Perfect True Guru, and all the cares and anxieties of my mind are dispelled.

The Lord, Har, Har, has placed the medicine of the Naam into my mouth; servant Nanak abides in peace. |4|12|62|

Sorat'h, Fifth Mehl:

Remembering, remembering God in meditation, bliss ensues, and one is rid of all suffering and pain.

Singing the Glorious Praises of God, and meditating on Him, all my affairs are brought into harmony. |1|

Your Name is the Life of the world.

The Perfect Guru has taught me, that by meditating, I cross over the terrifying world-ocean. |Pause|

You are Your own advisor; You hear everything, God, and You do everything.

You Yourself are the Giver, and You Yourself are the Enjoyer. What can this poor creature do? |2|

Which of Your Glorious Virtues should I describe and speak of? Your value cannot be described.

I live by beholding, beholding You, O God. Your glorious greatness is wonderful and amazing! |3|

Granting His Grace, God my Lord and Master Himself saved my honor, and my intellect has been made perfect.

Forever and ever, Nanak is a sacrifice, longing for the dust of the feet of the Saints. |4|13|63|

Sorat'h, Fifth Mehl:

I bow in reverence to the Perfect Guru.

God has resolved all my affairs.

The Lord has showered me with His Mercy.

God has perfectly preserved my honor. |1|

He has become the help and support of His slave.

The Creator has achieved all my goals, and now, nothing is lacking. |Pause|

The Creator Lord has caused the pool of nectar to be constructed.
The wealth of Maya follows in my footsteps,
and now, nothing is lacking at all.
This is pleasing to my Perfect True Guru. |2|

Remembering, remembering the Merciful Lord in meditation,
all beings have become kind and compassionate to me.
Hail! Hail to the Lord of the world,
who created the perfect creation. |3|

You are my Great Lord and Master.
These blessings and wealth are Yours.
Servant Nanak has meditated on the One Lord;
he has obtained the fruitful rewards for all good deeds. |4|14|64|

Sorat'h, Fifth Mehl, Third House, Du-Padas:
One Universal Creator God. By The Grace Of The True Guru:
Bathing in the nectar tank of Ram Das,
all sins are erased.
One becomes immaculately pure, taking this cleansing bath.
The Perfect Guru has bestowed this gift. |1|

God has blessed all with peace and pleasure.
Everything is safe and sound, as we contemplate the Word of the Guru's
Shabad. |Pause|

In the Saadh Sangat, the Company of the Holy, filth is washed off.
The Supreme Lord God has become our friend and helper.
Nanak meditates on the Naam, the Name of the Lord.
He has found God, the Primal Being. |2|1|65|

Sorat'h, Fifth Mehl:
The Supreme Lord God has established that home, in which He comes to
mind.

Section 13 - Raag Sorat'h - Part 032

I found the Guru, the ocean of peace, and all my doubts were dispelled. |1|

This is the glorious greatness of the Naam.
Twenty-four hours a day, I sing His Glorious Praises.
I obtained this from the Perfect Guru. |Pause|

God's sermon is inexpressible.
His humble servants speak words of Ambrosial Nectar.
Slave Nanak has spoken.
Through the Perfect Guru, it is known. |2|2|66|

Sorat'h, Fifth Mehl:
The Guru has blessed me with peace here,
and the Guru has arranged peace and pleasure for me hereafter.
I have all treasures and comforts,
meditating on the Guru in my heart. |1|

This is the glorious greatness of my True Guru;
I have obtained the fruits of my mind's desires.
O Saints, His Glory increases day by day. |Pause|

All beings and creatures have become kind and compassionate to me; my God has made them so.
Nanak has met with the Lord of the world with intuitive ease, and with Truth, he is pleased. |2|3|67|

Sorat'h, Fifth Mehl:
The Word of the Guru's Shabad is my Saving Grace.
It is a guardian posted on all four sides around me.
My mind is attached to the Lord's Name.
The Messenger of Death has run away in shame. |1|

O Dear Lord, You are my Giver of peace.
The Perfect Lord, the Architect of Destiny, has shattered my bonds, and made my mind immaculately pure. |Pause|

O Nanak, God is eternal and imperishable.
Service to Him shall never go unrewarded.
Your slaves are in bliss;
chanting and meditating, their desires are fulfilled. |2|4|68|

Sorat'h, Fifth Mehl:

I am a sacrifice to my Guru.
He has totally preserved my honor.
I have obtained the fruits of my mind's desires.
I meditate forever on my God. |1|

O Saints, without Him, there is no other at all.
He is God, the Cause of causes. |Pause|

My God has given me His Blessing.
He has made all creatures subject to me.
Servant Nanak meditates on the Naam, the Name of the Lord,
and all his sorrows depart. |2|5|69|

Sorat'h, Fifth Mehl:
The Perfect Guru has dispelled the fever.
The unstruck melody of the sound current resounds.
God has bestowed all comforts.
In His Mercy, He Himself has given them. |1|

The True Guru Himself has eradicated the disease.
All the Sikhs and Saints are filled with joy, meditating on the Name of the
Lord, Har, Har. |Pause|

They obtain that which they ask for.
God gives to His Saints.
God saved Hargobind.
Servant Nanak speaks the Truth. |2|6|70|

Sorat'h, Fifth Mehl:
You make me do what pleases You.
I have no cleverness at all.
I am just a child - I seek Your Protection.
God Himself preserves my honor. |1|

The Lord is my King; He is my mother and father.
In Your Mercy, You cherish me; I do whatever You make me do. |Pause|

The beings and creatures are Your creation.
O God, their reins are in Your hands.

Section 13 - Raag Sorat'h - Part 033

Whatever You cause us to do, we do.
Nanak, Your slave, seeks Your Protection. |2|7|71|

Sorat'h, Fifth Mehl:
I have woven the Lord's Name into the fabric of my heart.
All my affairs are resolved.
His mind is attached to God's feet,
whose destiny is perfect. |1|

Joining the Saadh Sangat, the Company of the Holy, I meditate on the Lord.
Twenty-four hours a day, I worship and adore the Lord, Har, Har; I have
obtained the fruits of my mind's desires. |Pause|

The seeds of my past actions have sprouted.
My mind is attached to the Lord's Name.
My mind and body are absorbed into the Blessed Vision of the Lord's
Darshan.
Slave Nanak sings the Glorious Praises of the True Lord. |2|8|72|

Sorat'h, Fifth Mehl:
Meeting with the Guru, I contemplate God.
All of my affairs have been resolved.
No one speaks ill of me.
Everyone congratulates me on my victory. |1|

O Saints, I seek the True Sanctuary of the Lord and Master.
All beings and creatures are in His hands; He is God, the Inner-knower, the
Searcher of hearts. |Pause|

He has resolved all of my affairs.
God has confirmed His innate nature.
God's Name is the Purifier of sinners.
Servant Nanak is forever a sacrifice to Him. |2|9|73|

Sorat'h, Fifth Mehl:
The Supreme Lord God created and embellished him.
The Guru has saved this small child.
So celebrate and be happy, father and mother.

The Transcendent Lord is the Giver of souls. |1|

Your slaves, O Lord, focus on pure thoughts.
You preserve the honor of Your slaves, and You Yourself arrange their affairs. |Pause|

My God is so benevolent.
His Almighty Power is manifest.
Nanak has come to His Sanctuary.
He has obtained the fruits of his mind's desires. |2|10|74|

Sorat'h, FIfth Mehl:
Forever and ever, I chant the Lord's Name.
God Himself has saved my child.
He healed him from the smallpox.
My troubles have been removed through the Lord's Name. |1|

My God is forever Merciful.
He heard the prayer of His devotee, and now all beings are kind and compassionate to him. |Pause|

God is Almighty, the Cause of causes.
Remembering the Lord in meditation, all pains and sorrows vanish.
He has heard the prayer of His slave.
O Nanak, now everyone sleeps in peace. |2|11|75|

Sorat'h, Fifth Mehl:
I meditated on my Guru.
I met with Him, and returned home in joy.
This is the glorious greatness of the Naam.
Its value cannot be estimated. |1|

O Saints, worship and adore the Lord, Har, Har, Har.
Worship the Lord in adoration, and you shall obtain everything; your affairs shall all be resolved. |Pause|

He alone is attached in loving devotion to God,
who realizes his great destiny.
Servant Nanak meditates on the Naam, the Name of the Lord.
He obtains the rewards of all joys and peace. |2|12|76|

Sorat'h, Fifth Mehl:
The Transcendent Lord has given me His support.
The house of pain and disease has been demolished.
The men and women celebrate.
The Lord God, Har, Har, has extended His Mercy. |1|

Section 13 - Raag Sorat'h - Part 034

O Saints, there is peace everywhere.
The Supreme Lord God, the Perfect Transcendent Lord, is pervading everywhere. |Pause|

The Bani of His Word emanated from the Primal Lord.
It eradicates all anxiety.
The Lord is merciful, kind and compassionate.
Nanak chants the Naam, the Name of the True Lord. |2|13|77|

Sorat'h, Fifth Mehl:
Here and hereafter, He is our Savior.
God, the True Guru, is Merciful to the meek.
He Himself protects His slaves.
In each and every heart, the Beautiful Word of His Shabad resounds. |1|

I am a sacrifice to the Guru's Feet.
Day and night, with each and every breath, I remember Him; He is totally pervading and permeating all places. |Pause|

He Himself has become my help and support.
True is the support of the True Lord.
Glorious and great is devotional worship to You.
Nanak has found God's Sanctuary. |2|14|78|

Sorat'h, Fifth Mehl:
When it was pleasing to the Perfect True Guru,
then I chanted the Naam, the Name of the Pervading Lord.
The Lord of the Universe extended His Mercy to me,
and God saved my honor. |1|

The Lord's feet are forever peace-giving.

Whatever fruit one desires, he receives; his hopes shall not go in vain. |1|Pause|

That Saint, unto whom the Lord of Life, the Great Giver, extends His Mercy - he alone sings the Glorious Praises of the Lord.
His soul is absorbed in loving devotional worship; his mind is pleasing to the Supreme Lord God. |2|

Twenty-four hours a day, he chants the Praises of the Lord, and the bitter poison does not affect him.
My Creator Lord has united me with Himself, and the Holy Saints have become my companions. |3|

Taking me by the hand, He has given me everything, and blended me with Himself.
Says Nanak, everything has been perfectly resolved; I have found the Perfect True Guru. |4|15|79|

Sorat'h, Fifth Mehl:
Humility is my spiked club.
My dagger is to be the dust of all men's feet.
No evil-doer can withstand these weapons.
The Perfect Guru has given me this understanding. |1|

The Name of the Lord, Har, Har, is the support and shelter of the Saints.
One who remembers the Lord in meditation, is emancipated; millions have been saved in this way. |1|Pause|

In the Society of the Saints, I sing His Praises.
I have found this, the perfect wealth of the Lord.
Says Nanak, I have eradicated my self-conceit.
I see the Supreme Lord God everywhere. |2|16|80|

Sorat'h, Fifth Mehl:
The Perfect Guru has done it perfectly.
He blessed me with forgiveness.
I have found lasting peace and bliss.
Everywhere, the people dwell in peace. |1|

Devotional worship to the Lord is what gives rewards.

The Perfect Guru, by His Grace, gave it to me; how rare are those who know this. |Pause|

Sing the Word of the Guru's Bani, O Siblings of Destiny.
That is always rewarding and peace-giving.
Nanak has meditated on the Naam, the Name of the Lord.
He has realized his pre-ordained destiny. |2|17|81|

Sorat'h, Fifth Mehl:

Section 13 - Raag Sorat'h - Part 035

I worship and adore the Perfect Guru.
All my affairs have been resolved.
All desires have been fulfilled.
The unstruck melody of the sound current resounds. |1|

O Saints, meditating on the Lord, we obtain peace.
In the home of the Saints, celestial peace is pervading; all pain and suffering is dispelled. |1|Pause|

The Word of the Perfect Guru's Bani
is pleasing to the Mind of the Supreme Lord God.
Slave Nanak speaks
the Unspoken, immaculate sermon of the Lord. |2|18|82|

Sorat'h, Fifth Mehl:
The hungry man is not ashamed to eat.
Just so, the humble servant of the Lord sings the Glorious Praises of the Lord. |1|

Why are you so lazy in your own affairs?
Remembering Him in meditation, your face shall be radiant in the Court of the Lord; you shall find peace, forever and ever. |1|Pause|

Just as the lustful man is enticed by lust,
so is the Lord's slave pleased with the Lord's Praise. |2|

Just as the mother holds her baby close,
so does the spiritual person cherish the Naam, the Name of the Lord. |3|

This is obtained from the Perfect Guru.
Servant Nanak meditates on the Naam, the Name of the Lord. |4|19|83|

Sorat'h, Fifth Mehl:
Safe and sound, I have returned home.
The slanderer's face is blackened with ashes.
The Perfect Guru has dressed in robes of honor.
All my pains and sufferings are over. |1|

O Saints, this is the glorious greatness of the True Lord.
He has created such wonder and glory! |1|Pause|

I speak according to the Will of my Lord and Master.
God's slave chants the Word of His Bani.
O Nanak, God is the Giver of peace.
He has created the perfect creation. |2|20|84|

Sorat'h, Fifth Mehl:
Within my heart, I meditate on God.
I have returned home safe and sound.
The world has become contented.
The Perfect Guru has saved me. |1|

O Saints, my God is forever merciful.
The Lord of the world does not call His devotee to account; He protects His
children. |1|Pause|

I have enshrined the Lord's Name within my heart.
He has resolved all my affairs.
The Perfect Guru was pleased, and blessed me,
and now, Nanak shall never again suffer pain. |2|21|85|

Sorat'h, Fifth Mehl:
The Lord abides in my mind and body.
Everyone congratulates me on my victory.
This is the glorious greatness of the Perfect Guru.
His value cannot be described. |1|

I am a sacrifice to Your Name.

He alone, whom You have forgiven, O my Beloved, sings Your Praises. |1|Pause|

You are my Great Lord and Master.
You are the support of the Saints.
Nanak has entered God's Sanctuary.
The faces of the slanderers are blackened with ashes. |2|22|86|

Sorat'h, Fifth Mehl:
Peace in this world, O my friends,
and bliss in the world hereafter - God has given me this.
The Transcendent Lord has arranged these arrangements;
I shall never waver again. |1|

My mind is pleased with the True Lord Master.
I know the Lord to be pervading all. |1|Pause|

Section 13 - Raag Sorat'h - Part 036

All beings are Yours, O Merciful Lord.
You cherish Your devotees.
Your glorious greatness is wonderful and marvellous.
Nanak ever meditates on the Naam, the Name of the Lord. |2|23|87|

Sorat'h, Fifth Mehl:
The Lord is always with me.
The Messenger of Death does not approach me.
God holds me close in His embrace, and protects me.
True are the Teachings of the True Guru. |1|

The Perfect Guru has done it perfectly.
He has beaten and driven off my enemies, and given me, His slave, the sublime understanding of the neutral mind. |1|Pause|

God has blessed all places with prosperity.
I have returned again safe and sound.
Nanak has entered God's Sanctuary.
It has eradicated all disease. |2|24|88|

Sorat'h, Fifth Mehl:

The True Guru is the Giver of all peace and comfort - seek His Sanctuary.
Beholding the Blessed Vision of His Darshan, bliss ensues, pain is dispelled, and one sings the Lord's Praises. |1|

Drink in the sublime essence of the Lord, O Siblings of Destiny.
Chant the Naam, the Name of the Lord; worship the Naam in adoration, and enter the Sanctuary of the Perfect Guru. |Pause|

Only one who has such pre-ordained destiny receives it; he alone becomes perfect, O Siblings of Destiny.
Nanak's prayer, O Dear God, is to remain lovingly absorbed in the Naam. |2|25|89|

Sorat'h, Fifth Mehl:
The Lord is the Cause of Causes, the Inner-knower, the Searcher of hearts; He preserves the honor of His servant.
He is hailed and congratulated throughout the world, and he tastes the sublime essence of the Word of the Guru's Shabad. |1|

Dear God, Lord of the world, You are my only support.
You are all-powerful, the Giver of Sanctuary; twenty-four hours a day, I meditate on You. |Pause|

That humble being, who vibrates upon You, O God, is not afflicted by anxiety.
Attached to the Feet of the True Guru, his fear is dispelled, and within his mind, he sings the Glorious Praises of the Lord. |2|

He abides in celestial peace and utter ecstasy; the True Guru has comforted him.
He has returned home victorious, with honor, and his hopes have been fulfilled. |3|

Perfect are the Teachings of the Perfect Guru; Perfect are the actions of God.
Grasping hold of the Guru's feet, Nanak has crossed over the terrifying world-ocean, chanting the Name of the Lord, Har, Har. |4|26|90|

Sorat'h, Fifth Mehl:

Becoming merciful, the Destroyer of the pains of the poor has Himself devised all devices.
In an instant, He has saved His humble servant; the Perfect Guru has cut away his bonds. |1|

O my mind, meditate forever on the Guru, the Lord of the Universe.
All illness shall depart from this body, and you shall obtain the fruits of your mind's desires. |Pause|

God created all beings and creatures; He is lofty, inaccessible and infinite.
In the Saadh Sangat, the Company of the Holy, Nanak meditates on the Naam, the Name of the Lord; his face is radiant in the Court of the Lord. |2|27|91|

Sorat'h, Fifth Mehl:
I meditate in remembrance on my Lord.
Day and night, I ever meditate on Him.
He gave me His hand, and protected me.
I drink in the most sublime essence of the Lord's Name. |1|

Section 13 - Raag Sorat'h - Part 037

I am a sacrifice to my Guru.
God, the Great Giver, the Perfect One, has become merciful to me, and now, all are kind to me. |Pause|

Servant Nanak has entered His Sanctuary.
He has perfectly preserved his honor.
All suffering has been dispelled.
So enjoy peace, O my Siblings of Destiny! |2|28|92|

Sorat'h, Fifth Mehl:
Hear my prayer, O my Lord and Master; all beings and creatures were created by You.
You preserve the honor of Your Name, O Lord, Cause of causes. |1|

O Dear God, Beloved, please, make me Your own.
Whether good or bad, I am Yours. |Pause|

The Almighty Lord and Master heard my prayer; cutting away my bonds, He has adorned me.
He dressed me in robes of honor, and blended His servant with Himself; Nanak is revealed in glory throughout the world. |2|29|93|

Sorat'h, Fifth Mehl:
All beings and creatures are subservient to all those who serve in the Lord's Court.
Their God made them His own, and carried them across the terrifying world-ocean. |1|

He resolves all the affairs of His Saints.
He is merciful to the meek, kind and compassionate, the ocean of kindness, my Perfect Lord and Master. |Pause|

I am asked to come and be seated, everywhere I go, and I lack nothing.
The Lord blesses His humble devotee with robes of honor; O Nanak, the Glory of God is manifest. |2|30|94|

Sorat'h, Ninth Mehl:
One Universal Creator God. By The Grace Of The True Guru:
O mind, love the Lord.
With your ears, hear the Glorious Praises of the Lord of the Universe, and with your tongue, sing His song. |1|Pause|

Join the Saadh Sangat, the Company of the Holy, and meditate in remembrance on the Lord; even a sinner like yourself will become pure.
Death is on the prowl, with its mouth wide open, friend. |1|

Today or tomorrow, eventually it will seize you; understand this in your consciousness.
Says Nanak, meditate, and vibrate upon the Lord; this opportunity is slipping away! |2|1|

Sorat'h, Ninth Mehl:
The mind remains in the mind.
He does not meditate on the Lord, nor does he perform service at sacred shrines, and so death seizes him by the hair. |1|Pause|

Wife, friends, children, carriages, property, total wealth, the entire world

- know that all of these things are false. The Lord's meditation alone is true. |1|

Wandering, wandering around for so many ages, he has grown weary, and finally, he obtained this human body.
Says Nanak, this is the opportunity to meet the Lord; why don't you remember Him in meditation? |2|2|

Sorat'h, Ninth Mehl:
O mind, what evil-mindedness have you developed?
You are engrossed in the pleasures of other men's wives, and slander; you have not worshipped the Lord at all. |1|Pause|

You do not know the way to liberation, but you run all around chasing wealth.

Section 13 - Raag Sorat'h - Part 038

In the end, nothing shall go along with you; you have entrapped yourself in vain. |1|

You have not meditated or vibrated upon the Lord; you have not served the Guru, or His humble servants; spiritual wisdom has not welled up within you.
The Immaculate Lord is within your heart, and yet you search for Him in the wilderness. |2|

You have wandered through many many births; you are exhausted but have still not found a way out of this endless cycle.
Now that you have obtained this human body, meditate on the Lord's Feet; Nanak advises with this advice. |3|3|

Sorat'h, Ninth Mehl:
O mind, contemplate the Sanctuary of God.
Meditating on Him in remembrance, Ganika the prostitute was saved; enshrine His Praises within your heart. |1|Pause|

Meditating on Him in remembrance, Dhroo became immortal, and obtained the state of fearlessness.

The Lord and Master removes suffering in this way - why have you forgotten Him? |1|

As soon as the elephant took to the protective Sanctuary of the Lord, the ocean of mercy, he escaped from the crocodile.
How much can I describe the Glorious Praises of the Naam? Whoever chants the Lord's Name, his bonds are broken. |2|

Ajaamal, known throughout the world as a sinner, was redeemed in an instant.
Says Nanak, remember the Chintaamani, the jewel which fulfills all desires, and you too shall be carried across and saved. |3|4|

Sorat'h, Ninth Mehl:
What efforts should the mortal make,
to attain devotional worship of the Lord, and eradicate the fear of death? |1|Pause|

Which actions, what sort of knowledge, and what religion - what Dharma should one practice?
What Name of the Guru should one remember in meditation, to cross over the terrifying world-ocean? |1|

In this Dark Age of Kali Yuga, the Name of the One Lord is the treasure of mercy; chanting it, one obtains salvation.
No other religion is comparable to this; so speak the Vedas. |2|

He is beyond pain and pleasure, forever unattached; He is called the Lord of the world.
He dwells deep within your inner self, O Nanak, like the image in a mirror. |3|5|

Sorat'h, Ninth Mehl:
O mother, how can I see the Lord of the world?
In the utter darkness of emotional attachment and spiritual ignorance, my mind remains entangled. |1|Pause|

Deluded by doubt, I have wasted my whole life; I have not obtained a stable intellect.

I remain under the influence of corrupting sins, night and day, and I have not renounced wickedness. |1|

I never joined the Saadh Sangat, the Company of the Holy, and I did not sing the Kirtan of God's Praises.
O servant Nanak, I have no virtues at all; keep me in Your Sanctuary, Lord. |2|6|

Sorat'h, Ninth Mehl:
O mother, my mind is out of control.
Night and day, it runs after sin and corruption. How can I restrain it? |1|Pause|

He listens to the teachings of the Vedas, the Puraanas and the Simritees, but he does not enshrine them in his heart, even for an instant.
Engrossed in the wealth and women of others, his life passes away uselessly. |1|

He has gone insane with the wine of Maya, and does not understand even a bit of spiritual wisdom.
Deep within his heart, the Immaculate Lord dwells, but he does not know this secret. |2|

Section 13 - Raag Sorat'h - Part 039

When I came to the Sanctuary of the Holy Saints, all my evil-mindedness was dispelled.
Then, O Nanak, I remembered the Chintaamani, the jewel which fulfills all desires, and the noose of Death was snapped. |3|7|

Sorat'h, Ninth Mehl:
O man, grasp this Truth firmly in your soul.
The whole world is just like a dream; it will pass away in an instant. |1|Pause|

Like a wall of sand, built up and plastered with great care, which does not last even a few days,
just so are the pleasures of Maya. Why are you entangled in them, you ignorant fool? |1|

Understand this today - it is not yet too late! Chant and vibrate the Name of the Lord.
Says Nanak, this is the subtle wisdom of the Holy Saints, which I proclaim out loud to you. |2|8|

Sorat'h, Ninth Mehl:
In this world, I have not found any true friend.
The whole world is attached to its own pleasures, and when trouble comes, no one is with you. |1|Pause|

Wives, friends, children and relatives - all are attached to wealth.
When they see a poor man, they all forsake his company and run away. |1|

So what should I say to this crazy mind, which is affectionately attached to them?
The Lord is the Master of the meek, the Destroyer of all fears, and I have forgotten to praise Him. |2|

Like a dog's tail, which will never straighten out, the mind will not change, no matter how many things are tried.
Says Nanak, please, Lord, uphold the honor of Your innate nature; I chant Your Name. |3|9|

Sorat'h, Ninth Mehl:
O mind, you have not accepted the Guru's Teachings.
What is the use of shaving your head, and wearing saffron robes? |1|Pause|

Abandoning Truth, you cling to falsehood; your life is uselessly wasting away.
Practicing hypocrisy, you fill your belly, and then sleep like an animal. |1|

You do not know the Way of the Lord's meditation; you have sold yourself into Maya's hands.
The madman remains entangled in vice and corruption; he has forgotten the jewel of the Naam. |2|

He remains thoughtless, not thinking of the Lord of the Universe; his life is uselessly passing away.

Says Nanak, O Lord, please, confirm your innate nature; this mortal is continually making mistakes. |3|10|

Sorat'h, Ninth Mehl:
That man, who in the midst of pain, does not feel pain,
who is not affected by pleasure, affection or fear, and who looks alike upon gold and dust;|1|Pause|

Who is not swayed by either slander or praise, nor affected by greed, attachment or pride;
who remains unaffected by joy and sorrow, honor and dishonor;|1|

who renounces all hopes and desires and remains desireless in the world;
who is not touched by sexual desire or anger - within his heart, God dwells. |2|

That man, blessed by Guru's Grace, understands this way.
O Nanak, he merges with the Lord of the Universe, like water with water. |3|11|

Section 13 - Raag Sorat'h - Part 040

Sorat'h, Ninth Mehl:
O dear friend, know this in your mind.
The world is entangled in its own pleasures; no one is for anyone else. |1|Pause|

In good times, many come and sit together, surrounding you on all four sides.
But when hard times come, they all leave, and no one comes near you. |1|

Your wife, whom you love so much, and who has remained ever attached to you,
runs away crying, "Ghost! Ghost!", as soon as the swan-soul leaves this body. |2|

This is the way they act - those whom we love so much.
At the very last moment, O Nanak, no one is any use at all, except the Dear Lord. |3|12|139|

Sorat'h, First Mehl, First House, Ashtapadees, Chau-Tukas:

One Universal Creator God. By The Grace Of The True Guru:

I am not torn by duality, because I do not worship any other than the Lord; I do not visit tombs or crematoriums.

I do not enter the houses of strangers, engrossed in desire. The Naam, the Name of the Lord, has satisfied my desires.

Deep within my heart, the Guru has shown me the home of my being, and my mind is imbued with peace and poise, O Siblings of Destiny.

You Yourself are all-knowing, and You Yourself are all-seeing; You alone bestow intelligence, O Lord. |1|

My mind is detached, imbued with detachment; the Word of the Shabad has pierced my mind, O my mother.

God's Light shines continually within the nucleus of my deepest self; I am lovingly attached to the Bani, the Word of the True Lord Master. |Pause|

Countless detached renunciates talk of detachment and renunciation, but he alone is a true renunciate, who is pleasing to the Lord Master.

The Word of the Shabad is ever in his heart; he is absorbed in the Fear of God, and he works to serve the Guru.

He remembers the One Lord, his mind does not waver, and he restrains its wanderings.

He is intoxicated with celestial bliss, and is ever imbued with the Lord's Love; he sings the Glorious Praises of the True Lord. |2|

The mind is like the wind, but if it comes to rest in peace, even for an instant, then he shall abide in the peace of the Name, O Siblings of Destiny.

His tongue, eyes and ears are imbued with Truth; O Lord, You quench the fires of desire.

In hope, the renunciate remains free of hopes; in the home of his own inner self, he is absorbed in the trance of deep meditation.

He remains content, satisfied with the charity of the Naam; he drinks in the Ambrosial Amrit with ease. |3|

There is no renunciation in duality, as long as there is even a particle of duality.

The whole world is Yours, Lord; You alone are the Giver. There is not any other, O Siblings of Destiny.

The self-willed manmukh dwells in misery forever, while the Lord bestows greatness upon the Gurmukh.

God is infinite, endless, inaccessible and unfathomable; His worth cannot be described. |4|

The consciousness in deep Samaadhi, the Supreme Being, the Lord of the three worlds - these are Your Names, Lord.
The creatures born into this world have their destiny inscribed upon their foreheads; they experience according to their destinies.
The Lord Himself causes them to do good and bad deeds; He Himself makes them steadfast in devotional worship.
The filth of their mind and mouth is washed off when they live in the Fear of God; the inaccessible Lord Himself blesses them with spiritual wisdom. |5|

Section 13 - Raag Sorat'h - Part 041

Only those who taste it know its sweet taste, like the mute, who eats the candy, and only smiles.
How can I describe the indescribable, O Siblings of Destiny? I shall follow His Will forever.
If one meets with the Guru, the Generous Giver, then he understands; those who have no Guru cannot understand this.
As the Lord causes us to act, so do we act, O Siblings of Destiny. What other clever tricks can anyone try? |6|

Some are deluded by doubt, while others are imbued with devotional worship; Your play is infinite and endless.
As You engage them, they receive the fruits of their rewards; You alone are the One who issues Your Commands.
I would serve You, if anything were my own; my soul and body are Yours.
One who meets with the True Guru, by His Grace, takes the Support of the Ambrosial Naam. |7|

He dwells in the heavenly realms, and his virtues radiantly shine forth; meditation and spiritual wisdom are found in virtue.
The Naam is pleasing to his mind; he speaks it, and causes others to speak it as well. He speaks the essential essence of wisdom.
The Word of the Shabad is his Guru and spiritual teacher, profound and unfathomable; without the Shabad, the world is insane.
He is a perfect renunciate, naturally at ease, O Nanak, whose mind is pleased with the True Lord. |8|1|

Sorat'h, First Mehl, Ti-Tukas:
Hope and desire are entrapments, O Siblings of Destiny. Religious rituals and ceremonies are traps.
Because of good and bad deeds, one is born into the world, O Siblings of Destiny; forgetting the Naam, the Name of the Lord, he is ruined.
This Maya is the enticer of the world, O Siblings of Destiny; all such actions are corrupt. |1|

Listen, O ritualistic Pandit:
that religious ritual which produces happiness, O Siblings of Destiny, is contemplation of the essence of the soul. |Pause|

You may stand and recite the Shaastras and the Vedas, O Siblings of Destiny, but these are just worldly actions.
Filth cannot be washed away by hypocrisy, O Siblings of Destiny; the filth of corruption and sin is within you.
This is how the spider is destroyed, O Siblings of Destiny, by falling head-long in its own web. |2|

So many are destroyed by their own evil-mindedness, O Siblings of Destiny; in the love of duality, they are ruined.
Without the True Guru, the Name is not obtained, O Siblings of Destiny; without the Name, doubt does not depart.
If one serves the True Guru, then he obtains peace, O Siblings of Destiny; his comings and goings are ended. |3|

True celestial peace comes from the Guru, O Siblings of Destiny; the immaculate mind is absorbed into the True Lord.
One who serves the Guru, understands, O Siblings of Destiny; without the Guru, the way is not found.
What can anyone do, with greed within? O Siblings of Destiny, by telling lies, they eat poison. |4|

O Pandit, by churning cream, butter is produced.
By churning water, you shall only see water, O Siblings of Destiny; this world is like that.
Without the Guru, he is ruined by doubt, O Siblings of Destiny; the unseen Divine Lord is in each and every heart. |5|

This world is like a thread of cotton, O Siblings of Destiny, which Maya has tied on all ten sides.

Without the Guru, the knots cannot be untied, O Siblings of Destiny; I am so tired of religious rituals.

This world is deluded by doubt, O Siblings of Destiny; no one can say anything about it. |6|

Meeting with the Guru, the Fear of God comes to abide in the mind; to die in the Fear of God is one's true destiny.

In the Court of the Lord, the Naam is far superior to ritualistic cleansing baths, charity and good deeds, O Siblings of Destiny.

Section 13 - Raag Sorat'h - Part 042

One who implants the Naam within himself, through the Guru's halter - O Siblings of Destiny, the Lord dwells in his mind, and he is free of hypocrisy. |7|

This body is the jeweller's shop, O Siblings of Destiny; the incomparable Naam is the merchandise.

The merchant secures this merchandise, O Siblings of Destiny, by contemplating the Word of the Guru's Shabad.

Blessed is the merchant, O Nanak, who meets the Guru, and engages in this trade. |8|2|

Sorat'h, First Mehl:

Those who serve the True Guru, O Beloved, their companions are saved as well.

No one blocks their way, O Beloved, and the Lord's Ambrosial Nectar is on their tongue.

Without the Fear of God, they are so heavy that they sink and drown, O Beloved; but the Lord, casting His Glance of Grace, carries them across. |1|

I ever praise You, O Beloved, I ever sing Your Praises.

Without the boat, one is drowned in the sea of fear, O Beloved; how can I reach the distant shore? |1|Pause|

I praise the Praiseworthy Lord, O Beloved; there is no other one to praise.

Those who praise my God are good, O Beloved; they are imbued with the Word of the Shabad, and His Love.

If I join them, O Beloved, I can churn the essence and so find joy. |2|

The gateway to honor is Truth, O Beloved; it bears the Insignia of the True Name of the Lord.
We come into the world, and we depart, with our destiny written and pre-ordained, O Beloved; realize the Command of the Commander.
Without the Guru, this Command is not understood, O Beloved; True is the Power of the True Lord. |3|

By His Command, we are conceived, O Beloved, and by His Command, we grow in the womb.
By His Command, we are born, O Beloved, head-first, and upside-down.
The Gurmukh is honored in the Court of the Lord, O Beloved; he departs after resolving his affairs. |4|

By His Command, one comes into the world, O Beloved, and by His Will, he goes.
By His Will, some are bound and gagged and driven away, O Beloved; the self-willed manmukhs suffer their punishment.
By His Command, the Word of the Shabad, is realized, O Beloved, and one goes to the Court of the Lord robed in honor. |5|

By His Command, some accounts are accounted for, O Beloved; by His Command, some suffer in egotism and duality.
By His Command, one wanders in reincarnation, O Beloved; deceived by sins and demerits, he cries out in his suffering.
If he comes to realize the Command of the Lord's Will, O Beloved, then he is blessed with Truth and Honor. |6|

It is so difficult to speak it, O Beloved; how can we speak, and hear, the True Name?
I am a sacrifice to those who praise the Lord, O Beloved.
I have obtained the Name, and I am satisfied, O Beloved; by His Grace, I am united in His Union. |7|

If my body were to become the paper, O Beloved, and my mind the inkpot; and if my tongue became the pen, O Beloved, I would write, and contemplate, the Glorious Praises of the True Lord.
Blessed is that scribe, O Nanak, who writes the True Name, and enshrines it within his heart. |8|3|

Sorat'h, First Mehl, Du-Tukas:
You are the Giver of virtue, O Immaculate Lord, but my mind is not immaculate, O Siblings of Destiny.
I am a worthless sinner, O Siblings of Destiny; virtue is obtained from You alone, Lord. |1|

O my Beloved Creator Lord, You create, and You behold.
I am a hypocritical sinner, O Siblings of Destiny. Bless my mind and body with Your Name, O Lord. |Pause|

Section 13 - Raag Sorat'h - Part 043

The poisonous Maya has enticed the consciousness, O Siblings of Destiny; through clever tricks, one loses his honor.
The True Lord and Master abides in the consciousness, O Siblings of Destiny, if the Guru's spiritual wisdom permeates it. |2|

Beautiful, beautiful, the Lord is called, O Siblings of Destiny; beautiful, like the deep crimson color of the poppy.
If man loves the Lord with detachment, O Siblings of Destiny, he is judged to be true and infallible in the Lord's court and home. |3|

You are pervading the realms of the underworld and the heavenly skies; Your wisdom and glories are in each and every heart.
Meeting with the Guru, one finds peace, O Siblings of Destiny, and pride is dispelled from the mind. |4|

Scrubbing with water, the body can be cleaned, O Siblings of Destiny, but the body becomes dirty again.
Bathing in the supreme essence of spiritual wisdom, O Siblings of Destiny, the mind and body become pure. |5|

Why worship gods and goddesses, O Siblings of Destiny? What can we ask of them? What can they give us?

The stone gods are washed with water, O Siblings of Destiny, but they just sink in the water. |6|

Without the Guru, the unseen Lord cannot be seen, O Siblings of Destiny; the world is drowning, having lost its honor.
Greatness is in the hands of my Lord and Master, O Siblings of Destiny; as He is pleased, He gives. |7|

That soul-bride, who talks sweetly and speaks the Truth, O Siblings of Destiny, becomes pleasing to her Husband Lord.
Pierced by His Love, she abides in Truth, O Siblings of Destiny, deeply imbued with the Lord's Name. |8|

Everyone calls God his own, O Siblings of Destiny, but the all-knowing Lord is known only through the Guru.
Those who are pierced by His Love are saved, O Siblings of Destiny; they bear the Insignia of the True Word of the Shabad. |9|

A large pile of firewood, O Siblings of Destiny, will burn if a small fire is applied.
In the same way, if the Naam, the Name of the Lord, dwells in the heart for a moment, even for an instant, O Siblings of Destiny, then one meets the Lord with ease, O Nanak. |10|4|

Sorat'h, Third Mehl, First House, Ti-Tukas:
One Universal Creator God. By The Grace Of The True Guru:
You always preserve the honor of Your devotees, O Dear Lord; You have protected them from the very beginning of time.
You protected Your servant Prahlaad, O Dear Lord, and annihilated Harnaakhash.
The Gurmukhs place their faith in the Dear Lord, but the self-willed manmukhs are deluded by doubt. |1|

O Dear Lord, this is Your Glory.
You preserve the honor of Your devotees, O Lord Master; Your devotees seek Your Sanctuary. |Pause|

The Messenger of Death cannot touch Your devotees; death cannot even approach them.
The Name of the Lord alone abides in their minds; through the Naam, the Name of the Lord, they find liberation.
Wealth and all the spiritual powers of the Siddhis fall at the feet of the Lord's devotees; they obtain peace and poise from the Guru. |2|

The self-willed manmukhs have no faith; they are filled with greed and self-interest.

They are not Gurmukh - they do not understand the Word of the Shabad in their hearts; they do not love the Naam, the Name of the Lord.

Their masks of falsehood and hypocrisy shall fall off; the self-willed manmukhs speak with insipid words. |3|

You are pervading through Your devotees, O Dear God; through Your devotees, You are known.

All the people are enticed by Maya; they are Yours, Lord - You alone are the Architect of Destiny.

Section 13 - Raag Sorat'h - Part 044

Overcoming my egotism and quieting the desires within my mind, I have come to realize the Word of the Guru's Shabad. |4|

God automatically does the work of those who love the Name of the Lord.

By Guru's Grace, he ever dwells in their minds, and He resolves all their affairs.

Whoever challenges them is destroyed; they have the Lord God as their Savior. |5|

Without serving the True Guru, no one finds the Lord; the self-willed manmukhs die crying out in pain.

They come and go, and find no place of rest; in pain and suffering, they perish.

But one who becomes Gurmukh drinks in the Ambrosial Nectar, and is easily absorbed in the True Name. |6|

Without serving the True Guru, one cannot escape reincarnation, even by performing numerous rituals.

Those who read the Vedas, and argue and debate without the Lord, lose their honor.

True is the True Guru, and True is the Word of His Bani; in the Guru's Sanctuary, one is saved. |7|

Those whose minds are filled with the Lord are judged as true in the Court of the Lord; they are hailed as true in the True Court.

Their praises echo throughout the ages, and no one can erase them.
Nanak is forever a sacrifice to those who enshrine the Lord within their hearts. |8|1|

Sorat'h, Third Mehl, Du-Tukas:
He Himself forgives the worthless, O Siblings of Destiny; He commits them to the service of the True Guru.
Service to the True Guru is sublime, O Siblings of Destiny; through it, one's consciousness is attached to the Lord's Name. |1|

The Dear Lord forgives, and unites with Himself.
I am a sinner, totally without virtue, O Siblings of Destiny; the Perfect True Guru has blended me. |Pause|

So many, so many sinners have been forgiven, O beloved one, by contemplating the True Word of the Shabad.
They got on board the boat of the True Guru, who carried them across the terrifying world-ocean, O Siblings of Destiny. |2|

I have been transformed from rusty iron into gold, O Siblings of Destiny, united in Union with the Guru, the Philosopher's Stone.
Eliminating my self-conceit, the Name has come to dwell within my mind, O Siblings of Destiny; my light has merged in the Light. |3|

I am a sacrifice, I am a sacrifice, O Siblings of Destiny, I am forever a sacrifice to my True Guru.
He has given me the treasure of the Naam; O Siblings of Destiny, through the Guru's Teachings, I am absorbed in celestial bliss. |4|

Without the Guru, celestial peace is not produced, O Siblings of Destiny; go and ask the spiritual teachers about this.
Serve the True Guru forever, O Siblings of Destiny, and eradicate self-conceit from within. |5|

Under Guru's Instruction, the Fear of God is produced, O Siblings of Destiny; true and excellent are the deeds done in the Fear of God.
Then, one is blessed with the treasure of the Lord's Love, O Siblings of Destiny, and the Support of the True Name. |6|

I fall at the feet of those who serve their True Guru, O Siblings of Destiny.

I have fulfilled my life, O Siblings of Destiny, and my family has been saved as well. |7|

The True Word of the Guru's Bani, and the True Word of the Shabad, O Siblings of Destiny, are obtained only by Guru's Grace.
O Nanak, with the Name of the Lord abiding in one's mind, no obstacles stand in one's way, O Siblings of Destiny. |8|2|

Section 13 - Raag Sorat'h - Part 045

Sorat'h, Third Mehl:
The Dear Lord is realized through the Word of His Shabad, O Siblings of Destiny, which is found only by perfect destiny.
The happy soul-brides are forever in peace, O Siblings of Destiny; night and day, they are attuned to the Lord's Love. |1|

O Dear Lord, You Yourself color us in Your Love.
Sing, continually sing His Praises, imbued with His Love, O Siblings of Destiny; be in love with the Lord. |Pause|

Work to serve the Guru, O Siblings of Destiny; abandon self-conceit, and focus your consciousness.
You shall be in peace forever, and you shall not suffer in pain any longer, O Siblings of Destiny; the Lord Himself shall come and abide in your mind. |2|

She who does not know the Will of her Husband Lord, O Siblings of Destiny, is an ill-mannered and bitter bride.
She does things with a stubborn mind, O Siblings of Destiny; without the Name, she is false. |3|

They alone sing the Lord's Praises, who have such pre-ordained destiny written upon their foreheads, O Siblings of Destiny; through the Love of the True Lord, they find detachment.
Night and day, they are imbued with His Love; they utter His Glorious Praises, O Siblings of Destiny, and they lovingly focus their consciousness on the Fearless Guru. |4|

He kills and revives all, O Siblings of Destiny; serve Him, day and night.
How can we forget Him from our minds, O Siblings of Destiny? His gifts are glorious and great. |5|

The self-willed manmukh is filthy and double-minded, O Siblings of Destiny; the finds no place of rest in the Court of the Lord.

But if she becomes Gurmukh, then she chants the Glorious Praises of the Lord, O Siblings of Destiny; the meets her True Beloved, and merges in Him. |6|

In this life, she has not focused her consciousness on the Lord, O Siblings of Destiny; how can she show her face when she leaves?

In spite of the warning calls which were sounded, she has been plundered, O Siblings of Destiny; she yearned only for corruption. |7|

Those who dwell upon the Naam, O Siblings of Destiny, their bodies are ever peaceful and tranquil.

O Nanak, dwell upon the Naam; the Lord is infinite, virtuous and unfathomable, O Siblings of Destiny. |8|3|

Sorat'h, Fifth Mehl, First House, Ashtapadees:

One Universal Creator God. By The Grace Of The True Guru:

The One who created the whole world, O Siblings of Destiny, is the Almighty Lord, the Cause of causes.

He fashioned the soul and the body, O Siblings of Destiny, by His own power.

How can He be described? How can He be seen, O Siblings of Destiny? The Creator is One; He is indescribable.

Praise the Guru, the Lord of the Universe, O Siblings of Destiny; through Him, the essence is known. |1|

O my mind, meditate on the Lord, the Lord God.

He blesses His servant with the gift of the Naam; He is the Destroyer of pain and suffering. |Pause|

Everything is in His home, O Siblings of Destiny; His warehouse is overflowing with the nine treasures.

His worth cannot be estimated, O Siblings of Destiny; He is lofty, inaccessible and infinite.

He cherishes all beings and creatures, O Siblings of Destiny; he continually takes care of them.

So meet with the Perfect True Guru, O Siblings of Destiny, and merge in the Word of the Shabad. |2|

Adoring the feet of the True Guru, O Siblings of Destiny, doubt and fear are dispelled.
Joining the Society of the Saints, cleanse your mind, O Siblings of Destiny, and dwell in the Name of the Lord.
The darkness of ignorance shall be dispelled, O Siblings of Destiny, and the lotus of your heart shall blossom forth.
By the Guru's Word, peace wells up, O Siblings of Destiny; all fruits are with the True Guru. |3|

Section 13 - Raag Sorat'h - Part 046

Give up your sense of mine and yours, O Siblings of Destiny, and become the dust of the feet of all.
In each and every heart, God is contained, O Siblings of Destiny; He sees, and hears, and is ever-present with us.
On that day when one forgets the Supreme Lord God, O Siblings of Destiny, on that day, one ought to die crying out in pain.
He is the all-powerful Cause of Causes, O Siblings of Destiny; he is totally filled with all powers. |4|

The Love of the Name is the greatest treasure, O Siblings of Destiny; through it, emotional attachment to Maya is dispelled.
If it is pleasing to His Will, then He unites us in His Union, O Siblings of Destiny; the Naam, the Name of the Lord, comes to abide in the mind.
The heart-lotus of the Gurmukh blossoms forth, O Siblings of Destiny, and the heart is illumined.
The Glory of God has been revealed, O Siblings of Destiny, and the earth and sky have blossomed forth. |5|

The Perfect Guru has blessed me with contentment, O Siblings of Destiny; day and night, I remain attached to the Lord's Love.
My tongue continually chants the Lord's Name, O Siblings of Destiny; this is the true taste, and the object of human life.
Listening with my ears, I hear and so I live, O Siblings of Destiny; I have obtained the unchanging, unmoving state.
That soul,which does not place its faith in the Lord shall burn, O Siblings of Destiny. |6|

My Lord and Master has so many virtues, O Siblings of Destiny; I am a sacrifice to Him.

He nurtures even the most worthless, O Siblings of Destiny, and gives home to the homeless.

He gives us nourishment with each and every breath, O Siblings of Destiny; His Name is everlasting.

One who meets with the True Guru, O Siblings of Destiny, does so only by perfect destiny. |7|

Without Him, I cannot live, even for an instant, O Siblings of Destiny; He is totally filled with all powers.

With every breath and morsel of food, I will not forget Him, O Siblings of Destiny; I behold Him ever-present.

In the Saadh Sangat, the Company of the Holy, I meet Him, O Siblings of Destiny; He is totally pervading and permeating everywhere.

Those who do not embrace love for the Lord, O Siblings of Destiny, always die crying out in pain. |8|

Grasping hold of the hem of His robe, O Siblings of Destiny, we are carried across the world-ocean of fear and pain.

By His Glance of Grace, He has blessed us, O Siblings of Destiny; He shall be with us until the very end.

My mind and body are soothed and calmed, O Siblings of Destiny, nourished by the food of the Naam.

Nanak has entered His Sanctuary, O Siblings of Destiny; the Lord is the Destroyer of sins. |9|1|

Sorat'h, Fifth Mehl:

The womb of the mother is an ocean of pain, O Beloved; even there, the Lord causes His Name to be chanted.

When he emerges, he finds corruption pervading everywhere, O Beloved, and he becomes increasingly attached to Maya.

One whom the Lord blesses with His kind favor, O Beloved, meets the Perfect Guru.

He worships the Lord in adoration with each and every breath, O Beloved; he is lovingly attached to the Lord's Name. |1|

You are the support of my mind and body, O Beloved; You are the support of my mind and body.

There is no other Creator except for You, O Beloved; You alone are the Inner-knower, the Searcher of hearts. |Pause|

After wandering in doubt for millions of incarnations, he comes into the world, O Beloved; for uncounted lifetimes, he has suffered in pain.
He has forgotten his True Lord and Master, O Beloved, and so he suffers terrible punishment.
Those who meet with the Perfect True Guru, O Beloved, are attached to the True Name.

Section 13 - Raag Sorat'h - Part 047

We are saved by following those, O Beloved, who seek the Sanctuary of the True Lord. |2|

He thinks that his food is so sweet, O Beloved, but it makes his body ill.
It turns out to be bitter, O Beloved, and it produces only sadness.
The Lord leads him astray in the enjoyment of pleasures, O Beloved, and so his sense of separation does not depart.
Those who meet the Guru are saved, O Beloved; this is their pre-ordained destiny. |3|

He is filled with longing for Maya, O Beloved, and so the Lord does not ever come into his mind.
Those who forget You, O Supreme Lord Master, their bodies turn to dust.
They cry out and scream horribly, O Beloved, but their torment does not end.
Those who meet the Guru, and reform themselves, O Beloved, their capital remains intact. |4|

As far as possible, do not associate with the faithless cynics, O Beloved.
Meeting with them, the Lord is forgotten, O Beloved, and you rise and depart with a blackened face.
The self-willed manmukh finds no rest or shelter, O Beloved; in the Court of the Lord, they are punished.
Those who meet with the Guru, and reform themselves, O Beloved, their affairs are resolved. |5|

One may have thousands of clever tricks and techniques of austere self-discipline, O Beloved, but not even one of them will go with him.

Those who turn their backs on the Lord of the Universe, O Beloved, their families are stained with disgrace.

They do not realize that they do have Him , O Beloved; falsehood will not go with them.

Those who meet with the True Guru, O Beloved, dwell upon the True Name. |6|

When the Lord casts His Glance of Grace, O Beloved, one is blessed with Truth, contentment, wisdom and meditation.

Night and day, he sings the Kirtan of the Lord's Praises, O Beloved, totally filled with Ambrosial Nectar.

He crosses over the sea of pain, O Beloved, and swims across the terrifying world-ocean.

One who is pleasing to His Will, He unites with Himself, O Beloved; he is forever true. |7|

The all-powerful Divine Lord is compassionate, O Beloved; He is the Support of His devotees.

I seek His Sanctuary, O Beloved; He is the Inner-knower, the Searcher of hearts.

He has adorned me in this world and the next, O Beloved; He has placed the Emblem of Truth upon my forehead.

I shall never forget that God, O Beloved; Nanak is forever a sacrifice to Him. |8|2|

Sorat'h, Fifth Mehl, Second House, Ashtapadees:

One Universal Creator God. By The Grace Of The True Guru:

They read scriptures, and contemplate the Vedas; they practice the inner cleansing techniques of Yoga, and control of the breath.

But they cannot escape from the company of the five passions; they are increasingly bound to egotism. |1|

O Beloved, this is not the way to meet the Lord; I have performed these rituals so many times.

I have collapsed, exhausted, at the Door of my Lord Master; I pray that He may grant me a discerning intellect. |Pause|

One may remain silent and use his hands as begging bowls, and wander naked in the forest.

He may make pilgrimages to river banks and sacred shrines all over the world, but his sense of duality will not leave him. |2|

Section 13 - Raag Sorat'h - Part 048

His mind's desires may lead him to go and dwell at sacred places of pilgrimage, and offer his head to be sawn off;

but this will not cause the filth of his mind to depart, even though he may make thousands of efforts. |3|

He may give gifts of all sorts - gold, women, horses and elephants.
He may make offerings of corn, clothes and land in abundance, but this will not lead him to the Lord's Door. |4|

He may remain devoted to worship and adoration, bowing his forehead to the floor, practicing the six religious rituals.
He indulges in egotism and pride, and falls into entanglements, but he does not meet the Lord by these devices. |5|

He practices the eighty-four postures of Yoga, and acquires the supernatural powers of the Siddhas, but he gets tired of practicing these.
He lives a long life, but is reincarnated again and again; he has not met with the Lord. |6|

He may enjoy princely pleasures, and regal pomp and ceremony, and issue unchallenged commands.
He may lie on beautiful beds, perfumed with sandalwood oil, but this will led him only to the gates of the most horrible hell. |7|

Singing the Kirtan of the Lord's Praises in the Saadh Sangat, the Company of the Holy, is the highest of all actions.
Says Nanak, he alone obtains it, who is pre-destined to receive it. |8|

Your slave is intoxicated with this Love of Yours.
The Destroyer of the pains of the poor has become merciful to me, and this mind is imbued with the Praises of the Lord, Har, Har. |Second Pause|1|3|

Vaar Of Raag Sorat'h, Fourth Mehl:
One Universal Creator God. By The Grace Of The True Guru:

Shalok, First Mehl:
Sorat'h is always beautiful, if it brings the True Lord to dwell in the mind of the soul-bride.
Her teeth are clean and her mind is not split by duality; the Name of the True Lord is on her tongue.
Here and hereafter, she abides in the Fear of God, and serves the True Guru without hesitation.
Discarding worldly adornments, she meets her Husband Lord, and she celebrates joyfully with Him.
She is adorned forever with the Name in her mind, and she does not have even an iota of filth.
Her husband's younger and elder brothers, the corrupt desires, have died, suffering in pain; and now, who fears Maya, the mother-in-law?

If she becomes pleasing to her Husband Lord, O Nanak, she bears the jewel of good karma upon her forehead, and everything is Truth to her. |1|

Fourth Mehl:
Sorat'h is beautiful only when it leads the soul-bride to seek the Lord's Name.
She pleases her Guru and God; under Guru's Instruction, she speaks the Name of the Lord, Har, Har.
She is attracted to the Lord's Name, day and night, and her body is drenched in the color of the Love of the Lord, Har, Har.
No other being like the Lord God can be found; I have looked and searched over the whole world.
The Guru, the True Guru, has implanted the Naam within me; my mind does not waver any more.
Servant Nanak is the Lord's slave, the slave of the slaves of the Guru, the True Guru. |2|

Pauree:
You Yourself are the Creator, the Fashioner of the world.
You Yourself have arranged the play, and You Yourself arrange it.
You Yourself are the Giver and the Creator; You Yourself are the Enjoyer.
The Word of Your Shabad is pervading everywhere, O Creator Lord.
As Gurmukh, I ever praise the Lord; I am a sacrifice to the Guru. |1|

Section 13 - Raag Sorat'h - Part 049

Shalok, Third Mehl:
In the flames of egotism, he is burnt to death; he wanders in doubt and the love of duality.
The Perfect True Guru saves him, making him His own.
This world is burning; through the Sublime Word of the Guru's Shabad, this comes to be seen.
Those who are attuned to the Shabad are cooled and soothed; O Nanak, they practice Truth. |1|

Third Mehl:
Service to the True Guru is fruitful and rewarding; blessed and acceptable is such a life.
Those who do not forget the True Guru, in life and in death, are truly wise people.
Their families are saved, and they are approved by the Lord.
The Gurmukhs are approved in death as in life, while the self-willed manmukhs continue the cycle of birth and death.
O Nanak, they are not described as dead, who are absorbed in the Word of the Guru's Shabad. |2|

Pauree:
Serve the Immaculate Lord God, and meditate on the Lord's Name.
Join the Society of the Holy Saints, and be absorbed in the Lord's Name.
O Lord, glorious and great is service to You; I am so foolish
- please, commit me to it. I am Your servant and slave; command me, according to Your Will.
As Gurmukh, I shall serve You, as Guru has instructed me. |2|

Shalok, Third Mehl:
He acts according to pre-ordained destiny, written by the Creator Himself.
Emotional attachment has drugged him, and he has forgotten the Lord, the treasure of virtue.
Don't think that he is alive in the world - he is dead, through the love of duality.
Those who do not meditate on the Lord, as Gurmukh, are not permitted to sit near the Lord.
They suffer the most horrible pain and suffering, and neither their sons nor their wives go along with them.
Their faces are blackened among men, and they sigh in deep regret.

No one places any reliance in the self-willed manmukhs; trust in them is lost.

O Nanak, the Gurmukhs live in absolute peace; the Naam, the Name of the Lord, abides within them. |1|

Third Mehl:

They alone are relatives, and they alone are friends, who, as Gurmukh, join together in love.

Night and day, they act according to the True Guru's Will; they remain absorbed in the True Name.

Those who are attached to the love of duality are not called friends; they practice egotism and corruption.

The self-willed manmukhs are selfish; they cannot resolve anyone's affairs.

O Nanak, they act according to their pre-ordained destiny; no one can erase it. |2|

Pauree:

You Yourself created the world, and You Yourself arranged the play of it.

You Yourself created the three qualities, and fostered emotional attachment to Maya.

He is called to account for his deeds done in egotism; he continues coming and going in reincarnation.

The Guru instructs those whom the Lord Himself blesses with Grace.

I am a sacrifice to my Guru; forever and ever, I am a sacrifice to Him. |3|

Shalok, Third Mehl:

The love of Maya is enticing; without teeth, it has eaten up the world.

The self-willed manmukhs are eaten away, while the Gurmukhs are saved; they focus their consciousness on the True Name.

Without the Name, the world wanders around insane; the Gurmukhs come to see this.

Section 13 - Raag Sorat'h - Part 050

Involved in worldly affairs, he wastes his life in vain; the peace-giving Lord does not come to abide in his mind.

O Nanak, they alone obtain the Name, who have such pre-ordained destiny. |1|

Third Mehl:

The home within is filled with Ambrosial Nectar, but the self-willed manmukh does not get to taste it.

He is like the deer, who does not recognize its own musk-scent; it wanders around, deluded by doubt.

The manmukh forsakes the Ambrosial Nectar, and instead gathers poison; the Creator Himself has fooled him.

How rare are the Gurmukhs, who obtain this understanding; they behold the Lord God within themselves.

Their minds and bodies are cooled and soothed, and their tongues enjoy the sublime taste of the Lord.

Through the Word of the Shabad, the Name wells up; through the Shabad, we are united in the Lord's Union.

Without the Shabad, the whole world is insane, and it loses its life in vain.

The Shabad alone is Ambrosial Nectar; O Nanak, the Gurmukhs obtain it. |2|

Pauree:
The Lord God is inaccessible; tell me, how can we find Him?

He has no form or feature, and He cannot be seen; tell me, how can we meditate on Him?

The Lord is formless, immaculate and inaccessible; which of His Virtues should we speak of and sing?

They alone walk on the Lord's Path, whom the Lord Himself instructs.

The Perfect Guru has revealed Him to me; serving the Guru, He is found. |4|

Shalok, Third Mehl:
It is as if my body has been crushed in the oil-press, without yielding even a drop of blood;

it is as if my soul has been cut apart into pieces for the sake of the Love of the True Lord;

O Nanak, still, night and day, my Union with the Lord is not broken. |1|

Third Mehl:
My Friend is so full of joy and love; He colors my mind with the color of His Love,

like the fabric which is treated to retain the color of the dye.

O Nanak, this color does not depart, and no other color can be imparted to this fabric. |2|

Pauree:

The Lord Himself is pervading everywhere; the Lord Himself causes us to chant His Name.

The Lord Himself created the creation; He commits all to their tasks.

He engages some in devotional worship, and others, He causes to stray.

He places some on the Path, while He leads others into the wilderness.

Servant Nanak meditates on the Naam, the Name of the Lord; as Gurmukh, he sings the Glorious Praises of the Lord. |5|

Shalok, Third Mehl:

Service to the True Guru is fruitful and rewarding, if one performs it with his mind focused on it.

The fruits of the mind's desires are obtained, and egotism departs from within.

His bonds are broken, and he is liberated; he remains absorbed in the True Lord.

It is so difficult to obtain the Naam in this world; it comes to dwell in the mind of the Gurmukh.

O Nanak, I am a sacrifice to one who serves his True Guru. |1|

Third Mehl:

The mind of the self-willed manmukh is so very stubborn; it is stuck in the love of duality.

He does not find peace, even in dreams; he passes his life in misery and suffering.

The Pandits have grown weary of going door to door, reading and reciting their scriptures; the Siddhas have gone into their trances of Samaadhi.

This mind cannot be controlled; they are tired of performing religious rituals.

The impersonators have grown weary of wearing false costumes, and bathing at the sixty-eight sacred shrines.

Section 13 - Raag Sorat'h - Part 051

They do not know the state of their own minds; they are deluded by doubt and egotism.

By Guru's Grace, the Fear of God is obtained; by great good fortune, the Lord comes to abide in the mind.

When the Fear of God comes, the mind is restrained, and through the Word of the Shabad, the ego is burnt away.

Those who are imbued with Truth are immaculate; their light merges in the Light.

Meeting the True Guru, one obtains the Name; O Nanak, he is absorbed in peace. |2|

Pauree:

The pleasures of kings and emperors are pleasing, but they last for only a few days.

These pleasures of Maya are like the color of the safflower, which wears off in a moment.

They do not go with him when he departs; instead, he carries the load of sins upon his head.

When death seizes him, and marches him away, then he looks absolutely hideous.

That lost opportunity will not come into his hands again, and in the end, he regrets and repents. |6|

Shalok, Third Mehl:

Those who turn their faces away from the True Guru, suffer in sorrow and bondage.

Again and again, they are born only to die; they cannot meet their Lord.

The disease of doubt does not depart, and they find only pain and more pain.

O Nanak, if the Gracious Lord forgives, then one is united in Union with the Word of the Shabad. |1|

Third Mehl:

Those who turn their faces away from the True Guru, shall find no place of rest or shelter.

They wander around from door to door, like a woman forsaken, with a bad character and a bad reputation.

O Nanak, the Gurmukhs are forgiven, and united in Union with the True Guru. |2|

Pauree:

Those who serve the True Lord, the Destroyer of ego, cross over the terrifying world-ocean.

Those who chant the Name of the Lord, Har, Har, are passed over by the Messenger of Death.

Those who meditate on the Lord, go to His Court in robes of honor.

They alone serve You, O Lord, whom You bless with Grace.
I sing continually Your Glorious Praises, O Beloved; as Gurmukh, my doubts and fears have been dispelled. |7|

Shalok, Third Mehl:
Upon the plate, three things have been placed; this is the sublime, ambrosial food of the Lord.
Eating this, the mind is satisfied, and the Door of Salvation is found.
It is so difficult to obtain this food, O Saints; it is obtained only by contemplating the Guru.
Why should we cast this riddle out of our minds? We should keep it ever enshrined in our hearts.
The True Guru has posed this riddle. The Guru's Sikhs have found its solution.
O Nanak, he alone understands this, whom the Lord inspires to understand.
The Gurmukhs work hard, and find the Lord. |1|

Third Mehl:
Those whom the Primal Lord unites, remain in Union with Him; they focus their consciousness on the True Guru.
Those whom the Lord Himself separates, remain separated; in the love of duality, they are ruined.
O Nanak, without good karma, what can anyone obtain? He earns what he is pre-destined to receive. |2|

Pauree:
Sitting together, the companions sing the Songs of the Lord's Praises.
They praise the Lord's Name continually; they are a sacrifice to the Lord.
Those who hear, and believe in the Lord's Name, to them I am a sacrifice.
O Lord, let me unite with the Gurmukhs, who are united with You.
I am a sacrifice to those who, day and night, behold their Guru. |8|

Shalok, Third Mehl:

Section 13 - Raag Sorat'h - Part 052

Without the Name of the Lord, everyone wanders around the world, losing.
The self-willed manmukhs do their deeds in the pitch black darkness of egotism.

The Gurmukhs drink in the Ambrosial Nectar, O Nanak, contemplating the Word of the Shabad. |1|

Third Mehl:
He wakes in peace, and he sleeps in peace.
The Gurmukh praises the Lord night and day.
The self-willed manmukh remains deluded by his doubts.
He is filled with anxiety, and he cannot even sleep.
The spiritually wise wake and sleep in peace.
Nanak is a sacrifice to those who are imbued with the Naam, the Name of the Lord. |2|

Pauree:
They alone meditate on the Lord's Name, who are imbued with the Lord.
They meditate on the One Lord; the One and Only Lord is True.
The One Lord is pervading everywhere; the One Lord created the Universe.
Those who meditate on the Lord's Name, cast out their fears.
The Lord Himself blesses them with Guru's Instruction; the Gurmukh meditates on the Lord. |9|

Shalok, Third Mehl:
Spiritual wisdom, which would bring understanding, does not enter into his mind.
Without seeing, how can he praise the Lord? The blind act in blindness.
O Nanak, when one realizes the Word of the Shabad, then the Naam comes to abide in the mind. |1|

Third Mehl:
There is One Bani; there is One Guru; there is one Shabad to contemplate.
True is the merchandise, and true is the shop; the warehouses are overflowing with jewels.
By Guru's Grace, they are obtained, if the Great Giver gives them.
Dealing in this true merchandise, one earns the profit of the incomparable Naam.
In the midst of poison, the Ambrosial Nectar is revealed; by His Mercy, one drinks it in.
O Nanak, praise the True Lord; blessed is the Creator, the Embellisher. |2|

Pauree:
Those who are permeated by falsehood, do not love the Truth.

If someone speaks the Truth, falsehood is burnt away.

The false are satisfied by falsehood, like the crows who eat manure.

When the Lord grants His Grace, then one meditates on the Naam, the Name of the Lord.

As Gurmukh, worship the Lord's Name in adoration; fraud and sin shall disappear. |10|

Shalok, Third Mehl:

O Shaykh, you wander in the four directions, blown by the four winds; bring your mind back to the home of the One Lord.

Renounce your petty arguments, and realize the Word of the Guru's Shabad.

Bow in humble respect before the True Guru; He is the Knower who knows everything.

Burn away your hopes and desires, and live like a guest in this world.

If you walk in harmony with the True Guru's Will, then you shall be honored in the Court of the Lord.

O Nanak, those who do not contemplate the Naam, the Name of the Lord - cursed are their clothes, and cursed is their food. |1|

Third Mehl:

There is no end to the Lord's Glorious Praises; His worth cannot be described.

O Nanak, the Gurmukhs chant the Glorious Praises of the Lord; they are absorbed in His Glorious Virtues. |2|

Pauree:

The Lord has adorned the coat of the body; He has embroidered it with devotional worship.

The Lord has woven His silk into it, in so many ways and fashions.

How rare is that man of understanding, who understands, and deliberates within.

He alone understands these deliberations, whom the Lord Himself inspires to understand.

Poor servant Nanak speaks: the Gurmukhs know the Lord, the Lord is True. |11|

Section 13 - Raag Sorat'h - Part 053

Shalok, Third Mehl:

Great men speak the teachings by relating them to individual situations, but the whole world shares in them.

One who becomes Gurmukh knows the Fear of God, and realizes his own self.

If, by Guru's Grace, one remains dead while yet alive, the mind becomes content in itself.

Those who have no faith in their own minds, O Nanak - how can they speak of spiritual wisdom? |1|

Third Mehl:

Those who do not focus their consciousness on the Lord, as Gurmukh, suffer pain and grief in the end.

They are blind, inwardly and outwardly, and they do not understand anything.

O Pandit, O religious scholar, the whole world is fed for the sake of those who are attuned to the Lord's Name.

Those who praise the Word of the Guru's Shabad, remain blended with the Lord.

O Pandit, O religious scholar, no one is satisfied, and no one finds true wealth through the love of duality.

They have grown weary of reading scriptures, but still, they do not find contentment, and they pass their lives burning, night and day.

Their cries and complaints never end, and doubt does not depart from within them.

O Nanak, without the Naam, the Name of the Lord, they rise up and depart with blackened faces. |2|

Pauree:

O Beloved, lead me to meet my True Friend; meeting with Him, I shall ask Him to show me the Path.

I am a sacrifice to that Friend, who shows it to me.

I share His Virtues with Him, and meditate on the Lord's Name.

I serve my Beloved Lord forever; serving the Lord, I have found peace.

I am a sacrifice to the True Guru, who has imparted this understanding to me. |12|

Shalok, Third Mehl:

O Pandit, O religious scholar, your filth shall not be erased, even if you read the Vedas for four ages.

The three qualities are the roots of Maya; in egotism, one forgets the Naam, the Name of the Lord.

The Pandits are deluded, attached to duality, and they deal only in Maya.

They are filled with thirst and hunger; the ignorant fools starve to death.

Serving the True Guru, peace is obtained, contemplating the True Word of the Shabad.

Hunger and thirst have departed from within me; I am in love with the True Name.

O Nanak, those who are imbued with the Naam, who keep the Lord clasped tightly to their hearts, are automatically satisfied. |1|

Third Mehl:

The self-willed manmukh does not serve the Lord's Name, and so he suffers in horrible pain.

He is filled with the darkness of ignorance, and he does not understand anything.

Because of his stubborn mind, he does not plant the seeds of intuitive peace; what will he eat in the world hereafter, to satisfy his hunger?

He has forgotten the treasure of the Naam; he is caught in the love of duality.

O Nanak, the Gurmukhs are honored with glory, when the Lord Himself unites them in His Union. |2|

Pauree:

The tongue which sings the Lord's Praises, is so very beautiful.

One who speaks the Lord's Name, with mind, body and mouth, is pleasing to the Lord.

That Gurmukh tastes the the sublime taste of the Lord, and is satisfied.

She sings continually the Glorious Praises of her Beloved; singing His Glorious Praises, she is uplifted.

She is blessed with the Lord's Mercy, and she chants the Words of the Guru, the True Guru. |13|

Shalok, Third Mehl:

The elephant offers its head to the reins, and the anvil offers itself to the hammer;

just so, we offer our minds and bodies to our Guru; we stand before Him, and serve Him.

Section 13 - Raag Sorat'h - Part 054

This is how the Gurmukhs eliminate their self-conceit, and come to rule the whole world.

O Nanak, the Gurmukh understands, when the Lord casts His Glance of Grace. |1|

Third Mehl:

Blessed and approved is the coming into the world, of those Gurmukhs who meditate on the Naam, the Name of the Lord.

O Nanak, they save their families, and they are honored in the Court of the Lord. |2|

Pauree:

The Guru unites His Sikhs, the Gurmukhs, with the Lord.

The Guru keeps some of them with Himself, and engages others in His Service.

Those who cherish their Beloved in their conscious minds, the Guru blesses them with His Love.

The Guru loves all of His Gursikhs equally well, like friends, children and siblings.

So chant the Name of the Guru, the True Guru, everyone! Chanting the Name of the Guru, Guru, you shall be rejuvenated. |14|

Shalok, Third Mehl:

O Nanak, the blind, ignorant fools do not remember the Naam, the Name of the Lord; they involve themselves in other activities.

They are bound and gagged at the door of the Messenger of Death; they are punished, and in the end, they rot away in manure. |1|

Third Mehl:

O Nanak, those humble beings are true and approved, who serve their True Guru.

They remain absorbed in the Name of the Lord, and their comings and goings cease. |2|

Pauree:

Gathering the wealth and property of Maya, brings only pain in the end.

Homes, mansions and adorned palaces will not go with anyone.

He may breed horses of various colors, but these will not be of any use to him.

O human, link your consciousness to the Lord's Name, and in the end, it shall be your companion and helper.

Servant Nanak meditates on the Naam, the Name of the Lord; the Gurmukh is blessed with peace. |15|

Shalok, Third Mehl:
Without the karma of good actions, the Name is not obtained; it can be obtained only by perfect good karma.

O Nanak, if the Lord casts His Glance of Grace, then under Guru's Instruction, one is united in His Union. |1|

First Mehl:
Some are cremated, and some are buried; some are eaten by dogs.

Some are thrown into water, while others are thrown into wells.

O Nanak, it is not known, where they go and into what they merge. |2|

Pauree:
The food and clothes, and all the worldly possessions of those who are attuned to the Lord's Name are sacred.

All the homes, temples, palaces and way-stations are sacred, where the Gurmukhs, the selfless servants, the Sikhs and the renouncers of the world, go and take their rest.

All the horses, saddles and horse blankets are sacred, upon which the Gurmukhs, the Sikhs, the Holy and the Saints, mount and ride.

All the rituals and Dharmic practices and deeds are sacred, for those who utter the Name of the Lord, Har, Har, the True Name of the Lord.

Those Gurmukhs, those Sikhs, who have purity as their treasure, go to their Guru. |16|

Shalok, Third Mehl:
O Nanak, forsaking the Name, he loses everything, in this world and the next.

Chanting, deep meditation and austere self-disciplined practices are all wasted; he is deceived by the love of duality.

He is bound and gagged at the door of the Messenger of Death. He is beaten, and receives terrible punishment. |1|

Section 13 - Raag Sorat'h - Part 055

Third Mehl:

They inflict their hatred upon the Saints, and they love the wicked sinners.

They find no peace in either this world or the next; they are born only to die, again and again.

Their hunger is never satisfied, and they are ruined by duality.

The faces of these slanderers are blackened in the Court of the True Lord.

O Nanak, without the Naam, they find no shelter on either this shore, or the one beyond. |2|

Pauree:

Those who meditate on the Lord's Name, are imbued with the Name of the Lord, Har, Har, in their minds.

For those who worship the One Lord in their conscious minds, there is no other than the One Lord.

They alone serve the Lord, upon whose foreheads such pre-ordained destiny is written.

They continually sing the Glorious Praises of the Lord, and singing the Glories of the Glorious Lord, they are uplifted.

Great is the greatness of the Gurmukhs, who, through the Perfect Guru, remain absorbed in the Lord's Name. |17|

Shalok, Third Mehl:

It is very difficult to serve the True Guru; offer your head, and eradicate self-conceit.

One who dies in the Word of the Shabad shall never have to die again; his service is totally approved.

Touching the philosopher's stone, one becomes the philosopher's stone, which transforms lead into gold; remain lovingly attached to the True Lord.

One who has such pre-ordained destiny, comes to meet the True Guru and God.

O Nanak, the Lord's servant does not meet Him because of his own account; he alone is acceptable, whom the Lord forgives. |1|

Third Mehl:

The fools do not know the difference between good and bad; they are deceived by their self-interests.

But if they contemplate the Word of the Shabad, they obtain the Mansion of the Lord's Presence, and their light merges in the Light.

The Fear of God is always on their minds, and so they come to understand everything.

The True Guru is pervading the homes within; He Himself blends them with the Lord.

O Nanak, they meet the True Guru, and all their desires are fulfilled, if the Lord grants His Grace and so wills. |2|

Pauree:

Blessed, blessed is the good fortune of those devotees, who, with their mouths, utter the Name of the Lord.

Blessed, blessed is the good fortune of those Saints, who, with their ears, listen to the Lord's Praises.

Blessed, blessed is the good fortune of those holy people, who sing the Kirtan of the Lord's Praises, and so become virtuous.

Blessed, blessed is the good fortune of those Gurmukhs, who live as Gursikhs, and conquer their minds.

But the greatest good fortune of all, is that of the Guru's Sikhs, who fall at the Guru's feet. |18|

Shalok, Third Mehl:

One who knows God, and who lovingly focuses his attention on the One Word of the Shabad, keeps his spirituality intact.

The nine treasures and the eighteen spiritual powers of the Siddhas follow him, who keeps the Lord enshrined in his heart.

Without the True Guru, the Name is not found; understand this, and reflect upon it.

O Nanak, through perfect good destiny, one meets the True Guru, and finds peace, throughout the four ages. |1|

Third Mehl:

Whether he is young or old, the self-willed manmukh cannot escape hunger and thirst.

The Gurmukhs are imbued with the Word of the Shabad; they are at peace, having lost their self-conceit.

They are satisfied and satiated within; they never feel hungry again.

Section 13 - Raag Sorat'h - Part 056

O Nanak, whatever the Gurmukhs do is acceptable; they remain lovingly absorbed in the Naam, the Name of the Lord. |2|

Pauree:
I am a sacrifice to those Sikhs who are Gurmukhs.
I behold the Blessed Vision, the Darshan of those who meditate on the Lord's Name.
Listening to the Kirtan of the Lord's Praises, I contemplate His virtues; I write His Praises on the fabric of my mind.
I praise the Lord's Name with love, and eradicate all my sins.
Blessed, blessed and beauteous is that body and place, where my Guru places His feet. |19|

Shalok, Third Mehl:
Without the Guru, spiritual wisdom is not obtained, and peace does not come to abide in the mind.
O Nanak, without the Naam, the Name of the Lord, the self-willed manmukhs depart, after having wasted their lives. |1|

Third Mehl:
All the Siddhas, spiritual masters and seekers search for the Name; they have grown weary of concentrating and focusing their attention.
Without the True Guru, no one finds the Name; the Gurmukhs unite in Union with the Lord.
Without the Name, all food and clothes are worthless; cursed is such spirituality, and cursed are such miraculous powers.
That alone is spirituality, and that alone is miraculous power, which the Carefree Lord spontaneously bestows.
O Nanak, the Lord's Name abides in the mind of the Gurmukh; this is spirituality, and this is miraculous power. |2|

Pauree:
I am a minstrel of God, my Lord and Master; every day, I sing the songs of the Lord's Glorious Praises.
I sing the Kirtan of the Lord's Praises, and I listen to the Praises of the Lord, the Master of wealth and Maya.
The Lord is the Great Giver; all the world is begging; all beings and creatures are beggars.
O Lord, You are kind and compassionate; You give Your gifts to even worms and insects among the rocks.
Servant Nanak meditates on the Naam, the Name of the Lord; as Gurmukh, he has become truly wealthy. |20|

Shalok, Third Mehl:

Reading and studying are just worldly pursuits, if there is thirst and corruption within.

Reading in egotism, all have grown weary; through the love of duality, they are ruined.

He alone is educated, and he alone is a wise Pandit, who contemplates the Word of the Guru's Shabad.

He searches within himself, and finds the true essence; he finds the Door of Salvation.

He finds the Lord, the treasure of excellence, and peacefully contemplates Him.

Blessed is the trader, O Nanak, who, as Gurmukh, takes the Name as his only Support. |1|

Third Mehl:

Without conquering his mind, no one can be successful. See this, and concentrate on it.

The wandering holy men are tired of of making pilgrimages to sacred shrines; they have not been able to conquer their minds.

The Gurmukh has conquered his mind, and he remains lovingly absorbed in the True Lord.

O Nanak, this is how the filth of the mind is removed; the Word of the Shabad burns away the ego. |2|

Pauree:

O Saints of the Lord, O my Siblings of Destiny, please meet with me, and implant the Name of the One Lord within me.

O humble servants of the Lord, adorn me with the decorations of the Lord, Har, Har; let me wear the robes of the Lord's forgiveness.

Such decorations are pleasing to my God; such love is dear to the Lord.

I chant the Name of the Lord, Har, Har, day and night; in an instant, all sins are eradicated.

That Gurmukh, unto whom the Lord becomes merciful, chants the Lord's Name, and wins the game of life. |21|

Section 13 - Raag Sorat'h - Part 057

Shalok, Third Mehl:

The filth of countless incarnations sticks to this mind; it has become pitch black.

The oily rag cannot be cleaned by merely washing it, even if it is washed a hundred times.

By Guru's Grace, one remains dead while yet alive; his intellect is transformed, and he becomes detached from the world.

O Nanak, no filth sticks to him, and he does not fall into the womb again. |1|

Third Mehl:

Kali Yuga is called the Dark Age, but the most sublime state is attained in this age.

The Gurmukh obtains the fruit, the Kirtan of the Lord's Praises; this is his destiny, ordained by the Lord.

O Nanak, by Guru's Grace, he worships the Lord night and day; he chants the Lord's Name, and remains absorbed in the Lord's devotional worship. |2|

Pauree:

O Lord, unite me with the Saadh Sangat, the Company of the Holy, so that with my mouth, I may speak the sublime Word of the Guru's Bani.

I sing the Glorious Praises of the Lord, and constantly chant the Lord's Name; through the Guru's Teachings, I enjoy the Lord's Love constantly.

I take the medicine of meditation on the Lord's Name, which has cured all diseases and multitudes of sufferings.

Those who do not forget the Lord, while breathing or eating - know them to be the perfect servants of the Lord.

Those Gurmukhs who worship the Lord in adoration end their subservience to the Messenger of Death, and to the world. |22|

Shalok, Third Mehl:

O man, you have been tormented by a nightmare, and you have passed your life in sleep.

You did not wake to hear the Word of the True Guru's Shabad; you have no inspiration within yourself.

That body burns, which has no virtue, and which does not serve the Guru.

I have seen that the world is burning, in egotism and the love of duality.

O Nanak, those who seek the Guru's Sanctuary are saved; within their minds, they meditate on the True Word of the Shabad. |1|

Third Mehl:

Attuned to the Word of the Shabad, the soul-bride is rid of egotism, and she is glorified.

If she walks steadily in the way of His Will, then she is adorned with decorations.

Her couch becomes beautiful, and she constantly enjoys her Husband Lord; she obtains the Lord as her Husband.

The Lord does not die, and she never suffers pain; she is a happy soul-bride forever.

O Nanak, the Lord God unites her with Himself; she enshrines love and affection for the Guru. |2|

Pauree:

Those who conceal and deny their Guru, are the most evil people.

O Dear Lord, let me not even see them; they are the worst sinners and murderers.

They wander from house to house, with impure minds, like wicked, forsaken women.

But by great good fortune, they may meet the Company of the Holy; as Gurmukhs, they are reformed.

O Lord, please be kind and let me meet the True Guru; I am a sacrifice to the Guru. |23|

Shalok, Third Mehl:

Serving the Guru, peace is produced, and then, one does not suffer in pain.

The cycle of birth and death is brought to an end, and death has no power over at all.

His mind is imbued with the Lord, and he remains merged in the True Lord.

O Nanak, I am a sacrifice to those who walk in the Way of the True Guru's Will. |1|

Third Mehl:

Without the Word of the Shabad, purity is not obtained, even though the soul-bride may adorn herself with all sorts of decorations.

Section 13 - Raag Sorat'h - Part 058

She does not know the value of her Husband Lord; she is attached to the love of duality.

She is impure, and ill-mannered, O Nanak; among women, she is the most evil woman. |2|

Pauree:
Be kind to me, Lord, that I might chant the Word of Your Bani.
May I meditate on the Lord's Name, chant the Lord's Name, and obtain the profit of the Lord's Name.
I am a sacrifice to those who chant the Name of the Lord, Har, Har, day and night.
May I behold with my eyes those who worship and adore my Beloved True Guru.
I am a sacrifice to my Guru, who has united me with my Lord, my friend, my very best friend. |24|

Shalok, Fourth Mehl:
The Lord loves His slaves; the Lord is the friend of His slaves.
The Lord is under the control of His slaves, like the musical instrument under the control of the musician.
The Lord's slaves meditate on the Lord; they love their Beloved.
Please, hear me, O God - let Your Grace rain over the whole world.
The praise of the Lord's slaves is the Glory of the Lord.
The Lord loves His Own Glory, and so His humble servant is celebrated and hailed.
That humble servant of the Lord meditates on the Naam, the Name of the Lord; the Lord, and the Lord's humble servant, are one and the same.
Servant Nanak is the slave of the Lord; O Lord, O God, please, preserve his honor. |1|

Fourth Mehl:
Nanak loves the True Lord; without Him, he cannot even survive.
Meeting the True Guru, one finds the Perfect Lord, and the tongue enjoys the sublime essence of the Lord. |2|

Pauree:
Night and day, morning and night, I sing to You, Lord.
All beings and creatures meditate on Your Name.
You are the Giver, the Great Giver; we eat whatever You give us.
In the congregation of the devotees, sins are eradicated.
Servant Nanak is forever a sacrifice, a sacrifice, a sacrifice, O Lord. |25|

Shalok, Fourth Mehl:

He has spiritual ignorance within, and his intellect is dull and dim; he does not place his faith in the True Guru.

He has deceit within himself, and so he sees deception in all others; through his deceptions, he is totally ruined.

The True Guru's Will does not enter into his consciousness, and so he wanders around, pursuing his own interests.

If He grants His Grace, then Nanak is absorbed into the Word of the Shabad. |1|

Fourth Mehl:

The self-willed manmukhs are engrossed in emotional attachment to Maya; in the love of duality, their minds are unsteady.

Night and day, they are burning; day and night, they are totally ruined by their egotism.

Within them, is the total pitch darkness of greed, and no one even approaches them.

They themselves are miserable, and they never find peace; they are born, only to die, and die again.

O Nanak, the True Lord God forgives those, who focus their consciousness on the Guru's feet. |2|

Pauree:

That Saint, that devotee, is acceptable, who is loved by God.

Those beings are wise, who meditate on the Lord.

They eat the food, the treasure of the Ambrosial Naam, the Name of the Lord.

They apply the dust of the feet of the Saints to their foreheads.

Section 13 - Raag Sorat'h - Part 059

O Nanak, they are purified, bathing in the sacred shrine of the Lord. |26|

Shalok, Fourth Mehl:

Within the Gurmukh is peace and tranquility; his mind and body are absorbed in the Naam, the Name of the Lord.

He contemplates the Naam, he studies the Naam, and he remains lovingly absorbed in the Naam.

He obtains the treasure of the Naam, and his anxiety is dispelled.

Meeting with the Guru, the Naam wells up, and his thirst and hunger are completely relieved.

O Nanak, imbued with the Naam, he gathers in the Naam. |1|

Fourth Mehl:
One who is cursed by the True Guru, abandons his home, and wanders around aimlessly.

He is jeered at, and his face is blackened in the world hereafter.

He babbles incoherently, and foaming at the mouth, he dies.

What can anyone do? Such is his destiny, according to his past deeds.

Wherever he goes, he is a liar, and by telling lies, he not liked by anyone.

O Siblings of Destiny, behold this, the glorious greatness of our Lord and Master, O Saints; as one behaves, so does he receive.

This shall be God's determination in His True Court; servant Nanak predicts and proclaims this. |2|

Pauree:
The True Guru has established the village; the Guru has appointed its guards and protectors.

My hopes are fulfilled, and my mind is imbued with the love of the Guru's Feet.

The Guru is infinitely merciful; He has erased all my sins.

The Guru has showered me with His Mercy, and He has made me His own.

Nanak is forever a sacrifice to the Guru, who has countless virtues. |27|

Shalok, First Mehl:
By His Command, we receive our pre-ordained rewards; so what can we do now, O Pandit?

When His Command is received, then it is decided; all beings move and act accordingly. |1|

Second Mehl:
The string through the nose is in the hands of the Lord Master; one's own actions drive him on.

Wherever his food is, there he eats it; O Nanak, this is the Truth. |2|

Pauree:
The Lord Himself puts everything in its proper place.

He Himself created the creation, and He Himself destroys it.

He Himself fashions His creatures, and He Himself nourishes them.

He hugs His slaves close in His embrace, and blesses them with His Glance of Grace.
O Nanak, His devotees are forever in bliss; they have burnt away the love of duality. |28|

Shalok, Third Mehl:
O mind, meditate on the Dear Lord, with single-minded conscious concentration.
The glorious greatness of the Lord shall last forever and ever; He never regrets what He gives.
I am forever a sacrifice to the Lord; serving Him, peace is obtained.
O Nanak, the Gurmukh remains merged with the Lord; he burns away his ego through the Word of the Shabad. |1|

Third Mehl:
He Himself enjoins us to serve Him, and He Himself blesses us with forgiveness.
He Himself is the father and mother of all; He Himself cares for us.
O Nanak, those who meditate on the Naam, the Name of the Lord, abide in the home of their inner being; they are honored throughout the ages. |2|

Pauree:
You are the Creator, all-powerful, able to do anything. Without You, there is no other at all.

Section 13 - Raag Sorat'h - Part 060

You Yourself created the world, and You Yourself shall destroy it in the end.
The Word of Your Shabad alone is pervading everywhere; whatever You do, comes to pass.
God blesses the Gurmukh with glorious greatness, and then, he finds the Lord.
As Gurmukh, Nanak worships and adores the Lord; let everyone proclaim, "Blessed, blessed, blessed is He, the Guru!"|29|1|SUDH|

Raag Sorat'h, The Word Of Devotee Kabeer Jee, First House:
One Universal Creator God. By The Grace Of The True Guru:
Worshipping their idols, the Hindus die; the Muslims die bowing their heads.

The Hindus cremate their dead, while the Muslims bury theirs; neither finds Your true state, Lord. |1|

O mind, the world is a deep, dark pit.
On all four sides, Death has spread his net. |1|Pause|

Reciting their poems, the poets die; the mystical ascetics die while journeying to Kaydaar Naat'h.
The Yogis die, with their matted hair, but even they do not find Your state, Lord. |2|

The kings die, gathering and hoarding their money, burying great quantities of gold.
The Pandits die, reading and reciting the Vedas; women die, gazing at their own beauty. |3|

Without the Lord's Name, all come to ruin; behold, and know this, O body.
Without the Name of the Lord, who can find salvation? Kabeer speaks the Teachings. |4|1|

When the body is burnt, it turns to ashes; if it is not cremated, then it is eaten by armies of worms.
The unbaked clay pitcher dissolves, when water is poured into it; this is also the nature of the body. |1|

Why, O Siblings of Destiny, do you strut around, all puffed up with pride?
Have you forgotten those days, when you were hanging, face down, for ten months? |1|Pause|

Like the bee which collects honey, the fool eagerly gathers and collects wealth.
At the time of death, they shout, "Take him away, take him away! Why leave a ghost lying around?"|2|

His wife accompanies him to the threshold, and his friends and companions beyond.
All the people and relatives go as far as the cremation grounds, and then, the soul-swan goes on alone. |3|

Says Kabeer, listen, O mortal being: you have been seized by Death, and you have fallen into the deep, dark pit.
You have entangled yourself in the false wealth of Maya, like the parrot caught in the trap. |4|2|

Listening to all the teachings of the Vedas and the Puraanas, I wanted to perform the religious rituals.
But seeing all the wise men caught by Death, I arose and left the Pandits; now I am free of this desire. |1|

O mind, you have not completed the only task you were given; you have not meditated on the Lord, your King. |1|Pause|

Going to the forests, they practice Yoga and deep, austere meditation; they live on roots and the fruits they gather.
The musicians, the Vedic scholars, the chanters of one word and the men of silence, all are listed on the Register of Death. |2|

Loving devotional worship does not enter into your heart; pampering and adorning your body, you must still give it up.
You sit and play music, but you are still a hypocrite; what do you expect to receive from the Lord? |3|

Death has fallen on the whole world; the doubting religious scholars are also listed on the Register of Death.

Section 13 - Raag Sorat'h - Part 061

Says Kabeer, those humble people become pure - they become Khalsa - who know the Lord's loving devotional worship. |4|3|

SECOND HOUSE|

With both of my eyes, I look around;
I don't see anything except the Lord.
My eyes gaze lovingly upon Him,
and now, I cannot speak of anything else. |1|

My doubts were removed, and my fear ran away,
when my consciousness became attached to the Lord's Name. |1|Pause|

When the magician beats his tambourine,
everyone comes to see the show.
When the magician winds up his show,
then he enjoys its play all alone. |2|

By preaching sermons, one's doubt is not dispelled.
Everyone is tired of preaching and teaching.
The Lord causes the Gurmukh to understand;
his heart remains permeated with the Lord. |3|

When the Guru grants even a bit of His Grace,
one's body, mind and entire being are absorbed into the Lord.
Says Kabeer, I am imbued with the Lord's Love;
I have met with the Life of the world, the Great Giver. |4|4|

Let the sacred scriptures be your milk and cream,
and the ocean of the mind the churning vat.
Be the butter-churner of the Lord,
and your buttermilk shall not be wasted. |1|

O soul-bride slave, why don't you take the Lord as your Husband?
He is the Life of the world, the Support of the breath of life. |1|Pause|

The chain is around your neck, and the cuffs are on your feet.
The Lord has sent you wandering around from house to house.
And still, you do not meditate on the Lord, O soul-bride, slave.
Death is watching you, O wretched woman. |2|

The Lord God is the Cause of causes.
What is in the hands of the poor soul-bride, the slave?
She awakens from her slumber,
and she becomes attached to whatever the Lord attaches her. |3|

O soul-bride, slave, where did you obtain that wisdom,
by which you erased your inscription of doubt?
Kabeer has tasted that subtle essence;
by Guru's Grace, his mind is reconciled with the Lord. |4|5|

Without Him, we cannot even live;

when we meet Him, then our task is completed.
People say it is good to live forever,
but without dying, there is no life. |1|

So now, what sort wisdom should I contemplate and preach?
As I watch, worldly things dissipate. |1|Pause|

Saffron is ground up, and mixed with sandalwood;
without eyes, the world is seen.
The son has given birth to his father;
without a place, the city has been established. |2|

The humble beggar has found the Great Giver,
but he is unable to eat what he has been given.
He cannot leave it alone, but it is never exhausted.
He shall not go to beg from others any longer. |3|

Those select few, who know how to die while yet alive, enjoy great peace.
Kabeer has found that wealth;
meeting with the Lord, he has erased his self-conceit. |4|6|

What use is it to read, and what use is it to study?
What use is it to listen to the Vedas and the Puraanas?
What use is reading and listening,
if celestial peace is not attained? |1|

The fool does not chant the Name of the Lord.
So what does he think of, over and over again? |1|Pause|

In the darkness, we need a lamp

Section 13 - Raag Sorat'h - Part 062

to find the incomprehensible thing.
I have found this incomprehensible thing;
my mind is illuminated and enlightened. |2|

Says Kabeer, now I know Him;
since I know Him, my mind is pleased and appeased.
My mind is pleased and appeased, and yet, people do not believe it.

They do not believe it, so what can I do? |3|7|

In his heart there is deception, and yet in his mouth are words of wisdom.
You are false - why are you churning water? |1|

Why do you bother to wash your body?
Your heart is still full of filth. |1|Pause|

The gourd may be washed at the sixty-eight sacred shrines,
but even then, its bitterness is not removed. |2|

Says Kabeer after deep contemplation,
please help me cross over the terrifying world-ocean, O Lord, O Destroyer
of ego. |3|8|

Sorat'h:
One Universal Creator God. By The Grace Of The True Guru:
Practicing great hypocrisy, he acquires the wealth of others.
Returning home, he squanders it on his wife and children. |1|

O my mind, do not practice deception, even inadvertently.
In the end, your own soul shall have to answer for its account. |1|Pause|

Moment by moment, the body is wearing away, and old age is asserting
itself.
And then, when you are old, no one shall pour water into your cup. |2|

Says Kabeer, no one belongs to you.
Why not chant the Lord's Name in your heart, when you are still young?
|3|9|

O Saints, my windy mind has now become peaceful and still.
It seems that I have learned something of the science of Yoga. |Pause|

The Guru has shown me the hole,
through which the deer carefully enters.
I have now closed off the doors,
and the unstruck celestial sound current resounds. |1|

The pitcher of my heart-lotus is filled with water;

I have spilled out the water, and set it upright.
Says Kabeer, the Lord's humble servant, this I know.
Now that I know this, my mind is pleased and appeased. |2|10|

Raag Sorat'h:
I am so hungry, I cannot perform devotional worship service.
Here, Lord, take back Your mala.
I beg for the dust of the feet of the Saints.
I do not owe anyone anything. |1|

O Lord, how can I be with You?
If You do not give me Yourself, then I shall beg until I get You. |Pause|

I ask for two kilos of flour,
and half a pound of ghee, and salt.
I ask for a pound of beans,
which I shall eat twice a day. |2|

I ask for a cot, with four legs,
and a pillow and mattress.
I ask for a quit to cover myself.
Your humble servant shall perform Your devotional worship service with love. |3|

I have no greed;
Your Name is the only ornament I wish for.
Says Kabeer, my mind is pleased and appeased;
now that my mind is pleased and appeased, I have come to know the Lord. |4|11|

Raag Sorat'h, The Word Of Devotee Naam Dayv Jee, Second House:
One Universal Creator God. By The Grace Of The True Guru:
When I see Him, I sing His Praises.
Then I, his humble servant, become patient. |1|

Section 13 - Raag Sorat'h - Part 063

Meeting the Divine True Guru, I merge into the sound current of the Naad. |1|Pause|

Where the dazzling white light is seen,
there the unstruck sound current of the Shabad resounds.
One's light merges in the Light;
by Guru's Grace, I know this. |2|

The jewels are in the treasure chamber of the heart-lotus.
They sparkle and glitter like lightning.
The Lord is near at hand, not far away.
He is totally permeating and pervading in my soul. |3|

Where the light of the undying sun shines,
the light of burning lamps seems insignificant.
By Guru's Grace, I know this.
Servant Naam Dayv is absorbed in the Celestial Lord. |4|1|

FOURTH HOUSE, SORAT'H:
The woman next door asked Naam Dayv, "Who built your house?
I shall pay him double wages. Tell me, who is your carpenter?" |1|

O sister, I cannot give this carpenter to you.
Behold, my carpenter is pervading everywhere.
My carpenter is the Support of the breath of life. |1|Pause|

This carpenter demands the wages of love, if someone wants Him to build their house.
When one breaks his ties with all the people and relatives, then the carpenter comes of His own accord. |2|

I cannot describe such a carpenter, who is contained in everything, everywhere.
The mute tastes the most sublime ambrosial nectar, but if you ask him to describe it, he cannot. |3|

Listen to the virtues of this carpenter, O sister; He stopped the oceans, and established Dhroo as the pole star.
Naam Dayv's Lord Master brought Sita back, and gave Sri Lanka to Bhabheekhan. |4|2|

SORAT'H, THIRD HOUSE:
The skinless drum plays.

Without the rainy season, the clouds shake with thunder.
Without clouds, the rain falls,
if one contemplates the essence of reality. |1|

I have met my Beloved Lord.
Meeting with Him, my body is made beauteous and sublime. |1|Pause|

Touching the philosopher's stone, I have been transformed into gold.
I have threaded the jewels into my mouth and mind.
I love Him as my own, and my doubt has been dispelled.
Seeking the Guru's guidance, my mind is content. |2|

The water is contained within the pitcher;
I know that the One Lord is contained in all.
The mind of the disciple has faith in the Guru.
Servant Naam Dayv understands the essence of reality. |3|3|

Raag Sorat'h, The Word Of Devotee Ravi Daas Jee:
One Universal Creator God. By The Grace Of The True Guru:
When I am in my ego, then You are not with me. Now that You are with
me, there is no egotism within me.
The wind may raise up huge waves in the vast ocean, but they are just
water in water. |1|

O Lord, what can I say about such an illusion?
Things are not as they seem. |1|Pause|

It is like the king, who falls asleep upon his throne, and dreams that he is a
beggar.
His kingdom is intact, but separated from it, he suffers in sorrow. Such is
my own condition. |2|

Section 13 - Raag Sorat'h - Part 064

Like the story of the rope mistaken for a snake, the mystery has now been
explained to me.
Like the many bracelets, which I mistakenly thought were gold; now, I do
not say what I said then. |3|

The One Lord is pervading the many forms; He enjoys Himself in all hearts.

Says Ravi Daas, the Lord is nearer than our own hands and feet. Whatever will be, will be. |4|1|

If I am bound by the noose of emotional attachment, then I shall bind You, Lord, with the bonds of love.
Go ahead and try to escape, Lord; I have escaped by worshipping and adoring You. |1|

O Lord, You know my love for You.
Now, what will You do? |1|Pause|

A fish is caught, cut up, and cooked it in many different ways.
Bit by bit, it is eaten, but still, it does not forget the water. |2|

The Lord, our King, is father to no one, except those who love Him.
The veil of emotional attachment has been cast over the entire world, but it does not bother the Lord's devotee. |3|

Says Ravi Daas, my devotion to the One Lord is increasing; now, who can I tell this to?
That which brought me to worship and adore You - I am still suffering that pain. |4|2|

I obtained this precious human life as a reward for my past actions, but without discriminating wisdom, it is wasted in vain.
Tell me, without devotional worship of the Lord, of what use are mansions and thrones like those of King Indra? |1|

You have not considered the sublime essence of the Name of the Lord, our King;
this sublime essence shall cause you to forget all other essences. |1|Pause|

We do not know what we need to know, and we have become insane. We do not consider what we should consider; our days are passing away.
Our passions are strong, and our discriminating intellect is weak; we have no access to the supreme objective. |2|

We say one thing, and do something else; entangled in endless Maya, we do not understand anything.

Says Ravi Daas, Your slave, O Lord, I am disillusioned and detached; please, spare me Your anger, and have mercy on my soul. |3|3|

He is the ocean of peace; the miraculous tree of life, the wish-fulfilling jewel, and the Kaamadhayna, the cow which fulfills all desires, all are in His power.
The four great blessings, the eighteen supernatural spiritual powers of the Siddhas, and the nine treasures, are all in the palm of His hand. |1|

You do not chant with your tongue the Name of the Lord, Har, Har, Har.
Abandon your involvement in all other words. |1|Pause|

The various Shaastras, Puranaas, and the Vedas of Brahma, are made up of thirty-four letters.
After deep contemplation, Vyaas spoke of the supreme objective; there is nothing equal to the Lord's Name. |2|

Very fortunate are those who are absorbed in celestial bliss, and released from their entanglements; they are lovingly attached to the Lord.
Says Ravi Daas, enshrine the Lord's Light within your heart, and your fear of birth and death shall run away from you. |3|4|

If You are the mountain, Lord, then I am the peacock.
If You are the moon, then I am the partridge in love with it. |1|

O Lord, if You will not break with me, then I will not break with You.
For, if I were to break with You, with whom would I then join? |1|Pause|

If You are the lamp, then I am the wick.
If You are the sacred place of pilgrimage, then I am the pilgrim. |2|

Section 13 - Raag Sorat'h - Part 065

I am joined in true love with You, Lord.
I am joined with You, and I have broken with all others. |3|

Wherever I go, there I serve You.
There is no other Lord Master than You, O Divine Lord. |4|

Meditating, vibrating upon You, the noose of death is cut away.

To attain devotional worship, Ravi Daas sings to You, Lord. |5|5|

The body is a wall of water, supported by the pillars of air; the egg and sperm are the mortar.
The framework is made up of bones, flesh and veins; the poor soul-bird dwells within it. |1|

O mortal, what is mine, and what is yours?
The soul is like a bird perched upon a tree. |1|Pause|

You lay the foundation and build the walls.
But in the end, three and a half cubits will be your measured space. |2|

You make your hair beautiful, and wear a stylish turban on your head.
But in the end, this body shall be reduced to a pile of ashes. |3|

Your palaces are lofty, and your brides are beautiful.
But without the Lord's Name, you shall lose the game entirely. |4|

My social status is low, my ancestry is low, and my life is wretched.
I have come to Your Sanctuary, O Luminous Lord, my King; so says Ravi Daas, the shoemaker. |5|6|

I am a shoemaker, but I do not know how to mend shoes.
People come to me to mend their shoes. |1|Pause|

I have no awl to stitch them;
I have no knife to patch them. |1|

Mending, mending, people waste their lives and ruin themselves.
Without wasting my time mending, I have found the Lord. |2|

Ravi Daas chants the Lord's Name;
he is not concerned with the Messenger of Death. |3|7|

Raag Sorat'h, The Word Of Devotee Bheekhan Jee:
One Universal Creator God. By The Grace Of The True Guru:
Tears well up in my eyes, my body has become weak, and my hair has become milky-white.

My throat is tight, and I cannot utter even one word; what can I do now? I am a mere mortal. |1|

O Lord, my King, Gardener of the world-garden, be my Physician,
and save me, Your Saint. |1|Pause|

My head aches, my body is burning, and my heart is filled with anguish.
Such is the disease that has struck me; there is no medicine to cure it. |2|

The Name of the Lord, the ambrosial, immaculate water, is the best medicine in the world.
By Guru's Grace, says servant Bheekhan, I have found the Door of Salvation. |3|1|

Such is the Naam, the Name of the Lord, the invaluable jewel, the most sublime wealth, which I have found through good deeds.
By various efforts, I have enshrined it within my heart; this jewel cannot be hidden by hiding it. |1|

The Glorious Praises of the Lord cannot be spoken by speaking.
They are like the sweet candies given to a mute. |1|Pause|

The tongue speaks, the ears listen, and the mind contemplates the Lord; they find peace and comfort.
Says Bheekhan, my eyes are content; wherever I look, there I see the Lord. |2|2|

RAAG DHANAASAREE

Section 14 - Raag Dhanaasaree - Part 001

Dhanaasaree, First Mehl, First House, Chau-Padas:
ONE Universal Creator God. Truth Is The Name. Creative Being Personified.
No Fear. No Hatred. Image Of The Undying. Beyond Birth. Self-Existent. By
Guru's Grace:
My soul is afraid; to whom should I complain?
I serve Him, who makes me forget my pains; He is the Giver, forever and
ever. |1|

My Lord and Master is forever new; He is the Giver, forever and ever.
|1|Pause|

Night and day, I serve my Lord and Master; He shall save me in the end.
Hearing and listening, O my dear sister, I have crossed over. |2|

O Merciful Lord, Your Name carries me across.
I am forever a sacrifice to You. |1|Pause|

In all the world, there is only the One True Lord; there is no other at all.
He alone serves the Lord, upon whom the Lord casts His Glance of Grace.
|3|

Without You, O Beloved, how could I even live?
Bless me with such greatness, that I may remain attached to Your Name.
There is no other, O Beloved, to whom I can go and speak. |1|Pause|

I serve my Lord and Master; I ask for no other.
Nanak is His slave; moment by moment, bit by bit, he is a sacrifice to Him.
|4|

O Lord Master, I am a sacrifice to Your Name, moment by moment, bit by
bit. |1|Pause|4|1|

Dhanaasaree, First Mehl:

We are human beings of the briefest moment; we do not know the appointed time of our departure.
Prays Nanak, serve the One, to whom our soul and breath of life belong. |1|

You are blind - see and consider, how many days your life shall last. |1|Pause|

My breath, my flesh and my soul are all Yours, Lord; You are so very dear to me.
Nanak, the poet, says this, O True Lord Cherisher. |2|

If you gave nothing, O my Lord and Master, what could anyone pledge to You?
Nanak prays, we receive that which we are pre-destined to receive. |3|

The deceitful person does not remember the Lord's Name; he practices only deceit.
When he is marched in chains to Death's door, then, he regrets his actions. |4|

Section 14 - Raag Dhanaasaree - Part 002

As long as we are in this world, O Nanak, we should listen, and speak of the Lord.
I have searched, but I have found no way to remain here; so, remain dead while yet alive. |5|2|

Dhanaasaree, First Mehl, Second House:
One Universal Creator God. By The Grace Of The True Guru:
How can I remember the Lord in meditation? I cannot meditate on Him in remembrance.
My heart is burning, and my soul is crying out in pain.
The True Lord creates and adorns.
Forgetting Him, how can one be good? |1|

By clever tricks and commands, He cannot be found.
How am I to meet my True Lord, O my mother? |1|Pause|

How rare is the one who goes out, and searches for the merchandise of the Naam.

No one tastes it, and no one eats it.

Honor is not obtained by trying to please other people.

One's honor is preserved, only if the Lord preserves it. |2|

Wherever I look, there I see Him, pervading and permeating.

Without You, I have no other place of rest.

He may try, but what can anyone do by his own doing?

He alone is blessed, whom the True Lord forgives. |3|

Now, I shall have to get up and depart, in an instant, in the clapping of hands.

What face will I show the Lord? I have no virtue at all.

As is the Lord's Glance of Grace, so it is.

Without His Glance of Grace, O Nanak, no one is blessed. |4|1|3|

Dhanaasaree, First Mehl:

If the Lord bestows His Glance of Grace, then one remembers Him in meditation.

The soul is softened, and he remains absorbed in the Lord's Love.

His soul and the Supreme Soul become one.

The duality of the inner mind is overcome. |1|

By Guru's Grace, God is found.

One's consciousness is attached to the Lord, and so Death does not devour him. |1|Pause|

Remembering the True Lord in meditation, one is enlightened.

Then, in the midst of Maya, he remains detached.

Such is the Glory of the True Guru;

in the midst of children and spouses, they attain emancipation. |2|

Such is the service which the Lord's servant performs,

that he dedicates his soul to the Lord, to whom it belongs.

One who is pleasing to the Lord and Master is acceptable.

Such a servant obtains honor in the Court of the Lord. |3|

He enshrines the image of the True Guru in his heart.

He obtains the rewards which he desires.

The True Lord and Master grants His Grace;
how can such a servant be afraid of death? |4|

Prays Nanak, practice contemplation,
and enshrine love for the True Word of His Bani.
Then, you shall find the Gate of Salvation.
This Shabad is the most excellent of all chanting and austere meditations.
|5|2|4|

Dhanaasaree, First Mehl:
My soul burns, over and over again.
Burning and burning, it is ruined, and it falls into evil.
That body, which forgets the Word of the Guru's Bani,
cries out in pain, like a chronic patient. |1|

To speak too much and babble is useless.
Even without our speaking, He knows everything. |1|Pause|

He created our ears, eyes and nose.
He gave us our tongue to speak so fluently.

Section 14 - Raag Dhanaasaree - Part 003

He preserved the mind in the fire of the womb;
at His Command, the wind blows everywhere. |2|

These worldly attachments, loves and pleasurable tastes,
all are just black stains.
One who departs, with these black stains of sin on his face
shall find no place to sit in the Court of the Lord. |3|

By Your Grace, we chant Your Name.
Becoming attached to it, one is saved; there is no other way.
Even if one is drowning, still, he may be saved.
O Nanak, the True Lord is the Giver of all. |4|3|5|

Dhanaasaree, First Mehl:
If a thief praises someone, his mind is not pleased.
If a thief curses him, no damage is done.
No one will take responsibility for a thief.

How can a thief's actions be good? |1|

Listen, O mind, you blind, false dog!
Even without your speaking, the Lord knows and understands. |1|Pause|

A thief may be handsome, and a thief may be wise,
but he is still just a counterfeit coin, worth only a shell.
If it is kept and mixed with other coins,
it will be found to be false, when the coins are inspected. |2|

As one acts, so does he receive.
As he plants, so does he eat.
He may praise himself gloriously,
but still, according to his understanding, so is the path he must follow. |3|

He may tell hundreds of lies to conceal his falsehood,
and all the world may call him good.
If it pleases You, Lord, even the foolish are approved.
O Nanak, the Lord is wise, knowing, all-knowing. |4|4|6|

Dhanaasaree, First Mehl:
The body is the paper, and the mind is the inscription written upon it.
The ignorant fool does not read what is written on his forehead.
In the Court of the Lord, three inscriptions are recorded.
Behold, the counterfeit coin is worthless there. |1|

O Nanak, if there is silver in it,
then everyone proclaims, "It is genuine, it is genuine."|1|Pause|

The Qazi tells lies and eats filth;
the Brahmin kills and then takes cleansing baths.
The Yogi is blind, and does not know the Way.
The three of them devise their own destruction. |2|

He alone is a Yogi, who understands the Way.
By Guru's Grace, he knows the One Lord.
He alone is a Qazi, who turns away from the world,
and who, by Guru's Grace, remains dead while yet alive.
He alone is a Brahmin, who contemplates God.
He saves himself, and saves all his generations as well. |3|

One who cleanses his own mind is wise.
One who cleanses himself of impurity is a Muslim.
One who reads and understands is acceptable.
Upon his forehead is the Insignia of the Court of the Lord. |4|5|7|

Dhanaasaree, First Mehl, Third House:
One Universal Creator God. By The Grace Of The True Guru:
No, no, this is not the time, when people know the way to Yoga and Truth.
The holy places of worship in the world are polluted, and so the world is drowning. |1|

In this Dark Age of Kali Yuga, the Lord's Name is the most sublime.
Some people try to deceive the world by closing their eyes and holding their nostrils closed. |1|Pause|

They close off their nostrils with their fingers, and claim to see the three worlds.

Section 14 - Raag Dhanaasaree - Part 004

But they cannot even see what is behind them. What a strange lotus pose this is! |2|

The K'shatriyas have abandoned their religion, and have adopted a foreign language.
The whole world has been reduced to the same social status; the state of righteousness and Dharma has been lost. |3|

They analyze eight chapters of (Panini's) grammar and the Puraanas. They study the Vedas,
but without the Lord's Name, no one is liberated; so says Nanak, the Lord's slave. |4|1|6|8|

Dhanaasaree, First Mehl, Aartee:
One Universal Creator God. By The Grace Of The True Guru:
In the bowl of the sky, the sun and moon are the lamps; the stars in the constellations are the pearls.
The fragrance of sandalwood is the incense, the wind is the fan, and all the vegetation are flowers in offering to You, O Luminous Lord. |1|

What a beautiful lamp-lit worship service this is! O Destroyer of fear, this is Your Aartee, Your worship service.
The sound current of the Shabad is the sounding of the temple drums. |1|Pause|

Thousands are Your eyes, and yet You have no eyes. Thousands are Your forms, and yet You have not even one form.
Thousands are Your lotus feet, and yet You have no feet. Without a nose, thousands are Your noses. I am enchanted with Your play! |2|

The Divine Light is within everyone; You are that Light.
Yours is that Light which shines within everyone.
By the Guru's Teachings, this Divine Light is revealed.
That which pleases the Lord is the true worship service. |3|

My soul is enticed by the honey-sweet lotus feet of the Lord; night and day, I thirst for them.
Bless Nanak, the thirsty song-bird, with the water of Your Mercy, that he may come to dwell in Your Name. |4|1|7|9|

Dhanaasaree, Third Mehl, Second House, Chau-Padas:
One Universal Creator God. By The Grace Of The True Guru:
This wealth is inexhaustible. It shall never be exhausted, and it shall never be lost.
The Perfect True Guru has revealed it to me.
I am forever a sacrifice to my True Guru.
By Guru's Grace, I have enshrined the Lord within my mind. |1|

They alone are wealthy, who lovingly attune themselves to the Lord's Name.
The Perfect Guru has revealed to me the Lord's treasure; by the Lord's Grace, it has come to abide in my mind. |Pause|

He is rid of his demerits, and his heart is permeated with merit and virtue.
By Guru's Grace, he naturally dwells in celestial peace.
True is the Word of the Perfect Guru's Bani.
They bring peace to the mind, and celestial peace is absorbed within. |2|

O my humble Siblings of Destiny, behold this strange and wonderful thing:

duality is overcome, and the Lord dwells within his mind.
The Naam, the Name of the Lord, is priceless; it cannot be taken.
By Guru's Grace, it comes to abide in the mind. |3|

He is the One God, abiding within all.
Through the Guru's Teachings, He is revealed in the heart.
One who intuitively knows and realizes God,

Section 14 - Raag Dhanaasaree - Part 005

O Nanak, obtains the Naam; his mind is pleased and appeased. |4|1|

Dhanaasaree, Third Mehl:
The wealth of the Lord's Name is immaculate, and absolutely infinite.
The Word of the Guru's Shabad is over-flowing with treasure.
Know that, except for the wealth of the Name, all other wealth is poison.
The egotistical people are burning in their attachment to Maya. |1|

How rare is that Gurmukh who tastes the sublime essence of the Lord.
He is always in bliss, day and night; through perfect good destiny, he obtains the Name. |Pause|

The Word of the Shabad is a lamp, illuminating the three worlds.
One who tastes it, becomes immaculate.
The immaculate Naam, the Name of the Lord, washes off the filth of ego.
True devotional worship brings lasting peace. |2|

One who tastes the sublime essence of the Lord is the Lord's humble servant.
He is forever happy; he is never sad.
He himself is liberated, and he liberates others as well.
He chants the Lord's Name, and through the Lord, he finds peace. |3|

Without the True Guru, everyone dies, crying out in pain.
Night and day, they burn, and find no peace.
But meeting the True Guru, all thirst is quenched.
O Nanak, through the Naam, one finds peace and tranquility. |4|2|

Dhanaasaree, Third Mehl:
Gather in and cherish forever the wealth of the Lord's Name, deep within;

He cherishes and nurtures all beings and creatures.
They alone obtain the treasure of Liberation,
who are lovingly imbued with, and focused on the Lord's Name. |1|

Serving the Guru, one obtains the wealth of the Lord's Name.
He is illumined and enlightened within, and he meditates on the Lord's Name. |Pause|

This love for the Lord is like the love of the bride for her husband.
God ravishes and enjoys the soul-bride who is adorned with peace and tranquility.
No one finds God through egotism.
Wandering away from the Primal Lord, the root of all, one wastes his life in vain. |2|

Tranquility, celestial peace, pleasure and the Word of His Bani come from the Guru.
True is that service, which leads one to merge in the Naam.
Blessed with the Word of the Shabad, he meditates forever on the Lord, the Beloved.
Through the True Name, glorious greatness is obtained. |3|

The Creator Himself abides throughout the ages.
If He casts His Glance of Grace, then we meet Him.
Through the Word of Gurbani, the Lord comes to dwell in the mind.
O Nanak, God unites with Himself those who are imbued with Truth. |4|3|

Dhanaasaree, Third Mehl:
The world is polluted, and those in the world become polluted as well.
In attachment to duality, it comes and goes.
This love of duality has ruined the entire world.
The self-willed manmukh suffers punishment, and forfeits his honor. |1|

Serving the Guru, one becomes immaculate.
He enshrines the Naam, the Name of the Lord, within, and his state becomes exalted. |Pause|

The Gurmukhs are saved, taking to the Lord's Sanctuary.
Attuned to the Lord's Name, they commit themselves to devotional worship.

The Lord's humble servant performs devotional worship, and is blessed with greatness.
Attuned to Truth, he is absorbed in celestial peace. |2|

Know that one who purchases the True Name is very rare.
Through the Word of the Guru's Shabad, he comes to understand himself.
True is his capital, and true is his trade.
Blessed is that person, who loves the Naam. |3|

God, the True Lord, has attached some to His True Name.
They listen to the most sublime Word of His Bani, and the Word of His Shabad.

Section 14 - Raag Dhanaasaree - Part 006

True is service to the True Lord God.
O Nanak, the Naam is the Embellisher. |4|4|

Dhanaasaree, Third Mehl:
I am a sacrifice to those who serve the Lord.
The Truth is in their hearts, and the True Name is on their lips.
Dwelling upon the Truest of the True, their pains are dispelled.
Through the True Word of the Shabad, the Lord comes to dwell in their minds. |1|

Listening to the Word of Gurbani, filth is washed off,
and they naturally enshrine the Lord's Name in their minds. |1|Pause|

One who conquers fraud, deceit and the fire of desire
finds tranquility, peace and pleasure within.
If one walks in harmony with the Guru's Will, he eliminates his self-conceit.
He finds the True Mansion of the Lord's Presence, singing the Glorious Praises of the Lord. |2|

The blind, self-willed manmukh does not understand the Shabad; he does not know the Word of the Guru's Bani,

and so he passes his life in misery.
But if he meets the True Guru, then he finds peace,
and the ego within is silenced. |3|

Who else should I speak to? The One Lord is the Giver of all.
When He grants His Grace, then we obtain the Word of the Shabad.
Meeting with my Beloved, I sing the Glorious Praises of the True Lord.
O Nanak, becoming truthful, I have become pleasing to the True Lord.
|4|5|

Dhanaasaree, Third Mehl:
When the mind is conquered, its turbulent wanderings are stopped.
Without conquering the mind, how can the Lord be found?
Rare is the one who knows the medicine to conquer the mind.
The mind is conquered through the Word of the Shabad; this is known to
the Lord's humble servant. |1|

The Lord forgives him, and blesses him with glory.
By Guru's Grace, the Lord comes to dwell in the mind. |Pause|

The Gurmukh does good deeds,
and so, he comes to understand this mind.
The mind is intoxicated, like the elephant with wine.
The Guru places the harness upon it, and rejuvenates it. |2|

The mind is undisciplined; only a rare few can discipline it.
If someone eats the uneatable, then he becomes immaculate.
As Gurmukh, his mind is embellished.
Egotism and corruption are eradicated from within. |3|

Those whom the Primal Lord keeps united in His Union,
shall never be separated from Him; they are merged in the Word of the
Shabad.
Only God Himself knows His own power.
O Nanak, the Gurmukh realizes the Naam, the Name of the Lord. |4|6|

Dhanaasaree, Third Mehl:
The ignorant fools amass false wealth.
The blind, foolish, self-willed manmukhs have gone astray.
Poisonous wealth brings constant pain.
It will not go with you, and it will not yield any profit. |1|

True wealth is obtained through the Guru's Teachings.

False wealth continues coming and going. |Pause|

The foolish self-willed manmukhs all go astray and die.
They drown in the terrifying world-ocean, and they cannot reach either this shore, or the one beyond.
But by perfect destiny, they meet the True Guru;
imbued with the True Name, day and night, they remain detached from the world. |2|

Throughout the four ages, the True Bani of His Word is Ambrosial Nectar.
By perfect destiny, one is absorbed in the True Name.
The Siddhas, the seekers and all men long for the Name.
It is obtained only by perfect destiny. |3|

The True Lord is everything; He is True.
Only a few realize the exalted Lord God.
He is the Truest of the True; He Himself implants the True Name within.

Section 14 - Raag Dhanaasaree - Part 007

O Nanak, the Lord Himself sees all; He Himself links us to the Truth. |4|7|

Dhanaasaree, Third Mehl:
The value and worth of the Lord's Name cannot be described.
Blessed are those humble beings, who lovingly focus their minds on the Naam, the Name of the Lord.
True are the Guru's Teachings, and True is contemplative meditation.
God Himself forgives, and bestows contemplative meditation. |1|

The Lord's Name is wonderful! God Himself imparts it.
In the Dark Age of Kali Yuga, the Gurmukhs obtain it. |1|Pause|

We are ignorant; ignorance fills our minds.
We do all our deeds in ego.
By Guru's Grace, egotism is eradicated.
Forgiving us, the Lord blends us with Himself. |2|

Poisonous wealth gives rise to great arrogance.
Drowning in egotism, no one is honored.
Forsaking self-conceit, one finds lasting peace.

Under Guru's Instruction, he praises the True Lord. |3|

The Creator Lord Himself fashions all.
Without Him, there is no other at all.
He alone is attached to Truth, whom the Lord Himself so attaches.
O Nanak, through the Naam, lasting peace is attained in the hereafter.
|4|8|

Raag Dhanaasaree, Third Mehl, Fourth House:
One Universal Creator God. By The Grace Of The True Guru:
I am just a poor beggar of Yours; You are Your Own Lord Master, You are
the Great Giver.
Be Merciful, and bless me, a humble beggar, with Your Name, so that I may
forever remain imbued with Your Love. |1|

I am a sacrifice to Your Name, O True Lord.
The One Lord is the Cause of causes; there is no other at all. |1|Pause|

I was wretched; I wandered through so many cycles of reincarnation. Now,
Lord, please bless me with Your Grace.
Be merciful, and grant me the Blessed Vision of Your Darshan; please grant
me such a gift. |2|

Prays Nanak, the shutters of doubt have been opened wide; by Guru's
Grace, I have come to know the Lord.
I am filled to overflowing with true love; my mind is pleased and appeased
by the True Guru. |3|1|9|

Dhanaasaree, Fourth Mehl, First House, Chau-Padas:
One Universal Creator God. By The Grace Of The True Guru:
Those Saints and devotees who serve the Lord have all their sins washed
away.
Have Mercy on me, O Lord and Master, and keep me in the Sangat, the
Congregation that You love. |1|

I cannot even speak the Praises of the Lord, the Gardener of the world.
We are sinners, sinking like stones in water; grant Your Grace, and carry us
stones across. |Pause|

The rust of poison and corruption from countless incarnations sticks to us; joining the Saadh Sangat, the Company of the Holy, it is cleaned away.
It is just like gold, which is heated in the fire, to remove the impurities from it. |2|

I chant the chant of the Name of the Lord, day and night; I chant the Name of the Lord, Har, Har, Har, and enshrine it within my heart.
The Name of the Lord, Har, Har, Har, is the most perfect medicine in this world; chanting the Name of the Lord, Har, Har, I have conquered my ego. |3|

Section 14 - Raag Dhanaasaree - Part 008

The Lord, Har, Har, is unapproachable, of unfathomable wisdom, unlimited, all-powerful and infinite.
Show Mercy to Your humble servant, O Life of the world, and save the honor of servant Nanak. |4|1|

Dhanaasaree, Fourth Mehl:
The humble Saints of the Lord meditate on the Lord; their pain, doubt and fear have run away.
The Lord Himself inspires them to serve Him; they are awakened within to the Guru's Teachings. |1|

Imbued with the Lord's Name, they are unattached to the world.
Listening to the sermon of the Lord, Har, Har, their minds are pleased; through Guru's Instruction, they enshrine love for the Lord. |1|Pause|

God, the Lord and Master, is the caste and social status of His humble Saints. You are the Lord and Master; I am just Your puppet.
As is the understanding You bless us with, so are the words we speak. |2|

What are we? Tiny worms, and microscopic germs. You are our great and glorious Lord and Master.
I cannot describe Your state and extent. O God, how can we unfortunate ones meet with You? |3|

O God, my Lord and Master, shower me with Your Mercy, and commit me to Your service.

Make Nanak the slave of Your slaves, God; I speak the speech of the Lord's sermon. |4|2|

Dhanaasaree, Fourth Mehl:
The True Guru is the Lord's Saint, the True Being, who chants the Bani of the Lord, Har, Har.
Whoever chants it, and listens to it, is liberated; I am forever a sacrifice to him. |1|

O Saints of the Lord, listen to the Lord's Praises with your ears.
Listen to the sermon of the Lord, Har, Har, for a moment, for even an instant, and all your sins and mistakes shall be erased. |1|Pause|

Those who find such humble, Holy Saints, are the greatest of the great persons.
I beg for the dust of their feet; I long for the longing for God, my Lord and Master. |2|

The Name of God, the Lord and Master, Har, Har, is the fruit-bearing tree; those who meditate on it are satisfied.
Drinking in the ambrosia of the Name of the Lord, Har, Har, I am satisfied; all my hunger and thirst is quenched. |3|

Those who are blessed with the highest, loftiest destiny, chant and meditate on the Lord.
Let me join their congregation, O God, my Lord and Master; Nanak is the slave of their slaves. |4|3|

Dhanaasaree, Fourth Mehl:
I am blind, totally blind, entangled in corruption and poison. How can I walk on the Guru's Path?
If the True Guru, the Giver of peace, shows His kindness, He attaches us to the hem of His robe. |1|

O Sikhs of the Guru, O friends, walk on the Guru's Path.
Whatever the Guru says, accept that as good; the sermon of the Lord, Har, Har, is unique and wonderful. |1|Pause|

O Saints of the Lord, O Siblings of Destiny, listen: serve the Guru, quickly now!

Let your service to the True Guru be your supplies on the Lord's Path; pack them up, and don't think of today or tomorrow. |2|

O Saints of the Lord, chant the chant of the Lord's Name; the Lord's Saints walk with the Lord.
Those who meditate on the Lord, become the Lord; the playful, wondrous Lord meets them. |3|

To chant the chant of the Lord's Name, Har, Har, is the longing I long for; have Mercy upon me, O Lord of the world-forest.
O Lord, unite servant Nanak with the Saadh Sangat, the Company of the Holy; make me the dust of the feet of the Holy. |4|4|

Section 14 - Raag Dhanaasaree - Part 009

Dhanaasaree, Fourth Mehl:
The Lord, Har, Har, is the rain-drop; I am the song-bird, crying, crying out for it.
O Lord God, please bless me with Your Mercy, and pour Your Name into my mouth, even if for only an instant. |1|

Without the Lord, I cannot live for even a second.
Like the addict who dies without his drug, I die without the Lord. |Pause|

You, Lord, are the deepest, most unfathomable ocean; I cannot find even a trace of Your limits.
You are the most remote of the remote, limitless and transcendent; O Lord Master, You alone know Your state and extent. |2|

The Lord's humble Saints meditate on the Lord; they are imbued with the deep crimson color of the Guru's Love.
Meditating on the Lord, they attain great glory, and the most sublime honor. |3|

He Himself is the Lord and Master, and He Himself is the servant; He Himself creates His environments.
Servant Nanak has come to Your Sanctuary, O Lord; protect and preserve the honor of Your devotee. |4|5|

Dhanaasaree, Fourth Mehl:

Tell me, O Siblings of Destiny, the religion for this Dark Age of Kali Yuga. I seek emancipation - how can I be emancipated?

Meditation on the Lord, Har, Har, is the boat, the raft; meditating on the Lord, the swimmer swims across. |1|

O Dear Lord, protect and preserve the honor of Your humble servant.
O Lord, Har, Har, please make me chant the chant of Your Name; I beg only for Your devotional worship. |Pause|

The Lord's servants are very dear to the Lord; they chant the Word of the Lord's Bani.
The account of the recording angels, Chitr and Gupt, and the account with the Messenger of Death is totally erased. |2|

The Saints of the Lord meditate on the Lord in their minds; they join the Saadh Sangat, the Company of the Holy.
The piercing sun of desires has set, and the cool moon has risen. |3|

You are the Greatest Being, absolutely unapproachable and unfathomable; You created the Universe from Your Own Being.
O God, take pity on servant Nanak, and make him the slave of the slave of Your slaves. |4|6|

Dhanaasaree, Fourth Mehl, Fifth House, Du-Padas:
One Universal Creator God. By The Grace Of The True Guru:
Enshrine the Lord within your heart, and contemplate Him. Dwell upon Him, reflect upon Him, and chant the Name of the Lord, the Enticer of hearts.
The Lord Master is unseen, unfathomable and unreachable; through the Perfect Guru, He is revealed. |1|

The Lord is the philosopher's stone, which transforms lead into gold, and sandalwood, while I am just dry wood and iron.
Associating with the Lord, and the Sat Sangat, the Lord's True Congregation, the Lord has transformed me into gold and sandalwood. |1|Pause|

One may repeat, verbatim, the nine grammars and the six Shaastras, but my Lord God is not pleased by this.

O servant Nanak, meditate forever on the Lord in your heart; this is what pleases my Lord God. |2|1|7|

Dhanaasaree, Fourth Mehl:

Section 14 - Raag Dhanaasaree - Part 010

Chant His Praises, learn of the Lord, and serve the True Guru; in this way, meditate on the Name of the Lord, Har, Har.
In the Court of the Lord, He shall be pleased with you, and you shall not have to enter the cycle of reincarnation again; you shall merge in the Divine Light of the Lord, Har, Har, Har. |1|

Chant the Name of the Lord, O my mind, and you shall be totally at peace.
The Lord's Praises are the most sublime, the most exalted; serving the Lord, Har, Har, Har, you shall be emancipated. |Pause|

The Lord, the treasure of mercy, blessed me, and so the Guru blessed me with the Lord's devotional worship; I have come to be in love with the Lord.
I have forgotten my cares and anxieties, and enshrined the Lord's Name in my heart; O Nanak, the Lord has become my friend and companion. |2|2|8|

Dhanaasaree, Fourth Mehl:
Read about the Lord, write about the Lord, chant the Lord's Name, and sing the Lord's Praises; the Lord will carry you across the terrifying world-ocean.
In your mind, by your words, and within your heart, meditate on the Lord, and He will be pleased. In this way, repeat the Name of the Lord. |1|

O mind, meditate on the Lord, the Lord of the World.
Join the Saadh Sangat, the Company of the Holy, O friend.
You shall be happy forever, day and night; sing the Praises of the Lord, the Lord of the world-forest. |Pause|

When the Lord, Har, Har, casts His Glance of Grace, then I made the effort in my mind; meditating on the Name of the Lord, Har, Har, I have been emancipated.
Preserve the honor of servant Nanak, O my Lord and Master; I have come seeking Your Sanctuary. |2|3|9|

Dhanaasaree, Fourth Mehl:

The eighty-four Siddhas, the spiritual masters, the Buddhas, the three hundred thirty million gods and the silent sages, all long for Your Name, O Dear Lord.

By Guru's Grace, a rare few obtain it; upon their foreheads, the pre-ordained destiny of loving devotion is written. |1|

O mind, chant the Name of the Lord; singing the Lord's Praises is the most exalted activity.

I am forever a sacrifice to those who sing, and hear Your Praises, O Lord and Master. |Pause|

I seek Your Sanctuary, O Cherisher God, my Lord and Master; whatever You give me, I accept.

O Lord, Merciful to the meek, give me this blessing; Nanak longs for the Lord's meditative remembrance. |2|4|10|

Dhanaasaree, Fourth Mehl:

All the Sikhs and servants come to worship and adore You; they sing the sublime Bani of the Lord, Har, Har.

Their singing and listening is approved by the Lord; they accept the Order of the True Guru as True, totally True. |1|

Chant the Lord's Praises, O Siblings of Destiny; the Lord is the sacred shrine of pilgrimage in the terrifying world-ocean.

They alone are praised in the Court of the Lord, O Saints, who know and understand the Lord's sermon. |Pause|

He Himself is the Guru, and He Himself is the disciple; the Lord God Himself plays His wondrous games.

O servant Nanak, he alone merges with the Lord, whom the Lord Himself merges; all the others are forsaken, but the Lord loves him. |2|5|11|

Dhanaasaree, Fourth Mehl:

The Lord is the Fulfiller of desires, the Giver of total peace; the Kaamad-haynaa, the wish-fulfilling cow, is in His power.

So meditate on such a Lord, O my soul. Then, you shall obtain total peace, O my mind. |1|

Section 14 - Raag Dhanaasaree - Part 011

Chant, O my mind, the True Name, Sat Naam, the True Name.
In this world, and in the world beyond, your face shall be radiant, by meditating continually on the immaculate Lord God. |Pause|

Wherever anyone remembers the Lord in meditation, disaster runs away from that place. By great good fortune, we meditate on the Lord.
The Guru has blessed servant Nanak with this understanding, that by meditating on the Lord, we cross over the terrifying world-ocean. |2|6|12|

Dhanaasaree, Fourth Mehl:
O my King, beholding the Blessed Vision of the Lord's Darshan, I am at peace.
You alone know my inner pain, O King; what can anyone else know? |Pause|

O True Lord and Master, You are truly my King; whatever You do, all that is True.
Who should I call a liar? There is no other than You, O King. |1|

You are pervading and permeating in all; O King, everyone meditates on You, day and night.
Everyone begs of You, O my King; You alone give gifts to all. |2|

All are under Your Power, O my King; none at all are beyond You.
All beings are Yours-You belong to all, O my King. All shall merge and be absorbed in You. |3|

You are the hope of all, O my Beloved; all meditate on You, O my King.
As it pleases You, protect and preserve me, O my Beloved; You are the True King of Nanak. |4|7|13|

Dhanaasaree, Fifth Mehl, First House, Chau-Padas:
One Universal Creator God. By The Grace Of The True Guru:
O Destroyer of fear, Remover of suffering, Lord and Master, Lover of Your devotees, Formless Lord.
Millions of sins are eradicated in an instant when, as Gurmukh, one contemplates the Naam, the Name of the Lord. |1|

My mind is attached to my Beloved Lord.

God, Merciful to the meek, granted His Grace, and placed the five enemies under my control. |1|Pause|

Your place is so beautiful; Your form is so beautiful; Your devotees look so beautiful in Your Court.
O Lord and Master, Giver of all beings, please, grant Your Grace, and save me. |2|

Your color is not known, and Your form is not seen; who can contemplate Your Almighty Creative Power?

You are contained in the water, the land and the sky, everywhere, O Lord of unfathomable form, Holder of the mountain. |3|

All beings sing Your Praises; You are the imperishable Primal Being, the Destroyer of ego.
As it pleases You, please protect and preserve me; servant Nanak seeks Sanctuary at Your Door. |4|1|

Dhanaasaree, Fifth Mehl:
The fish out of water loses its life; it is deeply in love with the water.
The bumble bee, totally in love with the lotus flower, is lost in it; it cannot find the way to escape from it. |1|

Now, my mind has nurtured love for the One Lord.
He does not die, and is not born; He is always with me. Through the Word of the True Guru's Shabad, I know Him. |1|Pause|

Section 14 - Raag Dhanaasaree - Part 012

Lured by sexual desire, the elephant is trapped; the poor beast falls into the power of another.
Lured by the sound of the hunter's bell, the deer offers its head; because of this enticement, it is killed. |2|

Gazing upon his family, the mortal is enticed by greed; he clings in attachment to Maya.
Totally engrossed in worldly things, he considers them to be his own; but in the end, he shall surely have to leave them behind. |3|

Know it well, that anyone who loves any other than God, shall be miserable forever.

Says Nanak, the Guru has explained this to me, that love for God brings lasting bliss. |4|2|

Dhanaasaree, Fifth Mehl:

Granting His Grace, God has blessed me with His Name, and released me of my bonds.

I have forgotten all worldly entanglements, and I am attached to the Guru's feet. |1|

In the Saadh Sangat, the Company of the Holy, I have renounced my other cares and anxieties.

I dug a deep pit, and buried my egotistical pride, emotional attachment and the desires of my mind. |1|Pause|

No one is my enemy, and I am no one's enemy.

God, who expanded His expanse, is within all; I learned this from the True Guru. |2|

I am a friend to all; I am everyone's friend.

When the sense of separation was removed from my mind, then I was united with the Lord, my King. |3|

My stubbornness is gone, Ambrosial Nectar rains down, and the Word of the Guru's Shabad seems so sweet to me.

He is pervading everywhere, in the water, on the land and in the sky; Nanak beholds the all-pervading Lord. |4|3|

Dhanaasaree, Fifth Mehl:

Ever since I obtained the Blessed Vision of the Darshan of the Holy, my days have been blessed and prosperous.

I have found lasting bliss, singing the Kirtan of the Praises of the Primal Lord, the Architect of destiny. |1|

Now, I sing the Praises of the Lord within my mind.

My mind has been illumined and enlightened, and it is always at peace; I have found the Perfect True Guru. |1|Pause|

The Lord, the treasure of virtue, abides deep within the heart, and so pain, doubt and fear have been dispelled.
I have obtained the most incomprehensible thing, enshrining love for the Name of the Lord. |2|

I was anxious, and now I am free of anxiety; I was worried, and now I am free of worry; my grief, greed and emotional attachments are gone.
By His Grace, I am cured of the disease of egotism, and the Messenger of Death no longer terrifies me. |3|

Working for the Guru, serving the Guru and the Guru's Command, all are pleasing to me.
Says Nanak, He has released me from the clutches of Death; I am a sacrifice to that Guru. |4|4|

Dhanaasaree, Fifth Mehl:
Body, mind, wealth and everything belong to Him; He alone is all-wise and all-knowing.
He listens to my pains and pleasures, and then my condition improves. |1|

My soul is satisfied with the One Lord alone.
People make all sorts of other efforts, but they have no value at all. |Pause|

The Ambrosial Naam, the Name of the Lord, is a priceless jewel. The Guru has given me this advice.
It cannot be lost, and it cannot be shaken off; it remains steady, and I am perfectly satisfied with it. |2|

Those things which tore me away from You, Lord, are now gone.

Section 14 - Raag Dhanaasaree - Part 013

When golden ornaments are melted down into a lump, they are still said to be gold. |3|

The Divine Light has illuminated me, and I am filled with celestial peace and glory; the unstruck melody of the Lord's Bani resounds within me.
Says Nanak, I have built my eternal home; the Guru has constructed it for me. |4|5|

Dhanaasaree, Fifth Mehl:
The desires of the greatest of the great kings and landlords cannot be satisfied.
They remain engrossed in Maya, intoxicated with the pleasures of their wealth; their eyes see nothing else at all. |1|

No one has ever found satisfaction in sin and corruption.
The flame is not satisfied by more fuel; how can one be satisfied without the Lord? |Pause|

Day after day, he eats his meals with many different foods, but his hunger is not eradicated.
He runs around like a dog, searching in the four directions. |2|

The lustful, lecherous man desires many women, and he never stops peeking into the homes of others.
Day after day, he commits adultery again and again, and then he regrets his actions; he wastes away in misery and greed. |3|

The Name of the Lord, Har, Har, is incomparable and priceless; it is the treasure of Ambrosial Nectar.
The Saints abide in peace, poise and bliss; O Nanak, through the Guru, this is known. |4|6|

Dhanaasaree, Fifth Mehl:
Nothing which this mortal being runs after, can compare to it.
He alone comes to have it, whom the Guru blesses with this Ambrosial Nectar. |1|

The desire to eat, to wear new clothes, and all other desires, do not abide in the mind of one who comes to know the subtle essence of the One Lord. |Pause|

The mind and body blossom forth in abundance, when one receives even a drop of this Nectar.
I cannot express His glory; I cannot describe His worth. |2|

We cannot meet the Lord by our own efforts, nor can we meet Him through service; He comes and meets us spontaneously.

One who is blessed by my Lord Master's Grace, practices the Teachings of the Guru's Mantra. |3|

He is merciful to the meek, always kind and compassionate; He cherishes and nurtures all beings.
The Lord is mingled with Nanak, through and through; He cherishes him, like the mother her child. |4|7|

Dhanaasaree, Fifth Mehl:
I am a sacrifice to my Guru, who has implanted the Name of the Lord, Har, Har, within me.
In the utter darkness of the wilderness, He showed me the straight path. |1|

The Lord of the universe, the Cherisher of the world, He is my breath of life.
Here and hereafter, he takes care of everything for me. |1|Pause|

Meditating on Him in remembrance, I have found all treasures, respect, greatness and perfect honor.
Remembering His Name, millions of sins are erased; all His devotees long for the dust of His feet. |2|

If someone wishes for the fulfillment of all his hopes and desires, he should serve the one supreme treasure.
He is the Supreme Lord God, infinite Lord and Master; meditating on Him in remembrance, one is carried across. |3|

I have found total peace and tranquility in the Society of the Saints; my honor has been preserved.
To gather in the Lord's wealth, and to taste the food of the Lord's Name - Nanak has made this his feast. |4|8|

Section 14 - Raag Dhanaasaree - Part 014

Dhanaasaree, Fifth Mehl:
You have made it your habit to practice those deeds which will bring you shame.
You slander the Saints, and you worship the faithless cynics; such are the corrupt ways you have adopted. |1|

Deluded by your emotional attachment to Maya, you love other things, like the enchanted city of Hari-chandauree, or the green leaves of the forest - such is your way of life. |1|Pause|

Its body may be anointed with sandalwood oil, but the donkey still loves to roll in the mud.
He is not fond of the Ambrosial Nectar; instead, he loves the poisonous drug of corruption. |2|

The Saints are noble and sublime; they are blessed with good fortune. They alone are pure and holy in this world.
The jewel of this human life is passing away uselessly, lost in exchange for mere glass. |3|

The sins and sorrows of uncounted incarnations run away, when the Guru applies the healing ointment of spiritual wisdom to the eyes.
In the Saadh Sangat, the Company of the Holy, I have escaped from these troubles; Nanak loves the One Lord. |4|9|

Dhanaasaree, Fifth Mehl:
I carry the water, wave the fan, and grind the corn for the Saints; I sing the Glorious Praises of the Lord of the Universe.
With each and every breath, my mind remembers the Naam, the Name of the Lord; in this way, it finds the treasure of peace. |1|

Have pity on me, O my Lord and Master.
Bless me with such understanding, O my Lord and Master, that I may forever and ever meditate on You. |1|Pause|

By Your Grace, emotional attachment and egotism are eradicated, and doubt is dispelled.
The Lord, the embodiment of bliss, is pervading and permeating in all; wherever I go, there I see Him. |2|

You are kind and compassionate, the treasure of mercy, the Purifier of sinners, Lord of the world.
I obtain millions of joys, comforts and kingdoms, if You inspire me to chant Your Name with my mouth, even for an instant. |3|

That alone is perfect chanting, meditation, penance and devotional worship service, which is pleasing to God's Mind.
Chanting the Naam, all thirst and desire is satisfied; Nanak is satisfied and fulfilled. |4|10|

Dhanaasaree, Fifth Mehl:
She controls the three qualities and the four directions of the world.
She destroys sacrificial feasts, cleansing baths, penances and sacred places of pilgrimage; what is this poor person to do? |1|

I grasped God's Support and Protection, and then I was emancipated.
By the Grace of the Holy Saints, I sang the Praises of the Lord, Har, Har, Har, and my sins and afflictions were taken away. |1|Pause|

She is not heard - she does not speak with a mouth; she is not seen enticing mortals.
She administers her intoxicating drug, and so confuses them; thus she seems sweet to everyone's mind. |2|

In each and every home, she has implanted the sense of duality in mother, father, children, friends and siblings.
Some have more, and some have less; they fight and fight, to the death. |3|

I am a sacrifice to my True Guru, who has shown me this wondrous play.
The world is being consumed by this hidden fire, but Maya does not cling to the Lord's devotees. |4|

By the Grace of the Saints, I have obtained supreme bliss, and all my bonds have been broken.
Nanak has obtained the wealth of the Name of the Lord, Har, Har; having earned his profits, he has now returned home. |5|11|

Dhanaasaree, Fifth Mehl:
You are the Giver, O Lord, O Cherisher, my Master, my Husband Lord.

Section 14 - Raag Dhanaasaree - Part 015

Each and every moment, You cherish and nurture me; I am Your child, and I rely upon You alone. |1|

I have only one tongue - which of Your Glorious Virtues can I describe?
Unlimited, infinite Lord and Master - no one knows Your limits. |1|Pause|

You destroy millions of my sins, and teach me in so many ways.
I am so ignorant - I understand nothing at all. Please honor Your innate nature, and save me! |2|

I seek Your Sanctuary - You are my only hope. You are my companion, and my best friend.
Save me, O Merciful Saviour Lord; Nanak is the slave of Your home. |3|12|

Dhanaasaree, Fifth Mehl:
Worship, fasting, ceremonial marks on one's forehead, cleansing baths, generous donations to charities and self-mortification

- the Lord Master is not pleased with any of these rituals, no matter how sweetly one may speak. |1|

Chanting the Name of God, the mind is soothed and pacified.
Everyone searches for Him in different ways, but the search is so difficult, and He cannot be found. |1|Pause|

Chanting, deep meditation and penance, wandering over the face of the earth, the performance of austerities with the arms stretched up to the sky

- the Lord is not pleased by any of these means, though one may follow the path of Yogis and Jains. |2|

The Ambrosial Naam, the Name of the Lord, and the Praises of the Lord are priceless; he alone obtains them, whom the Lord blesses with His Mercy.
Joining the Saadh Sangat, the Company of the Holy, Nanak lives in the Love of God; his life-night passes in peace. |3|13|

Dhanaasaree, Fifth Mehl:
Is there anyone who can release me from my bondage, unite me with God, recite the Name of the Lord, Har, Har,

and make this mind steady and stable, so that it no longer wanders around? |1|

Do I have any such friend?
I would give him all my property, my soul and my heart; I would devote my consciousness to him. |1|Pause|

Others' wealth, others' bodies, and the slander of others - do not attach your love to them.
Associate with the Saints, speak with the Saints, and keep your mind awake to the Kirtan of the Lord's Praises. |2|

God is the treasure of virtue, kind and compassionate, the source of all comfort.
Nanak begs for the gift of Your Name; O Lord of the world, love him, like the mother loves her child. |3|14|

Dhanaasaree, Fifth Mehl:
The Lord saves His Saints.
One who wishes misfortune upon the Lord's slaves, shall be destroyed by the Lord eventually. |1|Pause|

He Himself is the help and support of His humble servants; He defeats the slanderers, and chases them away.
Wandering around aimlessly, they die out there; they never return to their homes again. |1|

Nanak seeks the Sanctuary of the Destroyer of pain; he sings the Glorious Praises of the infinite Lord forever.
The faces of the slanderers are blackened in the courts of this world, and the world beyond. |2|15|

Dhanaasaree, Fifth Mehl:
Now, I contemplate and meditate on the Lord, the Saviour Lord.
He purifies sinners in an instant, and cures all diseases. |1|Pause|

Talking with the Holy Saints, my sexual desire, anger and greed have been eradicated.
Remembering, remembering the Perfect Lord in meditation, I have saved all my companions. |1|

Section 14 - Raag Dhanaasaree - Part 016

The Mul Mantra, the Root Mantra, is the only cure for the mind; I have installed faith in God in my mind.
Nanak ever longs for the dust of the Lord's feet; again and again, he is a sacrifice to the Lord. |2|16|

Dhanaasaree, Fifth Mehl:
I have fallen in love with the Lord.
My True Guru is always my help and support; He has torn down the banner of pain. |1|Pause|

Giving me His hand, He has protected me as His own, and removed all my troubles.
He has blackened the faces of the slanderers, and He Himself has become the help and support of His humble servant. |1|

The True Lord and Master has become my Saviour; hugging me close in His embrace, He has saved me.
Nanak has become fearless, and he enjoys eternal peace, singing the Glorious Praises of the Lord. |2|17|

Dhanaasaree, Fifth Mehl:
Your Name is the medicine, O Merciful Lord.
I am so miserable, I do not know Your state; You Yourself cherish me, Lord. |1|Pause|

Take pity on me, O my Lord and Master, and remove the love of duality from within me.
Break my bonds, and take me as Your own, so that I may never come to lose. |1|

Seeking Your Sanctuary, I live, almighty and merciful Lord and Master.
Twenty-four hours a day, I worship God; Nanak is forever a sacrifice to Him. |2|18|

Raag Dhanaasaree, Fifth Mehl:
One Universal Creator God. By The Grace Of The True Guru:
O God, please save me!
By myself, I cannot do anything, O my Lord and Master; by Your Grace, please bless me with Your Name. |1|Pause|

Family and worldly affairs are an ocean of fire.
Through doubt, emotional attachment and ignorance, we are enveloped in darkness. |1|

High and low, pleasure and pain.
Hunger and thirst are not satisfied. |2|

The mind is engrossed in passion, and the disease of corruption.
The five thieves, the companions, are totally incorrigible. |3|

The beings and souls and wealth of the world are all Yours.
O Nanak, know that the Lord is always near at hand. |4|1|19|

Dhanaasaree, Fifth Mehl:
The Lord and Master destroys the pain of the poor; He preserves and protects the honor of His servants.
The Lord is the ship to carry us across; He is the treasure of virtue - pain cannot touch Him. |1|

In the Saadh Sangat, the Company of the Holy, meditate, vibrate upon the Lord of the world.
I cannot think of any other way; make this effort, and make it in this Dark Age of Kali Yuga. |Pause|

In the beginning, and in the end, there is none other than the perfect, merciful Lord.
The cycle of birth and death is ended, chanting the Lord's Name, and remembering the Lord Master in meditation. |2|

The Vedas, the Simritees, the Shaastras and the Lord's devotees contemplate Him;
liberation is attained in the Saadh Sangat, the Company of the Holy, and the darkness of ignorance is dispelled. |3|

The lotus feet of the Lord are the support of His humble servants. They are his only capital and investment.

Section 14 - Raag Dhanaasaree - Part 017

The True Lord is Nanak's strength, honor and support; He alone is his protection. |4|2|20|

Dhanaasaree, Fifth Mehl:
Wandering and roaming around, I met the Holy Perfect Guru, who has taught me.
All other devices did not work, so I meditate on the Name of the Lord, Har, Har. |1|

For this reason, I sought the Protection and Support of my Lord, the Cherisher of the Universe.
I sought the Sanctuary of the Perfect Transcendent Lord, and all my entanglements were dissolved. |Pause|

Paradise, the earth, the nether regions of the underworld, and the globe of the world - all are engrossed in Maya.
To save your soul, and liberate all your ancestors, meditate on the Name of the Lord, Har, Har. |2|

O Nanak, singing the Naam, the Name of the Immaculate Lord, all treasures are obtained.
Only that rare person, whom the Lord and Master blesses with His Grace, comes to know this. |3|3|21|

Dhanaasaree, Fifth Mehl, Second House, Chau-Padas:
One Universal Creator God. By The Grace Of The True Guru:
You shall have to abandon the straw which you have collected.
These entanglements shall be of no use to you.
You are in love with those things that will not go with you.
You think that your enemies are friends. |1|

In such confusion, the world has gone astray.
The foolish mortal wastes this precious human life. |Pause|

He does not like to see Truth and righteousness.
He is attached to falsehood and deception; they seem sweet to him.
He loves gifts, but he forgets the Giver.
The wretched creature does not even think of death. |2|

He cries for the possessions of others.

He forfeits all the merits of his good deeds and religion.
He does not understand the Hukam of the Lord's Command, and so he continues coming and going in reincarnation.
He sins, and then regrets and repents. |3|

Whatever pleases You, Lord, that alone is acceptable.
I am a sacrifice to Your Will.
Poor Nanak is Your slave, Your humble servant.
Save me, O my Lord God Master! |4|1|22|

Dhanaasaree, Fifth Mehl:
I am meek and poor; the Name of God is my only Support.
The Name of the Lord, Har, Har, is my occupation and earnings.
I gather only the Lord's Name.
It is useful in both this world and the next. |1|

Imbued with the Love of the Lord God's Infinite Name,
the Holy Saints sing the Glorious Praises of the One Lord, the Formless Lord. |Pause|

The Glory of the Holy Saints comes from their total humility.
The Saints realize that their greatness rests in the Praises of the Lord.
Meditating on the Lord of the Universe, the Saints are in bliss.
The Saints find peace, and their anxieties are dispelled. |2|

Wherever the Holy Saints gather,
there they sing the Praises of the Lord, in music and poetry.
In the Society of the Saints, there is bliss and peace.
They alone obtain this Society, upon whose foreheads such destiny is written. |3|

With my palms pressed together, I offer my prayer.
I wash their feet, and chant the Praises of the Lord, the treasure of virtue.
O God, merciful and compassionate, let me remain in Your Presence.
Nanak lives, in the dust of the Saints. |4|2|23|

Section 14 - Raag Dhanaasaree - Part 018

Dhanaasaree, Fifth Mehl:
One who contemplates his Lord and Master - why should he be afraid?

The wretched self-willed manmukhs are ruined through fear and dread. |1|Pause|

The Divine Guru, my mother and father, is over my head.
His image brings prosperity; serving Him, we become pure.
The One Lord, the Immaculate Lord, is our capital.
Joining the Saadh Sangat, the Company of the Holy, we are illumined and enlightened. |1|

The Giver of all beings is totally pervading everywhere.
Millions of pains are removed by the Lord's Name.
All the pains of birth and death are taken away
from the Gurmukh, within whose mind and body the Lord dwells. |2|

He alone, whom the Lord has attached to the hem of His robe,
obtains a place in the Court of the Lord.
They alone are devotees, who are pleasing to the True Lord.
They are freed from the Messenger of Death. |3|

True is the Lord, and True is His Court.
Who can contemplate and describe His value?
He is within each and every heart, the Support of all.
Nanak begs for the dust of the Saints. |4|3|24|

Dhanaasaree, Fifth Mehl:
One Universal Creator God. By The Grace Of The True Guru:
At home, and outside, I place my trust in You; You are always with Your humble servant.
Bestow Your Mercy, O my Beloved God, that I may chant the Lord's Name with love. |1|

God is the strength of His humble servants.
Whatever You do, or cause to be done, O Lord and Master, that outcome is acceptable to me. |Pause|

The Transcendent Lord is my honor; the Lord is my emancipation; the glorious sermon of the Lord is my wealth.
Slave Nanak seeks the Sanctuary of the Lord's feet; from the Saints, he has learned this way of life. |2|1|25|

Dhanaasaree, Fifth Mehl:
God has fulfilled all my desires. Holding me close in His embrace, the Guru has saved me.
He has saved me from burning in the ocean of fire, and now, no one calls it impassible. |1|

Those who have true faith in their minds,
continually behold the Glory of the Lord; they are forever happy and blissful. |Pause|

I seek the Sanctuary of the feet of the Perfect Transcendent Lord, the Searcher of hearts; I behold Him ever-present.
In His wisdom, the Lord has made Nanak His own; He has preserved the roots of His devotees. |2|2|26|

Dhanaasaree, Fifth Mehl:
Wherever I look, there I see Him present; He is never far away.
He is all-pervading, everywhere; O my mind, meditate on Him forever. |1|

He alone is called your companion, who will not be separated from you, here or hereafter.
That pleasure, which passes away in an instant, is trivial. |Pause|

He cherishes us, and gives us sustenance; He does not lack anything.
With each and every breath, my God takes care of His creatures. |2|

God is undeceiveable, impenetrable and infinite; His form is lofty and exalted.
Chanting and meditating on the embodiment of wonder and beauty, His humble servants are in bliss. |3|

Bless me with such understanding, O Merciful Lord God, that I might remember You.

Section 14 - Raag Dhanaasaree - Part 019

Nanak begs God for the gift of the dust of the feet of the Saints. |4|3|27|

Dhanaasaree, Fifth Mehl:

The One who sent you, has now recalled you; return to your home now in peace and pleasure.
In bliss and ecstasy, sing His Glorious Praises; by this celestial tune, you shall acquire your everlasting kingdom. |1|

Come back to your home, O my friend.
The Lord Himself has eliminated your enemies, and your misfortunes are past. |Pause|

God, the Creator Lord, has glorified you, and your running and rushing around has ended.
In your home, there is rejoicing; the musical instruments continually play, and your Husband Lord has exalted you. |2|

Remain firm and steady, and do not ever waver; take the Guru's Word as your Support.
You shall be applauded and congratulated all over the world, and your face shall be radiant in the Court of the Lord. |3|

All beings belong to Him; He Himself transforms them, and He Himself becomes their help and support.
The Creator Lord has worked a wondrous miracle; O Nanak, His glorious greatness is true. |4|4|28|

Dhanaasaree, Fifth Mehl, Sixth House:
One Universal Creator God. By The Grace Of The True Guru:
Listen, O Dear Beloved Saints, to my prayer.
Without the Lord, no one is liberated. |Pause|

O mind, do only deeds of purity; the Lord is the only boat to carry you across. Other entanglements shall be of no use to you.
True living is serving the Divine, Supreme Lord God; the Guru has imparted this teaching to me. |1|

Do not fall in love with trivial things; in the end, they shall not go along with you.
Worship and adore the Lord with your mind and body, O Beloved Saint of the Lord; in the Saadh Sangat, the Company of the Holy, you shall be released from bondage. |2|

In your heart, hold fast to the Sanctuary of the lotus feet of the Supreme Lord God; do not place your hopes in any other support.

He alone is a devotee, spiritually wise, a meditator, and a penitent, O Nanak, who is blessed by the Lord's Mercy. |3|1|29|

Dhanaasaree, Fifth Mehl:
O my dear beloved, it is good, it is better, it is best, to ask for the Lord's Name.

Behold, with your eyes wide-open, and listen to the Words of the Holy Saints; enshrine in your consciousness the Lord of Life - remember that all must die. |Pause|

The application of sandalwood oil, the enjoyment of pleasures and the practice of many corrupt sins - look upon all of these as insipid and worthless. The Name of the Lord of the Universe alone is sublime; so say the Holy Saints.

You claim that your body and wealth are your own; you do not chant the Lord's Name even for an instant. Look and see, that none of your possessions or riches shall go along with you. |1|

One who has good karma, grasps the Protection of the hem of the Saint's robe; in the Saadh Sangat, the Company of the Holy, the Messenger of Death cannot threaten him.

I have obtained the supreme treasure, and my egotism has been eradicated; Nanak's mind is attached to the One Formless Lord. |2|2|30|

Section 14 - Raag Dhanaasaree - Part 020

Dhanaasaree, Fifth Mehl, Seventh House:
One Universal Creator God. By The Grace Of The True Guru:
Meditate in remembrance on the One Lord; meditate in remembrance on the One Lord; meditate in remembrance on the One Lord, O my Beloved.

He shall save you from strife, suffering, greed, attachment, and the most terrifying world-ocean. |Pause|

With each and every breath, each and every instant, day and night, dwell upon Him.

In the Saadh Sangat, the Company of the Holy, meditate on Him fearlessly, and enshrine the treasure of His Name in your mind. |1|

Worship His lotus feet, and contemplate the glorious virtues of the Lord of the Universe.

O Nanak, the dust of the feet of the Holy shall bless you with pleasure and peace. |2|1|31|

Dhanaasaree, Fifth Mehl, Eighth House, Du-Padas:

One Universal Creator God. By The Grace Of The True Guru:

Remembering, remembering, remembering Him in meditation, I find peace; with each and every breath, I dwell upon Him.

In this world, and in the world beyond, He is with me, as my help and support; wherever I go, He protects me. |1|

The Guru's Word abides with my soul.

It does not sink in water; thieves cannot steal it, and fire cannot burn it. |1|Pause|

It is like wealth to the poor, a cane for the blind, and mother's milk for the infant.

In the ocean of the world, I have found the boat of the Lord; the Merciful Lord has bestowed His Mercy upon Nanak. |2|1|32|

Dhanaasaree, Fifth Mehl:

The Lord of the Universe has become kind and merciful; His Ambrosial Nectar permeates my heart.

The nine treasures, riches and the miraculous spiritual powers of the Siddhas cling to the feet of the Lord's humble servant. |1|

The Saints are in ecstasy everywhere.

Within the home, and outside as well, the Lord and Master of His devotees is totally pervading and permeating everywhere. |1|Pause|

No one can equal one who has the Lord of the Universe on his side.

The fear of the Messenger of Death is eradicated, remembering Him in meditation; Nanak meditates on the Naam, the Name of the Lord. |2|2|33|

Dhanaasaree, Fifth Mehl:

The rich man gazes upon his riches, and is proud of himself; the landlord takes pride in his lands.

The king believes that the whole kingdom belongs to him; in the same way, the humble servant of the Lord looks upon the support of his Lord and Master. |1|

When one considers the Lord to be his only support,
then the Lord uses His power to help him; this power cannot be defeated. |1|Pause|

Renouncing all others, I have sought the Support of the One Lord; I have come to Him, pleading, "Save me, save me!"

By the kindness and the Grace of the Saints, my mind has been purified; Nanak sings the Glorious Praises of the Lord. |2|3|34|

Dhanaasaree, Fifth Mehl:
He alone is called a warrior, who is attached to the Lord's Love in this age.
Through the Perfect True Guru, he conquers his own soul, and then everything comes under his control. |1|

Section 14 - Raag Dhanaasaree - Part 021

Sing the Praises of the Lord and Master, with the love of your soul.
Those who seek His Sanctuary, and meditate on the Naam, the Name of the Lord, are blended with the Lord in celestial peace. |1|Pause|

The feet of the Lord's humble servant abide in my heart; with them, my body is made pure.
O treasure of mercy, please bless Nanak with the dust of the feet of Your humble servants; this alone brings peace. |2|4|35|

Dhanaasaree, Fifth Mehl:
People try to deceive others, but the Inner-knower, the Searcher of hearts, knows everything.
They commit sins, and then deny them, while they pretend to be in Nirvaanaa. |1|

They believe that You are far away, but You, O God, are near at hand.
Looking around, this way and that, the greedy people come and go. |Pause|

As long as the doubts of the mind are not removed, liberation is not found.
Says Nanak, he alone is a Saint, a devotee, and a humble servant of the Lord, to whom the Lord and Master is merciful. |2|5|36|

Dhanaasaree, Fifth Mehl:
My Guru gives the Naam, the Name of the Lord, to those who have such karma written on their foreheads.
He implants the Naam, and inspires us to chant the Naam; this is Dharma, true religion, in this world. |1|

The Naam is the glory and greatness of the Lord's humble servant.
The Naam is his salvation, and the Naam is his honor; he accepts whatever comes to pass. |1|Pause|

That humble servant, who has the Naam as his wealth, is the perfect banker.
The Naam is his occupation, O Nanak, and his only support; the Naam Is the profit he earns. |2|6|37|

Dhanaasaree, Fifth Mehl:
My eyes have been purified, gazing upon the Blessed Vision of the Lord's Darshan, and touching my forehead to the dust of His feet.
With joy and happiness, I sing the Glorious Praises of my Lord and Master; the Lord of the World abides within my heart. |1|

You are my Merciful Protector, Lord.
O beautiful, wise, infinite Father God, be Merciful to me, God. |1|Pause|

O Lord of supreme ecstasy and blissful form, Your Word is so beautiful, so drenched with Nectar.
With the Lord's lotus feet enshrined in his heart, Nanak has tied the Shabad, the Word of the True Guru, to the hem of his robe. |2|7|38|

Dhanaasaree, Fifth Mehl:
In His own way, He provides us with our food; in His own way, He plays with us.
He blesses us with all comforts, enjoyments and delicacies, and he permeates our minds. |1|

Our Father is the Lord of the World, the Merciful Lord.

Just as the mother protects her children, God nurtures and cares for us.
|1|Pause|

You are my friend and companion, the Master of all excellences, O eternal
and permanent Divine Lord.
Here, there and everywhere, You are pervading; please, bless Nanak to
serve the Saints. |2|8|39|

Dhanaasaree, Fifth Mehl:
The Saints are kind and compassionate; they burn away their sexual desire,
anger and corruption.
My power, wealth, youth, body and soul are a sacrifice to them. |1|

With my mind and body, I love the Lord's Name.
With peace, poise, pleasure and joy, He has carried me across the terrifying
world-ocean. |Pause|

Section 14 - Raag Dhanaasaree - Part 022

Blessed is that place, and blessed is that house, in which the Saints dwell.
Fulfill this desire of servant Nanak, O Lord Master, that he may bow in
reverence to Your devotees. |2|9|40|

Dhanaasaree, Fifth Mehl:
He has saved me from the awful power of Maya, by attaching me to His
feet.
He gave my mind the Mantra of the Naam, the Name of the One Lord,
which shall never perish or leave me. |1|

The Perfect True Guru has given this gift.
He has blessed me with the Kirtan of the Praises of the Name of the Lord,
Har, Har, and I am emancipated. |Pause|

My God has made me His own, and saved the honor of His devotee.
Nanak has grasped the feet of his God, and has found peace, day and night.
|2|10|41|

Dhanaasaree, Fifth Mehl:
Stealing the property of others, acting in greed, lying and slandering - in
these ways, he passes his life.

He places his hopes in false mirages, believing them to be sweet; this is the support he installs in his mind. |1|

The faithless cynic passes his life uselessly.
He is like the mouse, gnawing away at the pile of paper, making it useless to the poor wretch. |Pause|

Have mercy on me, O Supreme Lord God, and release me from these bonds.
The blind are sinking, O Nanak; God saves them, uniting them with the Saadh Sangat, the Company of the Holy. |2|11|42|

Dhanaasaree, Fifth Mehl:
Remembering, remembering God, the Lord Master in meditation, my body, mind and heart are cooled and soothed.
The Supreme Lord God is my beauty, pleasure, peace, wealth, soul and social status. |1|

My tongue is intoxicated with the Lord, the source of nectar.
I am in love, in love with the Lord's lotus feet, the treasure of riches. |Pause|

I am His - He has saved me; this is God's perfect way.
The Giver of peace has blended Nanak with Himself; the Lord has preserved his honor. |2|12|43|

Dhanaasaree, Fifth Mehl:
All demons and enemies are eradicated by You, Lord; Your glory is manifest and radiant.
Whoever harms Your devotees, You destroy in an instant. |1|

I look to You continually, Lord.
O Lord, Destroyer of ego, please, be the helper and companion of Your slaves; take my hand, and save me, O my Friend! |Pause|

My Lord and Master has heard my prayer, and given me His protection.
Nanak is in ecstasy, and his pains are gone; he meditates on the Lord, forever and ever. |2|13|44|

Dhanaasaree, Fifth Mehl:

He has extended His power in all four directions, and placed His hand upon my head.
Gazing upon me with his Eye of Mercy, He has dispelled the pains of His slave. |1|

The Guru, the Lord of the Universe, has saved the Lord's humble servant.
Hugging me close in His embrace, the merciful, forgiving Lord has erased all my sins. |Pause|

Whatever I ask for from my Lord and Master, he gives that to me.
Whatever the Lord's slave Nanak utters with his mouth, proves to be true, here and hereafter. |2|14|45|

Section 14 - Raag Dhanaasaree - Part 023

Dhanaasaree, Fifth Mehl:
He does not let His devotees see the difficult times; this is His innate nature.
Giving His hand, He protects His devotee; with each and every breath, He cherishes him. |1|

My consciousness remains attached to God.
In the beginning, and in the end, God is always my helper and companion; blessed is my friend. |Pause|

My mind is delighted, gazing upon the marvellous, glorious greatness of the Lord and Master.
Remembering, remembering the Lord in meditation, Nanak is in ecstasy; God, in His perfection, has protected and preserved his honor. |2|15|46|

Dhanaasaree, Fifth Mehl:
One who forgets the Lord of life, the Great Giver - know that he is most unfortunate.
One whose mind is in love with the Lord's lotus feet, obtains the pool of ambrosial nectar. |1|

Your humble servant awakes in the Love of the Lord's Name.
All laziness has departed from his body, and his mind is attached to the Beloved Lord. |Pause|

Wherever I look, the Lord is there; He is the string, upon which all hearts are strung.
Drinking in the water of the Naam, servant Nanak has renounced all other loves. |2|16|47|

Dhanaasaree, Fifth Mehl:
All the affairs of the Lord's humble servant are perfectly resolved.
In the utterly poisonous Dark Age of Kali Yuga, the Lord preserves and protects his honor. |1|Pause|

Remembering, remembering God, his Lord and Master in meditation, the Messenger of Death does not approach him.
Liberation and heaven are found in the Saadh Sangat, the Company of the Holy; his humble servant finds the home of the Lord. |1|

The Lord's lotus feet are the treasure of His humble servant; in them, he finds millions of pleasures and comforts.
He remembers the Lord God in meditation, day and night; Nanak is forever a sacrifice to him. |2|17|48|

Dhanaasaree, Fifth Mehl:
I beg for one gift only from the Lord.
May all my desires be fulfilled, meditating on, and remembering Your Name, O Lord. |1|Pause|

May Your feet abide within my heart, and may I find the Society of the Saints.
May my mind not be afflicted by the fire of sorrow; may I sing Your Glorious Praises, twenty-four hours a day. |1|

May I serve the Lord in my childhood and youth, and meditate on God in my middle and old age.
O Nanak, one who is imbued with the Love of the Transcendent Lord, is not reincarnated again to die. |2|18|49|

Dhanaasaree, Fifth Mehl:
I beg only from the Lord for all things.
I would hesitate to beg from other people. Remembering God in meditation, liberation is obtained. |1|Pause|

I have studied with the silent sages, and carefully read the Simritees, the Puraanas and the Vedas; they all proclaim that,

by serving the Lord, the ocean of mercy, Truth is obtained, and both this world and the next are embellished. |1|

All other rituals and customs are useless, without remembering the Lord in meditation.
O Nanak, the fear of birth and death has been removed; meeting the Holy Saint, sorrow is dispelled. |2|19|50|

Dhanaasaree, Fifth Mehl:
Desire is quenched, through the Lord's Name.
Great peace and contentment come through the Guru's Word, and one's meditation is perfectly focused upon God. |1|Pause|

Section 14 - Raag Dhanaasaree - Part 024

Please shower Your Mercy upon me, and permit me to ignore the great enticements of Maya, O Lord, Merciful to the meek.
Give me Your Name - chanting it, I live; please bring the efforts of Your slave to fruition. |1|

All desires, power, pleasure, joy and lasting bliss, are found by chanting the Naam, the Name of the Lord, and singing the Kirtan of His Praises.
That humble servant of the Lord, who has such karma pre-ordained by the Creator Lord, O Nanak - his efforts are brought to perfect fruition. |2|20|51|

Dhanaasaree, Fifth Mehl:
The Supreme Lord God takes care of His humble servant.
The slanderers are not allowed to stay; they are pulled out by their roots, like useless weeds. |1|Pause|

Wherever I look, there I see my Lord and Master; no one can harm me.
Whoever shows disrespect to the Lord's humble servant, is instantly reduced to ashes. |1|

The Creator Lord has become my protector; He has no end or limitation.

O Nanak, God has protected and saved His slaves; He has driven out and destroyed the slanderers. |2|21|52|

Dhanaasaree, Fifth Mehl, Ninth House, Partaal:
One Universal Creator God. By The Grace Of The True Guru:
O Lord, I seek the Sanctuary of Your feet; Lord of the Universe, Destroyer of pain, please bless Your slave with Your Name.
Be Merciful, God, and bless me with Your Glance of Grace; take my arm and save me - pull me up out of this pit! |Pause|

He is blinded by sexual desire and anger, bound by Maya; his body and clothes are filled with countless sins.
Without God, there is no other protector; help me to chant Your Name, Almighty Warrior, Sheltering Lord. |1|

Redeemer of sinners, Saving Grace of all beings and creatures, even those who recite the Vedas have not found Your limit.
God is the ocean of virtue and peace, the source of jewels; Nanak sings the Praises of the Lover of His devotees. |2|1|53|

Dhanaasaree, Fifth Mehl:
Peace in this world, peace in the next world and peace forever, remembering Him in meditation. Chant forever the Name of the Lord of the Universe.
The sins of past lives are erased, by joining the Saadh Sangat, the Company of the Holy; new life is infused into the dead. |1|Pause|

In power, youth and Maya, the Lord is forgotten; this is the greatest tragedy - so say the spiritual sages.
Hope and desire to sing the Kirtan of the Lord's Praises - this is the treasure of the most fortunate devotees. |1|

O Lord of Sanctuary, all-powerful, imperceptible and unfathomable - Your Name is the Purifier of sinners.
The Inner-knower, the Lord and Master of Nanak is totally pervading and permeating everywhere; He is my Lord and Master. |2|2|54|

Dhanaasaree, Fifth Mehl, Twelfth House:
One Universal Creator God. By The Grace Of The True Guru:
I bow in reverence to the Lord, I bow in reverence. I sing the Glorious Praises of the Lord, my King. |Pause|

By great good fortune, one meets the Divine Guru.
Millions of sins are erased by serving the Lord. |1|

Section 14 - Raag Dhanaasaree - Part 025

One whose mind is imbued with the Lord's lotus feet
is not afflicted by the fire of sorrow. |2|

He crosses over the world-ocean in the Saadh Sangat, the Company of the
Holy.
He chants the Name of the Fearless Lord, and is imbued with the Lord's
Love. |3|

One who does not steal the wealth of others, who does not commit evil
deeds or sinful acts
- the Messenger of Death does not even approach him. |4|

God Himself quenches the fires of desire.
O Nanak, in God's Sanctuary, one is saved. |5|1|55|

Dhanaasaree, Fifth Mehl:
I am satisfied and satiated, eating the food of Truth.
With my mind, body and tongue, I meditate on the Naam, the Name of the
Lord. |1|

Life, spiritual life, is in the Lord.
Spiritual life consists of chanting the Lord's Name in the Saadh Sangat, the
Company of the Holy. |1|Pause|

He is dressed in robes of all sorts,
if he sings the Kirtan of the Lord's Glorious Praises, day and night. |2|

He rides upon elephants, chariots and horses,
if he sees the Lord's Path within his own heart. |3|

Meditating on the Lord's Feet, deep within his mind and body,
slave Nanak has found the Lord, the treasure of peace. |4|2|56|

Dhanaasaree, Fifth Mehl:

The Guru's feet emancipate the soul.
They carry it across the world-ocean in an instant. |1|Pause|

Some love rituals, and some bathe at sacred shrines of pilgrimage.
The Lord's slaves meditate on His Name. |1|

The Lord Master is the Breaker of bonds.
Servant Nanak meditates in remembrance on the Lord, the Inner-knower, the Searcher of hearts. |2|3|57|

Dhanaasaree, Fifth Mehl:
The lifestyle of Your slave is so pure, that nothing can break his love for You. |1|Pause|

He is more dear to me than my soul, my breath of life, my mind and my wealth.
The Lord is the Giver, the Restrainer of the ego. |1|

I am in love with the Lord's lotus feet.
This alone is Nanak's prayer. |2|4|58|

One Universal Creator God. By The Grace Of The True Guru:
Dhanaasaree, Ninth Mehl:
Why do you go looking for Him in the forest?
Although he is unattached, he dwells everywhere. He is always with you as your companion. |1|Pause|

Like the fragrance which remains in the flower, and like the reflection in the mirror,
the Lord dwells deep within; search for Him within your own heart, O Siblings of Destiny. |1|

Outside and inside, know that there is only the One Lord; the Guru has imparted this wisdom to me.
O servant Nanak, without knowing one's own self, the moss of doubt is not removed. |2|1|

Dhanaasaree, Ninth Mehl:
O Holy people, this world is deluded by doubt.

It has forsaken the meditative remembrance of the Lord's Name, and sold itself out to Maya. |1|Pause|

Mother, father, siblings, children and spouse - he is entangled in their love.

Section 14 - Raag Dhanaasaree - Part 026

In the pride of youth, wealth and glory, day and night, he remains intoxicated. |1|

God is merciful to the meek, and forever the Destroyer of pain, but the mortal does not center his mind on Him.
O servant Nanak, among millions, only a rare few, as Gurmukh, realize God. |2|2|

Dhanaasaree, Ninth Mehl:
That Yogi does not know the way.
Understand that his heart is filled with greed, emotional attachment, Maya and egotism. |1|Pause|

One who does not slander or praise others, who looks upon gold and iron alike,
who is free from pleasure and pain - he alone is called a true Yogi. |1|

The restless mind wanders in the ten directions - it needs to be pacified and restrained.
Says Nanak, whoever knows this technique is judged to be liberated. |2|3|

Dhanaasaree, Ninth Mehl:
Now, what efforts should I make?
How can I dispel the anxieties of my mind? How can I cross over the terrifying world-ocean? |1|Pause|

Obtaining this human incarnation, I have done no good deeds; this makes me very afraid!
In thought, word and deed, I have not sung the Lord's Praises; this thought worries my mind. |1|

I listened to the Guru's Teachings, but spiritual wisdom did not well up within me; like a beast, I fill my belly.

Says Nanak, O God, please confirm Your Law of Grace; for only then can I, the sinner, be saved. |2|4|9|9|13|58|4|93|

Dhanaasaree, First Mehl, Second House, Ashtapadees:
One Universal Creator God. By The Grace Of The True Guru:
The Guru is the ocean, filled with pearls.
The Saints gather in the Ambrosial Nectar; they do not go far away from there.
They taste the subtle essence of the Lord; they are loved by God.
Within this pool, the swans find their Lord, the Lord of their souls. |1|

What can the poor crane accomplish by bathing in the mud puddle?
It sinks into the mire, and its filth is not washed away. |1|Pause|

After careful deliberation, the thoughtful person takes a step.
Forsaking duality, he becomes a devotee of the Formless Lord.
He obtains the treasure of liberation, and enjoys the sublime essence of the Lord.
His comings and goings end, and the Guru protects him. |2|

The swan do not leave this pool.
In loving devotional worship, they merge in the Celestial Lord.
The swans are in the pool, and the pool is in the swans.
They speak the Unspoken Speech, and they honor and revere the Guru's Word. |3|

The Yogi, the Primal Lord, sits within the celestial sphere of deepest Samaadhi.
He is not male, and He is not female; how can anyone describe Him?
The three worlds continue to center their attention on His Light.
The silent sages and the Yogic masters seek the Sanctuary of the True Lord. |4|

The Lord is the source of bliss, the support of the helpless.
The Gurmukhs worship and contemplate the Celestial Lord.
God is the Lover of His devotees, the Destroyer of fear.
Subduing ego, one meets the Lord, and places his feet on the Path. |5|

He makes many efforts, but still, the Messenger of Death tortures him.
Destined only to die, he comes into the world.

Section 14 - Raag Dhanaasaree - Part 027

He wastes this precious human life through duality.
He does not know his own self, and trapped by doubts, he cries out in pain. |6|

Speak, read and hear of the One Lord.
The Support of the earth shall bless you with courage, righteousness and protection.
Chastity, purity and self-restraint are infused into the heart,
when one centers his mind in the fourth state. |7|

They are immaculate and true, and filth does not stick to them.
Through the Word of the Guru's Shabad, their doubt and fear depart.
The form and personality of the Primal Lord are incomparably beautiful.
Nanak begs for the Lord, the Embodiment of Truth. |8|1|

Dhanaasaree, First Mehl:
That union with the Lord is acceptable, which is united in intuitive poise.
Thereafter, one does not die, and does not come and go in reincarnation.
The Lord's slave is in the Lord, and the Lord is in His slave.
Wherever I look, I see none other than the Lord. |1|

The Gurmukhs worship the Lord, and find His celestial home.
Without meeting the Guru, they die, and come and go in reincarnation. |1|Pause|

So make Him your Guru, who implants the Truth within you,
who leads you to speak the Unspoken Speech, and who merges you in the Word of the Shabad.
God's people have no other work to do;
they love the True Lord and Master, and they love the Truth. |2|

The mind is in the body, and the True Lord is in the mind.
Merging into the True Lord, one is absorbed into Truth.
God's servant bows at His feet.
Meeting the True Guru, one meets with the Lord. |3|

He Himself watches over us, and He Himself makes us see.

He is not pleased by stubborn-mindedness, nor by various religious robes.
He fashioned the body-vessels, and infused the Ambrosial Nectar into them;
God's Mind is pleased only by loving devotional worship. |4|

Reading and studying, one becomes confused, and suffers punishment.
By great cleverness, one is consigned to coming and going in reincarnation.
One who chants the Naam, the Name of the Lord, and eats the food of the Fear of God
becomes Gurmukh, the Lord's servant, and remains absorbed in the Lord. |5|

He worships stones, dwells at sacred shrines of pilgrimage and in the jungles,
wanders, roams around and becomes a renunciate.
But his mind is still filthy - how can he become pure?
One who meets the True Lord obtains honor. |6|

One who embodies good conduct and contemplative meditation,
his mind abides in intuitive poise and contentment, since the beginning of time, and throughout the ages.
In the twinkling of an eye, he saves millions.
Have mercy on me, O my Beloved, and let me meet the Guru. |7|

Unto whom, O God, should I praise You?
Without You, there is no other at all.
As it pleases You, keep me under Your Will.
Nanak, with intuitive poise and natural love, sings Your Glorious Praises. |8|2|

Dhanaasaree, Fifth Mehl, Sixth House, Ashtapadee:
One Universal Creator God. By The Grace Of The True Guru:
Whoever is born into the world, is entangled in it; human birth is obtained only by good destiny.
I look to Your support, O Holy Saint; give me Your hand, and protect me. By Your Grace, let me meet the Lord, my King. |1|

I wandered through countless incarnations, but I did not find stability anywhere.

I serve the Guru, and I fall at His feet, praying, "O Dear Lord of the Universe, please, show me the way."|1|Pause|

I have tried so many things to acquire the wealth of Maya, and to cherish it in my mind; I have passed my life constantly crying out, "Mine, mine!"

Section 14 - Raag Dhanaasaree - Part 028

Is there any such Saint, who would meet with me, take away my anxiety, and lead me to enshrine love for my Lord and Master. |2|

I have read all the Vedas, and yet the sense of separation in my mind still has not been removed; the five thieves of my house are not quieted, even for an instant.
Is there any devotee, who is unattached to Maya, who may irrigate my mind with the Ambrosial Naam, the Name of the One Lord? |3|

In spite of the many places of pilgrimage for people to bathe in, their minds are still stained by their stubborn ego; the Lord Master is not pleased by this at all.
When will I find the Saadh Sangat, the Company of the Holy? There, I shall be always in the ecstasy of the Lord, Har, Har, and my mind shall take its cleansing bath in the healing ointment of spiritual wisdom. |4|

I have followed the four stages of life, but my mind is not satisfied; I wash my body, but it is totally lacking in understanding.
If only I could meet some devotee of the Supreme Lord God, imbued with the Lord's Love, who could eradicate the filthy evil-mindedness from my mind. |5|

One who is attached to religious rituals, does not love the Lord, even for an instant; he is filled with pride, and he is of no account.
One who meets with the rewarding personality of the Guru, continually sings the Kirtan of the Lord's Praises. By Guru's Grace, such a rare one beholds the Lord with his eyes. |6|

One who acts through stubbornness is of no account at all; like a crane, he pretends to meditate, but he is still stuck in Maya.
Is there any such Giver of peace, who can recite to me the sermon of God? Meeting him, I would be emancipated. |7|

When the Lord, my King, is totally pleased with me, He will break the bonds of Maya for me; my mind is imbued with the Word of the Guru's Shabad.
I am in ecstasy, forever and ever, meeting the Fearless Lord, the Lord of the Universe. Falling at the Lord's Feet, Nanak has found peace. |8|

My Yatra, my life pilgrimage, has become fruitful, fruitful, fruitful.
My comings and goings have ended, since I met the Holy Saint. |1|Second Pause|1|3|

Dhanaasaree, First Mehl, Chhant:
One Universal Creator God. By The Grace Of The True Guru:
Why should I bathe at sacred shrines of pilgrimage? The Naam, the Name of the Lord, is the sacred shrine of pilgrimage.
My sacred shrine of pilgrimage is spiritual wisdom within, and contemplation on the Word of the Shabad.
The spiritual wisdom given by the Guru is the True sacred shrine of pilgrimage, where the ten festivals are always observed.
I constantly beg for the Name of the Lord; grant it to me, O God, Sustainer of the world.
The world is sick, and the Naam is the medicine to cure it; without the True Lord, filth sticks to it.
The Guru's Word is immaculate and pure; it radiates a steady Light. Constantly bathe in such a true shrine of pilgrimage. |1|

Filth does not stick to the true ones; what filth do they have to wash off?
If one strings a garland of virtues for oneself, what is there to cry for?
One who conquers his own self through contemplation is saved, and saves others as well; he does not come to be born again.
The supreme meditator is Himself the philosopher's stone, which transforms lead into gold. The true man is pleasing to the True Lord.
He is in ecstasy, truly happy, night and day; his sorrows and sins are taken away.
He finds the True Name, and beholds the Guru; with the True Name in his mind, no filth sticks to him. |2|

O friend, association with the Holy is the perfect cleansing bath.

Section 14 - Raag Dhanaasaree - Part 029

The singer who sings the Lord's Praises is adorned with the Word of the Shabad.

Worship the True Lord, and believe in the True Guru; this brings the merit of making donations to charity, kindness and compassion.

The soul-bride who loves to be with her Husband Lord bathes at the Triveni, the sacred place where the Ganges, Jamuna and Saraswaati Rivers converge, the Truest of the True.

Worship and adore the One Creator, the True Lord, who constantly gives, whose gifts continually increase.

Salvation is attained by associating with the Society of the Saints, O friend; granting His Grace, God unites us in His Union. |3|

Everyone speaks and talks; how great should I say He is?

I am foolish, lowly and ignorant; it is only through the Guru's Teachings that I understand.

True are the Teachings of the Guru. His Words are Ambrosial Nectar; my mind is pleased and appeased by them.

Loaded down with corruption and sin, people depart, and then come back again; the True Shabad is found through my Guru.

There is no end to the treasure of devotion; the Lord is pervading every-where.

Nanak utters this true prayer; one who purifies his mind is True. |4|1|

Dhanaasaree, First Mehl:

I live by Your Name; my mind is in ecstasy, Lord.

True is the Name of the True Lord. Glorious are the Praises of the Lord of the Universe.

Infinite is the spiritual wisdom imparted by the Guru. The Creator Lord who created, shall also destroy.

The call of death is sent out by the Lord's Command; no one can challenge it.

He Himself creates, and watches; His written command is above each and every head. He Himself imparts understanding and awareness.

O Nanak, the Lord Master is inaccessible and unfathomable; I live by His True Name. |1|

No one can compare to You, Lord; all come and go.

By Your Command, the account is settled, and doubt is dispelled.

The Guru dispels doubt, and makes us speak the Unspoken Speech; the true ones are absorbed into Truth.

He Himself creates, and He Himself destroys; I accept the Command of the Commander Lord.

True greatness comes from the Guru; You alone are the mind's companion in the end.

O Nanak, there is no other than the Lord and Master; greatness comes from Your Name. |2|

You are the True Creator Lord, the unknowable Maker.

There is only the One Lord and Master, but there are two paths, by which conflict increases.

All follow these two paths, by the Hukam of the Lord's Command; the world is born, only to die.

Without the Naam, the Name of the Lord, the mortal has no friend at all; he carries loads of sin on his head.

By the Hukam of the Lord's Command, he comes, but he does not understand this Hukam; the Lord's Hukam is the Embellisher.

O Nanak, through the Shabad, the Word of the Lord and Master, the True Creator Lord is realized. |3|

Your devotees look beautiful in Your Court, embellished with the Shabad.

They chant the Ambrosial Word of His Bani, savoring it with their tongues.

Savoring it with their tongues, they thirst for the Naam; they are a sacrifice to the Word of the Guru's Shabad.

Touching the philosopher's stone, they become the philosopher's stone, which transforms lead into gold; O Lord, they become pleasing to your mind.

They attain the immortal status and eradicate their self-conceit; how rare is that person, who contemplates spiritual wisdom.

O Nanak, the devotees look beautiful in the Court of the True Lord; they are dealers in the Truth. |4|

I am hungry and thirsty for wealth; how will I be able to go to the Lord's Court?

Section 14 - Raag Dhanaasaree - Part 030

I shall go and ask the True Guru, and meditate on the Naam, the Name of the Lord.

I meditate on the True Name, chant the True Name, and as Gurmukh, I realize the True Name.

Night and day, I chant the Name of the merciful, immaculate Lord, the Master of the poor.

The Primal Lord has ordained the tasks to be done; self-conceit is overcome, and the mind is subdued.

O Nanak, the Naam is the sweetest essence; through the Naam, thirst and desire are stilled. |5|2|

Dhanaasaree, Chhant, First Mehl:

Your Husband Lord is with you, O deluded soul-bride, but you do are not aware of Him.

Your destiny is written on your forehead, according to your past actions.

This inscription of past deeds cannot be erased; what do I know about what will happen?

You have not adopted a virtuous lifestyle, and you are not attuned to the Lord's Love; you sit there, crying over your past misdeeds.

Wealth and youth are like the shade of the bitter swallow-wort plant; you are growing old, and your days are coming to their end.

O Nanak, without the Naam, the Name of the Lord, you shall end up as a discarded, divorced bride; your own falsehood shall separate you from the Lord. |1|

You have drowned, and your house is ruined; walk in the Way of the Guru's Will.

Meditate on the True Name, and you shall find peace in the Mansion of the Lord's Presence.

Meditate on the Lord's Name, and you shall find peace; your stay in this world shall last only four days.

Sit in the home of your own being, and you shall find Truth; night and day, be with your Beloved.

Without loving devotion, you cannot dwell in your own home - listen, everyone!

O Nanak, she is happy, and she obtains her Husband Lord, if she is attuned to the True Name. |2|

If the soul-bride is pleasing to her Husband Lord, then the Husband Lord will love His bride.

Imbued with the love of her Beloved, she contemplates the Word of the Guru's Shabad.

She contemplates the Guru's Shabads, and her Husband Lord loves her; in deep humility, she worships Him in loving devotion.

She burns away her emotional attachment to Maya, and in love, she loves her Beloved.

She is imbued and drenched with the Love of the True Lord; she has become beautiful, by conquering her mind.

O Nanak, the happy soul-bride abides in Truth; she loves to love her Husband Lord. |3|

The soul-bride looks so beautiful in the home of her Husband Lord, if she is pleasing to Him.

It is of no use at all to speak false words.

If she speaks false, it is of no use to her, and she does not see her Husband Lord with her eyes.

Worthless, forgotten and abandoned by her Husband Lord, she passes her life-night without her Lord and Master.

Such a wife does not believe in the Word of the Guru's Shabad; she is caught in the net of the world, and does not obtain the Mansion of the Lord's Presence.

O Nanak, if she understands her own self, then, as Gurmukh, she merges in celestial peace. |4|

Blessed is that soul-bride, who knows her Husband Lord.

Without the Naam, she is false, and her actions are false as well.

Devotional worship of the Lord is beautiful; the True Lord loves it. So immerse yourself in loving devotional worship of God.

My Husband Lord is playful and innocent; imbued with His Love, I enjoy Him.

She blossoms forth through the Word of the Guru's Shabad; she ravishes her Husband Lord, and obtains the most noble reward.

O Nanak, in Truth, she obtains glory; in her Husband's home, the soul-bride looks beautiful. |5|3|

Section 14 - Raag Dhanaasaree - Part 031

Dhanaasaree, Chhant, Fourth Mehl, First House:

One Universal Creator God. By The Grace Of The True Guru:

When the Dear Lord grants His Grace, one meditates on the Naam, the Name of the Lord.

Meeting the True Guru, through loving faith and devotion, one intuitively sings the Glorious Praises of the Lord.

Singing His Glorious Praises continually, night and day, one blossoms forth, when it is pleasing to the True Lord.

Egotism, self-conceit and Maya are forsaken, and he is intuitively absorbed into the Naam.

The Creator Himself acts; when He gives, then we receive.

When the Dear Lord grants His Grace, we meditate on the Naam. |1|

Deep within, I feel true love for the Perfect True Guru.

I serve Him day and night; I never forget Him.

I never forget Him; I remember Him night and day. When I chant the Naam, then I live.

With my ears, I hear about Him, and my mind is satisfied. As Gurmukh, I drink in the Ambrosial Nectar.

If He bestows His Glance of Grace, then I shall meet the True Guru; my discriminating intellect would contemplate Him, night and day.

Deep within, I feel true love for the Perfect True Guru. |2|

By great good fortune, one joins the Sat Sangat, the True Congregation; then, one comes to savor the subtle essence of the Lord.

Night and day, he remains lovingly focused on the Lord; he merges in celestial peace.

Merging in celestial peace, he becomes pleasing to the Lord's Mind; he remains forever unattached and untouched.

He receives honor in this world and the next, lovingly focused on the Lord's Name.

He is liberated from both pleasure and pain; he is pleased by whatever God does.

By great good fortune, one joins the Sat Sangat, the True Congregation, and then, one comes to savor the subtle essence of the Lord. |3|

In the love of duality, there is pain and suffering; the Messenger of Death eyes the self-willed manmukhs.

They cry and howl, day and night, caught by the pain of Maya.

Caught by the pain of Maya, provoked by his ego, he passes his life crying out, "Mine, mine!".

He does not remember God, the Giver, and in the end, he departs regretting and repenting.

Without the Name, nothing shall go along with him; not his children, spouse or the enticements of Maya.

In the love of duality, there is pain and suffering; the Messenger of Death eyes the self-willed manmukhs. |4|

Granting His Grace, the Lord has merged me with Himself; I have found the Mansion of the Lord's Presence.
I remain standing with my palms pressed together; I have become pleasing to God's Mind.
When one is pleasing to God's Mind, then he merges in the Hukam of the Lord's Command; surrendering to His Hukam, he finds peace.
Night and day, he chants the Lord's Name, day and night; intuitively, naturally, he meditates on the Naam, the Name of the Lord.
Through the Naam, the glorious greatness of the Naam is obtained; the Naam is pleasing to Nanak's mind.
Granting His Grace, the Lord has merged me with Himself; I have found the Mansion of the Lord's Presence. |5|1|

Section 14 - Raag Dhanaasaree - Part 032

Dhanaasaree, Fifth Mehl, Chhant:
One Universal Creator God. By The Grace Of The True Guru:
The True Guru is merciful to the meek; in His Presence, the Lord's Praises are sung.
The Ambrosial Name of the Lord is chanted in the Saadh Sangat, the Company of the Holy.
Vibrating, and worshipping the One Lord in the Company of the Holy, the pains of birth and death are removed.
Those who have such karma pre-ordained, study and learn the Truth; the noose of Death is removed from their necks.
Their fears and doubts are dispelled, the knot of death is untied, and they never have to walk on Death's path.
Prays Nanak, shower me with Your Mercy, Lord; let me sing Your Glorious Praises forever. |1|

The Name of the One, Immaculate Lord is the Support of the unsupported.
You are the Giver, the Great Giver, the Dispeller of all sorrow.
O Destroyer of pain, Creator Lord, Master of peace and bliss, I have come seeking the Sanctuary of the Holy;

please, help me to cross over the terrifying and difficult world-ocean in an instant.

I saw the Lord pervading and permeating everywhere, when the healing ointment of the Guru's wisdom was applied to my eyes.

Prays Nanak, remember Him forever in meditation, the Destroyer of all sorrow and fear. |2|

He Himself has attached me to the hem of His robe; He has showered me with His Mercy.

I am worthless, lowly and helpless; God is unfathomable and infinite.

My Lord and Master is always merciful, kind and compassionate; He uplifts and establishes the lowly.

All beings and creatures are under Your power; You take care of all.

He Himself is the Creator, and He Himself is the Enjoyer; He Himself is the Contemplator of all.

Prays Nanak, singing Your Glorious Praises, I live, chanting the Chant of the Lord, the Lord of the world-forest. |3|

The Blessed Vision of Your Darshan is incomparable; Your Name is utterly priceless.

O my Incomputable Lord, Your humble servants ever meditate on You.

You dwell on the tongues of the Saints, by Your own pleasure; they are intoxicated with Your sublime essence, O Lord.

Those who are attached to Your feet are very blessed; night and day, they remain always awake and aware.

Forever and ever, meditate in remembrance on the Lord and Master; with each and every breath, speak His Glorious Praises.

Prays Nanak, let me become the dust of the feet of the Saints. God's Name is invaluable. |4|1|

Raag Dhanaasaree, The Word Of Devotee Kabeer Jee:

One Universal Creator God. By The Grace Of The True Guru:

Beings like Sanak, Sanand, Shiva and Shaysh-naaga - none of them know Your mystery, Lord. |1|

In the Society of the Saints, the Lord dwells within the heart. |1|Pause|

Beings like Hanumaan, Garura, Indra the King of the gods and the rulers of humans - none of them know Your Glories, Lord. |2|

The four Vedas, the Simritees and the Puraanas, Vishnu the Lord of Lakshmi and Lakshmi herself - none of them know the Lord. |3|

Says Kabeer, one who falls at the Lord's feet, and remains in His Sanctuary, does not wander around lost. |4|1|

Section 14 - Raag Dhanaasaree - Part 033

Day by day, hour by hour, life runs its course, and the body withers away.
Death, like a hunter, a butcher, is on the prowl; tell me, what can we do? |1|

That day is rapidly approaching.
Mother, father, siblings, children and spouse - tell me, who belongs to whom? |1|Pause|

As long as the light remains in the body, the beast does not understand himself.
He acts in greed to maintain his life and status, and sees nothing with his eyes. |2|

Says Kabeer, listen, O mortal: Renounce the doubts of your mind.
Chant only the One Naam, the Name of the Lord, O mortal, and seek the Sanctuary of the One Lord. |3|2|

That humble being, who knows even a little about loving devotional worship - what surprises are there for him?

Like water, dripping into water, which cannot be separated out again, so is the weaver Kabeer, with softened heart, merged into the Lord. |1|

O people of the Lord, I am just a simple-minded fool.
If Kabeer were to leave his body at Benares, and so liberate himself, what obligation would he have to the Lord? |1|Pause|

Says Kabeer, listen, O people - do not be deluded by doubt.
What is the difference between Benares and the barren land of Maghar, if the Lord is within one's heart? |2|3|

Mortals may go to the Realm of Indra, or the Realm of Shiva,
but because of their hypocrisy and false prayers, they must leave again. |1|

What should I ask for? Nothing lasts forever.
Enshrine the Lord's Name within your mind. |1|Pause|

Fame and glory, power, wealth and glorious greatness
- none of these will go with you or help you in the end. |2|

Children, spouse, wealth and Maya
- who has ever obtained peace from these? |3|

Says Kabeer, nothing else is of any use.
Within my mind is the wealth of the Lord's Name. |4|4|

Remember the Lord, remember the Lord, remember the Lord in meditation, O Siblings of Destiny.
Without remembering the Lord's Name in meditation, a great many are
drowned. |1|Pause|

Your spouse, children, body, house and possessions - you think these will
give you peace.
But none of these shall be yours, when the time of death comes. |1|

Ajaamal, the elephant, and the prostitute committed many sins,
but still, they crossed over the world-ocean, by chanting the Lord's Name.
|2|

You have wandered in reincarnation, as pigs and dogs - did you feel no
shame?
Forsaking the Ambrosial Name of the Lord, why do you eat poison? |3|

Abandon your doubts about do's and dont's, and take to the Lord's Name.
By Guru's Grace, O servant Kabeer, love the Lord. |4|5|

Dhanaasaree, The Word Of Devotee Naam Dayv Jee:
One Universal Creator God. By The Grace Of The True Guru:
They dig deep foundations, and build lofty palaces.
Can anyone live longer than Markanda, who passed his days with only a
handful of straw upon his head? |1|

The Creator Lord is our only friend.

O man, why are you so proud? This body is only temporary - it shall pass away. |1|Pause|

Section 14 - Raag Dhanaasaree - Part 034

The Kaurvas, who had brothers like Duryodhan, used to proclaim, "This is ours! This is ours!"
Their royal procession extended over sixty miles, and yet their bodies were eaten by vultures. |2|

Sri Lanka was totally rich with gold; was anyone greater than its ruler Raavan?
What happened to the elephants, tethered at his gate? In an instant, it all belonged to someone else. |3|

The Yaadvas deceived Durbaasaa, and received their rewards.
The Lord has shown mercy to His humble servant, and now Naam Dayv sings the Glorious Praises of the Lord. |4|1|

I have brought the ten sensory organs under my control, and erased every trace of the five thieves.
I have filled the seventy-two thousand nerve channels with Ambrosial Nectar, and drained out the poison. |1|

I shall not come into the world again.
I chant the Ambrosial Bani of the Word from the depths of my heart, and I have instructed my soul. |1|Pause|

I fell at the Guru's feet and begged of Him; with the mighty axe, I have chopped off emotional attachment.
Turning away from the world, I have become the servant of the Saints; I fear no one except the Lord's devotees. |2|

I shall be released from this world, when I stop clinging to Maya.
Maya is the name of the power which causes us to be born; renouncing it, we obtain the Blessed Vision of the Lord's Darshan. |3|

That humble being, who performs devotional worship in this way, is rid of all fear.

Says Naam Dayv, why are you wandering around out there? This is the way to find the Lord. |4|2|

As water is very precious in the desert, and the creeper weeds are dear to the camel,
and the tune of the hunter's bell at night is enticing to the deer, so is the Lord to my mind. |1|

Your Name is so beautiful! Your form is so beautiful! Your Love is so very beautiful, O my Lord. |1|Pause|

As rain is dear to the earth, and the flower's fragrance is dear to the bumble bee,
and the mango is dear to the cuckoo, so is the Lord to my mind. |2|

As the sun is dear to the chakvi duck, and the lake of Man Sarovar is dear to the swan,
and the husband is dear to his wife, so is the Lord to my mind. |3|

As milk is dear to the baby, and the raindrop is dear to the mouth of the rainbird,
and as water is dear to the fish, so is the Lord to my mind. |4|

All the seekers, Siddhas and silent sages seek Him, but only a rare few behold Him.
Just as Your Name is dear to all the Universe, so is the Lord dear to Naam Dayv's mind. |5|3|

First of all, the lotuses bloomed in the woods;
from them, all the swan-souls came into being.
Know that, through Krishna, the Lord, Har, Har, the dance of creation dances. |1|

First of all, there was only the Primal Being.
From that Primal Being, Maya was produced.
All that is, is His.
In this Garden of the Lord, we all dance, like water in the pots of the Persian wheel. |1|Pause|

Women and men both dance.

There is no other than the Lord.
Don't dispute this,
and don't doubt this.
The Lord says, "This creation and I are one and the same." |2|

Section 14 - Raag Dhanaasaree - Part 035

Like the pots on the Persian wheel, sometimes the world is high, and
sometimes it is low.
Wandering and roaming around, I have come at last to Your Door.
"Who are you?"
"I am Naam Dayv, Sir."
O Lord, please save me from Maya, the cause of death. |3|4|

O Lord, You are the Purifier of sinners - this is Your innate nature.
Blessed are those silent sages and humble beings, who meditate on my
Lord God. |1|

I have applied to my forehead the dust of the feet of the Lord of the
Universe.
This is something which is far away from the gods, mortal men and silent
sages. |1|Pause|

O Lord, Merciful to the meek, Destroyer of pride
- Naam Dayv seeks the Sanctuary of Your feet; he is a sacrifice to You.
|2|5|

Dhanaasaree, Devotee Ravi Daas Jee:
One Universal Creator God. By The Grace Of The True Guru:
There is none as forlorn as I am, and none as Compassionate as You; what
need is there to test us now?
May my mind surrender to Your Word; please, bless Your humble servant
with this perfection. |1|

I am a sacrifice, a sacrifice to the Lord.
O Lord, why are You silent? |Pause|

For so many incarnations, I have been separated from You, Lord; I dedicate
this life to You.

Says Ravi Daas: placing my hopes in You, I live; it is so long since I have gazed upon the Blessed Vision of Your Darshan. |2|1|

In my consciousness, I remember You in meditation; with my eyes, I behold You; I fill my ears with the Word of Your Bani, and Your Sublime Praise.
My mind is the bumble bee; I enshrine Your feet within my heart, and with my tongue, I chant the Ambrosial Name of the Lord. |1|

My love for the Lord of the Universe does not decrease.
I paid for it dearly, in exchange for my soul. |1|Pause|

Without the Saadh Sangat, the Company of the Holy, love for the Lord does not well up; without this love, Your devotional worship cannot be performed.
Ravi Daas offers this one prayer unto the Lord: please preserve and protect my honor, O Lord, my King. |2|2|

Your Name, Lord, is my adoration and cleansing bath.
Without the Name of the Lord, all ostentatious displays are useless. |1|Pause|

Your Name is my prayer mat, and Your Name is the stone to grind the sandalwood. Your Name is the saffron which I take and sprinkle in offering to You.
Your Name is the water, and Your Name is the sandalwood. The chanting of Your Name is the grinding of the sandalwood. I take it and offer all this to You. |1|

Your Name is the lamp, and Your Name is the wick. Your Name is the oil I pour into it.
Your Name is the light applied to this lamp, which enlightens and illuminates the entire world. |2|

Your Name is the thread, and Your Name is the garland of flowers. The eighteen loads of vegetation are all too impure to offer to You.
Why should I offer to You, that which You Yourself created? Your Name is the fan, which I wave over You. |3|

The whole world is engrossed in the eighteen Puraanas, the sixty-eight sacred shrines of pilgrimage, and the four sources of creation.

Says Ravi Daas, Your Name is my Aartee, my lamp-lit worship-service. The True Name, Sat Naam, is the food which I offer to You. |4|3|

Section 14 - Raag Dhanaasaree - Part 036

Dhanaasaree, The Word Of Devotee Trilochan Jee:
One Universal Creator God. By The Grace Of The True Guru:
Why do you slander the Lord? You are ignorant and deluded.
Pain and pleasure are the result of your own actions. |1|Pause|

The moon dwells in Shiva's forehead; it takes its cleansing bath in the Ganges.
Among the men of the moon's family, Krishna was born;
even so, the stains from its past actions remain on the moon's face. |1|

Aruna was a charioteer; his master was the sun, the lamp of the world. His brother was Garuda, the king of birds;

and yet, Aruna was made a cripple, because of the karma of his past actions. |2|

Shiva, the destroyer of countless sins, the Lord and Master of the three worlds, wandered from sacred shrine to sacred shrine; he never found an end to them.
And yet, he could not erase the karma of cutting off Brahma's head. |3|

Through the nectar, the moon, the wish-fulfilling cow, Lakshmi, the miraculous tree of life, Sikhar the sun's horse, and Dhanavantar the wise physician - all arose from the ocean, the lord of rivers;

and yet, because of its karma, its saltiness has not left it. |4|

Hanuman burnt the fortress of Sri Lanka, uprooted the garden of Raawan, and brought healing herbs for the wounds of Lachhman, pleasing Lord Raamaa;

and yet, because of his karma, he could not be rid of his loin cloth. |5|

The karma of past actions cannot be erased, O wife of my house; this is why I chant the Name of the Lord.

So prays Trilochan, Dear Lord. |6|1|

Sri Sain:
With incense, lamps and ghee, I offer this lamp-lit worship service.
I am a sacrifice to the Lord of Lakshmi. |1|

Hail to You, Lord, hail to You! Again and again, hail to You, Lord King, Ruler of all! |1|Pause|

Sublime is the lamp, and pure is the wick.
You are immaculate and pure, O Brilliant Lord of Wealth! |2|

Raamaanand knows the devotional worship of the Lord.
He says that the Lord is all-pervading, the embodiment of supreme joy. |3|

The Lord of the world, of wondrous form, has carried me across the terrifying world-ocean.
Says Sain, remember the Lord, the embodiment of supreme joy! |4|2|

Peepaa:
Within the body, the Divine Lord is embodied. The body is the temple, the place of pilgrimage, and the pilgrim.
Within the body are incense, lamps and offerings. Within the body are the flower offerings. |1|

I searched throughout many realms, but I found the nine treasures within the body.
Nothing comes, and nothing goes; I pray to the Lord for Mercy. |1|Pause|

The One who pervades the Universe also dwells in the body; whoever seeks Him, finds Him there.
Peepaa prays, the Lord is the supreme essence; He reveals Himself through the True Guru. |2|3|

Dhannaa:
O Lord of the world, this is Your lamp-lit worship service.
You are the Arranger of the affairs of those humble beings who perform Your devotional worship service. |1|Pause|

Lentils, flour and ghee - these things, I beg of You.

My mind shall ever be pleased.
Shoes, fine clothes, and grain of seven kinds - I beg of You. |1|

A milk cow, and a water buffalo, I beg of You,
and a fine Turkestani horse.
A good wife to care for my home
- Your humble servant Dhanna begs for these things, Lord. |2|4|

RAAG JAITSREE

Section 15 - Raag Jaitsree - Part 001

Jaitsree, Fourth Mehl, First House, Chau-Padas:
One Universal Creator God. By The Grace Of The True Guru:
The Jewel of the Lord's Name abides within my heart; the Guru has placed His hand on my forehead.
The sins and pains of countless incarnations have been cast out. The Guru has blessed me with the Naam, the Name of the Lord, and my debt has been paid off. |1|

O my mind, vibrate the Lord's Name, and all your affairs shall be resolved.
The Perfect Guru has implanted the Lord's Name within me; without the Name, life is useless. |Pause|

Without the Guru, the self-willed manmukhs are foolish and ignorant; they are forever entangled in emotional attachment to Maya.
They never serve the feet of the Holy; their lives are totally useless. |2|

Those who serve at the feet of the Holy, the feet of the Holy, their lives are made fruitful, and they belong to the Lord.
Make me the slave of the slave of the slaves of the Lord; bless me with Your Mercy, O Lord of the Universe. |3|

I am blind, ignorant and totally without wisdom; how can I walk on the Path?
I am blind - O Guru, please let me grasp the hem of Your robe, so that servant Nanak may walk in harmony with You. |4|1|

Jaitsree, Fourth Mehl:
A jewel or a diamond may be very valuable and heavy, but without a purchaser, it is worth only straw.
When the Holy Guru, the Purchaser, saw this jewel, He purchased it for hundreds of thousands of dollars. |1|

The Lord has kept this jewel hidden within my mind.

The Lord, merciful to the meek, led me to meet the Holy Guru; meeting the Guru, I came to appreciate this jewel. |Pause|

The rooms of the self-willed manmukhs are dark with ignorance; in their homes, the jewel is not visible.
Those fools die, wandering in the wilderness, eating the poison of the snake, Maya. |2|

O Lord, Har, Har, let me meet the humble, holy beings; O Lord, keep me in the Sanctuary of the Holy.
O Lord, make me Your own; O God, Lord and Master, I have hurried to Your side. |3|

What Glorious Virtues of Yours can I speak and describe? You are great and unfathomable, the Greatest Being.
The Lord has bestowed His Mercy on servant Nanak; He has saved the sinking stone. |4|2|

Section 15 - Raag Jaitsree - Part 002

Jaitsree, Fourth Mehl:
I am Your child; I know nothing about Your state and extent; I am foolish, idiotic and ignorant.
O Lord, shower me with Your Mercy; bless me with an enlightened intellect; I am foolish - make me clever. |1|

My mind is lazy and sleepy.
The Lord, Har, Har, has led me to meet the Holy Guru; meeting the Holy, the shutters have been opened wide. |Pause|

O Guru, each and every instant, fill my heart with love; the Name of my Beloved is my breath of life.
Without the Name, I would die; the Name of my Lord and Master is to me like the drug to the addict. |2|

Those who enshrine love for the Lord within their minds fulfill their pre-ordained destiny.
I worship their feet, each and every instant; the Lord seems very sweet to them. |3|

My Lord and Master, Har, Har, has showered His Mercy upon His humble servant; separated for so long, he is now re-united with the Lord.

Blessed, blessed is the True Guru, who has implanted the Naam, the Name of the Lord within me; servant Nanak is a sacrifice to Him. |4|3|

Jaitsree, Fourth Mehl:

I have found the True Guru, my Friend, the Greatest Being. Love and affection for the Lord has blossomed forth.

Maya, the snake, has seized the mortal; through the Word of the Guru, the Lord neutralizes the venom. |1|

My mind is attached to the sublime essence of the Lord's Name.

The Lord has purified the sinners, uniting them with the Holy Guru; now, they taste the Lord's Name, and the sublime essence of the Lord. |Pause|

Blessed, blessed is the good fortune of those who meet the Holy Guru; meeting with the Holy, they lovingly center themselves in the state of absolute absorption.

The fire of desire within them is quenched, and they find peace; they sing the Glorious Praises of the Immaculate Lord. |2|

Those who do not obtain the Blessed Vision of the True Guru's Darshan, have misfortune pre-ordained for them.

In the love of duality, they are consigned to reincarnation through the womb, and they pass their lives totally uselessly. |3|

O Lord, please, bless me with pure understanding, that I may serve the Feet of the Holy Guru; the Lord seems sweet to me.

Servant Nanak begs for the dust of the feet of the Holy; O Lord, be Merciful, and bless me with it. |4|4|

Jaitsree, Fourth Mehl:

The Lord's Name does not abide within their hearts - their mothers should have been sterile.

These bodies wander around, forlorn and abandoned, without the Name; their lives waste away, and they die, crying out in pain. |1|

O my mind, chant the Name of the Lord, the Lord within you.

The Merciful Lord God, Har, Har, has showered me with His Mercy; the Guru has imparted spiritual wisdom to me, and my mind has been instructed. |Pause|

In this Dark Age of Kali Yuga, the Kirtan of the Lord's Praise brings the most noble and exalted status; the Lord is found through the True Guru.
I am a sacrifice to my True Guru, who has revealed the Lord's hidden Name to me. |2|

By great good fortune, I obtained the Blessed Vision of the Darshan of the Holy; it removes all stains of sin.
I have found the True Guru, the great, all-knowing King; He has shared with me the many Glorious Virtues of the Lord. |3|

Section 15 - Raag Jaitsree - Part 003

Those, unto whom the Lord, the Life of the world, has shown Mercy, enshrine Him within their hearts, and cherish Him in their minds.
The Righteous Judge of Dharma, in the Court of the Lord, has torn up my papers; servant Nanak's account has been settled. |4|5|

Jaitsree, Fourth Mehl:
In the Sat Sangat, the True Congregation, I found the Holy, by great good fortune; my restless mind has been quieted.
The unstruck melody ever vibrates and resounds; I have taken in the sublime essence of the Lord's Ambrosial Nectar, showering down. |1|

O my mind, chant the Name of the Lord, the beauteous Lord.
The True Guru has drenched my mind and body with the Love of the Lord, who has met me and lovingly embraced me. |Pause|

The faithless cynics are bound and gagged in the chains of Maya; they are actively engaged, gathering in the poisonous wealth.
They cannot spend this in harmony with the Lord, and so they must endure the pain which the Messenger of Death inflicts upon their heads. |2|

The Holy Guru has dedicated His Being to the Lord's service; with great devotion, apply the dust of His feet to your face.
In this world and the next, you shall receive the Lord's honor, and your mind shall be imbued with the permanent color of the Lord's Love. |3|

O Lord, Har, Har, please unite me with the Holy; compared to these Holy people, I am just a worm.
Servant Nanak has enshrined love for the feet of the Holy Guru; meeting with this Holy One, my foolish, stone-like mind has blossomed forth in lush profusion. |4|6|

Jaitsree, Fourth Mehl, Second House:
One Universal Creator God. By The Grace Of The True Guru:
Remember in meditation the Lord, Har, Har, the unfathomable, infinite Lord.
Remembering Him in meditation, pains are dispelled.
O Lord, Har, Har, lead me to meet the True Guru; meeting the Guru, I am at peace. |1|

Sing the Glorious Praises of the Lord, O my friend.
Cherish the Name of the Lord, Har, Har, in your heart.
Read the Ambrosial Words of the Lord, Har, Har; meeting with the Guru, the Lord is revealed. |2|

The Lord, the Slayer of demons, is my breath of life.
His Ambrosial Amrit is so sweet to my mind and body.
O Lord, Har, Har, have mercy upon me, and lead me to meet the Guru, the immaculate Primal Being. |3|

The Name of the Lord, Har, Har, is forever the Giver of peace.
My mind is imbued with the Lord's Love.
O Lord Har, Har, lead me to meet the Guru, the Greatest Being; through the Name of Guru Nanak, I have found peace. |4|1|7|

Jaitsree, Fourth Mehl:
Chant the Name of the Lord, Har, Har, Har, Har.
As Gurmukh, ever earn the profit of the Naam.
Implant within yourself devotion to the Lord, Har, Har, Har, Har; sincerely dedicate yourself to the Name of the Lord, Har, Har. |1|

Meditate on the Name of the Merciful Lord, Har, Har.
WIth love, forever sing the Glorious Praises of the Lord.
Dance to the Praises of the Lord, Har, Har, Har; meet with the Sat Sangat, the True Congregation, with sincerity. |2|

Come, O companions - let us unite in the Lord's Union.
Listening to the sermon of the Lord, earn the profit of the Naam.

Section 15 - Raag Jaitsree - Part 004

O Lord, Har, Har, be merciful to me, and lead me to meet the Guru; meeting the Guru, a sincere yearning for the Lord wells up in me. |3|

Praise Him, the unfathomable and inaccessible Lord.
Each and every moment, sing the Lord's Name.
Be merciful, and meet me, O Guru, Great Giver; Nanak yearns for the Lord's devotional worship. |4|2|8|

Jaitsree, Fourth Mehl:
With love and energetic affection, praise the Lord, the storehouse of Nectar.
My mind is drenched with the Lord's Name, and so it earns this profit.
Each and every moment, worship Him in devotion, day and night; through the Guru's Teachings, sincere love and devotion well up. |1|

Chant the Glorious Praises of the Lord of the Universe, Har, Har.
Conquering mind and body, I have earned the profit of the Shabad.
Through the Guru's Teachings, the five demons are over-powered, and the mind and body are filled with a sincere yearning for the Lord. |2|

The Name is a jewel - chant the Lord's Name.
Sing the Glorious Praises of the Lord, and forever earn this profit.
O Lord, merciful to the meek, be kind to me, and bless me with sincere longing for the Name of the Lord, Har, Har. |3|

Meditate on the Lord of the world - meditate within your mind.
The Lord of the Universe, Har, Har, is the only real profit in this world.
Blessed, blessed, is my Great Lord and Master God; O Nanak, meditate on Him, worship Him with sincere love and devotion. |4|3|9|

Jaitsree, Fourth Mehl:
He Himself is the Yogi, and the way throughout the ages.
The Fearless Lord Himself is absorbed in Samaadhi.

He Himself, all by Himself, is all-pervading; He Himself blesses us with sincere love for the Naam, the Name of the Lord. |1|

He Himself is the lamp, and the Light pervading all the worlds.
He Himself is the True Guru; He Himself churns the ocean.
He Himself churns it, churning up the essence; meditating on the jewel of the Naam, sincere love comes to the surface. |2|

O my companions, let us meet and join together, and sing His Glorious Praises.
As Gurmukh, chant the Naam, and earn the profit of the Lord's Name.
Devotional worship of the Lord, Har, Har, has been implanted within me; it is pleasing to my mind. The Name of the Lord, Har, Har, brings a sincere love. |3|

He Himself is supremely wise, the greatest King.
As Gurmukh, purchase the merchandise of the Naam.
O Lord God, Har, Har, bless me with such a gift, that Your Glorious Virtues seem pleasing to me; Nanak is filled with sincere love and yearning for the Lord. |4|4|10|

Jaitsree, Fourth Mehl:
Joining the Sat Sangat, the True Congregation, and associating with the Guru,
the Gurmukh gathers in the merchandise of the Naam.
O Lord, Har, Har, Destroyer of demons, have mercy upon me; bless me with a sincere yearning to join the Sat Sangat. |1|

Let me hear with my ears the Banis, the Hymns, in praise of the Lord;
be merciful, and let me meet the True Guru.
I sing His Glorious Praises, I speak the Bani of His Word; chanting His Glorious Praises, a sincere yearning for the Lord wells up. |2|

I have tried visiting all the sacred shrines of pilgrimage, fasting, ceremonial feasts and giving to charities.
They do not measure up to the Name of the Lord, Har, Har.
The Lord's Name is unweighable, utterly heavy in weight; through the Guru's Teachings, a sincere yearning to chant the Name has welled up in me. |3|

All good karma and righteous living are found in meditation on the Lord's Name.
It washes away the stains of sins and mistakes.
Be merciful to meek, humble Nanak; bless him with sincere love and yearning for the Lord. |4|5|11|

Section 15 - Raag Jaitsree - Part 005

Jaitsree, Fifth Mehl, Third House:
One Universal Creator God. By The Grace Of The True Guru:
Does anyone know, who is our friend in this world?
He alone understands this, whom the Lord blesses with His Mercy.
Immaculate and unstained is his way of life. |1|Pause|

Mother, father, spouse, children, relatives, lovers, friends and siblings meet, having been associated in previous lives; but none of them will be your companion and support in the end. |1|

Pearl necklaces, gold, rubies and diamonds please the mind, but they are only Maya.
Possessing them, one passes his life in agony; he obtains no contentment from them. |2|

Elephants, chariots, horses as fast as the wind, wealth, land, and armies of four kinds
- none of these will go with him; he must get up and depart, naked. |3|

The Lord's Saints are the beloved lovers of God; sing of the Lord, Har, Har, with them.
O Nanak, in the Society of the Saints, you shall obtain peace in this world, and in the next world, your face shall be radiant and bright. |4|1|

Jaitsree, Fifth Mehl, Third House, Du-Padas:
One Universal Creator God. By The Grace Of The True Guru:
Give me a message from my Beloved - tell me, tell me!
I am wonder-struck, hearing the many reports of Him; tell them to me, O my happy sister soul-brides. |1|Pause|

Some say that He is beyond the world - totally beyond it, while others say that He is totally within it.

His color cannot be seen, and His pattern cannot be discerned. O happy soul-brides, tell me the truth! |1|

He is pervading everywhere, and He dwells in each and every heart; He is not stained - He is unstained.
Says Nanak, listen, O people: He dwells upon the tongues of the Saints. |2|1|2|

Jaitsree, Fifth Mehl:
I am calmed, calmed and soothed, hearing of God. |1|Pause|

I dedicate my soul, my breath of life, my mind, body and everything to Him: I behold God near, very near. |1|

Beholding God, the inestimable, infinite and Great Giver, I cherish Him in my mind. |2|

Whatever I wish for, I receive; my hopes and desires are fulfilled, meditating on God. |3|

By Guru's Grace, God dwells in Nanak's mind; he never suffers or grieves, having realized God. |4|2|3|

Jaitsree, Fifth Mehl:
I seek my Friend the Lord.
In each and every home, sing the sublime songs of rejoicing; He abides in each and every heart. |1|Pause|

In good times, worship and adore Him; in bad times, worship and adore Him; do not ever forget Him.
Chanting the Naam, the Name of the Lord, the light of millions of suns shines forth, and the darkness of doubt is dispelled. |1|

In all the spaces and interspaces, everywhere, whatever we see is Yours.
One who finds the Society of the Saints, O Nanak, is not consigned to reincarnation again. |2|3|4|

Section 15 - Raag Jaitsree - Part 006

Jaitsree, Fifth Mehl, Fourth House, Du-Padas:

One Universal Creator God. By The Grace Of The True Guru:
Now, I have found peace, bowing before the Guru.
I have abandoned cleverness, quieted my anxiety, and renounced my egotism. |1|Pause|

When I looked, I saw that everyone was enticed by emotional attachment; then, I hurried to the Guru's Sanctuary.
In His Grace, the Guru engaged me in the Lord's service, and then, the Messenger of Death gave up pursuing me. |1|

I swam across the ocean of fire, when I met the Saints, through great good fortune.
O servant Nanak, I have found total peace; my consciousness is attached to the Lord's feet. |2|1|5|

Jaitsree, Fifth Mehl:
Within my mind, I cherish and meditate on the True Guru.
He has implanted within me spiritual wisdom and the Mantra of the Lord's Name; Dear God has shown mercy to me. |1|Pause|

Death's noose and its mighty entanglements have vanished, along with the fear of death.
I have come to the Sanctuary of the Merciful Lord, the Destroyer of pain; I am holding tight to the Support of His feet. |1|

The Saadh Sangat, the Company of the Holy, has assumed the form of a boat, to cross over the terrifying world-ocean.
I drink in the Ambrosial Nectar, and my doubts are shattered; says Nanak, I can bear the unbearable. |2|2|6|

Jaitsree, Fifth Mehl:
One who has the Lord of the Universe as his help and support
is blessed with all peace, poise and bliss; no afflictions cling to him. |1|Pause|

He appears to keep company with everyone, but he remains detached, and Maya does not cling to him.
He is absorbed in love of the One Lord; he understands the essence of reality, and he is blessed with wisdom by the True Guru. |1|

Those whom the Lord and Master blesses with His kindness, compassion and mercy are the sublime and sanctified Saints.
Associating with them, Nanak is saved; with love and exuberant joy, they sing the Glorious Praises of the Lord. |2|3|7|

Jaitsree, Fifth Mehl:
The Lord of the Universe is my existence, my breath of life, wealth and beauty.
The ignorant are totally intoxicated with emotional attachment; in this darkness, the Lord is the only lamp. |1|Pause|

Fruitful is the Blessed Vision of Your Darshan, O Beloved God; Your lotus feet are incomparably beautiful!

So many times, I bow in reverence to Him, offering my mind as incense to Him. |1|

Exhausted, I have fallen at Your Door, O God; I am holding tight to Your Support.
Please, lift Your humble servant Nanak up, out of the pit of fire of the world. |2|4|8|

Jaitsree, Fifth Mehl:
If only someone would unite me with the Lord!
I hold tight to His feet, and utter sweet words with my tongue; I make my breath of life an offering to Him. |1|Pause|

I make my mind and body into pure little gardens, and irrigate them with the sublime essence of the Lord.
I am drenched with this sublime essence by His Grace, and the powerful hold of Maya's corruption has been broken. |1|

I have come to Your Sanctuary, O Destroyer of the suffering of the innocent; I keep my consciousness focused on You.

Section 15 - Raag Jaitsree - Part 007

Bless me with the gifts of the state of fearlessness, and meditative remembrance, Lord and Master; O Nanak, God is the Breaker of bonds. |2|5|9|

Jaitsree, Fifth Mehl:
The rainbird longs for the rain to fall.
O God, ocean of mercy, shower Your mercy on me, that I may yearn for loving devotional worship of the Lord. |1|Pause|

The chakvi duck does not desire many comforts, but it is filled with bliss upon seeing the dawn.
The fish cannot survive any other way - without water, it dies. |1|

I am a helpless orphan - I seek Your Sanctuary, O My Lord and Master; please bless me with Your mercy.
Nanak worships and adores the Lord's lotus feet; without Him, there is no other at all. |2|6|10|

Jaitsree, Fifth Mehl:
The Lord, my very breath of life, abides in my mind and body.
Bless me with Your mercy, and unite me with the Saadh Sangat, the Company of the Holy, O perfect, all-knowing Lord God. |1|Pause|

Those, unto whom You give the intoxicating herb of Your Love, drink in the supreme sublime essence.
I cannot describe their value; what power do I have? |1|

The Lord attaches His humble servants to the hem of His robe, and they swim across the world-ocean.
Meditating, meditating, meditating in remembrance on God, peace is obtained; Nanak seeks the Sanctuary of Your Door. |2|7|11|

Jaitsree, Fifth Mehl:
After wandering through so many incarnations, I have come to Your Sanctuary.
Save me - lift my body up out of the deep, dark pit of the world, and attach me to Your feet. |1|Pause|

I do not know anything about spiritual wisdom, meditation or karma, and my way of life is not clean and pure.
Please attach me to the hem of the robe of the Saadh Sangat, the Company of the Holy; help me to cross over the terrible river. |1|

Comforts, riches and the sweet pleasures of Maya - do not implant these within your mind.

Slave Nanak is satisfied and satiated by the Blessed Vision of the Lord's Darshan; his only ornamentation is the love of the Lord's Name. |2|8|12|

Jaitsree, Fifth Mehl:
O humble servants of the Lord, remember the Lord in meditation within your heart.

Misfortune does not even approach the Lord's humble servant; the works of His slave are perfectly fulfilled. |1|Pause|

Millions of obstacles are removed, by serving the Lord, and one enters into the eternal dwelling of the Lord of the Universe.

The Lord's devotee is very fortunate; he has absolutely no fear. Even the Messenger of Death pays homage to him. |1|

Forsaking the Lord of the world, he does other deeds, but these are temporary and transitory.

Grasp the Lord's lotus feet, and hold them in your heart, O Nanak; you shall obtain absolute peace and bliss. |2|9|13|

Jaitsree, Ninth Mehl: One Universal Creator God.
One Universal Creator God. By The Grace Of The True Guru:
My mind is deluded, entangled in Maya.

Whatever I do, while engaged in greed, only serves to bind me down. |1|Pause|

I have no understanding at all; I am engrossed in the pleasures of corruption, and I have forgotten the Praises of the Lord.

The Lord and Master is with me, but I do not know Him. Instead, I run into the forest, looking for Him. |1|

Section 15 - Raag Jaitsree - Part 008

The Jewel of the Lord is deep within my heart, but I do not have any knowledge of Him.

O servant Nanak, without vibrating, meditating on the Lord God, human life is uselessly wasted and lost. |2|1|

Jaitsree, Ninth Mehl:

O Dear Lord, please, save my honor!
The fear of death has entered my heart; I cling to the Protection of Your Sanctuary, O Lord, ocean of mercy. |1|Pause|

I am a great sinner, foolish and greedy; but now, at last, I have grown weary of committing sins.
I cannot forget the fear of dying; this anxiety is consuming my body. |1|

I have been trying to liberate myself, running around in the ten directions.
The pure, immaculate Lord abides deep within my heart, but I do not understand the secret of His mystery. |2|

I have no merit, and I know nothing about meditation or austerities; what should I do now?
O Nanak, I am exhausted; I seek the shelter of Your Sanctuary; O God, please bless me with the gift of fearlessness. |3|2|

Jaitsree, Ninth Mehl:
O mind, embrace true contemplation.
Without the Lord's Name, know that this whole world is false. |1|Pause|

The Yogis are tired of searching for Him, but they have not found His limit.
You must understand that the Lord and Master is near at hand, but He has no form or feature. |1|

The Naam, the Name of the Lord is purifying in the world, and yet you never remember it.
Nanak has entered the Sanctuary of the One, before whom the whole world bows down; please, preserve and protect me, by Your innate nature. |2|3|

Jaitsree, Fifth Mehl, Chhant, First House:
One Universal Creator God. By The Grace Of The True Guru:
Shalok:
I am thirsty for the Blessed Vision of the Lord's Darshan, day and night; I yearn for Him constantly, night and day.
Opening the door, O Nanak, the Guru has led me to meet with the Lord, my Friend. |1|

Chhant:

Listen, O my intimate friend - I have just one prayer to make.

I have been wandering around, searching for that enticing, sweet Beloved.

Whoever leads me to my Beloved - I would cut off my head and offer it to him, even if I were granted the Blessed Vision of His Darshan for just an instant.

My eyes are drenched with the Love of my Beloved; without Him, I do not have even a moment's peace.

My mind is attached to the Lord, like the fish to the water, and the rainbird, thirsty for the raindrops.

Servant Nanak has found the Perfect Guru; his thirst is totally quenched. |1|

O intimate friend, my Beloved has all these loving companions; I cannot compare to any of them.

O intimate friend, each of them is more beautiful than the others; who could consider me?

Each of them is more beautiful than the others; countless are His lovers, constantly enjoying bliss with Him.

Beholding them, desire wells up in my mind; when will I obtain the Lord, the treasure of virtue?

I dedicate my mind to those who please and attract my Beloved.

Says Nanak, hear my prayer, O happy soul-brides; tell me, what does my Husband Lord look like? |2|

O intimate friend, my Husband Lord does whatever He pleases; He is not dependent on anyone.

Section 15 - Raag Jaitsree - Part 009

O intimate friend, you have enjoyed your Beloved; please, tell me about Him.

They alone find their Beloved, who eradicate self-conceit; such is the good destiny written on their foreheads.

Taking me by the arm, the Lord and Master has made me His own; He has not considered my merits or demerits.

She, whom You have adorned with the necklace of virtue, and dyed in the deep crimson color of His Love - everything looks beautiful on her.

O servant Nanak, blessed is that happy soul-bride, who dwells with her Husband Lord. |3|

O intimate friend, I have found that peace which I sought.

My sought-after Husband Lord has come home, and now, congratulations are pouring in.

Great joy and happiness welled up, when my Husband Lord, of ever-fresh beauty, showed mercy to me.

By great good fortune, I have found Him; the Guru has united me with Him, through the Saadh Sangat, the True Congregation of the Holy.

My hopes and desires have all been fulfilled; my Beloved Husband Lord has hugged me close in His embrace.

Prays Nanak, I have found that peace which I sought, meeting with the Guru. |4|1|

Jaitsree, Fifth Mehl, Second House, Chhant:

One Universal Creator God. By The Grace Of The True Guru:

Shalok:

God is lofty, unapproachable and infinite. He is indescribable - He cannot be described.

Nanak seeks the Sanctuary of God, who is all-powerful to save us. |1|

Chhant:

Save me, any way You can; O Lord God, I am Yours.

My demerits are uncountable; how many of them should I count?

The sins and crimes I committed are countless; day by day, I continually make mistakes.

I am intoxicated by emotional attachment to Maya, the treacherous one; by Your Grace alone can I be saved.

Secretly, I commit hideous sins of corruption, even though God is the nearest of the near.

Prays Nanak, shower me with Your Mercy, Lord, and lift me up, out of the whirlpool of the terrifying world-ocean. |1|

Shalok:

Countless are His virtues; they cannot be enumerated. God's Name is lofty and exalted.

This is Nanak's humble prayer, to bless the homeless with a home. |2|

Chhant:

There is no other place at all - where else should I go?

Twenty-four hours a day, with my palms pressed together, I meditate on God.

Meditating forever on my God, I receive the fruits of my mind's desires.

Renouncing pride, attachment, corruption and duality, I lovingly center my attention on the One Lord.

Dedicate your mind and body to God; eradicate all your self-conceit.

Prays Nanak, shower me with Your mercy, Lord, that I may be absorbed in Your True Name. |2|

Shalok:

O mind, meditate on the One, who holds everything in His hands.

Gather the wealth of the Lord's Name; O Nanak, it shall always be with You. |3|

Chhant:

God is our only True Friend; there is not any other.

In the places and interspaces, in the water and on the land, He Himself is pervading everywhere.

He is totally permeating the water, the land and the sky; God is the Great Giver, the Lord and Master of all.

The Lord of the world, the Lord of the universe has no limit; His Glorious Virtues are unlimited - how can I count them?

I have hurried to the Sanctuary of the Lord Master, the Bringer of peace; without Him, there is no other at all.

Prays Nanak, that being, unto whom the Lord shows mercy - he alone obtains the Naam. |3|

Section 15 - Raag Jaitsree - Part 010

Shalok:

Whatever I wish for, that I receive.

Meditating on the Naam, the Name of the Lord, Nanak has found total peace. |4|

Chhant:

My mind is now emancipated; I have joined the Saadh Sangat, the Company of the Holy.

As Gurmukh, I chant the Naam, and my light has merged into the Light.

Remembering the Lord's Name in meditation, my sins have been erased; the fire has been extinguished, and I am satisfied.

He has taken me by the arm, and blessed me with His kind mercy; He has accepted me His own.

The Lord has hugged me in His embrace, and merged me with Himself; the pains of birth and death have been burnt away.

Prays Nanak, He has blessed me with His kind mercy; in an instant, He unites me with Himself. |4|2|

Jaitsree, Chhant, Fifth Mehl:

The world is like a temporary way-station, but it is filled with pride.

People commit countless sins; they are dyed in the color of the love of Maya.

In greed, emotional attachment and egotism, they are drowning; they do not even think of dying.

Children, friends, worldly occupations and spouses - they talk of these things, while their lives are passing away.

When their pre-ordained days have run their course, O mother, they behold the Messengers of the Righteous Judge of Dharma, and they suffer.

The karma of their past deeds cannot be erased, O Nanak, if they have not earned the wealth of the Lord's Name. |1|

He makes all sorts of efforts, but he does not sing the Lord's Name.

He wanders around in countless incarnations; he dies, only to be born again.

As beasts, birds, stones and trees - their number cannot be known.

As are the seeds he plants, so are the pleasures he enjoys; he receives the consequences of his own actions.

He loses the jewel of this human life in the gamble, and God is not pleased with him at all.

Prays Nanak, wandering in doubt, he does not find any rest, even for an instant. |2|

Youth has passed, and old age has taken its place.

The hands tremble, the head shakes, and the eyes do not see.

The eyes do not see, without vibrating and meditating on the Lord; he must leave behind the attractions of Maya, and depart.

He burnt his mind and body for his relatives, but now, they do not listen to him, and they throw dust on his head.

Love for the infinite, Perfect Lord does not abide in his mind, even for an instant.

Prays Nanak, the fort of paper is false - it is destroyed in an instant. |3|

Nanak has come to the Sanctuary of the Lord's lotus feet.

God Himself has carried Him across the impassable, terrifying world-ocean.

Joining the Saadh Sangat, the Company of the Holy, I vibrate and meditate on the Lord; God has made me His own, and saved me.

The Lord has approved of me, and blessed me with His Name; He did not take anything else into consideration.

I have found the infinite Lord and Master, the treasure of virtue, which my mind had yearned for.

Prays Nanak, I am satisfied forever; I have eaten the food of the Lord's Name. |4|2|3|

Jaitsree, Fifth Mehl, Vaar With Shaloks:

One Universal Creator God. By The Grace Of The True Guru:

Shalok:

In the beginning, He was pervading; in the middle, He is pervading; in the end, He will be pervading. He is the Transcendent Lord.

The Saints remember in meditation the all-pervading Lord God. O Nanak, He is the Destroyer of sins, the Lord of the universe. |1|

Section 15 - Raag Jaitsree - Part 011

See, hear, speak and implant the True Lord within your mind.

He is all-pervading, permeating everywhere; O Nanak, be absorbed in the Lord's Love. |2|

Pauree:

Sing the Praise of the One, the Immaculate Lord; He is contained within all.

The Cause of causes, the Almighty Lord God; whatever He wills, comes to pass.

In an instant, He establishes and disestablishes; without Him, there is no other.

He pervades the continents, solar systems, nether worlds, islands and all worlds.

He alone understands, whom the Lord Himself instructs; he alone is a pure and unstained being. |1|

Shalok:

Creating the soul, the Lord places this creation in the womb of the mother.

With each and every breath, it meditates in remembrance on the Lord, O Nanak; it is not consumed by the great fire. |1|

With its head down, and feet up, it dwells in that slimy place.
O Nanak, how could we forget the Master? Through His Name, we are saved. |2|

Pauree:
From egg and sperm, you were conceived, and placed in the fire of the womb.
Head downwards, you abided restlessly in that dark, dismal, terrible hell.
Remembering the Lord in meditation, you were not burnt; enshrine Him in your heart, mind and body.
In that treacherous place, He protected and preserved you; do not forget Him, even for an instant.
Forgetting God, you shall never find peace; you shall forfeit your life, and depart. |2|

Shalok:
He grants our hearts' desires, and fulfills all our hopes.
He destroys pain and suffering; remember God in meditation, O Nanak - He is not far away. |1|

Love Him, with whom you enjoy all pleasures.
Do not forget that Lord, even for an instant; O Nanak, He fashioned this beautiful body. |2|

Pauree:
He gave you your soul, breath of life, body and wealth; He gave you pleasures to enjoy.
He gave you households, mansions, chariots and horses; He ordained your good destiny.
He gave you your children, spouse, friends and servants; God is the all-powerful Great Giver.
Meditating in remembrance on the Lord, the body and mind are rejuvenated, and sorrow departs.
In the Saadh Sangat, the Company of the Holy, chant the Praises of the Lord, and all your sickness shall vanish. |3|

Shalok:

For his family, he works very hard; for the sake of Maya, he makes countless efforts.
But without loving devotional worship of the Lord, O Nanak, he forgets God, and then, he is a mere ghost. |1|

That love shall break, which is established with any other than the Lord.
O Nanak, that way of life is true, which inspires love of the Lord. |2|

Pauree:
Forgetting Him, one's body turns to dust, and everyone calls him a ghost.
And those, with whom he was so much in love - they do not let him stay in their home, even for an instant.
Practicing exploitation, he gathers wealth, but what use will it be in the end?
As one plants, so does he harvest; the body is the field of actions.
The ungrateful wretches forget the Lord, and wander in reincarnation. |4|

Shalok:
The benefits of millions of charitable donations and cleansing baths, and countless ceremonies of purification and piety,

O Nanak, are obtained by chanting the Name of the Lord, Har, Har with one's tongue; all sins are washed away. |1|

I gathered together a great stack of firewood, and applied a tiny flame to light it.

Section 15 - Raag Jaitsree - Part 012

When the True Lord and Master abides in one's mind, O Nanak, all sins are dispelled. |2|

Pauree:
Millions of sins are totally erased, by meditating on the Lord's Name.
The fruits of one's heart's desires are obtained, by singing the Glorious Praises of the Lord.
The fear of birth and death is eradicated, and one's eternal, unchanging true home is obtained.
If it is so pre-ordained, one is absorbed in the Lord's lotus feet.

Bless me with Your mercy, God - please preserve and save me! Nanak is a sacrifice to You. |5|

Shalok:
They are involved in their beautiful houses, and the pleasures of the mind's desires.
They never remember the Lord in meditation; O Nanak, they are like maggots in manure. |1|

They are engrossed in ostentatious displays, lovingly attached to all their possessions.
That body which forgets the Lord, O Nanak, shall be reduced to ashes. |2|

Pauree:
He may enjoy a beautiful bed, countless pleasures and all sorts of enjoyments.
He may possess mansions of gold, studded with pearls and rubies, plastered with fragrant sandalwood oil.
He may relish in the pleasures of his mind's desires, and have no anxiety at all.
But if he does not remember God, he is like a maggot in manure.
Without the Lord's Name, there is no peace at all. How can the mind be comforted? |6|

Shalok:
One who loves the Lord's lotus feet searches for Him in the ten directions.
He renounces the deceptive illusion of Maya, and joins the blissful form of the Saadh Sangat, the Company of the Holy. |1|

The Lord is in my mind, and with my mouth I chant His Name; I seek Him in all the lands of the world.
O Nanak, all ostentatious displays are false; hearing the Praises of the True Lord, I live. |2|

Pauree:
He dwells in a broken-down shack, in tattered clothes,
with no social status, no honor and no respect; he wanders in the wilderness,
with no friend or lover, without wealth, beauty, relatives or relations.

Even so, he is the king of the whole world, if his mind is imbued with the Lord's Name.

With the dust of his feet, men are redeemed, because God is very pleased with him. |7|

Shalok:
The various sorts of pleasures, powers, joys, beauty, canopies, cooling fans and thrones to sit on

- the foolish, ignorant and blind are engrossed in these things. O Nanak, desire for Maya is just a dream. |1|

In a dream, he enjoys all sorts of pleasures, and emotional attachment seems so sweet.

O Nanak, without the Naam, the Name of the Lord, the beauty of Maya's illusion is fake. |2|

Pauree:
The fool attaches his consciousness to the dream.

When he awakes, he forgets the power, pleasures and enjoyments, and he is sad.

He passes his life chasing after worldly affairs.

His works are not completed, because he is enticed by Maya.

What can the poor helpless creature do? The Lord Himself has deluded him. |8|

Shalok:
They may live in heavenly realms, and conquer the nine regions of the world,

but if they forget the Lord of the world, O Nanak, they are just wanderers in the wilderness. |1|

In the midst of millions of games and entertainments, the Lord's Name does not come to their minds.

O Nanak, their home is like a wilderness, in the depths of hell. |2|

Pauree:
He sees the terrible, awful wilderness as a city.

Gazing upon the false objects, he believes them to be real.

Section 15 - Raag Jaitsree - Part 013

Engrossed in sexual desire, anger and egotism, he wanders around insane.
When the Messenger of Death hits him on the head with his club, then he regrets and repents.
Without the Perfect, Divine Guru, he roams around like Satan. |9|

Shalok:
Power is fraudulent, beauty is fraudulent, and wealth is fraudulent, as is pride of ancestry.
One may gather poison through deception and fraud, O Nanak, but without the Lord, nothing shall go along with him in the end. |1|

Beholding the bitter melon, he is deceived, since it appears so pretty
But it is not worth even a shell, O Nanak; the riches of Maya will not go along with anyone. |2|

Pauree:
It shall not go along with you when you depart - why do you bother to collect it?
Tell me, why do you try so hard to acquire that which you must leave behind in the end?
Forgetting the Lord, how can you be satisfied? Your mind cannot be pleased.
One who forsakes God, and attaches himself to another, shall be immersed in hell.
Be kind and compassionate to Nanak, O Lord, and dispel his fear. |10|

Shalok:
Princely pleasures are not sweet; sensual enjoyments are not sweet; the pleasures of Maya are not sweet.
The Saadh Sangat, the Company of the Holy, is sweet, O slave Nanak; the Blessed Vision of God's Darshan is sweet. |1|

I have enshrined that love which drenches my soul.
I have been pierced by the Truth, O Nanak; the Master seems so sweet to me. |2|

Pauree:
Nothing seems sweet to His devotees, except the Lord.
All other tastes are bland and insipid; I have tested them and seen them.

Ignorance, doubt and suffering are dispelled, when the Guru becomes one's advocate.

The Lord's lotus feet have pierced my mind, and I am dyed in the deep crimson color of His Love.

My soul, breath of life, body and mind belong to God; all falsehood has left me. |11|

Shalok:

Leaving the water, the fish cannot live; the rainbird cannot live without the raindrops from the clouds.

The deer is enticed by the sound of the hunter's bell, and shot through with the arrow; the bumble bee is entangled in the fragrance of the flowers.

The Saints are entranced by the Lord's lotus feet; O Nanak, they desire nothing else. |1|

Show me Your face, for even an instant, Lord, and I will not give my consciousness to any other.

My life is with the Lord Master, O Nanak, the Friend of the Saints. |2|

Pauree:

How can the fish live without water?

Without the raindrops, how can the rainbird be satisfied?

The deer, entranced by the sound of the hunter's bell, runs straight to him; the bumble bee is greedy for the flower's fragrance; finding it, he traps himself in it.

Just so, the humble Saints love the Lord; beholding the Blessed Vision of His Darshan, they are satisfied and satiated. |12|

Shalok:

They contemplate the Lord's lotus feet; they worship and adore Him with each and every breath.

They do not forget the Name of the imperishable Lord; O Nanak, the Transcendent Lord fulfills their hopes. |1|

He is woven into the fabric of my mind; He is not outside of it, even for an instant.

O Nanak, the True Lord and Master fulfills my hopes, and always watches over me. |2|

Pauree:

My hopes rest in You, O Lord of the universe; please, fulfill them.

Meeting with the Lord of the world, the Lord of the universe, I shall never grieve.

Grant me the Blessed Vision of Your Darshan, the desire of my mind, and my worries shall be over.

Section 15 - Raag Jaitsree - Part 014

By body is sanctified, by the dust of Your feet.

O Supreme Lord God, Divine Guru, You are always with me, ever-present. |13|

Shalok:

With my tongue, I chant the Lord's Name; with my ears, I listen to the Ambrosial Word of His Shabad.

Nanak is forever a sacrifice to those who meditate on the Supreme Lord God. |1|

All concerns are false, except those of the One Lord.

O Nanak, blessed are those, who are in love with their True Lord. |2|

Pauree:

I am forever a sacrifice to those who listen to the sermon of the Lord.

Those who bow their heads before God are perfect and distinguished.

Those hands, which write the Praises of the infinite Lord are beautiful.

Those feet which walk on God's Path are pure and holy.

In the Society of the Saints, they are emancipated; all their sorrows depart. |14|

Shalok:

One's destiny is activated, when one chants the Lord's Name, through perfect good fortune.

Fruitful is that moment, O Nanak, when one obtains the Blessed Vision of the Darshan of the Lord of the Universe. |1|

Its value cannot be estimated; it brings peace beyond measure.

O Nanak, that time alone is approved, when my Beloved meets with me. |2|

Pauree:

Tell me, what is that time, when I shall find God?

Blessed and auspicious is that moment, and that destiny, when I shall find the Lord of the Universe.

Meditating on the Lord, twenty-four hours a day, my mind's desires are fulfilled.

By great good fortune, I have found the Society of the Saints; I bow and touch their feet.

My mind thirsts for the Blessed Vision of the Lord's Darshan; Nanak is a sacrifice to Him. |15|

Shalok:

The Lord of the Universe is the Purifier of sinners; He is the Dispeller of all distress.

The Lord God is Mighty, giving His Protective Sanctuary; Nanak chants the Name of the Lord, Har, Har. |1|

Renouncing all self-conceit, I hold tight to the Lord's Feet.

My sorrows and troubles have departed, O Nanak, beholding God. |2|

Pauree:

Unite with me, O Merciful Lord; I have fallen at Your Door.

O Merciful to the meek, save me. I have wandered enough; now I am tired.

It is Your very nature to love Your devotees, and save sinners.

Without You, there is no other at all; I offer this prayer to You.

Take me by the hand, O Merciful Lord, and carry me across the world-ocean. |16|

Shalok:

The Merciful Lord is the Savior of the Saints; their only support is to sing the Kirtan of the Lord's Praises.

One becomes immaculate and pure, by associating with the Saints, O Nanak, and taking the Protection of the Transcendent Lord. |1|

The burning of the heart is not dispelled at all, by sandalwood paste, the moon, or the cold season.

It only becomes cool, O Nanak, by chanting the Name of the Lord. |2|

Pauree:

Through the Protection and Support of the Lord's lotus feet, all beings are saved.

Hearing of the Glory of the Lord of the Universe, the mind becomes fearless.

Nothing at all is lacking, when one gathers the wealth of the Naam.

The Society of the Saints is obtained, by very good deeds.

Twenty-four hours a day, meditate on the Lord, and listen continually to the Lord's Praises. |17|

Shalok:

The Lord grants His Grace, and dispels the pains of those who sing the Kirtan of the Praises of His Name.

When the Lord God shows His Kindness, O Nanak, one is no longer engrossed in Maya. |1|

Section 15 - Raag Jaitsree - Part 015

The burning fire has been put out; God Himself has saved me.

Meditate on that God, O Nanak, who created the universe. |2|

Pauree:

When God becomes merciful, Maya does not cling.

Millions of sins are eliminated, by meditating on the Naam, the Name of the One Lord.

The body is made immaculate and pure, bathing in the dust of the feet of the Lord's humble servants.

The mind and body become contented, finding the Perfect Lord God.

One is saved, along with his family, and all his ancestors. |18|

Shalok:

The Guru is the Lord of the Universe; the Guru is the Lord of the world; the Guru is the Perfect Pervading Lord God.

The Guru is compassionate; the Guru is all-powerful; the Guru, O Nanak, is the Saving Grace of sinners. |1|

The Guru is the boat, to cross over the dangerous, treacherous, unfathomable world-ocean.

O Nanak, by perfect good karma, one is attached to the feet of the True Guru. |2|

Pauree:

Blessed, blessed is the Divine Guru; associating with Him, one meditates on the Lord.

When the Guru becomes merciful, then all one's demerits are dispelled.

The Supreme Lord God, the Divine Guru, uplifts and exalts the lowly.

Cutting away the painful noose of Maya, He makes us His own slaves.

With my tongue, I sing the Glorious Praises of the infinite Lord God. |19|

Shalok:

I see only the One Lord; I hear only the One Lord; the One Lord is all-pervading.

Nanak begs for the gift of the Naam; O Merciful Lord God, please grant Your Grace. |1|

I serve the One Lord, I contemplate the One Lord, and to the One Lord, I offer my prayer.

Nanak has gathered in the wealth, the merchandise of the Naam; this is the true capital. |2|

Pauree:

God is merciful and infinite. The One and Only is all-pervading.

He Himself is all-in-all. Who else can we speak of?

God Himself grants His gifts, and He Himself receives them.

Coming and going are all by the Hukam of Your Will; Your place is steady and unchanging.

Nanak begs for this gift; by Your Grace, Lord, please grant me Your Name. |20|1|

Jaitsree, The Word Of The Devotees:

One Universal Creator God. By The Grace Of The True Guru:

O my Lord and Master, I know nothing.

My mind has sold out, and is in Maya's hands. |1|Pause|

You are called the Lord and Master, the Guru of the World.

I am called a lustful being of the Dark Age of Kali Yuga. |1|

The five vices have corrupted my mind.

Moment by moment, they lead me further away from the Lord. |2|

Wherever I look, I see loads of pain and suffering.

I do not have faith, even though the Vedas bear witness to the Lord. |3|

Shiva cut off Brahma's head, and Gautam's wife and the Lord Indra mated; Brahma's head got stuck to Shiva's hand, and Indra came to bear the marks of a thousand female organs. |4|

These demons have fooled, bound and destroyed me.
I am very shameless - even now, I am not tired of them. |5|

Says Ravi Daas, what am I to do now?
Without the Sanctuary of the Lord's Protection, who else's should I seek? |6|1|

33702416R00408

Made in the USA
Lexington, KY
07 July 2014